The Empowered Christian Road Map

by Brian S. Holmes

Brian S. Holmes is the Pastor, Founder, and President of MPowered Christian Ministries, a division of MPowered Living, Inc. MPowered Christian Ministries is dedicated to global revival by the Kingdom of God in every city. They provide a variety of services, products, and resources to mobilize disciples to advance the Kingdom of God globally.

For information, visit https://MPoweredChristian.org

First Edition published in Clearwater, Florida by MPowered Christian Publishing in June 2020. First Edition of *book concept* published as an Adobe PDF Ebook in November 2019.

ISBN 978-1-7352423-0-9 (Paperback, Standard Edition)
ISBN 978-1-7352423-1-6 (Paperback, Full Color Edition)
ISBN 978-1-7352423-2-3 (Ebook, Adobe PDF Edition)
ISBN 978-1-7352423-3-0 (Ebook, EPUB Edition)
ISBN 978-1-7352423-5-4 (Ebook, Mobi Edition)
ISBN 978-1-7352423-4-7 (Audiobook Edition)

This book is manufactured in the United States of America.

Unless otherwise indicated, all Scripture quotations are taken from:
The Holy Bible, Berean Study Bible, BSB
Copyright © 2016, 2018 by Bible Hub
Used by Permission. All Rights Reserved Worldwide.
View translation at https://bereanbible.com. Compare with others at https://biblehub.com/bsb/

Edited by Brian S. Holmes
Cover and book design by Brian S. Holmes
Proofreading by Theresa L. Holmes

Library of Congress Control Number: 2020911564

DISCLAIMER: This book is intended for informational purposes only, with the understanding that no one should rely upon this information as the basis for medical decisions. Anyone requiring medical or other health care should consult a medical or health care professional. Any actions based on the information provided are entirely the responsibility of the user and of any medical or other health care professionals who are involved in such actions. Although every effort to ensure that the information in this book was correct at press time and while this publication is designed to provide accurate information in regard to the subject matter covered, the publisher and the author assume no responsibility for errors, inaccuracies, omissions, or any other inconsistencies herein and hereby disclaim any liability to any party for any loss, damage, or disruption caused by errors or omissions, including but not limited to special, incidental, consequential, or other damages, whether such errors or omissions result from negligence, accident, or any other cause. This publication is not meant as a substitute for direct expert assistance. If such level of assistance is required, the services of a competent professional should be sought.

DEDICATION

This book is dedicated to my Heavenly Father, and my Lord and Savior, Jesus Christ, without whom this book would not only be impossible to make, but totally unnecessary to make. Without Your gracious salvation, adoption, and commission, me, and countless others like me, would still be lost, aimlessly wandering the tumultuous paths of life searching for meaning.

I pray that this work is full of spirit and truth, and that it glorifies You, elevates Christ, and magnifies the gospel. I pray You would use it to abundantly advance your Kingdom and to set people free, bring restoration, build unshakable faith, and give encouragement to many.

I also pray that it reaches far, wide, and deep, and empowers Your bride, the Church, to fully embrace all of her potential.

FOREWARD

Over the past twenty-two years I've experienced, overcome, learned, and grown a lot. And over the past nine years, the LORD has led me on a personal journey of restoration, rededication, reeducation, and commission to be more and do more. In many ways this work is the fruit of the many lessons I've learned.

I was raised Roman Catholic by loving parents but fell into mischief, ungodly behavior, drugs and gangs for several years. After hitting my rock bottom, I got my life back in order, restored my relationship with my parents, was working, was in love with a girlfriend, and pushing myself to get the best grades ever to graduate high school. On paper everything was great but something was missing. I cried out to the universe searching for what I still lacked. Jesus told me it was Him. I'd forsaken my first love and hadn't even realized He once was. I reaffirmed my faith from that point on, unfortunately, God remained far from the *center* of my life.

After thirteen years as a "lukewarm" evangelical the Lord convicted me and called me out at age thirty, gradually completely uprooting, and simultaneously building upon, much of who I was prior. He's blessed and empowered me with the time, opportunity, talent, personality, and desire to venture the roads less traveled. Never one to pursue the status quo, I didn't want to just become a church pastor. The world is broken and it desperately needs revival. I've been an ambitious, serial entrepreneurial roadrunner, venturing out into many directions, starting many projects, while also being a sponge, soaking up all the knowledge, experience, and wisdom I could along the way. My lack of focus has, perhaps, hindered my success, at least worldly success. The world rewards the specialist, not the self-actualized and balanced, knowing a little about a lot. However, a love of this is how the Lord designed me, and I think this quirk comes with it contentment, wisdom, and fulfillment, and greater potential to teach, coach, and help others. This diverse journey, and the things I've learned on it, have been a blessing to me personally, and I pray that, through this work, they'll be a blessing to you as well.

It's the goal of this book to share with the rest of the Christian world, my brothers and sisters in Christ, many of the things I've learned so far that are helpful in navigating the Christian life and living up to your highest potential. It's with the big picture in focus, and with the important details outlined for easy reference, that our journey can be traveled with confidence and drive. Though tomorrow is not promised for any of us, it's my belief and optimistic hope that my journey, as well as each of yours, is just getting started. We only get to travel this journey once, so let's make it count! Enjoy the ride!

With Love,
Brian S. Holmes

PREFACE: HOW TO USE THIS BOOK

This book has been designed to be used in a variety of ways. It could be read from beginning to end for a broad survey of the Christian life. But it could also easily be used for *topical* independent or group study, or as a topical reference book. Since each chapter covers a different key principle in depth each chapter could be used as an independent curriculum. Additionally, chapters are divided into main *Sections (I, II, III)*, and within these broken down into smaller **Subsections (A, B, C, etc.)**.

For example, consider this condensed version of the Table of Contents of Chapter One below, which is about getting a new map. (See page 7 for full version) The *purpose* of life, *why* we need a new map, could be studied separately in *Section I*, beginning on page 8, whereas *Section III* is about the *final destination*, beginning on page 60. As a Christian you should know there's more than one destination. There's both Heaven and Hell. So, if you'd like to study or defend that specific topic you can choose to go right to the final section: **Section (P)**, beginning on page 69. There you'll get teaching, supplementary Bible verse references to look up, and even many whole verses used to prove the validity of the historical Christian doctrines on that topic. Suppose you've already read this chapter but just want to reevaluate your knowledge, confidence, faith, application, etc. just go to *Section IV*, beginning on page 76. There you'll find a personal evaluation tool, group discussion questions, and a place to take notes or plan to-do tasks for the week.

BIBLE QUOTATIONS. Throughout this book over a hundred Scripture verses are quoted—in full—in stand apart areas, and sometimes within the main copy (*in a font like this*) to support the teachings provided. Occasionally, I quote partial verses that have excess content irrelevant to my point. When I seldom do this the verse includes an "a" if it shows the entire first half of the verse, or "b" if the latter half. This way you still get to read God's Word rather than mine. I don't think it's best to bounce between many translations picking those that fit best with *my* words. If what I'm saying is biblical then all good translations will reflect it; they don't need my effort to help it agree. To make the book uniform, scholarly yet user-friendly, and easy to study further, I did what no one does: I used a *single* translation: the Berean Study Bible. I've found it to be a great translation with high literal accuracy on par with the NASB and ESV, easy readability like the NIV, with structure often like the KJV. You can read it in full at (https://bereanbible.com) or effortlessly compare it side-by-side with your preferred translation as you read this book at (https://biblehub.com), which also incorporates many other Bible study tools.

THE EMPOWERED CHRISTIAN

Looking for something specific? A brief summary of each chapter is in the Introduction starting on page 1. Also, a summary of each subsection (ABC, etc.) is provided in its subtitle. There's also a Topic Index on page 385.

ROAD MAP — Table of Contents

Introduction

Hey Siri... Am I even going in the right DIRECTION?!?!

Were you told God loves you just as you are and has a wonderful plan for your life? Perhaps your favorite TV preacher tells you God just wants you to be happy, healthy, and wealthy? Did you know most people believe they're already a good person and they'll go to Heaven? Did you know that we're all sinners and that without repentance, faith, and a right walk with Jesus we won't? Jesus said in Matthew 7:13-14, *"For wide is the gate and broad is the way that leads to destruction, and many enter through it. But small is the gate and narrow the way that leads to life, and only a few find it."* It's our faith in the gospel that saves us—the good news that Jesus is the eternal Son of God who died for our sins on the cross and then rose from the dead. Your journey begins there. This book will help you understand, with deep clarity and fresh insights, this truth and hundreds of others. My goal is to not only guide you through the narrow way but empower you to success— total lasting success! I want you to be an *empowered* Christian, who does great things, but here's the harsh truth: Many who call themselves Christians aren't even saved yet!

Matthew 7:21 *[Jesus]* "Not everyone who says to me, 'Lord, Lord,' will enter the kingdom of heaven, but the one who does the will of my Father who is in heaven. ²²On that day many will say to me, 'Lord, Lord, did we not prophesy in your name, and cast out demons in your name, and do many mighty works in your name?' ²³And then will I declare to them, 'I never knew you; depart from me, you workers of lawlessness.'

> NOTE: ALL VERSE QUOTATIONS IN THIS BOOK ARE FROM THE BEREAN STUDY BIBLE. SEE COPYRIGHT AND PREFACE PAGES FOR INFO.

Don't get mad at me—those are Jesus's words, not mine! And that's about people that were *actively* following Him enough to be prophesying, casting out demons, and doing works in His name. How much worse off are some of us: the Sunday-only Christians, the Christmas-only Christians, the living-in-perpetual-sin Christians? Some of you picked up this book thinking you're starting this journey in the middle but you're actually closer to the starting line. That's okay though! *Real* empowerment comes from being equipped with everything you need to be successful. This begins with clarity of what is true. It means knowing the truth about God and His plan of redemption, even if it's not inclusive or politically correct. It means knowing the truth about who you are, and where you currently are, even if in all its brutal honesty it's not a very good place. It means having a true and clear road map of how to get from where you are to where you want to go.

For better or worse, your *past* beliefs and efforts have brought you to the present. Whether you're in a great place right now - or not - in order to be more and do more, you must continue to learn and grow

> ### Quick thought
> Are you defining "success" the world's way, your own way, or God's way?

and move into new territories. Life isn't stagnant, it's always moving. If you're not moving forward, you're moving backward. If you're not growing, then you're dying. If you're not improving, then you're getting worse. And if you're not moving towards God, and His plan for your life, then you're moving away from God and His plan for your life. We all want success, but rarely do we define or really understand the success we seek before trying to get it. If we want to be *truly* successful in life, we're going to have to redefine "success" God's way, and then actively pursue it God's way. *The Empowered Christian Road Map* does just this. It helps you properly see the terrain ahead accurately, define success rightly, and measure your progress towards it. My goal for this book is for it to be used like a manual that provides the outline of the most critical parts of your journey. This will make it easier to diagnose areas you have less certainty about so you can learn more about them and work on them. To know and not to do is really not to know. I wish I would've had this: a blueprint and guidebook of the Christian life that didn't just help me know what to *believe*, but also what to *do* next. One that helped me develop the skills to think through tough subjects and have the mindset and emotional resolve to identify concerns to course-correct. This book is organized sequentially so each chapter, and each subsets within chapters, build upon the previous. However, each subtopic has its own section so you can also easily reference them separately later. Each chapter provides lots of indicators and guide posts you can use to review your own personal progress throughout your Christian journey, so you can make adjustments as needed.

The journey will still be difficult, but the map shouldn't be. Know *where* you're going and *how* to get there!

CHAPTER 1: THE RIGHT ROAD MAP

To be successful you must start with the right map. It doesn't matter how fast you're traveling, or how much progress you make along the way—if you're going in the wrong direction! In Mark 8:34-36 Jesus said we needed to pick up our crosses, follow Him, and lose our lives for the sake of Him and the gospel, then we'd find true life. *That's* Jesus's example of the right direction! God *does* want you to be successful, to "find life," and have "abundant life." *(Matt. 10:37-39, John 10:10)* But God has a different definition of success and abundant life. After this book I think you will too. This chapter is a broad survey of Christian theology and essential doctrine. You'll learn the purpose for it all, the reason we exist, God's nature: Holy Trinity, the necessity of absolute truth, how and why we're made in God's image, the benefits of the Fall, the dynamics of human free will, why Jesus is the only way to be saved, how He fulfilled the Law of God, how to interpret the Law today, why we need to be born again and how, the nuances of baptism, God's desire to make us like Jesus, our adoption by God the Father, and all about our two possible destinations: eternal life on New Earth or eternal death in Hell.

CHAPTER 2: REBUILT AND HEADED IN A NEW DIRECTION

This chapter provides greater detail about why and how we become a rebuilt car (born again) before our journey can even start. Part 1 describes different aspects of the fallen human condition. Part 2 is about Soteriology, the study of *how* we're saved, going deeper in topics briefly covered in chapter one including God's grace, humility, repentance, faith, atonement, forgiveness, and imputation. Part 3 provides insights into your new nature, covering the necessity of regeneration and sanctification, and how to get the most out of it! Section O gives an overview of the Bible and its reliability for guidance. This will give your Christian faith some muscle! You'll learn why to trust God's Word and how to rely on the Holy Spirit inside of you to venture towards your destination with confidence.

CHAPTER 3: DUMPING THE GARBAGE BAGGAGE

Building off of the foundations of the previous, even the new car can still be bogged down with garbage baggage that needs to be removed. This spiritual warfare and counter-cult apologetics manual will teach you about Satan's true nature as a saboteur and equip you for victory! Part 2 describes bad drivers and passengers to throw out of your car including beliefs from harmful philosophies, false religions, legalism, demonic spirituality posing as the Holy Spirit, sinful lifestyles and identities incompatible with godliness, and unbiblical beliefs about Jesus espoused from Islam, the New Age, or Christian cults. The Holy Spirit must be driving instead of one of *these* to affirm that you're truly a new car! Detailed comparisons and documentation of the divinity and humanity of Jesus provided. Part 3 teaches about different types of open doors that need to be closed including hyper-grace beliefs, false repentance, sinful behavior, toxic habits, toxic relationships, soul ties, curses, cursed objects, emotional brokenness, and unforgiveness. Driving with this junk in your car will hinder your journey, making it less enjoyable, fruitful, or successful.

CHAPTER 4: THE ATMOSPHERE IN THE CAR

Now you're moving along but the journey is long with plenty of bumps in the road ahead. How will you control the *vibe in* the car? What's playing on the radio? What's the conversation about? I cover how your thoughts and beliefs affect how you feel, and how you feel affects what you do. Part 1 deals with beliefs: how to crucify old patterns, reaffirm your new identity and righteousness in Christ, understand your election and what the unpardonable sin is, confirm your salvation, and renew your mind using God's Word. Part 2 deals with emotions: good vs. bad, and living with gratitude, optimism, and a conqueror mentality. Part 3 deals with behavior: how the Holy Spirit empowers us to overcome and persevere, and how to use prayer, warfare prayer, worship, activations, and declarations to rebuke Satan. Includes an 11-page exposé on Word of Faith (Health & Wealth) beliefs that pervade the Church so you're not misdirected by a counterfeit New Age-influenced faith, but empowered by genuine faith!

CHAPTER 5: THE NEW DIRECTION IS VERY FRUITFUL

Next, you'll get your compass: fruitfulness. You'll use the fruit of your life and decisions for navigation to know if you're going in the right or wrong direction. Part 1 looks at the significance of fruit and why it needs to be an expression of God's character to be good, and attributes of those in God's Kingdom, like humility and childlike faith. Part 2 examines the aspects of fruits of righteousness such as: God's Law to govern Israel, its relation to repentance, how it manifests first inwardly in the heart and then flows outwardly through individuals into families and society. Next, I cover biblical justice and both the godly and demonic aspects of the modern social justice movement, including how certain supposedly-good cultural trends will be used by the Antichrist. Part 3 covers how good fruit must be humble, merciful, obedient, and driven by right motives. You'll learn how: works don't assist in salvation but faith without them is dead, they're evidence of saving faith, sanctification, and being Jesus's disciple. You'll learn how they must be built on Jesus to have eternal significance because He's the vine and foundation, and can merit eternal rewards later!

THE GREAT COMMISSION
Matthew 28:18-20

CHAPTER 6: OUR MISSION AS DISCIPLES

The Gospel-centered worldview reveals the differences between fruit and our mission as a follower of Jesus. Part 1 covers how good fruit is only a byproduct, isn't eternal, and may even seem unloving to the world. You'll learn in Part 2 that the Holy Spirit gives us power for a *reason*: for our mission to be an ambassador for Christ, a light in the darkness, and to preach the gospel, make disciples, and advance the Kingdom of God. You'll learn how Jesus reigns now with all authority, what Satan still has authority over, and what we have authority over. In Section (F) I refute the Catholic Church's claim to be the true Church and several of their practices as unbiblical. Part 3 covers how to run the race, be a good and faithful servant, receive rewards at the BEMA judgment, and endure, persevere, and witness during the Tribulation and Last Days.

CHAPTER 7: THE AUTO CLUB (THE CHURCH)

This chapter will shift your perspective of what and who the church is, and what it's for. Part 1 describes the global Church, the Elect, the Body of Christ, and the local congregation. In Part 2 you'll learn Jesus's intended function of the Church was to be united in a common Spirit and mission. To be a community for fellowship, baptism, Lord's Supper, prayer, preaching and study of God's Word, and community outreach and service. Some tips provided to empower churches. Part 3 covers what I call the higher calling of the church: living more like a spiritual family; making discipleship a universal, active, missional lifestyle rather than a class; and equipping and empowering mutual collaboration towards discipleship, total restoration, and advancement of the Kingdom of God. Includes a survey and critical analysis of spiritual gifts in the church today.

CHAPTER 8: SAME DESTINATION, ALTERNATE ROUTES

We're all going to the same destination but we each take a unique path there. Part 1 builds off the previous chapter to discover your unique identity and calling in the Body of Christ. You'll learn a simple framework to follow and use exercises to determine *your* highest values, personality type, spiritual gifts, and S.H.A.P.E. You'll learn the A.P.E.S.T. roles in the Global church (and APEST *categories* - my unique take!), and gain insights into how you can be most fulfilled and effective in the local church. You'll learn ways to be more empowered for your unique calling by putting God's presence first, getting regular updates from the Holy Spirit, focusing on your circle of influence and local community, and creating your own vision, mission, and S.M.A.R.T. action plan!

FEATURES FOR STUDY AND APPLICATION

To help the many topics in this book be fully digested and acted upon, I've added many features for personal or small group study, reflection, evaluation, and application. Every chapter is organized sequentially for comprehension, and broken down into numerical sections, making it easier to refer to specific topics later. Chapters end with an evaluation for grading yourself - your current level of understanding of main points, as well as your current level of trust, commitment, or personal application. You'll be able to revisit these later and re-grade yourself as you progress throughout your journey (your entire life). I've also included deeper questions for personal reflection or group study. Indexes of Scriptures and Topics are also included.

The Empowered Christian Road Map is here for YOU!

Don't worry if this seems like a lot! It is! But I'll begin at the starting line with you and we'll walk through it together, step-by-step. This book is for new and mature Christians. My hope is that pastors will consider it a great resource to recommend, helping get it into the hands of every Christian. This book will help you understand and live out Biblical Christianity! I won't promise it'll be an *easy* read because it's jam-packed full of deep spiritual truths, but it's worth it! Decide today to commit to searching for absolute truth and following Jesus wholeheartedly! Jesus expects your best. Like all meaningful activities, if you'll commit yourself to the process of doing important things, consistently, whether you *feel* like it or not, it will change your life! So be ready to learn, grow, and be challenged to live out what is taught. This book will give you lots of insights, direction, and tools for success, but you still need to take the initiative, be proactive, and push yourself to your limits. I promise - IF you commit yourself to Jesus in this life, HE will empower you and YOU WILL be successful. Buckle up and prepare for an amazing journey!

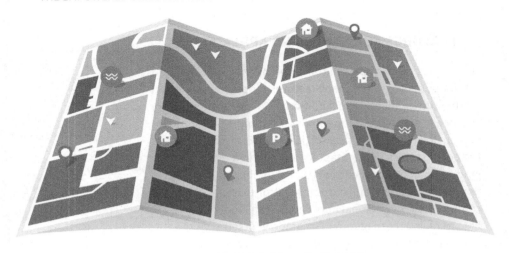

CHAPTER ONE

RECALCULATING.....
The Right Road Map

To arrive successfully at the desired destination you need to start with the right map!

Chapter Contents

I. The Purpose of It All

a. They're Not Our Roads
The one eternal God, created everything else, and did so for His own glory.

There is only one God. *(Deuteronomy 3:39, John 5:44-47)* He is eternal. He had no origin. He is the self-existent One. He had no beginning. He has always existed, has always been God, and was never anything else. *(Psalm 90:2)* There has always been and will only be, one God, in all places, at all times. *(Isaiah 43:10, Ephesians 4:6, 1 Chr. 17:20)* He is the Alpha and Omega, the Beginning and the End. *(Isaiah 45:18, 45:21-22, 44:6-8)* God is omniscient (all-knowing), omnipotent (all-powerful), and omnipresent (all-present). *(Acts 17:29, Exodus 33:20)* God is also perfect, good, holy, loving, and just. God is One. We are to worship God alone, and to do so with all our heart, mind, soul, and strength. *(Luke 4:8, Mark 12:29, 1 Cor. 8:4-6)*

Everything that has been made, was created by Him, and for Him. Ask yourself this: Why would *you* paint a painting, start a business, raise a family, develop a talent, or choose to do any other kind of optional activity? You would do it for your own pleasure, right? If you didn't have to, the only reason you would is because you actually wanted to. The *result* of your activity would be an expression of you. It'd be a reflection of you. Let's use you painting something as an example. Your painting could never be more intrinsically valuable than you are. It is your intrinsic value that you possess, and *your* self-expression, through your talent, creativity, skill, discipline, etc. that gives the painting itself any potential value it might have. And I'm not talking about value to sell it for. Let's say you live on a deserted island by yourself and there's no one else to buy it from you. I'm talking about the inherent value that it provides to you, just for creating it and having it as your work of art. The better you are as an artist, or the more the painting represents the most or best of you, the more glorious it is, and the more glory and pride it gives you to have made it. The more the painting reflects the least or worst of you, the less glorious it is, and the more dishonor, shame, and disgust it gives you to have made it. And then what if it were to permanently and prominently hang in the center of the living room.

Just as the painting is an expression of the painter, and has potential to bring either glory or shame to the painter, all of creation is an expression of God, and has potential to bring either glory or shame to God. He's the artist who made it all for His own pleasure. God made both the angels and humans with free will and we have abused that will to profane the glory of God. We've become a vile work that doesn't bring God glory and pleasure. We certainly understand why a terrible painting deserves to be destroyed. Why not trash it and start over? But we rarely consider this perspective from God's point of view about us. What prerogative does God have, letting that which defiles His glory, to continue to exist forever? Especially a dynamic, progressive painting like us, not one that just stayed in its original bad form, but kept getting worse and worse. He really doesn't!

It is only because of His love, mercy, justice, and glorious grace (unmerited favor) that He hasn't immediately and permanently destroyed us. Fortunately for us, God is loving, merciful, and forgiving. Because of this, it actually reflects His nature to show kindness to us and give us a way, and time, to repent. So even though we're evil, God receives glory in the present, by being patient with us, for a time. He cannot, and will not, allow it forever though. But He will allow it until the full maximum of all those who will turn from their evil, do. In this way, He will transform into good those who do, and receive glory as being One who forgives, saves, restores, and transforms. Then they will be transformed and made glorious as well, which in turn magnifies His glory. Then He will share His glory, with those who also recognize and value His glory, forever.

In the end, everything that brings God glory will continue to multiply in glory forever. Everything that doesn't bring God *direct* glory, will do so at the time He judges and condemns it. It also gives God glory to demonstrate justice, to punish evil and destroy things that are wicked. In God's universe everything will give Him glory one way or another. These are the two destinations at the end of the road map. One of existence that gives Him glory, and one of destruction that gives Him glory. One where objects go through restoration, progression, and transformation, into something good *like* Him, and it gives Him glory to save and mold them. Or one where objects go through decay, regression, and mutation, into something awful completely *unlike* Him, and it gives Him glory to destroy them. To be on the right side of history, our existence and transformation—rather than our destruction—need to glorify God. The right road map is the former.

In order for us to be on the right side of history, our existence and transformation—rather than our destruction—need to glorify God.

Isaiah 48:9 *[God]* For the sake of My name I will delay My wrath; for the sake of My praise I will restrain it, so that you will not be cut off. [10]See, I have refined you, but not as silver; I have tested you in the furnace of affliction. [11]For My own sake, My very own sake, I will act; for how can I let Myself be defamed? I will not yield My glory to another.

Isaiah 43:6b *[God]* "Bring My sons from afar, and My daughters from the ends of the earth—[7]everyone called by My name and created for My glory, whom I have indeed formed and made."

Isaiah 42:8 *[God]* I am the LORD; that is My name! I will not give My glory to another or My praise to idols.

b. Celebrating God's Glory

God's about His own glory, we need to be about His glory too.

Since God is rightly preoccupied with the celebration and proliferation of His own glory, we need to be so too. The entire universe proclaims the glory of God. Every galaxy, solar system, sun, planet, animal, plant, cell, and atom does. *(Ps 19:1, 8:1, 97:6)* But they proclaim His glory in their *mere existence*, the same way that a painting's existence proclaims the glory of the painter. And in a sense, our existence does as well. But we also have intellect, emotions, talents, and the ability to choose and act. We are also made in God's image so we're actually an exquisite design. So we have greater potential—for both good or evil. Unlike the other creations God made, that lack sophistication and choice, the goodness of our superior design is offset by the wickedness we use our design for. Imagine if your painting was not only a bad painting but also raped, murdered, and tortured, your other paintings for fun, and influenced them to hate you and do evil too!

God did foresee and know this would happen, but despite this potential harm, the creation of free beings was still worth it to Him in the grand scheme of things. God had a higher purpose and calling for living beings. God never intended us to be automatons, mindless robots that just praised Him constantly. He desired intelligent, emotional, capable, spiritual, beings with free will. First for the spirit beings (angels) and then for human beings. Unlike everything else He created, we would uniquely have the opportunity to experience God *personally*. We would be capable of knowing Him, and loving Him, and being known by Him, and loved by Him. God's Word teaches us that God *is* love. *(1 Jn 4:16)* Love isn't possible without free will. So He created beings freely capable of love, with the caveat that they would also be capable of hate. And they would also have the potential to love themselves, more than they love God or others, or even to hate God or others. It was love of ourselves that led eventually to idolatry and to originally-beautiful paintings that gradually devolved and twisted into something wicked, entirely unlike God.

John 5:44 *[Jesus]* How can you believe if you accept glory from one another, yet do not seek the glory that comes from the only God?

1 Corinthians 10:31 So whether you eat or drink or whatever you do, do it all to the glory of God.

God's glory is multiplied through a shared intimate relationship with beings capable of witnessing, experiencing, and rejoicing in His divine majesty. With beings who can see His glory and enjoy Him just for who He *is*. Not what He can *do* necessarily, and especially not what He can do for us—but just for who He *is*. Because there truly is nothing greater.

People sometimes insult the Christian understanding of God, thinking less of Him, claiming that He only cares about His own ego. That He is selfish and egotistical and flawed or unrealistic as a result. But they're looking at this with no introspection and flawed reasoning. Humans instinctively know that selfishness is bad. Why? Because deep down in the core of our being we know we aren't God. The universe doesn't revolve around us and when we act like it does we have conflicting emotions because we know we're living a lie. No matter how bad we want it all to be about us, deep down we all know it's not about us. We're fragile, finite beings living for a few years on a blue rock flying through space surrounded by billions of other galaxies. Another reason we know selfishness is bad is because we experience empathy: how others feel. We know what it feels like to be hurt by other people who were themselves acting selfishly. Selfishness is a bad quality, to us, *because* the selfishness of other people prevents *our* selfishness! Isn't it ironic the same people who claim that God is egotistical for wanting our worship, refuse to worship Him and instead they worship themselves. They do for themselves the very thing that God desires us to do for Him, all while protesting that He's wrong for wanting it! That is selfish. Egotistical. Ignorant. This is love of self, over love of God.

God desires us to witness, experience, rejoice, worship, and celebrate, in His glory. But the reality and truth is that He has the right to. And He is right to do so. There is literally not a single thing that is greater than He is! There's nothing in all of creation that is greater! There's nothing, that has any beauty, that is more beautiful. Nothing with power, that is more powerful. Nothing that loves, that is more loving. Nothing that is good, or just, or wise, with more goodness, or justice, or wisdom. There is not a single painting that is better than the painter! It's impossible, illogical, and unreasonable to think there is.

So when we, as free will beings recognize this, we have the opportunity to join in God with the celebration of His glory. And as we will learn later God is very relational. The invitation isn't to just celebrate Him. It's to become *like* Him, in a way that glorifies Him, and deepens the bonds

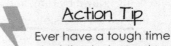

Action Tip

Ever have a tough time deciding between two different options? Just ask yourself a simple question: "Which of the two options will bring more glory to God?"

of love between us into ever-increasing, glorious, eternal, intimate relationship. I like the way Pastor John Piper describes what he calls *Christian hedonism*: "God is most glorified in us when we are most satisfied in Him."[1] The right road map is fixed on God being glorified through *our* knowledge and celebration of Him and relationship with Him.

"God is most glorified in us when we are most satisfied in Him." - Pastor John Piper[1]

c. God's Triune Nature

The Holy Trinity reveals that God is eternally relational within His very nature.

One of the perplexing mysteries about God, that was hinted at throughout the Old Testament, but revealed explicitly in the New Testament, is His triune nature. I don't want to provide an entire apologetic for this doctrine here, I have other offerings for that, but I want to make sure you fully and clearly understand what it is and why it's important. I also want to provide a few examples from the Bible to demonstrate that it's an authentic biblical truth. Then I'll share a few ways that this truth, that was not invented by the Church but rather revealed to us by God, is more glorious than any unitarian view. Lastly I'll explain how God's trinitarian nature reveals that God is relational in His very nature.

Matthew 28:19 [Jesus] Therefore go and make disciples of all nations, baptizing them in the name of the Father, and of the Son, and of the Holy Spirit...

Notice there's only one NAME (not names) there? There is one God, and this one God exists as one (ousia) "essence/substance" in three (hypostasis) "persons" — God the Father, God the Son (Jesus Christ), and God the Holy Spirit (also called Holy Ghost). God is one absolute perfect divine BEING in three "persons." His being is what God *is*—in relation to the universe that He created. He is One in essence and everything else is created by Him. Don't get too caught up in the word persons. The three are called "persons" (merely for the lack of a better word) just because they relate to each other *in personal ways*. However, all three distinctions are the one, singular God, co-eternal, and co-equal. There is a clear (not separation) but *distinction* between them. The Father is not the Son is not the Spirit. The persons are each distinct. However, they are all God. There are not three gods. There is not one person, or one God doing all three as separate "modes." *(Jn 14:26, Jn 17:1-5, 1 Jn 2:1, 2 Jn 1:3)* All three are equally co-eternal. *(Rom 16:26, Rev 1:17, Heb 9:14)* In every action of God all three "persons" work together as one, with a single divine Will as they are in absolute perfect agreement.

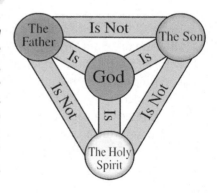

Prayer to God may be helpful to think of in the following way. Christians usually pray *to* the Father, *in* the name of and *through* the Son, *by* the power of the Holy Spirit. But because they are all God, you can pray to any individually, and they all (God) receives it. The works of God are also performed by all three simultaneously. God the Father *wills*

it, the Son of God (the logos/Word of God) is the essence of the directive of His creative expression, and the Spirit of God is the power that causes it to *be*. The Son, the logos/Word of God, is who was incarnated as the man, Jesus Christ, becoming both fully God and fully human. *(Isa 9:6, Col 1:15-20, 2:8-9, Phil 2:5-11, Heb 1:1-13, Tit 2:13)* The Holy Spirit is the Spirit of God. *(Acts 5:3-4, Eph 4:30, 2 Pet 1:21, 1 Cor 6:11, 1 Cor 2:10-11, Heb 9:14, Zech 4:6, 1 Cor 3:16)*

John 1:1 In the beginning was the Word, and the Word was with God, and the Word was God. ²He was with God in the beginning. ³Through Him all things were made, and without Him nothing was made that has been made... ¹⁴The Word became flesh and made His dwelling among us. We have seen His glory, the glory of the one and only Son from the Father, full of grace and truth.

Colossians 2:15 The Son is the image of the invisible God, the firstborn over all creation. ¹⁶For in Him all things were created, things in heaven and on earth, visible and invisible, whether thrones or dominions or rulers or authorities. All things were created through Him and for Him.

Ephesians 4:30 And do not grieve the Holy Spirit of God, in whom you were sealed for the day of redemption.

1 John 5:20 And we know that the Son of God has come and has given us understanding, so that we may know Him who is true; and we are in Him who is true—in His Son Jesus Christ. He is the true God and eternal life.

It's true the word "Trinity" does not appear in the Bible, but it is still a Bible-based belief. The word "Trinity" refers to this "Godhead" and is used to explain the eternal relationship between the Father, the Son, and the Holy Spirit. The doctrine of the "Trinity" was defended by church fathers early on including: Clement, third bishop of Rome, AD 96; Justin Martyr, great Christian writer, AD 155; Theophilus, the sixth bishop of Antioch, AD 168; and Tertullian, early church leader, AD 197.[2] The Trinity can be a difficult concept to understand, but this is not an argument against its validity—rather it's an argument for its truth. The Bible is the self-revelation of an infinite God. Therefore, we are bound to encounter concepts which are difficult to understand–especially when dealing with an incomprehensible God who exists in all places at all times. So, when we view descriptions and attributes of God revealed in the Father, Son, and Holy Spirit, we discover that a completely comprehensible and understandable explanation of God's nature is not possible. What we've done, however, is derive from the Scripture truths that we can grasp and combine them into the doctrine we call the Holy Trinity. The Trinity is, to a large extent, a mystery. After all, we are dealing with God Himself. It is the way of man-made religions and cults to reduce biblical truth to make God comprehensible and easily understandable. To this end, they subject God's revelation to their own simplicity and reasoning and thereby distort the truth. They also worship a false Jesus, who becomes an elevated—but still created—being. But remember, God said He will not yield HIS glory to any other! In Isaiah 45:23, *"To ME [GOD] every knee shall bow and every tongue swear allegiance."* Paul even quotes this verse in Romans 14:11 so he had and confirmed this truth, but in Philippians 2:10-11 Paul writes, *"at the name of JESUS every knee should bow... and every tongue confess that Jesus Christ is Lord, to the glory of God the Father."*

Without the Holy Trinity there is no way to have ONE God and worship Him ALONE, and worship Jesus as Lord, without committing idolatry by worshipping something *created*.

The revelation of the truthfulness of the Holy Trinity brings us to many fascinating conclusions. Humans are three dimensional, not surprisingly God has infinitely more dimensions. Humans are simple and singular, God is complex and pluralistic. The Trinity shows God's majesty in His infinite uniqueness. This is actually the definition of *holy*. Distinct. Set apart. The Trinity also helps us understand how certain attributes of God's character, that He claims have always been true, can be *eternally* true. For example, God was not lonely before creating personal beings. He has always had perfect harmonious relationship internally between the Father, Son, and Spirit. I mentioned earlier that God *is* love. *(1 Jn 4:16)* Yet, for any form of unitarian monotheism this can't be true. How could God be love an eternity before creating anything *to* love? He would have been void of both giving love and receiving love. In the same way, additional attributes come into question such being eternally just, eternally generous, eternally gracious, etc. No, the true God has not lacked a single thing for all of eternity! It glorifies God for us to recognize this. Rather than diminishing His glory, the doctrine of the Holy Trinity glorifies Him.

In Romans, chapter 8, there is a passage that shows both the entire Holy Trinity as well as well as the relational aspect of God. It is through the new spiritual rebirth (more later on that) that we become "born again" and receive the Holy Spirit, the Spirit of God—in us. *(Jn 3:3-8)* It is also when we are put *in* Christ *(Gal 3:27)*, and at the same time Christ is put *in* us. *(Gal 2:20)* This passage also shows God the Father, as the One who raised Jesus from the dead, is *also* somehow living in us. In these three verses we see that by the Holy Spirit being inside of us, in a mysterious way we also have the Father and the Son in us as well. And it is through this indwelling that we are given life and transformed by the imputed righteousness of Christ. Any religion, God, Jesus, or gospel that doesn't teach the doctrine of the Holy Trinity is a false religion, god, Jesus, or gospel—and is a false map.

Romans 8:9 You, however, are controlled not by the flesh, but by the Spirit, if the Spirit of God lives in you. And if anyone does not have the Spirit of Christ, he does not belong to Christ. [10]But if Christ is in you, your body is dead because of sin, yet your spirit is alive because of righteousness. [11]And if the Spirit of Him who raised Jesus from the dead is living in you, He who raised Christ Jesus from the dead will also give life to your mortal bodies through His Spirit, who lives in you.

---

d. Invitation to Eternal Relationship
We're invited, in Christ, to enter into eternal family relationship with God.

Through learning of the Holy Trinity we learn that God wasn't lacking *anything* prior to making free beings. For all of eternity God already had all the benefits of relationship but with absolute, pure, totally-selfless, love and devotion. And this at the highest depths of intimacy, without blemish, yielding, or conflict via selfish interest. Certainly far beyond the best of the flawed and broken relationship capabilities we're able to provide. So, if God already had it all, everything He could ever possibly need or want within His very own nature—why create us? The answer: For more. There are no bounds to God's glory! God is continually seeking to increase His glory and pleasure. There was potential glory for Him in our existence, and through the future relationship He would have with us. And since God is omniscient He already foreknew the successful outcome even prior to starting.

So if He knows the end before the beginning, and sees the evil, havoc, and deaths that ensue, why do it? Especially since God is love and says outright, *"I take no pleasure in the death of anyone."* (Ezekiel 18:32) Why make beings that you know will rebel and sin and many will need to be destroyed? The answer again: There is for God more glory gained than lost, both during the process, and in the end result, of all of those who will inherit eternal life with Him and through Him. Why? Basically, because it will be worth it! The good outweighs the bad. The ends justify the means. The Bible teaches that God is not pleased by the loss of even a single life, but that ALL would repent and live. *(2 Pet 3:9)* But just because He doesn't *desire* any losses doesn't mean it's not worth it despite losses. God sees eternity-future at the same time as eternity-past. He foreknows a future life with those who are saved, and rejoices that the glory to come, that we share with Him, is exceedingly abundantly greater than the unfortunate loss of those who undoubtedly refuse the invitation to repent and join. Jesus taught that it's definitely the will—and even the *joy*—of the Father that all of us would repent and return to Him, including the well known parables of the Lost Sheep, the Lost Coin, and the Prodigal Son. (See Luke 15)

---

2 Corinthians 4:17 For our light and momentary affliction is producing for us an eternal glory that is far beyond comparison.

Ezekiel 33:11 *[God]* Say to them: 'As surely as I live, declares the Lord GOD, I take no pleasure in the death of the wicked, but rather that the wicked should turn from their ways and live. Turn! Turn from your evil ways! For why should you die, O house of Israel?'

Luke 15:7 *[Jesus]* In the same way, I tell you that there will be more joy in heaven over one sinner who repents than over ninety-nine righteous ones who do not need to repent... [10] In the same way, I tell you, there is joy in the presence of God's angels over one sinner who repents."... [32]But it was fitting to celebrate and be glad, because this brother of yours was dead and is alive again; he was lost and is found.'"

2 Peter 3:9 The Lord is not slow to fulfill His promise as some understand slowness, but is patient with you, not wanting anyone to perish but everyone to come to repentance.

God foreknew all of us who would repent and be saved. *(Rom 8:29)* This is foreknowledge: God knowing in advance before us. I believe He already knows us from eternity-future. His plan of redemption of us through Christ, and ultimately even in His relationship with each of us individually, appealed to Him. This plan, and our ultimate destiny with Him, is what God predestined for us. *(Rom 8:29, 1 Cor 2:7)* And because of this, He made all of creation, gave us free will, and allowed the fall to happen. Romans 11:32 says, *"For God has consigned all men to disobedience so that He may have mercy on them ALL."*

It is by considering things from God's point of view, and from this paradigm of eternal *relationship*, that certain aspects of the New Covenant era take on new and powerful relational attributes. These go far beyond even what God did with His first people that He foreknew (Israel). For starters, God reveals Himself explicitly in the person of Jesus, who is *"the exact representation of His nature."* *(Heb 1:3)* And Jesus takes on flesh, *adding* human nature *to* His divine nature, making Him more like us and more relatable to us. He's also the first to be resurrected, becoming the firstfruits of the resurrection, relationally leading the way before us. Jesus reveals relational aspects of God's nature in the Trinity. We learn that the Father *sends* the Son and the Spirit to us. *(1 Jn 4:14, Gal 4:4-6)* The Son speaks to us, not on His own, but on behalf of the Father. *(Jn 8:28)* The Spirit speaks to us, not on His own, but on behalf of Jesus. *(Jn 16:13-15)* The Father loves the Son, and the Son loves the Father. *(Jn 3:35, 5:20)* We learn the Son is our Advocate before the Father, *(1 Jn 2:1)* the Spirit is our Advocate that Jesus sends to be with us forever, who is also Christ in us. *(Jn 14:16, 26, Rom 8:9)* There's interpersonal intimacy on every level.

And then Jesus makes sure that every single one of His followers would know about the doctrine of the Holy Trinity by putting it into the "new convert" baptismal formula. (Matthew 28:19) This also puts His Church in relationship with each other as well, because all officially become part of His visible Church through their public declaration of faith and water baptism. And again relationship is emphasized afterwards through the Lord's Supper, which is spiritual communion with Him and each other, at His table. For deeper relationship is why no one can see or enter the Kingdom of God unless He first *regenerates* us spiritually with His Spirit inside of us. *(Jn 3:3-8)* For relationship is why we need to be in the Son, and the Son needs to be in us. We know the Son is in the Father, the Father is in the Son, and God the Father adopts us, in Christ, so that He is our father, too. And all of us are brothers and sisters. The Father, Son, and Holy Spirit have been engaging in a beautiful, intimate type of dance for all of eternity. And through Jesus, we are being invited to join them in the eternal dance. We're invited into the eternal family relationship with God!

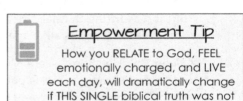

Empowerment Tip

How you RELATE to God, FEEL emotionally charged, and LIVE each day, will dramatically change if THIS SINGLE biblical truth was not only believed but REALIZED.

II. The Opportunity and Invitation

e. The Necessity of Truth

Our love of, desire for, and capacity for truth, will determine our destination.

If you love truth, desire truth, can cope with truth, and are willing to submit yourself to the truth, you will find your way to eternal life with God. I don't mean any and everything people *think* is true, or that is subjectively true for them, i.e. *relative* truth. I'm talking about objective reality, it's true whether you think it's true or not, true whether you like it or not, true whether you ever even knew about it or not, i.e. *absolute* truth. The gravitational force of the earth is an example of this. It was true before we discovered that gravity was happening, or learn what caused it. It is still true even if the person in the insane asylum doesn't think it is. It is true even if a person has so much faith that they are willing to jump off the Empire State building just to prove that it's false. It's true regardless. It's truth is an absolute. It's not dependent on any other variables.

The reality of God is the same way. His existence is absolutely true, whether we acknowledge it or not. Before we had the revelation of God through the prophets and compiled the Bible we didn't know how we came into existence or what caused it, but we can look into the stars and know something did. It was big, powerful, beautiful and creative. We didn't know yet about Adam and Eve or the Fall. Yet, all of us know instinctively we're sinful. This is because we don't even live up to our *own* standards perfectly, much less a perfect ideal, that we all somehow instinctively yearn for. We didn't know what the meaning and purpose of life was, but we yearn and desire meaning and purpose. As a result we search for it, and create our own. And we all absolutely experience pain, brokenness, suffering, and death, and humans have always sought a way to escape this seemingly never-ending cycle. So, because of these four elements: (1) Origin, (2) Morality, (3) Meaning, and (4) Death, we look for answers and solutions. And so philosophy and religion is born. Either the search and quest for absolute truth—or the invention of a relative truth that satisfies our needs and is good enough, whether it's true or not.

Like I said before, I'm convinced that every person that loves truth, desires truth, can cope with truth, and submits their own desires *to* the truth, will ultimately find God. Or, perhaps better stated, if they do so, then *God* will make sure that He is found *by* them. It is God's will to save us, for eternal relationship, for His own glory after all. That might sound like an astoundingly simple statement that seems too simple to be true, but I think it is. For this to be the case we must make three assumptions that I believe are existentially verifiable: (1) there is absolute truth, (2) absolute truth is knowable by humans, and (3) God, in His prevenient grace, has provided a way for all to know and receive truth and so be saved by it. I believe the Bible teaches all these presuppositions.

> John 18:37b ... Jesus answered. "For this reason I was born and have come into the world, to testify to the truth. Everyone who belongs to the truth listens to My voice."

It is our love of and desire for worshipping ourselves, and for wickedness, that causes us to suppress the truth about God, reality, ourselves, morality, and the purpose of our lives. We were created *by* God, *for* God, and to be *with* God. *This* is where our highest fulfillment would be found. *This* is our meaning and purpose. The less in harmony we are with this, the more we search for purpose in other things. We have the ability to reject this truth and become our own god, or to worship and live for other created things.

> Romans 1:18 The wrath of God is being revealed from heaven against all the godlessness and wickedness of men who suppress the truth by their wickedness. [19]For what may be known about God is plain to

them, because God has made it plain to them. ^{20}For since the creation of the world God's invisible qualities, His eternal power and divine nature, have been clearly seen, being understood from His workmanship, so that men are without excuse.

^{25}They exchanged the truth of God for a lie, and worshiped and served the creature rather than the Creator, who is forever worthy of praise! Amen.

The enemy of humanity, Satan, is the father of lies. *(Jn 8:44)* The way that he enslaves us is through lies. The other fallen angels (demons) are also described as lying spirits *(1 Jn 4:1)* who do false wonders *(2 Thes 2:9)*, as are humans that have been deceived and now deceive others. *(2 Tim 3:13, Acts 13:10, Mt 24:24)* They are following philosophies, human traditions, demonic lies, and empty deception—rather than truth. *(Col 2:8, Gal 2:4, 2 Pet 2:1)* If we love and desire his lies and choose to believe him, rather than God, we will do as Adam and Eve did in the Garden of Eden. *(Gen 3)* Inevitably we will end up worshipping something created, whether ourselves, angels, nature, sun, pleasure, hobbies, etc., rather than the Creator. But if we loved truth, we would love God. And if we loved God, we would love truth. If we belonged to God we'd be drawn to the truth. We'd continuously seek to know truth, and desire to conform ourselves to it. We wouldn't resist change. We wouldn't persist in lies just because they are good enough, or because they're comfortable. We'd be willing to change so that we'd have *integrity*—our inner being would be integrated to what is absolutely true, and therefore to God, the Father of all truth. If we love righteousness we'll love truth. And if we love truth we'll be drawn to Jesus.

John 8:42 Jesus said to them, "If God were your Father, you would love Me, for I have come here from God. I have not come on My own, but He sent Me. ^{43}Why do you not understand what I am saying? It is because you are unable to accept My message. ^{44}You belong to your father, the devil, and you want to carry out his desires. He was a murderer from the beginning, refusing to uphold the truth, because there is no truth in him. When he lies, he speaks his native language, because he is a liar and the father of lies. ^{45}But because I speak the truth, you do not believe Me! ^{46}Which of you can prove Me guilty of sin? If I speak the truth, why do you not believe Me? ^{47}Whoever belongs to God hears the words of God. The reason you do not hear is that you do not belong to God."

[Hardness in the End Times prophesied] 2 Thessalonians 2:10 and with every wicked deception directed against those who are perishing,

because they refused the love of the truth that would have saved them. For this reason, God will send them a powerful delusion so that they will believe the lie, in order that all those not having believed the truth but having delighted in unrighteousness should be judged.

The eternal triune God revealed in biblical Christian orthodoxy is the truth. Notice how much truth is emphasized. Jesus, the eternal Word of God that became incarnated as a human, *(Jn 1:1-3, 14)* is called "the truth." *(Jn 14:6)* The apostles saw *"His glory, the glory of the one and only Son from the Father, full of grace and truth." (Jn 1:14)* "For the law was given through Moses; grace and truth came through Jesus Christ." (Jn 1:17)* The Holy Spirit is numerously called "the Spirit of Truth." *(Jn 15:26, 14:17, 16:13)*

In order to be on the path to truth, and to be fully set free from the enslavement caused by Satan's web of lies, you must follow, surrender to, be redeemed by, and become a disciple of Jesus. This isn't a one-time event. Jesus says you must *"continue in His Word," (Jn 8:31)* which is also called *"the word of truth." (Eph 1:13)* You must allow the Holy Spirit, which is also referred to as the Spirit of Christ and the Spirit of God *(Rom 8:9)* to sanctify (purify) every area of your being: your thoughts, feelings, and behaviors. We must worship God in both spirit and truth. *(Jn 4:24)* Not only in the right way, and with the right motivations, but also with the right understanding. We must be born again, and *in* Christ, who is true, who has given us understanding, and through whom we may know Him who is the true God and eternal life. Consider the centrality of "truth" in these:

John 4:24 *[Jesus]* "God is Spirit, and His worshipers must worship Him in spirit and in truth."

John 8:31 So He *[Jesus]* said to the Jews who had believed Him, "If you continue in My word, you are truly My disciples. Then you will know the truth, and the truth will set you free."

John 14:6 Jesus answered, "I am the way, and the truth, and the life. No one comes to the Father except through Me."

1 John 5:20 And we know that the Son of God has come and has given us understanding, so that we may know Him who is true; and we are in Him who is true--in His Son Jesus Christ. He is the true God and eternal life.

Ephesians 4:21 Surely you heard of Him and were taught in Him, in keeping with the truth that is in Jesus, to put off your former way of life, your old self, which is being corrupted by its deceitful desires; to be renewed in the spirit of your minds

Decide today that you will love absolute truth and dedicate yourself to the pursuit of it, no matter how uncomfortable. Love truth so much that you humble yourself regularly, and continue to seek God's will. Refine why you believe what you believe and challenge yourself with the viewpoints of others. Check your own cognitive biases and make sure you're not being influenced by things beyond absolute truth. It's okay to change your mind! It's okay to have been wrong before. Love the truth more than your own comfort! And before you spend countless hours trying to persuade people to come to Jesus, first ask them a few questions to find out if *they care* about truth. If they don't *care* what is true, then all the arguments in the world won't matter, even if you could prove that Jesus is the true way! Many don't deny Jesus because they've genuinely evaluated the evidence and remain unpersuaded. They deny Him because they hate the truth and want to be their own god. Start by asking them, "IF Christianity was TRUE, would you follow Jesus?"

f. Made In God's Image
An unbiblical understanding of human nature leads to many false beliefs.

There are all kinds of false ideas about the nature of humanity. False ideas include everything from the belief that all of reality is just an illusion, that we aren't truly individuals or even physical at all, but merely an "idea" in the mind of "the universe." Others say that we are merely more-evolved animals with higher intelligence and we just invented the idea of spirituality for meaning. Still others say we are actually only souls but are trapped in a physical body and we need to do religious activities to be released. And still even some "Christians" believe that we once existed as a soul, an angel, etc. before receiving bodies at conception. And there are many other false beliefs. The truth is that humans *are* complex beings and if we don't both know, and properly interpret, and then trust, our Bible we will end up with a myriad of false beliefs. These might seem innocent enough at first but they have a trickle-down effect. What we believe about human nature directly impacts what we believe about many other things. This includes what exactly is dead or broken in our current sinful condition, how we view "the flesh" and its relation to the Spirit, the specifics of Jesus's incarnated nature, how a person can exist or function while demon-possessed and what happens when it's exorcised out, what changes when we become "born again" by the Holy Spirit, where and how sanctification happens within us afterwards, what do we become and what happens to us when we die, and what happens during the physical resurrection later. It also directly correlates to how we see, utilize, and care for ourselves now in the present.

After the previous sections you see how essential it is for mankind to have free will in order for God to have a people for Himself, to have eternal relationship with them. A people who knew good and evil, and experienced truthhood and falsehood, and have loved and chosen that which is good and true, and *became* good through Christ. At the same time, we know that there were ongoing consequences after the Fall of Adam. All humans would have the curse of death and the cumulative effects of sin. *(Gen 3)* The Bible teaches that humans are "*dead* in our trespasses and sins" and "fulfilling the cravings of our flesh and indulging its desires and thoughts." *(Eph 2:2-3)* It teaches that sin dwells in all of us, in our flesh, producing death, enslaving us, and inclining us to do evil. *(Rom 7:14-25)* Does this mean our physical bodies are evil, and our souls are a good prisoner inside of them? No, but certainly I can see how Satan can twist the interpretation of Scripture to help people come to this conclusion. The "flesh" needs to be understood, and this book will help you in that regard. In order to know how the rest of our transformation—from evil to good—happens we need to understand how we begin. We will start with the fact that every single human being is made in the image of God.

Understanding Creation. The first chapter of Genesis records the big-picture narrative of creation. Genesis 1:1 describes God creating the entire known spiritual and physical universes at an undisclosed time. Then it zooms in the camera from that point forward, and describes what happens specifically on the planet earth, from the vantage point of the surface of the earth. (Gen 1:2-31) God takes the earth through multiple progressive stages of creation, separated by *yoms*, most commonly translated as "days." Some interpret these as literal 24-hour periods, some as long-but-finite periods of time. Both views are biblical and fine as the word yom does have several different meanings. Regardless of which position you hold, it's possible we're still in God's seventh "rest" day - the start and end of the seventh day is not described in the narrative. We learn that men and women are created in the latter-half of the sixth "day." In the *second* chapter of Genesis we get another camera zoom in that gives us a more detailed perspective about these *same* events that happened during the latter half of the sixth creation day.

Genesis **1:26** Then God said, "Let Us make man in Our image, after Our likeness, to rule over the fish of the sea and the birds of the air, over the livestock, and over all the earth itself and every creature that crawls upon it." ²⁷So God created man in His own image; in the image of God He created him; male and female He created them.

Genesis 2:4 This is the account of the heavens and the earth when they were created, in the day that the LORD God made them. ⁷Then the LORD God formed man from the dust of the ground and breathed the breath of life into his nostrils, and the man became a living being. ²¹So the LORD God caused the man to fall into a deep sleep, and while he slept, He took one of the man's ribs and closed up the area with flesh. ²²And from the rib that the LORD God had taken from the man, He made a woman and brought her to him. ²³And the man said: "This is now bone of my bones and flesh of my flesh; she shall be called 'woman,' for out of man she was taken." ²⁴For this reason a man will leave his father and mother and be united to his wife, and they will become one flesh.

Man? First, God made man in His image and in His likeness. And when I say "man" I mean HU*MAN*. Homo sapien. Every race. Every ethnicity. Every country. Every color. Every size, shape, and age, whether highly intelligent or an ignoramus, whether able-bodied or disabled. The fact that woman was created from man also doesn't negate this. Both men and women are in God's image and likeness. Insert the word "*human*" for "man" and reread it and see it's the same. The word "man" in Genesis 1:27 is also the plural "them" in 1:27, which includes both sexes. Male and female are also the *only* two genders.

How *exactly* are we in God's image? Some think our dominion over the earth and our ruling over the other animals here, or in possessing intellect and emotions, as attributes of God's likeness. Certainly I would *include* these things, and others, as ways we're like God, but they're not the main thing. He appoints us "to rule over..." right afterwards, so saying that would be redundant. Plus, we don't need to be *just* like Him to rule over animals. It says multiple times "*Our* image" and "*His own* image." These are clues. It's plural, and it means something more personal. It's also not the physical design of humankind (whether male or female) that makes us like God. It's something else entirely. God doesn't even *have* a physical image. Ephesians 4:6 says "God is over all and through all and in all." God is a spirit, *(Jn 4:24, 2 Cor 3:17)*, He's invisible, *(1 Tim 1:17, Rom 1:20, Col 1:15)*, He has no image like the idols, *(Deut 4:14-20, Acts 17:29)*, He has no limitations. *(Job 11:7)* "No one can measure the depths of His understanding." *(Isa 40:28)* God is "the first and the last." *(Isa 44:6, 43:10)* He existed prior to physicality. Prior to a creation. God is more like an infinitely powerful *mind* without any boundaries, than He is like a physical human. He is omnipresent, intelligent, spiritually deep, and emotionally and relationally complex. And God created us to be "in His likeness." Humans have many of these attributes, just in a limited way. Just as God is spirit, so are we—well, partially. He made us spiritual too, capable of having a renewed spirit, communing with Him in spirit, and worshipping Him in spirit and in truth. *(Jn 4:23-24)* God is singular in essence, but triune—He's *complex in His unity*. Like God, we are singular in essence, but complex in our unity. We're not triune, but I personally believe that we *are* tripartite: spirit, soul, body.

You *are* a soul, united with spirit, and a body.

It is our spiritual nature that is most like God. Not our *physical* nature, since we know that God doesn't even have a body. We also know that the body is carbon-based, made out of the "dust" of the earth, and then God breathed life into it. Our body is "dust" just like all the animals. As archaeology, biology, and genetics show our bodies are similar to other animals, especially other bipedal primates like the great apes or the Neanderthals. So, it's not our bodies. What about being like Him in our *soulish* nature? In many ways, yes. We have will, intellect, desire, emotions, personality, talents, etc. These are soulish attributes that give us personhood, i.e. individual identity. This is necessary, as without it we wouldn't be able to know God or have any kind of meaningful relationship with Him. However, for several reasons not even our soulish nature is the *most* like God.

The Soul. God created many *soulish* (nephesh) creatures. Many of the animals created in Genesis 1 are also described as soulish. So even though the "soul" is thought of by many as a "thing" inside of a person, something that can be lost, trapped in a body, sold to the devil, etc., this is not biblical. A "soul" (nephesh) is a living being, a life, a *self*, an individualized entity that has intellect, emotions, desires, talents, passions, memories. In order words, we don't *have* a soul—we *are* a soul! You've probably had a close bond with a pet. They are living, breathing, thinking, feeling creatures. They aren't emotionless rocks. They are soulish, too. And like I noted with the Neanderthals, who have a similar body plan, they possessed some of our soulish qualities, too. The more intelligent and physically capable the animal the more personality and potential it has as an individualized soul. I'm not saying that animals are an *eternal* soul, like humans are, but they're still a soul, that lives and thinks and feels. However, none of these other animals seek higher meaning and purpose in life, transcend the spiritual plane and commune with God or other spirit beings, worship, create music, develop societies, etc—only human beings do. These other animals don't have a *spirit* (pneuma), at least not beyond merely just being alive. But humans are unique, we are a soul-*spirit* with a body.

You don't *have* a soul—you *are* a soul!

Two parts or three? Throughout history many Christian theologians have combined the human soul and spirit into one entity, so that humans are duopartite (two-parts). Here the "flesh" referred to in the Bible is the body, and then the soul-spirit are a separate combined entity. That's option one. Option two is that God united the spirit and body together and made them a single, integrated (unified) soul. Either of these views is okay.

They are biblical, but there's a third option I think is even *more* biblical: the trichotomic or tripartite (i.e. three-part) view: that the body, soul, and spirit are all distinct but integrated together in humans. If you're not sure keep these different views in mind to see how they affect other things later. When we get to secondary doctrines I think you'll find the three part view fits best with what the Bible teaches. But what matters *most* for the right map now is knowing humans are a unity of material (physical) and immaterial (spiritual) aspects, and all are good, but all have been tarnished by sin.

Three-part view. Before I move on I just want to do a quick defense of the three part view. First argument, this view corresponds to several passages in Scripture which make clear distinctions between all three parts, like 1 Thessalonians 5:22-24. Here, Paul prays that the Holy Spirit would sanctify *every* part of us completely (*holoteleis*) and entirely (*holokleron*): (*pneuma*) spirit, (*psyché*) soul, and (*soma*) body. Unlike the other verses often cited by the opponents of this view, this verse is *specifically* talking about describing all of the parts of our human nature that the sanctification process occurs in, specifically in "born-again" Christians. So it really doesn't get more specific than that!

---

1 Thessalonians 5:23 Now may the God of peace Himself sanctify you completely, and may your entire spirit, soul, and body be kept blameless at the coming of our Lord Jesus Christ.

Second argument. The Bible does sometimes use "body" and "soul" interchangeably, and "spirit" and "soul" interchangeably. However, I've found that anywhere this occurs it can easily be understood by interpreting the text with a trichotomic view. Meaning the trichotomic view incorporates all other Biblical doctrine, but the reverse isn't true. For example, in Ezekiel 18:20 God says, "The *soul* who sins shall die." We wouldn't understand this to be saying the "soul and spirit" will die but the body will live. Neither would we understand this saying the "soul and body" will die but the spirit will live. No, God is just saying that "the *person* who sins will die"—and that includes every living part of them. Another example of where others claim soul and spirit are used interchangeably is Luke 1:46-47, *"Then Mary said: 'My soul magnifies the Lord, and my spirit rejoices in God my Savior!'"* Here we can see both "parts" are in agreement, but is this *really* teaching that they are the same entity? First, she uses two different words, that alone should give us pause to think these are two distinct things, even if closely related. This actually shows her *soul* (i.e. her life, emotions, and thoughts) as her *being*—while her *spirit* is the driving internal connection and communion between her and God. Doesn't it make sense interpreted this way: "My entire soul (*being and all of my heart, mind, and emotions*) magnifies the Lord, and my spirit (*spiritual-life-force within me*) rejoices in God my Savior!"

I want to leave a few additional thoughts that I think will help us all, regardless of opinions, to remain united on this, by offering some important concessions. One, both the soul and the spirit are immaterial. Because of this they have spiritual commonalities. I see the realms of our *being*, our soul (different aspects of our life, thoughts, emotions, desires, etc.) as spiritual things. We can't organize all of our emotions and stack them in a pile. Two, the spirit and soul are also both deeply interconnected and inseparable. If your spirit dies, your soul (i.e. "you") die too. It is your life essence. Likewise, if any part of *you* die, your spirit dies with it. If you lose your life essence, the "you" that is you, ceases to exist as well. I believe they are *distinct* things but make no mistake about it

25

they are still inseparable. There is nothing wrong with thinking of your soul—you—as a spiritual being with a body. When we die the body goes into the ground and the rest of us (soul-and-spirit) goes somewhere else until the resurrection. So, in many instances I think of soul and spirit as a single, combined unit as well. However, the rest of this section, and throughout the book, I'm going to assume a tripartite view. I just ask you to keep an open mind and consider it as you see how it interrelates to everything else later.

The Body. Listen up brethren: the body is *good*. I hear too much about "the flesh" being evil. This is usually by the same Christians who deny that demons are still active in the world, or deny that demons have the ability to influence or cohabitate in the hearts and minds of people, so "the flesh" gets ALL the blame for every sinful thing! Or they interpret passages such as "*dead* in our sins and trespasses" *(Eph 2:1, 5, Col 2:13)* to mean that we're *actually* and *totally* dead. Meaning that the physical body isn't capable of anything at all. I think this is false. The flesh is demonized—instead of *actual* demons! The flesh is getting all the blame, for things that are our own choices that we *are* capable of changing and are responsible for! And if demons or curses or spiritual things are the cause, they won't be resolved because we're always blaming the body. Something we all have for life! So it's an endless cycle of perpetual victimhood. That's not empowering!

Caveat, we *are* spiritually dead—rather, *dying*— meaning that we are naturally in active rebellion to God, living wickedly and immorally. We began in an unsaved state, cut off and estranged from God, the source of life. We had no fellowship with God, and were under His wrath, and we are dead in *that* sense. Our spiritual nature and our conscience are seared and are dead-dying, and we're dead in *that* sense. And our physical body is under the curse of original sin, is absolutely sinful and depraved, is predisposed and inclined to desire that which is wicked, and is literally decaying, and we're dead in *that* sense. However, our "deadness" is not all the body part of us. And, despite this, we're still responsible. We're response-able. At the end of the Parable of the Prodigal Son the rebellious prodigal returns home to his father who graciously forgives and welcomes him back into the family. He exclaims, twice, "*For this son of mine was DEAD and is ALIVE again!*" *(Luke 15:24, 32)* The son was dead in one sense, but not like bones in a grave. He was still actually quite alive and doing sinful activities. He wasn't unable to be humbled or to repent and return. As it is with us. We all start life in the pigpen.

To be clear, the flesh *does* deserve *some* of the blame, and we do need to rightly understand the consequences of the Fall on our nature (all parts). We will get to that later. It's worth repeating that even in our best efforts we can *never* be "good enough" on our own. We need Jesus. We need the cross. We need His righteousness. We need His indwelling presence to sanctify us from our uncleanness, and His spiritual life to restore every part of our deadness. But for right now, as it relates to our "deadness" I want to make it clear that despite the many limitations we have in the flesh, we are STILL capable of being humble and repenting to God. Humility and repentance is not something we're unable to do, nor is it a "work." It wasn't when the prodigal realized he was foolish and miserable in his filthy pigpen and returned home to grovel at his father's feet. We are all (hopefully-former) prodigals, no doubt. But God, in His grace, has given us all the ability in our deadened state to still recognize our need to return home to our Father.

I also want to empower you through a shift in perspective, to have better discernment and recognize what the true sources of our problems are. When we blame the flesh for everything, and continually talk about it as though it's not capable of anything good at all, we *empower* the sinful aspects of our flesh, or demons and other spiritual things, to have more power over us than they should. The same with empowering our bad habits, as though they are unchangeable, lifelong issues, or are more difficult than they actually are. We have a BIG God! And yet many Christians struggle with the same besetting sins for YEARS! They have empowered their own sin nature, or demons, through disempowering lies, beliefs, emotions, and practices. And when we deny the reality of—or the ability of, or the great extent of—demonic influence in people's lives, then demons get a free pass to stay and continue to destroy, while we counsel-to-death the flesh with obviously limited success. Too many in the Church are far from holy, sanctified, and empowered in large part because they're either making excuses for the flesh, or misdiagnosing it as the cause. In chapter three I go into detail on this, but for now, just know the body isn't *all* bad.

There are religions who say the body is evil. I expose these later on. God created the human body and said "it was very good." *(Gen 1:31)* It's part of God's good design for humans to be body, soul, and spirit. We didn't exist as souls prior to getting a body. The body is not evil. Adam was unique, who was first a body and then God breathed life (soul and spirit) into him uniting them as one living being. But all the rest of us became a living person when body, soul, and spirit were united together, at the moment of our conception, and the breath of life from God was passed down to us. The body isn't bad, it is still the vehicle for life on earth. The tongue has *both* death and life in it. The Word of God became incarnated into body as the man Jesus. That wouldn't have happened if flesh, itself, was bad. Jesus rose from the dead in His same-yet-transformed-and-glorified physical body. We will all be resurrected one day also in a physical body. Jesus and all the rest of us will eternally have a physical body. The "flesh," despite its weaknesses, still has intrinsic value.

Christians need to value our bodies, they are the temple of the Holy Spirit! *(1 Cor 3:16, 6:19)* Take care of yourself! Take care of your health, exercise, eat healthy, get plenty of rest, get medical check-ups, don't work yourself to death, don't allow yourself to become overburdened and overstressed, etc. or otherwise neglect your physical, mental, and emotional needs. Your body was given to you by God as a gift. Just like every other thing in your life, it is your Christian responsibility to be grateful for it and *steward* it wisely for the glory of God! Way too many Christians neglect this. They legalistically forbid smoking cigarettes or drinking alcohol, yet do not see the hypocrisy of gluttony, harmful addictions, unhealthy diet habits, lack of exercise, obesity, or working 80 hours a week to stressful exhaustion. These may be socially acceptable in the church but they're bad stewardship.

Yes, our bodies are broken because of sin and we need to wage war against the sinful desires of the flesh. *(1 Pet 2:11, Rom 7:13-25)* Yes, because of sin, our bodies are continuously decaying and dying and nothing we do via maintenance or good stewardship is going to stop that. Yes, regardless of what happens to us physically in this life, we're going to get our body back one day renewed, awesome, and glorified. Still, love on your body! Be grateful for it. Take care of it. Use it to glorify God! Discover your unique talents. Discover God's unique purpose for designing you the way He did. There was a plan for ALL of it. There is an ideal you, with amazing potential for all of us. Don't let Satan destroy your self esteem and get you to hate your body. To be consumed with the way you look compared to others. Your talents, etc., compared to others. No! God formed you in your innermost being. He knit you together in your mother's womb. You are fearfully and wonderfully made! *(Jer 1:5, Ps 139:14)* Marvelous are His works, and you are no exception! Respond with praise! Do your best to stay attractive for your spouse and serve them lovingly by meeting their physical needs. Stay healthy so you can have more time on earth for your family, your church, your community. Discover and develop your talents, and stay learned, healthy, and strong so you can fulfill your unique calling in the world. You only get one body in this life—so take care of it!

Rightly understood, the body is weak but good. It's a Christian's duty to be grateful for theirs and to steward it well for the glory of God.

The Spirit. Last but not least is our *spirit* nature. This is the most important part of our nature when it comes to understanding how we're made God's image, how we've been affected by sin, and how that changes after we're born again in Christ. I'll go into more detail on these things later, so let me just summarize what's special and unique about our spirit nature that's distinct from our soul. Our soul is "us," our identity, our individuality. Our *spirit* is the part of us most like God. It's also the part of us that's like the angels (and fallen angels, i.e. demons) who are *spirit* beings. There's also a spiritual realm on earth. I believe this is also called the Abyss and the "second heaven." See my notes[3] for an article I wrote for more on that. It's only because we have a spiritual nature that we can interact with, pray to, or receive from either God or other spiritual beings.

Our spiritual nature was given to us by God who desired us to have a relationship with Him. Unfortunately, it also gives us access to everything else that is spiritual as well. It is the various false spiritual practices of fallen humanity that provide an artificial spirituality. Through these mechanisms people embrace this important part of our nature, but they do so to their own destruction by communing with demons. We have the ability to commune with demons, in our spirit, which *affects* our souls, but it does not change the fact that we remain an individual. Even fully demon-possessed people in the Bible are people *with* a demon. They don't become a demon themselves. They are still a unique soul, with a spirit being cohabiting them, *in* their soul and body. And those of us who have become born-again and received the Holy Spirit, we didn't stop being an individual soul right after either. Our "soulish" attributes—our thoughts, emotions, talents, memories, desires, etc.—don't get instantly erased! No, our "spirit" nature *alone* was born again. Our soul and body aren't *immediately* or fully affected when we are justified and regenerated. They're affected through sanctification, which is the ongoing process of the Holy Spirit changing the rest of us to make us more like Christ. *(1 Thes 5:23, Eph 5:25-27)* Because we don't cease to be a unique soul by either having a demonic spirit, or by receiving the Holy Spirit, our soul and spirit *cannot logically* be the same thing.

Another important difference between the soul and spirit, is our spirit nature is where the human conscience is. The conscience is not our soul. We are not our conscience. It is independent from us and is external to who we are. Often, our conscience testifies against us and makes us feel guilty for what we're already doing or did, that our soul *wanted* to do. The soul drove our action, our instinct, that is "us." The conscience is separate, as it is not the part responsible for *causing* the very thing that it is also making us feel guilty for *doing*. That would be contradictory. It cannot both love and hate the action simultaneously. No, the sinful desires come from us, our soul, or they come from the dead-dying body or spirit. The conscience is lawful, it comes from the part of us still *alive*, the part of us that is *still* obeying God. The conscience is the Law of God that is written into every single person. This is how even unregenerate heathens, who do not have the law, can still do by nature what the law requires, as Romans 2 teaches. God's moral law has been given to every person, and their consciences bear witness against them, either accusing or defending them, so they're without excuse on Judgment Day.

The conscience is an essential part of the human makeup that convicts us of our own sinfulness and draws us to our need for a Savior. It's only those who: (1) hate the truth, (2) love wickedness, and (3) suppress the truth in unrighteousness, who don't *rejoice* to hear the glorious gospel about Jesus bearing their guilt and punishment on their behalf. This isn't good news to them, so they reject Him, because they've convinced themselves they're already good by their own standards. They've rejected God as their god, and have become their own god. They reject God's moral law as their law, opting to creating their own law with their own preferences. Yes, God can choose to "give us over," meaning He stops *externally* trying to convict us. He does so because we choose to suppress our conscience, hardening our hearts, rejecting its prompting. But no one is without the *ability* to respond to it. If it were so then anyone could blame God of wrongdoing on Judgment Day, for they were without ability to do anything else but evil. No, God's Word declares that there is none without excuse! All humans are responsible for responding to God's grace via the conscience and to circumcise our own hearts. More on this later.

God is spirit. Humans are spirit, soul, body. It's in our spirit nature where we're *most* like God's image and likeness.

Romans 2:14 Indeed, when Gentiles, who do not have the law, do by nature what the law requires, they are a law to themselves, even though they do not have the law, [15]since they show that the work of the law is written on their hearts, their consciences also bearing witness, and their thoughts either accusing or defending them. [16]This will come to pass on that day when God will judge men's secrets through Christ Jesus, as proclaimed by my gospel.

[28]A man is not a Jew because he is one outwardly, nor is circumcision only outward and physical. [29]No, a man is a Jew because he is one inwardly, and circumcision is a matter of the heart, by the Spirit, not by the written code. Such a man's praise does not come from men, but from God.

Jeremiah 4:4 *[God]* Circumcise yourselves to the LORD, and remove the foreskins of your hearts, O men of Judah and people of Jerusalem. Otherwise, My wrath will break out like fire and burn with no one to extinguish it, because of your evil deeds."

Summary. The correct road map on this has us viewing all of us as God's image bearers. This will dramatically affect how we see, interact with, and treat all other human beings. Every human has a conscience, regardless of how dead it is due to suppressing the truth in unrighteousness. All are capable of being convicted of their sinfulness and seeing their need for Jesus. Since all humans are made in God's image and likeness, as a soul united to spirit and body, our *physical* appearance is irrelevant. This truth alone should eradicate any perceived significance of race, color, ethnicity, or racial superiority or inferiority. It should change the cultural philosophies and political policies we support. Since we receive God's breath of life at conception that means every human life is sacred and valuable, especially our most vulnerable. Therefore, abortion is unacceptable, as it's the willful killing of an innocent human soul and spirit, regardless of the level of development of the body. All humans have a spiritual nature, this is how unsaved people can still have spiritual experiences. But without Scripture to guide them to truth, they are very likely to end up in error and become ensnared by the lies of Satan. Christians are temples of the Holy Spirit and we need to take care of every part of our being. We need to allow the Holy Spirit to sanctify us completely: all of our spirit, soul, and body.

g. Understanding Free Will
To love God, or not to love God, that is the question...

Let's summarize a few things we've learned so far. God created angels and humans. God is a loving and relational being and He created us with the capacity to freely love and have relationship with Him. By creating truly free beings there would be the potential for them to sin against Him. God foreknew that there would be both an angelic and a human rebellion into sin, which would displease Him. However, this would enable Him to predetermine, establish, and then fulfill a glorious plan of redemption by which many will be graciously saved, by Himself, by bearing on Himself the just punishment that they deserve. He would be glorified in at least the following four ways: (1) through the grace He extends to all rebellious creatures by not destroying them instantly after sinning, (2) through the offer of a plan of redemption, (3) through the self-sacrificial way He became the very Savior of many, and (4) through the interpersonal restoration process. Free will, choice, and faith, are the *vehicles* that God is using to determine if we actually love Him, or not. If we desire to live a reality around His attributes, or not.

The plan of redemption (through salvation, by His grace, through their faith in Jesus) will not only glorify God, and determine if we love Him, it has another benefit: it teaches the people being saved *who God is*. Rather than just telling us that He is loving, He is showing us that He is. Rather than just telling us how holy and distinct He is, and how the world isn't (as demonstrated by the fact that it will hate you if you're holy too) He is showing us. Rather than just saying sin/rebellion to Him leads to death and separation from Him, He lets us experience a dying-life first *without* Him. And then teaches us that we will need to die to our old life of sin that leads to death, and find our new life with Him in Christ, that leads to eternal life. Rather than just saying how He is just and will judge all sin, He executes His wrath on sin in front of us—on His Son on the cross at calvary. The cross was the intersection of perfect love and perfect justice. The execution of God's full wrath on all evil, but received by the perfect, blameless, sinless, Son of God.

In all of these things, God teaches us about Himself, and DRAWS us to Himself, through them. They are like guideposts to Him, pointing to our need for Him ultimately, and to our Savior, Jesus. Rather than just commanding orders to obey Him and love Him whether we want to or not—like the "god" of Islam does—He shows WHY He is worthy of all of our love and worship. He reveals His awesome and beautiful attributes to us. He shows us that He *actually is* a loving Father to us. Rather than just saying "Love Me, because I said so, I created you and you have to", God shows us His beauty, in the Gospel, so that if there is ANY goodness in us at all, we can't help but repent and love Him in response! Why is "goodness in us" a requirement? Because it is remaining goodness in us that looks at the brokenness and suffering in the world, and the sinfulness of our own hearts, that becomes the catalyst for humility and our confession of our need of a Savior.

**Rather than just saying "Love Me, because I said so,
I created you and you have to" God reveals the depths
of His Love and Beauty in the Gospel,
so if there's any goodness in us, we *can't help*
but repent and love Him in response!**

In the final analysis, those who will inherit eternal life will love God, not arbitrarily, but because they know who He *is*, and love that about Him. They will also feel loved by God, who they will know, personally, as their gracious and beautiful Savior. They will be able to recall being lost in their former lives, drowning in the depths of their sin, and God's gracious mercy overwhelming them in the moment they cried out to Jesus. They will have experienced relationship and sanctification and walked with God through life. They will have voluntarily surrendered their own free will to sin, in submission to God's will. More on the purpose of free will to know, love, and choose good, in the next section.

h. Knowing Good and Evil
The Fall helps us know evil, but have the opportunity to love and choose good.

I've heard many Christians say that our goal is to get back to Eden. Back to where we were innocent. "If *only* Adam and Eve hadn't sinned, we could've lived there forever!" This is just not deeply biblical once you go below the surface. I get their sentiment on the surface level, but philosophically speaking, it shows a very shallow understanding of God and the human story. Something I'm hoping this book has already begun to change. Was that God's intention, for us to live in Eden forever? Was the fall an accident? Did God not foresee of that possibility in creating free will beings? Not foreknow it was going to happen? Not allow it to happen and plan to use it for His own glory? Of course He did! Could God have made them and not even put a forbidden tree there in Eden at all? Yep! Could He not have allowed Satan to go and tempt them? Yep!

Let's back up one level before beings were made. If God could create us with free will, with *full* knowledge and revelation of who He is, and live with us for all eternity in perfect loving relationship, wouldn't He? Why create this relatively-short period (compared to all the rest of eternity) with so much death and pain and confusion and eternal consequence for so many? We've already looked at many passages that show that God is *also* grieved by the things we've done, and the separation, suffering, and death as a result. If God doesn't enjoy every aspect of it either, and He was in a position to create everything in an entirely different way, a way that accomplished the *exact same end result*, He probably would have! For us to think otherwise is to have a perspective that limits God's foreknowledge, or power, or goodness. We shouldn't concede that unless it's out of logical necessity. One thing we can have confidence of: God knows what He's doing. He's God! Trust that *this* reality and timeline we find ourselves in is the *absolute best* reality and timeline possible to achieve His ultimate goal. The reality and timeline with maximum good results and minimum bad. The timeline with maximum glory to God. The timeline with God's glory revealed to His creations the best possible way. If the *very first* two humans sinned we can be sure that it was part of God's overarching plan to allow for that. Matter of fact, did you ever stop and think why the very first two people? Why not their children, or their great grandchildren, or even ten thousand years later? God didn't *have* to let the tempter in there, right from the beginning, nor did there even need to exist a forbidden-yet-easily-accessible tree either. No, it was part of the plan! It wasn't an accident. God knew it was going to happen as soon as He gave free will creatures the ability to sin, with a strong enough temptation to sin.

It was our free will that led to the Fall, that is absolutely on us (humanity). I am NOT saying that God set us up to fail. He didn't. He gave us everything we needed to succeed. Adam and Eve knew God, and they walked and talked with Him. *(Gen 3:8)* Adam knew God as his father that both loved him and was powerful and generous enough to voluntarily offer to make his wife for him. And gave her to him as a *gift. (Gen 2:22)* Someone who pleased him immensely. And He gave them rule over the whole garden. They weren't under the impression that God was holding out on them. Yet, despite this, God *knew* they would give in to Satan's temptation. And not only would *they* do it, all humans would. They can represent all of humanity because of this, we are in Adam's likeness. *(1 Cor 15:49)*

Make no mistake about it, the fall was not an unforeseen, unfortunate accident that took God by surprise. Humanity inevitably falling was *included* in God's plan *before* He even created us. He foreknew that it was going to happen and then afterwards still created us, cast Satan to the earth to allow *his* sinful rebellion to God to act as our first tempter, and then allowed the fall to happen. Now, it didn't *have* to be the very first two people, lol! I mean humanity could have been obedient and successful longer than that, but it was still going to happen eventually. God foresaw the same exact thing before He created the angels. He knew Lucifer/Satan would become depraved and lead a fall there as well. All these things are part of God's long-term plan. The sooner we understand that, the sooner we have a more robust and grounded worldview and adjust our maps accordingly.

Ephesians 1:4 For He chose us in Him *[Christ]* before the foundation of the world to be holy and blameless in His presence... [10]as a plan for the fullness of time, to bring all things in heaven and on earth together in Christ.

Matthew 25:34 *[Jesus]* Then the King will say to those on His right, 'Come, you who are blessed by my Father, inherit the kingdom prepared for you from the foundation of the world.

Free will is real. So God is writing a long-term story, an eternal one actually. I believe genuine free will is an essential part of the creation-fall-redemption-restoration story that God is writing. Not just the illusion of free will. Not just partial free will. Not "everything except for salvation" free will. Without genuine free will we would just be going through the motions. We would just be puppets on the stage, that He is ultimately controlling. What a deterministic and fatalistic thought! Is there *highest* glory in that? God making the puppets believe, think, and feel it's real, that they are being saved from *their own* sin, because He loves them and calls them, and wants to have relationship eternally. But He is the only One who chooses to effectually cause them to begin to hate sin and repent and have faith? I don't think that's what the Bible teaches, or the heart of the true gospel, or what the person of Jesus reveals to us. It also makes God the author of all sin, Satan, the fall, etc. What a terrible suggestion that not only makes God the author of sin, it also suggests that He receives glory because of it! If His intention was to be glorified by revealing His true nature to us in that way, but He had to effectually cause it, I believe He could have just designed us for eternity *already knowing* this about Him.

There is a BIG difference between ALLOWING sin to happen and then *using* it—and CAUSING it to happen!

No, God does not need to author sin just so that He can receive glory by judging it. That's not true sovereignty. God is infinite, powerful, all-knowing and all-seeing. I fully believe that He could make beings capable of free will, who choose to sin on their absolute own. He endures with much patience our rebellion, and is sovereign over allowing for everything. We receive His grace or His judgment. And does it in a way that it ultimately leads some of them to have a deeper and more intimate and beautiful relationship with Him in the end. Sinner's are *without excuse! (Rom 1:20)* Adam and Eve undoubtedly encountered Jesus and were saved and restored back to God through what He accomplished at Calvary. And after experiencing this much deeper knowledge of who God is, and how merciful He is, and how much He loves them, they will forever be changed by that knowledge. Their relationship with God is better *after* the Fall! Now they know good and evil. The tree, tempter, temptation, fall, redemption, and restoration, gave them knowledge and wisdom, which begins with the fear of the Lord. *(Prov 9:10)* Their relationship is much deeper now—as it is for all of us who have been saved! Every single one of us has experienced the exact same salvation. This is no coincidence. The guiltiness and conviction of our sin against God, remorse and then repentance, and then the receipt of His gracious gift of salvation by faith in Christ, the satisfaction for our sins. And then even the ongoing forgiveness of our shortcomings throughout our lives on our way towards perfection. We are called to live our lives loving and striving towards goodness, and God molds us to become like Him along that journey. Yes, there is something nice about the idea of having never fallen in the first place. About never having tasted sin or suffering or death or separation from God. However, now that we have experienced it we more highly esteem its opposite, and we know and love and value our Savior for delivering us from it! This means that the fall, ultimately, has a *net positive* effect.

As difficult as our life in a fallen world is, it was actually a *net positive* gift from God, to be used to reveal Himself to us as our Savior!

Knowledge of good and evil. Let me dispel a myth. People have messaged me accusing God of doing evil in the Garden of Eden. They claim that Adam and Eve didn't know any better *before* they ate so it was unfair that God punished them, and the rest of humanity, as a result. That until they *ate* from the tree of "the knowledge of good and evil" they had no knowledge of these things. The truth is that they did have *knowledge* of good and evil prior to the Fall, they just didn't have the *experience* of evil prior to the Fall. They knew the difference between "what we're permitted to do and not permitted to do." That's knowledge. They had that the moment God gave them instructions about the tree. Doing what God wants is good, not doing what God wants is evil. They even *knew* of the consequences if they did evil: they would die. They had knowledge, just not firsthand experience. And we could take this even one step farther. As soon as Satan (the serpent) came to them and accused God of evil of lying to them, having selfish motives, and not loving them, he gave them *even more* knowledge of evil! They had the ability to decide who to trust and who not to. Who really cared for them and who didn't. Which action was good for them, and which action was evil for them. All this before even touching or eating the fruit. They had all the benefits of knowledge, without having firsthand experience of the consequence. God said the pot was hot, don't touch it, it'll burn your hand. Satan said the pot isn't hot, it won't burn your hand, you'll receive wisdom if you touch it. They did *know* not to touch it, they'd just never been burned before. They had a choice. Trust God or trust the serpent. Trust the one they actually *knew*, who was their father, the one who gave them the entire garden to cultivate, the one who created Eve and gave them each another to love. Or trust the new guy they just met, and his enticing temptation to become like God themselves. So that they don't have to submit to God or answer to anyone else but themselves. It is EXACTLY like the human temptation we all face. We choose who we will believe and trust. Either God (His Word/Bible) or Satan, the world, or ourselves.

God was then, and is now, looking for FAITH (trust) in Him, demonstrated through obedience.

The foundation of this lie is this: opponents claim that the story is telling us that the tree *provided* the knowledge of good and evil. That, when they eat of it, they would *gain* this knowledge. All kinds of cults are based on this idea, that God wanted to keep them *from* gaining knowledge. From ancient Gnosticism the early church went up against (which comes from the Greek work gnosis, which means knowledge) to many modern false religions and teachings. We all know knowledge is good so we struggle with that. But like everything else Satan inspires, it's truth-twisting. Adam and Eve *already knew* the difference between good and evil *before* the Fall! What they didn't have was the experience of *having done* evil. The tree itself did NOT provide this knowledge. The human conscience did, and subsequently God did directly through the verbal command to avoid it. The tree was just the *object* for which the real imperative could be directed at.

For example, let's say God says to you and me, "Thou shall not murder. If you do you will die." We know that murder is evil and we know our death is the consequence. It's not that we have to murder someone, and then at the very moment that we do, we receive the knowledge of murder being evil. No, we already knew that if we believed God when He said it. Committing murder would just be the moment we personally *experienced* the evil firsthand, having committed the action itself, with it now bearing witness to our conscience. This same scenario happened with their son Cain, who also gave in to this temptation. *(Gen 4:7)*

Romans 5:19 For just as through the disobedience of the one man the many were made sinners, so also through the obedience of the one man the many will be made righteous. [20]The law came in so that the trespass would increase; but where sin increased, grace increased all the more, [21]so that, just as sin reigned in death, so also grace might reign through righteousness to bring eternal life through Jesus Christ our Lord.

2 Peter 3:13 But in keeping with God's promise, we are looking forward to a new heaven and a new earth, where righteousness dwells.

After committing evil Adam and Eve had to be removed from God's presence because He is righteous and cannot tolerate the presence of sin. But God taught them how to get right with Him using the sacrificial system right away. All this pointing already to Jesus. Have you ever noticed that God Himself does the very first sacrifice? He even clothes Adam and Eve with the skins of the animal afterwards. *(Gen 3:21)* In the next chapter we see Cain and Abel offering sacrifices to the Lord as well. *(Gen 4:3-4)* Though they were already fallen, dead in their sins too, God offers the opportunity to love goodness and do what is right, and so be accepted by Him. We don't even have to be guilty of the outward action of sin yet for us to decide to love good. Even the *temptation* of the heart to love evil is enough for us to choose. God says to Cain in Genesis 4:7, "If you do what is *right*, will you not be accepted? But if you refuse to do what is right, sin is crouching at your door; it desires you, but you must master it." We can do what is right and be accepted, or we can refuse to do what is right and become mastered by sin.

Even though the sins of man have brought death and separation from God, the plan of redemption through Christ brings life and restoration with God. It is through the plan of redemption in Christ that humans receive the deeper revelation of God. The Fall and the temptations help us *know* evil—but hopefully love and choose good. So now, all those being saved receive all of the following: (1) the full knowledge of good and evil, (2) having personally committed and experienced the consequences of evil, (3) experienced the grief and sorrow as a result of being a sinner, and repented of their evil, (4) having loved what is good and chosen to become a slave to righteousness, and (5) are being renewed daily into the good image of righteousness in Christ. We are now *declared* good (justified), and are *being made* good (sanctified), and one day we will be resurrected and established as *actually* good (glorified). *(Rom 8:28-31)* All this we play a role in, with Jesus as the author and perfecter of our faith. *(Heb 12:2)* This is the eternal benefit of the fall. Without *experiencing* evil we wouldn't *know* what is good and love it eternally the same way. What is good? Anything that is *like* God's character. All that which glorifies Him.

i. What Do You Want?
Do you love goodness and truth, and want glory, honor, and immortality?

Let's get personal. What do YOU want? Really. Seriously. The universe, and everything in it, including you, was created for God's glory. Is that what you want, to participate in and celebrate God's glory? God made us in His image and likeness, gave us a spiritual nature, revealed His triune, interpersonal nature, and invited us into a relationship with Himself for eternity through Christ. Is that what you want to be doing? Knowing God, being known by God, and celebrating His glory? His Word tells us that if we love goodness and truth we will be drawn to this. Do you feel drawn to this? What do you *really* want?

If I say often "I want to be in great physical shape," and then I neglect the gym and healthy eating and continue to get in worse shape, would you still *believe* me? Sure, I may desire to be in good shape, don't we all, but the truth is that I have stronger desires that contradict that one. What if I said "Having a healthy marriage is very important to me." But then because it's football season, I neglect to spend time with my spouse doing any relationship-bonding activities I could be doing. And when my spouse proposes the idea of a marriage retreat for some alone time to work on us, I shoot the idea down without much consideration. Would you still believe me? Or do my actions speak louder than my words? The truth is obvious. It's not what we say, or even what we desire. Our actions reveal our true desires.

You see because of our conscience, the law of God written on our hearts, we all have some idea of what we *should* do. What is most good. This is often a vague "ideal," the thing we talk about having, perhaps even do wish we had, even though our actions show what we *really* want. We all want things if we don't have to change our behavior to get them. All of us would check the "be in great physical shape" box on the checklist if that's all it took to get it. But anything worth having comes with effort. And unless you are actively trying to achieve it, and failing daily, and then trying again, and then trying new and different ways, it's because you really don't want what you say you want, as bad as you think you do. I know this is a harsh truth, but you *are* on a search for truth...... right?

Truth Bomb: Our actions reflect what we actually value much more than our thoughts or words do.

When we're honest with ourselves we know this is true. And if *we* know it, don't you think God does too? You bet! This is why God doesn't judge us foremost by our words, but by our actions. Our words *do* matter, because our words proceed from our heart. If the heart is good then the words are, too. But actions demonstrate more. But it's not only our *outward* actions that matter. It's the inner motivations of our heart, that provoke us to act, that matter. It's not enough that we just do what is good and right, it's that we *actually love* what is good and right, and desire to do it for the right *reasons*. But take heart, we aren't expected to be perfect this side of Heaven. The right reason and motivation is *our desire to be like Christ*, to actually be perfect. To please our Heavenly Father and live for His glory. To actually love goodness and truth and continually seek to grow deeper in both. To want glory and honor and immortality. If we want these things we will be drawn to Jesus. He is the ONLY way to perfection. No other religion can even attempt to offer an alternative way. Our recognition of how far we fall short of not only our own standards, but God's glory, and our humble and sincere heart's desire to please Him, is what God is looking for. We demonstrate this through genuine repentance over our sinfulness, and total trust in Jesus for His sacrifice and imputed righteousness, as evidenced by our life of faithfulness, obedience, and good works.

So, is this what you have done? Is this what you are doing daily? It's essential that you realize that you can't just talk the talk, you've got to walk the walk. And you've got to be in communion with God, and with His Church, and always seeking for God to help take you to the next level. God *will* change you but you have to really submit, fight the good fight, run the race. Be on a daily mission to extinguish every trace of falsehood and wickedness in you, because that's what the Holy Spirit wants to do if He is in you! Jesus hates lukewarm; it's not even an option. Settling for "decent enough" is a major red flag, especially in our vastly sinful and corrupt world. If you're not or barely different than the unsaved people around you that should concern you. The Bible teaches that we are to shine like lights in a dark world. So, decide now what you REALLY want. And remember if you really actually want it there will be evidence of it! Do you seek glory? Do you seek honor? Do you seek immortality? If you do, put your desire in these things to action. A good tree bears good fruit. Neither can a bad tree bear good fruit. *(Mt 7:15-20)* I pray that you persevere in doing good *because* you seek glory, honor, and immortality!

Romans 2:4 Or do you disregard the riches of His kindness, tolerance, and patience, not realizing that God's kindness leads you to repentance?

⁵But because of your hard and unrepentant heart, you are storing up wrath against yourself for the day of wrath, when God's righteous judgment will be revealed. ⁶God "will repay each one according to his deeds."

⁷To those who by perseverance in doing good seek glory, honor, and immortality, He will give eternal life. ⁸But for those who are self-seeking and who reject the truth and follow wickedness, there will be wrath and anger.

---

j. The Greatest Commandment
The essence of God's Law, and how Jesus helps us become obedient to it.

Perhaps that last section rattled you. It should rattle all of us at least a little. If we've put our trust in Jesus then we should be confident of our salvation, the blessed hope. And if you're saved and are already walking on the narrow path that leads to life, I don't want you to live in constant doubt and fear of damnation. You shouldn't. Your *faith* is what saves you. As long as you have faith in Christ, and your faith is a genuine faith as evidenced by obedience, righteousness, and good works. But it's also good for us to question our spiritual condition and our motivations regularly. Verse 7 before said "to those who by *perseverance* in..." Meaning your salvation and your faith are not something to take for granted. You don't receive it and then put it on a shelf somewhere. You must persevere *in it* until the end. The gift of salvation through Christ is a gift that you don't, and can't, earn. However—your *faith in that gift*—needs to be "continuously worked out with fear and trembling." (Philippians 2:12) Paul tells us to examine ourselves, to see whether we are in the faith, to test ourselves. *(2 Cor 13:5)* He also says to run our race in such a way as to show that we are trying to get the prize at the finish line. *(1 Cor 9:24)* So let your walk be your testimony!

Even before the New Covenant era the Law of God was given to be a tutor for us. *(Gal 3:24)* To help us know God in truth and to teach us the goodness of God so that we could walk in His ways. When God delivered Abraham's descendants from slavery in Egypt and called them to be a people for Himself, the Israelites, He gave them many laws to live by. Choosing to obey them would bring relationship with God and inevitable blessings, and choosing not would bring separation from God and inevitable curses. *(Deut 28)* There were 613 specific laws in total, but they could be summarized into ten "pillar" laws, which God wrote onto stone tablets, what we call the Ten Commandments. *(Ex 20:1-17, Deut 5:6-21)* These were first given, not by asking *from* them, but first by God revealing what He had *already* done *for* them—which was delivering them from slavery and setting them free. You see, before God asks us to obey Him, He shows us how He is good, how He has loved us and been good to us through no doing of our own. And *then* He gives us the law to obey, with the caveat that if we are unwilling to obey His laws, we will be left to our own devices, and the natural consequences thereof. In these Ten Commandments, the first four were about how we relate to God, and the last six were about how we relate to one another. Of the 613 total laws, some of them were *moral* laws about personal ethical behavior, but the vast majority of these laws were *civil* and *ceremonial.* Their purpose was to govern the nation state of Israel so it would be moral, ritually clean and sinless; holy, separate, and different from the wicked surrounding pagan nations. They would be governed, by God, through a king, priests, and prophets. They were to be a light to the nations that drew people to God. The laws were important but applied to a specific people, in a specific location, for specific purposes, and was a covenantal arrangement. Called the Mosaic Covenant: God's covenant with Israel given to them through Moses.

There were already 613 laws of God, and by Jesus's time there were also abuses of, and man-made traditions added to, God's law by many of the religious leaders. Fortunately, Jesus made the path clear to us. During Jesus's ministry He was asked by a scribe (an expert in the Jewish law) which commandment was the most important of all?

Mark 12:29 Jesus replied, "This is the most important: 'Hear O Israel, the Lord our God, the Lord is One. [30]Love the Lord your God with all your heart and with all your soul and with all your mind and with all your strength.' [31]The second is this: 'Love your neighbor as yourself.' No other commandment is greater than these." [32]"Right, Teacher," the scribe replied. "You have stated correctly that God is One and there is no other but Him, [33]and to love Him with all your heart and with all your understanding and with all your strength, and to love your neighbor as yourself, which is more important than all burnt offerings and sacrifices." [34]When Jesus saw that the man had answered wisely, He said, "You are not far from the kingdom of God."

This is the *essence* of the Law. It is foremost vertical, about a right relationship upward between us and God alone, who is to be our all-encompassing desire. And then it's horizontal, about a right relationship between us and all others as fellow equals. The other laws God gave to the Israelites did have their purpose and they were to be followed in obedience. The laws also reveal truths about God, about us, and about God's will for humanity. So there is always a benefit of studying and knowing what God has said and done in the past. The laws were also good—when used properly. *(1 Tim 1:8, Rom 7:12-16)* I'll say that again. Every law of God is good. If God gave it then there is some benefit to it. However, it's most important for Christians to understand God's heart *behind* the Law, best summarized by Jesus above.

We also need to know that Jesus fulfilled—not changed or abolished—but *fulfilled* the Law, on our behalf. This means that all who are in Christ meet the full requirements of the entire Law. The Law of God, summarized by the teachings in the first five books of the Bible, is also called the *Torah* in Hebrew, meaning the "Teaching" or the "Instruction". Beware, in most Christian cults, and even in some Christian denominations, the Law of God is *misunderstood* and *misappropriated*. Sometimes seen as the eternal, unchanging decree of God, obligatory for all time. This includes mandatory Sabbath-keeping, dietary restrictions, tithing regulations, and other forms of religious asceticism. This is false. This is a perversion of the gospel, which embraces a new freedom found in Christ, and worse it sometimes quite subtly adds religious works to what is necessary to be saved. Some even add beyond the original 613, such as total abstinence from alcohol and ultra-conservative dress for women. As though *we* can improve upon God's Law! This doesn't mean we are to be totally lawless. That is also a perversion of the truth! The truth is the narrow road that leads to life, which is in the middle of these two demonic extremes.

We just need to properly understand the Law and by doing so determine *which* parts of the Law have been fulfilled already in Christ, and which parts are for Christians to continue to observe within the New Covenant. Hebrews 10:1 says, *"For the law is only a shadow of the good things to come, not the realities themselves."* (Heb 7:11, 7:19, 8:5, Col 2:16-17) The Law was a picture that pointed to the reality, like a picture of your family points to your family. When you're on the road you embrace the picture. But when you get home, and you now have your family, you don't ignore your real family to focus on the picture. You have the real thing to enjoy and celebrate in. The Law was fulfilled by Jesus on the cross. As Hebrews 10:10 and 14 say all who put their trust in Him, *"have been sanctified through the sacrifice of the body of Jesus Christ once for all... Because by a single offering He has made perfect for all time those who are being sanctified."* (Heb 10:9-10, 14, 7:27)

I sometimes hear Christians, who are willfully living in sin, saying that Jesus did away with the Law so that they don't have to obey it. But understand this: the Law still stands. Jesus did not erase the Law, so that we don't have to be obedient or good or moral or loving. He *fulfilled* the Law for us so that: (1) we *could* be perfect, under the Law, through

Him, and (2) He could fill us with His Spirit so that we could be empowered to be *more* obedient, good, moral, and loving. It's not about *reducing* God's standards, it's actually about *raising* them! Not having to do all 613 laws doesn't mean God stopped caring about His law. It means Christ fulfills these laws for us, so that we can use all of our energy and focus on those specific laws, as a way of life, that are most closely connected to God's heart: loving Him with all of our being, and then loving our neighbors as ourselves.

Matthew 5:17 *[Jesus]* Do not think that I have come to abolish the Law or the Prophets. I have not come to abolish them, but to fulfill them. [18]For I tell you truly, until heaven and earth pass away, not a single jot, not a stroke of a pen, will disappear from the Law until everything is accomplished.

[16]In the same way, let your light shine before men, that they may see your good deeds and glorify your Father in heaven.

There are three categories of laws: (1) *Civil laws.* These were how the nation state of Israel was to function under divinely-appointed kings, prophets, and priests and remain holy/distinct from other nations. (2) *Ceremonial laws.* These were procedural, for guiding temple maintenance and the sacrificial system of cleansing both the nation and individuals of their sins through the levitical priesthood. (3) *Moral laws.* These were about how we relate to God and to one another. All these laws were governed through the king, priests, and prophets. Jesus has now perfectly fulfilled each of these three types of laws. Ephesians 5:2 says, *"Christ loved us and gave Himself up for us as a fragrant sacrificial offering to God."* Hebrews 1:3 says, *"The Son is the radiance of God's glory and the exact representation of His nature, upholding all things by His powerful word. After He had provided purification for sins, He sat down at the right hand of the Majesty on high."*

Those born again in Christ are now declared innocent according to the Law. They are also self-directed—by Him—as their eternal King, Prophet, and High Priest. They are holy and distinct, not by nationality or law-keeping, but by being *in* Him. We are to still be holy and separate from the world, but not through Sabbath-keeping, clothing, or dietary restriction, but by moral and spiritual purity and a transformed mind, heart, and soul through the reality of the gospel. *(Col 2:16-17, 21-23, Mk 7:14-23)* Jesus also fulfilled all of the ceremonial duties and cleansed us of all our sins and unrighteousness. It is not our outward law keeping and ceremonial cleansing that makes us clean enough to enter God's temple. We now *are* God's temple. *(1 Cor 3:16-17, 6:19)* And it is not our animal sacrifices and sin offerings that atones for our sins, but our faith in Jesus, who is our once and for all sacrifice. As Romans 12:1 says we become a *living sacrifice* now. You see, this is not less worship, it is more. It is not less sacrifice, it is more. Instead of outward changes, it is inward changes, ones that produce a different kind of outward change. Not religious ritual, but genuine acts of love and devotion. Not in order to be saved, but out of response of having already been saved. And it is not our submission to priests, or *external* systems of religious laws and ordinances that cleanse us or make us more godly or *permit* us to get closer to God. No, those that still exist in the world these are legalistic bondages of demonic lies and man-made religion, that Christ has so graciously rescued us from. We are brought NEAR to God by the blood of Jesus, and He cleanses us of all unrighteousness, in the past and present. He is our great Advocate and Intercessor with our Father. *(1 Jn 2:1-2, Rom 5:10, 8:34, 1 Tim 2:5, Heb 7:25)* All the born again in Christ are now a holy priesthood. *(1 Pet 2:5, 9, Rev 1:6, 5:10)* And our cleansing comes not from external washing, but from the *internal* sanctifying work of the Holy Spirit. *(Heb 9:14, Acts 15:9, Rom 15:16)*

Jesus fulfilled the Law, so that in Him, we could be not less but *MORE* godly, moral, and loving.

In Christ, we must still abide by the MORAL laws. There are moral laws commanded in the Torah. There are moral laws commanded in the New Testament. And there are moral laws being written on our hearts by the Holy Spirit. We must obey these, and we should *desire* to. Because it is THESE that show that our *repentance* of sin was genuine, that our *faith* in Jesus was genuine, that our spiritual *regeneration* by the Holy Spirit was genuine. Our outward desire and obedience to the moral law indicate that our guilty conscience has been cleansed, and that our salvation in Christ is indeed secure. Not only our willingness to obey God's moral law, but our desire to, because both show that in fact God's law HAS now been written on our hearts! If we do not desire a morality like God's then, guess what, we are still of our old nature. We still have yet to repent—much less be saved! We are yet to have God's Law written on our hearts and minds! And *this* Moral Law is the Law that God writes on us. He is not writing the ceremonial or the civil laws on hearts and minds. What would be the need for that? There is no temple. No priesthood. We are not Jews living in Israel. No way to obey most of it without completely reinterpreting the *purpose* of those laws! We cannot offer a greater sacrifice than Jesus. No, it's the moral law that is key. The obedience to, and even desire for, God's Moral Law, is the *evidence* of the genuine faith that saves. How we think and how we live. How we relate to God and to one another. Our vertical and horizontal relationships. It is THIS—God's Moral Law on our hearts and minds—that is the lynchpin of how we are ABLE to best love God with all our heart, mind, soul, and strength, and then love our neighbors as ourselves.

Hebrews 10:15 The Holy Spirit also testifies to us about this. First He says: [16]"This is the covenant I will make with them after those days, declares the Lord. I will put My laws in their hearts and inscribe them on their minds." [17]Then He adds: "Their sins and lawless acts I will remember no more."

[19]Therefore, brothers, since we have confidence to enter the Most Holy Place by the blood of Jesus, [20]by the new and living way opened for us through the curtain of His body, [21]and since we have a great priest over the house of God, [22]let us draw near with a sincere heart in full assurance of faith, having our hearts sprinkled to cleanse us from a guilty conscience and our bodies washed with pure water.

[26]If we deliberately go on sinning after we have received the knowledge of the truth, no further sacrifice for sins remains, [27]but only a fearful expectation of judgment and of raging fire that will consume all adversaries. [28]Anyone who rejected the law of Moses died without mercy on the testimony of two or three witnesses. [29]How much more severely do you think one deserves to be punished who has trampled on the Son of God, profaned the blood of the covenant that sanctified him, and insulted the Spirit of grace?

[35]So do not throw away your confidence; it holds a great reward. [38]"But My righteous one will live by faith; and if he shrinks back, I will take no pleasure in him." [39]But we are not of those who shrink back and are destroyed, but of those who have faith and preserve their souls.

---

k. New Hearts, New Minds
The New Birth provides access to God and righteousness, from the inside-out.

Quite frankly, if you don't have a desire to be moral, according to God's standards, you most likely have not been born again yet. There is no room for unrighteousness in God's Kingdom. If you want to serve yourself as god, live for all of your own idols, and live according to your own standards or the world's standards, you're still probably on the path that leads to eternal separation from God and damnation. If you still fit right in and live as the rest of the world does, and are all about your own glory, rather than God's glory, you still have the old map. Those who still live in willful sinful rebellion to God, or "Christians" who have ignored, rewritten, or reinterpreted what God *clearly* calls forbidden sin in the Bible, so that they can keep doing what seems right to them, are just lying to themselves. They're "suppressing the truth in their unrighteousness." (Romans 1:18)

This is why we start the map with understanding the absolute centrality of God's glory. All of God's Law, but most important to our discussion here, God's *Moral* Law, is related to His glory. Are we going to live according to His good design, and with Him alone, as our God? Or are we going to do it our way, and with a "who cares what God says" kind of attitude? This is where the *belief leading to action* I mentioned earlier comes into play. This is where the "born again" stands out from the "cultural Christian." The true follower of Jesus will be exactly that—an *actual follower*. Jesus said to be His disciple we must deny ourselves, take up our cross, and follow Him. *(Mt 16:24)* He said that anyone who loves their parents, or their children, more than Him is not worthy of Him! *(Mt 10:37)* Obedience to the moral law is *faith demonstrated*. Jesus calls us to still pick up *our* crosses and follow Him. His true followers will stop living as the world does. That means we might be hated by some, making enemies for proclaiming righteousness. Those living sinfully will not be happy with us saying that what they are doing is not good. And we will be different, and not doing all the same activities that godless society does around us, if those activities dishonor God or diminish His glory in any way.

Those who love God's Law—or at least desire to and are striving to—will welcome the New Birth. What exactly is the New Birth? Humans are tripartite: body, soul, and spirit. Because of sin, both the sin nature we inherited from our parents, as well as our own sins, all three parts of us are dead-dying. When we *truly* repent and put our faith in Jesus to atone for our sins on the cross, and believe that He did so, died, was buried, and was raised three days later, we become spiritually born again. The technical term for this is regeneration, because the Holy Spirit of God *regenerates* our dead spirit nature and takes up residence in us. He quickens it, doing a miracle that causes our dead-dying spirit to become alive again. This is called the New Birth, or being "Born Again." Jesus said in John 3:3 that "no one can see the Kingdom of God unless he is born again." The New Birth is absolutely essential to salvation, faith, life, and right beliefs. But there is confusion as to exactly *how* and *when* this happens. Let's debunk some more unbiblical teachings.

> Ezekiel 36:26 I will give you a new heart and put a new spirit within you; I will remove your heart of stone and give you a heart of flesh. [27] And I will put My Spirit within you and cause you to walk in My statutes and to carefully observe My ordinances.
>
> Romans 7:6 But now, having died to what bound us, we have been released from the law, so that we serve in the new way of the Spirit, and not in the old way of the written code.

New Spiritual Birth. Despite what some teach, this does NOT happen during water baptism (called *baptismal* regeneration). Water doesn't cause it. A baptism ceremony doesn't cause it. We can't say yes to Jesus and cause it ourselves. Even in our faith *we* don't cause it. It happens outside of us. It occurs according to God's grace and HIS timing alone, but it does occur the moment we *truly* have saving faith. This is not necessarily the first, or even the most-significant time, we said "Yes" to Jesus. We don't see it happen, we just have to trust that it has happened, by faith. Although this isn't an all-or-nothing decision on our part to have faith either. Some believe that it's all God provoking it. I'm willing to concede that it's probably *almost all* God. We are dead in our sins and we love them. It is His prevenient (provisional) grace that He has extended to all of us undeserving sinners. The Father draws us to faith in Jesus. *(Jn 6:44, 65)* Jesus draws us all to Himself. *(Jn 12:32)* In the drawing process, it's *almost* all Him. His grace draws.

In the actual New Birth though, it's 100% God. We do not participate in that at all. It's sad that I even have to say this—but we're NOT able to initiate, cause, or assist in our own births! Lol. Just as a human child has zero say so in its own birth, neither do we have any say so in our spiritual birth. Ultimately the Holy Spirit determines when—and if—the New Birth happens. Not you. Not me. Not the church. Not our parents. Not when we were water baptized as an infant or chose to be on our own later, if it was all ritual and our hearts were unrepentant and our faith was never true. Consider Simon the Sorcerer who was water baptized by Philip, but was never born again, and never received the Holy Spirit. *(Acts 8:9-24)* The new births of Ananias and Sapphira is also questionable. They would've been water baptized prior to selling their possessions, but then, right after acted wickedly and were immediately struck down by the Holy Spirit. *(Acts 5:1-10)* A person can't be born again against their will, by being forced into water. The presence of water and the formula alone aren't effectually changing anyone. A person could even be born again because Jesus came to them in a dream and they believed the gospel, even if the person was stranded about to die in the middle of a desert without a single drop of water nearby. The Ethiopian eunuch was saved by faith when Philip shared the gospel with him. His water baptism was a *response* in obedience to His decision to trust in Jesus. *(Acts 8:26-39)* Faith always comes before baptism. And God exercises His totally sovereignty over who HE decides to adopt and regenerate and when. I'm not saying we can do nothing. We choose to repent. We choose to believe. But God causes our new birth.

You must be Born Again. And it's not your choice when, or if, it happens. God decides when to "birth" you. It is His gracious response to your saving faith in Jesus.

Jesus said, "It is My Father's will that everyone who *looks* to the Son and *believes* in Him shall have eternal life." *(Jn 6:40)* It is faith in the Son that saves, not even obedience to the Son's command to be water baptized that does. And I said faith-*in* not faith-*that*. It is not just believing *that* the gospel is true as a type of fact. Rather, it is believing *in* the gospel, and staking your life on it, and putting your full personal trust in Jesus, that saves. You can't just believe *that* the parachute exists and *that* it saves. You have to believe *in* it, actually put it *on*, and actually jump out of the plane! It is our faith alone, coinciding with the will and response of God's grace alone, that causes the new birth. *(1 Jn 4:15, 5:1, 4)* It is an act of the grace of God. When the New Birth happens, we do not see it occurring. Jesus said it is like the wind, we see its *effects* afterwards, but have no control over when or where it comes from. Just as you can feel the wind and see the leaves blowing, you can see the effects of the New Birth. There will be faith in Jesus, there will be godliness, there will be good fruit. It is the New Birth, that *causes* a good tree to be planted in us, that now grows good fruit, which can now be seen. The planting comes before the fruit. Your good fruit, outward deeds, and religious rituals do not *cause* the planting. They are possible *evidences* that the good tree has already been planted by the Holy Spirit.

John 3:6 Flesh is born of flesh, but spirit is born of the Spirit. ⁷Do not be amazed that I said, 'You must be born again.' ⁸The wind blows where it wishes. You hear its sound, but you do not know where it comes from or where it is going. So it is with everyone born of the Spirit."

John 1:12 But to all who did receive Him, to those who believed in His name, He gave the right to become children of God— ¹³children born not of blood, nor of the desire or will of man, but born of God.

1 Peter 1:3 Blessed be the God and Father of our Lord Jesus Christ! By His great mercy He has given us new birth into a living hope through the resurrection of Jesus Christ from the dead,

---

Water Baptism. If water baptism doesn't cause the New Birth what's it for? Water baptism is important, but it's ideally done AFTER repentance of sin, belief in the gospel, confession of faith in Jesus, one's pledge of allegiance to surrender to Jesus as Lord and Savior, etc. As we've seen, we cannot know, for sure, when the New Birth has occurred, but it's most certainly not before any of those things happen. This is why full immersion "believer's baptism" is best. Genuine faith in Jesus and the desire to give a public confession of faith to surrender one's life to Him, is the *catalyst* that drives a person's decision to be water baptized. It is in obedience to Jesus's command to be baptized, and to officially enter the visible expression of His Church. If someone professes to be a follower of Jesus and outwardly rejects being baptized, I would highly doubt the validity of their conversion. Jesus was baptized in water! (Although it should be noted that this was John the Baptist's "baptism of repentance," which represented a confession of one's sinfulness and a desire to be right with God). This baptism is different than "Jesus's" triune-formula water baptism, which represents *both* repentance and belief in the gospel and entrance into His Church.) Nonetheless, Jesus taught His disciples to water baptize all new believers in the name of the Father, Son, and Holy Spirit. THIS is the "Jesus" baptism. It is not just baptizing in Jesus's name alone. That's a false teaching. *(Jn 3:26, 4:2, Mt 28:19, Acts 8:12, 16-17; 19:1-6)* The early church fathers have been using the triune formula since the beginning. Records of this include the Didache, Tatian, Tertullian, and Origen.[4] All Christians are to be water baptized by a born-again believer using the triune formula. Water baptism is a *picture* of the baptism of the Holy Spirit, that occurs by faith. It's also a *symbol* of our burial with Him in death and rising with Him in new life. *(Rom 6:3-4)* It's a representation, not the reality of these things. 1 Peter 3:21 says, *"And this water symbolizes the baptism that now saves you also--not the removal of dirt from the body, but the pledge of a clear conscience toward God--through the resurrection of Jesus Christ."*

Infant Baptism. Some Protestant denominations do infant baptism. This doesn't really represent either the New Birth or a person's personal identification with the death and burial of Jesus and their public confession of faith in Him before the Church. Infant baptism is more symbolic of a child's entrance into the covenant community of the global Church, just like infant circumcision was for Israel. What it *does* is represent the faithfulness of one's parents to officially dedicate their children to the Lord, more so than anything for the child. I suppose it's *possible* that God does a special work of grace in that child's life as a result of the blessing of the faithfulness of the parents, or the prayers of the church community. This may help to keep them nearer to God, but it's no guarantee. And however inferred, that is still basically theoretical. There's no explicit teaching of that revealed in Scripture. We also need to be mindful that the purpose of baptism has been perverted by the Roman Catholic Church to teach water baptism both removes the "stain" of original sin *and* causes the New Birth. This is totally unbiblical. We're not "stained" by original sin, we're totally depraved and dead-dying in all ways because of it. And water baptism doesn't correct this. What does, and puts us on the track to eternal life, is NOT religious ritual observance, rather, it is: (1) God's gracious drawing, followed by (2) our humility and repentance, followed by (3) our faith and trust in Jesus, which (4) coincides with the New Birth. Every single aspect of our salvation is by God's grace alone, through faith alone, and not by any religious work, lest anyone should boast. Always remember this, and prevent beautiful sacraments the Lord gave, like baptism, to be perverted into something we do to *earn or merit* salvific benefits. *(Eph 2:8-10)* In infant baptism what *actually* counts is the parent's commitment to be faithful and raise up their children in godly ways, with biblical instruction, to know and love the Lord, and to be in fellowship with His Church. There *is* tremendous spiritual blessing in this. The alternative practice of doing a *child dedication ceremony*, in which the parents promise in front of the congregation to do all of this, with the church also anointing the head of the children with water using the triune baptismal formula, and then having them individually receive believer's baptism later in life by their own confession, is the best of both, in my opinion.

Baptism (Filling) of the Holy Spirit. There is another type of baptism mentioned in Scripture: the baptism of the Holy Spirit. This baptism is not *itself* the New Birth either. There are some different aspects of this for us to consider but the most important takeaway is this: There is only ONE "New Birth" spiritual baptism—and it is *into* Jesus Christ! *(Eph 4:5, 1 Cor 12:13)* You are either in Christ, or you are not. Christ is either in you, and you have been born of the Holy Spirit, or you have not. You have either repented of your sins and put all of your trust in Jesus, or you have not. FAITH is what determines the New Birth—not any *outward* experience. We are commonly born again and thus "*receive* the Holy Spirit" in a way that is not *outwardly* supernatural. (See John 20:22)

Jesus is the one who baptizes with the Holy Spirit and fire. *(Mt 3:11, Lk 3:16, Mk 1:8, Acts 1:5, Jn 1:33)* This baptism—or *filling* if you prefer that language—is described in Scripture, and confirmed through personal testimonies, to feel like an overwhelming, immersive "baptism" experience. It either coincides at the same time as the New Birth, or comes later at a future time. *(Lk 24:49, Acts 1:4-8)* The New Birth likely occurs prior with this supplemental empowering in response to prayer and earnestly seeking, or to fulfill one's calling. This experience may be noticeably distinct, especially if faith in Jesus came long before. It doesn't happen to unregenerate unbelievers. Since only believers can receive this baptism it *could* also be an indicator of genuine faith and salvation as well. In Acts 11:15-18, the Gentiles receive the baptism of the Holy Spirit visibly and Peter proclaimed that God had granted them "repentance unto life." So it's possible to be baptized in the Holy Spirit and born again at the same time. Whether or not you've experienced this doesn't mean you're not saved or that the Holy Spirit won't empower you with other spiritual gifts later. Paul tells us to eagerly desire the gifts *(1 Cor 14:1, 12, 12:31)* and to not quench the Holy Spirit. *(1 Thes 5:19)* The Holy Spirit can give you new abilities anytime.

Empowerment Tip

He won't empower us to sit on our couch and watch TV! Put yourself out there, for the sake of the Kingdom and the gospel, and give Him a *reason* to empower you!

I'd also like to provide a caution here. The baptism of the Holy Spirit (or what you *think* is that) and spiritual gifts and miracles are not a guarantee that someone is saved, is more spiritually mature, or is necessarily believing or doing or teaching what is right. Satan *does* offer counterfeit supernatural experiences and powers—even to Christians! I've personally cast demons out of plenty of people who were deceived in believing that they were hearing from God. Others had genuinely been baptized by the Holy Spirit, spoke in tongues, heard from God audibly, etc. and yet still *also* had demons. Others had the Holy Spirit and supernatural gifting but were still deceived in a myriad of other ways. Still other genuine believers hadn't yet had the baptism, and had no noticeable supernatural gifting at all, but still had demons. It's not all or nothing! Another caution. There are some Christians who teach that if you haven't had this immersive experience, or haven't yet spoken in tongues or gained a prayer language, that you're either not saved or not mature. This is false. The Bible is clear that these experiences are not an absolute confirmation that one has genuine faith or that they have been born again. Even in Christ, not everyone will be gifted in the same ways. Not everyone will speak in tongues. *(1 Cor 12:4, 10, 13, 27-31)* Tongues are not even the greatest gift we should seek, much less the litmus test for either saving faith *(1 Cor 13-14)* or for possessing knowledge and truth.

Do not put your *trust in* spiritual experiences, like these as the guarantee of your position as a born again believer! Your faith must be in Christ *alone*. Your faith must be in your TRUST in HIM alone—through faith—not in your trust of your personal experiences. Additionally, persevering faith, godliness, and love, bearing good fruit in keeping with repentance, is a MUCH more reliable indicator of your secure position in Christ!

The Purpose of the New Birth. Why do we have to be born again? It's because God knows that our flesh is depraved and dying and sinful and weak and obeying His Law is difficult. He also doesn't want us to just obey His Law externally. He wants to change us internally. It's not just *do*— it's *desire* to do! Not just try to be, but *actually be*! That's always been the plan. But He wants our free will involved. He didn't want to just make us perfect at the outset. There's no real "us" in that. There's no real love of Him if there's no real choice. There's no real obedience to Him if there's no real choice. God wants us to be *like* Him, but it has to be something that we want, too. And I don't mean like Him, as in we want to be God. That's demonic. I mean like Him, as in like Him in *character*. In His manifest attributes: Loving, just, merciful, generous, hopeful, peaceful, etc. The New Birth is the beginning of us starting to *become* like Him. The New Birth is the crucifixion of the old us, where we die to our old sin nature and its wicked desires. *(Gal 6:14-15)* This is the beginning of our new good tree, a tree that bears good fruit that leads to holiness, and the outcome is eternal life. (See John 15:1-8)

Romans 6:2 How can we who died to sin live in it any longer? [3]Or aren't you aware that all of us who were baptized into Christ Jesus were baptized into His death?... [6]We know that our old self was crucified with Him so that the body of sin might be rendered powerless, that we should no longer be slaves to sin.

[22]But now that you have been set free from sin and have become slaves to God, the fruit you reap leads to holiness, and the outcome is eternal life. [23]For the wages of sin is death, but the gift of God is eternal life in Christ Jesus our Lord.

1 John 5:1 Everyone who believes that Jesus is the Christ is born of God, and everyone who loves the Father also loves the one born of Him. [2]By this we know that we love the children of God: when we love God and keep His commandments. [3]For this is the love of God,

that we keep His commandments. And His commandments are not burdensome, ⁴because everyone born of God overcomes the world. And this is the victory that has overcome the world: our faith.

1 John 3:9 Anyone born of God refuses to practice sin, because God's seed abides in him; he cannot go on sinning, because he has been born of God. ¹⁰By this the children of God are distinguished from the children of the devil: Anyone who does not practice righteousness is not of God, nor is anyone who does not love his brother.

Our transformation process—after being "reborn" anyways—isn't instant though. Even after we've received Jesus as our Lord and Savior, and the New Birth occurs, He doesn't change us all at once. Otherwise we're almost back to where we started, God forcing it to happen, just one single decision removed. No, it's got to be gradual. There are exceptions to this rule, the thief on the cross for example, who died and was saved the same day as his confession of faith. He didn't even have the opportunity to return to His old life of sin. *(Lk 23:43)* But for most of us this process occurs gradually. God sanctifies us and renews our minds in such a way wherein we *voluntarily give up* our free will, willingly! So slowly we get changed. I'm not saying we're *always* happy about it, lol. We are still waging war with our old nature, so there will be a struggle sometimes. We may protest to being changed the way that a child protests eating their vegetables. But He is patient and a good disciplinarian and we eventually eat them, and we know deep down that He loves us, and is right, and that it's good for us. We're usually happy we listened after the fact. We enjoy the fruits of a clear conscience before God. We enjoy the love of our Heavenly Father and the peace and joy of our guarantee of Heaven. Of course, we still stumble along the way. We *do* start out as *infants* in godliness after all. We start on spiritual milk before we get to whole foods, but we eventually grow and mature. *(1 Pet 2:2, 1 Cor 3:2, Heb 5:12)* But remember this brethren—*stumbling* does NOT equal running hard and fast in the wrong direction! *That* is a lack of genuine repentance. Stumbling is the act of continuously moving forward in the *right* direction, but having moments of weakness and struggling while doing so. Stumbling occurs while moving forward.

Stumbling ≠ Running Hard and Fast in Wrong Direction!

Perseverance of the Saints. God changes us, guaranteed. Once He's moved in, it's going to happen. We eventually become the person that He wants us to be. Part of the change happens in this life, the rest happens in the resurrection. But of course, this is only *genuine* spiritual regeneration. I've already said multiple times that a person can be baptized, call Jesus "Lord," etc., and that doesn't guarantee anything. Only God knows if the New Birth happened or not. Speaking in tongues, casting out demons, getting baptized, being a pastor, knowing the Lord and being obedient a long time, etc. None of these things guarantees anything. They may give us evidence we've been born again. They may increase our faith that we have been. None of us, including me, can actually see into a person's soul and tell if the New Birth occurred or not *definitely*. Thus, we MUST have faith and persevere. I personally believe that Scripture teaches that after the New Birth occurs, God's Spirit in us preserves us by *assisting in* the process of us "working out our salvation with fear and trembling," guaranteeing that we will persevere in the faith until the end, and so be saved. *(Phil 2:12)* This doctrine also goes by the names "Once Saved, Always Saved" or "Eternal Security." Because these doctrines are both widely misunderstood, and widely abused by false teachers, I'll elaborate further.

I don't think it's possible to be lost after being born again. If someone falls away from the faith later, I think they were never *truly* born again when they were trying to walk with Jesus. Some Christians do believe that it's possible to be genuinely born again and still *apostacize* later. Note, "apostatizing" does not mean to lose our salvation accidentally, or to go back and forth between being saved and lost daily. Rather, apostasy is to decide formally to absolutely reject one's salvation altogether and so damn themselves. I see their argument, there are certainly many strong warnings against tasting God's sweet offer of salvation and then later rejecting Jesus. We DO need to take these warnings seriously! Both the moral commands *(1 Tim 6:9-10, 2 Pet 2:20-22, Jam 5:19-20)* and in keeping with right doctrine. *(Mk 4:16; 1 Tim 4:1, 6:20-21, 1:18-21; 2 Pet 2:1, 3:17; 2 Jn 1:8-9)* However, I think a good argument can be made that if someone continues to live in sin, or stops for awhile but then returns to sin, or if they fall away from the true faith at a later date, then they were never truly born again and of us to begin with. *(1 Jn 2:19, 3:5-10)* The *sealing* of the Holy Spirit to preserve and lead God's children to the finish line is a biblical fact. *(Eph 4:30)* However, I understand not everyone sees the "sealing" this way. And I'm not saying that you have to believe what I believe here to have a right map. Both are permissible. What matters MOST is the output of the "saving lifestyle" that bears the fruit of a genuine conversion. You, and others in the Body of Christ, need to be able to look at your life and have confidence that you have *been* saved, and are *being* saved. Godly Christians on both sides of this discussion ALL agree that if you go from knowing the truth and then rejecting Jesus later and persisting in your rebellion then that would unquestionably mean surefire damnation. No one who rejects Jesus as Lord and Savior—or who claims Him as Lord but still lives in hypocrisy persisting in their outright sinfulness—is going to be saved. (See Hebrews chapter 10 quotes, pg 48-49). *(See also: Heb 6:4-6, 10:26-39; Gal 5:4; Rom 11:19-23; Rev 2:4-5, 3:5, 3:16-17)*

**You either have a NEW Heart and Mind—or you don't.
You're either DEAD to your Sin—or you're not.**

I've written these sections to make a very clear distinction between being an "outward follower" of Jesus—and being "born of God." I think it's absolutely true a person can be a follower of Jesus and then apostatize later. *(Mt 7:21-23, Lk 13:25-27)* We ALL need to be born again *(Jn 3:3)* and persevere in our faith and obedience until death. We cannot say a one-time prayer to Jesus and live in sinful rebellion to God the rest of our lives and still believe we're saved. That's deceived wishful thinking. This doctrine has been perverted by false teachers more commonly under the name "Once Saved, Always Saved" or "Eternal Security" to teach that we can reject Jesus or even live in sin indefinitely, and still be saved, if at any one point in time we confessed Jesus. I've heard of a pastor who led the funeral for a violent gangster who was selling hardcore drugs, committing crime, living grossly immoral, etc. And he proclaims to an entire room full of his gangster friends that because decades ago he "said a prayer and gave Jesus his life" that he was in Heaven! Absolutely heretical! What a wolf in sheep's clothing that pastor is! Pastors who would teach this need to be publicly outed. I would have had no confidence in that gangster's eternal state, and he should have given the real gospel to that audience.

A license to sin? I've heard other opponents of this view claim that it is a license to sin, but this is not the case. The doctrine is not that "because you're saved already you can live however sinful you want." It is that "you need to persevere until the very end to be saved, but if the Holy Spirit is genuinely in you, you won't have to do it on your own, and He will ensure that you finish strong." It's not how you start, it's how you finish! But none of us knows when our time is up. To better understand the difference we could reword it. I personally think it would be better understood if it was renamed from "Once Saved, Always Saved" to be: "ONCE redeemed, saved, adopted by God, spiritually born-again, with us in Christ and He is in us, being empowered by Him to be holy and persevere —ALWAYS redeemed, saved, adopted by God, spiritually born again, with us in Christ and He is in us, being empowered by Him to be holy and persevere." And if there's not good fruit as evidence that *that* has actually happened, then it probably hasn't happened yet. When I see supposed Christians living in willful sin I don't tell them they're still saved anyways. I tell them they need to repent and tell them the gospel again, because I don't know if they've actually received it! There are some more on Hyper-grace later) who *do* misinterpret this doctrine as a license to sin, but they're still unregenerate. Rather than tossing out the truthfulness of this doctrine, that has the potential to be very empowering in the right hands, let's just proclaim the truth of Scripture while also disavowing those still suppressing the truth in unrighteousness. It's unfortunate there are those still well on their way to Hell who think that they're saved. And that's a damn shame. Literally.

God wants us to be like Him, but we have to want it too. We must repent and gradually consent to the inevitable loss of our ability to sin.

The purpose, again. To properly understand this doctrine we have to reflect on what we've already learned about what God desires to do in us. Why does He come live in us in the first place? What's His goal? To make us more like Christ. Are we to think that if He genuinely comes in that He will decide to abandon us later? Or that He would be there but fail to "hold" us? I don't think so. But that also means we do not, and cannot, stay the SAME either. It is my belief that everyone that *has* been truly born of God, it is in *this* sanctification process, that we are consenting to and being groomed for, eternal life with God. I believe the New Birth *is* the beginning of our new life, a new life that will look very different if the New Birth has occurred. I think the Lord chose this metaphor of "New Birth" for a reason. If we have become born again then we cannot become unborn. If we are *truly* a new creation, I don't think we can choose to stay the old creation. We are either new—or we are still the old! We HAVE to come into agreement with God that we don't want to be the sinful way that we were and are, and want Him to take away our ability to be that way. All sinfulness and unrighteousness must be eradicated! We have to daily "die to ourselves." We have to think and live in such a way that we demonstrate a *genuine* desire for a future in which He actually takes away part of our free will, the part capable of sinning against Him. For our own good, we know we can't have it! We will still remain an individual with freedom of the will, but both the desire and the ability to sin will be absolutely removed. In the life to come, there will never again be the possibility of another sinful rebellion. I don't want to leave you with the impression that this process is all up to us in our own strength. God helps us to do this, and that is *really empowering!*

Philippians 1:6 being confident of this, that He who began a good work in you will continue to perfect it until the day of Christ Jesus.

1 Corinthians 1:8 He will sustain you to the end, so that you will be blameless on the day of our Lord Jesus Christ. [9]God, who has called you into fellowship with His Son Jesus Christ our Lord, is faithful.

1 Thessalonians 5:23 Now may the God of peace Himself sanctify you completely, and may your entire spirit, soul, and body be kept blameless at the coming of our Lord Jesus Christ. [24]The One who calls you is faithful, and He will do it.

Ephesians 1:13 And in Him, having heard and believed the word of truth—the gospel of your salvation—you were sealed with the promised Holy Spirit, [14]who is the pledge of our inheritance until the redemption of those who are God's possession, to the praise of His glory.

So we need to be faithful, but God Himself is also faithful in preserving us too. Let's get back to how this process works, and how it helps us get to our end goal: to be like God and have relationship with Him forever. It begins with humility which leads to repentance.

When we genuinely humble ourselves and repent (which means to change your mind and go the opposite direction), it means we've made an active decision, in our own free will, that we want the same thing God does. When we put our trust in Jesus alone, we acknowledge that we understand God is perfect, and He wants us to be perfect too. (See Sermon on the Mount quotes, page 57) We're not, and we can never be on our own. Get beyond believing you can do good deeds and that erases all the sins you've committed, or nullifies the wicked desires of our hearts that we still have to resist. We've got to stop thinking we can do good deeds and tip the scales to be a heavier than our bad deeds. That's what Islam falsely teaches. God isn't impressed with us for only being 49% evil! Or even with us being 99% good, as if that were possible anyways. The truth is the more we recognize God's as infinitely good, and rightfully glorify Him, the less we ignorantly boast of our own self-righteousness. The less we see a good work, for example helping the poor, as actually *earning* something. God desires us to be like Him, to *naturally* do good, for goodness sake. Not by compulsion because we think we're going to get something out of it. Because that really isn't that good, if you think about it! We have to arrive at that place where we see ourselves as a miserable wretch that needs Jesus to save us, and desires God to make us more like Him. We're drowning in our sin, dead in the water. Even when we choose to do the right thing, we're *choosing it*—which means we don't automatically!! Only wicked creatures have to *decide* not to be wicked. God doesn't decide to do what is right, He just does. It's His nature. When we finally get this, we stop trying to earn our righteousness and trust in Jesus to receive it imputed to us by Him, through faith alone. And we've been given the offer of the free gift of salvation in Christ through God's grace (His unmerited forgiveness and favor) alone, to the glory of God alone.

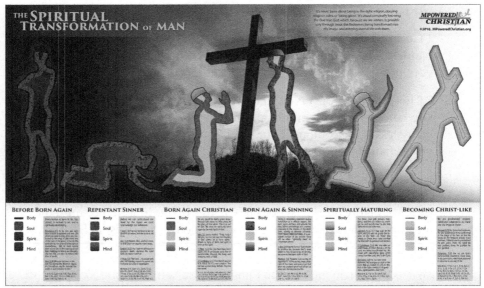

This is a poster I designed to help illustrate the new birth gradual transformation. You can view the small text in the full size version at: https://mpoweredchristian.org/wall-art-transformation

God gives us everything we need to get to the finish line, right from the outset, but we consent to it all along the way. He transforms us little by little, and we gradually consent to our desire to die to our sin and our ability to sin. When we put our faith in Jesus we become spiritually born again with the Spirit of God in us. We are adopted into the family of God. God the Father becomes our father. We now have the ability to commune with God. Our sins from the past or the present are not barriers between us. We're justified (declared blameless) through the imputed righteousness of Christ, put upon us. We are in Christ, and He is in us. Because we are in Christ, and His blood is continually cleansing us, we can always go to the Father. We receive a new heart and a new mind. This happens immediately. We get a brand new spirit: the Holy Spirit. However, we still have the old soul and body (the "flesh") that is still broken and inclined towards sin. These still need a lot of work! And so the Holy Spirit gets right to work in us, sanctifying us, transforming us. He puts the moral Law of God on our hearts and minds so that we love it and follow it. He slowly removes our false beliefs, bad habits, sinful desires, and heals our brokenness. All from the inside-out! I believe this is a synergy that we participate in. Not that our roles are equal in any way. He is still God. He leads, we follow. He prompts, we obey. He heals, we seek healing. He forgives, we seek forgiveness. He teaches, we seek truth. He transforms, we seek transformation. He empowers, we fight. Ultimately He wins in all ways, but we consent to it, desire it, and strive and persevere towards the same goal.

Romans 8:1 Therefore, there is now no condemnation for those who are in Christ Jesus. [2]For in Christ Jesus the law of the Spirit of life has set you free from the law of sin and death. [3]For what the law was powerless to do in that it was weakened by the flesh, God did by sending His own Son in the likeness of sinful man, as an offering for sin. He thus condemned sin in the flesh, [4]so that the righteous standard of the law might be fulfilled in us, who do not walk according to the flesh but according to the Spirit.

[9]You, however, are controlled not by the flesh, but by the Spirit, if the Spirit of God lives in you. And if anyone does not have the Spirit of Christ, he does not belong to Christ. [10]But if Christ is in you, your body is dead because of sin, yet your spirit is alive because of righteousness. [11]And if the Spirit of Him who raised Jesus from the dead is living in you, He who raised Christ Jesus from the dead will also give life to your mortal bodies through His Spirit, who lives in you.

[12]Therefore, brothers, we have an obligation, but it is not to the flesh, to live according to it. [13]For if you live according to the flesh, you will die; but if by the Spirit you put to death the deeds of the body, you will live. [14]For all who are led by the Spirit of God are sons of God.

l. The Way, The Truth, and The Life.

Jesus is the only way to be saved, by faith alone. Period.

God desires to have relationship with us, yet He is perfect, righteous, and holy. As one who is righteous, He cannot tolerate the presence of wickedness. So He separates Himself from us, because we are not. God is perfect, and He desires us to be perfect. Yet, none of us is. We are all sinners who have fallen short of the glory of God. There's no way for us to do good deeds, meditate, or do anything else to build a bridge capable of crossing this infinite chasm. Jesus is the only way. That sounds exclusive. It is. But it's still true. It's only offensive to people who think they are *already* good. Or they have an idolatrous "god" that is not *that* good, so it's really not too hard to meet its standards. It's all about how we view God. If God is very, very, very good—in fact, absolutely totally perfect—then you need Jesus. Period. Every false religion has a common denominator, they all teach: "You can get to God by doing XYZ because God isn't really much better than you."

Matthew 5:20 *[Jesus]* For I tell you that unless your righteousness exceeds that of the scribes and Pharisees, you will never enter the kingdom of heaven. [21]You have heard that it was said to the ancients, 'Do not murder, and anyone who murders will be subject to judgment.' [22]But I tell you that anyone who is angry with his brother will be subject to judgment... [27]You have heard that it was said, 'Do not commit adultery.' [28]But I tell you that anyone who looks at a woman to lust after her has already committed adultery with her in his heart... [38]You have heard that it was said, 'Eye for eye and tooth for tooth.' [39]But I tell you not to resist an evil person. If someone slaps you on your right cheek, turn to him the other also... [48]Be perfect, therefore, as your Heavenly Father is perfect.

Can any humble human being actually read those words of Jesus and *not* see their NEED for Him? None of us can claim perfection. None of us can stand before God and think that we actually deserve to be there. God's standards are higher than ours. And that would be absolutely terrifying if the story ended there, but it doesn't. We aren't judged on our own merit, we're judged by the merit of Jesus. And thank God for that! Plus, aren't you happy that your God is morally perfect? Would you want any less than that? Our confidence must not be in us, or in anything we can do, but in Jesus alone. Nothing we do can accomplish making us perfect. Not belonging in the denomination or individual church we belong to. Not the "anointing" of the pastors or prophets that speak into our lives. Not confession to a priest, fasting, sacraments, or any other religious rituals. Not prayers to Mary or saints, or even prayers to God. No, it is our individual faith in Christ alone and in the Gospel. It is believing in Him and trusting in Him alone. And that is such a beautiful thing. God forgives us despite all our flaws, grants us life by merely trusting in Jesus, and then empowers us to become the best possible version of ourselves.

John 3:16 "For God so loved the world, that He gave His only begotten Son, that whoever believes in Him shall not perish, but have eternal life... [36]"He who believes in the Son has eternal life; but he who does not obey the Son will not see life, but the wrath of God abides on him."

John 14:6 Jesus answered, "I am the way, and the truth, and the life. No one comes to the Father except through Me.

Acts 4:12 Salvation exists in no one else, for there is no other name under heaven given to men by which we must be saved."

Salvation is by grace alone, through faith alone, in Christ alone, to the glory of God alone. Let me unpack that a little bit more. Salvation, which is being saved from God's wrath in His right judgment of our sinfulness, is available only because of God's grace alone. Grace is unmerited or undeserved favor. Grace is the act of giving mercy to those who don't deserve mercy. God doesn't owe us His favor or His mercy. We're guilty, we've broken the law, we deserve judgment. He would be perfectly just to condemn us. But He's loving and merciful so He offers to us this free gift. What is the gift? Christ, who is our means of salvation. How do we receive this free gift? Through faith alone. By personally trusting in Him. By giving our lives to Him as our Lord and Savior. And this has been offered to us for the glory of God alone. God is glorified in that He has graciously provided us a way to be redeemed. Lest we err by adding even a single deed to this and think that our cooperation, or good works (deeds or efforts or rituals), help in any way.

Good works may be the *evidence* of our salvation. But in no way do they *contribute* to our salvation.

For us to take any credit at all is to defame God's grace. We're drowning in sin so God throws us Jesus like a life preserver to grab on to. As He is pulling us to the boat, we give a small tug of practically insignificant help here and there towards the boat. Imagine us trying to take credit for helping to save ourselves because of those tugs! Shameful. We *should* give our tugs of help, it shows that we really want to be saved! Our tugs and effort *do* count. They *are* good, but they're almost nothing when compared to perfection. They show that we appreciate what God is doing for us! They confirm we want to go in the same direction! But if we think we're actually HELPING to save ourselves we're delirious and arrogant and probably still drowning, and the boat there to rescue us is just a mirage in our mind as a result of the loss of oxygen from drowning!

Ephesians 2:4 But because of His great love for us, God, who is rich in mercy, ⁵made us alive with Christ, even when we were dead in our trespasses. It is by grace you have been saved! ⁶And God raised us up with Christ and seated us with Him in the heavenly realms in Christ Jesus, ⁷in order that in the coming ages He might display the surpassing riches of His grace, demonstrated by His kindness to us in Christ Jesus. ⁸For it is by grace you have been saved through faith, and this not from yourselves; it is the gift of God, ⁹not by works, so that no one can boast. ¹⁰For we are God's workmanship, created in Christ Jesus to do good works, which God prepared in advance as our way of life.

So good works *are* good. We're created in Christ to do them. It's what God saved us for, prepared in advance to do as our way of life. But they're not what saves us, at all. What about repentance? Doesn't repentance count as a "work" since it's something we have to *do* to be saved? What about faith? We have to believe in Jesus still. Does that count as a "work?" No. Neither of these are works. Neither of these are good deeds, loving acts, or religious rituals. They are both *spiritual responses* to God's grace. Remember the parable of the Prodigal Son in Luke 15)? Our ability to repent of our sin and trust in what Jesus accomplished on the cross on our behalf, doesn't *earn* us salvation any more than the prodigal son's return and groveling to his father *earned his* forgiveness. *(Lk 15:17-24)* No, the forgiveness and acceptance of the father, as well as his provision of sonship and restoration back into the family, was all a generous gift from the father because of his own grace and mercy. The father would've been justified to reject his wicked son. His extension of mercy is the grace that is like God's grace toward us in Christ. Humility and repentance are necessary, but they're not works. They're the other side of the faith coin. Anyone who claims that repentance of sin is not necessary is telling a demonic lie! This is like trying to *continue* to be financially supported by their father *while also continuing* to reject him personally and relationally and staying in their pigpen of filth! No, our repentance is the catalyst that drives us back to God to seek His forgiveness and restoration.

Faith is not a "work" either. This is proved by the fact that *"faith by itself, if it is not complemented by action, is dead."* (James 2:17) The mere fact that genuine, saving, *living* faith must always be accompanied by works, speaks to the fact that the faith cannot *itself* be a work. Genuine faith is always accompanied by action that demonstrates that the faith is real. James tells us of the foolishness in putting faith in good works alone, as well as a faith alone without works. He says, *"Show me your faith without deeds, and I will show you my faith by my deeds."* (James 2:18) Faith is the act of the will to accept the *means* that God has provided to be restored to Him. Our faith is our trust in God, and our actions complement our faith, and attest to it. Let's return to our previous analogy of drowning. Is it a "work" of my own merit to come to the realization that I'm drowning? Of course not. Is it a "work" of my own merit to want to be saved from drowning? Of course not. Is it a "work" of my own merit to grab the life preserver that God has thrown out to me in Jesus Christ? Of course not. Is it a "work" of my own merit to hang on to the life preserver as it is being pulled slowly towards the boat? Of course not. I'm not earning anything at all. The whole entire process is a *gift* from start to finish! Is it any surprise that we should sing praises of God and live a transformed life now, as we're being pulled towards the boat? No way! Joy is the natural fruit of a person that is being saved!

III. The Final Destination

m. Conformed Into Christ's Image
The final destiny, of every person saved, is to become like Jesus.

The purpose of human life is to glorify God. God has created humans, in His image and likeness, each with a spiritual nature and a conscience and the effectual ability to respond to His grace. God's grace is provided for all, in Christ, so that all have the ability to be restored to relationship with Him and receive eternal life. It is God's desire that we desire this same goal, and so accept this gift by faith in pursuit of the same desire. In doing so, we enter into the New Covenant that Christ has established, with His own blood. Christ is the Mediator of this New Covenant with humanity and He preserves all who enter into it by faith in Him. The Holy Spirit seals the believer, causes the new spiritual rebirth of their spirit nature, and begins to sanctify (purify) the rest of their soul and body. His work of sanctification is enjoined by our desire to *be* sanctified. It is now that we are in Christ, that we're actually empowered by His Spirit for this job, and are able to bear genuine transformation and good fruit as a result. *(Jn 15:1-8)* This process continues for the rest of the believer's life—even into eternity. Upon death we leave the sinful desires of the soul behind and go to be with Jesus in Heaven where we will reign with Him. In the resurrection, we are reunited to our new eternal bodies, similar to the one that Jesus was resurrected in, and made even more glorious. *(Phil 3:20)* At the BEMA judgment Christians will receive rewards for their deeds on earth, and made even more glorious. (More on that in chapter six) But in the New Earth to come there is no death or decay or sorrow. It will be perpetual *increase.* Perpetual growth. With eternity to spend with our Father, Lord and Savior, bearing continuous fruit for *their* glory, we will continue to increase in our own glory as well. All this is possible because Jesus has made it possible. As we increase in our knowledge of Him we mature to the full measure of becoming like Him. There actually is wisdom to asking WWJD?!

Romans 8:28 And we know that God works all things together for the good of those who love Him, who are called according to His purpose. [29]For those God foreknew, He also predestined to be conformed to the image of His Son, so that He would be the firstborn among many brothers. [30]And those He predestined, He also called; those He called, He also justified; those He justified, He also glorified.

2 Corinthians 3:18 And we, who with unveiled faces all reflect the glory of the Lord, are being transformed into His image with intensifying glory, which comes from the Lord, who is the Spirit.

n. The Blessed Adoption
To be spiritually born again means being adopted as a child of God the Father.

Our position in Christ is not just one of "believer" or "member of Kingdom." It's so much more than that! We're actually spiritually-adopted by God the Father. In Jesus, who is the eternal Son of God the Father, we also become sons and daughters of the Father. Really let that sink in. We become co-heirs of the Kingdom that has been entrusted to Him. Do you really think of God as your father? Do you think, pray, talk, act, and live as though God is your father? The Holy Spirit in us is our seal, our guarantee, the pledge of our *inheritance* until we receive our new bodies later. We cry out "Abba!" (Daddy)

John 1:12 But to all who did receive Him, to those who believed in His name, He gave the right to become children of God— [13]children born not of blood, nor of the desire or will of man, but born of God.

Ephesians 1:5 In love [5]He predestined us for adoption as His sons through Jesus Christ, according to the good pleasure of His will, [6]to the praise of His glorious grace, which He has freely given us in the Beloved One.

[13]And in Him, having heard and believed the word of truth—the gospel of your salvation—you were sealed with the promised Holy Spirit, [14]who is the pledge of our inheritance until the redemption of those who are God's possession, to the praise of His glory.

Romans 8:23 Not only that, but we ourselves, who have the firstfruits of the Spirit, groan inwardly as we wait eagerly for our adoption as sons, the redemption of our bodies.

Galatians 4:4 But when the time had fully come, God sent His Son, born of a woman, born under the law, ⁵to redeem those under the law, that we might receive our adoption as sons. ⁶And because you are sons, God sent the Spirit of His Son into our hearts, crying out, "Abba, Father!" ⁷So you are no longer a slave, but a son; and since you are a son, you are also an heir through God.

Do you think you need special "holy" or "anointed" people or "ordained" pastors, prophets, or priests, etc. to confess sins or to pray to God? You don't if you *actually* believe the gospel! I was raised Catholic, and I have an issue with multiple things they do. Catholics are taught they need to go to a priest for confession to be forgiven, as though a *child* needs an "official representative" *between* them and their own parent. As though our Heavenly Father does not care about His own children enough to hear from them directly. And this concept goes against *everything* we have looked at so far in this chapter. The entire *point* is for God to have an intimate relationship with us. This is why the plan of restoration is eternal. This is why He *adopts* us! This is why He "births" us. It's why He gives us His own Spirit! The Church is also called "the Bride of Christ," another relational metaphor. It's all about relationship, connection, and intimacy. Having intermediaries in the middle as go-betweens is the exact OPPOSITE of the entire reason for the gospel!

Scripture is clear, God does not show favoritism. *(Gal 2:6, Rom 2:11, Acts 10:34)* Does anyone who believes that they have a very far, distant relationship with God, sound like they even *believe* that they are *already* children of God? *Already* co-heirs with Christ? Not words-only belief, but real belief, as demonstrated by action? Doesn't this sound like a lack of faith? I think it does. Decide today if you will believe God's Word and trust in the gospel: the good news that you've been *fully* restored to God through Christ. If you do believe this then immediately abandon all of these other beliefs. They are hindrances to your relationship with God. If you believe them, but still happen to have an intimate relationship with God, that's good—but it is *despite* these things, not because of them.

They also teach to pray to Mary or the saints, so that *they* could then pray to God or Jesus for them. I've heard a priest recently say that "our prayers sound *sweeter* to Jesus coming from His mother." As though our Lord, Savior, Brother, and co-heir to the Kingdom, Jesus, is unwilling, or less-favorably willing, to hear from us directly. His own brothers and sisters He suffered and died for! All His sheep that He loves and is the Good Shepherd for! As though it's God's eternal plan for Mary to be the one we all think of as the gracious, loving one to relate to! Because God and Jesus are what? Too hard, cold, distant?! As though Jesus didn't say to love GOD with ALL our heart, mind, soul, and strength. How could we love God with everything when our attention is shared with Mary? How can we read all these passages about the entire plan of salvation teaches us of GOD's grace, and then abandon that by thinking that Mary is who God wants us to go to for grace and help. Mariolatry comes from an idolatrous desire for *some form* of female goddess worship. It is paganism. It's not biblical, gospel-centered, or God-honoring. No, Jesus promises us that He hears us in whatever we ask *(1 Jn 5:14)* and that if we ask Him anything in His name He will do it. *(Jn 14:13-14)* And the entire Bible teaches to pray to and worship God alone!

Plus, this whole entire belief system implies that God and Jesus are very, very far away from us. That He is in a distant place in Heaven with Mary and the Saints and the Priests all in-between us in the middle. No, Jesus is very near! He is in us, and we have fellowship with Him. Jesus's spirit is already in us, and we are already children of the Father through Him. *(Jn 14:18-20, Rom 8:9, 1 Jn 1:6, 2:24)* There is ONLY ONE Mediator between God and men: Jesus! *(1 Jn 2:1, 1 Tim 2:5)* We, who were once far away have been brought NEAR by His blood, *(Eph 2:13)* and we are now *already* seated with Him in the heavenly realms. *(Eph 2:6)* Your closeness to God is dependent, not upon good works, or sacraments, or intermediaries, or religious rituals, but on how much time you invest into your relationship with Him! The more time you actually spend with God *(Jam 4:8)*, and in His Word *(Jn 17:17)*, and worshiping Him in spirit and in truth *(Jn 4:24)* the more you will know Him. In Christ, you are a child of God. Never let anyone rob your intimacy with God directly and try to enslave you again to religious systems just to get closer to God.

Your closeness to God is dependent upon how much time you invest in YOUR relationship WITH Him!

Be confident in this, in the promises of God's Word that you are His child. And if you lack certain confidence of this, then invest in and stir up your faith in Jesus and in the gospel. Rather than trusting in human traditions and the false doctrines of pagan religion that once again enslaves you to believe of your vast separation between you and God, and to enslave you to religious works of bondage, and the necessity of relying on *them* as intermediaries. No, pour your heart and mind into the gospel. Do whatever it takes to stir up and strengthen your faith in Jesus alone, and in trusting God's WORD, so that your confidence comes from trusting in HIM alone for your salvation and adoption.

Ephesians 2:13 But now in Christ Jesus you who once were far away have been brought near through the blood of Christ.

[18]For through Him [Christ] we both have access to the Father by one Spirit. [19]Therefore you are no longer strangers and foreigners, but fellow citizens of the saints and members of God's household,

Ephesians 3:12 In Him [Christ] and through faith in Him [Christ] we may enter God's presence with boldness and confidence.

o. Eternal Life With God

The future New Earth, in God's presence, without separation, sin, sorrow, or death.

As we press on towards our destination, and run with endurance the race set out for us *(Heb 12:3)*, we need to reflect often what we are running *towards*. We are running *towards* goodness, glory, honor, peace, praise, and immortality. *(Rom 2:7, 10, 1 Pet 1:7)* We run towards the joy of the revelation of—and fellow partaker of—the glory of Christ. *(1 Pet 4:13, 5:1)* We run towards the joy of *"seeing God face to face,"* and when *"we shall be like Him, because we shall see Him as He is."* *(Mt 5:8, Rev 22:4, 1 Jn 3:2)* We run towards eternal rewards, like the crown of glory, that will never fade away, *(1 Pet 5:4)* and the crown of life that God has promised to those who love Him. *(Jam 1:12)* We run towards the victory of accomplishment, and the right to sit with Jesus on His throne, just as He overcame and sat down with His Father on His throne! *(Rev 3:21)*

We run towards being in the *"Paradise of God,"* *(Rev 2:7)* where Jesus confesses our name before His Father and the angels. *(Rev 3:5)* We run towards the experience of the *"fullness of joy"* and *"pleasures forevermore."* *(Ps 16:11)* We run towards the opportunity to *"dwell in God's presence,"* *"feast on the abundance of His house,"* and *"drink from the river of His delights."* *(Ps 140:13, 36:8)* The crowns we race towards are imperishable, undefiled, unfading ones, reserved in Heaven for us. *(1 Pet 1:4)* A crown of righteousness is waiting for you, me, and all the saints—all who have longed for the Lord's appearing! *(2 Tim 4:8)* We can even receive the morning star, which is a title likely related to the attribute of brightness, that was previously only given to the angels. (See Rev. 2:28) And then we will shine like the brightness of the heavens, shining like the stars forever. *(Dan 12:3)*

Ezekiel 37:26 And I will make a covenant of peace with them; it will be an everlasting covenant. I will establish them and multiply them, and I will set My sanctuary among them forever. ²⁷My dwelling place will be with them; I will be their God, and they will be My people.

Revelation 21:1 Then I saw a new heaven and a new earth, for the first heaven and earth had passed away, and the sea was no more. ²I saw the holy city, the new Jerusalem, coming down out of heaven from God, prepared as a bride adorned for her husband. ³And I heard a loud voice from the throne saying:

"Behold, the dwelling place of God is with man, and He will dwell with them. They will be His people, and God Himself will be with them as their God. ⁴He will wipe away every tear from their eyes, and there will be no more death or mourning or crying or pain, for the former things have passed away."

> ⁷The one who is victorious will inherit all things, and I will be his God, and he will be My son.
>
> ²²But I saw no temple in the city, because the Lord God Almighty and the Lamb are its temple. ²³And the city has no need of sun or moon to shine on it, because the glory of God illuminates the city, and the Lamb is its lamp.
>
> Revelation 22:3 No longer will there be any curse. The throne of God and of the Lamb will be within the city, and His servants will worship Him. ⁴They will see His face, and His name will be on their foreheads. ⁵There will be no more night in the city, and they will have no need for the light of a lamp or of the sun. For the Lord God will shine on them, and they will reign forever and ever.

What wonderful promises we just read from God's Word! So what will eternity be like? Will we just float on clouds and play harps? Where did that even come from? It's definitely not in the Bible! No, we will get to do great things! This is such an important and neglected part of the typical Christian map. If we fail to set our eyes on the greatness of our prize, we are more likely to stumble during the journey. We need a map in our minds that shows how great the destination is! The annoying and painstakingly slow drive through rush hour traffic, the long lines and wait at the airport, the long uncomfortable flight with the child screaming, etc. are all worth it when the plane touches down in Hawaii. So let's have a real idea of what eternity might be like. Let's examine the good attributes of *this* life that we enjoy—that God also made—and parallel them with some of the things the Bible describes about the age to come. Consider for a moment the implications of these two verses about the New Jerusalem in the New Earth:

> Revelation 21:24 By its light the nations will walk, and into it the kings of the earth will bring their glory. ²⁵Its gates will never be shut at the end of the day, because there will be no night there.
>
> ²⁶And into the city will be brought the glory and honor of the nations. ²⁷But nothing unclean will ever enter it, nor anyone who practices an abomination or a lie, but only those whose names are written in the Lamb's Book of Life.

Note that it does say that there are still separate nations and kings. *(Rev 21:24-26)* It's *possible* that we may even get to become kings or presidents of our own countries, if we would like to, and have shown that we could be responsible with such a task. *(Lk 19:11-*

27) It is safe to presume we will get to be used to the *absolute fullness* of our gifts, talents, and abilities. For those who love to lead and govern and build and create and maintain, they will likely be able to do such things. After all, it was God's original design that we would steward the earth. *(Gen 1:26-28)* This same thing may extend towards entrepreneurs who want to build businesses and create products and services. Or in teachers and worship leaders and inventors and builders. Why not?! We *are* made in God's image and likeness. Bearing good fruit towards one another and the creation is not only the way that He created and established things, but also part of our calling in Christ. *(Jn 15:1-8)* Stewardship is good, creating things and doing things is good. We are just supposed to do them in communion with God, and in a way that is pleasing to Him and glorifies Him!

And others may be full or part time priests. Even now we are said to be priests of God and of Christ, a royal priesthood, and that we reign with Christ. *(1 Pet 2:9, 2 Tim 2:12, Rev 1:6, 5:10, 20:6)* Every day we offer up our own bodies as living sacrifices to God, which is our holy and pleasing form of spiritual worship. *(Rom 12:1)* How much more so in the life to come! Some may do this from wherever they live by running a nation or a business in a way that glorifies God. Revelation 21:24 says, *"into it* [the New Jerusalem] *the kings of the earth will bring their glory."* So some bring in their glory to give it to God. Even though we will all be able to enter the holy city and bring our glory to God, some may choose to live and work there. Perhaps some get to help "deliver" this glory to God somehow. Jesus even describes different types of rewards related to our desires. To some, who desire to rule, He says we can have authority over others. In Revelation 2:26 Jesus says, *"And to the one who is victorious and continues in My work until the end, I will give authority over the nations."* But to others, in Revelation 3:12, Jesus promises them to be made, *"a pillar in the temple of My God, and he will never again leave it."*

To another, Jesus promises in Revelation 2:17 to, *"give a white stone inscribed with a new name, known only to the one who receives it."* This is a really interesting promise that has profound meaning if we really meditate on it. We value things that are rare. Gold is valuable because of how rare it is. Diamonds are even more rare and valuable. Original paintings that were created by famous artists can be worth millions. Why? Yes, because we value the item itself, but also because of its exclusivity. It's greater because it's an original. Because we have something no one else does, or can. Now, imagine having something one-of-a-kind, made not only by mere human hands, but in all of the entire universe. Now, imagine that infinitely-rare object was also custom-designed just for you. Awesome! Now, let's go even further. Imagine that *that* custom-designed, infinitely-rare object was custom designed, for you—by GOD! And not only that, but only you and He know what it says. It is a personal secret known only between you and the Almighty God of the universe! How awesome is that!

I feel like there's someone who will read this and think I wonder what I could sell that for. Ah, our idolatrous nature. First, remember this, since all things will be available for us in the life to come, money is irrelevant. We can *already* have and do whatever we want. Whatever else you want you can just get anyway. Whatever your heart's desire is. They will all be good, godly desires, that glorify God, remember? So God will grant them. Also, what will you sell it for anyways? It's not like you could sell it to get something else *more* valuable. What you already have, the greatest One in the universe (God) has given you as a personalized gift. It is, in actuality, *the* most valuable thing, for you, ever. And, it will be the gift and reward—for what *you did*—in *this* life. So, regardless of whatever we accomplish in the life to come, for everyone in the New Earth, whatever they could go on to get, earn, or build in *that* life, no one can ever go back to their first life and redo it. The time for this life is, you get it, this life! So that gift that God gives you as a reward for your accomplishment in this life is absolutely irreplaceable. This seemingly simple statement by Jesus, to offer the victor a stone inscribed with a name known only to the one who receives it, is *amazingly* profound when you really ponder it. Meditating on this has taught me a very, very valuable lesson:

God knows EXACTLY how to create a Paradise for us!

When people scoff that Heaven for eternity will be boring, as though we float on clouds playing harps for a trillion years, I know that they have not actually studied Scripture or philosophically thought this through. God made THIS world! That means any good thing that you, or anyone, has *ever* experienced, it was a broken, fallen version of its true potential! Think about that. Every single good thing that you have *ever* enjoyed was something good that God made that you got a *partial sampling of* because it was also tainted by sin. In the New Earth, the potential will be unlimited! There are no limits to God.

Whatever good things we enjoy about this fallen world are NOTHING compared to the life to come!

It's reasonable to me to believe that we will get to enjoy whatever our heart's desire is, because there will be no sin, no death, no entropy, no decay, no struggle. All of this is from the curse of the ground after the Fall, see Genesis 3:17-19. No more sin management. No maintenance, or repair, of brokenness. Only *forward* growth! Only *increase* of glory! Eating will be only for pleasure, not maintenance of the body. You will never have to eat food again just for your health to maintain a broken body or stave off hunger pains. I personally see a whole lot of chocolate in my future! Lol. And no gluttony, obesity, heart disease, judgment from others, etc. No negative effects at all. Can you imagine it? God, who invented our taste buds, will recreate it all, but perfectly. Likewise, jobs will be for pleasure, not sustenance or survival. Homes will be for enjoyment and parties, not protection. There is no night or thieves or evil doers or harsh weather or ravenous animals. Sleep will be for pleasure, or might not even exist. But our bodies won't break down so we may have all the energy we always need for whatever we want to do that would please us. Rest will never be a necessity, but only for pleasure, as well. Likewise, work, even hard work, will be for pleasure. For growth and improvement and achievement. Relationships will be for mutual-pleasure, not self-serving or getting ahead. Sports and competitions will be for pleasure of the game itself, of continual improvement of our skills, not our ego against others. A loss is winning a small amount rather than winning a large amount! There is no backwards, only forwards. There is no decay, only growth. Whether you win or lose the game, you have eternity to play again. Always playing a little better than you previously did. No injuries, no pain. There is no hostility, so selfishness, no ego, because there is no sin. All the good benefits of ANY activity that could potentially glorify God, minus all of the sinful emotions that often come along with it! Traveling, exercise, starting businesses, rock climbing, shopping, praise and worship, flying planes, arts and crafts, playing with animals, swimming, going to the beaches without sunscreen or cancer or sunburns, you name it, it's possible. Oh, did I mentioned that we can teleport like Jesus did? Go skiing in the mountains and then meet friends on the beach instantly and then spend some time with God in His temple.

Or perhaps Jesus will be with us in Spirit no matter where we are! That will probably still be true, too. It's true now, why not? We will live in peace and harmony with all people, and all animals, and they will also live in peace with each another too. All good activities are possible and can be enjoyed for God's glory! God's Spirit is with you doing it with you. All of it will be to His glory and praise. You can't hike a mountain without appreciating God's design of nature and celebrating Him for it. Like Paul said in 1 Corinthians 10:31, "Whether you eat or drink or whatever you do, do it all to the glory of God." All interactions are with your brothers and sisters and all have one Lord and one Father and there is perfect love. Our currency will be God's glory! And there will be perpetual inflation! Different ways, and types, and methods for us to enjoy our lives and give God glory.

---

2 Corinthians 4:17 For our light and momentary affliction is producing for us an eternal glory that is far beyond comparison.

Romans 8:18 I consider that our present sufferings are not comparable to the glory that will be revealed in us.

1 Peter 5:1 As a fellow elder, a witness of Christ's sufferings, and a partaker of the glory to be revealed, I appeal to the elders among you

Matthew 19:29 And everyone who has left houses or brothers or sisters or father or mother or wife or children or fields for the sake of My name will receive a hundredfold and will inherit eternal life.

p. Two Maps, Two Destinations
There are two destinations: Eternal life and glory, or eternal death and torment.

The previous section focused on the wonderful destination that all of us should strive towards. It truly will be marvelous. However, a good map to a good destination cannot be presented without also providing a warning about the old bad map to a bad destination. Satan has been very active through false prophets and teachers to mislead and remove the doctrine of Hell. Why? Because without it we don't rightly fear God. The reason is this: *fear* of God is the beginning of wisdom. Without fear there's no humility before God, no conviction of sin, no remorse or repentance of sin, no true knowledge of God's justice, and ultimately no real need for a Savior from God's wrath on sin. *(Prov 9:10, Ps 36:1, Rom 3:18, Rev 14:7, 2 Cor 7:1, Eph 5:21)* But Scripture is clear. Jesus was clear. The warnings are clear—and severe. There are *only* two destinations and they are both final and permanent. Because of the many lies I want to thoroughly demonstrate that eternal Hell is biblical, and then share some additional insights to wrap our head and heart around it.

It *is* tempting, for all of us with a heart anyways, to desire a way for all to be saved, or at least all those who *we* know, who we hope would be saved. Many false religions, Christian cults, and even once orthodox (traditional) believers have drifted into heretical (false) ideas about the afterlife. One of these ideas is *annihilationism*, where those who don't enter Heaven just stay dead and just cease to exist. This means there's rewards for trusting in Jesus or for doing good, but there's no punishment beyond just staying dead for not doing so. On the opposite end of the spectrum is *universalism*, the idea that all people will ultimately be reconciled to God, regardless of whether they repented, trusted in Jesus, lived a "good" life, etc. That everyone gets saved. Both of these positions find support because of our empathy for others. They appeal to God's goodness, love, and mercy, and thus our desire for none to go to Hell eternally. However pure and good these motives may be, the fact remains: both are false. More than false, they are the "doctrines of demons" that distort important truths, such as what is our authority for doctrine, and the righteousness and justice of God. For the *biblical* Christian—whose faith is rooted and grounded in trusting God at His Word—the Bible is our God-breathed, inspired, and inerrant authority, and it's clear on this matter. There are two destinations and both are conscious and eternal. We've already imagined God's potential for an eternal paradise. Imagining God's potential for an eternal punishment takes new horrific form.

A key aspect of this is understanding God's righteousness and justice. It is *because of* God's justice, against all sin, that Jesus had to bear the consequences for our sin on the cross. Sin can't be ignored. *That* would be unjust. The judge that says to the guilty child molester "you can go free, because I'm a loving and merciful judge" is NOT a good judge! He's a depraved, corrupt judge. That is a perversion of justice and an act of hatred against all *that* person's victims. It is God's *goodness* that demands there be a punishment. God will not send people to Hell *because* He's bad. He will do so *because* He's good.

The judge who ensures that every single sin is answered for is the good judge. That would be a good thing—if all of us weren't guilty sinners! All of us have sins piled up to the sky. Sins against ourselves, sins against others, sins against the creation, and worst of all, sins against God. In fact our greatest sin is the rejection of God as our god in the first place, even though He gives us as a gift every single breath, every heartbeat, and every good thing we've ever experienced. But then also, against many of us, is the rejection of Jesus as our Savior once we hear of the good news that He has willfully taken our punishment, and offered to redeem us and purchased for us eternal life. What an incredible free gift to have been offered! God essentially says, "Trust in My Son and I will forgive every single one of your sins against Me, and continue to forgive them going forward whenever you slip; receive a new heart and spirit from Me that will help you know Me, bless others, and become righteous; come back into relationship with Me as my child, and persevere in this blessed hope and I will give you a new, blessed, eternal life." What is our excuse for rejecting this? Seriously!? The rejection of *this* news—what others receive as the greatest life-giving news ever—is the greatest sin. In fact it's the *only* unpardonable sin.

God is just, much more than we are, so He *is* going to punish all sin. Either He punishes our sin, on Jesus, on the cross—or He punishes our sin, on us, in Hell. Hell is not inconsistent with the boundless love of God, it is an expression of His righteousness and justice. God is BOTH loving and just, not either/or. The cross teaches us this best. It is the perfect symbol. The cross was the intersection of *perfect* love and *perfect* justice. Perfect sacrificial love and mercy for those who don't deserve it, perfect wrathful justice for those who do. An eternal Heaven and eternal Hell are the exact same: perfect love and perfect justice. Beautiful, joyous, eternal life received by undeserving, sinful creatures who don't deserve it—or horrific, tormenting, eternal death received by sinful creatures who do. We all receive one or the other. We either receive God's offer of mercy, or His offer of justice. We just have to decide WHERE we receive God's justice. Are we going to receive His justice against sin on the cross with Christ—or in Hell?

God is BOTH loving and just. Not either/or. The cross teaches us this best. It is the intersection of perfect love and perfect justice.

It is God's love and mercy that the offer of salvation is available to us all. If we hate God and truth and righteousness so much that we persist in our sin, that's our choice. If we don't *actually* want a life with God as our god. If we don't actually want eternity to worship Him. If we don't actually want eternity to grow closer to Him, that's our choice. God is not going to force us to. It's *this* life that we show God we *want* Him as our God and Father and Savior for eternity. It's this relatively short life of usually 100 years or less that we show God who we are and what we want. I hate the thought of people I know and love going to Hell, but I also see it from God's perspective. Imagine some parents you know, raising their child, taking care of all their needs, loving them in every way. And then the child becomes an ungrateful adult, moves out, hates them, wants nothing to do with them. Those parents continue to fully support them, sending them enough money to live on and continually seek a relationship with them, offering love and support and providing for 100% of their needs. But their child *despises* their affection and uses their money to curse their parents and society and do immense evil. They use the money and resources being given to them by their parents to fund horrendous evils, like murder, gang rape, and the sex trafficking of children. They take the blessings given to them, and use them to curse others. So the blessing of the parents is not only rejected, but also harnessed to hurt others. See how wicked that is on so many levels? That's an extreme example, but when contrasted to God's holiness, even our "minor" sins are nearly as awful. Even if we are socially "good" but blaspheme God's name, and reject Jesus, this is really very evil! And the truth is some *do* use God's blessing to do the same evils like those I mentioned. God is patient with us, wanting us to repent, but we cannot defame His glory forever. God gives us this life to decide what we will be, and where we will go. And if we use *this* life, to basically say in every possible way, that we don't want to spend eternity with God, doing things that glorify God, then God is not going to force us to. He will let us get what we want, though I believe the alternative in the life to come will be a LOT worse than people think. I have the FEAR of God! They don't. This is the beginning of knowledge and wisdom. *(Rom 3:18, Rev 14:7, 2 Cor 7:1, Deut 25:18, Prov 36:1, 9:10, 111:10)*

If we don't want to spend eternity with God, He's not going to force us to.

I'm convinced, both through Scripture and through the heart of God revealed through the illumination of the Holy Spirit, that every person receives enough grace and light from God in this life to respond to His offer for salvation. God's offer is extended to all. God loved *"the world"* and sent His Son *"to save the world through Him." (Jn 3:17)* Jesus, *"the true light that gives light to everyone,"* (cf. John 1:9) *"but men loved the darkness rather than the Light, because their deeds were evil."* (cf. John 3:19) However, John 3:21 assures us, *"But whoever practices the truth comes into the Light, so that it may be seen clearly that what He has done has been accomplished in God."*

John 3:36 Whoever believes in the Son has eternal life. Whoever rejects the Son will not see life. Instead, the wrath of God remains on him."

I want to make sure you are convinced beyond all doubt that there is an eternal Hell. As Heaven is eternal, so also is Hell, its counterpart. *(Mt 25:46, 2 Thes 1:9, Dan 12:2)* Hell was originally prepared for the Devil and his fallen angels, *(Mt 25:41)* and not intended for man, but men who die in their sins by refusing the work of redemption on the Cross of Calvary through the shed blood of the Lord and Savior Jesus Christ, would have no other choice than to have Hell as their abode. *(Mt 25:1-46)* It is described as a destination *"of outer darkness," "where there will be weeping and gnashing of teeth."* (Mt 25:30, 13:42, 13:50, 8:12) Jesus gives severe warnings about sin, and about avoiding Hell from our sin, saying that even if your eye causes you to sin it would be better to gouge it out than for your whole *body* to be thrown *into* Hell. *(Mt 5:29-30, Mt 18:6-9, Mk 9:42-48)*

Hell is an eternal destination without God's presence. This is physical, mental, emotional, and spiritual torment. It is also eternal death, where every part of our being (body, soul, and spirit) that comes from God, slowly dies, eternally, until whatever is left eventually ceases to exist. *(Mt 10:28)* I am not saying that it is, even eventually, annihilated, but Scripture is clear that it *is* death. There is likely still some form of existence, as without existing it wouldn't be eternal, but the *form* of existence, your *identity*, would probably cease to be recognizable eventually from your original. Because of the absence of God's presence, and life and grace, the ravages of sin which would now be completely unrestrained. This perpetual decay would eventually diminish all that is good, and all that is alive. All attributes of God's likeness—all that is holy, righteous, pure, loving, hopeful, gracious, peaceful, forbearing, kind, faithful, merciful, and generous—would extinguish. The conscience, God's law on the heart of man, would go from seared to absent, as would any restraint a person has from giving in to every form of vileness and moral degradation. The inevitable result is perpetual death of all that is good, all that comes from God in His good design. The remnant remaining would be pure, unadulterated evil. A miserable end indeed to imagine a place so horrific where God does not exist and has intentionally been made absent of all that the free being was initially made to enjoy.

Many times Hell is associated with fire such as *"the lake of fire," "the fiery furnace,"* the *"fiery lake of burning sulfur,"* or *"where the fire is never quenched."* (Mt 13:42, Mt 13:50, Mk 9:48, Rev 14:10-11, 19:20, Rev 20:10, Rev 20:15, Rev 21:8) Whether this is physical fire or metaphorical fire is unknown, but either way the picture painted is clear. It is a destination of vast *consumption.* Fire feeds off of something else. It maintains its "life" through the destruction of something else that is living. It *takes* life in order for it to continue on. For fire to keep burning, something alive must keep dying. This is how Hell is described. A place that continues on eternally by feeding off of the decay of the life that was cast into it. Revelation 14:10-11, speaking of when the Antichrist is thrown into Hell says, *"he will be tormented in fire and brimstone," "and the smoke of their torment rises forever and ever."* This same *continuous burning* picture is given in Isaiah 34:9-10, speaking of the Lords' day of vengeance against Zion's enemies. *"Her streams will be turned into tar, and her soil to sulfur; her land will become a blazing pitch. It will not be quenched—day or night. Its smoke will ascend forever."* And again in Revelation 19:3, when the great prostitute, who represents the world's sinful kingdoms is destroyed and God's people respond, *"Hallelujah! Her smoke ascends forever and ever."* (Rev 17:3-6, 15-18) The following list of passages brings home the point that we don't need to like this truth to realize it is what the Bible teaches. Rebuke all false teachers who say otherwise.

John 5:28 *[Jesus]* Do not be amazed at this, for the hour is coming when all who are in their graves will hear His voice [29]and come out—those who have done good to the resurrection of life, and those who have done evil to the resurrection of judgment.

Mark 9:43 *[Jesus]* If your hand causes you to sin, cut it off. It is better for you to enter life crippled than to have two hands and go into hell, into the unquenchable fire.[44] [45]If your foot causes you to sin, cut it off. It is better for you to enter life lame than to have two feet and be thrown into hell.[46] [47]And if your eye causes you to sin, pluck it out. It is better for you to enter the kingdom of God with one eye than to have two eyes and be thrown into hell, [48]where 'their worm never dies, and the fire is never quenched.'

Daniel 12:1b But at that time your people—everyone whose name is found written in the book—will be delivered. [2]And many who sleep in the dust of the earth will awake, some to everlasting life, but others to shame and everlasting contempt.

2 Thessalonians 1:8 He *[the Antichrist]* will inflict vengeance on those who do not know God and do not obey the gospel of our Lord Jesus. [9]They will suffer the penalty of eternal destruction, separated from the presence of the Lord and the glory of His might...

Revelation 19:20b Both the beast and the false prophet were thrown alive into the fiery lake of burning sulfur.

Revelation 20:10 And the devil who had deceived them was thrown into the lake of fire and sulfur, into which the beast and the false prophet had already been thrown. There they will be tormented day and night forever and ever.

Revelation 20:12 And I saw the dead, great and small, standing before the throne. And there were open books, and one of them was the Book of Life. And the dead were judged according to their deeds, as recorded in the books. [13]The sea gave up its dead, and Death and Hades gave up their dead, and each one was judged according to his deeds. [14]Then Death and Hades were thrown into the lake of fire. This is the second death—the lake of fire. [15]And if anyone was found whose name was not written in the Book of Life, he was thrown into the lake of fire.

Revelation 21:8 "But to the cowardly and unbelieving and abominable and murderers and sexually immoral and sorcerers and idolaters and all liars, their place will be in the lake that burns with fire and sulfur. This is the second death."

Revelation 22:11 Let the unrighteous continue to be unrighteous, and the vile continue to be vile; let the righteous continue to practice righteousness, and the holy continue to be holy." [12]"Behold, I am coming quickly, and My reward is with Me, to give to each one according to what he has done... [14]Blessed are those who wash their robes, so that they may have the right to the tree of life and may enter the city by its gates. [15]But outside are the dogs, the sorcerers, the sexually immoral, the murderers, the idolaters, and everyone who loves and practices falsehood.

Matthew 13:40 As the weeds are collected and burned in the fire, so will it be at the end of the age. [41]The Son of Man will send out His angels, and they will weed out of His kingdom every cause of sin and all who practice lawlessness. [42]And they will throw them into the fiery furnace, where there will be weeping and gnashing of teeth. [43]Then the righteous will shine like the sun in the kingdom of their Father. He who has ears, let him hear.

Matthew 25:46 "And they will go away into eternal punishment, but the righteous into eternal life."

Let these many warnings be a word of caution for us. Here's a few takeaways and action steps: First, let's praise God for delivering us from His wrath through Christ! Hallelujah! Every single day know that your sins against God were piled up to Heaven, and you were on your way to Hell, and Jesus bore the weight of their due punishment on your behalf. God gets all the glory for doing that. He is so gracious! Love Him for it! Praise Him for it! Proclaim His glory to the world! Second, know that all of eternity in the world to come, and every single day today, is a gift from God. Cherish it! Internalize this truth. If you believe it then you will live it out and you will think and live and feel differently. Your life will be marked by one of peace and joy—if you have genuine faith in the promise of this gospel. Third, take these biblical truths to those who claim to be a Christian yet deny these realities. They don't yet know the true God and worship Him in spirit and in truth. Share it and be an apologist for it. And fire, demote, or publicly out any false preacher, teacher, prophet, or elder who is teaching contrary doctrine. People need to know the love of God but *not* at the expense of the fear of God. Proclaim both God's love and His justice. God's love is *so* much sweeter when we appreciate His justice! Fourth, let this horrific description of Hell motivate you, in love for *all of them* out there, to overcome our fears and hesitations that keep us from sharing the gospel with others. We need to be about our Father's business, which is to be part of the plan of restoration. He's using us to do it! Let the Apostle Paul's words below inspire you. If you're convinced then your destination is set. You're on your way towards Heaven, and you're an ambassador for Christ in the world, as though God is making His appeal to *them*—through you!

> 2 Corinthians 5:18 All this is from God, who reconciled us to Himself through Christ and gave us the ministry of reconciliation: [19]that God was reconciling the world to Himself in Christ, not counting men's trespasses against them. And He has committed to us the message of reconciliation. [20]Therefore we are ambassadors for Christ, as though God were making His appeal through us. We implore you on behalf of Christ: Be reconciled to God. [21]God made Him who knew no sin to be sin on our behalf, so that in Him we might become the righteousness of God.

HAS THIS CONTENT BEEN HELPFUL?
SHARE IT WITH OTHERS FOR FREE!

I believe everyone needs the new map so they can learn everything they need to be saved, so this entire chapter is available as a free download on our website.

This ENTIRE Chapter is available as a FREE PDF download at
https://MPoweredChristian.org/TECRM-FREE

IV. Chapter Summary and Evaluation

Chapter Summary
You need to always know where you're going, and where you currently are.

God created us with an amazing purpose in mind. God has invited us to join in eternal relationship with the Father, Son, and Holy Spirit. And our destiny has amazing *potential* but our course is not set for us. *Fate* is a lie of Satan. None of our final destinations have been predetermined in advance. All that has been predetermined is that those *who belong* to Jesus *will* inherit eternal life through Him, and none of them will be lost. Everyone found in Christ has been predestined for glory. Jesus is the Anointed One, the elect one, and everyone found in Him is also elect, i.e. chosen, in Christ. No one is elect apart from Christ, our election *is found in* Christ. Draw near to God, and Christ as your Shepherd, and so be His sheep. The invitation and *calling* (the offer of salvation through Christ) is available to all, *"but small is the gate and narrow the way that leads to life, and only a few find it."* (Matthew 7:14) *"Many are called, but few are chosen."* (Mt 22:14) As the Apostle Paul writes, *"we know that He has chosen you, because our gospel came to you... And you became imitators of us and of the Lord when you welcomed the message with the joy of the Holy Spirit, in spite of your great suffering."* (1 Thes 1:4-6) See also: (Lk 18:7-8, Mt 24:22, 2 Tim 2:10, 1 Cor 1:21) So let us take the advice below from the Apostle Peter to heart. In fact, even if you already knew and believed everything from this entire chapter, he tells us *"it is right to refresh your memory,"* (2 Pet 1:13) and make every effort that *"you will be able to recall these things at all times."* (2 Pet 1:15) In other words, have a clear map in your mind!

---

2 Peter 1:10 "Therefore, brothers, be all the more eager to make your calling and election sure. For if you practice these things you will never stumble, ¹¹and you will receive a lavish reception into the eternal kingdom of our Lord and Savior Jesus Christ."

With a confidence in your election in Christ, based on your faith alone, you can press on forward wholeheartedly—towards a destination, not of wrath, but of salvation. *(1 Thes 5:9)* Press on and be described by the Lord as one of His called (invited) and chosen (elect, who choose to follow) and faithful (believing, obedient, persevering) ones! *(Rev 17:4)*

Press on toward the destination, and be described as one of "His called and chosen and faithful ones."

There are a lot of important aspects of the Christian life, and life in general, so it's easy to get lost in the day-to-day shuffle. In order to have focus; not to mention direction, hope, and peace in the midst of obstacles; we need to know and be mindful of the journey where we're going. The car sickness on the way there, the flat tire, the other driver that almost killed you with their reckless driving, the annoying and hurtful people in the car with you, these things are all easier to keep in perspective and cope with when our eyes are always fixed on the joy we will have at our final destination. And if you think about it, the *greater* the destination ahead, the more we need to make sure that we don't allow *anything* on the drive to break our focus or our joy during the journey. Or even worse, provoke us to just turn around and give up the trip altogether! I refuse to allow that to happen to me. I will press on. I will love those who hate me. I will overcome every obstacle before me because I believe God is with me and *"I can do all things through Christ who gives me strength."* (Phil 4:13) Do you believe this too? Do you commit today to do the same?

It is so easy for us to get immersed in daily minutia, the ebb and flow of life, and even in the secondary and of lesser-importance, matters of the Christian life. I'm sure I've said some things that you disagree with already. Hopefully none of those things were matters of life-or-death, essential Christian doctrine required for salvation. As long as that's the case, then we are free to agree to disagree, agreeably. We are still on the *same* journey, towards the *same* destination, together. And sometimes our different perspectives are even a gift from God because it forces us to come together in love, despite them, and show ourselves approved as children of God. Reflect upon the massive amount of information in this chapter. It's key to having a clear map. It's key that you know who God is and what the purpose of your life is. It is key that you know who the true Jesus is and how you receive salvation. From all of this as the bedrock, the foundation, you can build upon other things later. Too many Christians run forward too quickly. They want the exciting stuff. They want to fight demons, or fight others about doctrine. They want to start making converts before they even know their own doctrines well. They want to tell others what *they* are doing wrong or sinful and they haven't even gotten the log out of their own eyes. *(Mt 7:1-6)* They will even hypocritically quote *that* verse against others, not realizing it's about *them*! Work on YOURSELF first. The verse I previously provided about calling in 2 Peter 1:10, he said to *"practice* these things *so that* you will never stumble." Which things to practice? I have them below. Don't just learn them—*actively* practice them!

---

2 Peter 1:5 For this very reason, make every effort to add to your faith virtue; and to virtue, knowledge; ⁶and to knowledge, self-control; and to self-control, perseverance; and to perseverance, godliness; ⁷and to godliness, brotherly kindness; and to brotherly kindness, love. ⁸For if you possess these qualities and continue to grow in them, they will keep you from being ineffective and unproductive in your knowledge of our Lord Jesus Christ.

The Purpose of Chapter Evaluations

An important part of discipleship into spiritual maturity is continuous refinement. Your goal should be regular education, followed by personal evaluation and personal application. It's not just about learning, it's about *doing.* You need to continue honestly evaluating your current state, and then challenging yourself to keep learning, refining, applying, changing, or else you won't grow. The Holy Spirit, from the moment He came in, wants to conform you into the image of Christ. Commit today to *submit* in obedience and play an active role in this process. As we've already seen, Scripture is clear that those in Christ *will* change. They *will* bear fruit of repentance. They *will* begin conforming to the will of God. They *will* persevere in faith and good works. These things are NOT optional!

These evaluations will help you keep an eye on important areas throughout your journey. At the end of every chapter there are a few simple guides to help you assess where you currently are (both now, and again later at any given point in time) so you can refer back later, periodically, as you continue to progress forward. Think of this as a GPS tool that helps you keep an eye on all the important navigational instruments so you can monitor your current position on the road map. You want to make sure you're always going the right direction, with an eye on everything. May God bless your journey!

Evaluation Directions.

On a scale from 1-10, how knowledgeable, certain, and confident, are you in the following declarations? Using a pencil select the corresponding number. A lower number means you have no confidence, major confusion, major doubts, or other emotional obstacles that are keeping you from fully embracing this truth as a reality right now. A higher number means you understand it well, believe it's true, have confidence in its truthfulness, and allow its reality to impact the way you think, feel, worship, and live. This book's content should be enough to get you to a 5 on each unless you have presuppositional beliefs that hinder it. If you score a 4 or less on any, I recommend starting with further study in those topic areas first. If you score a 5 or greater on all, continue to chapter two. But if you score less than a 7 in any, I recommend re-reading those sections again first (see letter key on the left of each).

Chapter 1 Evaluation
I UNDERSTAND WHY, BELIEVE, HAVE CONFIDENCE THAT:

Scale: False — Partially False — Mostly True — True (1 to 10)

Statement	1	2	3	4	5	6	7	8	9	10
a) There's only One eternal God, He created everything else.	1	2	3	4	5	6	7	8	9	10
a) God created and sustains everything for His own glory	1	2	3	4	5	6	7	8	9	10
b) I exist to glorify God and celebrate and share in His glory .	1	2	3	4	5	6	7	8	9	10
b) My greatest satisfaction will be found in God's glory..........	1	2	3	4	5	6	7	8	9	10
c) God exists eternally as a Trinity: Father, Son, Holy Spirit ...	1	2	3	4	5	6	7	8	9	10
c) Jesus is God, the eternal Word of God that became flesh..	1	2	3	4	5	6	7	8	9	10
c) If Jesus isn't God then worship of Him is idolatry	1	2	3	4	5	6	7	8	9	10
d) God has invited me into eternal intimate relationship	1	2	3	4	5	6	7	8	9	10
d) Though many reject it, God desires all to receive His gift...	1	2	3	4	5	6	7	8	9	10
e) I understand all Truth is intimately connected with God ...	1	2	3	4	5	6	7	8	9	10
e) I value, love, and desire Truth wherever it can be found....	1	2	3	4	5	6	7	8	9	10
f) Every human is made in God's image and has value	1	2	3	4	5	6	7	8	9	10
f) Humans are an eternal soul united to spirit and body	1	2	3	4	5	6	7	8	9	10
f) Humans (spirit and conscience) are response-able to God	1	2	3	4	5	6	7	8	9	10
g) God is most glorified in us when we freely love Him	1	2	3	4	5	6	7	8	9	10
h) The Fall gives us the opportunity to love and choose good	1	2	3	4	5	6	7	8	9	10
h) God didn't cause evil; moral beings with free will did	1	2	3	4	5	6	7	8	9	10
i) My actions show that I live for glory, honor, immortality ...	1	2	3	4	5	6	7	8	9	10
j) Jesus did not replace the Law, but fulfills it perfectly for us	1	2	3	4	5	6	7	8	9	10
j) Christians are to obey the Moral Law and should love it	1	2	3	4	5	6	7	8	9	10
k) The New Birth provides access to God and righteousness.	1	2	3	4	5	6	7	8	9	10
k) Water baptism is important but it doesn't merit salvation	1	2	3	4	5	6	7	8	9	10
k) We cannot know if we're born again so we must persevere	1	2	3	4	5	6	7	8	9	10
l) Through Jesus is the only Way to receive eternal life	1	2	3	4	5	6	7	8	9	10
l) Salvation is received by Faith in Christ alone, not works ...	1	2	3	4	5	6	7	8	9	10
m) My destiny is to be conformed into the image of Christ	1	2	3	4	5	6	7	8	9	10
m) Becoming more like Christ now is inevitable if we're in Him	1	2	3	4	5	6	7	8	9	10
n) In Christ, I'm an adopted child of God, who is my Father...	1	2	3	4	5	6	7	8	9	10
n) God's children, in Christ, don't need other intermediaries	1	2	3	4	5	6	7	8	9	10
o) Eternal life in Paradise with God awaits those in Christ......	1	2	3	4	5	6	7	8	9	10
p) Eternal death (Hell) awaits those who reject God's offer....	1	2	3	4	5	6	7	8	9	10

Date Last Taken: _____

Questions for Reflection or Group Study:

1) What *would* you have scored lowest in? What part of the "new map" was different than you had previously thought? How had it negatively affected your journey or destination?

2) How does the *purpose* of your life change when considering it from God's perspective, you being created for *His* glory, rather than by trying to decide what you want out of life?

3) Section (F) provided a complex view of what it means to be made in God's image. Discuss how we would think and behave differently ourselves, or with others, if we believed this.

4) Section (K) details how to be *Born Again* and how it changes us permanently. Do you have evidence of this? How could you recommit your faith in Jesus today?

Explore Chapter 1 Deeper:

For additional resources related to the topics discussed in this chapter see our companion website at **https://MPoweredChristian.org/Road-Map-Book-Resources**

- Free printable pdf of this chapter evaluation for personal or classroom use
- List of related online courses, e-coaching programs, personal coaching services
- List of related videos, articles, and recommended books
- List of related live webinars and ways to ask questions

Notes/Reflections:

_____
_____
_____
_____
_____
_____
_____
_____
_____
_____
_____
_____
_____
_____
_____
_____
_____
_____
_____
_____
_____
_____
_____
_____
_____
_____
_____
_____
_____
_____
_____
_____

To-Do List: Date: _____

MY TASKS FOR **THIS UPCOMING WEEK...**

✔ **My Big 1-3:**
_____
_____
_____

✔ **For Personal Growth:**
_____
_____
_____

✔ **For Key Roles:**
_____
_____
_____

✔ **For Calling/Ministry Service:**
_____
_____
_____

✔ **Pray for/Request prayer about:**
_____
_____
_____

✔ **Learn more about:**
_____
_____
_____

✔ **Other:**
_____
_____
_____

CHAPTER TWO

REBUILT and headed in a NEW DIRECTION

You need more than a new map but also a new car, new driver, new mechanic—a NEW EVERYTHING!

Chapter Contents

I. Understanding the Old

a. We've Got A Bad Map
Our "direction" is completely off and we need an entirely different direction.

I spent the entire first chapter really driving this point home. We do not start out "okay but a little off." We don't just need to *tweak* things a little to move in the right direction. Many false religions are based on this idea: that humans are generally pretty good. The opposite is true. We are actually more bad than good. The nature of sin is all consuming. It is like a cancer that has spread to every cell of the body. It has completely poisoned the well. Every aspect of our being has been tarnished and influenced, even what we consider the good parts of us. It began with the sin of Adam and Eve in the Garden of Eden and the effects have compounded (like compound interest in the bank) through every generation since then. This is the doctrine of "original sin." We inherit the sin nature, passed down through our parents. This includes the consequences of sin, such as struggle, pain, decay, and death. It also includes the presence and power of sin, such as wicked and wrong desires, that sometimes seem good and right to us. So we must not think that we can trust most of what seems right to us, or what necessarily *feels* good. The truth is that humans are wicked, and the thoughts and desires of our hearts are wicked. Our conscience testifies to us the truth of this but we often suppress it. We need to trust God when He tells us this plainly in His Word. We need to trust Him when He tells us that we're sick. It is only when we are humble enough to realize, acknowledge, and confess to ourselves and to God that we are sick, that we can be healed. To see our sinfulness and depravity, to recognize our own brokenness and the inner struggle within to do good. This is why there is a struggle and a choice to do good, because there are parts of our nature that don't want to. If there wasn't we would always just do what is right and best. But we don't. We need to stop being self-righteous, and denying this reality, and just be humble enough to accept this truth. Then we can then turn to Jesus, who is our Great Physician! Jesus not only heals us, He completely rebuilds us from the ground up. It starts with the new map. The entirely new direction that was very different from our old direction. Chapter one was the new map. Now it's time to start the journey! But it is crucial that you understand we don't travel the journey in our old nature, and in our own strength. God gives us a set of new everything for the journey.

b. We've Got A Broken Car
We don't need a "tune-up," we need an entirely new vehicle.

For your journey you will need a vehicle. You—your body, mind, will, emotions, spirit, etc.—is the vehicle that you travel through life in. Think of yourself as the vehicle. You are the car. But you're busted. You're broken. Don't feel bad, we all are! And it's not your fault. You were born that way. King David acknowledges this in Psalm 51:5, *"Surely I was brought forth in iniquity; I was sinful when my mother conceived me."* After the Fall humanity was cursed with death. *(Gen 3:16-19)* The toil of the ground that we have to labor with that continues to decay, the pain of childbirth, the decay of our bodies and minds, these are all related to the curse of death. Which is related to the presence of sin. If anyone thinks that we are not a sinner, or that we have no sin, do we still decay? Will we die, and are we dying in a small way every day? Yes. Then there is sin in us.

Romans 5:12 Therefore, just as sin entered the world through one man, and death through sin, so also death was passed on to all men, because all sinned.

Romans 3:23 states that, *"All mankind has sinned and falls short of the glory of God."* Even when we try to do good we will inevitably still fall short of God's perfection. Remember Jesus's Sermon on the Mount in Matthew 5? Our Father desires us to become perfect. *(Mt 5:48)* Ecclesiastes 7:20 acknowledges our imperfection saying, *"Surely there is no righteous man on earth who does good and never sins."* Isaiah 53 and 59 speak in detail of our corrupt nature and then prophesy of the Redeemer to come who intercedes to make us new. We now know that this is Jesus. Because every person is a sinner, is under the curse of sin which is death, and has a sin nature and an inclination to continue to sin more, we all need Jesus to save us and to make us new. We need a brand new car, designed by God for the journey. The old car isn't going to get us to where we want to go.

Romans 3:10 As it is written: "There is no one righteous, not even one. [11]There is no one who understands, no one who seeks God. [12]All have turned away, they have together become worthless; there is no one who does good, not even one."

Ephesians 2:1 As for you, you were dead in your trespasses and sins, [2]in which you used to walk when you conformed to the ways of this world and of the ruler of the power of the air, the spirit who is now at work in the sons of disobedience. [3]At one time we all lived among them, fulfilling the cravings of our flesh and indulging its desires and thoughts. Like the rest, we were by nature children of wrath.

---

c. We've Got Poor Eyesight
What seems good and right to us is, by God's standards, often wicked and wrong.

The way that we think, and feel, and act, is all influenced by our sin nature. Sin hasn't only caused physical death but also spiritual death, which is separation from God and from being like God in moral character. We inherited a nature of flesh, that is pre-corrupted by, and naturally inclined toward, sin. Even when we fully submit and obey all the law and righteousness of God we're unable to stand fully blameless before God. So all who know God's Law, and try to obey it, this is good, but we still stand guilty. We are guilty of all the sins we *have* committed, and we're guilty of the wicked thoughts and desires of our hearts that we secretly enjoy. The law merely brings awareness of sin.

Romans 3:9 What then? Are we any better? Not at all. For we have already made the charge that Jews and Greeks alike are all under sin.

[19]Now we know that whatever the law says, it says to those who are under the law, so that every mouth may be silenced and the whole world held accountable to God. [20]Therefore no one will be justified in His sight by works of the law. For the law merely brings awareness of sin.

And while all people have some moral code they live by, whether it's based on God's Law or not, because of our own sin nature, we often view the law through distorted eyesight. We submit only to certain parts of the law, parts we find comfortable, while condemning others for doing the same. It is not uncommon to see religious people who condemn others for *their* sins, while ignoring the different kinds of sins that they themselves are committing. They condemn homosexuals while ignoring their own adultery, fornication, pornography, lust. But sexual immorality is sexual immorality. They condemn tobacco use because it is bad stewardship of the body while ignoring overeating, gluttony, and obesity, which causes even more deaths. I could give numerous more examples. The point is that we are all partially blind. We don't see clearly the reality. We see through a skewed lens. This is the effect of sin. It is blinding. It is deceptive. This is why Jesus taught us to first focus on ourselves, to first remove the log from our own eyes. With a log still in our own eye we cannot see clearly enough to help remove the speck from our brother's eye. *(Mt 7:1-7)* It is also not a coincidence that what is in our own eye is much larger. It is a log, rather than a speck. Christians are told by opponents often that Jesus said not to judge. But the truth is that we are to judge. Without judging at all we cannot detect and avoid sin. Without judging we cannot discover truth and avoid lies. Without judging we cannot help each other grow and mature in holiness. But we are to judge without being a hypocrite. And without condemnation in our hearts. We are to judge with discernment, and personal humility, and with love and grace and empathy and longsuffering, knowing how easy it is to have a log in our own eye about some other type of sin. We need to come alongside one another in love and encouragement.

Our commitment to our own relationship with God, and His holiness, and our dedication to being conformed into Christ-likeness is needed to remove these logs. As-is the sanctifying presence of, and our regular submission to, the Holy Spirit. Without which, we would still be blind. And of course, if we are blind, with bad eyesight and a massive log in our eyes, we cannot trust ourselves to see clearly for the journey before us. No, we need entirely new eyes. We cannot keep our old eyesight and then decide to follow the law of God. This only leads to Pharisaism. It leads to inwardly-spiritually-dead sinners trying to muster up the strength and obedience to obey God outwardly. This won't cut it. It only adds to our guiltiness. It makes us even more blind. The more we *do*, in the way of the Pharisee, the more we will judge others for not doing. The harder our hearts will become towards people struggling with sin. We will not love our neighbors, nor are we really loving God. Blinder and blinder we become. And self-deceived. We must be spiritually reborn and get brand new infant eyes, and then we also need to continue to mature and let the Holy Spirit teach us how to use them. We all still have remnants of our old eyesight in the flesh, that we must crucify, and give way to the new way of seeing.

Luke 18:9 *[Jesus]* To some who trusted in their own righteousness and viewed others with contempt, He also told this parable: ¹⁰"Two men went up to the temple to pray. One was a Pharisee and the other a tax collector. ¹¹The Pharisee stood by himself and prayed, 'God, I thank You that I am not like the other men—swindlers, evildoers, adulterers—or even like this tax collector. ¹²I fast twice a week and pay tithes of all that I acquire.'

¹³But the tax collector stood at a distance, unwilling even to lift up his eyes to heaven. Instead, he beat his breast and said, 'God, have mercy on me, a sinner!' ¹⁴I tell you, this man, rather than the Pharisee, went home justified. For everyone who exalts himself will be humbled, but the one who humbles himself will be exalted."

---

d. You Must Be Born Again
You need to become a new creation, an entirely new car, to succeed your journey.

You need to become a brand new car! And this is not of your own doing, it is the work of the Holy Spirit. It is only by the grace of God, through your faith and trust in Jesus as your Lord and Savior. I can't tell you how to make this happen, I can only tell you that it must happen. You can't force it to happen. It is God's decision if, when, and how. All you can do is die to your old plans, and your old way, and repent of your sins, and humble yourself before God, and fully surrender your life to Jesus. And then trust that it has happened, by faith alone. I can assure that if God does not rebuild your car, and He is not the one driving your car, then you will never get to the desired destination. And you will be a miserable replica during the entire journey. You will still do many of the things the other changed cars will do, but you will never have peace or joy or contentment. You will never have the inner witness of the Holy Spirit confirming that you have been saved.

You won't have the strength to stand in the midst of the storms and persevere. So how do you know that you have been born again? FAITH. You trust that you have. You trust in Jesus. You trust in God's goodness. Times will come when the enemy comes and tries to beat you down, and he will try to make you doubt your faith and your conversion. What do you do? You, once again—like you have done a million times before that—drop to your knees at the foot of the cross and put your trust in the gospel. We never outgrow the gospel. We only mature in our understanding of just how dependent we are upon it.

We never outgrow the gospel. We only mature in our understanding of just *how* dependent we are upon it.

We have to be made new, and then continuously pursue newness. We don't know when it first begins, unless we have a dramatic salvation experience of course, but we will look back during the journey and see transformation having occurred. If we are continuously pursuing newness we will see evidence of our change and consistency in our seeking. This will increase your faith to continue to walk—or *drive*, if you will—in newness.

John 3:3 Jesus replied, "Truly, truly, I tell you, no one can see the kingdom of God unless he is born again... ⁶Flesh is born of flesh, but spirit is born of the Spirit."

Mark 2:21 *[Jesus]* "No one sews a patch of unshrunk cloth on an old garment. If he does, the new piece will pull away from the old, and a worse tear will result. ²²And no one pours new wine into old wineskins. If he does, the wine will burst the skins, and both the wine and the wineskins will be ruined. Instead, new wine is poured into new wineskins."

Romans 6:4 We therefore were buried with Him through baptism into death, in order that, just as Christ was raised from the dead through the glory of the Father, we too may walk in newness of life.

Galatians 6:14 But as for me, may I never boast, except in the cross of our Lord Jesus Christ, through which the world has been crucified to me, and I to the world. [15]For neither circumcision nor uncircumcision means anything. What counts is a new creation.

John 20:21 Again Jesus said to them, "Peace be with you. As the Father has sent Me, so also I am sending you." When He had said this, He breathed on them and said, "Receive the Holy Spirit."

II. Understanding the Process

e. By Grace God Calls
The common, prevenient, provisional grace of God draws all of us to Jesus.

So we've got a bad map, a broken car, and poor eyesight, and we need to be born again and made new by the Holy Spirit. Our journey actually *starts* there! So how does this process happen? Grace, which comes from the Greek word *charis*, means "favor, blessing, or kindness." It is the unmerited favor of God upon us sinners that He extends to us first, ways to restrain our evil. Because we're all sinners, who love our sin, it requires a "Common grace" of God that is given to all, that helps to restrain human sinful behavior, have civil authorities instituted by God to maintain order and punish wrong-doing, etc. Also called "Divine Providence," this common grace offered by God continues to provide for His creation, *"causing His sun to rise on the evil and the good, and sends rain on the righteous and the unrighteous."* (Matthew 5:45) The human conscience is also another example of this common or universal grace given to all. *(Rom 2:15-15)* It is by grace alone that beings who sin at all are not immediately destroyed.

It's also because of God's grace that He continually pursues us. God doesn't just make an offer and say "There, I put it in Jerusalem, some might find it, others won't." No, He is continually both sending us all out, and drawing all of us towards, that offer. He is spiritually working in all, and around all, and throughout all of our lives to impress upon each of us our need for, and towards, that offer. Everyone hearing from the God of Israel will be drawn to Jesus, and of those who come to Him, He will never drive them away. Prior to Jesus, God used this same description of *drawing* when speaking of how He continually pursued Israel. *(Jer 31:3, Hos 11:4)* Jesus describes the Holy Spirit coming to convict the world in regard to sin, for not believing in Him; in regard to righteousness, because He is going to Heaven; and in regard to judgment, because Satan has been condemned. *(Jn 16:7-11)* The Holy Spirit is continually drawing us, as is Jesus. In John 12:32 Jesus says, *"And I, when I am lifted up from the earth, will draw all men to Myself."* The Bible teaches that the Father, the Son, and the Holy Spirit are all drawing people to Jesus.

John 6:44 No one can **come** to Me unless the Father who sent Me **draws** him, and I will raise him up at the last day. [45]It is written in the Prophets: 'And they will all be taught by God.' Everyone who has heard the Father and learned from Him **comes** to Me.

John 6:65 Then Jesus said, "This is why I told you that no one can **come** to Me unless the Father has **granted** it to him."

John 6:37 Everyone the Father **gives** Me will **come** to Me, and the one who **comes** to Me I will never drive away.

So we've seen three different types of intervention by God all relying on His grace first. First, Scripture clearly teaches that God, by His grace, draws us to Jesus. Second, we know it's by God's grace that there even is a Jesus to save us at all! And three, we're saved through Jesus, not by any good thing we've done, but by trusting in Him, which is also a gift of God's grace. Which means that *no matter how* we arrive at being saved, if a person gets saved at all it's by God's grace alone! So now that that's settled, the next question is *how much of* God's grace in the drawing of us, is necessary for us to come to faith to be saved? Meaning how much of this *drawing* is God's doing vs. how much of it is our own doing in response to His prompting? In other words, just how depraved (dead) in our sins are we? Are we *so* dead that we're literally corpses and we can't come to Jesus at all unless God effectually causes us to? Does He do everything, literally waking *some* up from the dead, compelling us irresistibly to believe in Jesus without our involvement at all? This belief is called "Total Depravity" and is held in Calvinism or Reformed theology (named after reformer John Calvin).[1] Since all biblical Christians believe in *some* level of human depravity we may think of this view as "Total Inability." Calvinists believe God is 100% responsible for causing a person's faith in Jesus, in fact causing the new birth *before* faith that itself enables their faith. God *causes* faith through an "Irresistible Grace," an undeniable compelling for them to believe and be saved.

Another view is called Arminianism (named after Jacob Arminius) which teaches that God provides "Prevenient grace" (meaning grace that "preceeds") which then restores man's free will to be able to choose to come to Jesus. This means man freely chooses themselves to respond in faith but God plays a role in softening their heart beforehand. This can be understood to happen on an individual basis, by each person through hearing the gospel, or universally, to every single person. This grace would be a resistable grace though and could be rejected by free will. There's a third option that I think best captures the heart of the gospel and the whole biblical witness. This is an Arminian-leaning view held by many in the Southern Baptist Convention called "Traditionalism" or "Provisionism," based on the belief that God provides absolutely all that every person needs to come to salvation. I believe God, by His grace, has universally and preveniently made *every* single person responsible (response-able) to His appeals for reconciliation through Jesus. Does God's grace come apart from, prior to, or in conjunction with receiving the gospel? I believe the Gospel, and God's Word, and God's truths, each have illuminating power to break down our resistance and draw us closer to salvation. This "illuminating grace" helps to compel those who would respond in faith upon their hearing. I also believe that once we are spiritually born again we are eternally secured, and that God preserves us, leading to our eventual glorification. This *last part is* a work of "irresistible grace" that compels and empowers us to be victorious. But I don't believe God forces us to believe, we must choose to. For more on this view see (https://Soteriology101.com).

PROTESTANT - Salvation by GRACE Alone	(+ Works)

Calvinism
- Total Inability
- God chooses only some (the elect)
- Gives irresistable grace to believe; none reject

Provisionism
- Human Depravity
- God graciously provides for all in the Atonement and through the Gospel
- All can freely choose to believe or reject

Arminianism
- Total Depravity
- God preveniently softens all (grace)
- All can *then* freely choose to believe or reject

Catholicism
(Semi-Pelagianism, Born with original sin, cleansed by baptism, grace enables works)

Pelagianism
(Born without sin)

Being Drawn vs. Coming To Jesus. Jesus made it clear that no one can come to Him unless the Father draws them to Him first. But Scripture does not say the inverse: that all that are drawn to Him will come to Him. The Bible says all who come to Jesus, Jesus will not cast them away. But just because Jesus won't cast any that *come* to Him away, does not mean that all will willingly come to Him. The Father *sends us all to* Jesus— and Jesus is ready to receive us—but that doesn't guarantee that *we* will receive *Him!* As we looked at numerous times in Chapter One, we can suppress the truth, love wickedness, hate God, and reject His drawing. Jesus is willing to be the Lord and Savior of all, but that doesn't mean that all will repent and surrender their lives to Him. There's a decision in the middle, between God's drawing us to Him, and our actually coming to Him: our free surrender. Only that those who actually come to Jesus will not be cast away by Him. This is not saying God's irresistible grace predetermines, then draws, and then compels our coming to Jesus so that we have no choice. Rather, it's saying that if we go to Jesus we didn't do it on our own because God's grace was needed to. James 4:8 says, *"Draw near to God, and He will draw near to you. Cleanse your hands, you sinners, and purify your hearts, you double-minded."*

John 6:39 And this is the will of Him who sent Me, that I shall lose none of those He has **given** Me, but raise them up at the last day. [40]For it is My Father's will that **everyone** who looks to the Son and believes in Him shall have eternal life, and I will raise him up at the last day."

John 17:12 While I was with them, I protected and preserved them by Your name, the name You gave Me. Not one of them has been lost, except the son of destruction, so that the Scripture would be fulfilled.

Being Drawn vs. Being Given. Scripture does say that everyone the Father GIVES to Jesus, Jesus will not cast them away. *(Jn 6:37)* And in John 17:12 and John 18:8-9 Jesus said that none of those the Father GAVE Him have been lost, except for Judas. This is speaking of the Twelve Apostles. These were the twelve the Father had given Him. Review all the passages I've quoted carefully, and even all of John 6, 17, and 18. I've bolded the key words so it's easier to see. There are major differences between: (1) being *drawn* (helkyse) by God, (2) actually deciding and *coming* (erchetai) to Jesus, (3) and being *given* (dedōken) by the Father to Jesus. *All* are drawn—but only some will come. And think of the word "given" being replaced with the word "delivered" meaning *provided*, or "actually handed over" to. All people are being drawn to Jesus by God's grace, but only some of us (come) will actually go to Him and surrender. But remember the seed in shallow soil, *(cf. Matt 13:20-21)* not everyone who hears with joy and believes is saved, only those who are born again and persevere until the end. They *came* to Jesus but were not actually *given* (delivered) to Him. Those who *are* being saved are those who were GIVEN, provided, delivered over to Him—not all those who were drawn. The Father has actually given us to Him, once we actually *belong* to Him. In John 17, Jesus testified that these other eleven apostles had been given to Him, all those the Father gave Him, all besides Judas. He confirms that they've been delivered to Him, and they do belong to Him. They first belonged to the God of Israel and then believed Jesus came from God (see v. 6-8). Jesus's prayer indicates that those given to Him, the *them* in "not one of them has been lost" is referring to the twelve. Verse 20 says, *"I am not asking on behalf of them alone, but also on behalf of those who will believe in Me through their message."*

God has provided for all. He draws all. Only some will come. Those who come will not be rejected. They will be given/delivered over, if their repentance and faith is genuine, then they will be born again. Since the Father draws all to Jesus, and Jesus draws all to Himself, and the Holy Spirit convicts all in regards to sin, righteousness, and judgment, and their need for Jesus, God's provision of salvation cannot be available only to a few elect people predetermined in advance. I believe it's available to all. God so loved the entire world. *(Jn 3:16)* And *regardless* of what percent God does in drawing vs our choice to respond in faith, we're ALL saved by God's grace alone either way. This should give us joy that God is loving, gracious, and forgiving. It should also give us faith and hope that we would continue to pray for those who have not yet surrendered to Jesus, that they would, and press on in our Great Commission! God has committed to us the message of reconciliation. *(2 Cor 5:19-20)* These three: faith, hope, and love are greatest and we need to continue in them. Don't adopt disempowering beliefs that have the potential to detract us in any way from having love, faith, or hope, for the salvation of all. *(1 Cor 13:13)*

God's drawing isn't about predeterminism—it's about the Gospel! God's grace and willingness to both draw and receive everyone who puts their trust in Jesus.

f. By Grace God Forgives
God's provision of Christ, and our preservation in Him, is not granted by our merit.

My Calvinist brothers and sisters might respond that we could only be saved by God's grace *if* it were irresistible. Meaning that if we play any role at all, however small, providing any level of consent in choosing to believe in Jesus, then we're being saved by our choice, rather than God's grace. The previous section describes how this isn't true because the Bible teaches that it's precisely God's grace that He bothers to first draw any of us to Jesus to even be saved by Him. Therefore, we are all dependent upon God's grace first—even if we have the ability to reject or accept His offer. In fact, this being the case, the longer we rebelled and rejected it, the more of His grace we have to be grateful for once we surrender. After all, it would have been our legitimate choice to reject it.

It's also by God's grace that He has made an offer of forgiveness, reconciliation, restoration, and eventual glorification. We don't deserve it. We can't earn it. And we don't meet God halfway or at all. God would be perfectly good and just to allow us to suffer the consequences of our sin. He's not required to pardon us. He doesn't have a moral commitment to provide a way for guilty people to be forgiven. No, He lavishes His grace upon us because of *His* goodness, not ours. It's merely by God's grace that *any* offer is available to us at all. God is glorified in this fact: that He's gracious. He's glorified by extending to sinful humanity the *offer* of salvation through Jesus. Even if God's grace was not preveniently given to draw us to Christ at all. Even if we were less dead in our sins and actually able to make the spiritual decision to surrender to Christ and trust in Him apart from God's grace. Or even if we had to genuinely seek Him out 100% on our own, and really desire in us to be saved and have a relationship with God, entirely on our own, He doesn't have to give us this! The fact that a Christ has been given to us *at all*, as a way of atonement available for us, is proof alone of salvation by God's grace. Even our estranged friends in the Roman Catholic and Eastern Orthodox Church will acknowledge this. We all need a Savior, and it is *only* by God's grace that we have been provided One!

Furthermore, God's continual forgiveness of our sins, and our continual preservation in Christ is God's grace working upon and in us. Daily, the Father is forgiving our sins. Grace. Daily the Son is interceding for us. Grace. And daily the Holy Spirit is sanctifying, preserving, and empowering us. Grace! All this is available and possible only because of God's grace. So let us not think that if we play a role at all in our free will that we are earning or meriting anything, or that it somehow diminishes God's grace. It doesn't. In fact, our ability to freely choose to do otherwise, against God's will, is evidence of His grace all the more as He endures and preserves us! The last verse quoted in Section (B) was Ephesians 2:1-3, ending by saying that we were, by nature, children of wrath. The passage continues below. Note it's not in our predetermined election before time where God's grace is demonstrated. Rather, the surpassing riches of His grace is demonstrated by His kindness to us IN Christ. His grace is revealed *in* Christ, not before Christ.

> Ephesians 2:4 But because of His great love for us, God, who is rich in mercy, [5]made us alive with Christ, even when we were dead in our trespasses. It is by **grace** you have been saved! [6]And God raised us up with Christ and seated us with Him in the heavenly realms in Christ Jesus, [7]in order that in the coming ages He might **display the surpassing riches of His grace, demonstrated by His kindness to us in Christ Jesus.**

g. By Humility We Repent
Before faith, before obedience, comes repentance—and before it, humility.

Lest any think we can boast of being already good enough, or by earning our salvation by law keeping, let me remind us, we're not our own Savior. There's only One Savior, Jesus our Lord. And He doesn't save those who think they don't need saving. Those who boast of their righteousness. They may need Him the most, but He's farthest from them. No, our salvation comes from recognizing our sinfulness, brokenness, flaws, and imperfections, and then viewing them in light of God's infinite majesty. If we saw ourselves as we truly were, drenched in sin and uncleanness, we wouldn't do anything but bow our head, prostrate ourselves on the floor, and cry out the way that Isaiah did in Isaiah 6:5, *"Woe is me, for I am ruined, because I am a man of unclean lips dwelling among a people of unclean lips; for my eyes have seen the King, the LORD of Hosts."* But what happened next? A prophetic picture of God's grace, and of our atonement and cleansing through Jesus! Verses 6-7 read, *"Then one of the seraphim flew to me, and in his hand was a glowing coal that he had taken with tongs from the altar. And with it he touched my mouth and said: "Now that this has touched your lips, your iniquity is removed and your sin is atoned for."*

What a beautiful picture of God's grace to forgive us of our sins! But first we must humble ourselves. We need to see ourselves as we truly are—as God's Word says we are. Believing in what God's Word says is an act of faith. Seeing it as personally true in our own conscience is a sign of illuminating grace in us. The ability and decision to not be prideful and allow the weight of this reality to sink our hearts into grievance is humility. The Holy Spirit says in Hebrews 3:7-8, *"Today if you hear His voice, do not harden your hearts, as you did in the rebellion, in the day of testing in the wilderness."* Our humility is what leads to repentance in the first place, which gives way for faith in Jesus. Repentance means a change of mind and heart. It means to turn around, 180 degrees, and go in the opposite direction. This is why we must be humbled. If we don't lay down our pride and arrogance before God, then we'll never be convicted in our hearts that we're wicked, wrong and broken, and need His help, healing, and salvation. Humility leads to repentance and repentance leads to faith. Recall the parable of the tax collector from Luke 18:9-14. It's on page 85. Jesus teaches us that we're closer to our salvation in Him when we're a worse sinner, but humble and seeking forgiveness, than we are as less of a sinner but prideful and arrogant about it. God gave His Law and He expects us to obey it. But it wasn't given so we can accomplish our own righteousness through it. Romans 3:20 says, *"no one will be justified in His sight by works of the law. For the law merely brings awareness of sin."* The law was given to compare ourselves against, to make us humble. Jesus assures us in Matthew 23:12, *"For whoever exalts himself will be humbled, and whoever humbles himself will be exalted."* Why does God allow bad things to happen? They humble us.

And we don't grow out of this truth, by the way. We must never become arrogant, no matter how long we've been saved. Our humility is an indicator of many things. First, that our salvation and conversion were genuine. A repentance without humility is not a true acknowledgement of guilt and the contrite heart that God desires. *(Isa 57:15, 66:2; Ps 34:17-18, 51:17)* Second, our humility is evidence that we are *IN* Jesus later. Our level of humility is a guidepost we can use to determine that our heart is *still* humble before God, lest we ever forget that salvation is a gift by God's grace alone. Our fear of God's rejection and wrath should be greater than our overinflated confidence, in our interpretation of Scripture, that says we can never lose our salvation. I don't *believe* we can—but I *know* God will not be mocked! Remember humility in your evangelism and apologetics with others, and in your prayers, declarations, and proclamations. Read James 4. God gives grace to the humble, but He opposes the proud. Third, our humility enables us to continue to grow and mature in the faith, to be sanctified, and to be molded into Christ's image. Hebrews chapter 3 repeats these same warnings. Not to harden our hearts in verse 15. In verse 13 told to exhort (i.e. to encourage or plead) with one another daily, as long as it is called today, so we won't be hardened by sin's deceitfulness. Verse 14 makes it clear that this is a warning for those already in Christ. Humility is essential for both the initial path that leads to salvation, as well as a key attribute modeled throughout the Christian life. Be confident, but humble! Humility is not only the right heart before God it's also the right heart towards others, wherein love, empathy, and compassion must flow.

James 4:6 But He gives us more grace. This is why it says: "**God** opposes the proud, but **gives grace to the humble.**"... [10]Humble yourselves before the Lord, and He will exalt you.

1 Peter 5:4b And all of you, clothe yourselves with humility toward one another, because, "God opposes the proud, but gives grace to the humble." Humble yourselves, therefore, under God's mighty hand, so that in due time He may exalt you.

---

h. By Faith We're Saved
We're saved by faith alone (in Christ and the Gospel), but not by faith that is alone.

Let's recap. By grace God provides Jesus. By grace God calls and draws us to Jesus.

By grace God sends the Holy Spirit who convicts us of sin, of righteousness, of Satan. I would also add that God has also graciously allowed all things that have happened, ever, either to us or to others, whether good or evil, as things that help to bring us to Jesus. And God is patient with us, not wanting anyone to perish, but everyone to come to repentance. *(2 Pet 3:9)* Because regardless of how long it takes us to repent and turn from our evil rebellion, we know that *"God works all things together for the good of those who love Him, who are called according to His purpose."* (Romans 8:28) So all things play a role, but what is the determining factor? It is our faith. It is our faith in Jesus, specifically. It's our faith in Him as the Messiah, the only begotten Son of the only God, the eternal Word/Son of Yahweh, that became a human being, God-incarnate, the God-man. It's our faith in the fact that He lived a perfect sinless life, died on a cross for the sins of the world, and for our own sins personally, and was then resurrected in the same but glorified body three days later, conquering sin, death, and Hell. It's belief that faith in Him as the atoning sacrifice for our sins we are restored to God and given the gift of eternal life. It's our faith in *all* of that saves us. If we deny any of those things we are missing a fundamental aspect of the gospel. Because Jesus is the eternal, uncreated Son of God, and the Holy Spirit is the Spirit of God in us, by necessity, belief in the Holy Trinity is essential. Unfortunately, this means many who identify as Christians do not yet possess a saving faith.

So that's the minimum that we need to have faith *in*, but what exactly *is* faith? Is faith blind? Faith is better understood as *trust,* which for most will help us see that it is really trust in Jesus, more so than belief in Jesus, that saves us. But I can do even better than that. Think of "Genuine Faith" as the intersection of knowledge, belief, and trust. In order to believe and trust the gospel you have to *know* of it. There needs to be some level of intellectual understanding. But you can't just know it, you have to also *believe* it. You have to believe that it's true, that it really happened. That Jesus was real, and was God, and died for your sins, and that He's now alive. And you have to also *trust* Him. You have to have a personal relationship with Him. He has to be your Lord and your Savior. You can't just know about Him, and believe that He exists, you have to *walk* with Him. He has to be experientially known by you. No one of these three can be absent. You can't know of Him, and believe in Him, and not trust Him. You can't believe in Him and trust in Him and not know of Him. And you can't know of Him, and trust in Him, without believing in Him. You must know, believe, and trust. And if you do, you have genuine faith.

"Genuine Faith" is at the intersection of Knowledge, Belief, and Trust.

However, there is a difference between genuine faith and *Saving* faith. And it is this: saving faith corresponds to true repentance and change of behavior. For example, I could have genuine faith in a car seat belt. I could have knowledge and know that it saves lives if worn. I could believe that it saves lives if worn. I could even trust that if I wore it I would be statistically better off in the event of a car accident. But that doesn't necessarily mean I will put it on. I could have knowledge, belief, and trust in it, and still decide not to put it on. Likewise, I could know the gospel, believe the gospel, and trust that the gospel saves, and then still not receive Jesus as my Lord and Savior. Or, what more commonly happens, is that we accept Jesus as our Savior but not our Lord. We put on the seatbelt because we care about our life, but then we drive twice as recklessly, because we can afford to now that we have the seatbelt on. The truth is that if we *really* believed we were going to get into a crash that day that would total our car and paralyze us completely, but we wouldn't die because we had the seatbelt on, we wouldn't drive recklessly. Our faith may be in the seatbelt, but we have greater faith that we won't get into a wreck at all, and if we did it wouldn't be a bad one. Faith in the gospel is like that. Being completely paralyzed from head to toe in a car accident is less severe than eternity in Hell, yet many people that call themselves Christians still live recklessly. But if we truly had faith in what the Bible teaches we would be much more cautious and careful. We would be much more obedient and righteous. We would be much more loving and sacrificial. We would be much more concerned with our knowledge of, and relationship with, Jesus than on our TV shows, or our career, finances, relationships, or where we're going on vacation this year. Real faith produces a corresponding behavior change.

Saving faith produces fruit, in other words, outward evidence of an inward change of who we now are and what we now care about. Saving faith is demonstrated by a life that reflects a genuine change. The Bible often uses the metaphor of us as trees, those that thrive and bear good fruit, or those that either die or bear bad, diseased fruit. John the Baptist put it this way in Luke and Matthew 3:8, *"Produce fruit in keeping with repentance."* Our beliefs, heart, emotions, desires, lifestyle, and actions all give evidence of our faith—or lack thereof. This is why the Protestant Reformer Martin Luther said, "We are saved by faith alone, but the faith that saves is never alone." For if we claim to have a saving faith but live outwardly like a wicked heathen then we are self-deceived. Jesus said in John 15:2 that the Father cuts off every branch in Him that bears no fruit. In verse 5 He says that the ones who remain in Him, and He in them, *will* bear much fruit. In verse 8 He says all of this is to the Father's glory, and that by remaining in Him, and bearing much fruit, we prove ourselves to be His disciples.

"Saving Faith" always produces outward fruit (good works) as evidence of the inward change.

These are important distinctions. The Roman Catholic Church rejected the doctrine of salvation by faith alone at the Council of Trent. They teach that we are saved by *both* faith and our works (observance to religious sacraments and good deeds). The error in this is that we are then contributing towards salvation. We would be assisting the process and helping to earn Heaven through our good works. The Bible flat out contradicts this. I fully acknowledge that many have claimed to be saved by faith alone, and then lived immoral, ungodly lives. And there are other unbiblical movements such as the Hyper Grace camp which actually promotes godlessness intentionally. I understand that the Protestant doctrine of salvation by faith alone has helped these unfortunate errors come about, and I sincerely grieve because of that. However, all abuses aside, God's Word remains clear on this and the truth of the gospel is at stake. We shall not take any credit for assisting in our own salvation. Salvation is a gift. A gift by the grace of God alone, by faith alone, in Christ alone, to the glory of God alone! This is the biblical witness. It is clear that we are to do good works, in fact we are created to do them! We are to do them, and this is to the Father's glory, but that they in no way help to save us. Jesus said in John 15:4-6 that we cannot bear fruit unless we *remain* in Him. That we are utterly fruitless unless we are already a branch that is first in the vine (i.e. Him). It is only those already in Him by faith alone that are in the vine. Then, and only then, can we bear fruit. Fruit, i.e. "good works" are the *result* of our salvation, not the *cause* of it. Good works are the *effect* of our saving faith that saves us, not a contributor towards our salvation. We've already read in section (B) Ephesians 2, verses 1-3; and in section (F) verses 4-7, and now we continue with the next:

Ephesians 2:8 For it is **by grace** you have been **saved through faith**, and this not from yourselves; it is the **gift of God,** [9]**not by works**, so that no one can boast. [10]For we are God's workmanship, created in Christ Jesus **to do good works**, which God prepared in advance as our way of life.

John 15:1 *[Jesus]* "I am the true vine, and My Father is the keeper of the vineyard. [2]He cuts off every branch in Me that bears no fruit, and every branch that does bear fruit, He prunes to make it even more fruitful... [4]Remain in Me, and I will remain in you. Just as no branch can bear fruit by itself unless it remains in the vine, neither can you bear fruit unless you remain in Me. [5]I am the vine and you are the branches. The one who remains in Me, and I in him, will bear much fruit. For apart from Me you can do nothing. [6]If anyone does not remain in Me, he is like a branch that is thrown away and withers. Such branches are gathered up, thrown into the fire, and burned... [8]This is to My Father's glory, that you bear much fruit, proving yourselves to be My disciples."

Romans 3:23 for all have sinned and fall short of the glory of God, [24]and are justified freely by His grace through the redemption that is in Christ Jesus. [25]God presented Him as the atoning sacrifice through faith in His blood... [26]He did this to demonstrate His righteousness at the present time, so as to be just and to justify the one who has faith in Jesus. [27]Where, then, is boasting? It is excluded. On what principle? On that of works? No, but on that of faith. [28]For we maintain that a man is justified by faith apart from works of the law.

i. Legal Fines Paid-in-Full
Atonement: Our total sin debt was paid-in-full, voluntarily, by Christ on the cross.

Imagine you're about to begin a 10,000-mile road trip knowing that there's a warrant for your arrest. You're wanted in six states for murder, adultery, and more, and there's a APB out on you. Highway Patrol is out looking for you! Plus, as if it couldn't be any worse, you also have a glove box full of a billion dollars of speeding tickets and parking violations! Oh, and did I mention that your car bumper is falling off and it's dragging on the road causing sparks to fly behind you? Basically, you're a moving target, you're going to get caught soon, and everything is working against you. Alright, enough with the car metaphors. The point is clear, right? You're guilty and they're on your trail. Your road trip is going nowhere fast unless you take care of these things first. Fortunately, that is exactly what Jesus did! Without Him and the cross, taking your trip is a point in futility.

You need to know that EVERYTHING against you was dealt with by Jesus on the cross. Everything! The punishment for your sins. The guilt of your conscience over your sinfulness. Your guilty standing before God. Your separation with the Father. The right for Satan to hold your sins against you and attack you. The consequences of your sin, such as decay, death, demons, and damnation. The presence of sin, and its hold, bondage, and power over you. All of it. On the cross, before yielding His spirit to God, Jesus said "It is finished"—and He meant it. *(Jn 19:30)* He has triumphed over everything by the cross!

John 8:34 Jesus replied, "Truly, truly, I tell you, everyone who sins is a slave to sin. [35]A slave is not a permanent member of the family, but a son belongs to it forever. [36]So if the Son sets you free, you will be free indeed."

Colossians 2:13 When you were dead in your trespasses and in the uncircumcision of your sinful nature, God made you alive with Christ. He forgave us all our trespasses, [14]having canceled the debt ascribed to us in the decrees that stood against us. He took it away, nailing it to the cross! [15]And having disarmed the powers and authorities, He made a public spectacle of them, triumphing over them by the cross.

Wonderful news indeed! This is the gospel that we place our trust in Jesus for. The journey will get rough at times. We need to have this gospel firmly resolved in mind and our spirit. The more faith you have in this gospel, the more empowered you will be. Your empowerment, strength, peace, courage, holiness, freedom, love, joy, these don't come from outside—they come from within. They are rooted in your faith. This does not mean that you will never stumble and you'll always have perfect confidence. As long as you're still living in the sinful flesh, and in the sinful world, there will be a struggle. You must continue to crucify the flesh daily, renew your mind daily, and continuously press in to the Lord daily. But expect it, it's part of the journey. Without the cross we are still dead in our sins, and everything is against us. Through the cross, God is for us. And as Romans 8:31 says, *"If God is for us who can be against us?"* Trust in the gospel is everything. Everything. It really is all about this: faith. We will keep touching on many aspects of the Christian life but they are ALL built on this foundation of faith in the gospel. If this is weak then the house that is built upon it will crumble. Be sure not to have faith in the cross, but then distort what the cross actually stands for! Or to add to the cross other things that you are putting your faith in, things that you're doing, in addition to the cross. No, all other things you could even add are only buildings that grow on the foundation. The foundation is that Christ paid for everything already. He dealt with it all. It is finished! He has paid it all as the perfect sacrifice. The unblemished *"Lamb of God who takes away the sins of the world."* (Jn 1:29, 36; Heb 2:9, 1 Pet 2:24) His one-time sacrifice accomplished it all!

Hebrews 9:25 Nor did He *[Jesus]* enter heaven to offer Himself again and again, as the high priest enters the Most Holy Place every year with blood that is not his own. ²⁶Otherwise, Christ would have had to suffer repeatedly since the foundation of the world. But now He has appeared **once for all at the end of the ages to do away with sin by the sacrifice of Himself**... ²⁸so also Christ was offered once to bear the sins of many...

Hebrews 10:10 And by that will, we have been sanctified through the sacrifice of the body of Jesus Christ once for all... ¹²But when this priest had offered for all time one sacrifice for sins, He sat down at the right hand of God... ¹⁴**because by a single offering He has made perfect for all time those who are being sanctified.**

So *how* did Jesus accomplish paying for all of the debt of all of our sins while on the cross? What exactly happened there? Generally speaking, this is called atonement. **Atonement**, think of it like "at-one-ment" is how we can become "one" again with God, how we get reunited with God by means of reconciliation. This happens through something called propitiation. **Propitiation** means the turning away of wrath by an offering, by appeasing the wrath of the offended person and then reconciling with them. In this case, it is an offering being made to God to satisfy His wrath against our sin. Jesus atoned for the sins of humanity so that God is satisfied that justice has been served and satisfied, and reconciliation is accomplished for all being redeemed. I'm not saying that Jesus paid for the sins of the world as though every person automatically receives what Jesus accomplished and is universally forgiven because of it. Jesus paid for all sin to the utmost degree, so that an infinite number of sinful people could be forgiven through Him. He has provided for all that God is calling to Himself, and I believe He accomplished all that was necessary and more, as the provision for ALL. However, it's ONLY those who put their trust in Him that *enter into* Him, and thus receive His atonement on *their* behalf. He didn't atone for universal forgiveness for all. He made it accessible and available, without limit, to those who will put their trust in Him. In John 8:24 Jesus said, *"For unless you believe that I am He, you will die in your sins."* And who is He? He's the eternal Son of God from the Father, the Lamb that was slain, who takes away the sins of the world! In verse 58 Jesus identifies Himself as God saying, *"before Abraham was born, I am!"* using the divine name of God. Those who reject Jesus don't have their sins forgiven.

The predominant and most important way this forgiveness was accomplished is called **Penal Substitutionary Atonement.** Penal just means that it is related to penalty, as in an act or offense punishable by law. Substitutionary is because Jesus was *our* substitute, and atonement we've already looked at. This is the doctrine that Christ died on the cross as a substitute for sinners. God imputed the GUILT of our sins onto Christ, and He, in our place, bore the punishment that we deserve. This was a full payment for sins, which satisfied both the wrath and the righteousness of God, so that He could forgive sinners without compromising His own holy standard. This is how Jesus pays our legal fines so we are blameless. *(Isa 53:6, 12; Rom 3:25, 2 Cor 5:21, Gal 3:13, Heb 2:17, 10:1-4, 1 Pet 3:18)*

Hebrews 2:17 For this reason He *[Jesus]* had to be made like His brothers in every way [...] to make atonement for the sins of the people.

Romans 3:10 As it is written: "There is no one righteous, not even one... ²⁵God presented Him *[Jesus]* as **the atoning sacrifice through faith in His blood,** in order to demonstrate His righteousness, because in His forbearance He had passed over the sins committed beforehand. ²⁶He did this to demonstrate His righteousness at the present time, so as to be just and to **justify the one who has faith in Jesus.**

Revelation 1:5b To Him *[Jesus]* who loves us and has **released us from our sins** by His blood...

Ephesians 1:7 In Him *[Jesus]* we have redemption through His blood, **the forgiveness of our trespasses,** according to the riches of His grace..

Jesus paid our total debt, to satisfy God's wrath, by being our substitute and bearing the punishment we deserve.

Other views on the Atonement. The view we've just covered, Penal Substitutionary Atonement, is the *primary* way Christians should view what occurred on the cross. But I want to also survey, and deemphasize, some other views on the atonement. The problem with these theories is not that they have no truth at all, because they do. The problem, and greatest harm, is when they're advocated as the primary way to view what the cross accomplished. Worse yet, there are some dangerous false teachers, Brian Zahnd as one example, that distort biblical truth about Jesus and the Gospel and deny Penal Substitution completely.[2] Penal Substitutionary Atonement has been attacked and slandered, calling it "unjust," or "a form of cosmic child abuse," or by suggesting that it implies a universalism, that all will be saved. For detailed responses to these accusations see the videos cited by Pastor Mike Winger and American Gospel: Christ Crucified documentary. I want to provide a few of these different views on the atonement so you can consider and examine the differences.[3] Guard yourself against all perverted distortions, so that your faith may be biblical, grounded, centered, and able to withstand all trials. As Paul advises in 2 Corinthians 10:5, *"We tear down arguments, and every presumption set up against the knowledge of God; and we take captive every thought to make it obedient to Christ."*

The *Moral-Example Theory (or Moral-Influence Theory)* teaches that the purpose of Christ's death was to influence mankind toward moral improvement, by impressing mankind with a sense of God's love to persuade them to right action. Of course the gospel does have this effect, but that is not the primary purpose of the cross. And to say it was *only* for this purpose is heretical (false). This is what New Age cults teach, that Christ was just an "enlightened man" who was here to teach us or to be an "example" for us. As we've read, Christ's death was not just an object lesson for us, it was effectual at *actually* finishing something—at providing a satisfactory offering for the punishment of the sins of the world. He does become a model for His disciples to follow, even telling us to "take up our cross and follow Him." *(Matt 16:24)* Yet, it's a grave error to think example alone is all that occurred, or even that example is a primary way to view the cross.

Another theory laid out by Gustaf Aulén, *Christus Victor* (Christ the Victor), built on ideas from the early church's *Ransom theory,* states that Christ's death was "first and foremost a victory over the powers which hold mankind in bondage: sin, death, and the devil." Of course, again, Christ as victorious over these are true realities to be celebrated as well. Nevertheless, we saw in Colossians 2 (page 96) that though Christ *has* triumphed over our enemies, He has *also* canceled the debt that stood against us. Remember also that it isn't until the last day that God will judge and condemn all of His enemies at that time, eternally, when they are cast into the eternal lake of fire. *(Rev 20)* Furthermore, 1 Corinthians 15:24-26 teaches us that Christ's enemies, including all dominions, authorities, powers, and the last enemy, death, are not fully destroyed until the very end of the age. So nearly two thousand years ago, on the cross, was not *chiefly* about Christ defeating His enemies, rather it was about *rescuing the victims of* His enemies. In fact this is exactly what Jesus says in Luke 4:18. The cross, therefore, is less about His victory over His enemies now (which are being permitted to exist by the will of God anyways) and more about God's self-revelation of His own glorious nature to those being saved. In eternity, the saved will not look at the holes in Jesus's hands and be most concerned about His triumph over death and Satan. We will be most concerned and overwhelmed by His voluntary sacrifice on our behalf because of His love for us. See John 3:16. It was first and foremost, because of LOVE, that God sent His only begotten Son into the world!

For the same reason we must deemphasize the *Satisfaction (or Commercial) Theory* formulated by the medieval theologian Anselm. In this view, the emphasis is on giving God the glory and HONOR due Him, by Christ obeying God and repaying this honor on our behalf. The emphasis being Christ obeying how we should've obeyed—rather than Penal Substitution which emphasizes Him being punished how we should've been punished. This is similar to the *Recapitulation Theory of Atonement,* that originated with early church father Irenaeus. Here the emphasis is on Christ, who is the new Adam, who rather than disobeying God as Adam did, was obedient to God and undoes what Adam did. It's true our sins are an offense to God and we have robbed Him of honor through our disobedience. It's true that Adam did what all of humanity has done, and that Jesus did what all of humanity should do. It's true that Jesus is our model for being obedient to God, and His selfless sacrifice on our behalf does give God the glory and honor He's due. However, like the previous examples, this is not the primary purpose of the cross. The cross is not merely an object for God to receive back the honor He should've had. Nor is it the central theme of the cross to be just a reversal of Adam's wrongs and a "summing up" of human life. If God's supreme goal was receiving honor, and sin dishonors Him, or if God's supreme goal was humans being 100% obedient to Him, He could have chosen not to create beings capable of sinning at all! Also if His supreme goal was His *honor,* He could have corrected the problem to restore His honor without humbling Himself and becoming a man and dying on a cross in our place. These actions teach us that honor is not God's *highest value*, and therefore not the chief reason for the cross.

The earliest theory of all, **The Ransom Theory**, claims that Christ offered Himself as a ransom. This wording is found in Mark 10:45 and Matthew 20:28. The word translated ransom, *lytron,* literally meant the "liberty-price" paid to free a slave. Often people were slaves because they were indebted. In debt to the kingdom that conquered them in battle, offering slavery as an alternative to death. Or selling themselves into slavery, via indentured servitude to pay off their own debt. Jesus says that He came to give Himself as a ransom for us, to pay for our freedom. Where it's not clear is exactly to whom this ransom was paid. Many in the early church viewed the ransom being paid to Satan. However, God does not owe Satan anything, and neither does humanity. Satan and his demons are more guilty of sin than we are because they've contributed to our sinfulness.

I'd argue we've been set free, not principally from Satan—but rather from the bondage of sin and death—our ransom paid for by the blood of Jesus. Sin, and the wages of sin, death, are what is owed as our debt, and owed to none other than God alone. This is because of God's *just* nature. God is not only the Creator and Father, He's also the Judge of the universe. If there are crimes that demand justice He's the supreme judge, jury, and executioner. To be responsible to punish evil, and not, is unjust. By His very nature God must ensure that justice is served. Scripture suggests that God uses Satan's own free will rebellion against Him, to then voluntarily play the role of our adversary and accuser. This is even what the word "satan" means. So, perhaps we may view one of Satan's many roles, as similar to a prosecutor who is continuously arguing for the guiltiness of the plaintiff. In this courtroom drama, God is the judge, jury, and executioner, making all ultimate decisions. Each of us is the defendant, presently on trial, guilty of transgression, fighting for our own freedom. Our prison: enslavement by sin, and the consequence of sin which is death. Because of this, we are also, in a sense, enslaved to the one who holds the power of death, Satan. (Hebrews 2:14) Satan, the prosecutor, accuses us, argues for our ongoing punishment now, and also later for our ultimate damnation. But God makes the ultimate decision. We also have an Advocate, a defense attorney: Jesus, *(1 Jn 2:1)* and the Holy Spirit who's also called our Advocate. *(Jn 14:16)* Therefore, it might look like:

---

1 Timothy 2:5 For there is one God and one mediator between God and men, the man Christ Jesus, ⁶**who gave Himself as a ransom for all...**

Romans 6:22 But now that you have been **set free from sin** and have become slaves to God, the fruit you reap leads to holiness, and the outcome is eternal life. ²³For the **wages of sin is death**, but the gift of God is eternal life in Christ Jesus our Lord.

Hebrews 2:14 Now since the children have flesh and blood, He [*Jesus*] too shared in their humanity, so that by His death He might destroy him who holds the power of death, that is, the devil, ¹⁵and **free those who** all their lives **were held in slavery** by their fear of death.

Revelation 12:9 ...Satan, the deceiver of the whole world... ¹⁰ ...For the accuser of our brothers has been thrown down—he who accuses them day and night before our God. ¹¹They have conquered him by the blood of the Lamb and by the word of their testimony.

This debt and slavery, and then ransom/payment and freedom, metaphor is used throughout Scripture. Acts 20:28 says *God purchased* the church with His own blood. Revelation 5:9 says Jesus was slain, and men from every tribe and tongue and people and nation were *purchased* for God with His blood. But rather than thinking that this is *only* or even primarily about our ransom or a purchase, we must consider *why* we need to be ransomed or purchased in the first place. It is our debt and slavery to SIN, which we are guilty of. We are not unjustly in bondage to sin. We are guilty. We do deserve all of the consequences of our sin. If we are sick and dying, and there are curses upon us, and if Satan is accusing and attacking us, then, technically, we do deserve it. These things are all bad, and we don't want them, but that doesn't make them unjust. If the demons are bound in misery in the Abyss in torment for committing their sins why do we not think that we shouldn't be punished for ours? So yes, Jesus purchases our freedom from these things but we must keep in focus WHY we have this bondage in the first place: SIN!

The ransom for our freedom is paid for, by the Son, to God, on behalf of our debt, for the penalty of our sin.

The Ransom theory brings us back around full circle to why Penal Substitutionary Atonement is most biblical and why it must be your primary view of the atonement going forward. It is our own sinfulness against God that is our *primary* enemy. When we finally get this we will stop blaming Adam and Eve, and the flesh, and Satan, and other people inside and outside of the church, for all of our problems. SIN is our chief enemy. Without sin there is no death or Satan or Hell, etc. I promise you that if you begin to hate sin you will have much greater victory over all of these other things in your life as well! Satan still accusing you of wrongdoing? He can't if that sin was in your past and you've put it under the blood of Jesus! Satan still attacking you? He can't unless there's still sin in your life you're still walking in! Satan still using your emotions and your brokenness to torment you? He can't unless there's your sin, or the hurt of someone else's sin that you haven't dealt with and allowed the Holy Spirit to heal! Sin is the root of all of our other enemies. Deal with sin and you will have victory over everything else. And how do we deal with sin? FAITH. We give it to Jesus, because He has already dealt with all of our sin on the cross. It is finished. And if it is finished, then we should not have it in our lives as though it hasn't been finished. And if we do, it is lack of knowledge or faith or desire or perseverance to eradicate it. So fix your eyes on the cross, and never take them off.

Each of these views of the atonement, and the many other views I didn't cover, offer unique perspectives of the total triumph of Jesus on the cross. We can and should know and celebrate all of them! Any way we can give God glory by elevating Jesus is a good thing. But unfortunately some of these views can and have been used, to distort, distract and confuse what exactly the gospel that saves actually *is!* They make what Jesus did on the cross very complicated. The gospel "good news" that saves us, that we've been commissioned to share, is *not* complicated! You can be a witness and share the simple gospel with someone in a few minutes, and thoroughly enough to lead them to salvation in a single conversation. As you go forward and think of the cross, keep foremost in your mind, Jesus dying in your place to pay for the penalty of your sins, and not only your sins but everyone who will come to Him, and you'll always have the unfiltered gospel. Then your faith will be a firm foundation for you to continually draw from for renewal and growth, and when you share the gospel with others it will be easy for them to understand the gospel and repent and believe and accept Jesus as their Savior.

Primary purpose of Jesus's death on the cross	
Penal Substitutionary Atonement	Jesus stood in our place as our substitute and took the penalty (penal) for our sins upon Himself. His death thus paid our total sin debt, satisfying God's wrath, and reconciling those in Christ to God.
Secondary aspects:	
The Ransom Theory	Gave Himself as ransom to purchase our freedom from SIN/Satan.
Christ the Victor Theory	Victory over all of His enemies including sin, death, and Satan.
Moral-Example Theory	A moral example for us to live by. Dying to ourselves to love others.
Satisfaction Theory	Demonstrated obedience to God, giving Him the honor due Him.
Recapitulation Theory	Obedience to God, as a reversal of Adam's disobedience to God.

j. Imputed Righteousness
Jesus He gave us His righteousness, crediting His perfect life to our accounts.

The previous section covered many aspects of the atonement Jesus provided on our behalf. He: (1) paid the ransom price for our freedom from sin, (2) accomplished a reversal of Adam and all of humanity's rebellion to God, (3) modeled submission and obedience to God, (4) triumphed as victorious over sin, death, Hell, and Satan, and (5) gave God the honor and glory He was due. A sixth thing happened though. He took upon Himself the guilt and consequence of our sins. They were *imputed* to Him. Imputation means counted or reckoned to. He wasn't guilty of our sin, but it was counted, attributed, credited, or imputed *to* Him, so that He received it as *though* it was. So that His suffering and death on the cross actually was the just penalty our sins deserved. This imputation worked both ways. Not only was our sin imputed to His account, His righteousness was imputed to our account! This marvelous reversal took place! It's not only that Christ paid for all of our sins, and our justification, thereby leaving us neutral and innocent. Beyond that, His righteousness was imputed to us, leaving us actually righteous! Theologians say it this way: upon repentance and belief in Christ, we are forensically declared righteous. We have the righteousness of Christ! *Imputed* righteousness is in contrast to the Roman Catholic doctrine of justification of *Infused* righteousness. Meaning righteousness is infused into a person initially through sacraments of baptism and penance, and is either increased through good works or reduced through sin. The cults have this in common as well. God's grace, therefore, is not God's unmerited provision for us through our FAITH in what Jesus DID, but rather through our own WORKS and what we DO. This is unbiblical.

The imputation of Christ's righteousness is a glorious aspect of the gospel. Jesus merits for us not only to not be punished, but also to receive blessings and rewards. It is our focus on this righteousness, that we have already received by faith, that empowers us to persevere through difficult seasons. We do not stumble at one point and then lose our favor with God, only to have to re-earn it through ongoing penance and sacraments. As though on a continuous cycle of up and down, still being led by fear that at any point we could lose it all. No, as Romans 8:15 says, *"For you did not receive a spirit of slavery that returns you to fear, but you received the Spirit of sonship, by whom we cry, "Abba! Father!""* Furthermore, Galatians 5:1 says, *"It is for freedom that Christ has set us free. Stand firm, then, and do not be encumbered once more by a yoke of slavery."* And Ephesians 3:12 says, *"In Him [Christ] and through faith in Him we may enter God's presence with boldness and confidence."* If you are in Christ, then you are not cast out because of your momentary sin, nor is there a veil still between you and God, because of your sin. You are justified by faith and you receive the imputed righteousness of Christ.

---

2 Corinthians 5:21 God made Him who knew no sin to be sin on our behalf, so that in Him we might become the righteousness of God.

Romans 3:21 But now, apart from the law, the righteousness of God has been revealed, as attested by the Law and the Prophets. [22]And this righteousness from God comes through faith in Jesus Christ to all who believe.

Philippians 3:9 and be found in Him [Christ], not having my own righteousness from the law, but that which is through faith in Christ, the righteousness from God on the basis of faith.

Romans 10:4 For Christ is the end of the law, to bring righteousness to everyone who believes.

In Jesus' parable of the wedding banquet in Matthew 22:1-14 it is only those who show up in "wedding clothes" that are permitted to stay. This is a beautiful picture of imputation. They show up clothed in the pure white robes of Christ's righteousness. I do not mean to suggest that Christ's righteousness is the *only* righteousness we are to have. We are to become righteous as well. But Christ's righteousness, that is imputed to us by faith, is the only one that we are to have our confidence in for salvation and life! We are to be perfect, as our Heavenly Father is perfect. *(Mt 5:48)* We cannot attain this righteousness, either on our own doing, or even by it being infused into us. However good we can become in this life, even by the grace of God in our lives, none of us has become actually perfect. Not one person. As Romans 9:30-33 says that we have pursued—and obtained—

a righteousness that is by faith. And those who are still trying to pursue it by obedience to the law, or as if it were by works, have stumbled over the stumbling stone. But if our full trust is in Christ alone then we are secure. As 1 Corinthians 1:30 says, it is because we are IN Christ who has become OUR righteousness, holiness, and redemption. And in Him, we walk in the light, and the blood of Jesus cleanses us from all sin. And not only does He forgive us our sins, He also cleanses us from all unrighteousness. *(1 Jn 1:7-9)* And as it says in Romans 6:18, by His Spirit operating in us we have "*been* [past tense] set free from sin and have become [present tense] slaves to righteousness."

III. Understanding the New

k. Our New Car
We are a new creation in Christ, God's workmanship, created to do good works.

You already know from section (B) how our car is busted and we need a new one for our journey. Using this road map metaphor that I've developed, *you* are the car. The car has the three primary components we've looked at several times already. First is your body, which is the transportation vehicle you get around in. Second is yourself, your soul, the essence of who you are as an individual. And third is your spirit, the very life force of your vehicle, the part that animates the soul and body, and the part that determines which direction you're going in. Your spirit and soul are the "inside" of the car. Your journey begins with the rebirth of your spirit by the Holy Spirit. You've repented and put your faith in Jesus and surrendered your life to Him. The spirit part of the car has been rebuilt!

You are now a brand new vehicle, fresh out of the "Kingdom of God" manufacturing facility, model type: "God's masterpiece," serial number "one out of one." You belong to God. He built you. He owns you. Your VIN label says, "Made in Christ." The license plate reads "Child of God." The Kingdom of God is where you belong to, Heaven is your new home, the country you're registered in. Your title says "Owner: Jesus." There's no lien, you've been fully redeemed, paid-for-in-full, by His blood. You're one-of-a-kind. There's only one of you and God has a unique plan and purpose for how He's going to use you for His Kingdom and for His glory. The look of your exterior is now different. Now, you look the same physically in the world, but every part of your new design and DNA has access to the Spirit of God in it. In the spiritual realm, that God and the angels and demons can see, you're full of light now, and you shine bright in the world full of darkness. You're part of an elite squad of vehicles, each one custom-made. The high beams are always on. Wherever you go, it brings the light of Christ there. Whatever you focus on has the potential to be transformed, for good, through the illuminating light now in you.

2 Corinthians 5:17 Therefore if anyone is in Christ, he is a new creation

1 Corinthians 6:19 Do you not know that your body is a temple of the Holy Spirit who is in you, whom you have received from God? You are not your own; [20]you were bought at a price. Therefore glorify God with your body.

Ephesians 2:10 For we are God's workmanship, created in Christ Jesus to do good works, which God prepared in advance as our way of life.

l. Our New Driver
We're no longer in control, Jesus our Lord, by His Spirit, leads and guides in all ways.

In our former way of life, we were in control. And that led to disobedience, sin, separation from God, and all the other consequences of sin. But now, as a new creation, we are no longer in control. We don't belong to ourselves anymore. Well, we never really did. Before, we were a slave to sin, though we weren't fully aware of it. But now, we are slaves of Christ. *(Eph 6:6)* We are slaves to righteousness. *(Rom 6:18)* Christ is Lord. But He is not just our Lord that we now have to obey, in our own will, and in our own strength. He has sent His Spirit, the Holy Spirit, the Spirit of Christ and of God, to lead and guide us. He is in the driver seat! He is in control! We *will* go in the right direction, because He is driving, not us. We are in the passenger seat, sitting "shotgun." Jesus, take the wheel!

There are things we can do to cause problems for ourselves during the journey. There are things we can do to grieve the Holy Spirit. There are things we can do that slow down our progress moving forward, things that limit our fruitfulness during the journey, things that invite bad passengers into the car with us and cause pain and suffering and hardship. The one thing we *cannot* do is decide to turn around and drive in the opposite direction. If we could do that, then I am convinced that we had never surrendered the driving seat to Jesus in the first place. It's not as though we can give up the control and let Him drive for awhile, and then take it back, and then we drive for awhile, and then give it back, so on and so on. No, this is evidence that we are not a new car at all. Either He is the owner and the driver, or we are still a broken old car and sin is our driver. The choice to genuinely repent and surrender our lives to Jesus is ours. But once it has been done, it is done. We are a new car and we have a new driver.

What if we are genuinely born again but then fall away into a season of sinful rebellion? Does this mean that we were never truly born again? John does give us a stern warning in 1 John 3:5-6 saying, *"But you know that Christ appeared to take away sins, and in Him there is no sin. No one who remains in Him keeps on sinning."* Again, does this mean we were never born again? Not necessarily. I will not say this cannot happen. It *should* not happen, but Scripture teaches us that it can and does happen. 1 John 2:1

says, *"My little children, I am writing these things to you so that you will not sin. But if anyone does sin, we have an advocate before the Father—Jesus Christ, the Righteous One."* We may stumble at times, or even for a whole season, but during and afterwards, we trust in God's grace and mercy to hold us. We trust that Jesus will forgive us and cleanse us, and that we are preserved by His imputed righteousness during our period of testing. For more on how Christ's righteousness is imputed to us, see Section (J).

So, how can we visualize the reality of this using my road map metaphor? I would say that if we are in a season of serious sinful rebellion, the Holy Spirit pulls the car over to the side of the road. We stop moving forward and growing into Christ's likeness, we stop producing good fruit in the world. We stop bringing the light to the darkness. In fact, our sin allows darkness to come in to the car with us. We stop shining as bright. We are not in the driver seat but we can still open the doors to allow wickedness in. And our sin brings along with it natural consequences of such actions—and the Holy Spirit LETS it! He lets the consequences of our thoughts and decisions negatively affect us. For our short term displeasure yes—but for our long-term benefit. This is a form of loving discipline. He lets us be hurt by our own sin so that we will be humbled by it and repent and confess our sins to Jesus and have our "car" cleansed. But He does not leave us during this. He doesn't just get out of the car and leave us alone. We don't lose our salvation during every moment of imperfection. In Ephesians 4:30 says not to do sinful things, *"And do not grieve the Holy Spirit of God, in whom you were sealed for the day of redemption."* The reason we aren't to grieve Him with these things is because He is still there. We're sealed! Jude 1:19 says the unsaved, the scoffers, are *"worldly and devoid of the Spirit."* There is a major difference between being devoid of the Spirit, and having the Spirit, but grieving Him. Brethren, He is patient with us! James 4:4-6 says, *"..Therefore, whoever chooses to be a friend of the world renders himself an enemy of God. Or do you think the Scripture says without reason that the Spirit He caused to dwell in us yearns with envy? But He gives us more grace..."* He will not leave us nor forsake us. He will not fail at making us a masterpiece. However, our own sin will cause us much trouble and suffering if we don't crucify it. Let us then make every effort to walk by—or rather, to be driven by—the Spirit. He is the driver of the car, you are the passenger. Submit to Him!

John 10:16b I must bring them in as well, and they will listen to My voice. Then there will be one flock and one shepherd... [27]My sheep listen to My voice; I know them, and they follow Me.

John 16:13 However, when the Spirit of truth comes, He will guide you into all truth.

Romans 8:8 Those controlled by the flesh cannot please God. [9]You, however, are controlled not by the flesh, but by the Spirit, if the Spirit of God lives in you. And if anyone does not have the Spirit of Christ, he does not belong to Christ.

Galatians 5:16 So I say, walk by the Spirit, and you will not gratify the desires of the flesh. [17]For the flesh craves what is contrary to the Spirit, and the Spirit what is contrary to the flesh. They are opposed to each other, so that you do not do what you want. [18]But if you are led by the Spirit, you are not under the law... [24]Those who belong to Christ Jesus have crucified the flesh with its passions and desires. [25]Since we live by the Spirit, let us walk in step with the Spirit.

m. Our New Mechanic
Jesus, by the Holy Spirit, heals, repairs, restores, renews, corrects, and establishes.

Here's another interesting aspect of having Jesus, via the Holy Spirit, as not only the owner of your car (you), and your driver: He's also your new mechanic! He may have to pull over to the side of the road now and again and rebuke you if you're causing problems during the journey by allowing sin to creep in. However, you won't have to worry about the car breaking down and no one to repair it. Nope, repairing you is one of His main jobs. But if you're brand new then why do you need repair? The answer is that only your spirit is new—not your soul, not your body. The car itself is new. The frame, the engine, the paint job, the skeleton of the car is new. But everything *in* the car is still "old you." Your mind, will, desires, emotions, memories, habits, patterns, addictions, curses, thoughts, beliefs, current interpersonal relationships, past soul connections, behaviors, etc. are all a part of you, and all of these carry over into the new you. And every form of ungodliness, falsehood, brokenness, or poor stewardship of your life not dealt with prior to your faith and conversion, still needs to be dealt with after your conversion. Because of the glorious gospel these things aren't required to be fixed *before* being saved. However, they're not things God is okay with you continuing to remain in. They still need to be fixed up in order for you to be God's masterpiece! The best version of you possible in Christ Jesus is yet to come, so God begins to bring restoration in you right way, so He can do good works in and through you as your way of life! See Ephesians 2:10.

Later in the book we will explore in greater detail the many facets of life where the Holy Spirit acts like our mechanic, but for now let me just briefly describe some of the major categories. The first category of repair work is your false beliefs. Many false beliefs about God, sin, righteousness, etc. needed to be corrected just to bring you to be saved by faith in Jesus. However, they don't stop there. Your entire life until this point you developed beliefs, some true, some false. You will not walk in complete freedom and power still believing lies of the enemy. I've even written this book with this truth in mind.

The more truth I can pack into this book, the more freedom and empowerment you will get as a result of believing it and aligning your life according to it. And of course nothing I say means anything if it is not grounded in what God has revealed to us in His Word. His Word is truth. *(Jn 17:17)* And the truth sets us free. *(Jn 8:32)* And the Word is living and active, piercing even to dividing soul and spirit, judging the thoughts and intentions of the heart. *(Heb 4:12)* The Holy Spirit is always illuminating the mind, confirming the Word of God, to set you free from the bondage of the lies of the enemy. *(Jn 16:13)* This is why I've showed so much Christian theology into the first two chapters. You need to know this stuff in order to be unshakeable later!

The second category of repair is your brokenness. We all come with a lot of baggage. This is what Chapter 3 is all about. Our emotional, physical, or mental trauma, pain, and our past that was never brought healing can significantly affect our journey. It is a shame that often in the church it's taught that we are a new creation in Christ without realizing that not *every* part of us as been brought into this "newness." Jesus is our Great Physician, our Healer—or for the sake of the metaphor, our Mechanic—but this is not automatic. We must intentionally approach the throne of grace and surrender *each* broken part to God and ask Him to heal it. Unlike salvation, which is by faith alone, this process, sanctification, must be intentional. We must be determined to cooperate with the Holy Spirit for our healing and repair. He will fix us, in His way, and in His perfect timing, it's what He does. But we must diligently pursue it.

And lastly is our poor stewardship of our lives. He helps us repair these as well. No stone is left unturned. The light will be brought to every area of darkness. God is writing a story in us and through us. In us, because we are each individually His masterpiece. And through us, because we each play a small part in the master story He's writing. The question we must ask ourselves is this? Will we spend more of our time submitting to Him and letting Him repair more and more—or will we spend more of our time resisting Him and being an obstacle that slows down progress in ourselves and in the world?

---

1 Thessalonians 5:23 Now may the God of peace Himself sanctify you completely, and may your entire spirit, soul, and body be kept blameless at the coming of our Lord Jesus Christ.

Philippians 4:7 And the peace of God, which surpasses all understanding, will guard your hearts and your minds in Christ Jesus.

1 Peter 5:10 And after you have suffered for a little while, the God of all grace, who has called you to His eternal glory in Christ, will Himself restore you, secure you, strengthen you, and establish you. [11]To Him be the power forever and ever. Amen.

n. Our New Fuel System
We have a new, renewable, supernatural, nuclear powerhouse living in us.

An exciting new part of our rebuild is this: we get an entirely new fuel system. That is, we get an entirely different type of energy system to power us for the drive! So how does the fuel system in a car typically work? Well, we have to first get to a gas station and pump gas into a large tank in our car that holds a significant quantity of gas. A fuel pump then takes gas out of the tank, pushing it through hard metal fuel lines along the car that carry the gas to the engine. Before it gets to the engine the gas must pass through a fuel filter to remove impurities or debris. Then, either a carburetor or a fuel injection system draws in the gas, and the appropriate amount of outside air, for ignition in the combustion chamber. Within this chamber, a spark plug fires which ignites the fuel, creating an explosion which then creates the power necessary for the rest of the mechanical assembly to operate. What an amazing system that most of us take for granted! However, it does still have many limitations.

First off, we have to mine for crude oil/petroleum, of which there is a limited supply of in the earth. And that is the recycling of remains that were once living animals. Then that crude oil still has to be manually processed and have other things added to it. So this is a *limited* natural resource, available only because something else died, that we have to then extract, and then process before it can be used. Next, we have many working parts, fuel tanks, lines, injectors, spark plugs, and dozens of other parts I didn't even mention, all that wear down, or can work incorrectly, and need to be repaired or replaced. In a lot of ways, the human body is the same way. We have a limited supply of energy and we need to continue to replenish it with fuel, i.e. food, that actually comes from something else living that needs to die. The body's mechanisms that convert food into energy can *also* break down and fall apart, leading to diabetes, insulin resistance, etc. or even needing to be repaired or even replaced. We also need daily rest time in order to give everything a break. And this is just the physical part of our body. The same is needed for our spiritual, mental, and emotional states as well. Because of sin, the entire human condition is naturally decaying and dying. Meaning that beyond the age preprogrammed into our DNA to be optimal, anywhere from age 25 to 30, after that we're all on a downward trend trying to slow down our decay rate as much as possible. What I'm trying to say is this: all our natural systems have limitations and they all fall apart.

I'm certainly not saying this to be a bummer! If the story ended there it would be. But it doesn't. First, we will get a whole new eternal everything one day. Second, as it pertains to us right now during our journey, this is our *natural* condition. However, we have been born again which means we are not fully natural any more! We have been rebuilt supernaturally and now have a supernatural supplement: the Spirit of the Living God! The caveat is that His presence is *primarily* spiritual. I say primarily because He can, and does, bring physical healing and energy to the body. However, His primary concern, as it relates to us individually, is the spiritual wellbeing of our soul. The spirit is the place where our mind, emotions, and everything else—can and should—draw from. So if our spirit is strengthened by the presence of the Holy Spirit, and our soul is being renewed and even growing daily, then though our outer self (our body) is wasting away, we will be full of joy and peace and vitality in our innermost being!

The natural man (the person who hasn't been born again) must continuously go to metaphorical gas stations to fill up because their energy comes from "outside" themselves. It is their lives, their relationships, their vacations, their hobbies, their careers, dining out, dessert, etc. that makes them *feel* good. It is what energizes them. It is where they get their joy from. They have to, it's the only option! They must find a way to fill up in the world because they are still of the world. But it is not so with us. At least it doesn't have to be and shouldn't be! Unlike the natural man, our primary fuel tank is a *renewable energy source within*. It's more like we are a battery operated car and our energy comes from a self-recharging battery! But you know, a battery has a "full" capacity and a limitation too. We're talking about God! So there is no "full." There is no limit. We also don't have to worry about recharging. God doesn't get tired or need to refill the tank! So we're really *not* like a battery-operated car either. It's really more like an internal nuclear power plant that is being fed continuous nuclear power directly from Heaven! And within us we have an infinite number of explosions of supernatural, atomic-sized energy capable of allowing us to do all that we could ever desire and more! And since our energy is spiritual, rather than physical, it doesn't run out, or wear out the fuel lines, or need a new fuel filter, spark plugs, etc. It just works and it doesn't break. The Holy Spirit is our mechanic. He ensures that our "energy system" is always in tip-top shape, ready for whatever the task is at hand. We need to know this and let it encourage us!

Have you ever noticed that Jesus began His earthly ministry by first fasting in the wilderness for 40 days? *(Matt 4:1-2)* This is even though, physically speaking in His human nature, He was just as human as we are with the same limitations. He was hungry, but the Holy Spirit sustained Him. I think one of the reasons He did this is to develop His spiritual muscles, to learn how to depend on the Holy Spirit. We still know that it wore Him out. He ended His fast by receiving additional ministering from angels. *(Matt 4:11)* I'm not saying that you should try such a long fast, but try to fast by skipping a single meal to start, using that time to pray and seek God, and over time work your way up to build your tolerance to increased durations. Fasting (temporary abstinence from food and even occasionally other recreational activities) is a spiritual discipline activity that helps us to hone our ability to be dependent upon God. This is because we are depriving ourselves of something that we do need and then spending that time, energy, and focus that would have been used to eat, to be with God in a dedicated pursuit towards spiritual growth. Scripture speaks repeatedly about fasting as an approved method of drawing closer to God, seeking His direction and guidance about something, and God rewards this type of activity. It is such a staple that Jesus didn't even *tell* us to do it. He just *assumes* we will. He says "*when* you fast..." *(Matt 6:17)* and later, after our bridegroom has been taken away, *then* they will fast. *(Mark 2:20)* While I think fasting is worth mentioning here, I don't want you to think that fasting is the primary goal of my creating this section in the book. It is not necessary to fast in order to draw energy, power, and strength from God. You can and should do it at any time, and all the time, especially whenever you really need it, not just when fasting. But fasting is a deliberate way for you to practice the exercise of learning to sharpen your mind's focus on the Spirit, and to do it regularly, and by doing it regularly will eventually help you turn the discipline into a powerful habit.

Of even more importance though is just that you recognize that the Holy Spirit's presence is not *only* about leading you to truth, holiness, righteousness, or even just experiencing God's presence. He also empowers us internally for whatever lies before us. He is there to give you the power to do any God-given task or pursuit or desire that the Lord brings you to. By saying you have this massive resource of internal power I do not mean to suggest that you should not be taking breaks, or sleep, or taking vacations, etc. Not at all. We should also steward our body well by realizing it's natural limitations and not putting undo stress on ourselves. Especially not for worldly pursuits. But when it comes to matters of our faith, that is different. Your struggle with sin conflicting with your Christ-likeness, or your role in advancing God's Kingdom, or your Gospel proclamation to the lost, or your ministering to someone during a critical time, or any other moments in your journey when you will be put to the test, challenged beyond your normal, natural capabilities we have an infinite power source to draw from! Christians often live defeated because they don't trust in the truths of their faith deep enough. You know this as a truth revealed in the Bible, so it is an act of your faith for you to believe it live it out. Remember this, when you're pushed to your limit at a critical junction, but you know for a fact that it is God's will for you to be a conqueror over that matter, rather than retreating to rest defeated, saying you'll try again tomorrow, do this. Stop, pray, envision traveling in your mind to the depth of your spirit, where the Holy Spirit resides, and ask Him for an explosion of power and energy and confidence and boldness so that you can be strong enough to do God's will in that moment. And then see what happens! Your car is a V12, and it has a turbo charger, and even a nitrous tank! Don't live like you're in a 4-cylinder!

Acts 1:8 But you will receive power when the Holy Spirit comes upon you, and you will be My witnesses in Jerusalem, and in all Judea and Samaria, and to the ends of the earth."

John 7:38 Whoever believes in Me, as the Scripture has said: 'Streams of living water will flow from within him.'" [39]He was speaking about the Spirit, whom those who believed in Him were later to receive...

Colossians 1:29 To this end I also labor, striving with all His energy working powerfully within me.

---

o. Our New Owner's Manual
The Holy Bible is our Holy Spirit-inspired guide to all that we need for faith and life.

It should come as no surprise by now that the owner's manual for our cars, for each of us, and the manual for how we should be doing "church" is the Holy Bible. The Bible is our foundational source, providing all that we need to know for life, including the path to salvation and eternal life, as well as how to practically live out our faith in the here and now. The Bible is a collection of warnings to humanity to prepare them of God's judgment and wrath to come, and to God's people to guide them through the perilous times ahead of them. However, it's also a love letter from God to humanity, sharing His heart and affection for us, and teaching us the way to be reconciled to Him. Just like a car owner's manual the Bible teaches us how to operate ourselves individually and how to operate the auto club (the church). But unlike an owner's manual we need the Bible for more than just knowing how to getting started and for troubleshooting. We need to draw from it daily for guidance through the drive through the rough terrain that lies ahead of us. The Bible is our GPS, our weather forecast, our shield, our sword, and so much more. If the Holy Spirit provides the fuel and power for our journey, then the Bible, God's living Word, is the additive and high octane boost that amplifies that fuel. The Holy Spirit both inspired and preserves the words in the Bible. He is there, illuminating His own Word to our mind and spirit, opening it up to us as we humbly and hungrily consume it. And all the while His Word simultaneously does the reverse, the Word itself confirming His presence in us, testifying to the majesty and lordship of Jesus, empowering our faith and walk, and testifying of its own self-revealing divine authenticity.

Brief History. Much could be said about the technical aspects of the Bible. "Bible" is simply a transliteration of the Greek word bíblos (βίβλος), meaning "book."[4] The Bible is a collection of 66 different books, poems, and letters, that were written over 1600 years (from approximately 1500 BC to AD 100) by more than 40 kings, prophets, leaders, and followers of Jesus.[5] The Hebrew Scriptures (the "Old Testament") has 39 books (written approximately 1500-400 BC) and the New Testament has 27 books (written approximately AD 45-100).[5] The books of the Bible were collected and arranged and recognized as inspired sacred authority by councils of rabbis and councils of church leaders based on careful guidelines.[5] The entire collection of all 39 universally-accepted Old Testament books now included in Bibles were established as authentic Hebrew Scriptures by Jewish rabbis around AD 90 at the Council of Jamnia.[13] And of our current 27 New Testament books, no fewer than 19 were always universally agreed to as authoritative.[13] Twenty-three appear listed on the fragment of Muratori in the mid-second century.[13] All 27 books, as they are now recognized throughout the modern world, are listed in a letter by early church father Athanasius in AD 367.[13] These were *last* assembled together into a single set canon (rule of faith and truth) and formally confirmed at the Synod of Carthage in AD 397.[6] The collection was first referred to as *ta biblia* (the books), the Latin form of biblos, in the fourth century by John Chrysostom.[5] Other than the matter of how to deal with the portion of the Bible called the Apocrypha, which I will touch on shortly, the Bible has remained remarkably unchanged in over 1600 years!

Canon (Book Selection/Order). The entire New Testament canon and the universally-accepted Hebrew Bible (39 books of the Old Testament canon) have not changed, however there are 7 books that remain in the Catholic and Eastern Orthodox canons that have been excluded from the Protestant canon since the Reformation. These 7 historical books were written during the second temple period between the last prophet in the Old Testament and the New Testament. These are called the *Apocrypha* by Protestants and the *Deuterocanonical books* by Catholics. They've been excluded for a variety of reasons, all related to the lack of evidence of their being inerrant and inspired by God. These reasons include: (1) their rejection by Jesus and the Apostles, (2) their rejection by the Jewish Community, (3) their rejection by many in the Catholic Church, (4) false teachings found in them, and (5) their lack of prophetic fulfillment or foresight.[7,8,9] Protestants are Sola Scriptura, meaning they base their beliefs on "Scripture alone," whereas the Catholic Church interprets Scripture through "Tradition" and the teaching authority of its "Magisterium."[10] Because of this dedication to the absolute authority of Scripture, it's crucial only unquestionable books are included in the Protestant canon. These other historical books may offer insight into the beliefs and practices of Jews during the second temple period, and possibly even wisdom or supplementary sacred truths to consider and wrestle with. But for the reasons listed above and others, I recommend only the universally-accepted 66 books as your *authoritative manual* for faith and life. The apocryphal books, and any other pseudepigraphal sacred writings should be seen as secondary, supplementary, and considered with extreme caution, and outright rejected if they contradict anything in the authoritative books.

Reliability. There is much evidence that the Bible we have today is remarkably true to the original writings. Of the thousands of copies made by hand prior to the invention of the printing press in AD 1455 more than 5,900 Greek manuscripts from the New Testament alone still exist today.[5] And this is not even including the tens of thousands of extant (surviving) manuscripts translated into other languages. In fact, the Bible had already been translated into 7 languages by AD 200 and 13 languages by AD 500.[5] In addition to this, there are a vast number of quotations of the Biblical text by early church fathers preserved in their writings. There is an inventory of 270,000 entries published in the volumes of Biblia Patristica, which have all been scientifically verified.[12] Because of the high volume and high variety of ancient manuscripts, as well as the great contributions from the fields of archaeology, carbon dating techniques, linguistical analysis of ancient languages, and modern textual criticism, we can have a very high degree of confidence in the accuracy of modern translations. While human scribes are capable of error or bias it has been evidenced that we could trust the Holy Spirit as He has continued to preserve the essential spirit and truth of His Word, despite Satan's attempts to alter or distort it. The discovery of the Dead Sea Scrolls in the 20th century found manuscripts of hundreds of books from the Old Testament that had been hidden in a cave, untouched and hidden away for over 2,000 years. This confirmed the amazing reliability of the Old Testament as it had also been very well-preserved. And despite scribal errors and spelling variations, no variation affects basic Bible doctrines![5]

So the Bible we have today is an accurate representation and translation of the original writings to a high degree of certainty. Still, even if we now have a good copy of the originals, how do we know that the original authors were trustworthy? That they were who they claimed to be, were eyewitnesses, were honest? Or that their writings were passed down reliably for the first two hundred years? Many excellent historians, scholars, and Christian apologists could be recommended. Let me briefly list some of the evidenced-based conclusions of J. Warner Wallace outlined in his book, *Cold-Case Christianity*. He concludes the gospels *are* reliable and were written by authors writing what *they* observed. They were: (1) verified and corroborated by other contemporaries, (2) accurately delivered, (3) attested to have no ulterior motives, (4) written very early by eyewitnesses present to the events recorded, and (5) there is a reliable chain of custody between the original writers and what was passed down to other reliable early church fathers.[11] Therefore, we can be confident that the Bible contains reliable eyewitness accounts that were then reliably preserved and passed down to other known and reliable people.

Summary. The Bible is a type of warning, love letter, and owner's manual from God to guide us. The books considered authentic and authoritative sacred writings were organized relatively early, very close to the formation of the early church. We have many reasons to trust in the writings of the original authors, and in the process of transmission and translation down through history up to the present day. The Bible itself teaches us that, while each book was written by human authors with their own unique literary styles and historical intentions for writing, they were also under the divine inspiration of the Holy Spirit. This makes the Bible a unique collection of both the historical writings of men, as well as a cohesive narrative and instruction authored by God. Additionally, because God is the author and He intends to use His Word to redeem humanity the Holy Spirit has also preserved the Word to keep it from being lost or corrupted. Because God is the ultimate author those who profess faith in Jesus Christ as Lord and Savior are called to humbly and faithfully believe and obey God's written Word. This leads me to my final point in this section: *biblical inerrancy*. Biblical inerrancy is the belief that the Bible is without error in its foundation and instructions for faith and life.

I believe the most precise summary of the key points of biblical inerrancy were put together by the International Council on Biblical Inerrancy in Chicago, Illinois, USA on October 28, 1978. The resulting confessional statement was called *The Chicago Statement on Biblical Inerrancy*. The goal of this statement was to establish the basis for the belief in the divine inerrancy of Scripture, as it is our chief authority for all doctrine and way of life. Since our commitment to be obedient to Scripture is only as real as our ability to *understand* the meaning of Scripture, a second statement was prepared the following year to clarify the appropriate ways to *interpret* Scripture. This was called *The Chicago Statement on Biblical Hermeneutics*. I recommend you read these short summaries. They, along with supporting educational material, can be found at (DefendingInerrancy.com). God's Word is what everything else we believe and do is governed by. It's essential that you trust in His Word and allow it to guide you.

Deuteronomy 18:18 I will raise up for them a prophet like you from among their brothers. I will put My words in his mouth, and he will tell them everything I command him.

2 Samuel 23:2 The Spirit of the LORD spoke through me; His word was on my tongue.

2 Peter 1:20 Above all, you must understand that no prophecy of Scripture comes from one's own interpretation. [21]For no prophecy was ever brought forth by the will of man, but men spoke from God as they were carried along by the Holy Spirit.

Matthew 4:4 But Jesus answered, "It is written: 'Man shall not live on bread alone, but on every word that comes from the mouth of God.'"

Matthew 22:29 Jesus answered, "You are mistaken because you do not know the Scriptures or the power of God.

Hebrews 4:12 For the word of God is living and active. Sharper than any double-edged sword, it pierces even to dividing soul and spirit, joints and marrow. It judges the thoughts and intentions of the heart.

2 Timothy 3:15 From infancy you have known the Holy Scriptures, which are able to make you wise for salvation through faith in Christ Jesus. [16]All Scripture is God-breathed and is useful for instruction, for conviction, for correction, and for training in righteousness, so that the man of God may be complete, fully equipped for every good work.

Psalm 119:105 Your word is a lamp to my feet and a light to my path.

p. Dying To The Old Daily
The Christian Life is a daily denial of the Old and embrace of the New.

An interesting part of the Christian life, of human *born-again* experience, is having to live with this profound new reality, this complicated and dynamic type of dualism. We're now simultaneously a new spiritual creation, but we're still also the same old flawed person we've always been. We're now a spiritually-adopted child of God the Father and heir of all things that belong to God the Son, but we're also still in our same earthly family we've always had with all of its dysfunction. We're now a member of God's heavenly council and a citizen and priest in the Kingdom of God, but we're also still in the world with a citizenship to a country and governing authorities. We're now a holy temple of the Spirit of the Living, Almighty God that spoke the universe into existence, but we're also in a weak body of decaying flesh that's susceptible to all kinds of sinful desires and temptations. This is a profound reality. We're navigating life in many ways like everyone else, but we also began a very different journey after putting our trust in Jesus. The truth is that, this side of Heaven, we never escape the "old *man*" aspects of our journey. These are part of our journey, part of our story, part of God's story in us and through us. During the Early and Middle Ages, the role of "monk" was developed, as was the institution for monks to live in, called the monastery. By separating themselves from the rest of society, and all of its distractions and ways of life, monks were able to then fully dedicate themselves to studying, seeking God, and pursuing spiritual growth. This is not a bad thing, in and of itself, but this is not God's ultimate intention for us in this life. While temporary reprieve and isolation can be very helpful, and at times even necessary for personal renewal, it should only be temporary. God has not called us out of the world physically, He has called us out of the world spiritually. We have not been called to abandon all worldly human institutions, we've been called to endure them, and to seek to bring influence and transformation within them.

God has left us here for reasons and we need to discover and embrace those reasons. We do need to be careful though not to be ensnared by our flesh, the world, the enemy, and the sinful passions that war within us. As long as we are in the body, and in the world, the struggle will be harder, but God has designed it this way and He provides everything we need to be victorious. This is the vehicle He is using to mature us to become His eternal people. Our struggle is what helps to make us. Our struggle is what helps to prepare us. Our struggle is what creates in us an appreciation for who God is, and for who He is to each one of us. It is through this life, and our struggle, that we develop a relationship with God. As we die to our old selves, and begin to embrace our new identity in Christ, we will be shaped and molded into the unique version of ourselves that knows and glorifies God. We're not just called to be *generically like* Christ, we're called to be our special and unique way of being like Christ. We become like Him and simultaneously become the best of our unique self in the process. We must continue to crucify the sinful and selfish desires of our flesh. Our old self, and the struggles we face, are *our* crosses.

We don't take up Jesus's cross, we take up our own cross and follow Him.

The struggles you face are not really your enemy, they are God's sculpting tools that He is using to remove the dead parts of you. Let Him. Submit to the process. They are *our* crosses. We each have one. They might look very different. Accept it and pray for His grace, pray for grace to appreciate your cross, pray for grace to endure your cross. You can pray that He takes away some of your cross, He might answer, but He won't take the whole cross away. There will always be some type of cross. Pray, rather, that He comes near you, like Simon of Cyrene, and helps you to carry your cross. *(Matt 27:32)* This He has promised to do. *(Matt 11:28-30)* Stop praying relentlessly that God takes you *out* of your problems, and start praying that He would draw near to you, and take you *through* your problems, and do whatever it takes to strengthen your relationship and to make you more like Jesus! Do this, and you will take advantage of every opportunity to grow in all the right ways in your relationship with Him, and as a person. If you're prepared to endure and He delivers you from the problem then you will immediately recognize it has a gift and a blessing to appreciate. But your love for Him isn't dependent upon Him first giving something to you. Continue to die to the old you, every day, and appreciate the process. Every day, look for opportunities to crucify some old part and embrace the new.

Luke 14:27 *[Jesus]* And whoever does not carry his cross and follow Me cannot be My disciple.

Romans 6:6 We know that our old self was crucified with Him so that the body of sin might be rendered powerless, that we should no longer be slaves to sin.

Galatians 5:24 Those who belong to Christ Jesus have crucified the flesh with its passions and desires. [25]Since we live by the Spirit, let us walk in step with the Spirit.

IV. Chapter Summary and Evaluation

Chapter Summary
The New Journey BEGINS with not only a New Map but also a New You.

We start out this new journey by understanding that everything we previously had needs to be completely revamped. Our old map was completely wrong. It would've taken us down a completely different path that ended at a wrong, and bad, destination. The map didn't just need to be tweaked, it needed to be thrown out. We needed an entirely new map. In the same way, we've got a broken car. It didn't need to be fixed, it needed to be rebuilt from the ground up. It needed to be regenerated. The way that we see the world, and spiritual truths, and morality, is also very distorted. We needed to receive new eyes. Essentially, we needed to be "born again." This needs to happen at the outset just to get started on our journey. We can't begin the journey until after this has happened.

We learned of different aspects of this process. By God's grace alone He willingly and lovingly calls us to Himself. By God's grace alone He is willing to forgive us of our sins. The way that God extends us the offer of forgiveness is through His Son, and His sacrificial death, on our behalf, on the cross. Through the internal conviction of our sin and guiltiness, as well as the weight of sheer gratitude after hearing the gospel, we are humbled and drawn to repentance. By our faith in who Jesus is and what He did we're saved, justified (declared blameless), received His imputed righteousness, and adopted as a child of God, in Christ. Now in Christ, we become born again, regenerated, as a new car. We receive a new driver for our car, the Holy Spirit that we've been sealed by. He also becomes our new mechanic that fixes, heals, and restores us along the journey. He becomes our new fuel system, an internal source of renewable energy and power for the specific calling and tasks laid out before us. We learned that the Bible is like our new owner's manual. And that it is inspired, preserved, and provided by God to us to give us all that we *need* for faith and life, and it is our highest authority. And since we remain in this old world, and in the same old body, we must continually die to the nature of our old selves and focus on embracing our new identity and life purpose.

If we fail to constantly remind ourselves, and therefore remember, all of these essential truths, we risk making the mistake of trying to do this journey in our own will, and our own strength. And in so doing we will be miserable replicas and inevitably fall away.

Evaluation Directions.

On a scale from 1-10, how do the following truths guide your personal walk?
Using a pencil select the corresponding number. A lower number means you are just now learning this truth and you haven't fully reflected on it and applied it in any significant way. A higher number means you understand it well, believe it's true and already live in accordance with it allowing it to impact the way you think, feel, worship, and live. This book's content should be enough to get you to a 5 on each unless you have presuppositional beliefs that hinder it. If you score a 4 or less on any, I recommend starting with further study in those topic areas first. If you score a 5 or greater on all, continue to chapter two. But if you score less than a 7 in any, I recommend re-reading those sections again first (see letter key on the left of each).

Chapter 2 Evaluation

I UNDERSTAND WHY, BELIEVE, HAVE CONFIDENCE THAT:

	False		Partially False				Mostly True			True
a) I've abandoned my Old Map and wholly trust in God's Map	1	2	3	4	5	6	7	8	9	10
b) I understand why people are not "basically good"	1	2	3	4	5	6	7	8	9	10
c) I humbly accept my sight/discernment is blinded by my sin	1	2	3	4	5	6	7	8	9	10
d) I understand and believe that people must be born again	1	2	3	4	5	6	7	8	9	10
e) It is only by God's grace that He calls us all to Himself	1	2	3	4	5	6	7	8	9	10
f) It is only by God's grace that He offers us forgiveness	1	2	3	4	5	6	7	8	9	10
g) Only the humble before God have truly repented	1	2	3	4	5	6	7	8	9	10
h) It is only by faith alone, in Christ alone, that I'm saved	1	2	3	4	5	6	7	8	9	10
h) We're saved to do good works, but works don't help save us	1	2	3	4	5	6	7	8	9	10
h) I'm confident that I have been born again	1	2	3	4	5	6	7	8	9	10
i) I'm confident all my past sins have already been paid for .	1	2	3	4	5	6	7	8	9	10
j) I'm confident that though I fail, I have Christ's righteousness	1	2	3	4	5	6	7	8	9	10
k) I must first be a new car, belonging to Jesus, for this journey	1	2	3	4	5	6	7	8	9	10
l) The Holy Spirit is the driver; I allow/trust Him in control ...	1	2	3	4	5	6	7	8	9	10
m) I trust/allow the Holy Spirit to restore, heal, repair, etc.	1	2	3	4	5	6	7	8	9	10
n) I trust/receive spiritual renewal, energy, power, talent, etc	1	2	3	4	5	6	7	8	9	10
n) In Christ, I am an adopted child of God, who is my Father .	1	2	3	4	5	6	7	8	9	10
o) I'm confident in the Bible as the authoritative Word of God	1	2	3	4	5	6	7	8	9	10
o) I regularly read, study, pray on, submit to the Word of God	1	2	3	4	5	6	7	8	9	10
p) My struggle with my flesh doesn't mean that I'm not saved	1	2	3	4	5	6	7	8	9	10
p) I'm dedicated to dying to the old and embracing the new	1	2	3	4	5	6	7	8	9	10

Date Last Taken: _____

Questions for Reflection or Group Study:

1) What are some ways to identify parts of our old selves still playing a role in our lives?
2) Why is it important for us to understanding the role of God's grace in our salvation?
3) In what ways is "blind faith" different from a faith based on knowledge, belief, and trust?
4) If the Bible is our primary way to discern truth and God's will, and it is the only authoritative source, why do so many Christians neglect it? Why do you?
5) How can we be better at taking the log out of our own eye first before judging others?
6) If we must be saved by grace through faith why do you think that all other religions teach that we can do things to work out our own salvation?
7) Since humility is essential to repentance and a right walk with God, what are some areas that you could work on being more humble in?
8) What does Satan gain by Christians downplaying Penal Substitutionary Atonement?
9) How will remembering that you're a new car headed in the right direction, even if you stumble, help your faith and confidence going forward?

Subjects I plan to study more of: Strategy, Plan, Deadline:

1. _____
2. _____
3. _____

Explore Chapter 2 Deeper:

For additional resources related to the topics discussed in this chapter see our companion website at **https://MPoweredChristian.org/Road-Map-Book-Resources**

- Free printable pdf of this chapter evaluation for personal or classroom use
- List of related online courses, e-coaching programs, personal coaching services
- List of related videos, articles, and recommended books
- List of related live webinars and ways to ask questions

Notes/Reflections:

_____
_____
_____
_____
_____
_____
_____
_____
_____
_____
_____
_____
_____
_____
_____
_____
_____
_____
_____
_____
_____
_____
_____
_____
_____
_____
_____
_____
_____
_____
_____
_____
_____
_____
_____
_____

To-Do List: _Date:_ _____

MY TASKS FOR **THIS UPCOMING WEEK...**

✔ **My Big 1-3:**

✔ **For Personal Growth:**

✔ **For Key Roles:**

✔ **For Calling/Ministry Service:**

✔ **Pray for/Request prayer about:**

✔ **Learn more about:**

✔ **Other:**

CHAPTER THREE

DUMPING THE GARBAGE BAGGAGE

Regular examination of your car will confirm you're rebuilt, and enhance and protect your journey.

Chapter Contents

I. Evidence and Remnants of the Old

a. The Old Road Map
Examine your life regularly for evidence of the Old Map.

As we read in Chapter 2, especially in section (P), we are called to die daily to our old selves and embrace our new identity. To say this is difficult is an understatement. It does not come naturally. In fact, it only comes *supernaturally*. The natural part of us, the "old" part, will *always* feel more natural! It *is* natural. So we must be deliberate. You must examine your life regularly, with humility, with introspection, and in submission to the inner promptings of the Holy Spirit. As you make decisions that affect your life, or the lives of others around you, or the society as a whole, ask yourself, what would God have me do? How do I approach this from an "eternal treasures" perspective? Am I just satisfying my worldly needs or wants? Am I glorifying God through this? How could I handle this differently, with pleasing my Heavenly Father and Lord as my primary motive? Remind yourself and reflect upon the truths revealed in Chapter One regularly. Make sure that these essential truths are guiding pillars of your life.

b. The Old Car
Examine your life regularly for evidence of the Old Car.

You must be born again. There should be no confidence in your salvation if you're not confident in your spiritual regeneration. For more on this read Chapter 2, especially Subsection II, (G-J). As I document in detail there we are saved by God's grace through faith alone in Christ alone. If you wholeheartedly repent of your sin, and wholeheartedly believe that Jesus is the Son of God, that He died for your sins and rose again, and you have willingly surrendered your life to Him, then you CAN be confident in your salvation! You may have had a dramatic salvation moment at a specific time where God convicted you of your sins, touched your heart and brought you to Him in tears. Or maybe your mind recalls having a unique spiritual or supernatural encounter with the Lord or where you were baptized in the Holy Spirit and you spoke in tongues or prophesied. Or maybe it was more of a gradual process that occurred over months or even years without any kind of dramatic outward encounter with a date attached, but you know in your heart-of-hearts that God is real, that Jesus is the way and truth, and His peace and confidence of your salvation has entered you. No one type of encounter is more true or false than the others, and reject those who say it is. Your faith is between you and the Lord. YOU must KNOW for YOURSELF. No one else can tell you if you are saved. You must know that you are, by faith alone.

If there is ever ANY doubt in your mind then repeat the same steps we've already covered. Humble yourself, repent of your sins, and trust in Jesus. It is never more complicated than this, but some seasons of life may have us needing to do this more frequently. But know, that you know that you know, that *you are* saved! And if you have any doubts take your doubts and fears to the Lord Jesus and lay them at His feet in prayer. Ask Him if He knows you....

It's not about *SOMETHING* you need still to *DO*, it's about *SOMEONE* you need still to TRUST.

c. The Old Driver
Examine your life regularly for evidence of the Old Driver.

Of course, that last statement is only true if you've already previously repented of your sins and are living a somewhat sanctified and godly life. If you're already being obedient then you just need to trust the Lord and develop your relationship with Him. But if that's not the case, and you're not being obedient in some significant way, then you might still be the "*old* you." That's no good. When we first give ourselves to Jesus, but even on a regular basis, we need to examine ourselves and confirm that we are, in fact, a Christian—a "Christ *follower.*" That might sound like nonsense to some, but some need to hear this: if you *still live* like a heathen (an ungodly pagan who doesn't know or obey God) then you're probably still unsaved. I could give modern examples of the attributes of so-called Christians who are probably still unsaved, but let's just let the Bible broadly define these attributes for us:

---

1 Corinthians 6:9 Do you not know that the wicked will not inherit the kingdom of God? Do not be deceived: Neither the sexually immoral, nor idolaters, nor adulterers, nor men who submit to or perform homosexual acts, [10]nor thieves, nor the greedy, nor drunkards, nor verbal abusers, nor swindlers, will inherit the kingdom of God.

Revelation 21:8 "But to the cowardly and unbelieving and abominable and murderers and sexually immoral and sorcerers and idolaters and all liars, their place will be in the lake that burns with fire and sulfur. This is the second death."

Ephesians 5:3 But among you, as is proper among the saints, there must not be even a hint of sexual immorality, or of any kind of impurity, or of greed. [4]Nor should there be obscenity, foolish talk, or crude joking, which are out of character, but rather thanksgiving. [5]For

> of this you can be sure: No immoral, impure, or greedy person (that is, an idolater), has any inheritance in the kingdom of Christ and of God.

People who do such things are acting ungodly, unchristian. This does not mean a born again person cannot stumble into temptation and so fall into such behaviors, they can. However, it is a clear violation of God's Word, and is contrary to God's character and His will for His children. His Spirit does not lead, nor does His Spirit enjoy or entertain such behavior. Immoral behavior can only be considered a genuine *stumble* if it was preceded by a noticeably godly lifestyle prior to the stumble. If it is not a stumble, but rather a *persistent state* of unrepentant behavior then the evidence implies that the person has not been born again. They have denied the faith with their actions. Regardless of their "profession" of faith in Jesus they are not born again. They are self-deceived. They are a hypocrite at best, and a wolf-in-sheep's-clothing at worst. By removing such people from church fellowship we can preserve the sanctity of the church so it can be beyond reproach. The Apostle Paul gives clear instructions not to associate with such people:

> 1 Corinthians 5:2 And you are proud! Shouldn't you rather have been stricken with grief and removed from your fellowship the man who did this?... [9]I wrote you in my letter not to associate with sexually immoral people. [10]I was not including the sexually immoral of this world, or the greedy and swindlers, or idolaters. In that case you would have to leave this world. [11]But now I am writing you not to associate with anyone who claims to be a brother but is sexually immoral or greedy, an idolater or a verbal abuser, a drunkard or a swindler. With such a man do not even eat. [12]What business of mine is it to judge those outside the church? Are you not to judge those inside? [13]God will judge those outside. "Expel the wicked man from among you."

Examine yourself. If this is you, then realize that you are living in a very ungodly way. Your church may let you fellowship and not know how you live or hold you accountable if they do. But I will say to you what they should. You need to repent now! You need to realize that God is righteous and holy—and just—and the guilty will not go unpunished. Do not trample on the grace of God and assume that you are okay and that you can continue to live in sin and still be saved because you believe in Jesus. That desire to even do such a thing is evidence that you have not been born again. Fear God, fear Hell, fear His wrath, and repent today! Humble yourself. Examine yourself. Test yourself. And if you fail the test, repent! I get it, I was there once too. The old man, the sinner part of us, wants us to "have our cake and eat it too" but this cannot happen. If our old driver is still in control, he needs to die, we need to evict him! And if you're ever not sure, and you feel like your old driver might be trying to get back into the driver seat, remind yourself to throw him back out of the car! We will explore this in greater detail shortly.

> 2 Corinthians 13:5 Examine yourselves to see whether you are in the faith; test yourselves. Can't you see for yourselves that Jesus Christ is in you—unless you actually fail the test?

d. The Saboteur
Examine your life regularly for evidence of the Saboteur.

Let's say that you've already got your new map, your new car, and your new driver, but there's one other major player you need to be on the look out for. This is Satan, Lucifer, the Devil, AKA the "Saboteur."

Satan is a cherub, a type of angelic being, which was originally created good by God in Heaven, but became prideful by his own beauty and wickedly sought to be worshipped by others, like God. He inspired other angels to sin against God, and to follow him. He led a rebellion against God, eventually being defeated and they were all cast down to the spiritual realm on earth. There is only one chief demon "Satan/Lucifer," who is not omnipresent and can only be in one location at a time. The vast majority of people do not encounter the literal biblical Satan but rather other demons who might still identify as Satan, etc. The word *satan* literally just means "adversary." It is not actually a proper name.[1] Neither is *Lucifer*, which is just a 4th-century AD Latin translation of words meaning "light bearer" or "shining one", referring to a text in Isaiah 14:12 of Satan's pre-fall beauty and brightness as an angel.[2] These are just descriptions of his their attributes. But for consistency and simplicity sake I will continue to refer to both the chief fallen angel (Satan/Lucifer) or any of his follower minions (demons), who all operate in a very similar way, simply as "Satan." Of course, Satan and his other fallen angels (demons), the chief enemies and adversaries of humanity and especially the Church, attack us in many ways throughout the Christian life. However, I want to focus on a specific role in this section, and that is of him/them as saboteurs.

A saboteur is someone who engages in sabotage,[3] which is the act of deliberately destroying, damaging, or obstructing (something), especially for political or military advantage.[4] Of particular interest to us at this junction in our study is the Saboteur's (Satan's/demons') use of subversion against us. Subversion is the systematic attempt to overthrow or undermine a government or political system by person's working secretly from within.[5] In this case, Satan seeks to infiltrate individuals, marriages, families, homes, churches, institutions, governments, etc. to overthrow or undermine the healing, deliverance, restoration, or other advancement of the Kingdom of God in those things. Saboteur is a good analogy because Satan's tactics are not always obvious. In fact they often are quite undetected, especially in the lost world where most things are being actively influenced by Satan regularly. But Satan gets a lot of influence even in the lives of Christians who are not biblically astute, introspective, or spiritually discerning. Satan has been at this for thousands of years as he is quite good at it so we need to be on guard.

For my clients and ministry partners who are familiar with me and my ministry (MPowered Christian Ministries) it may come as a surprise that I have waited until the third chapter of this book to mention Satan, demons, and spiritual warfare. This may be even more surprising to you once I reveal this fact: I'm also a deliverance minister, or perhaps a title you may be more familiar with: an exorcist. I am on a fairly regular basis helping people identify how Satan has infiltrated their lives and empowering and assisting them to overcome their spiritual oppression and find freedom in the name of Jesus. Given my belief that this is an important, and often neglected area of the Christian life, and the fact that I have greater knowledge and expertise in this area than most pastors, why have I waited until after a third through my book to first bring up the topic of spiritual warfare? Well the truth is, I haven't. I've been teaching you essential aspects of spiritual warfare this entire time!

Satan is a saboteur. He rarely comes out in the open and tells you he's Satan, that he's evil, that he hates you, that he wants to destroy you, and that he's deeply involved in almost every aspect of your life. He's rarely going to openly reveal his true nature and his intent, tell you where he's hiding, tell you how long he's been there and how he stays there, and tell you that you that he's actively working to sabotage all of your efforts in many ways. He's not going to tell you that he won't leave unless you make him, that you should be much more concerned with your sanctification, and that you should identify, reject, and expel him because if he stays there, he's only going to keep lying to you, damaging you, sabotaging you, and deceiving you so you ultimately reject Jesus and get thrown into Hell with him! That would just be way too easy! No, most of the time he hides in the background skillfully and plays the long game. Making you think that all of your problems are *your* fault, even reminding you to feel guilty about what *you've* done.

---

1 Peter 5:8 Be sober-minded and alert. Your adversary the devil prowls around like a roaring lion, seeking someone to devour.

Occasionally they get detected, or their pride and arrogance provoke them to boastfully reveal themselves to us, or they can gain greater influence through direct contact, then often claiming to be something good. Surely, even a part of Satan actually believes he is the good one and God the bad one. Sin has perverted and twisted his mind to believe they have something to offer us. Often they know full well they hate us and want to destroy us but put on a friendly veneer to get closer and more deeply embedded. Just as a political saboteur can do more damage if they remain undetected and work their way up to become the president, Satan can do more damage if he works his way up undetected to influence us, or others through us, at a high level. The Apostle Paul acknowledges this facade that Satan puts on, and not only the chief Satan, and his demons, but also their human counterparts, the false apostles, teachers, and servants that they have deceived to do their will and teach their lies.

---

2 Corinthians 11:13 For such men are false apostles, deceitful workers, masquerading as apostles of Christ. [14]And no wonder, for Satan himself masquerades as an angel of light. [15]It is not surprising, then, if his servants masquerade as servants of righteousness. Their end will correspond to their actions.

Most people that have demons don't even know that they do. This is because demons usually hide in the background. Though we're justified through faith, none of us are fully sanctified yet, which means there are still areas of our beliefs and lives that are vulnerable. Much of what you've learned so far are not only solid biblical truths, they're also truths that will guard you from Satan's lies. As the previous verse indicates, Satan's primary vehicle to gain influence is through lies and deception. Paul wrote in 2 Corinthians 2:9, *"My purpose in writing you was to see if you would stand the test and be obedient in everything."* And he tells us why in verse 11, *"in order that Satan should not outwit us. For we are not unaware of his schemes."* Jesus said in John 8:44 that Satan, the devil, is *"a murderer from the beginning, refusing to uphold the truth, because there is no truth in him. When he lies, he speaks his native language, because he is a liar and the father of lies."* This is what Satan does, he lies, and one of the ways he is a murderer is because his lies lead to death. Just as we could extract from this that Satan is the false way, the lie, and the death, Jesus call Himself in John 14:6, *"the way, the truth, and the life."* Jesus said in John 8:31-32, to those *who believed in Him, "If you continue in My word, you are truly My disciples. Then you will know the truth, and the truth will set you free."*

Before you study Satan or learn tactics or strategies or study anything spiritual warfare related you need to have sound doctrine. You need to be firmly established in the truth of who God is, who Jesus is, what the gospel is, etc. and have faith in that. This is what I do in personal deliverance ministry sessions. You need to believe in and know Jesus and have eternal life before dealing with the secondary concern of how to be free in this temporary life. I've taken the same approach in this book. All permanent deliverance comes from Jesus and so if we want to be fully free then it needs to happen His way, and as an appeal to Him, in faith, through the gospel. I've been teaching you the truth because if you know the truth then you will reject the lies, and the liar who gives them! This is why you need a new map, based on the truth of the gospel and on God's Word. There are many aspects of spiritual warfare but the most important is knowing truth and having faith in Jesus, the truth, and the author of all truth. Next we'll take a look at some of Satan's schemes so that you are not unaware of them.

II. Bad Drivers and Bad Passengers

I've identified four broad categories that Satan uses to deceive people from knowing the true God, believing in the true gospel, and giving their lives to and being saved by the true Jesus. These include: (1) false religion, (2) false spirituality, (3) carnal compromise, and (4) counterfeit Jesuses. It is essential for our journey in the right direction that we're able to identify these in our car and evict them if we find them. I've included two different forms they could take in our car. The first is a "bad driver." This means they're driving the car, they're leading the way and choosing the direction. If this is the case then you're not saved yet! If you find one of these driving the car then you need to decide whether you're going to trust that driver—or the Bible. And your life depends on it, so choose wisely. The second is more subtle, and that is a "bad passenger." This means that you're still saved, still born again and going in the right direction, yet there's a demonic infiltration in the car. They know you're going in the right direction and are being led by the Holy Spirit, but they're seeking to persuade you, mislead you, cause misery, hamper your success, and keep you from being truly fruitful and successful in all of the things God is calling you to. If this demonic passenger is allowed to be in the car at all, then they have what we call a *foothold*. This means that they're there and can grab ahold of you in some way. If they're deeply embedded in your car, and have a strong, secure position there, and you can't easily remove them, then they have a *stronghold*. Whether they're driving—or are a passenger with either a foothold or a stronghold—you need to remove them! They need to be totally evicted and locked outside! *Every* part of you (every part of your car) should be dedicated to Christ and led by the Holy Spirit.

Ephesians 4:26 "Be angry, yet do not sin." Do not let the sun set upon your anger, [27]and do not give the devil a foothold.

2 Corinthians 10:3 For though we live in the flesh, we do not wage war according to the flesh. [4]The weapons of our warfare are not the weapons of the world. Instead, they have divine power to demolish strongholds.

---

e. False Religion
A distorted understanding of God and/or a distorted way to be reconciled to God.

There are many types of false religion, all inspired by Satan. They can be vastly different from one another but they all have common element: they all reject the God of the Bible and/or salvation by faith through Jesus the Son of God. Satan is happy to let people believe anything else. I want to give you a bird's eye view of the primary types of religions just so you can be more protected from them, know the differences so you can help guide others out of them, and notice if any of these beliefs are lingering around in your car.

First there is monotheism (*mono*, "one," and *theos*, "god"). This is what Christianity teaches but it teaches a *trinitarian* monotheism. By contrast, Islam, Judaism, Jehovah's Witnesses, and Oneness Pentecostals all teach a *unitarian* monotheism. Both teach that there is only one God, but the latter teaches God is singular, unitarian, and simple in nature, rather than tripartite, triune, and complex in nature. In so doing also reject the deity of Jesus as the eternal Word/Son of God that became flesh to die for the sins of the world. *Polytheism* (*poly*, "many," and *theism*, "god") is the belief in many gods or divine beings. Examples of this include the Greco-Roman, Canaanite, and Egyptian pantheons, the millions of manifestations of the Hindu gods, and even Mormonism, though Mormons claim they worship only the one over this planet.[9] Next there is *pantheism* (from *pan*, "all," and *theos*, "god") which is a way of seeing that identifies everything with God and God with everything. The largest example of this belief today is Hinduism. *Panentheism* (*en*, "in") also holds that the world and universe are included in God but maintains that God is more than these things, and that the divine can be both transcendent (out there) as well as the "divine within." The last category of religious beliefs I'll mention here is *animism* (from *animae*, "spirits") which is the belief in myriad spirit beings who are concerned with human affairs and are capable of helping or harming people's interests. Popular modern examples of this include New Age, tribal religions, Wicca, Shamanism, Paganism, and Native American beliefs.[6]

Belief	Summary	Example
Monotheism	One God	Christianity, Judaism, Islam
Polytheism	Many gods	Greco-Roman Pantheon
Pantheism	All is god	Hinduism, Some New Age
Panentheism	All is within god	Buddhism, Some Hinduism
Animism	Many spirits	New Age, Shinto, Wicca
Atheism	No gods	Naturalism, Secularism

But what about atheism? The word atheism as a belief system dates back to the 1570s. It comes from (*atheos*, "godless, ungodly" from *a-*, "without" + *theos*, "god").[7] Atheists often argue human beings are religious creatures. We were designed as not only physical and soulish but also spiritual. We *are* religious. We *do* worship. The self-aware atheists acknowledge this, the specific behaviors that religious people do can be replaced with secular (irreligious) activities but the behaviors themselves are still being performed. For example, we can worship God, many gods or spirit beings, ourselves like a god, nature like a god, ourselves like we are all that there is, or any enjoyable intellectual or emotionally stimulating activity like that's all that there is to life. But our heart, mind, and soul *will* be devoted to something. And for it to be fulfilling long term it will need to be a cause that is beyond ourselves that connects us to something larger. We will develop beliefs about that thing, we will organize with others who share those beliefs, and we will dedicate ourselves to improving our knowledge and experience of that thing. This pursuit is spiritual. It is a form of worship to dedicate ourselves, and essentially the meaning of our lives, to serve whatever we view to be a worthwhile goal or a higher purpose. These organized sets of beliefs and accompanying practices *are,* at their essence, religion. Satan knows this. In fact any time we worship something, anything, other than God, it is a form of idolatry. I'm not suggesting that all careers, hobbies, and interests are all idols, but they certainly *can* be. And if they come before God, or if aspects of them have greater devotion from us than God does, then it is serving as an idol in our lives. Remember that any potential idol in our lives is a foothold, and any form of idolatry actually indirectly gives worship to Satan. We are worshipping the world, and the things in the world, of that which he is the prince of. This type of idolatry Christians are more likely to be susceptive to because of how easily Satan can influence us to do so and our acquiescence often goes unnoticed.

All false religions and religious beliefs distort or undermine essential truths necessary to properly know who God is, who we are, what the purpose of life is, why there is suffering and death in the world, and what can be done about it. Since every human longs for answers to these questions, every religion and sociological philosophy attempts to answer them, and Satan has provided some common denominators amongst them. Religions seek to reconcile the chasm between where-we-are-now-with-suffering to where-we-would-like-to-be-without-suffering through: (1) earning rewards through loving acts, good deeds, or religious efforts, (2) gaining knowledge or enlightenment through mystical means, (3) loss of the self/ego/individual through meditation and spiritual discipline, or (4) hedonism, making the most of life now through an emphasis on temporary, worldly pleasure-seeking without concern for eternal spirituality or deeper meaning.

Philosophy	Description of Behavior
Legalism	EARN salvation through law keeping, good deeds, or religious efforts
Gnosticism	FIND salvation through secret or hidden external knowledge and mysticism
Enlightenment	UNLOCK salvation within by destroying the ego (self) and all human desires
Hedonism	INDULGE in carnal pleasures and pursue natural desires in this life alone

All of these worldview philosophies deny the biblical foundations we've learned so far. At their core they all lack the entire premise of the simple gospel, the basis of us being separated from the one true God, due to our sin, and our restoration back to God, achieved through faith in the sacrificial death, burial, and resurrection of Jesus. This simple declaration, the gospel, cuts to the heart of every single false worldview. If you remember this fact alone you will be able to see through all of these other philosophies. They get quite complex, hundreds of categories could be listed, but I boiled it down so you can see their foundations.

Legalism. The first of these, and perhaps the best one of the four ultimately-false options, religious legalism, at least recognizes that loving acts, good deeds, and religious efforts are part of the solution. This at least gets people listening to their conscience, trying to do good, and seeking meaning, purpose, and maybe even the true God. The problem is that it can often lead to *legalism* rather than Christ. The true path to restoration with God is freedom from monotonous, religious law-keeping in an effort to earn favor with God. If Satan can't get us "completely off the reservation" then he will settle for us not seeing the beauty of God, and of the gospel, and have us putting our trust in our own efforts instead. Our faith would then be in ourselves, rather than God. We need to believe what God says, that we are worse sinners than we think. We need more than just a little religious effort—we need a Savior! And then spiritual empowerment to live it out! This philosophy also grossly distorts who God is and why we were created. We were made for God's glory, and for relationship, not just to be mindless, obedient robots that follow all the rules. Religious legalism will only make us a miserable replica doing outward good, perhaps, but inwardly still a wreck who is actually still spiritually dead and very far from God. Our desire in religious obedience would be to avoid punishment, or perhaps we would rightly believe that God's way is best. However, it still wouldn't be interpersonal or relational. We would not be seeking relationship with God, because being created for God's glory, and knowing God through the glory of the Son, for eternity is not even being considered as the purpose of our existence. We are not to know God primarily through the law, it is through grace we are justified and set free from the slavery of sin. "Christianized" religious legalism is one of the great threats to your journey. Satan uses it to deceive believers, who are not trusting in faith, to believe they're saved. It can easily creep in, or remain in. Throw it out!

Galatians 5:1 It is for freedom that Christ has set us free. Stand firm, then, and do not be encumbered once more by a yoke of slavery. [2]Take notice: I, Paul, tell you that if you let yourselves be circumcised, Christ will be of no value to you at all. [3]Again I testify to every man who gets himself circumcised that he is obligated to obey the whole law. [4]You who are trying to be justified by the law have been severed from Christ; you have fallen away from grace.

One other type of religious legalism takes the form of restoration of *order*, rather than moral justice, through religious rituals. This may be done for the sake of making things "straight" or orderly, more in balance or in harmony, or more pure or in peaceful coexistence. And this could be a realignment of forces either in the natural world, like the natural elements, or in the spiritual world. One example of this is Shinto which is more of a Japanese cultural expression, a way of seeing the world, than it is a transcendent and complete religion. Prayers as well as purification and cleansing rituals are performed regularly for people by priests at Shinto shrines, not to be purified of moral evil, or to repent of sin, but rather to "restore natural order." The goal is "peaceful coexistence," order, and balance by appealing and soothing impersonal spiritual forces. Essentially animistic practices like these are a form of legalism that seeks to deal with the problems in the world without addressing human moral failure. It seeks to treat only the symptoms, while the Bible reveals the cause of disorder, the problem of sin, as well as the solution, faith in Jesus unto restoration.[10] Legalism takes many different forms but they all identify problems and then seek to restore them through false spiritual activities.

f. False Spirituality
The demonic deception behind "spiritual but not religious."

While false *religion* usually takes the form of either false god(s), a false view of the true God, or some form of religious legalism to help bridge the gap to God, false *spirituality* focuses more on the hidden or mystical side of having faith. This is best represented by the next two worldview philosophies I mentioned in the last section: Gnosticism and Enlightenment.

Gnosticism. The Gnostic philosophy is one in which adherents seek to find pleasure or salvation or knowledge or power through secret or hidden external knowledge and mysticism. Gnostic comes from the Greek word *gnosis,* (a Koine Greek word meaning "secret knowledge"), or "knowledge of transcendence arrived at by way of internal, intuitive means."[8] A heretical religion called Gnosticism developed in the second century AD that taught that all matter, whether the physical universe or the human body, was evil, and only the spirit was good. The Gnostics taught that there was a Fall, but it was a fall into matter. They taught that "as long as spirits are trapped in physical bodies and materiality, they will be subject to sin, which is caused by ignorance of their true nature and home."[8] It is by learning or receiving this knowledge, either externally from God or other spirits, or internally as self-knowledge, they can be awakened and begin their journey back home. Because this was just a more well-developed version of another of Satan's lies, which all have a common thread, we can see the antecedent to it even in the first century AD. Both the apostles Paul and John warned of such false teachers, and even the lying spirits behind their beliefs.

---

1 Timothy 6:20 O Timothy, guard what has been entrusted to you. Avoid irreverent, empty chatter and the opposing arguments of **so-called "knowledge,"** [21]which some have professed and thus swerved away from the faith. Grace be with you all.

1 John 4:1 Beloved, do not believe every spirit, but test the spirits to see whether they are from God. For many false prophets have gone out into the world. [2]By this you will know the Spirit of God: Every spirit that confesses that Jesus Christ **has come in the flesh** is from God, [3]and every spirit that does not confess Jesus is not from God. This is the spirit of the antichrist, which you have heard is coming and which is already in the world at this time.

It's important to note that Gnostics, both in the second century and today, called themselves Christians. They believed in Jesus, who they saw as a heavenly messenger, but was not God incarnate, who did not become a man, die, and then rise bodily. The Masonic movement has been referred to as a Gnostic movement. The ideas that lay at the foundation of Gnosticism go far beyond just a single religion so by calling it a philosophy, I'm using the term in its broadest definition. The fascination with trying to connect with the spiritual realm is still in existence today in various secretive cults, in the New Age, Scientology, Freemasonry, Kabbalah (Jewish mysticism), Shamanism, tribal or nature religions; they are found in all divination practices such as astrology, alchemy, psychics, tarot cards, palm readings, Ouija boards, seeking angels, channeling, etc.[8]

All of these religions and practices seek to gain hidden or secret knowledge in one way or another. They all emphasize paying less attention to the physical world by further connecting with, or trying to contact other beings in, the spiritual world. Humans are spiritual so there's an alluring attraction to this. To gain knowledge, power, wisdom, or become like God in some other way. Satan knows this. He's been offering this as bait to humanity since the Garden of Eden, and it continues to work! But the "knowledge" that he's offering is the knowledge of *being* a sinner - *by* sinning against God. Any part of this philosophy driving your car is a major red flag that you're headed in the wrong direction. Even if it's not driving but is just a passenger in the car, it's something that needs to be removed immediately. Search your heart. Are you drawn to secret knowledge? Do you read the Bible and seek to understand what God was communicating to those people there and then—*or* are you looking for hidden clues to secret meaning? Do you have supposedly "Christian" tarot cards? Burn 'em! Do you look to your astrological sign or the alignment of the stars for hidden meaning? That's demonic and it will make you vulnerable. Repent of this and seek deliverance from it. These types of beliefs and practices will not only cause you to stumble they will also attract demons into your life.

Genesis 3:1 Now the serpent was more crafty than any beast of the field that the LORD God had made. And he said to the woman, "Did God really say, 'You must not eat from any tree in the garden?'" ²The woman answered the serpent, "We may eat the fruit of the trees of the garden, ³but about the fruit of the tree in the middle of the garden, God has said, 'You must not eat of it or touch it, or you will die.'" ⁴"You will not surely die," the serpent told her. ⁵"For God knows that in the day you eat of it, your eyes will be opened and you will be like God, knowing good and evil." ⁶When the woman saw that the tree was good for food and pleasing to the eyes, and that it was desirable for obtaining wisdom, she took the fruit and ate it. She also gave some to her husband who was with her, and he ate it. ⁷And the eyes of both of them were opened, and they knew that they were naked; so they sewed together fig leaves and made coverings for themselves.

Leviticus 19:31 You must not turn to mediums or spiritists; do not seek them out, or **you will be defiled by them.** I am the LORD your God.

Deuteronomy 18:9 When you enter the land that the LORD your God is giving you, do not imitate the detestable ways of the nations there. ¹⁰Let no one be found among you who sacrifices his son or daughter in the fire, practices divination or conjury, interprets omens, practices sorcery, ¹¹casts spells, consults a medium or spiritist, or inquires of the dead. ¹²For whoever does these things is detestable to the LORD. And because of these detestable things, the LORD your God is driving out the nations before you.

Acts 16:16 One day as we were going to the place of prayer, we were met by a slave girl with a spirit of divination, who earned a large income for her masters by fortune-telling. ¹⁷This girl followed Paul and the rest of us, shouting, "These men are servants of the Most High God, who are proclaiming to you the way of salvation." ¹⁸She continued this for many days. Eventually Paul grew so aggravated that he turned and said to the spirit, "In the name of Jesus Christ I command you to come out of her!" And the spirit left her at that very moment.

Powerful words. I was tempted to include some of the passages, like Exodus 22:18 and Leviticus 20:27, where God said people who do such practices should be put to death! It is that serious. Now in the New Covenant era of grace we shouldn't be stoning to death people who do such practices (nor should *"Christians" ever* have!) but we should still realize how serious these practices are from a spiritual perspective. They are not "slap-on-the-wrist-sins," they are major. People doing such things are either not saved at all or they are being seriously deceived by demons to do something so obviously in rebellion to God. For more on this topic see Leviticus 19-20, Deuteronomy 12 and 18, Jeremiah 27, 2 Kings 21:6, 1 Chronicles 33:6, and Isaiah 8:19.

Notice something interesting about that last passage I quoted from Acts 16. The demon inside the girl *rightly* professed that Paul was a servant of God and was proclaiming the way of salvation. Would a demonic spirit say something true that even leads people to hear the true gospel? No, right? False. Obviously the answer is yes! That is exactly what happened. Why? It is because if the demon could use Paul's fame to gain for itself credibility then it could continue to deceive people for years long after Paul left. Once trust has been established it could teach contrary things later that completely contradict Paul's original teaching. Demons play the long game. They're often smart. If you have engaged in any of these demonic divination practices and spirits you've contacted, or the teachings from spirits that influenced the religion, confirm *some* of the biblical truth that does NOT mean that they are from God. The same is true for any psychic, tarot card, astrological prediction, etc. that was right about something. First, God has explicitly forbidden these practices. That means neither God, nor any good heavenly angel, is going to communicate to humanity this way. Second, these demons are building your trust in THEM—rather than God and His Word. Once trust has been established and built up into a habit it is harder to reject future guidance. Demons play the long game, they rarely show their true colors up front. Remember, Satan is a saboteur! And he knows that if he can create a false system that allows you to remain enjoying your sins while still getting some type of spirituality then he is willing the battle for your soul!

The popular book and movie *The Da Vinci Code* by Dan Brown promoted Gnostic ideas, as do many of today's movies and music coming out of Hollywood and celebrated by pop culture. The culture of the world is saturated with false beliefs. A few ministries that expose false religions and Christian cults I'd recommend for additional information: *Watchman Ministries* (watchman.org), *Bob Larson Ministries* (boblarson.org), *Good Fight Ministries* (goodfight.org), *Bible Thinker* (biblethinker.org) and *Christian Apologetics & Research Ministry* (carm.org). And I've also written pretty extensively as well on my website, blogs, and social media. Links can be found at (MPoweredChristian.org).

Enlightenment. The Enlightenment philosophy is one in which adherents unlock salvation from within by destroying the ego (self) and all human desires. I am referring to those having a philosophical worldview dedicated to *spiritual* enlightenment not related to The Enlightenment period, which was an intellectual renaissance in Europe in the 15th and 16th centuries. This philosophy is that human suffering is not caused by sin or evil but rather by the *illusion* of the individual self. As a pantheistic and panentheistic belief, everything is believed to be God, and all things, including humans, are themselves manifestations of God. In Hinduism this is called Brahman. The individual self is one with Brahman, and our minds, the immaterial part of us, is identical to Brahman, not just a manifestation of Brahman. Essentially, it's the belief that we are God and are a part of God. And suffering, war, death, etc. is all a consequence of being trapped in the illusion that we're a separate self with a separate identity. The goal, the Hindu belief called *moksha*, is to overcome the illusion that one is separate from Brahman. To overcome one's "ignorance" not only learning of their true Brahman nature but also experiencing "one-ness" with it. This is found through (1) religious devotion and rituals, (2) attaining wisdom, and (3) selfless service or good works. All forms of Buddhism also believe that it's the "attachment to desires" that cause suffering, and systems of religious beliefs and practices, have been developed to find freedom from these attachments.

The good thing about this philosophy is that if people followed it they would be less selfish and egotistical. If people truly sought to think less of getting more for themselves, because *self* is just an illusion anyways, and personal *desire* is what leads to problems, that would indeed lead to less sin and evil hurting others for the sake of selfish gain. There is a certain degree of this also taught in Christianity. You are to love your neighbors as yourselves. Yet, you are not to do this without first knowing the truth about God and loving Him first and foremost, with all of your heart, mind, soul, and strength. *(Mark 12:29-31)* We certainly cannot be doing this if there *is* no self. The truth is that we *do* exist! This is why every human believes that they do exist as an individual, because every aspect of our reality confirms it. We have to go through mental gymnastics to force ourselves to forget this obviously-true reality. We would have to deny our own experiences.

If it's obvious we exist, where does the belief that the individual doesn't exist come from? Satan, who seeks to steal, kill, and destroy. *(Jn 10:10)* By willfully denying our self, and all aspects of self, and denying the transcendant, personal, righteous God, a person enters a godless false spirituality. Every step towards losing one's self, emptying themselves of all personal desire, and seeking to connect with the unknown spiritual forces is a step toward demonic possession. This type of environment is perfect for it. It's like intentionally choosing to empty your car on purpose so that "the universe" can come in and drive it. And you don't even care *what's* driving or *where* it's going because "it's spiritual" so it *must* be going in the right direction! It may be more "spiritual" but it is not more of God. All important truths and doctrines given to protect us from demons are intentionally dismissed in this philosophy because these beliefs are just parts of the illusion! All spiritual practices warned to avoid in the Bible, because they connect us with things that will defile us, become tools for intentionally achieving connection and one-ness with Brahman. It's a demonic philosophy that's a deliberate reversal of what Christians are to do that denies all the ways to safeguard ourselves. All of this is said to help find "enlightenment." It's phrased in such a way that to achieve it is a good thing, when it's far from good, or enlightening. It's the *loss* of true intellect, knowledge, and wisdom.

> Colossians 2:8 See to it that no one takes you captive through philosophy and empty deception, which are based on human tradition and the spiritual forces of the world rather than on Christ.

However sort-of nice a philosophy that purports to be about selflessness may sound, we need to remember this philosophy goes all the way back to Satan's first temptation in the Garden. First, it's an attempt to be our own God and to decide what is good and evil for ourselves. It *is* sinful to think that we *are* God. We would be forsaking our own individuality, not for the sake of loving others more than ourselves, but for the sake of remembering that we are a part of God. Two, it is sinful to see our own evil deeds and desires as merely the consequences of believing the illusion of our own individuality. We don't need to meditate and gain wisdom or enlightenment or discipline ourselves with "intentionally-emptying" religious exercises (i.e. yoga, meditation, mantras, chanting, etc.) in the effort to *lose* oneself. Meditation that is mindful (mind-*full*) by a focus on God's truth, is different than meditation that is mind-*less*). Instead of emptying our mind and losing our personhood we need to understand that we *are* individuals, we *have* sinned, we *are* sinners, we *need* to feel remorse, repent, and seek forgiveness! Because we are not truly God, and believing so is to make an idol of ourselves and reject the true God, our own sinfulness, our need for a Savior, and faith in Jesus. All effort to find "freedom" in this way takes us further *away* from true freedom and more into bondage to sin and Satan. The closer we get to achieve a loss of our "self" in this way, the closer we actually get to the place where that goal's accomplished, where people *will* lose their self: Hell.

> Colossians 2:23 Such restrictions indeed have an appearance of wisdom, with their self-prescribed worship, their false humility, and their harsh treatment of the body; but they are of no value against the indulgence of the flesh.
>
> Ephesians 6:14 Stand firm then, with the belt of truth buckled around your waist, with the breastplate of righteousness arrayed
>
> 1 Peter 5:8 Be sober-minded and alert. Your adversary the devil prowls around like a roaring lion, seeking someone to devour.

Be sober-minded and alert. Dismiss all spiritual beliefs and activities that encourage lowering your guard. This brings me to the topic of **"Christian" Hyper-Spirituality**. There are some in the church today, even some that are very popular recognizable names, that embrace a type of exacerbated spirituality and mysticism very similar to the eastern beliefs and practices I've described. Of course a Christian veneer covers it but the foundation is questionable and sometimes disturbing. I've seen "Christian" versions of yoga, mindless meditation, controlled breathing exercises, repetitive mindless worship, mindless emotionalism, "one-ness" teaching, uncontrolled and highly disorderly church services, and an embrace of all kinds of spiritual experiences without discernment. I've seen videos of "Christian" services with outward manifestations of clearly demonic possessions taking place! People barking like dogs, convulsing on the floor, slithering like a snake, all being called "the Holy Spirit working!" No! No! No! This is demonic. We must be *way* more discerning! Just because something is spiritual does not mean that it's of God. Pursue intimacy with God, His presence, and the higher gifts of the Holy Spirit—but proceed with biblical discernment and caution!

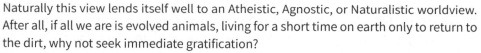

g. Carnal Compromise
The subtle deception of pleasure, leading to compromising with the lusts of the sinful flesh.

The fourth category of dangerous, false philosophical worldviews is that of Hedonism. This is the belief that the purpose of life is to be happy, or to experience and increase pleasure, while avoiding discomfort and pain. Naturally this view lends itself well to an Atheistic, Agnostic, or Naturalistic worldview. After all, if all we are is evolved animals, living for a short time on earth only to return to the dirt, why not seek immediate gratification?

However, God's Word tells us that this is a lie of Satan. Of course, it is normal to not want to experience unpleasant things but this shouldn't be the overarching purpose of life. Neither should that drive us to the extreme end to develop an entire worldview that the purpose of life is all about whatever makes us feel good. This isn't even sustainable because often what makes one person feel good conflicts with another person and makes them feel bad. This philosophy isn't true and in order to believe it we have to suppress all kinds of moral conflicts within our conscience. Even truly evil people still *live* as though there is more meaning to life that transcends just their own immediate pleasure. But they do still appeal to this worldview ("You only live once!") whenever they want to enjoy something that the Bible or the human conscience calls sinful. There is often an appeal to the notion that "it doesn't hurt anyone else" without regard to the long-term consequences of such actions on others, which *do* hurt others. Our collective sin against God, and against His moral order for society, has far-reaching consequences on everyone else. And the more our beliefs and actions help influence the moral decay of society, into newer and more-perverse societal norms, the greater the challenges will be for future generations to adhere to God's way in the future. In other words they will have a harder time to be godly in the future because of our decisions today. I'm not going to rehash everything I've already about the necessity of righteousness, holiness, godliness. I'm not going to tell you again that unless you put to death the fruitless deeds of the flesh you won't inherit eternal life. I'm not going to tell you that we can't just believe in Jesus and go to church and still live immorally and think we're okay. You should know better. And if you don't, re-read the first part of this book! What I will remind you is that the lusts of the sinful flesh are sometimes *subtle.* And so is Satan. And so is the sinful world which is always perverting God's standards and leading us towards sinful beliefs and behaviors. The sinful world proclaims that the Bible is antiquated, written by goat herders, that there is nothing wrong with these things and you just need to catch up with the 21st century. No. You need to be vigilant. You need to be dedicated and stand firm in the biblical truth, with the breastplate of righteousness. *(Eph 6:14)*

Sinful Identity. Can you be a "*gay* Christian?" What about a "*transgender* Christian," or any other type of pseudo gender besides either the predominantly male or female you were born as? No, to believe so is to believe a lie. That can't exist because the two terms contradict one another. Can a person be a murderous Christian or a drunkard Christian? No. They can be a *former* homosexual, transgender, murderer, or drunkard who *became* a Christian. Or, they can be a Christian who *struggles* with sinful sexual desires, identity dysmorphia, rage, or alcohol. But no one who is truly in Christ, and living for Him, can *persist in* a lifestyle or have a core identity that is incompatible with God's design and moral order. We must believe what GOD says about human sexuality and identity, how He designed it, and how we're to rightfully express it. If you've believed any contrary thing then your identity is built on a lie from Satan that you believed, and it has perverted and distorted the way you see yourself. It's like if the Church told Adam and Eve in the Garden, God made you good just as you are! Then Satan showed up and said no, you aren't good, you need to eat the forbidden fruit. In other words, you need to believe *me*, not God, and then obey me, and *then* you will feel better. No, they'd feel better if they didn't believe his lie in the first place! I'll say it plainly: God did *not make you* that way. You weren't born gay. You weren't born in the wrong body. God made you good, in His image. Am I denying how you feel? Not at all. So why do you have those feelings? The *sin nature* you inherited is what has made you feel that way, meaning *it—* sin—is responsible for the sinful desires and/or distorted identity you have. It's not who you *truly* are. That's a lie. So God isn't asking you to deny your true self. Sin has its grip on you now and God is asking you to overcome or endure it by His help through your trust in Him. It's no different than going through any of the other trials in life. In the next chapter we talk about suffering and illness. You can apply a lot of those same challenges to any identity struggles. You cannot embrace a core identity and lifestyle about yourself that is in direct *rebellion* to God and at the same time be *reconciled* to God. This is evidence of a false conversion (no true repentance) or at best, a massive open door.

How you *feel* doesn't determine your identity. Your faith in *who* you choose to believe about your identity does.

Mutual Empathy. Are you having heterosexual fornication with someone you're not married to? Then you're also living in sexual immorality and are no less sinful than those living in homosexuality. Are you racist against other groups? Then you're also living with a false *identity* and are no less sinful than those living with false sexual identity. I hope all of us will humble ourselves and realize our struggles aren't all the same. The sin in your flesh might provoke *different desires* in you than they do in another, but they're all influenced by the *same sin*. The sin that causes death. The sin that separates us from God. The sin that makes us think and *feel* one way, when God's Word tells us that those thoughts and feelings are not good and not to be trusted. I don't doubt you feel a certain way, maybe as long as you can remember - it doesn't make it true. The sins of your brothers and sisters in Christ may be different, and you may not understand *exactly* what *they're* going through. We all have a unique story, unique desires, unique struggles. But you understand your own temptations and failings. When you think of *their* struggle with *their* sin, relate it to *your* struggle with *your* sin. The sinful hedonistic desires must be crucified. In all their various forms, whether society is advocating for them or not, whether we still enjoy and desire them or not. It leads to death. It'll lead to your death. Don't love *it* more than you love God! As for how we relate to others, know that some sins are more external and easier for others to see. This is no excuse to focus on those sins more than others. Focus on removing the log from your own eye first. And after that, rather than judging, accusing, or condemning, come alongside those trying but struggling, and give each other the grace, love, support, and encouragement to help them be faithful to God. Our struggles aren't easy, especially when first starting or doing it alone, but God's grace is sufficient for all of us. (cf. 2 Corinthians 12:9) Trust in God and *rely* on Him for strength to live according to His will. His grace will be sufficient!

Sexual immorality isn't the only feels-physically-good form of hedonism we need to resist. Recreational drug use? Drunkenness? Pornography? Strip clubs? Crude behavior? Blasphemy of the Lord's name and using it as a curse word? Living in any sinful way, while identifying as Christian, thus defaming Christ as a result? Having a foul mouth full of hatred, envy, or vulgar language? Gossip or slander? Perjury or telling of lies? Do you neglect, criticize, slander, or hate the Church—the Bride of Christ? Do you lust after others sexually, or covet their possessions? Have you committed murder? How about an abortion? Same thing. Even if you never would yourself, do you still support a woman's "right to *choose*" (..to murder her child?) Do you use your voting power to put people in power who will continue to make this a common and acceptable practice in society? The blood of those children is also on your hands then. You're an accomplice to murder. You're not the one who drove the nails into Jesus's hands, you're just one who voted for His crucifixion to be legal by saying "Crucify Him." Have you ever repented of being complicit in these abortion murders and asked God's forgiveness for it? This is something more need to do. What about gluttony? Does your body's physical composition testify against you, that you treat it as a house of selfish, hedonistic, indulgence—rather than the temple of the Living God? Or perhaps you're not overweight but you're still physically unhealthy. Maybe you're addicted to junk food, fast food, tobacco, pharmaceutical drugs, gambling, or something else that *feels* good? Even basic selfishness in non-sinful ways can be a form of hedonism. Are you motivated daily by what you want more than how you could be a blessing for others? That's a tough one we all struggle with. Do you steward your body, time, talents, and treasure for God's glory? Or do you earn as much as you can so that you can spend all of your money and time on your own hobbies and pleasures? It's not about what you *say*, it's about what you *do.* Do you profess to be a Christ-follower but live for your own glory, your own pleasure, your own interests—like a hedonist? If your thinking and your life's actions are no different than the unsaved then guess what, you might still be. Repent! Change! Lay down yourself on the altar. Be a *living* sacrifice that is holy and pleasing to God. *This* is your spiritual service of worship.

Romans 12:1 Therefore I urge you, brothers, on account of God's mercy, to offer your bodies as living sacrifices, holy and pleasing to God, which is your spiritual service of worship. [2]Do not be conformed to this world, but be transformed by the renewing of your mind. Then you will be able to test and approve what is the good, pleasing, and perfect will of God. [3]For by the grace given me I say to every one of you: Do not think of yourself more highly than you ought, but think of yourself with sober judgment, according to the measure of faith God has given you.

Please note that I began this section describing some ways that *strongly* suggest if a person continues to walk in them then they are not saved. But I've also mentioned some things that are so broad that they will challenge all of us, including me. Am I equating a lifelong homosexual relationship without repentance and going out for fast food once as the same level of sin? Of course not. They are not the same level of sinful defiance to God, or to what is a good use of our bodies for His glory. I merely mention these latter, less-consequential ways, here to remind us all that our *posture* before God needs to be right. What matters most is not that we follow all the religious rules. That just gets us to religious legalism. In both the very serious sinful lifestyles leading to damnation, and the lesser sinful desires of the flesh, both relate to a common desire to love and serve ourselves, and our own desires, more than God and His desires. Question your *motives* about what's most important to you. Let's say "Person A" is living in long-term sexual sin, and is serving *themselves* in serious, core-identity forming, life-patterning ways, while serving God in ways of lesser importance. And then "Person B" has their core identity in Christ, with God at their center, but still has occasional struggles in ways of lesser importance. The Bible would describe Person A as unrepentant and unsaved and Person B as saved and *working out* their salvation. If you still live like a hedonist then you haven't *truly* repented yet. Satan still *has* you!

You must put to death the desires of the flesh. I know that they *feel natural* - that's the point! You're not the same after you're born again. Sin needs to start feeling unnatural to you! We all struggle with some, or many, of these things I listed. But they must be crucified. Do not *walk* in them and still believe that you're a Christian. You're not a *follower* of Christ doing these things. I'm not saying that if you stumble then you're lost. I'm saying that if you're not actively fighting against these desires, knowing that they lead to death, then you have a false comfort. And Satan's behind that deceiving you to believe you can continue as you are and still be saved. And that's more wicked than even him attacking you with physically. Because it's more subtle, it's more dangerous. Don't let this get in your car! The Holy Spirit will empower you to accomplish God's will. He'll empower you to crucify these natural sinful desires, but you must *choose* to *submit* to Jesus as Lord.

Galatians 5:16 So I say, walk by the Spirit, and you will not gratify the desires of the flesh. [17]For the flesh craves what is contrary to the Spirit, and the Spirit what is contrary to the flesh. They are opposed to each other, so that you do not do what you want. [18]But if you are led by the Spirit, you are not under the law. [19]The acts of the flesh are obvious: sexual immorality, impurity, and debauchery; [20]idolatry and sorcery; hatred, discord, jealousy, and rage; rivalries, divisions, factions, [21]and envy; drunkenness, orgies, and the like. I warn you, as I did before, that those who practice such things will not inherit the kingdom of God. [22]But the fruit of the Spirit is love, joy, peace, patience, kindness, goodness, faithfulness, [23]gentleness, and self-control. Against such things there is no law. [24]Those who belong to Christ Jesus have crucified the flesh with its passions and desires. [25]Since we live by the Spirit, let us walk in step with the Spirit.

1 John 3:3 And everyone who has this hope in Him purifies himself, just as Christ is pure. [4]Everyone who practices sin practices lawlessness as well. Indeed, sin is lawlessness. [5]But you know that Christ appeared to take away sins, and in Him there is no sin. [6]No one who remains in Him keeps on sinning. No one who continues to sin has seen Him or known Him. [7]Little children, let no one deceive you: The one who practices righteousness is righteous, just as Christ is righteous. [8]The one who practices sin is of the devil, because the devil has been sinning from the very start. This is why the Son of God was revealed, to destroy the works of the devil. [9]Anyone born of God refuses to practice sin, because God's seed abides in him; he cannot go on sinning, because he has been born of God. [10]By this the children of God are distinguished from the children of the devil: Anyone who does not practice righteousness is not of God, nor is anyone who does not love his brother.

h. Counterfeit Jesus'

Unable to prevent people from hearing about Jesus, Satan invented false versions of Him that distort the gospel.

It is essential to know exactly who Jesus is, as best we can, because a right understanding of Him is necessary to *know* Him and be known *by* Him. We cannot be saved by a counterfeit, imposter Jesus. Many false ones have come claiming to be the Messiah, the Christ, and even bearing the name Jesus.

Biblical Jesus	The Eternal Logos/Word of God, Second person of the Holy Trinity, Was then supernaturally conceived in the womb of the virgin Mary by the Holy Spirit, Now has two natures: divine and human, Son of God, Son of Man, Image of the Invisible God, "Christ" = Anointed/Messiah
Counterfeit Jesus's	**Who is Jesus?**
Jehovah's Witnesses	First creation of God, AKA Archangel Michael, Resurrected as spirit only
Church of Jesus Christ of Latter Day Saints (Mormon)	Spirit child of copulation between "Heavenly Father" ("God") & Mother (who were both once human), born human as are all spirit children
Christian Science	Human only, Enlightened Teacher, Had "Christ-consciousness"
Unity School of Christianity	Human only, Enlightened Teacher, "Christ" is the idea of God
Unitarian Universalist	Human only, Teacher; Some believe divine (but so are all people)
Islam	Human only, Prophet, Born of Virgin, "Messiah" but not Savior
New Age	Human only, Enlightened Teacher, Had "Christ-consciousness"
Gnosticism	Spirit only, Not Human/Material, An emanation of "God" (all people are)
Bahá'ism	Only one of Many Manifestations of "God", as are figures in other religions
Hinduism	Son of "God" (many are), Guru/Avatar (Incarnation of Vishnu)
Oneness Pentecostals	Became "God" in the flesh - NOT Eternal SON of God (Denial of Trinity)
"Emerging" Churches	Contemporary "Evangelical churches" adopting false ideas from above

As you can see from the list above, which is far from exhaustive, Satan has unleashed a variety of false ideas about Jesus into the world in order to muddy the pool. In the modern age of relativism people seek to have their own version of Jesus rather than belief or disbelief in the account of the historical person. These distortions all have a common goal: to minimize exactly who Jesus is, why He came, and what He did. This is because without the true Jesus you don't have the true gospel, salvation, or the presence and power of the Holy Spirit. For a refresher about the Holy Trinity see Chapter 1, Section (C) of this book. You will notice that the counterfeit Jesuses will generally fall into one of four categories: Jesus a divine/spiritual-but created being, Jesus a human prophet of God, Jesus a human and enlightened teacher, and Jesus as god but so is everything else.

Jesus a divine/spiritual-but-created being. The first category of counterfeit Jesuses do claim that Jesus is Lord and Savior, but is not of the same divine essence as the one true God of the entire universe. That He is an angel, spirit, etc. or some other type of lower, *created* being. That He had an origin. That He was *made*. The Church rejected this definitively early. The Nicene Creed (c. 325 AD) states, Jesus is *"true God from true God, begotten, not made, of the same essence as the Father."*[11] Jehovah's Witnesses teach that God's first creation was the archangel Michael, who was then "used" somehow to create everything else through him, and then later became the incarnate Jesus.[12] This is unbiblical and even nonsensical for many reasons shown in the charts below. The Church of Jesus Christ of Latter-Day Saints (called "Mormons" by traditional Christians) teaches that Jesus is a literal spirit child produced through copulation by "God" ("Heavenly Father") and Mother. Jesus is therefore just the elder brother of all other spirit children who were also then later born into human bodies, which also include Lucifer and all the rest of us. Another important difference is "Heavenly Father" and Mother were both also once humans born to human parents who progressed and ascended into godhood. So God in Mormonism was once a human and is only god of the planet Earth. There are also gods of other planets throughout the universe, and there will continue to be more in the future. When we consider all of this, the Mormon Jesus, looking at primary attributes alone, has little in common with the Jesus of biblical Christianity. He is a false Jesus, that was created, through copulation, by a false god, who didn't create either the earth or the universe, and really is no god at all. Both Jehovah's Witnesses and Mormons may profess to be Christians, and claim themselves to be biblical, but their core doctrines are found first and foremost *outside* of the Bible. The Bible is then used, selectively, to support their religion's presuppositional doctrines. These beliefs are not found *in* the Bible, but the Bible is broad enough that it's teachings can be used, often out of context, or through odd forms of interpretation in order to support them. Most of the false religions and spiritual systems do this. Another reason why you need to know your Bible and your doctrine. If you don't, you're either still lost, or you're easy pickings for satanic attack later.

Jesus a human and prophet of God. The second category of counterfeit Jesuses claim that Jesus was only a human, and not God or divine at all, but was still a special person with a unique role in history. One way is to say that Jesus was just a prophet of God. The largest religion by far that teaches this is Islam, relying on their founder Muhammad's testimony alone. He came nearly 600 years after Jesus lived, in Saudi Arabia some 800 miles away from Israel. This revelation was given to Muhammad, an illiterate trader, in an entirely unique society, language, culture, and religious background. Satan (operating under the disguise of being the angel Gabriel) came to Muhammad telling him to recite messages. Muhammad's first impression was that it was a demon and it drove him mad and later to multiple suicide attempts. After some convincing by his wife that he was a prophet of God he accepted this and eventually continued to be deceived by Satan to found the world's largest false religion. While it is monotheistic, and does claim to be Abrahamic, it also denies the promise of God to Abraham to bless all nations through Isaac and Jacob. It also denies and is hostile to the chosen Jewish people, and accepts *some* things about Jesus while simultaneously denying all of the essential aspects of the gospel. Muhammad's Quran, which is supposedly directly from Allah ("God"), refutes several times the Christian doctrine of the Holy Trinity, several passages in the Quran reveal that neither Muhammad, nor its spiritual author, never truly understood what it even was. (Surah 4:171, 5:17, 5:73, 5:116) Early Islamic commentaries confirm that Muhammad and the Quran were rejecting a false version of the Trinity that thought Christians believed in three separate gods, one of which was Jesus's mother Mary.[13] The fact that Christianity had existed for over 500 years by then, and even had multiple church councils, several official creeds, and an official Old and New Testament canon for hundreds of years prior to this, reveals that Muhammad didn't have a clue what he was talking about. At best, he was confronting the theology in response to some local gnostic or heretical cults he encountered in Arabia. But if his revelations were from God then surely God would have known that the vast majority of Christians globally don't believe what those few heretics believed. Satan is behind this attack of the Trinity because without it Jesus is no longer divine and the rest of the gospel becomes null and void. All this leaving a monotheistic, yet anti-Jewish, anti-Israel, anti-Christ, and counter-Christianity global movement of idolatry, religious legalism.

This system is also both capable of, and intentionally designed, to stoke the desire for continuous religious and political domination and ongoing expansion. This creating the perfect recipe for later ushering in the Antichrist. Satan has also introduced another important-yet-telling lie about Jesus into Islam. Sharing commonality with the category we'll examine next it changes the meaning of Christ. That Jesus (they would use the name "Isa") *is* the Messiah (Christ). But they deny all of the biblical requirements necessary for being Christ, making him even more of an Islamic counterfeit. And Islam relates to our eschatology (end times) their Islamic Jesus comes *second*, confirms to the Christian world that they were wrong, that he *was* just a prophet, and that Islam is true, and does miracles to confirm this. He also plays a role, alongside the leader called the Mahdi, in either convincing to abandon our faith, or persecuting those who refuse to submit to Sharia (Islamic government)—especially Christians and Jews. In other words, the Mahdi sounds a lot like the biblical Antichrist, and the Islamic Jesus has a lot more in common with 'The False Prophet' figure alongside the Antichrist than he does the true, biblical Jesus. It's important that you understand these important distinctions because Satan is subtle in his deception. He's a saboteur. People wouldn't fall for it if it was easy to tell it was a lie. Muslims continue to profess that they believe in and cherish Jesus as their Messiah, and also that they hate the Antichrist who opposes him—the problem is that they have a counterfeit Jesus, not the One we worship. And their entire system is a flawed perversion from the ground up. Continue to learn about this so your house is built on the solid rock, the true Jesus, and so that you can share the truth in love with your Muslim friends and neighbors. *(Lk 6:46-49)* For more information check out my workshop and online course *Counterattack Islam* (https://MPoweredChristian.org). Muhammad has no credibility as an eye witness of Jesus, any knowledge of genuine Christianity, nor was he even a knowledgeable Israelite who understood the Jewish people or the Hebrew Scriptures, like the biblical authors do. It is their revelations and testimonies that are to be trusted.

Jesus a human and enlightened teacher. The next most common way to say that Jesus was only human, and not God at all, but was still a special person with a unique role in history, is to say that he was just an enlightened teacher. That He may have received this knowledge by going through some type of spiritual evolution by gaining spiritual knowledge and wisdom. This awareness is called by many cults "Christ-consciousness." This enlightenment supposedly exists outside of the man Jesus, He just so happened to achieve it, just like how the Buddha supposedly did. And by doing the same esoteric practices they did we can achieve it too. Essentially the very beliefs and practices that their worldview embraces, Jesus is said to have done these things too. They blaspheme against God by saying that Jesus did mysticism and witchcraft! This belief is a subtle invention of Satan to help encourage more people to practice a false spirituality. It also encourages a desire to be like God—to be like this modified new version of Jesus even—all while denying the biblical, historical witness of who Jesus was, what He taught, what He stood for, and what He did. As we looked at in Section (F) of this chapter, these types of mystical practices lead to high levels of demonic influence, oppression, and possession. It's no wonder Satan really likes this teaching and it has spread like wildfire throughout the last 150 years, sneaking its way in subtle forms even into individual Christians and churches. In calling this enlightenment "Christ-consciousness," "Christ," in this system, refers to a spiritual reality, a way of thinking and being, a way of becoming more divine or spiritually deep yourself—rather than a person. This is a totally historically ignorant, false, New Age butchering of the original meaning and the historical facts. The word Christ comes from the Greek word *Christos,* which means "Anointed One, Messiah." There was to be only one who was the fulfillment of all of the prophecies of God's Promised One to come. Not many. Neither can Christ be a way of thinking or spiritual reality to receive. Luke 9:20 says, *"But what about you?" Jesus asked. "Who do you say I am?" Peter answered, "The Christ of God."* Likewise, Matthew 16:20 says, *"Then He admonished the disciples not to tell anyone that He was the Christ."* Luke 23:35 mentions people mocking Jesus while He was on the cross saying, *"He saved others; let Him save Himself if He is the Christ of God, the Chosen One."* In John 20:31 he writes, *"But these are written so that you may believe that Jesus is the Christ, the Son of God, and that by believing you may have life in His name."* The New Testament makes it abundantly clear who and what the "Christ" is: the promised Jewish Messiah. The idea it's a type of consciousness to attain is utter nonsense. It's a fable, pulled out of thin air, with no historical support or even logical coherency.

Jesus is God—but so is everything else. The fourth category of counterfeit Jesuses claim that Jesus *is* God. Of course we Christians do believe that Jesus is God, at least in the sense that He is of the same divine nature, though He is distinct from the Father. But when false religions say Jesus is God they mean something else. Remember most of them are pantheistic or panentheistic, meaning they believe "God" *is* everything, and everything *is* "God/Brahma." This means not only is Jesus "God," all other people are also God, the trees are God, the animals are God, the wind is God, the sun and stars are God, etc. This effectively robs any actual meaning out of the phrase "We believe Jesus is God too." And this is true whether everything is *actually* God, or whether everything we think is real is just an illusion. All of it makes God a not-truly-unique being distinct and separate from us. And it makes all of the creation *a part of* Him, rather than what the Bible teaches: creation is something distinct and separate from God, outside of Him. All of these false variations of Jesus, and the false worldviews they are a part of, do what Paul describes in Romans 1:25, *"They exchanged the truth of God for a lie, and worshiped and served the creature rather than the Creator."* Whether Jesus is being worshiped as a created angel, as a created spirit, as the spirit child offspring of a god that was a created human, as a created human that reached higher consciousness, or any other variation the same truth applies: people are worshipping a *created* thing. You cannot worship a created thing— ANY created thing! Only the single God of the universe is to be worshipped! And it's only because the Son and Holy Spirit are one with the Father that they are worshipped too.

Romans 1:20 For since the creation of the world God's invisible qualities, His eternal power and divine nature, have been clearly seen, being understood from His workmanship, so that men are without excuse... [22]Although they claimed to be wise, they became fools, [23]and exchanged the glory of the immortal God for images of mortal man and birds and animals and reptiles.

And it is faith in Jesus having the same divine essence as God that makes His sacrifice on the cross effectual for the sins of the world. It is also how He could be sinless, How He could be perfect, and how it went against God's justice to keep Him in Sheol. Denying the divinity of Jesus negates the entire gospel. It means that even to put faith in Him is to *still* worship a *created* being. It is not faith in anything that saves, or faith in any Jesus that saves, it is faith in the true Jesus that is the eternal Son of God that saves. Our faith can be in no other Jesus than the Jesus that is the eternal Word of God that became man. Without being fully human and fully divine, Jesus could not pay the price for humanity's sin. He needed to be divine to have the power to save us, and he needed to be human in order to adequately represent us. A different Jesus is a different gospel. Examine your heart and mind and make sure that Satan has not deceived you to put your faith in a false Jesus. And extinguish in you any type of compromise in this area. For your benefit and future study I've provided additional descriptions and Scripture references in the table below to help you learn more and have greater confidence in the fact that Jesus is truly of the same substance as the eternal God.

Acts 20:28 Keep watch over yourselves and the entire flock of which the Holy Spirit has made you overseers. Be shepherds of the church of **God**, which He purchased with **His own blood.**

2 Corinthians 11:2 I am jealous for you with a godly jealousy. For I promised you to one husband, to present you as a pure virgin to Christ. ³I am afraid, however, that just as Eve was deceived by the serpent's cunning, your minds may be led astray from your simple and pure devotion to Christ. ⁴For if someone comes and proclaims **a Jesus other than the One we proclaimed**, or if you receive a different spirit than the One you received, or a different gospel than the one you accepted, you put up with it way too easily.

Jesus was called Human

- "He became **flesh**, and dwelt among us" (Jn 1:14)
- "One mediator also between God and men, the **man** Christ Jesus," (1 Tim 2:5)
- He shared his grief that (He must go and suffer) but knew these were **man's** concerns (Mt 16:21-23)
- He emptied and humbled himself, taking the form of a slave, made in **human likeness** (Phil 2:7)
- Made for a little while **lower** than the angels... flesh and blood, shared in their **humanity** (Heb 2:9, 14)
- He was born of a **woman**, born under the law (Gal 4:4)
- He was in appearance as a man, and became **obedient to the point of** death (Phil 2:8)
- He was born of a descendant of David according **to the flesh** (Rom 1:3)
- He has come in the **flesh** (1 Jn 4:2)
- He became **poor** (weak/corruptible) so through his poverty we might become rich. (2 Cor 8:9)
- He came in the likeness of sinful **flesh**, as a sin-offering, He condemned sin in the flesh (Rom 8:3)

Jesus was/is fully Human

- He was born and raised as a child. *(Lk 2:5-7, 22-23, 42, Mk 6:3)*
- He grew physically, intellectually, socially, and spiritually. *(Lk 2:40, 2:52)*
- He got worn out, sweat, got tired, and slept. *(Jn 4:6, Mt 8:24)*
- He got hungry and thirsty. *(Mt 4:2, Lk 4:2, Lk 24:41-43, Jn 19:28)*
- He felt temptation. *(Mt 4:1-11, Lk 4:2, Mt 16:21-23, Heb 2:18, 4:15)*
- He felt emotions, grief, and sorrow. *(Jn 11:33, Lk 22:42)*
- He wept, and felt fear and anguish. *(Jn 11:35, Mk 11:12, Mt 26:36-44, Lk 22:42-44)*
- He felt suffering and physical pain. *(Mt 16:21, Heb 2:9-10, Gen 3:15)*
- He bled and died, his body was buried. *(Jn 19:28-42)*
- After rising from the dead, he ate and drank. *(Lk 24:41-43, Jn 20:27-29)*
- After rising from the dead, they saw his scars and touched his body. *(Mt 28:9, 1 Jn 1:1-2)*
- Jesus said, *"Look at My hands and My feet. It is I Myself. Touch Me and see—for a spirit does not have flesh and bones, as you see I have."* *(Lk 24:39-40)*

Jesus was called God	Scripture
"The Word was with God, and the Word was God… The Word became flesh… among us"	Jn 1:1, 14
"You are the most handsome of men… since God has blessed you forever… Your throne, O God, endures forever and ever… therefore God, your God, has anointed you"	Ps 45:2, 6-7, Heb 1:8, 9
"For unto us a child is born, unto us a son is given… He will be called Wonderful Counselor, Mighty God, Everlasting Father, Prince of Peace… there will be no end."	Isa 9:6-7
"of our great God and Savior Jesus Christ."	Tit 2:13
"of Christ, who is God over all, blessed forever."	Rom 9:5
"We are in Him who is true—in His Son Jesus Christ. He is the true God and eternal life."	1 Jn 5:20
"Jesus said to Thomas… Stop doubting… Thomas replied, "My Lord and my God!"	Jn 20:27-28
"For in Christ all the fullness of the Deity dwells in bodily form."	Col 2:9
"We are not stoning You for any good work," said the Jews, "but for blasphemy, because You, who are a man, declare Yourself to be God."	Jn 10:33
"His Son… through whom also He made the universe… The Son is the radiance of God's glory… the exact representation of His nature, upholding all things by His word"	Heb 1:2-3
"The Son is the image of the invisible God, the firstborn over all creation. For in Him all things were created, things in heaven and on earth, visible and invisible, whether thrones or dominions or rulers or authorities. All things were created through Him and for Him. He is before all things, and in Him all things hold together."… "For God was pleased to have all His fullness dwell in Him,"	Col 1:15-17, 19

Jesus possessed traits unique to only God

UNCHANGING & Eternal – GOD: *(Ps 90:2, 102:26-27; Mal 3:6)* JESUS: *(Jn 8:58, Col 1:17, Heb 1:11-12, 13:8)*

DIVINE GLORY, Worshiped by All Angels – GOD: *(Isa 42:8, 48:11; Ex 20:3-5, Deut 6:13-14, Ps 97:7, 29:1-2, 103:20, 148:1-2)* JESUS: *(Jn 17:5, Heb 1:6, Phil 2:10-11, Jn 9:35-38, 20:28; Mt 2:11, 14:33, 28:16-17; Rev 4:8-9)*

CREATION is "the work of God's hands" ALONE – GOD: *(Gen 1:1, Ps 102:25, 33:6, 9; Isa 44:24, Neh 9:6)* JESUS: *(Jn 1:3, 1:10, Col 1:16, Heb 1:2, 10, 1 Cor 8:6)*

HAS TITLE "The first and the last" & "Lord of lords" – GOD: *(Isa 44:6, Deut 10:17, Ps 136:3)* JESUS: *(Rev 1:17, 22:13; 17:14, 19:16, 1 Tim 6:15)*

FORGIVE SINS ONLY God CAN – GOD: *(Ex 19:5, Lev 16:20-22, 26:40-42, 2 Sam 12:13, Is 55:7, Ez 18:21)* JESUS: *(Mt 9:6, Mk 2:5, Lk 5:21, Jn 3:36, 8:11, Acts 13:38-39, Tit 2:14)*

JUDGE of All People – GOD: *(Gen 18:25, Ps 94:2, 96:13, 98:9)* JESUS: *(Jn 5:22, Acts 17:31, 2 Cor 5:10, 2 Tim 4:1)*

THE ONLY SAVIOR – GOD: *(Isa 43:11, 45:21-22, Hos 13:4)* JESUS: *(Jn 4:42, Acts 4:12, Tit 2:13, 1 Jn 4:14)*

HEARS & ANSWERS PRAYER – GOD: *(Ps 86:5-8, Isa 55:6-7, Jer 33:3, Joel 2:32, Jn 15:16, 16:23; Mt 18:19)* JESUS: *(Jn 14:14, Rom 10:12-13, 1 Cor 1:2, 2 Cor 12:8-9)*

Jesus possesses unique equalities with God

He called God His own Father, and said that knowing Him *is* knowing the Father. *(Jn 5:18, 8:19)*

Perfect representation of God; Seeing Him *is* seeing the Father. *(Jn 12:45, 14:8-9, 15:23-25; Mt 13:16-17)*

Pre-existed in the form of God, equality with God, but lowered Himself. *(Phil 2:5-7, Jn 3:13, 17:4-5, 24)*

There's only ONE on God's throne, yet (the Lamb) is in CENTER of the SAME throne. *(Rev 3:21; 4:2-3, 8-11; 5:6-8, 13-14; 7:9-10, 14-17; 11:15-17; 19:4-5; 20:6, 11; 21:5-7, 22-23; 22:1-5; Heb 1:8, 4:16)*

III. Open Doors and Unlocked Doors

If you have made it this far without having to shift how you think, and what you believe, you are quite rare. Nonetheless, do not think that you can let down your guard. Satan will not stop trying to get you. The Apostle Paul reminds us our struggle is ongoing.

Ephesians 6:11 Put on the full armor of God, so that you can make your stand against the devil's schemes. [12]For our struggle is not against flesh and blood, but against the rulers, against the authorities, against the powers of this world's darkness, and against the spiritual forces of evil in the heavenly realms. [13]Therefore take up the full armor of God, so that when the day of evil comes, you will be able to stand your ground, and having done everything, to stand.

Several translations including the KJV and the ESV say, "we do not *wrestle*" against flesh and blood. It's a little more ambiguous but perhaps a more accurate translation of the Greek word, *palé*, which means a wrestling bout, fight, conflict, contest. I like this picture. Paul is telling us our struggle is close. It's not a far-away attack. It's up front and personal. We are hands-on wrestling against our opponent, our adversary. Now it's not always close. He also tells us in verse 17 to *"take up the shield of faith, with which you can extinguish all the flaming arrows of the evil one."* So some attacks will be close personal attacks that will cause pain, causing fear, anxiety, or pressure, and other attacks will come from much farther away and be much more subtle. Remember though, it is the smaller attacks, those little arrow tips that sneak that are often the deadly blows. Only one needs to get through your guard to pierce through and cause a fatality. We need to be prepared for both.

I believe we will be victorious if we're doing all that the Spirit is calling us to do. However, the best of us may still stumble, and either way, the struggle never ceases. Fortunately, we have one advantage. Just as doing resistance training, lifting heavier weights the right way, challenging our muscles, will cause our muscles to get bigger and stronger, and therefore easier the next time, the same is true for our spirit. If we allow the pressure of the struggles to be used like a type of resistance training then we *will* get stronger and more capable. Every time we stumble, we rest, we learn, we get back up, and we're stronger as a result. We prepare to fight again, this time more confident. We were down but not out. We felt the struggle—it hurt—but it didn't kill us. And if we persist in our faith in Jesus for the glory of God then it didn't work either. Are you still here? Are you still standing? Then guess what—you are winning! It doesn't matter if you've taken a lot of blows on the way. Satan's goal is to pin you and finish you, to knock you out cold, KO—not make you tired.

As this section has taught he needs to be removed as the driver or even as a passenger ASAP. And remember, he's subtle. He might be quietly in your background, right now, in a way that you hadn't realized. We will examine a few subtle ways he could be operating behind the scenes in the next few sections. But let's say that you successfully remove him from your car. Remember, even after this, your struggle is not over. You should scan your vehicle frequently to see if he's trying to climb back in—because he is! He's not done with you. He's Hell-bent (literally) and fully dedicated to stealing, killing, and destroying you and doing whatever he can to hinder the Kingdom of God on earth however he can. So he *is* trying to get back in. Assume it. The next question to ask yourself is, "Is he gaining success anywhere?" You need to realize that as life goes by we can lose our focus and realize he's gaining ground on us in some way. Now to be clear, Satan is never to be our focus. Jesus is our focus—always. But we do need to make sure that Satan is not interfering with our *ability* to focus on and live for Jesus! It's not enough that Satan is thrown outside. Those opened doors need to be shut and locked!

i. False Beliefs
Continually renew your mind and guard your thoughts.

Throughout your life you are holding on to beliefs about reality. We often feel that this is just "the way it is" but the truth is it's actually more about "the way *we* are." You see, what we believe about things is influenced by a variety of things: how we were raised, our society, our culture, our religious upbringing, our past experiences, where and how we received our education, etc. We have a particular paradigm, or way of seeing the world. It's like our own set of glasses that filters all of the data. We have an overall worldview that has been further shaped and molded by our own unique views. We often view the beliefs and opinions of others as either the same as ours, or *wrong.* This can often be bad because our views and opinions may not be *objectively* correct. They are only *subjectively* correct, meaning that they seem right, according to the subject, or us, in this instance. We need an objective standard to measure our own beliefs against. God has provided His Word (the Bible) to help us have this standard. We must also be aware of our own cognitive biases because these can influence us greatly, including whether we will accept the Bible at all, which translation we will use, and the way that we will try to interpret the Bible.

"We see the world, not as it is, but as we are—or, as we are conditioned to see it." - Stephen R. Covey[14]

A cognitive bias is a systematic error in thinking that affects the decisions and judgments that people make.[15] Common causes of cognitive bias include individual motivations, social pressure, and emotional drivers. The takeaway is to accept that there are many ways that our thinking can become distorted. And this is for otherwise fully healthy people. If we then factor in emotional trauma, physical chemical imbalances, psychological disabilities, mental health disorders, or demonic interference, we see that our thinking is far from always-true-and-trustworthy. As soon as you humble yourself and accept this, you can press in and work on *improving* your ability to see things as they *really* are. If you can continue in this it will make you a discernment warrior, a truth seeker who questions everything. You'll blow past your own, and others', presuppositions. You'll expose all biases, false conclusions, and logical fallacies (irrational forms of logical arguments), and be able to detect when other people or demonic belief systems are trying to force them upon you against biblical truths. God's Spirit, if you allow Him to, will guide you through this process. In so doing, you will renew your mind, see reality clearly, and expose darkness hiding wherever it is hiding. Over time, your doors will be closed and locked and you'll see them coming. You will increase in both strength and ability and Satan won't stand a chance.

Empowerment Tip

We all have cognitive biases and distortions in how we believe, but only truth-loving people overcome their own. Learn more about them at: https://YourBias.is

---

Ephesians 4:21 ...in keeping with the truth that is in Jesus... [23]to be renewed in the spirit of your minds... [25]Therefore each of you must put off falsehood... [27]and do not give the devil a foothold.

2 Corinthians 10:4 The weapons of our warfare are not the weapons of the world. Instead, they have divine power to demolish strongholds. [5]We tear down arguments, and every presumption set up against the knowledge of God; and we take captive every thought to make it obedient to Christ.

---

j. False Repentance and Faith

Continually renew your repentance of sin and your faith in the gospel of Christ.

I remember a story of a young Catholic man who had a major lust problem. He would compulsively sleep around with different women and also watch pornography and masturbate every day. Then he would, every single week like clockwork, go to the confessional booth and confess his sins to his priest. The priest would absolve him of his sins and tell him to do penance by saying some "Our Father'" and "Hail Mary" prayers. Rinse and repeat. Every week. For years and years. Now according to the official catechism of the Roman Catholic Church this is not acceptable, but let's be honest, it happens more than they would like to admit. The priest's role in the confessional is meant to be an intercessor and grace-dispenser, not a biblical counselor, but quite frankly, I think a lot of Catholics need both. Perhaps many priests themselves do as well. The fact is this is FAR from biblical repentance. God doesn't want us acknowledging that our sin is, in fact sin, while *still* doing it. As Paul says in Romans 6:2, *"How can we who died to sin live in it any longer?"* Are you dead, and dying, to your sins—or not?

Without even having an established institution for sin-confession in the Protestant Church I'm afraid that the situation may not be much better here. At least in the Catholic Church sin is explicitly to be brought out *somewhere.* It can't remain in that person alone. Here's the cold, hard reality: if you continue to live committing the same sin habitually, perpetually, then you haven't repented! And if you think you have, you're living in denial. You have a false sense of security. Christians can still be tempted to sin so we might invent or embrace certain scenarios or situations it's okay to. Or we may seek out pastors that tell us what we *want* to hear, that allow us to compromise God's standards. *(2 Tim 4:3)* LGBTQ Christian churches are a good example of this. Rather than denying their sin they just find a place that will tell them it isn't sin. You might be doing this in less obvious ways. Be your own toughest critic. Examine your life. Make sure you don't have any opened or unlocked doors! Expose and share them with others you can trust and confide in and have accountability and help from. Don't lose all hope when you find something —just change it! Right away. Repentance means to change your mind and do a 180° turn in the opposite direction. Take Jesus's warnings below to heart. Then demonstrate your faith in the gospel by believing that through your confession, and your faith alone, that you *are* forgiven in Jesus's name. The gospel should impact your life on a regular basis. Every examination of yourself is an opportunity for either sin discovery and sanctification or joy and gratitude for all that God has already done in your life. Either way, it's good!

Revelation 2:5 Therefore, keep in mind how far you have fallen. Repent and perform the deeds you did at first. But if you do not repent, I will come to you and remove your lampstand from its place.

3:1b I know your deeds; you have a reputation for being alive, yet you are dead. ²Wake up and strengthen what remains, which was about to die; for I have found your deeds incomplete in the sight of My God. ³Remember, then, what you have received and heard. Keep it and repent. If you do not wake up, I will come like a thief, and you will not know the hour when I will come upon you... ¹⁹Those I love, I rebuke and discipline. Therefore be earnest and repent.

k. Sinful Behavior
Continually examine your external behavior, and the desires of your heart, for sin.

All sin is falling short of the glory of God. All sin leads to separation from God and to death. All sin should be rooted out. Not just externally, but also internally. Examine your own heart. What do you live for? What do you desire? Why? What motives you? Get to the root of your habits and behaviors. Don't just treat the symptoms. Don't just be a legalist that cleans up the outside. Jesus called the pharisees who did this "whitewashed tombs." *(Mt 23:27)* Don't just be content with other people not seeing or judging your sin. They aren't your judge anyways. God sees the heart. All of us will need to continually examine and grow in this. None of us have reached perfection yet. We don't have to be unsaved to still keep trying to remove sin from our lives. Satan is looking for an open door - don't leave him one! And if he finds a closed, but unlocked door, he's going to send you temptation in that area knowing that it is less secure than other areas. Satan sees the things we don't see. Demons have been examining you your whole life from a very in-depth vantage point, so you need to be introspective and diligent. You are a potential masterpiece that God is working on, don't let any part be defiled. See Section (G) *'Carnal Compromise'* in this chapter for some specific examples of the sins of the flesh.

---

2 Corinthians 6:16 What agreement can exist between the temple of God and idols? For we are the temple of the living God. As God has said: "I will dwell with them and walk among them, and I will be their God, and they will be My people." [17]"Therefore come out from among them and be separate, says the Lord. Touch no unclean thing, and I will receive you." [18]And: "I will be a Father to you, and you will be My sons and daughters, says the Lord Almighty." 7:1 Therefore, beloved, since we have these promises, let us cleanse ourselves from everything that defiles body and spirit, perfecting holiness in the fear of God.

1 Peter 1:13 Therefore prepare your minds for action. Be sober-minded. Set your hope fully on the grace to be given you at the revelation of Jesus Christ. [14]As obedient children, do not conform to the passions of your former ignorance. [15]But just as He who called you is holy, so be holy in all you do, [16]for it is written: "Be holy, because I am holy." [17]Since you call on a Father who judges each one's work impartially, conduct yourselves in reverent fear during your stay as foreigners. [18]For you know that it was not with perishable things such as silver or gold that you were redeemed from the empty way of life you inherited from your forefathers, [19]but with the precious blood of Christ, a lamb without blemish or spot.

l. Emotional Brokenness
Continually examine your life and heart, for areas to seek God's healing in.

It's extremely unfortunate, and it can seem unfair, but one of the most common areas Satan can access us is through the open door of our emotional wounds. We all deal with emotional pain during life and some of us have dealt with extreme abuse or suffering. That doesn't make it your sin. It's not something you need to repent over. It wasn't your fault. It was someone else's sin, that just happened to be directed towards you, and left a deep wound in the process. We understand that this is just a consequence of living in a fallen world full of sinners who make sinful choices. We may not have personally hurt anyone else in the exact same way, or to the same degree, but we've all sinned against and hurt someone else, whether intentionally or unintentionally. We've all fallen short. It's just the way it is. Find it in your heart to forgive them. You need to. Not for *their* sake, but for yours. God commands us to, and for our own good. We can't harbor that pain, that suffering, that unforgiveness, that anger, that hatred, that desire for revenge, that pity for ourselves, a depression because that had happened, or an unwillingness to move on from that emotional state.

It is good for you to get healing. It is good for you to bring those emotional skeletons and feelings out of the dark closet and expose them to the light of Christ. It is good for you to get biblical pastoral counseling, mental health therapy, psychological assistance, spiritual deliverance from demonization or oppression, or inner spiritual healing from trauma. All these things are good to do and if they apply to your current needs then you need to be willing to go there. Whatever you need to be fully healed and totally restored that's what you need to do. God cares about you. He wants you to take care of yourself! YOU are the temple of the Holy Spirit. If you are emotionally broken down then how can you love Him with all of your heart, mind, soul, and strength? *(Mk 12:30)* You can't! We can only give away to God those pieces of us that we have control of. If there are parts of us, aspects of our being that are deeply broken and traumatized that we refuse to give up, not only will we stay miserable, we're limiting our fruitfulness and our joyfulness. It's not God's best for you. The Holy Spirit doesn't usually just fix everything for you. He can, He's God, but usually He just guides us along the healing the process. Perhaps there will be miraculous divine intervention, but not always. And none of Jesus's healings were for people that were pushing Him away and trying to get away from Him! No, they were those who were desperate, those who were seeking, those who were knocking, that He answered the door for. If you're not going to commit to your healing then He's not going to force you to against your will. Your dedication to continuous examination and restoration will improve the quality of your life, improve your relationship with God, strengthen your walk with Jesus, make you a better witness in the world, make you personally happier, and make you more useful in the Kingdom of God.

Emotional Trauma and Demons. Another aspect of emotional brokenness I want to touch on, that may shed a completely new light on for most, is that Satan uses our trauma as a massive open door into our lives. In deliverance circles we find, especially in America, that emotional trauma is the leading cause of cases of demonization. In other countries, say India for example, it might be more contributed to idolatry, due to their entire culture built around Hindu beliefs and temples, and their false spiritual practices such as meditation or yoga. But in "Christian America" the largest access point for Satan is the breakdown of marriage and the nuclear family unit, and the increased secularization, and all of their subsequent consequences on our society. As the church weakens or loses more of its influence in society, the moral compass of each next generation continues to disintegrate. Examples include rampant sexual immorality, pornography, child molestation or abuse, rape, sex trafficking, drug use and gangs, increased propensity for violence in music and entertainment, and consumer materialism fueled by greed and envy. All of this openly embraced sinfulness has influenced more people to act very evil, hurting people, and causing painful experiences and memories. These actions open up doors.

In order for demons to enter our lives in a significant way they need a *legal right*, an access point of entry, due to some type of sin, either ours or someone else's. They're allowed to enter in this way because we're guilty. It's just. This is how they *get in.* But this is not where demons operate from, within the soul and within our lives. They need a place to operate in from a position of strength and domination. This is called a *stronghold.* A legal right is how they get in, a stronghold is how they stay in. To break a demon's legal rights to come in to your life and oppress you all you need to do is stop living in sin, repent of your sins in Christ, break the curses over you in the name of Jesus, and put everything under the blood of Jesus. There can be deeper aspects of it to deal with, but that's the simplified version that we all need to do for starters. I often get people who have spent years trying constantly breaking curses and fighting witchcraft and completely entangled in matters of daily spiritual warfare unable to do anything else. That's not typically the way it works. The demon's aren't "*out* there" if the personal attacks are that relentless. They are "*in* there." They have a stronghold. You know, that area of your life that is totally dysfunctional but instead of getting the healing that you need and dealing with it, you keep trying not to think about it and focus on other things. Go to the point of the pain. If you've got demons, that's where they're probably hiding. Your pain, your suppressed memories, traumatic events that you never dealt with, never talked about with a confidant, never fully processed and get healing for. That area that you haven't let Jesus into yet. And you *know* it. A dead giveaway is that you can't talk about it or even think about it. Demons love that stuff. It's a stronghold fortress. As long as it still stands they can live there forever, up close and personal, and torment and hinder your walk in all kinds of ways. Don't let them win!

You might be thinking "why the heck did he start talking about people getting actual demons?!" Because it's real. And it's a lot more common than most Christians think it is! If you have deep emotional trauma then you need to get help because it's no doubt hindering your life, your relationship with God, your fruitfulness, your happiness, and your sanctification. But it should put a fire under your butt if you've been procrastinating in this area to know that you can also get demons from not dealing with it! In fact you might still be struggling with besetting sins, bad habits, compulsive behaviors, dysfunctional lifestyles, and much more *because* you *already* do! Remember Satan is a saboteur. Your "demons" (what people call their hang-ups sometimes) might *actually* be demons! If you're not living the way that you're supposed to be, ask yourself "why?" And whether it's in the natural or the spiritual—deal with it! Don't ignore this. You are the temple of the Holy Spirit and he doesn't want demons in His temple, living across the hall, trespassing on God's property. Darkness *shouldn't* be in us but that doesn't mean that it *can't* be in us. Scripture is clear that it *shouldn't*, see 2 Corinthians 6:14-16, but that doesn't mean it can't. It can if you are not sanctified. We know that in Christ there is no darkness (cf. 1 John) and that everyone in Him, who has this hope of being like Him, purifies himself, just as Christ is pure. (1 John 3:2-3)

Therefore, leave no stone unturned. If you give it to the Lord and pursue your sanctification with greater dedication than you do figuring out where this year's vacation will be, all darkness will be forced out! If demons, they will be cast out. If brokenness, it will receive healing. If anxiety, it will receive peace. If depression, it will receive joy. If fragmentation, it will receive restoration and wholeness. If there are open doors, they will be closed. Seek your own wholeness as though it is one of your primary objectives. We must take care of our basic needs before we can help to meet the needs of others. We must put on our own oxygen mask before we help others get theirs on. If we don't we won't have enough oxygen ourselves to help very many people before we pass out. We must wait until the drowning person stops fighting before we grab them to pull them to shore. If we don't, in their panic, they will pull us down with them. I want you to be fully empowered to do great things for the Lord to advance His kingdom in significant ways. But get your own house in order first! If it's personal emotional challenges then give yourself some rest to get the healing you need. It's not selfish—it's wise, and biblical.

Matthew 11:28 *[Jesus]* Come to Me, all you who are weary and burdened, and I will give you rest. ²⁹Take My yoke upon you and learn from Me; for I am gentle and humble in heart, and you will find rest for your souls. ³⁰For My yoke is easy and My burden is light."

2 Corinthians 1:3 Blessed be the God and Father of our Lord Jesus Christ, the Father of compassion and the God of all comfort, ⁴who

comforts us in all our troubles, so that we can comfort those in any trouble with the comfort we ourselves have received from God.

---

m. Toxic Relationships

Continually examine your life for toxic relationships that are poisoning your walk.

To get the most out of your journey you'll want to pay close attention to the company you keep while on it. We want to surround ourselves with people that are a complement to us, *adding* to our lives in some way, being involved in the purpose and calling God has for you. But there will be others who can be a detriment to it, acting in no way as a contributor towards good, but merely as an obstacle and hindrance. Don't make the mistake of thinking people will be either always good or always bad. People are flawed so you'll rarely find this. What we are to do then is step back and look at the big picture and examine the way the pendulum swings over time. A person can still make mistakes and let you down from time to time but do they generally love and care for you and lift you up, rather than put you down? Do they put your needs above theirs? Are they willing to help you, even if it will be an inconvenience to them and they don't really want to? Do they want you to be happy and fulfilled and do they rejoice when you are? Do they want what's best for you? Do they care about the relationship itself, as opposed to just getting what they want out of it? All of these questions should help you examine your relationships, to see if others are acting right towards you, but also to see if you're treating others the way that you should be.

If you are in a situation with any type of dangerous or physically, mentally, or emotionally abusive spouse, partner, friend, employer, etc. you need to get out of it. Abusive situations are not those we have been called to remain in, in the name of Christian love and dedication. You may be able to help such people later on in life, but first you need to separate yourself from it and take care of yourself. Remember, put your own oxygen mask on first! Toxic people or relationships are not only drawn to other toxic people, they are also drawn to healthy people. This is because there is often a genuine part of them that wants the "light." However, they do not have control over their own darkness. And what will happen is not you bringing your light to their darkness. What will happen is their darkness will crowd, smother, and dim your light. You need to care for your own needs, your own temple, your own relationship with God, your own witness and calling, first. Then, if it's possible, either you, or a third party intermediary could try to minister to their needs—from the *outside*. But you cannot help them from the inside. Your departure and separation may be exactly the wake up call they need to start taking care of their own needs. Even Jesus did not "fix" everybody He encountered. Many still wanted to kill Him. So why do Christians think it is our job to fix everyone in our lives? Only God can truly restore them. And we can't be an effective witness of His light if we're in the active process of being smothered and darkened. Almost always the bad one is rubbing off on the good one. Continue to love them, pray for them, and try to help them, but if it's abusive get out of there. Get therapeutical help, deliverance help, help through law enforcement and courts, etc. Whatever is necessary, but deal with it. Don't just let whatever happens happen, be in control. One definition of insanity is doing the same thing over and over again and expecting a different result. God does not judge us based on what others do. We are judged based on what *we* do, and on how we *respond* to what others do. Respond well. Wisely. If you know being around a certain person, or continuing in a certain abusive situation, is causing you to sin, hurting your walk with God, etc. then it is sin for you to continue to do it. You cannot drag them kicking and screaming into the light. You must be willing to leave and go towards the light—hopefully they will follow.

Another toxic aspect of relationships, that is even more common than abuse, are unhealthy dependencies and cross-generational coalliances. God's design for the family structure is to be this: God the Father is the head of Christ, who is the head of all other things. Husband and wife, who have each left their parents, come together in marriage to unite as one. The husband bears the role of head and leader of their union, and the wife submits to him, based on the promise that he is also in submission to Christ and will lead the marriage and home accordingly. Both of the parents are then co-equal as a united front that heads over the children. All children are on equal status unless the age gap is significant and older children are endowed with additional responsibilities over their younger siblings. All household pets are then under the children, as well as everyone in the hierarchy above them. If grandparents or other family members are also present in the home they are to submit under this same structure. They may be given a larger voice in important decisions, and certainly more respect as elders, but they are still *under* the headship of, and in submission to, the united front of the husband and wife together. This is God's design and it is the structure most blessed and protected. Of course, in single parent homes, or in homes led by grandparents or others because the parents are either unable or unreliable, the situation isn't optimal. In these cases, it is best for people to *assume* all necessary roles until the appropriate people are present and capable of stepping up and fulfilling their proper role satisfactorily. This should be the goal for all people involved. By focusing on helping each person strive towards the objective of being the best they can be at *their* God-given role, we can remove unhealthy family dynamics from continuing to worsen. Additionally, it is to be clear for all people to know which roles and responsibilities they have, and are expected of them. Everyone should know which roles *should* be fulfilled, and by whom, so that proactive steps can be made to encourage each person is growing towards achieving success there.

If godly family dynamics are not within focus all kinds of unhealthy problems can develop. For example, if a husband and wife are not a united front when dealing with all children equally then a child and one parent could form close bonds that usurp the role of the parents united has head. This might seem innocent enough at first, with a child going to the other parent crying, because the other parent told them "no," only to be told "yes" by the other parent who felt sorry for them. This undermines the structure of both the marriage as a united relationship, and also the parent-child relationship. Years of this dynamic could lead to parents on the verge of divorce while the one parent complains about the other parent to the child, who has become their confidant, person to vent to, and person they get emotional support from—instead of the other spouse. This could cause further resentment and problems between that child and the other parent—all because the dynamic has been distorted over time. The other parent has become villainized and the other parent sympathized with. This also places undo stress and anxiety on the child who is now stuck in the middle, and has to fulfill an emotional support role for their parent. This is toxic for not only the parent but for the child. And if not treated will also carry forward to that child's future dysfunctional family, repeating the cycle. Another common example is when a grandparent moves in and begins to take sides with either the husband or the wife in decision making. Rather than the spouses learning how to work together like a team to meet each other's needs, which is difficult, the easier solution is to get "support" or confirmation of rightness from an outside party. Repetition of this gradually could become an unhealthy two-vs-one dynamic between one spouse and the parent, who often side together, against the other spouse. This further destroys the marriage and the appropriate unity of the marriage, as well as the husband's ability to lead. The grandparent is given then role of the other side of united front and the other spouse is reduced to a subordinate role. The balance of power is off which leads to dysfunction in all the other areas. This also creates additional unhealthy dynamics between in-laws and often trickles down to affect others, such as children in the home. These toxic situations not only hurt personal relationships they also "program" the way each person sees the world, relationships, God, their own walk, etc. We cannot function at our highest ability or serve God appropriately while living this way.

Another aspect of toxic relationships is intimate union with nonbelievers. This may not always be unavoidable, for instance if a person comes to faith in Jesus while they're already being married. Though many people see them not following Jesus as a good enough reason to get divorced, this belief comes from the selfish flesh. This is wrong, and it is the sin of adultery to divorce for this reason. Scripture is clear on this, as long as the unbelieving spouse remains faithful they are to remain married. *(1 Cor 7:10-16)* The gospel should be shared with them, prayer, etc. Don't hamper your witness. Not at all. In fact, I would argue that God would have you *increase* your witness. However, this does not mean to keep annoyingly pestering them, trying to convert them. It means be the loving, sacrificial, devoted, generous, joyful, hopeful, servant who models Christ to them. Serve your spouse as though they were Christ Himself. Be the best you that you can be towards them, and perhaps you will eventually win them over. Whether you win them over or not, you will have glorified God and served Christ faithfully by honoring your commitment to the union that God has united.

Now, if you're not married but are in a committed relationship, or perhaps are just single and dating, you should be approaching relationships in a different way. If you are not married, and again Scripture is *very* clear on this: You are not to be in a spiritually unequally-yoked relationship with a nonbeliever. Remember how I said earlier in the book that we're always moving. We're either moving closer to God or we're moving further away from Him. We're never just stagnant. In the same way, in any intimate relationship, we're bonding ourselves to someone else, and we're both moving. So either they are going in the same direction, towards the Lord, with us, or they're moving away from the Lord, and dragging us away with them. If we know that they don't believe in, have faith in, know the Lord, or care about the Lord—and we still want to be with them anyways—that is a major red flag! There should not be anything else more important to us. No amount of physical attraction, personality, charisma, hobbies, interests, common goals, etc. should add up to be more important to us that we are willing to risk sacrificing either our eternal destination, or the fruitfulness of our walk, just to have those other things. We must examine our hearts to see if we're allowing other idols to cloud our judgment and the flesh to be persuading us more than the Spirit. I know that this is tough, but we must realize that we're in a spiritual battle and we need to be with someone who's going to be fighting on the same team. We need to be with someone who has similar eternal goals before we concern ourselves with whether or not they have similar earthly goals. *(1 Cor 7; 2 Cor 6:14-18)*

So much more could be said about this topic. Interpersonal relationships have a dramatic impact on so many areas of our lives. You could be fully on board with everything I've said so far in the book and then still be completely derailed from your faith through the lashing out of an abusive person, a dysfunctional family dynamic leading to serious marital or parenting problems, or being yoked with a person who hates Jesus and wants nothing to do with your faith. These areas of life are massive open doors for all kinds of sin, bad habits, depression, anxiety, drug and alcohol abuse, addiction, financial irresponsibility, adultery, lust, and so much more. The people in our lives, and the toxic relational dynamics we allow ourselves to be a part of, can derail our faith causing people to fall away from the faith, or to live miserably despite it. If I said Satan *sometimes* uses toxic relationships to get to us it would be an understatement. He does often. Even if we are sanctified and seemingly "untouchable" he can still get to us through *them*. Other people, who are much more easily accessed and influenced, that we are unwilling to distance ourselves from, can be used to destroy us. This has been used as an attempt to destroy a lot of people, myself included. Satan has tried to destroy me and my ministry before using other people like pawns in a game of chess. Examine your life for toxic relationships and decide what is best, whether to remove them or improve them. If you're guilty of playing a role in dysfunctional family dynamics stop it and begin to restructure them towards healthy, godly function. If you've been praying for God to heal brokenness there, while simultaneously actively contributing to the problems yourself, you know why it hasn't improved. It requires your repentance and an actively different approach on your part. Start moving inline with God's will and you just might start noticing those prayers *are* being answered.

n. Toxic Connections

Continually examine your life for signs of "open doors" for demonic entry.

I wanted to briefly mention a few other types of *less-obvious* toxic attachments that we could have that open the doors for demonic entry. Do you have an ex-spouse, ex-lover, or pornographic image in your mind that you still think about or fantasize about? Regarding the former real-relationships, do you still own keepsakes, pictures of them, gifts they gave you, that remind you about them? Are they a toxic person that you need to let go of anyways, or perhaps someone that is married now, or perhaps you're married now, so you know that there can be no godly way to revisit this relationship and therefore fantasizing about them is definitely wrong? Or perhaps it's someone from your past who abused or hurt you, that now haunts your memories? Does the memory of them trigger feelings of anxiety, depression, fear, hatred, rage, murder, envy, unforgiveness, etc.? The reason you are unable to let them go is likely because there is still a soul-tie or soul-bond with them. This is an emotional, and/or spiritual, and/or physical connection with someone else. These ties can be caused through sexual intercourse, covental agreements, oaths, vows, authority relationships, or through deeply emotional or traumatizing experiences.

We can have both godly and ungodly soul ties. Godly ties don't harm us. You know which connections are causing bad fruit in your life, these are ungodly ties that need to be destroyed. Satan will use these ties as an open door to harass and oppress. This is an example of an emotional stronghold. As long as that hold exists it is a revolving door to all kinds of sin and to demons. It is closely connected to a certain person as well as certain feelings, experiences, and memories. You can, and probably do, live in denial to some extent, but it isn't healed yet. If the healing *had* occurred then there wouldn't be an ongoing tormenting memory. We can know them by their fruits. Follow the symptoms. Healing has occurred when it's not just "out of sight, out of mind." We don't want to suppress our traumas or hide them in the back of our minds. That's actually what humans generally do anyways and while it's a reasonable coping mechanism at first it is a terrible long term solution. These parts of us that never get their healing go and live on in torment and cause interpersonal struggles later in life. This often leads to disassociated altar states, a fragmented personality, and even dissociated identity disorder (DID), which used to be called multiple personality disorder. No, we want to unify the mind, soul, emotions, and bring definitive healing to them, in the name and power of Jesus.

Accursed Objects. Another type of toxic connection is related to the partially-limited access of all of the primary demonic categories I described early on in this chapter. For example, let's say you used to believe in a False Religion (see Section E). If you still own books about it, still honor the founder, have a tattoo about it, still have some connections there, whether literal or spiritual, then there may still be an open door. Those books should be destroyed. Some discernment is needed here though. If all you have is the books and use them to write content exposing it as a false religion then that is a different purpose for owning it and you may be okay. But if there is still the occasional draw to think "maybe it wasn't all false" then demons are trying to use it against you and you should cut it out completely. Same thing with False Spirituality (see Section F) or Counterfeit Jesus' (see Section H). Even if you don't believe what you used to, if there is still a nagging draw back, or other internal discontentments or conflicts within, then there may still be an open door there. Close it!

This principle of the toxic connection, or internal or external open door, is perhaps most clearly demonstrated using the example of witchcraft, which is another thing I've helped people overcome. Any form of witchcraft in the home is an open door to the demonic to have access to your home. This could be an external haunting, that anyone coming in could experience supernatural phenomena, or more commonly, it could be greater oppression within an individual while they are at their home. Examples include books of the occult, Ouija boards, dream catchers; sage burning, crystals, salts, bones, ropes, sticks, used for "cleansing" purposes; tarot cards; false idol icons, paintings, or artwork; buddha statues, yoga or chakra posters, snake and owl images, demonic bands' or music posters. Some things, like souvenirs of religious iconography while traveling abroad in third world countries or mystical-looking artifacts, or jewelry associated with astrology or birth colors may have been actually *designed* with spiritual significance. I know that some indigenous artwork is actually created for false gods and blessed (or cursed depending upon how you think about it) before given to the shops to sell. The examples are broad and numerous, but you get the idea. The demonic access cannot be removed until we first removed and destroyed the items. Then we do the house blessing, anointing the doors, windows, and every room with holy oil in the name of the Father, Son, and Holy Spirit, consecrating the entire home to the Lord Jesus. I've barely scratched the surface here all the things that could be problematic. Now that you're aware, if you have anything in your home, car, office, etc. that doesn't glorify God and is a clear open door, or even a potential one, don't gamble with it. Just remove it. Better safe than sorry. Pray to God and ask the Holy Spirit to bring to your mind questionable objects that you should consider removing. Like the previous example, trace the symptoms. Consider first those items related to areas that you may be struggling in. There could be a connection. Let God help you to root it out. Get rid of everything that defiles! Consecrate yourself and your home to the Lord!

Curses. One other type of toxic connection, that is closely related to the previous, is curses. Curses are essentially the consequences of God's temporal judgment against sin. Basically, whenever there is sin it brings with it a curse. And with the curse it brings with it death and reduced protection from the demonic realm, which is also under a curse. The easiest biblical example of this is the curse of death, which was brought by the sin of Adam. It has passed down to every generation since. The curse is embedded in the person's bloodline, I like to picture it spiritually embedded in the DNA. Blessings are opposite of this. A consequence of God's favor passed down to future generations. We all have curses and blessings that we inherited from those who came before us. These are called generational curses. Most of the curses that hang over us do not have any power over us—that is unless demons can successfully influence us to commit that particular type of sin. For example, we could have a 50-generation curse of witchcraft in our bloodline that demons know about. If they can influence us to commit witchcraft it will give them a powerful stronghold in our lives in this area. However, God has built into this system protections, also based on spiritual justice. The demons don't get any special favors either, they are more guilty than we are. So this door doesn't open up to them unless we are also guilty. As God describes in Ezekiel 18:4 and 20, *"The soul who sins is the one who will die."* However, we *will* be drawn heavily towards this type of sin more so than other types. We will be inclined towards it. But unless we give in it and commit the sin we will not open that door. It is perhaps just an unlocked door prior to that.

To dismantle these we lead clients through a variety of curse-breaking prayers, which are very simple and easy to do. A prayer like this is not about communicating *to* God, but rather is a declaration made in the spirit realm, *with* God, in the name of Christ. It's a a verbal declaration, putting into tangible means, an intangible faith, in the substance of the declaration being made. Paul describes this in Romans 10:8-10 for more detail. Much in the same way that your verbal confession to God before baptism is an outward expression of your inward faith in the gospel, curse breaking prayers are an outward expression of your inward faith in the gospel, in your right standing in Christ, and confidence in Jesus' power and authority to break curses through what He accomplished on the cross. The entire process is an act of faith and without personal saving faith in Jesus, and in the reality of curses, and in His ability to break curses, it won't do anything. To break curses just declare out loud and with faith, *"In the name of Jesus Christ, the Son of God, I break all curses of 'blank' going all the way back to Adam and Eve and all future generations."* For a good book that goes through the biblical theology behind this, and gives 25 pages of curse breaking prayers see Rev. Bob Larson's book *Curse Breaking*. (https://mpoweredchristian.org/book-cursebreaking). I've had numerous occasions where I've lead people, sometimes long time Christians who don't think they have any demons by the way, through these prayers, with demonic manifestations coming up. I remember one time I was leading someone through this and as she was declaring, interjections would sporadically pop up and yell "Noooo!!!" *through* her mouth! Wild experience! She was fully cognizant and we both heard it. And it happened over a dozen times during that time. It was scary but also kind of funny. We were both laughing a bit because of how awkward it was. No one is expecting that - to hear something in them disagree with doing something like this. There's not a good natural explanation for that. We ended up later discovering specific demons attached and accessing those specific curses to stay in her life that she had always assumed were "outside". You know, because it's impossible for Christians to have demons! How many times have I heard that by pastors who have never actually dealt with any of this stuff. I should mention also that we were just doing a "general housekeeping" kind of ministry. I've done several of these on myself over the years, and occasionally will just to make sure I'm dotting all the I's and crossing all the T's. You never know what's hiding in the background and I would rather find something that unknowingly crept in and deal with it than have it and not know it! Have I told you yet that Satan is subtle?! God did not give us a spirit of fear! *(2 Tim 1:7)* Anyways, she had no idea anything was back there. Neither one of us did. But once it's exposed then it's possible to deal with it. And you can too. Don't let Satan hide in the background in you or in your life. And don't let curses linger around in your bloodline. Break them so that you don't even have the drawings to those sins in the first place.

Dedicate yourself to your sanctification. We are more complex than the Church typically treats us like we are. All of these things are not stuff in your born again spirit. That belongs to Jesus. This is stuff in the soul, the old you. The parts that still need work, so work on them. Clean up shop! Don't give the devil a foothold! The good news is that no matter what it is it can be broken through faith in the gospel and by the power of Jesus! If you have an ungodly soul-tie, it is declared and broken the exact same way as a curse is. And you destroy all objects that connect you to an ungodly soul tie the same way that you would an occult object in your home. You cut off all the access points and then pray to God and ask Him to remove that person and to sanctify the memory of them to honor Him. The book I recommended also walks you through how to do that in greater detail. It is worth mentioning that the more specific you can get with the actual details of the soul ties, accursed objects, ancestral curses, etc. the better. So if you do this I would recommend checking that out, and my other writing on this topic, so that you can give it greater depth. But this all makes us appreciate just how much evil and sin there is in the world. Just how much infiltration Satan has into so many spheres of our being that we take for granted. Don't let this depress you or scare you or cause you anxiety. Let this information empower you! Satan's ways are exposed! And Jesus is Lord over all! It can all be broken in His name and you have all of the authority and power available to you right now, through faith. The gospel here has a profound practical application in the here and now. You are bringing relevant things in your life to the cross to be crucified. Be empowered to fight the good fight today. And as you close, and lock, every door, you will gain more blessing, more holiness, more confidence, more faith, and so much more!

o. Toxic Habits

Continually examine your behavior for unhealthy habits or unfruitful patterns.

What is a habit? A habit is a settled, usual way of behaving, or regular tendency or practice that one is settled into. We have both good and bad habits. Good habits are learned behaviors we have put into practice that help us be productive and move us towards our goals. These may have been difficult to begin at first, because change is difficult, but over time they became routine and effortless. They now have a net positive outcome on our lives but now require very little emotional or mental force to do them. They're now automatic. Create more of these!

Bad habits are the opposite. They have a net negative outcome on our lives. They are common behaviors that move us in the wrong direction and away from our goals. When creating any type of behavior modification it's important to examine the *needs* that lay at the root of habits. We have needs and wants and we naturally try to meet those needs. Sometimes we do this in a way that is unfruitful, unhelpful, unhealthy, or counterproductive in the long term. Rather than focus on the habit itself, consider the need/desire that first *initiated* the activity that then, over time, became a bad habit. Recognize that the behavior did, correctly, solve the immediate problem and satisfy your needs. Acknowledge it had that positive effect for you. However, you will want to determine two things. First, ask yourself was it a godly, Christ-exalting need/desire in the first place? If it wasn't, then this need/desire is sinful or worldly and it needs to crucified, laid on the altar. But if it was a godly need/desire then ask yourself why you choose to satisfy the desire the way that you did? Usually we look for quick solutions, taking the easier or faster solution in the short term, without thinking about the long term consequences of that behavior compounded over time. Another common reason we may have chosen a particular solution was to make someone else happy, or perhaps as a means to end a fight with someone, or perhaps to end a conflict within an immediate situation. Perhaps we are just being lazy or selfish and settling, rather than putting in the work towards seeking a godly, win-win solution, with the highest potential for long term gain. Whichever you determine to be the case you will want to retrace your steps, spend some time being introspective, reflecting on your own hearts desires that initiated these habits. Then give yourself healthier, more constructive replacements for those behaviors. Don't just try to "stop" them, meet your needs with better alternatives. Set up alternatives that are very easy, effortless really, to start doing, that have triggers built in that remind you to begin them connected to other healthy activities you are already doing habitually. Choose godly alternatives that are also enjoyable, satisfying, and rewarding. This will make it easier to start and to maintain.

What does it mean to be toxic? It means poisonous, harmful, dangerous. Toxic habits are those that go beyond just "bad" habits. They are those that slide into the territory of sinful, malicious, deadly, dangerous, demonic. So I'm not talking about things like watching too much TV, smoking cigarettes, or eating unhealthy. These are bad habits, that you should work on, but they're not immediately toxic to your soul. I'm talking those behaviors and habits that if you don't get a check on them they will do more than just make you less happy, less fruitful, less productive—they will outright jeopardize your salvation! An example of this includes any type of compulsion or addiction to *sinful* activities. You need to deal with these right now. Today, not tomorrow.

Satan is either: (1) the instigator of the toxic *desire* in the first place, (2) the instigator of the toxic *solution* to an otherwise godly desire, or (3) the cheerleader on the sideline encouraging your continuance of the toxic habit. He is also being a type of prosecutor, who is holding up your sins against you, to proclaim your guiltiness before God. In line with this, his demons are using your toxic habit as a stronghold in your life. As long as you permit them to continue they can use every infraction as another legal right to remain there. Discontent to have only one area of your life, they will continue to draw strength from their current stronghold, and seek to influence, and eventually to dominate, other areas of your life as well. Satan will always seek to dominate you but that does not mean that he automatically gets to. Consider what God told Cain in Genesis 4:7, *"If you do what is right, will you not be accepted? But if you refuse to do what is right, sin is crouching at your door; it desires you, but you must master it."* It is imperative that you recognize that this is a war for your soul, which is your life. Picture it like a war map. Wars are not fought with an entire army of a million charging at another army of a million head on. They are a series of individual strategic battles, each in a different region. You must focus on winning each battle, one at a time, and eventually you will have victory in the war. If you focus on the war, by neglecting each individual battle, then your distraction will lead to many small battle failures which will lead to eventual loss of the war. Each toxic habit is a stronghold for them, and is a battleground to wage war in. If you win that specific battle, you gain position and strength that will help you go into the next battles with greater confidence and firepower. So focus on the most pressing, most immediately necessary, most deadly of your toxic habits—i.e. battle— first. Win victory there. Then go after the next toxic habit after that one has been conquered, and the Holy Spirit fills the place where darkness once occupied. Set up your own godly habit there. Your own stronghold. A solid fortress for the Kingdom of God, with the banner of Christ waving on its flag.

Everything we do we do it to meet a need/desire. So the process to detect, identify, correct, and replace it is the same as any other habit. Replace each toxic habit with healthy, godly alternatives. Don't try to do them all at once. That will lead to stress, anxiety, and burnout and feelings of inevitable failure. Focus all of your energy and intensity on the most crucial one first and work your way down the list over time. Pray diligently into each one and make sure God is leading and empowering you through the whole process. If you win the battle, and do it without God, then you have lost the battle. Make sure it's a victory conquered by Christ working in and through you.

p. Hyper-Grace
Continually rebalance both gratitude for, and a healthy level of fear of, the Lord.

There is a very dangerous, demonic, and perverted version of Christianity that has crept into the Church I want to warn you to look out for. If this is being taught in your local church you should leave that church, especially if you're a newer believer. If you have been there for some time and some influence in the church I would perhaps distance yourself from the church but remain connected enough to perhaps bring this to their attention and influence their leadership to reconsider their positions. But either way, make sure that these teachings are not something that is driving you, or that it has an open door in your life. It is often presented nice, even "gracious," but just like all of Satan's other subtle lies, it is straight up false, demonic, and evil. This is otherwise orthodox Christianity, meaning all the same beliefs about God and Jesus and salvation, but with one twist: God's grace covers all sin and does so much so that it doesn't even matter if you keep living in sin!

Hyper-Grace, also called "Radical Grace," is a new (and yet historically old) type of teaching that emphasizes the grace of God to the exclusion of other vital teachings such as repentance and confession of sin. Hyper-grace teachers proclaim that all sin, past, present, and future has already been forgiven, so there is no need for a believer to confess it. They teach that God only sees holy and righteous people when He looks at us, regardless of how we live. They teach that we're not under the Law, not responsible for our sin, and to disagree with this is to be a Pharisee or a Legalist. These preachers ignore and discount the entire Old Testament about sin, the Ten Commandments, Jesus's teachings against sinfulness, and all of the admonitions against sin throughout the letters and Revelation. They may claim that Jesus's words spoken before His resurrection are just part of the Old Covenant so they are not applicable to us in the New Covenant. However, Jesus said His words will never pass away (cf. Mark 13:31) and He said the Holy Spirit would remind them of everything He taught them. (cf. John 14:26)

Jude 1:4 For certain men have crept in among you unnoticed—ungodly ones who were designated long ago for condemnation. They **turn the grace of our God into a license for immorality,** and they deny our only Master and Lord, Jesus Christ.

2 Peter 2:18 With lofty but empty words, they appeal to the sensual passions of the flesh and entice those who are just escaping from others who live in error. ¹⁹They promise them freedom, while they themselves are slaves to depravity. For a man is a slave to whatever has mastered him. ²⁰If indeed they have escaped the corruption of the world through the knowledge of our Lord and Savior Jesus Christ, only to be entangled and overcome by it again, their final condition is worse than it was at first. ²¹It would have been better for them not to have known the way of righteousness than to have known it and then to turn away from the holy commandment passed on to them.

Romans 6:1 What then shall we say? Shall we continue in sin so that grace may increase? ²Certainly not! How can we who died to sin live in it any longer?... ¹¹So you too must count yourselves dead to sin, but alive to God in Christ Jesus. ¹²Therefore do not let sin reign in your mortal body so that you obey its desires... ¹⁴For sin shall not be your master, because you are not under law, but under grace. ¹⁵What then? Shall we sin because we are not under law, but under grace? Certainly not! ¹⁶Do you not know that when you offer yourselves as obedient slaves, you are slaves to the one you obey, whether you are slaves to sin leading to death, or to obedience leading to righteousness? ¹⁷But thanks be to God that, though you once were slaves to sin, you wholeheartedly obeyed the form of teaching to which you were committed. ¹⁸You have been set free from sin and have become slaves to righteousness.

The born-again Christian *has* been set free from sin, but this is not the freedom TO sin—it's the freedom FROM sin! We *have* been saved by grace, and in Christ, God's grace *does* cover our sins. But as 1 John 1:8 tells us, *"If we say we have no sin* [meaning, no sin at all] *we deceive ourselves, and the truth is not in us."* Verse 10 says, *"If we say we have not sinned, we make Him out to be a liar, and His word is not in us."* We are to recognize our sinfulness and seek to walk in both the freedom we have in Christ, as well as the power to overcome our sins by the Holy Spirit. And when we fall short we are to confess those sins, not be blind or ignorant to them, as though they didn't occur or don't matter. Verse 9 says, *"IF we confess our sins, He is faithful and just to forgive us our sins and to cleanse us from all unrighteousness."* Galatians 6:7 reminds us, *"Do not be deceived: God cannot be mocked. Whatever a man sows, he will reap in return."* As 1 John 3:9 says, *"Anyone born of God refuses to practice sin..."* So let us not distort the purpose of our liberty, which is for freedom, not for sin. Titus 1:16 says of wicked people: *"They profess to know God, but by their actions they deny Him..."* Remember, God is holy and righteous. Any beliefs that allow for God's people to act contrary to this does not come from God.

IV. Chapter Summary and Evaluation

Chapter Summary

Regular examination of your car, and dumping of all garbage baggage will confirm that you're rebuilt, and serve to enhance and protect you on your journey.

Let this be an ongoing activity throughout your journey. A type of double-checking that the gas is full, that the fluids are topped off, that the tire pressure is good, etc. Satan not driving the car is common sense, but he also cannot be permitted to ride in the backseat either. He needs to be thrown out and locked out! You don't even have to stop the car first. Throw him out of your moving car! ;-P Your journey can't be started with confidence without first examining your car to make sure that all evidence of the Old, and remnants of the Old are gone (*I*). Make sure that old map is gone (A), that old car is gone (B), that old driver is gone (C), and the saboteur is not operating there in a major way (D). Once this has been accomplished you can be sure that you're beginning on the right path but there are still things you need to watching for as you proceed. Next, you will want to be looking for evidence of his *influences* as a driver or as a passenger (*II*). It only takes a little bit of poison to eventually work its way through your entire body leading to progressive death. If there is poison in your car you need to remove it. It's going to get worse. You need to do an immediate surgery and cut out the diseased parts. Examine your worldview, beliefs, culture, lifestyle, and behavior. Make sure that you are biblical and that your essential beliefs are being shaped by a biblical and godly worldview. Make sure that there's no trace or remnants of false religion (E), false spirituality (F), carnal compromise (G), or counterfeit Jesus's (H).

Lastly, remember that Satan is always trying to open your doors. Strive to have a zero tolerance policy for false beliefs (I), false repentance and faith (J), sinful behavior (K), emotional brokenness (L), toxic relationships (M), toxic connections (N), toxic habits (O), or hyper-grace beliefs (P). You need to remain on *offense*, always seeking new ways to discover open doors so that you can close them. I don't mean to be paranoid or consumed by spiritual warfare. This doesn't need to take much time, that is unless you discover something. If you do, battle vigorously, win, and then get back to your normal routine. Jesus warned us to "beware of the leaven," which was the false and destructive teachings of others. *(Mt 16:5-12, Mk 8:15, Lk 12:1)* This is because it's *pervasive*, meaning that it only takes a little to spread itself around and modify everything else around it. The Apostle Paul further elaborated on His analogy. In Galatians 5:7-9 he says, *"You were running so well. Who has obstructed you from obeying the truth? Such persuasion does not come from the One who calls you. A little leaven works through the whole batch of dough."* 1 Corinthians 5:6-7 says, *"..Do you not know that a little leaven works through the whole batch of dough? Get rid of the old leaven, that you may be a new unleavened batch..."*

Chapter 3 Evaluation
AFTER THOROUGH, CAREFUL EXAMINATION, RIGHT NOW:

Statement	False			Partially False			Mostly True			True
3) I'm dedicated to living offensively in the battle against Satan	1	2	3	4	5	6	7	8	9	10
3) I'm proactive and seeking to grow in my sanctification daily	1	2	3	4	5	6	7	8	9	10
3) I'm humble, open, responsive to correction from others...	1	2	3	4	5	6	7	8	9	10
3) I'd rather my error, sin, brokenness revealed, so I can heal	1	2	3	4	5	6	7	8	9	10
3) I care more about being like Christ, than hiding my shame	1	2	3	4	5	6	7	8	9	10
a) There is no evidence in my life of the old Road Map...........	1	2	3	4	5	6	7	8	9	10
b) There is no evidence in my life of the old Car......................	1	2	3	4	5	6	7	8	9	10
c) There is no evidence in my life of the old Driver	1	2	3	4	5	6	7	8	9	10
d) There is no evidence in my life of the Saboteur	1	2	3	4	5	6	7	8	9	10
e) There is no evidence in my life of False Religion	1	2	3	4	5	6	7	8	9	10
f) There is no evidence in my life of False Spirituality	1	2	3	4	5	6	7	8	9	10
g) There is no evidence in my life of Carnal Compromise......	1	2	3	4	5	6	7	8	9	10
h) There is no evidence in my life of Counterfeit Jesus'..........	1	2	3	4	5	6	7	8	9	10
i) There is no evidence in my life of False Beliefs....................	1	2	3	4	5	6	7	8	9	10
j) There is no evidence in my life of False Repentance / Faith	1	2	3	4	5	6	7	8	9	10
k) There is no evidence in my life of Sinful Behavior	1	2	3	4	5	6	7	8	9	10
l) There is no evidence in my life of Emotional Brokenness ..	1	2	3	4	5	6	7	8	9	10
m) There is no evidence in my life of Toxic Relationships........	1	2	3	4	5	6	7	8	9	10
n) There is no evidence in my life of Toxic Connections	1	2	3	4	5	6	7	8	9	10
o) There is no evidence in my life of Toxic Habits...................	1	2	3	4	5	6	7	8	9	10
p) There is no evidence in my life of Hyper-Grace	1	2	3	4	5	6	7	8	9	10

Date Last Taken: _____

Questions for Reflection or Group Study:

1) Why do many Christians hide their mistakes, faults, sins, or pain from others rather than seeking for ways to share them so that they could receive prayers, ministry, and healing?
2) What has been the most significant—yet subtle—way that Satan has attacked you personally during your journey so far? What or who did you blame/take it out on instead?
3) What section of this chapter did you struggle with the most? Why?
4) Have open doors been revealed? Take turns verbally renouncing false beliefs, confessing sins, forgiving others, laying hands on and praying over one another for healing.
5) What area did you score lowest in? Why? How could overcoming this be a unique calling in your life? Discuss strategies for you to gain victory in that area.
6) What area did you score highest in? Why? Could this be connected to a gift of the Holy Spirit you've received? How could you partner with someone low in this area to help them?
7) Have you gone through curse-breaking? Consider doing this on your own, as a small group together, or by breaking up into pairs leading one another through them. (see Section N)

Subjects I plan to study more of: Strategy, Plan, Deadline:

1. _____
2. _____
3. _____

Explore Chapter 3 Deeper:

For additional resources related to the topics discussed in this chapter see our companion website at **https://MPoweredChristian.org/Road-Map-Book-Resources**

- Free printable pdf of this chapter evaluation for personal or classroom use
- List of related online courses, ecoaching programs, personal coaching services
- List of related videos, articles, and recommended books
- List of related live webinars and ways to ask questions

Notes/Reflections:

_____
_____
_____
_____
_____
_____
_____
_____
_____
_____
_____
_____
_____
_____
_____
_____
_____
_____
_____
_____
_____
_____
_____
_____

To-Do List: *Date:* _____

MY TASKS FOR **THIS UPCOMING WEEK...**

✔ **My Big 1-3:**
_____
_____
_____

✔ **For Personal Growth:**
_____
_____
_____

✔ **For Key Roles:**
_____
_____
_____

✔ **For Calling/Ministry Service:**
_____
_____
_____

✔ **Pray for/Request prayer about:**
_____
_____
_____

✔ **Learn more about:**
_____
_____

✔ **Other:**
_____
_____

CHAPTER FOUR

The Atmosphere in the Car

Control the atmosphere in the car and it'll make your journey way more fruitful and pleasurable.

Chapter Contents

I. Thoughts & Beliefs

The journey is supposed to be enjoyable! Did you hear that? Many Christians live out their faith miserable and defeated but it's not supposed to be that way! I'm not saying it will always be easy. I'm not saying the road isn't rough and paved with lots of pot holes, downed trees, careless and aggressive drivers, bad weather, and the like. It is. You only have so much control in the direction you're driving—especially if you're letting God drive. But you have A LOT of control on the atmosphere IN the car.

The Holy Spirit is driving, and at least in this analogy, His eyes are on the road, getting you to the final destination. So that leaves you in the front passenger seat. You're not driving so it's your job to co-pilot and help manage the other things that need to happen. It's your job to keep the doors shut and locked and to keep an eye out for Satan trying to get back in. It's your job to monitor and manage what's playing on the radio. It's your job to monitor and manage the internal atmosphere during the journey. What kind of conversation is happening? What's everyone thinking about? How does everyone feel? If you manage these things well, it could be Hell-on-Earth outside the car but still be at peace and joy and fulfillment inside the car. But if you manage these things poorly it could be relatively smooth driving outside but you could be having Hell-on-Earth inside the car. How you manage the atmosphere inside the car will determine the inner life you experience and profoundly shape both your fruitfulness and your happiness in life.

a. Crucifying Old Patterns
The old you is dead, so stop allowing your old patterns to continue.

Do you believe the gospel? If you do, why do you continue to allow your old patterns to continue as though you have not been changed? The truth is that sometimes the *memory* of our old nature seems more real to us, or more strong to us, than our faith in our new nature. This belief empowers the old us to persist on long past its recommended expiration date—which is the day that we were saved and born again. I know, the struggle is real! But it is all the old nature. That old way of thinking about life. That old way of feeling day to day. Those old habits, lifestyles, preferences, thoughts, desires, etc. They feel natural to us still. But we know they aren't good, God's Word tells us so. You've gotten rid of the really bad stuff. It's outside the car now. You no longer live the way that you used to, or you're actively pursuing this in all areas. But there's still another level.

It's not enough that you've done your best to throw it out of the car. Get rid of it *in* the car too. For example, let's say you struggle with anger. I used to have an anger problem and I had a hard time learning how to constructively harness those emotions. I would get really upset and punched several holes into walls and doors! Aside from the benefit of learning how to do a wall patch there wasn't much good that came out of this.

Now, there is a worse end to the spectrum of anger. Some let it get pent up and then take out their rage on others by getting into fights at bars and such. Some become physically abusive and take it out their spouses or children. Some people allow it to get so out of control that it pushes them to commit murder. But it's not enough to just determine not to let it get that far. See it for the poisonous sin that it is.

Sin is not a disease that needs to be managed. It's a cancer that needs to be removed.

I became conscious of my anger problem and became determined to get a control of my anger. I learned a valuable lesson from *The 7 Habits of Highly Effective People*: "between stimulus and response, there's a pause." Between what happens to you, and how you decide to respond to it, there is a pause, a moment where you can decide how to respond. Take a breath or two. Decide. Don't just react. Choose.

Within months I had learned to control my anger so I didn't take it outwards. However, it was still frustrating inside. I still *felt* anger I could just sit on it internally or walk it off. It took longer over time to learn how to turn to God in those moments, intentionally at first, and seek His peace. To step outside of myself, and my situation, and my feelings, and just give it to Him. To choose to be the kind of person that acted the right way in response regardless of how I felt. My commitment to *BE* who I wanted to be eventually led to me seeking God to change my heart. I didn't want to be a person that had anger. I wanted to be a man of peace. I wanted to feel peace. I wanted to be able to have peace whenever I wanted it, regardless of what happened to me or in life. The gospel provides us with this, but we don't believe it all the time. Not practically speaking. We don't think on the gospel in those moments, we react in the moment first. But we have the choice not to. We *can* use that pause to remind ourselves of what's really important, who we really are, and then use our response to it to glorify God. By doing so, we give the Holy Spirit an opportunity to change us.

Over time this became a habit, an unconscious behavior that I did instinctually. I eventually could even drive in rush hour traffic (and here near Tampa, FL it's pretty bad!) and not be filled with road rage the whole time. I realized how far I had come when I noticed reckless, irresponsible drivers would nearly kill me (like seriously!) with their dangerous, selfish driving and instead of getting mad, or even saying or *even thinking* curse words at them, I would just feel sorry for them. I would just pray for them to find Jesus. I could've just died, thank you Lord for giving me some more time here. Lord, give that person salvation and peace so they don't hurt themselves or someone else. When *that* is your *first* response you can rejoice. God's peace truly surpasses all understanding.

My past struggles with pornography, lust, greed, envy, gossip, fear, covetousness, and any other sins have all been overcome in similar ways. I'm far from perfect but I know who I used to be and it's night-and-day different than how I am now. And life has thrown me some pretty bad storms to walk through and my new nature has helped me weather them a whole lot easier. You can do the same. You can have the fruit of the Spirit flowing in and through you, filling up your car to the brim. This is God's will for you. Believe this. Act on this. Abandon the false belief that you have to do *sin-management* for life. It is that belief that has kept it around as long as it has been around. God has empowered you to overcome your sins. The question is: do you trust in God's promises?

In chapter 3, Section (O), "Toxic Habits," I talked about how we can have habits that are habitual, automatic, routine. This also applies to our thought life. Do your thoughts just run on autopilot, or are you conscious about them? Not only *should* you not let them run on autopilot, your "autopilot sensor" is the *old* you. The way you think is often your old programming still running its program. If you continue to *think* the way that you've always thought, you will continue to *believe* what you've always believed. And if you continue to believe what you've always believed, you will continue to *feel* what you've always felt. And if you continue to feel what you've always felt, you will continue to *act* the way that you've always acted. And if you continue to act the way that you've always acted, you will continue to *be* who you've always been! One definition of insanity is doing the same thing over and over again and expecting a different result.

That old person who thinks, believes, feels, and acts those old ways is supposed to be dead! You are now a new creation. So you must live your life analyzing every link in the chain. It's human nature to compensate. To take the path of least resistance. To do things efficiently, the way that's typical, normal, the way that you're used to doing things. To be at a place of normalcy, to achieve homeostasis. This is easier. This is comfortable. And certainty/comfort is one of the top four fundamental human needs. So there are forces, even good and natural ones, that want us to stay as we are. But we must change. It's not going to *feel* normal. It's not normal. It's not going to *feel* comfortable. It's not comfortable. It's going to feel odd, and uncertain, and foreign, and difficult, and even stressful or painful sometimes. Change is painful. Most people never fix their bad habits until the pain of change is less than the pain of staying the same! Consider physical fitness as an example. It's easier to deal with the pain of not liking how you look and feel than it is to adopt a new and more disciplined way of diet and exercise. But the truth is that a lifetime of being out of shape, and all that comes along with it, physically, emotionally, mentally, etc., carries much more pain with it in the long run. In all of our challenges we must keep our eyes on the goal and develop discipline to press through the pain to the other side. And when we commit to doing that, pain is not a problem, pain isn't a sign that there's something wrong. The pain of overcoming our own defects, and becoming all that we can be, is a pain signal that there's something right!

So how *do* we change? Where do you start? How do you keep an eye on things once you're going? Analyze the chain. There could be a breakdown or disconnect anywhere in the chain: **Think → Believe → Feel → Act → Be**. Who we are is what we repeatedly do. And what we do begins with thoughts. Our thoughts initiate and drive the rest of the chain via cause-and-effect. You won't *feel* depression unless you first *think* about depressing things and then *believe* them. You won't *be* an angry person if you don't first *feel* angry and then *act* angry. You won't *act* on lust if you don't first allow yourself to *think* about things that produce lust and then stir up the *feelings* of lust. The good thing is that you can stop up the process at any point in the chain. You could think a lustful thought and then instead of believing on it, and allowing it to take root and entertain it in your mind, cast it away immediately instead. Choose to think about something else, and then allow *that* to go through the chain. Think about something else that is good and pure, something you believe is true and good, something you want to feel, and to act on, and to become. And if you allow the Holy Spirit to empower you in this process, and become disciplined in it, you will eventually gain mastery over it. Now your energies are not going to be used up daily in this rigorous struggle to manage your sin disease. The cancer will have been removed. You'll have peace and your energy can be used to live in a way that glorifies God and advancing His Kingdom instead! **Think → Believe → Feel → Act → Be**

b. Clothed in Christ
Forget your faults and failures and think on your newfound righteousness.

If everything begins with our thought life, what should we think? We need to forget our past. We need to forget our faults and our failures. We need to forget our mistakes. We need to embrace our new position in Christ. We are nestled in Him. No longer living for ourselves, but living in Him. This is good news! It means that all of that junk that we hold on to, the junk from our past that weighs us down, the junk thinking that keeps us thinking about what is *wrong* with us, we need to drop it. All of that was wrong, but it was also crucified with Christ. We don't have to live in it anymore. And we don't have to atone for it either. We sometimes feel as though we should keep beating ourselves up about it forever, and if we don't, then it's like we aren't repentant. But this is wrong. Repentance is not the same thing as *penance*. Repentance means "to change your mind," but penance means "paying for." But it is not up to us to pay for our old sins. Jesus paid for them already. We're not supposed to *suffer* now for what we've done. Jesus suffered for us on our behalf. If we continue to try to pay for them, or allow ourselves to suffer now, even if we're doing it unintentionally and subconsciously, we're still walking around with an ankle weight dragging us down, but we're not supposed to. Our trust in the gospel is our trust in the very reason for us not to carry around our past! So let your past mistakes go and let the peace of Christ wash over you today! Don't forget them entirely, like what you did and the lessons you learned, but forget it in the sense that you're still guilty for it and you still deserve to be punished for it. This is a lie! Jesus paid for it already—no matter what it is!

We all carry around some things, but we shouldn't. Examine your thoughts and your heart. What are you still carrying around? Give it to Jesus. If you haven't already done so, make it right with any persons still alive that you've sinned against. Go somewhere isolated and quiet, reflect on that thing. Picture it in your mind. Let the weight of its terrible reality be fully present so that you feel it. If you haven't already done so, confess the sin to God. Make your remorse officially known to Him. He knows your heart but it's cathartic to specifically give it to Him. Then take that whole entire memory, all the facts, all the thoughts, all the feelings, all the consequences, and put it all into a box. Hand the box in your mind to Jesus. Envision Him having it with Him when He went to the cross. It was with Him when He was up there. It was with Him, nailed to the cross. Tell Him today how grateful you are to Him for His love for you and for doing that for you. Tell Him how much you trust Him, and how much you trust *in* Him, having completely and permanently resolved that for you. Ask Him to purge your mind and heart of this sin and all guilt, pain, fear, etc. related to it. Declare that you trust in Him and that you will not let Satan try to remind you of this anymore, to feel guilty again, to try to use it against you. Decide and declare that if Satan does try to remind you of it later, or if you remind yourself later, that you will immediately rebuke it down as soon as you are aware of it. Ask the Holy Spirit to give you the discernment to see when this is happening quickly and the wisdom to respond to it accordingly. Then ask Him to purify your thoughts continually with the mind of Christ. This is your new reality. Rejoice and be glad! Be filled with peace. Do not let your car be filled with condemnation and guilt.

Galatians 3:27 For all of you who were baptized into Christ have clothed yourselves with Christ.

Philippians 4:4 Rejoice in the Lord always. I will say it again: Rejoice! [5]Let your gentleness be apparent to all. The Lord is near. [6]Be anxious for nothing, but in everything, by prayer and petition, with thanksgiving, present your requests to God. [7]And the peace of God, which surpasses all understanding, will guard your hearts and your minds in Christ Jesus.

---

c. New Identity in Christ
Whatever you hate about yourself has died, discover your new identity in Christ.

That's a provocative subtitle, no? The truth is that we all have things about ourselves that we don't like. Things about our past we wish we did differently. Things about our body, or our habits, behaviors, talents, career, family, etc. that we wish were different. It's easy to focus on these things. We may catch ourselves wanting to be like someone else, to have what they have, to live the way that they live. Sometimes this can be healthy, perhaps driving us to work harder to achieve more of what we want in life. But other times it can fuel insecurities, depression, envy, covetousness, anger, or hatred. It's critical for your journey to be productive and fruitful to focus on YOU, not others. Your story is different than theirs. God is doing something unique in and through you. He's not comparing you to them—He's comparing you to the *old* you. That is also how you should measure your success. How are you doing on your journey to become less like the old you, the sinner version, and more like the new you, the Christlike version? You're not meant to follow *their* calling, you're meant to discover and fulfill your calling. That is where your highest purpose will be achieved and where your highest fulfillment will be found!

How do you see yourself? What's your identity? Father, mother? Brother, sister? Realtor, teacher, architect, janitor, mechanic, manager, entrepreneur? American, German, African, Israeli, Brazilian, Russian, Japanese? Young, old, middle-aged? White, Black, Asian, Hispanic? Beautiful, ugly, insightful, wise, smart, creative, athletic, strategic? When you think of *who* you are what are the qualities and attributes you describe yourself as? Pause reading and think about this now for a minute or two and create a short list.

After you've done this little exercise, let me ask you a question. Did you list "child of God?" How about "disciple of Jesus?" You see we may believe these things but still not really think about them much. Or at the very least, we aren't thinking about them at the critical times when it matters most. We need to think these things instinctively, habitually. When the thoughts come from Satan or from ourselves to depress us, to make us compare ourselves with others, that is when we need to think it. We need to think it before our emotions are even triggered because we didn't. Once we *feel* like less we have already missed our opportunity. If my identity is foremost wrapped up in any of these other things in life, I will let them influence how I feel. Then when I decide to think "but I'm a child of God and I should be content with that" even if that's true, I won't *feel* it right away. We need to be better guards of what enters our minds and hearts. But here's a profound truth when it comes to thoughts: a good offense is our best defense. If we are constantly reminding ourselves of our true identity as a child of God then we will be prepared when the inevitable doubts come later. *This* is who you *are.* This transcends what you do now, your current status in life, your career, your family, the future. Whatever you would like to change about your life will be better accomplished built UPON this foundation, rather than instead of this foundation. Fix your eyes and thoughts on your new identity in Christ, and be all that you can be in Christ, which may look very different.

---

1 John 3:2 Beloved, we are now children of God, and what we will be has not yet been revealed. We know that when Christ appears, we will be like Him, for we will see Him as He is.

---

d. Understanding Your Election

We *become* "the elect" *by* being in Christ, not by being elected first *to* be in Christ.

I don't want to be a broken record on this point but I feel in this chapter it is important to reiterate a teaching I've already mentioned elsewhere in the book, and that is on the topic of election. For a more thorough explanation of election, or what it means for us "to be *elect*" or "to be *chosen* before the foundations of the world" see Chapter 1, (*IV*) *Summary* section, and Chapter 2, Section (E). I'm not trying to cause division between my Calvinistic brothers and sisters by disagreeing with them on this topic, but there is a very real threat in the *practical* application of their theology. So this message is applicable to anyone influenced by the Calvinistic interpretation of election, Calvinists and non-Calvinists alike.

When you provide counseling to a broad range of people, and pastoral counseling to a wide spectrum of Christians across denominational lines like I do, you deal with all kinds of different theological problems. One that I've encountered numerous times is people struggling with their own salvation because they've been led to believe that they are not of *'the elect.'* I know for my Reformed professors and pastor friends they understand the complexity of the Calvinistic systematic and would never teach that a person could be a faithful follower of Jesus and still be one of the reprobates. Nonetheless, many people still struggle deeply with this and it affects their journey immensely. We need to take this seriously; there are souls on the line.

And as a deliverance minister who's encountered this *a lot*, I can provide another perspective: Satan uses this often! I've had many people come to me with demons who are hounded day and night by tormenting demons convincing them that they are not of the elect and for them to throw in the towel and give up all faith and hope in Jesus. That they are not of the elect and therefore Jesus didn't die for *them*, doesn't care about *them*, that *they* have not been born again, that *they* are still in all their sins, and no matter what they do *they* on their way to Hell. And then I have to fight an uphill battle against these voices by trying to convince these struggling souls that the Bible is clear on this: if they believe in Jesus and trust in Him then they ARE of the elect! But Calvinists cannot really guarantee a person's salvation in this regard with absolute assuredness. They will try to minister to them and tell them to put their faith in Jesus and trust in Him, but will also say, pistol to the head, that they cannot know, for sure, who is of the elect or not. And this only feeds into the fears and doubts of people struggling with this.

So, whether you are a Calvinist or not, I want you to REJECT any beliefs, thoughts, or feelings that God doesn't love you, that Jesus didn't die for you, or that you're not saved. My advice is to put your faith in the gospel, that Jesus died to purchase the salvation of EVERYONE, and that anyone who puts their trust in Him will be saved. Do not give Satan this foothold in your life! If you have, it has already halted your confidence, your peace, and your joy. Take it back! Jesus's arms are wide open for you! The water of life is available to you. If you believe in Jesus and the gospel you can have confidence you are of the elect of God. You *become and/or are* the elect by being found in Jesus! Let your heart be settled on this matter once-and-for-all, completely and permanently.

John 3:15 that everyone who believes in Him may have eternal life. [16]For God so loved the world that He gave His one and only Son, that everyone who believes in Him shall not perish but have eternal life.

Revelation 22:16 "I, Jesus, have sent My angel to give you this testimony for the churches... [17]The Spirit and the bride say, "Come!" Let the one who hears say, "Come!" And let the one who is thirsty come, and the one who desires the water of life drink freely.

---

e. Losing Your Salvation
Salvation can be unreceived, or intentionally forsaken, but not accidentally lost.

Another routine area of depression, joylessness, and hopelessness are Christians under the impression that they have already lost their salvation, or who walk on eggshells with the fear that they will do something to lose it. This is similar to the previous section, Satan has tormented some with these thoughts relentlessly. Just as he has gone after the theology of some Calvinists to convince them they are not of the elect, and are thus not saved, this is the equivalent of how he goes after my Arminian brothers and sisters. Since most Arminians believe Christians can lose their salvation all he has to do is convince them that they already have, and that there's nothing they can do about it. A very different type of subtle strategy, with equally effective results. Beyond our theological differences, Calvinists and Arminians (and everyone else) need to zoom out and see the bigger picture, how their mutual enemy is using both of their theological beliefs to hurt members of the Body of Christ. We should all be united in this common goal: to proclaim the gospel and assure believers that they ARE saved by faith alone!

Salvation can be *unreceived*, meaning that we could not hear about how to be saved in the first place, or choose not to believe it and receive it if we do hear about it. Or, we could have it and then intentionally *forsake* it and abandon it. But we cannot accidentally lose it. We don't stumble and sin once and lose it. We don't even commit a major (what Catholics call a *mortal*) sin and lose it. No, what Protestants believe isn't Romanism. Though Arminians tend to lean towards the belief that we can lose our salvation, certainly all Protestants agree that we don't lose it and then gain it back every time we fall short and then repent, yo-yo'ing between being saved and unsaved. No, it is therefore not actually *lost*, it is either had, or it is intentionally forsaken. This means that if you believe in Jesus and put your faith in Him then you are saved. And provided that you're not a total hypocrite, and are walking the talk, and bearing fruit, then you can be confident in your salvation. And every day is another day. If you look back and doubt whether or not you *used* to be saved—that is in the past. Today is the day of salvation! If you believe in Jesus and trust in Him TODAY then you are saved today. Do not worry about your past. Live today, repent today, live faithfully today, do what is right today, trust in the gospel today, draw near to God today. Live each day this way and if voices come to tell you otherwise, reaffirm your commitment to Jesus. Let every voice, whether Satan's or yours, that tries to cause doubt or fear, to be a catalyst for you to reaffirm your trust in the gospel. In doing this, every attack to cause you to fear losing your salvation becomes an additional boost to your confidence that you do have your salvation!

Hebrews 3:6 But Christ is faithful as the Son over God's house. And we are His house, if we hold firmly to our confidence and the hope of which we boast.

Hebrews 10:35 So do not throw away your confidence; it holds a great reward.

---

f. The Unpardonable Sin
Not something you *did* in the past, but something you can *do* in the present.

In the same vane as the previous two sections, I want to come against another common, terribly harmful belief that assaults the confidence and peace of many Christians. This is the belief that perhaps they have committed the unpardonable sin, either long before they became a Christian, or sometime after becoming a Christian. I've had numerous people come to me in deliverance sessions who were plagued by tormenting demons trying to convince them of this as well. Do you see the common denominator here? Satan convinces that we're not of the elect, or that we lost our salvation, or that we committed the unpardonable sin. The best defense is a good offense. Why am I teaching deep biblical theology to "regular, everyday" Christians? Because if we understood deep theology we would have a robust, persevering faith able to stand firm against all of the attacks of the enemy! And our journey would be full of so much more peace and joy! That is what God wants for you and it's what I want for you.

So, where does this phrase come from? It's a summary of a teaching of Jesus found in Mark 3:28-30 and Matthew 12:31-32. The 'The Unpardonable Sin,' also called 'Blasphemy against the Holy Spirit,' is the one sin that Jesus said would never be forgiven. Because we know that every other type of sin, including murder, adultery, and every other kind of terrible thing we can commit *can* be forgiven, this particular teaching has stood out in Scripture. It's shocking nature has made it easy to abuse by evil people and by Satan. Let's take a look at it and examine it more closely.

Mark 3:28 *[Jesus]* Truly I tell you, the sons of men will be forgiven all sins and blasphemies, as many as they utter. ²⁹But whoever blasphemes against the Holy Spirit will never be forgiven; he is guilty of eternal sin." ³⁰Jesus made this statement because they were saying, "He has an unclean spirit."

Matthew 12:31 *[Jesus]* Therefore I tell you, every sin and blasphemy will be forgiven men, but the blasphemy against the Spirit will not be forgiven. ³²Whoever speaks a word against the Son of Man will be forgiven, but whoever speaks against the Holy Spirit will not be forgiven, either in this age or in the one to come.

This response was given by Jesus to address Pharisees who watched Jesus cast a demon out of a man and heal him of blindness and muteness. They saw Jesus, experienced His glory, and watched Him heal and deliver a person made in God's image, to the glory of God, and their response is recorded in Matthew 12:24, *"Only by Beelzebul, the prince of the demons, does this man drive out demons."* To experience the epitome of God's hand with such a good work and then attribute it to Satan is to be truly blinded and wicked and hardened to the things of the Spirit of God. Besides perhaps seeing Jesus after the resurrection, they would never experience such a thing later that has greater potential to open them up to the things of the Kingdom of God. Imagine how much less it took to convince you to have faith in Jesus. Now imagine having a much more personal and tangible experience with Him, and witnessing Him do His miracles before your very eyes, and then not only rejecting Him, but calling *Him* Satan! *This* is the depth of wickedness required to blaspheme the Holy Spirit.

So, can we commit this sin today? Yes, but I'm convinced it is not as easy or prevalent as Satan would have us believe it is. Many have come to me, having seen or experienced weird and questionable charismatic phenomena doubting that it was the Holy Spirit causing it. They are plagued by tormenting thoughts of if they blasphemed the Holy Spirit by not having faith that what they witnessed was truly the Holy Spirit's doing. First of all, *many* of the things done in the name of the Holy Spirit *should* be questioned! I've seen outright demonic manifestations that Christians were claiming was the Holy Spirit. When people are barking like dogs, slithering on the ground like a snake, and having violent convulsions on the floor I struggle to see how these could be the fruits of the same Spirit who calls us to self-control and gentleness. *(2 Pet 1:6, Gal 5:23, 2 Tim 1:7, 3:3, Tit 2:2)*

Second, consider how this type of manifestation is different than what Jesus gave. He brought healing of blindness and muteness. He casted out a demon. He loved a person, and brought about restoration for them, and did it in front of people, in the open, so that they praised God, had increased faith in God, and then followed Jesus and listened to His teachings. What does a closed-setting of barking and violent convulsions accomplish? Where is the fruit? Where is the healing? Where is the deliverance of evil? Where is the gospel? Where is the discipleship? This is not to put "God in a box" and limit Him from being able to do things that are unorthodox or peculiar, but by examining the lack of fruit that is consistent with the purpose of the Kingdom of God we have not only a right, but a *duty*, to question it. It is good to be cautious and discerning, and not rush into accepting odd practices without first being a wise Berean, examining the Scriptures, praying on it, evaluating the teachings alongside those practices, and testing everything. This goes in both directions too! It is *equally* blaspheming the Spirit to see truly demonic things and attribute them to the Holy Spirit, too. So, no, this is not blasphemy of the Holy Spirit. You have not committed the unpardonable sin by doing this. If you have any guilt or remorse still then simply confess your sin—or *potential* sin—to Jesus and trust that He dealt with it already on the cross.

I've also had numerous people who thought they had blasphemed the Holy Spirit in a different way, by insulting or blaspheming Him directly, or by slandering God at some point in the past before coming to faith. This is not what this is talking about. First, notice that Jesus will forgive those who speak against Him. Second, the Pharisees, the very people Jesus was speaking about here, hadn't even mentioned the words "Spirit" or "Holy Spirit." It was not what they *said*, it was what they *did*. New Testament professor D.A. Carson summarized it this way: He said this blasphemy of the Holy Spirit is the rejection of the "truth in full awareness that is exactly what one is doing—thoughtfully, willfully, and self-consciously rejecting the work of the Spirit even though there can be no other explanation of Jesus' exorcisms than that. For such a sin there is no forgiveness."[1]

This is a hardness of heart that is beyond redemption, not something we can feel remorse for later and repent about. *Every* Christian who was once not a Christian would be guilty of it otherwise. Examples of others in Scripture who initially rejected the Spirit's testimony of Jesus as the Christ, but later accepted it, include Jesus's brother James and the Apostle Paul. It's clear that an initial or temporary rejection of the prompting of the Holy Spirit is not the same thing as when one knowingly, unambiguously, intentionally, and *permanently* rejects the Holy Spirit's testimony to Jesus. New Testament professor Darrell L. Bock sums it up well: "The blasphemy of the Spirit might be regarded as the by-product of rejecting the Son of Man. The difference between blaspheming the Son of Man and blaspheming the Spirit is that blasphemy of the Son of Man is an instant rejection, while blasphemy of the Spirit is a permanent rejection... Once the Spirit's testimony about God's work through Jesus is permanently refused, then nothing can be forgiven, since God's plan has been rejected."[2] So if you have not abandoned your belief in Jesus and the gospel, and your trust in Him, then you have not committed this eternal sin. As with the other pervasive thoughts that come against your faith and walk, reject this one as well. Let the very thought of it cause an instant reaffirmation of your faith in Jesus and ignite your confidence in your salvation. "You have committed the unpardonable sin.." Oh no, I haven't! Jesus is my Lord and Savior!

g. How Sin Separates
Sin creates barriers of separation between us and God but it doesn't cut us off.

One of the most common obstacles between Christians who live full of peace and joy, and those who don't, is how they understand how sin in the present affects our immediate relationship with God. You know by now that we cannot, nor should we want to, just live in willful sin against God. This is evidence that we have not been reborn and that we are still the old car. But what about when we're generally holy and righteous, but occasionally stumble, get caught up in our emotions, the temptations of the flesh, etc.? We know that sin, all sin, causes separation from God. Yet, we also know that those who are in Christ are already justified and forgiven for their sins. It's a mistake to forget this, and think that if we sin then we are immediately either lost, or at the very least "God is mad at us," or doesn't want anything to do with us - at least until we repent. This is not accurate. We do not cease to be a child of God, even if we sin. Sin is not something we always do consciously. We are sinners. We live in a flesh of sin. Sin will still feel natural and normal to us whenever we are walking by our flesh. Our natural predisposition is not to be holy and then *choose* to sin—our natural predisposition is to be a sinner and then *choose* to be holy! God knows this. It is why He has given us the Holy Spirit as a deposit. Notice I said deposit—a deposit of what is to come in the future. You shouldn't expect yourself to be fully done already. The "perfect" has not come yet. God could have made you perfect instantly, but He chose to do it this way. He is glorified in your *struggle*.

God is glorified in your struggle with sin! Accept that it's normal and good. He doesn't expect you to be perfect, He expects you to trust in the One who is.

So how might I provide you with a proper analogy of this dynamic? You might think that if you sin, or *mortally* (seriously) sin, then you become the old car again. That's false. You might think that God cuts you off until you repent. After all, Isaiah 59:2 says, *"But your iniquities have built barriers between you and your God, and your sins have hidden His face from you, so that He does not hear."* And there are truths to this that we must deal with. However, in the same chapter it prophesies of the coming of Jesus. It says in Isaiah

59, verses 15-17, *"The LORD looked and was displeased that there was no justice. He saw that there was no man; He was amazed that there was no one to intercede. So His own arm brought salvation, and His own righteousness sustained Him. He put on righteousness like a breastplate, and a helmet of salvation on His head; He put on garments of vengeance and wrapped Himself in a cloak of zeal."* (Isa 59:15b-17)

It is God Himself that accomplishes the perfect righteousness that we need. It should give us some peace of mind to know that not only can't we do it on our own, but if we had the desire to do it on our own it actually robs God of glory. So when you fall short, glorify Christ as the One who doesn't, and who carries you. And when you walk upright and steady, glorify the Holy Spirit as the One who sustains you and makes it possible. Let this take the pressure off of you. You're not your own savior, you know this intellectually. Yet, many Christians live day-to-day as though they must act like it. You never outgrow the gospel! Walk in the confidence of your trust in Christ and it will not give Satan a foothold in your life. He wants you to feel that you have to *earn* it, and to feel guilt and shame and fear whenever you aren't measuring up. If we listen to these lies they will drag us down emotionally and spiritually like a massive anchor in the soul. Rather, fix your eyes each day on Jesus, "the author *and perfector* of your faith." (Heb 12:2)

When we sin it does grieve the Holy Spirit, and so we should strive never to sin and to be fully blameless. (Eph 4:30) But our sin does not cut us off from our Heavenly Father. You are still His child. And you still have Jesus as your advocate with the Father, you are in Him, and *He* is your righteousness. (1 Jn 2:1) Sin will hamper your walk though. Though the Holy Spirit is driving your car, your sin will blunt your ability to hear His guidance and prompting. It will blunt your closeness with God. It will hinder your ability to produce good fruit, blunt your spiritual gifts, and distract you from the work of the Kingdom. Sin permitted to continue will create an entirely different atmosphere in the car. It will unlock and open doors that were once closed. It can even invite harmful passengers back into the car. And the more harmful passengers in the car the harder it is to hear from, and be led by, the Holy Spirit, rather than those passengers. However, if this happens, these passengers can be removed again, and the doors can be shut and locked once again. The intimacy with God and the atmosphere of your car can be restored again. But it is better if you never let it get off the tracks in the first place. Keep a close eye on your life and strive for perfection, in the sense that it is good and best, while also knowing that your perfection will *only* be truly fulfilled by Christ. And rest in the peace of that reality.

---

1 John 2:1 My little children, I am writing these things to you so that you will not sin. But if anyone does sin, we have an advocate before the Father—Jesus Christ, the Righteous One. ²He Himself is the atoning sacrifice for our sins, and not only for ours but also for the sins of the whole world.

> Romans 8:33 Who will bring any charge against God's elect? It is God who justifies. [34]Who is there to condemn us? For Christ Jesus, who died, and more than that was raised to life, is at the right hand of God—and He is interceding for us.

h. Renewing the Mind
Let God's thoughts and beliefs become your thoughts and beliefs.

> Romans 12:2 Do not be conformed to this world, but be transformed by the renewing of your mind. Then you will be able to test and approve what is the good, pleasing, and perfect will of God.

So how exactly do we renew our minds? We know what the old thoughts and beliefs are, what comes from our old nature. We know what Satan wants us to think and believe and to focus on. What is the *source* of information with which to renew our minds *by*? The answer is God's WORD. In John 17:17 Jesus told us that we can be sanctified by the truth; God's Word is truth. We can be sanctified, purified, just by hearing (or reading), thinking, believing, and receiving internally the Word of God in our spirit. Jesus told the apostles in John 15:3, *"You are already clean because of the word I have spoken to you."* In Ephesians 5:25 it says Christ gave Himself up for the church, and in verse 26-27 it says, *"to sanctify her, cleansing her by the washing with water through the word, and to present her to Himself as a glorious church, without stain or wrinkle or any such blemish, but holy and blameless."* Lest we make the mistake of trying to interpret these verses metaphorically Hebrews 4:12 tells us, *"For the word of God is living and active. Sharper than any double-edged sword, it pierces even to dividing soul and spirit, joints and marrow. It judges the thoughts and intentions of the heart."* The living and active Word of God is powerful. It is sanctifying, renewing, restoring—in the person who, by faith, *believes in* the truths and promises revealed therein. So this is our primary defense against our flesh and the enemy, but it is not only defensive, it is also offensive. Ephesians chapter 6 teaches us how to wage spiritual warfare with verse 17 describing the Word of God as "the sword of the Spirit."

This is why I'm constantly preaching and counseling for Christians to read their Bibles. Get on a daily reading plan that takes you through the entire Bible every year. That will take you less than 95 hours per year, averaging 25 minutes a day. If it includes videos or other educational materials, even better. This is not just extra credit. It is the lifeblood of the believer. You need God's Word living in you. You need to hear God's truths in your mind and in your thoughts throughout your day. The small amount you hear in church on Sundays or on Wednesdays is not enough. The small amount present in the worship music you listen to is not enough. The few verses included in your daily devotional is not enough. Though these are all good things that you should utilize as well. But they are supplements. They are vitamins and shakes to supplement where you get your "meat and potatoes." They aren't the solid meal. The solid meal is your direct reading and study and application of God's Word yourself. You will never grow to become mature in your faith if you never graduate from the introductory tools created to help new believers to get started. You need to take ownership of your own walk with Christ.

I've been asked what I use. I recommend a free Bible reading app called *Read Scripture*. I believe I first heard about it from Pastor Francis Chan. I like it because it is simple and very easy to use. It uses the ESV translation; includes introductory videos for every book and major themes by *The Bible Project*; a checklist format to keep track of what has been read; and easily allows you to set a custom start date. The custom date allows newcomers to your Bible study or home group to just plug in the same date and jump right in where everyone else is so they are on the same schedule. I also like to use the *YouVersion Bible App*. I primarily use this for its free audiobook feature. I like the NIV translation read by Max McLean. I like to walk my dog and listen to my daily readings, reaping the spiritual benefits, as well as the physical, mental, and emotional benefits. I also use long drives to and from work, or running errands, or even while doing thinkless chores like mowing the lawn or housecleaning as opportunities to multitask and get my reading in. Stop making excuses not to do it, and find excuses *to* do it! Depending on the section of Scripture, its complexity, and your familiarity with it, you might have to reread it in order to make sure you fully grasp the meaning, or to study it deeper, but often this won't even be necessary. I like the BSB, ESV, NASB, NIV, CSB, and NKJV but use whatever Bible translation you like best, and the apps and websites you enjoy so that you stay consistent. Consistency is what matters most! And for you to be consistent you need to develop the habit by incorporating your reading (or listening) into enjoyable activities in your daily routine. The point is this: it's important to do. Do it! Find a way - any way that works for you - to get it in. You will be blessed by it and happy you did.

Daily Bible reading (or listening) is another way to continually impress your thoughts with the thoughts of God. Additional examples include listening to Christian and worship music throughout the day. You need to manage and regulate all of the thoughts and beliefs that go through your mind during the day. See yourself as the co-conductor of your symphony, as the co-pilot of your car. What you allow to be said, and believed, and entertained, in the car will shift the atmosphere in the car. It is your job to see to it that it is an environment that is conducive to godliness, to righteousness, to good fruit; to growing, building, and edifying the Church; to advancing the Kingdom of God. Think on *these* things. If you focus on these things, and fill your car up with them, you won't even have *room* in the car to allow space for the bad stuff to come in and make a home there!

Philippians 4:8 Finally, brothers, whatever is true, whatever is honorable, whatever is right, whatever is pure, whatever is lovely, whatever is admirable—if anything is excellent or praiseworthy— think on these things.

II. Emotions & Feelings

i. Good vs Bad Fruit

How you feel, is a produce (fruit) of what you think (plant), believe (root), and feed (water).

This is true of all emotions and feelings, but let me provide an example to illustrate this truth. If you *feel* shameful consistently, it is because you have allowed yourself to *think* about something that causes shame, then *believed* it to be true about yourself and so held on to it, and then *fed* it to nurture it to grow. That growth has allowed it to develop and become fruit. If you had extinguished it, rather than nurturing it and growing it, then it would never have bore fruit. You believed that you should feel shame and so now you do. What we think and believe, and then nurture, becomes what we feel. It becomes our reality. We often don't feel these feelings because they *are* our reality— rather they're often our reality *because* we have allowed and fed their precursors, to these feelings, those things that made them possible. If you want to change how you feel, you have to change what you think about and/or whether or not you want to believe and nurture the thoughts that come into your mind. That is what the previous section was all about: controlling your thoughts so that you are thinking rightly.

I didn't cover every single type of thought or belief possible. Once you learn this principle you'll be able to apply it to your specific situation. So what about all of the other types of feelings? What about those related to marriages, or parenting, or career, or ministry, or your calling? What about your personal struggles or emotional challenges? You know now that in order to change what you feel you have to change what you think, believe, and feed (water). But what if you're not sure if your thoughts and beliefs are right? Is there a way to cut through all of the uncertainty and narrow it down if something is good or bad? Yes! You will know it by its fruit! Good thoughts, lead to good beliefs, which lead to good behavior, which leads to good fruit. Bad thoughts, lead to bad beliefs, which lead to bad behavior, which leads to bad fruit. Examine the fruit. If it's bad, then trace it all the way back to its origin and correct it at the source. It's as simple as that! If you fail to do this then you will make the mistake of trying to treat the *symptom*, rather than the root cause of the problem. Identify bad fruits to then go back and pull up by their roots. And continue to feed the good fruits and you will grow into a healthy plant.

You must remember that there is bad (i.e. wicked, sinful, demonic) fruit, that we need to avoid at all costs, but then there is also what we might call "unfruitful" fruit. Fruit that is not necessarily ungodly but it's not of God, or loving, or helpful, or beneficial either. These are often the sources of our anxieties, worries, fears, feelings connected to bad habits, and our other unhelpful emotional states. Chapter 5 is all about living a life of fruitfulness so if you're eager to learn more about this topic just know that it's coming up next. But, in the meantime, just remember that how you feel day-to-day is directly related to what you think (plant), believe (root), and feed (water). You can begin to change how you feel immediately, right now, and the entire atmosphere of your car can rapidly shift overnight! Take back control of your car! Don't believe the lies of the enemy and feed into them, believe the truth of the Word of God and feed into it. Do it consistently and before you know it you will feel the grace of God overflowing in your spirit and empowering you with joy no matter what life is throwing at you.

Luke 10:38 As they traveled along, Jesus entered a village where a woman named Martha welcomed Him into her home. [39]She had a sister named Mary, who sat at the Lord's feet listening to His message. [40]But Martha was distracted by all the preparations to be made. She came to Jesus and said, "Lord, do You not care that my sister has left me to serve alone? Tell her to help me!" [41]"Martha, Martha," the Lord replied, "you are worried and upset about many things. [42]But only one thing is necessary. Mary has chosen the good portion, and it will not be taken away from her."

---

j. Gratitude as a Constant
Gratitude to God should be the foundation under everything you think and feel.

Gratitude is simply the quality or feeling of being grateful or thankful. It is a strong feeling of appreciation to someone or something. When asking ourselves what feelings are fruitful for the Christian, gratitude tops the list. We are grateful for Jesus, for salvation, for our adoption, for eternal life. Gratitude is a fruitful *feeling*, and as taught in section (I) is therefore the product of fruitful thoughts, beliefs, and behaviors that came before it. This is especially true when we rightly acknowledge God as the chief aim *of* our gratitude. Despite what is popular in culture and New Age philosophy it's not enough that we just have gratitude—we need to have *rightly placed* gratitude. We can certainly be grateful for other people, things, movements, events, blessings, etc. but even these, ultimately, also come from God. God is responsible for enabling these other things to have occurred. So we should praise God all the more for all that is good and right in our lives. But we should do even more than this. We should be grateful for even the bad and wrong things in our lives. Why? Because even those bad things, ultimately serve an important purpose—one that is still for our good. I often quote Romans 8:28, *"And we know that God works all things together for the good of those who love Him, who are called according to His purpose."* This verse teaches us that ALL things work together for the good of those who love God. It's not only the *good* things that work together for our good. All things do. The good and the bad. So whether we *see* the good that comes about through our endurance through our trials in *this* life or not, through faith and hope, we can still trust that good fruit is being formed and good is being accomplished. God is not allowing bad things to happen in the world, and to us, for no reason. Everything has purpose. Everything has a purpose—*for good eventually.* In this we can always rejoice.

Just because we know all things work for good, and so we should always be grateful, doesn't mean that we need to remain in the dark about how. We should pray for the wisdom to understand the good purpose of even bad things in this life. God has revealed a lot of these things to me already. I've come to see the good out of the bad and it has made me so much more grateful. We should be grateful for the big and the small, the good and the bad. We tend to think that only the good is good and the bad is bad. The healings are good, the diseases are bad. The prosperity is good, the poverty is bad. In a sense this is true, but in another deeper sense it is also spiritually immature. God calls us to go deeper in our philosophy than this type of simplicity. He wants us to appreciate all of the things that are obviously and only good, but not to only be grateful during seasons of prosperity. We should be grateful regardless, in harvest or in famine, in sickness or in the health. After acknowledging in 1 Thessalonians 3:3-4 that the church in Thessolonica would, and was destined to, go through trials and persecutions, Paul tells them in chapter 5 verse 18, to, *"Give thanks in every circumstance, for this is God's will for you in Christ Jesus."* Thankfulness is part and parcel with the Christian life. Likewise, James tells us not only to be grateful, but even *joyful* to encounter trials. And he tells us why, because it is good for us ultimately in the long run. And that which causes *eventual* good is still good, with the right perspective, even if it is bad in the short term.

James 1:2 Consider it pure joy, my brothers, when you encounter trials of many kinds, ³because you know that the testing of your faith develops perseverance. ⁴Allow perseverance to finish its work, so that you may be mature and complete, not lacking anything.

This may not come naturally, or easily, but the Holy Spirit does empower us to think and feel and live in such a way. Gratitude is not listed as one of the "fruits" of the Spirit, rather I think it's more like the roots of the whole tree. Gratitude is part of the very structure itself that everything else flows outward from. This is because our gratitude is so closely connected with the gospel. As we fix our eyes on Jesus, and our gratefulness for the gospel and our adoption, new identity, and purpose, gratitude inevitably overflows. And from this good fruit, things like love, joy, peace, faithfulness, etc. flow outward. Focus on that which you are grateful for and the rest will follow naturally.

"Gratitude unlocks the fullness of life. It turns what we have into enough, and more. It turns denial into acceptance, chaos to order, confusion to clarity. It can turn a meal into a feast, a house into a home, a stranger into a friend." — Melody Beattie[3]

Sometimes it's hard to find the good in the midst of the bad. And in these times it can be difficult to be grateful. Like I said before, we should pray for the wisdom so that God will help us see the bigger picture so we could focus on that instead of the hiccups of life. James continues to say this, from where we left off before, in James 1:5-8, *"Now if any of you lacks wisdom, he should ask God, who gives generously to all without finding fault, and it will be given to him. But he must ask in faith, without doubting, because he who doubts is like a wave of the sea, blown and tossed by the wind. That man should not expect to receive anything from the Lord. He is a double-minded man, unstable in all his ways."* So this process of trust, gratitude, faith, prayer, etc. allows God to share His heart and mind with us, and it grows us into spiritual maturity. As we encounter challenges that test our resolve we must lean in to Him in order to maintain our gratitude. And each step we take forward, in this pursuit towards our trust in Him, helps us to become more and more grateful. Our gratitude not only glorifies God it also produces within us a wellspring of joy and peace. We are making a habit of creating a deep reservoir of things that we are thankful for—one that we can pull from whenever things aren't going our way. Our gratitude, therefore, lays the foundation for our thoughts to be stable, fixed on what is good, so that we aren't double-minded. And with our thoughts stable, and focused on God, and with our feelings fixed on being grateful, faithful, hopeful, and joyful, we can build on that foundation, a life of fruitfulness. Anxiety, depression, and the like can't form roots in this kind of place. There's not enough focus on them. Your dedication to always have gratitude in your heart towards God will make you a firm tower in the storms.

Colossians 2:6 Therefore, just as you have received Christ Jesus as Lord, continue to walk in Him, [7]rooted and built up in Him, established in the faith as you were taught, and overflowing with thankfulness.

Colossians 3:17 And whatever you do, in word or deed, do it all in the name of the Lord Jesus, giving thanks to God the Father through Him.

k. Optimism vs Pessimism

Optimism is the outlook that moves faith, that produces good fruit, into action.

The empowered Christian life is one filled with optimism. Optimism has many definitions, but I am referring specifically to the disposition or tendency to look on the more favorable side of events or conditions and to expect the most favorable outcome. This relates to the Christian way of living specifically in two main ways. First, our optimism of the future is grounded in our *faith* (knowledge, belief, and trust) in God's promises. I'm referring to our faith in the following beliefs: (1) ultimately good wins over evil, (2) death and suffering will be destroyed forever, (3) sin, Hell, and death will be abolished, and (4) all separation from God is ultimately and permanently restored in the life to come. And if we believe this, and if our daily emotions are being influenced by these beliefs, they will produce in us a bright outlook of hopefulness. To be pessimistic, by contrast, is to believe, and/or to live as though you believe, that these biblical truths are really not true. To live such a way is not only unenjoyable, it's also counterproductive to your faith. To allow such an attitude into your daily life is to try to possess faith while simultaneously living with a hopeless and faithless despair as someone who doesn't have faith. Don't let Satan have this foothold in your life! Take back your hope by believing God's promises and feeling and living as though you actually trust them!

> John 16:33 *[Jesus]* I have told you these things so that in Me you may have peace. In the world you will have tribulation. But take courage; I have overcome the world!"
>
> 1 Peter 1:13 Therefore prepare your minds for action. Be sober-minded. Set your hope fully on the grace to be given you at the revelation of Jesus Christ.

The second type of optimism, a *general* optimistic disposition, is available to everyone, whether they are Christian or not. Optimism is also a philosophical worldview, and an emotional and psychological mindset that is favorable to a pessimistic one, regardless of beliefs. Pessimism is a toxic attitude and easily contributes to the rest of the toxic beliefs, behaviors, and habits described in Chapter 3. People prefer to be around others who are generally *positive* people who lean towards expecting the best and seeing the best in things. People don't want to be around *downers*, negative, toxic people who are always complaining and focusing on what is wrong. This is true of your friends, family, employers, clients, and colleagues. It's true of the people in your church. It's also true of the people that you're trying to reach with the gospel. It really hurts the witness of the Church when those who are still lost experience Christians as pessimistic, hopeless, depressed, anxious, and negative. You could speak for hours on end about the good news but if you *live the reality* of a person that does not feel the impact of the good news on the soul your witness will fall on deaf ears. After all, if you really had the keys to eternal life and inner peace of the soul would you still be a negative, pessimistic person? Do not underestimate the value of what I'm saying here. The early church rapidly exploded in growth because of the sheer joy experienced when people heard and received the good news and then spontaneously shared it with others. Examine your own thoughts, emotions, and habits, and extinguish any trace of pessimism you find in yourself. Realign your beliefs with the biblical truth about God's sovereignty. Take control of what thoughts you focus on. Shift your disposition to an optimistic one. And set your expectations for the future on the optimism of being used in wonderful, and maybe even surprising or unexpected ways for the Lord.

Psalm 118:24 This is the day that the LORD has made; we will rejoice and be glad in it.

Matthew 5:14 *[Jesus]* You are the light of the world. A city on a hill cannot be hidden. [15]Neither do people light a lamp and put it under a basket. Instead, they set it on a stand, and it gives light to everyone in the house. [16]In the same way, let your light shine before men, that they may see your good deeds and glorify your Father in heaven.

Phase	Optimism	Pessimism
Perspective	Glass is half-full (it could be empty)	Glass is half-empty (it could be full)
BELIEFS	All things work for good (Rom. 8:28)	Life is pain/suffering, no meaning to it
	God/Christ is sovereign, in control	Satan and demons are in control
	God/Christ/Life ultimately wins	Satan/Sin/Death seem to win right now
	Good ultimately triumphs over evil	Evil seems to triumph right now
FOCUS	Gratitude (grateful for what I have)	Ingratitude (about what I don't have)
	I'm Blessed, Called, Chosen, Saved	I'm Cursed (dealt a tough hand in life)
	Sin, Death, Pain will be destroyed	Sin, Death, Pain still exist right now
DISPOSITION	Feelings of Hopefulness	Feelings of Hopelessness
	Joy (regardless of what is wrong)	Depression (regardless of what is right)
	Peace (despite external hostility)	Anxiousness (despite available peace)
	There is potential good in everyone	There is potential evil in everyone
	They could love me/bless me back	They could hate me/harm me if I try
	Better to have love and lost...	Better to not try and not get hurt
EXPECTATION	Best is yet to come; Good is coming	Worst is yet to come; Bad is coming
	Hopeful to see the good of others	Anticipating to see the bad of others
	If bad happens, I'll survive and grow	When bad happens, it'll be even worse

l. Conqueror vs Victim Mentality

You need to think, believe—and feel—like a victor, rather than a victim.

Romans 8:35 Who shall separate us from the love of Christ? Shall trouble or distress or persecution or famine or nakedness or danger or sword? [36]As it is written: "For Your sake we face death all day long; we are considered as sheep to be slaughtered." [37]No, in all these things **we are more than conquerors through Him** who loved us. [38]For I am convinced that neither death nor life, neither angels nor principalities, neither the present nor the future, nor any powers, [39]neither height nor depth, nor anything else in all creation, will be able to separate us from the love of God that is in Christ Jesus our Lord.

When life sends us trials we will be tempted to believe we are a victim, and to feel like a victim. Sometimes this is a form of self-indulgence, to feel sorry for ourselves, to throw our own "pity party." By doing this, we can feel a sense of importance. It can actually make us feel *significant* to be the victim of someone or something. It's not a *good* form of significance but it is significance nonetheless. It is a human need to feel significant, important, like we matter, and if we're not meeting this need in a healthy way we will subconsciously meet it in an unhealthy way. Are you playing the victim? Do you identify as a victim? Have you struggled with something for a long time, and if so, has it become part of your identity? Reflect deeply on it—do you get a sense of significance out of it? Does it make you unique or different or special in some way to have dealt with it? It's important to identify this. To be empowered you will need to stop this pattern. As a beloved child of God, a beloved disciple of Christ, and an essential, unique, and important member of the Church, we have all the significance we need. Make sure that you get your need for significance met by this and other healthy and fruitful identities, values, and achievements.

Life can be cruel in a fallen world. We've all been victimized by someone or something. Maybe you've gone through such painful experiences that your victim mentality is fully warranted. In these instances most people will not fault you for feeling the way that you do. There is certainly a time and a place where it is okay to feel like a victim, to take your time processing the events that occurred, and to work through the emotions. You should not just push those thoughts and feelings to the corner of your mind and just try to "think positive." See Chapter 3, Section (N) where I talked about the harms of disassociation. You can do more harm than good by not processing those feelings, by not giving them to the Lord, by not getting the healing that you need. It is better to allow yourself to "think negative" if that means getting the help in counseling, therapy, or ministry necessary to receive healing first before moving on.

That being said, you need to make sure you're not *staying* in victim mode. If you were victimized in the past, or were to get victimized in the future, allow yourself to be weak with people you can trust, and go through the process of healing, but don't stay in that state. Take care of yourself in such a way that you're moving towards the goal of freedom of the mind and emotions. And then eventually graduate and enter the conqueror mindset again. In fact, you need to remember that it is *because* you're *already* a conqueror through Christ that you *will* conquer your victimhood. Aim to forgive those who sinned against you, just as your Heavenly Father forgave you for sinning against Him. Seek reconciliation with them—if possible, wise, and fruitful for you to do so. If not, just forgive them in your heart, and pray that God would bring them to a knowledge of the truth.

Even if how you were victimized legitimately warrants you to continue to feel like a victim, and people will indulge that, make sure that you're not subconsciously finding significance in it. Just because you may have a more legitimate reason doesn't mean that you're immune to hanging on to it longer just for this reason. We can have serious emotional traumas we claim to be unable to overcome, or even simple hangups or bad habits we claim to be unable to overcome, either can satisfy our need for significance. To be fully empowered for the advancement of the Kingdom of God you need to stop seeing yourself as the victim of sin, and see yourself as a conqueror of sin. You need to see the victim mentality as thoughts that we can choose to either believe or disbelieve, which then either bears the fruit of the emotions of a victim: depression, anxiety, phobias, pessimism, etc. or the fruit of the emotions of a conqueror: hope, joy, peace, confidence, boldness, and optimism. The choice is yours. Which will you believe and feed? There is no benefit in feeling like a victim long term. It can even open bad doors and lead to other toxic problems. But the one who chooses to trust in the Lord will be victorious. Take hold of this victory in your heart, and set your focus on it, and experience freedom in the soul, regardless of your past or your future circumstances.

"Everything can be taken from a man but one thing: the last of human freedoms - to choose one's attitude in any given set of circumstances, to choose one's own way." — Victor E. Frankl[4]

III. Words and Behaviors

So we've examined the thoughts we should have and not have, and the feelings we should have and not have, now let's put these things to practical action. In this next section, we will briefly survey eight different lifestyle behaviors that will help you to create and maintain the right atmosphere in your car. These actionable behaviors are to be an ongoing part of your lifestyle as ways to help keep your thoughts and emotions on the right track, focusing on the right things.

m. Prayer and Intimacy
Prayer, via intimacy with God, is the hallmark behavior of the Christian life.

Just as daily Bible reading (or listening), and Christian and/or worship music is another way to continually impress your thoughts with the thoughts of God, so is prayer. Prayer, at its core, is simply *communication with God.* It is you talking with God and God talking with you. Because of this it can happen at any time, in any place, whether verbally or silently, with a specific goal in mind or with no goal in mind. Prayer can take many forms: asking for help in some way, just sharing your thoughts or feelings, asking for wisdom or guidance, just saying thanks in gratitude, offering direct praise and worship, to discuss with God a difficult situation you're wrestling with, to intercede on the behalf of others' needs, or just to spend time in quiet reflection while inviting God to lay on your heart whatever He wants. The key thing is that the point of prayer is to develop the intimacy between you and God. You taking the time to talk with God, and to listen to Him talking to you, will develop your personal relationship. More important than *what* you say, is *how* you say, and *why* you say.

Prayer is communication with God. It is you talking with God and God talking with you.

Let me provide a few guidelines to effective prayer. The most important thing is not that you pray long; Jesus told us this was unnecessary. Our Father knows what we need even before we ask. It's also not necessary that we pray loud or aggressive, or so that others can hear our prayers and be impressed by them. Our motive in this case is pride through the admiration of others. This doesn't impress God. God wants our heart to be sincere. Your goal should be the conversation between us and Him, not the esteem of others. If your cries and pleas are loud and passionate, while genuine, sincere and from the heart, that's okay. *(Mt 6:5-18, Lk 11:1-13)* You need to forgive others who have sinned against you. Holding onto bitterness and unforgiveness can limit your prayer. *(Mt 5:23-24, 6:12-15; Mk 11:25)* You need to seek the Lord with all your heart, don't just "do it to do it." Be sincere. *(Jer 29:13, Deut 4:29)* You need to repent of your sins, and strive to be righteous, knowing that sin hampers your intimacy with God. *(Isa 59:2; Ps 34:15, 66:18; Lam 3:42-44)* You need to be concerned with the things that God cares about. You cannot serve yourself, neglect justice and those in need around you, and still expect God to bless you with abundance. That is wicked. *(Prov 21:13, Isa 58:1-7)* You need to have a healthy, reverent fear of the Lord. You can speak to the Father like your father; and Jesus like your king, brother, and best friend; but not like "your *homeboy.*" There needs to always be a reverence and a humility in your words and tone, that you understand that it is the God of the universe you're speaking to. Never get so comfortable that you forget that! *(Lk 18:9-14, Mt 8:8, Ps 51:16-17, Isa 1:15-17)* You need to push aside doubt and have faith in your prayer. Have faith in who God is and trust in what He has promised in His Word about prayer. *(Jam 1:6-7, Matt 21:21-22, Mk 11:22-24, Lk 7:1-10, Jn 14:12-14)* You need to ask with pure, godly motives, those led by the Holy Spirit. Sinful, selfish, or worldly-indulgence requests will not be honored. *(Jam 4:3-10)* God may choose to answer "No" or "Yes, but later" but we must have faith that He does hear our prayer, and that if it is in accordance with His will He will do it.

Prayer is not to be your last resort.
It should be your first response.

There are several ways to begin to incorporate prayer into your daily routine. That is great if you dedicate a period of time for prayer each day, but don't think that it's this or nothing. An easy way to get started is to pray for a few minutes before each meal. This is an easy-to-remember and convenient way to not only show gratitude for your sustenance, and ask God to bless it, but also to pray for things that have come up in the last few hours that are still on your mind. Your prayer doesn't need to be an hour long but you can still do better than a cookie-cutter, 4-second statement you've repeated a million times. Remember gratitude? Take a minute or two of sincerity to thank God for your provision. Not only the food itself, but the sun, rain, nutrients, and all the plants, animals, farmers, businesses, and technologies that made it possible to bring it to your plate. Reflect on the situations you just learned about on social media and pray for those in need. I use a daily calendar from *The Voice of the Martyrs* which helps me to pray for a different situation the global persecuted Church is dealing with every day. Invite and acknowledge God during your day. Ask God to guide your thoughts, emotions, footsteps, and interactions. If you have the time, sit in quiet reflection and ask God - "Who needs prayer?," "Who needs an encouraging phone call?," "How can I be or share Jesus with someone today?" God's always there. Remind yourself of this. It will strengthen your walk and you will find that talking with Him will get easier and more personal over time.

---

1 John 3:22 we will receive from Him whatever we ask, because we keep His commandments and do what is pleasing in His sight.

1 John 5:14 And this is the confidence that we have before Him: If we ask anything according to His will, He hears us.

n. Worship Way of Life
Worship is a way of life, an ongoing attitude and posture, to always have.

It bothers me when I hear churches reinforce the common belief that the only, or primary way, for believers to worship God is through a live musical performance. The only reason individual believers think this way is because churches are espousing it. It really is a shame that many churches have no budget for evangelism or missions because they have prioritized the Sunday "performance." This shift has not come from God, it has come from the influence of the popular secular entertainment culture on the church. And even if churches are only doing it to keep up with the wants of the people, they shouldn't be. The church is not here to cater to the worldly passions of people, they are to help influence them to replace those worldly passions in exchange for godly ones. Worship is the feeling or expression of reverence and adoration for God. Worship *can* be provided through shared participation in a live musical performance in a large gathering of people. But it can also be done silently and imperceptibly in the heart of a single individual on a park bench reflecting on who God is. Get away from thinking that if we aren't doing a big performance then we aren't worshipping God. Worship is not a shared and celebrated musical performance to God—but a shared and celebrated musical performance to God is worship. Did you catch that? We have to flip our understanding. Worship to God is not always music and singing, but music and singing to God is always worship. You can worship God through music and singing *sometimes*, but you should be worshipping God in other ways *always*.

Our worship has more to do with *who* and *why* and *what* we are doing than how. God is not impressed by our extravagance if our hearts are not engaged. Or if we're not worshipping Him in spirit and in truth. Jesus said in John 4:23-24, *"But a time is coming and has now come when the true worshipers will worship the Father in spirit and in truth, for the Father is seeking such as these to worship Him. God is Spirit, and His worshipers must worship Him in spirit and in truth."* This is worth mentioning because some of the so-called "worship" music in churches today is man-centered, rather than God-centered. Full of nice sounds, rhymes, and harmonious melodies, but full of empty platitudes and lacking in any real biblical truth or spiritual substance. More geared towards our desire to *be spiritual with* God, than to offer our worship *to* God. Of course, these things are not mutually exclusive, but we should embrace the former without neglecting the latter. God's Word tells us that worship should be accompanied with reverence, rejoicing, and trembling *(Ps 2:11, 96:9)*, with sacrifices of righteousness *(Ps 4:5)*, with extolling, praise, blessing, glory, and thanks *(Ps 22:22, 100:4, 107:32; Heb 13:15)*, which may include instruments, singing, or dancing *(Ps 149:3)*. In Matthew 15:1-9 Jesus rebuked the Pharisees for honoring God with their lips but worshipping Him in vain. Their worship was unacceptable because their hearts were far from Him, as were their doctrines. Jesus was quoting from Isaiah 29 here, where God was rebuking people who *live* one way, and then *worship* another way. This is why Jesus called the Pharisees in this interaction hypocrites. In Isaiah 29:15 God says, *"In darkness they do their works and say, "Who sees us, and who will know?"* Yet, God says of His redeemed in verse 23, *"they will honor My name, they will sanctify the Holy One of Jacob, and they will stand in awe of the God of Israel."* It's far more important that we know and glorify God—in spirit and in truth—and with the right heart, attitude, and posture, than to live one way that is contrary to God's nature, and then meet up to offer so-called worship extravagantly in church meetings.

The REAL worship we offer to God is what we do with the other 167 hours of the week!

We have to align our *daily* thoughts, emotions, and behaviors with that of worship to God. He is more glorified in our way of life, our ongoing attitude and posture towards Him, than He is in our scheduled appointments. Imagine if a husband told his wife, *"I'm going to do whatever I want the rest of the week but I'll give you one hour per week where I'll give you 100% of my focus. I'll even worship and sing to you during our appointment. I'm going to sleep with other people, and do a wide variety of activities you disapprove of during the week, but I'll be a perfect gentlemen during our appointments. Aren't you pleased by me for being so dedicated to our appointments? We have a great relationship."* Sounds ridiculous, right? Yet, many Christians think about God and worship this way. No, we are to worship God with our *entire* lives! This doesn't mean that we need to continuously sing lol! It means that we want everything we do to be pleasing to God. When we watch TV, listen to music, dance, play sports, go to the gym, eat a meal, clean the house, do yard work, drive our car, perform at work, walk the dog, watch a sunset, and anything else, we do it to the glory of God! It doesn't mean that we think about *only* God every second of the day, it means that every second of the day, regardless of what we're doing, we're doing something with God *in mind*. He may not be in the foreground at every moment, but we know He's still in the background and He's not unpleased with whatever we're doing. You're still only doing things that He would approve of, and in spirit, you're always aware of the fact He is still with you while you do them. You don't have to always, but you *could* think of or even talk to God, at any instant. This happens to me. I'll do something stupid, or some interesting thing will happen to me, and I'll give a chuckle and smile to God, as though He was in the room with me. A lifestyle like this is more like the husband who has a dedicated date with his wife where she gets all of his focus one day a week but the rest of the week he is still living in a way that would please her, and he always has her on his mind. Because the rest of the week is built up of many moments like this, their dedicated time together is much more significant and meaningful. Approach your relationship with God in such a way. Worship God as a lifestyle. Make every breath you take, and every word or deed you do, be an offering to God that pleases

Him. This means more to Him and it will to you too. Don't fall for the trap of thinking that your worship is lacking if you're not the most vocal or extravagant on Sunday, with hands raised the highest! Relationship and level of worship are about quantity and quality, and *both* of these are measured throughout the entire week. Then when you set aside time, in church on Sundays, or any other time during the week, to sing, praise, dance, prostrate yourself, or more exuberantly worship Him in any other way, it will be an activity that further reinforces the intimacy you already share. It will be like a special date night you look forward to every week, rather than the meaning and substance of your relationship.

Ephesians 5:19 Speak to one another with psalms, hymns, and spiritual songs. Sing and make music **in your hearts** to the Lord, [20]always giving thanks to God the Father for everything in the name of our Lord Jesus Christ.

Colossians 3:16 Let the word of Christ richly dwell within you as you teach and admonish one another with all wisdom, and as you sing psalms, hymns, and spiritual songs with gratitude in your hearts to God. [17]And **whatever you do**, in word or deed, do it all in the name of the Lord Jesus, giving thanks to God the Father through Him.

---

o. Repentance and Confession
Expect and encourage your beliefs and desires to change throughout your journey.

Remember when you first felt conviction of your sins? What about when you confessed out loud that you were a sinner? What about when you finally gave up one of those "lingering" or besetting sins? You know, those ones that stick around for awhile because you've deceived and convinced yourself it's not a *real* sin. What are yours? What are those things that the rest of the Church calls a sin but you're not ready to give it up yet?

For me it was pornography and abortion. I was raised by personally-conservative but politically-liberal parents. Most of my family falls into this category. I bought into the "pro-choice" lie for a long time. If you struggle with this topic some resources I recommend include (http://180Movie.com), the nonprofit *Live Action, Unplanned* movie. I also have a YouTube video playlist at (https://MPoweredChristian.org/YouTubeAbortion). Pornography was another area it took longer to convict me than it really should have. It wasn't until I really started to understand God's holiness, and value myself as the temple of the Holy Spirit, and see the bad fruit of that industry, which is full of sex trafficking, drug addiction, degradation of the meaning of sex, marriage, purity, etc. And the spiritual and emotional consequences of pornography on intimacy with God, leading to broken marriages, and uncontrollable lust. Even the physical consequences of the chemical alterations of the brain due to the rewiring of the neural networking and the physical addiction to the flood of the pleasure hormone dopamine. For a good secular resource on the harmful effects of pornography check out (https://FightTheNewDrug.org).

It has been many years since I've repented and changed my beliefs and behavior on these things and it all seems so black-and-white to me now. It's not a temptation at all. I just see them both as pure evil. But you might still be in the beginning or in the denial or excuse stages on these issues. Or you might struggle or still entertain something else entirely that is questionable. My point here is that we're always changing. Expect it and even encourage it. This is sanctification. We're *supposed* to keep growing and maturing in our understanding. As we grow closer to God we're supposed to keep improving our discernment to a greater degree, which will inevitably lead us to realizing that we've been doing or supporting things that are sinful. Listen to your brothers and sisters around you, learn from them, especially those more knowledgeable, experienced, older, or wiser than you. As someone who tends to walk to the beat of my own drum I've been guilty of being reluctant to hear people out when they disagreed with me, too. But we need to remain humble. We need to remain open and teachable.

Follow your conscience, yes, but also realize that your conscience is in the process of changing. Don't slow down its progress down through your arrogance or stubbornness. Listen to the Holy Spirit driving the car, not the old you still in the back trying to be a backseat driver! Remember, we do not naturally want to change. Change is painful. You have to *force* yourself to change because you see the value in it! For more on this see Section (A) of this chapter. My eyes were opened once I became dedicated to knowing and submitting to the truth—whichever direction that went. Maybe I'm right and the majority is wrong, maybe I'm biased or ignorant and wrong. Right or wrong didn't matter, what matters is what is true? So I didn't just do what I'd always done, or what *seemed* right, or what others around me thought. I *invested myself* into really going deep and exploring every side of the issues, really listening to the best defenses on each side, carefully weighing all of the arguments, and really praying into it. This is the behavior of people who really want to do what is right. This gives tremendous peace later because your conscience is not in constant conflict and you're not always second guessing your beliefs and behaviors. And this also gives tremendous confidence. That's empowering.

Lastly, don't just acknowledge your past sins, confess them. Confess them to God and ask for forgiveness, wisdom, healing, deliverance, courage, power—whatever you need. You can also confess them to other believers, not as though they were the one you sinned against, or like they're an intermediary you have to go through like Catholicism teaches. Rather, this is so that they can walk alongside you, praying for you, and strengthening and encouraging you in your new direction. Confession to God is so that those sins can be "officially" put under the blood of Jesus. Confession to others in the church is so that you can get support, fellowship, community. This is for your benefit and theirs.

Romans 10:10 For with your heart you believe and are justified, and with your mouth you confess and are saved.

1 John 1:9 If we confess our sins, He is faithful and just to forgive us our sins and to cleanse us from all unrighteousness.

James 5:16 Therefore confess your sins to each other and pray for each other so that you may be healed. The prayer of a righteous man has great power to prevail.

---

p. Word of Faith vs Biblical Faith
Eradicate every trace of Word of Faith; believe and practice only biblical faith.

During your journey you need to be reinforcing the right *thoughts* (Section I), the right *feelings* (Section II), and the right *behaviors* (Section III). I want to introduce you to an often subtle, false belief and behavior, that you may even be embracing right now, and that is combining your good biblical faith with "word of faith." I've heard different definitions of what "word faith" is so I will be detailing the beliefs I am referring to explicitly. Word of Faith theology distorts the map (see Chapter 1 for the true map). It also negatively influences what a person believes faith *is* (see Chapter 2, Section H) for more on what biblical faith is. And it can even radically distort who Jesus was and *how* and *why* He was able to perform the miraculous during His earthly ministry. Word of Faith theology can even influence what Christians believe they can do today and distort how we should think and live. This includes what we think about sickness, health, and prosperity, which we'll cover in some detail because these are the most prevalent forms today. Word of Faith theology is more than just a different *take* on historical Christianity, it actually shares common beliefs with the *False Spirituality* (Chapter 3, Section F) and *Counterfeit Jesus'* (Chapter 3, Section H) sections described in the previous chapter. In fact, it even finds its origins in these false and demonic belief systems! First we will look at a demonic spiritual philosophy called New Thought. It's here we see the clear contrast between it and a biblical worldview. It's important to realize that Word of Faith theology didn't originate anywhere in the Church. It's a spring that flows out of New Thought.

New Thought. "The Prosperity Gospel [Word of Faith] is built upon a quasi-Christian heresy known as the New Thought movement, an ideology that gained popularity in the late nineteenth and early twentieth century."[5a] So before we get to the modern forms of this theology it's important to understand where it came from. "American psychologist and philosopher William James noted in 1905 that New Thought drew not only from the Gospels but also from Hinduism, philosophical idealism, transcendentalism, popular science evolution, and the optimistic spirit of progress. New Thought was a mashup of pagan philosophies."[5a] Four influential figures emerge including Emanuel Swedenborg

(1688-1772), considered the grandfather of New Thought, who was a seventeenth century clairvoyant who claimed to have met God, the apostle Paul, the Reformer Martin Luther, and Moses. He believed he had the power to look into heaven, hell, and other dimensions of the spirit world. He rejected orthodox Christian beliefs, the Trinity, the deity of Jesus, and salvation by grace through faith alone.[5a] Then there was Phineas Parkhurst Quimby (1802-1866), the intellectual father of New Thought, who denied the deity and bodily resurrection of Jesus. He developed the idea of "mental healing," believing that "all disease is in the mind or belief" and the cure is to correct false reasoning is in the mind. Mary Baker Eddy, the founder of the Christian Science cult discussed in Chapter 3, Section (H), conducted healing classes based on his teachings.[5b] Then there

New Thought		Biblical Truth
Distorted View of God and Reality	• Pantheism, Panentheism (Ch. 3, E) • Rejection of the Holy Trinity (Ch. 1, C) • God is an impersonal life force or creative energy that must be harnessed in order to be successful • Universal laws govern the world/reality • Goal: Align mind with laws that govern reality	• Monotheism • Holy Trinity • God is personal & sovereign To be appealed to by prayer • God governs His creation • Align mind with God's mind
Elevation of Mind over Matter	• Thoughts are forces that can and do create reality • Thoughts, spirit, and mind are real • Physical world is an illusion • The reason people are unhealthy or unsuccessful is because of their negative thoughts • Think positive, visualize what you want, and you will create it in reality; Law of attraction • Humans are godlike, can change the future	• Thoughts are just thoughts • The body is real (Ch. 1, F) • The world is real (Ch. 3, E) • We don't always have control of circumstances • Results from actual effort, not thoughts, and God's sovereignty and blessing
Exalted View of Humans	• Humans are intrinsically good, spiritual beings • Humans are one with Infinite Spirit, to become more godlike through properly oriented thought • No mention of sin, fallen nature, or redemption • Human divinity is not related to being made in the image of God or the indwelling of the Holy Spirit	• Humans are fallen sinners • Humans are separate from God, restored only through faith in Jesus and the gospel • In Image of God (Ch. 1, F) • Must be Born Again (Ch. 2, D)
Focus on Health and Wealth	• Disease, lack of financial prosperity, and personal success is caused by negative thoughts in mind or misalignment with the "Infinite Divine" inside • Consistently, clearly visualize, think positive, have faith, speak right words, and it will change	• Disease, poverty, and evils are consequence of sin/fall • The meaning and focus of our life is greater than simple self-centered pleasures
Non-Orthodox View of Salvation	• Works-based Salvation (see Ch. 3, section F) • Salvation = process of learning to love neighbor • Salvation is a mystical, self-generated experience in order to receive health, wealth, success • Jesus was just a religious man whose spirit was raised from dead; not the only way to salvation	• Grace-by-Faith Salvation • Salvation is God rescuing us from Sin, Death, Hell, to have eternal life with Him • Jesus is the only Son of God • Jesus is the only Savior

Content borrowed heavily from the book Health, Wealth, and Happiness [5]

was Ralph Waldo Trine (1866-1958), an influential evangelist of New Thought, who was a universalist that believed every religion leads to God. Though he denied faith in and salvation through Jesus, and the uniqueness of the inspiration of the Bible, nonetheless his writings were popular among Christians. Books inspired by New Thought ideas include Napoleon Hill's *Think and Grow Rich* and Wallace D. Wattles's *The Science of Getting Rich.* Trine's work focused on helping people achieve health and success with "key recurring elements of the Prosperity Gospel: speaking the right words, invoking a universal law of success with words, and having faith in oneself."[5c] Lastly there is Norman Vincent Peale (1898-1993), a New York City pastor who readily admits that he had been influenced by various metaphysical teachers. His 1952 book, *The Power of Positive Thinking,* popularized New Thought ideas and techniques in America. According to David Jones, the director of the ThM program at Southeastern Baptist Theological Seminary, the five pillars of the New Thought movement include: (1) a distorted view of God, (2) an elevation of mind over matter, (3) an exalted view of humankind, (4) a focus on health and wealth, and (5) an unorthodox view of salvation.[5] These New Thought ideas are often taught using biblical words and justified by distorting Scripture. In this way Satan has deceived people and used them to distort biblical truth in the Church. See table for a brief overview of these pillars, and examples, in clear contrast with biblical truths.

A poison in the Church. New Thought is clearly demonic and not Biblical Christianity at all. But since these beliefs would be called New Age today, we're really focused on how that morphed into the modern Word of Faith beliefs. In some cases it's clearly just New Age with a Christian veneer, and should be totally rejected. But in other cases, it's biblical Christianity with small doses of this mixed in. When so, I believe it's a poisonous stream *within* the true Church. That's why I didn't address this as a false Christianity per se in Chapter 3 and consider it an "atmosphere" issue, rather than a "false religion" one. It could go either way, but I'll give all Christians the benefit of the doubt. Most of the time you'll find it's more like a false, toxic poison floating through the bloodstream of an otherwise potentially healthy believer. What determines whether or not it's a false Christianity, or just a false stream of beliefs *within* an orthodox Christianity is whether or not there's *so much of* this poison that they aren't a new car at all, rather than just a new car with a toxic passenger. Some "Christians" are still in an old car because their entire worldview is shaped by this counterfeit, whereas others have a biblical worldview and a bad passenger or open door because of these beliefs. But as Paul warned Timothy in 1 Timothy 4:16, *"Pay close attention to your life and to your teaching. Persevere in these things, for by so doing you will save both yourself and those who hear you."*

As we go through this section you might find that your church is a heavy proponent of these things, fully embracing a lot of them, in which case you might be best off finding a new church. But you might find that only one or two of these beliefs are embraced and they don't play a significant role. In this case, they're still present but there's minimal damage. This calls for knowledge, discernment, and wisdom. You want to make sure you're positioning yourself in a healthy environment and not unintentionally allowing yourself to adopt false beliefs or behaviors. They will negatively hinder your journey and the atmosphere of the day-to-day life in your car. If you've fallen for any of these beliefs, just study them carefully, test what I'm saying, compare it with Scripture. Once convinced it's wrong just repent and stop. Also, if you find these beliefs in others don't be quick to label them as not saved, or false prophets or teachers. Especially if they're not leaders, but lay members in your local church and are otherwise godly and biblical. I do know true believers who unfortunately haven't been convinced yet that these beliefs are just not biblical. I still consider them brothers and sisters. I think they have left themselves vulnerable to the enemy though because they're continuing to believe his lies, but they're still family! If others around you still believe this stuff, get to know why, love on them, and gently lead them to the full truth so they can walk in total victory!

History. Word of Faith theology comes in a variety of names including Word-Faith, Faith movement, positive confession, the "health and wealth" gospel, and prosperity gospel (a term that applies to a broad range of teachers). It has been derogatorily called the "name-it-and-claim-it" or "blab-it-and-grab-it" gospel. It's push of "faith-cure" teachings (the belief that faith is necessary for healing) has spread largely throughout the Pentecostal and charismatic world, especially through the "Latter-Rain" movement, a "healing" revival of the late 1940s and 1950s.[6] The movement has no one, specific denomination but its teachings have had a large and far-reaching impact influencing many Christian groups, churches, and individuals. Prominent figures include E.W. Kenyon, Kenneth Hagin, Kenneth and Gloria Copeland, Aimee Semple McPherson (founder of the International Church of the Foursquare Gospel, a major Pentecostal denomination), William Branham, Paul Crouch (and his TV network the Trinity Broadcasting Network), Joyce Meyer, Joel Osteen, Benny Hinn, and Fred Price.[6] Others include Bethel Church (Redding, CA), Bill Johnson, Todd White, Hillsong Church, T.D. Jakes, Paula White, Robert Tilton, and Creflo Dollar. A. B. Simpson (founder of the Christian & Missionary Alliance) has also been listed but there are important distinctions between classic faith and holiness leaders like Simpson and others in the modern movement.[67] Some emphasize Word of Faith beliefs more than others. I mention the above because they're all prominent figures with large followings, and ministries have identified them teaching some type of harmful Word of Faith belief. Some of the above are guilty more than others. Some seem genuine and who I otherwise like. They may even have good teachings in other areas but they're still wrong to spread these beliefs. But it's not my goal here to focus on them and what *they're* doing. Most of the global Church has been exposed to these beliefs, in one degree or another. They're provided as an example and head's up. What matters is exactly *what you* believe and why. I *do* believe in divine healing but not *every* belief about healing is biblical or fruitful. Desire pure, biblical truth so your faith and focus is rightly aligned!

"Unfiltered" Word of Faith. The table here outlines some of the characteristics of the "full strength" version of these beliefs. These are disturbing, but remember you're more likely to encounter *watered-down variations* of these beliefs that mix biblical truth with greater or lesser amounts of these errors. The modern Word of Faith movement is built upon New Thought teachings but with a greater degree of Christian veneer. If there was a faith spectrum, with New Thought on the far left, and biblical Christianity on the far right, Word of Faith is an ideology in the middle between the two. The majority of Word of Faith proponents today hold to mostly biblical Christian doctrines about God, Jesus, and salvation, while also trying to keep the beliefs about how we're supposed to have a life of health, wealth, and success. And this type of carnal worldly success, that is believed to be for us today, is received by directing our positive thoughts, words, and the New Thought reinterpretation of *what Faith is*. This understanding of "faith" has nothing to do with real biblical faith at all. The "faith" in Word of Faith is an entirely different concept, with an entirely different goal and focus. As prosperity preacher Kenneth Copeland said, "faith is a spiritual force, a spiritual energy, a spiritual power... There are certain laws governing prosperity in God's Word. Faith causes them to function."[5d] In this New Thought/New Age worldview it is faith (or belief in) spiritual laws, faith in yourself, or even faith in faith itself. This is in contrast to where your faith should be directed at: *faith in God*. In Chapter 2, Section (H) we explored biblical faith in detail. Please review this section for a deeper understanding of what faith is from a biblical perspective. The Bible does provide many examples of when a person was healed because of their faith. Some of these include Matthew 8:5-13, 9:19-22, and Mark 9:14-29. However, the object *of* their faith was always in Jesus and what He could do. It was their *trust in Him*, not trust in spiritual laws or principles. Faith is nothing if not directed at a reliable object of faith. I could have all the faith in the world that I can jump out of a plane with a parachute made of Legos, and fly; it doesn't mean I'll actually be able to! The faith that God desires is a faith that comes *from* Him to begin with. It's our own soul's *willing consent to trust in* God. It's the spiritual promptings of the Holy Spirit drawing us to trust in God. When we jump out of the plane our trust is in our parachute—Jesus. We don't have belief in spiritual principles of the universe. We have trust in a personal God.

**Faith is not a spiritual force to obtain what we desire.
Faith is trust. Trust in a personal God who is trustworthy.**

Prosperity Gospel. A major feature is better understood by the term "Prosperity Gospel." It's one of prosperity—not in the life to come—in *this* life. *This* is its focus. It's the *reason* to have the so-called faith. It's the desired object to put one's "faith" in. It's the desire to have everything you want in *this* life, and is thus motivated by greed and the carnal desires of the flesh. It's not about God, His glory, His will, or His Kingdom purposes. It's about humans, our glory, our will, and worldly purposes. If our purpose, desire, focus, and motivation in life is all about ourselves we have a very wrong map!

Doctrines	Word of Faith	Biblical Faith
Authority	There are "anointed" apostles and prophets today that God will punish if they are questioned or criticized.	The Bible is our chief authority, received from anointed and inspired apostolic eyewitnesses of Jesus and their followers.
God's words of faith	God has a *literal* mouth that He uses to speak "words of faith." The world was created only because He believed in His heart that whatever He spoke would come to pass.	God does not have a body. God created the world by simply *willing* it to happen. God does not have "faith," (confidence beyond what one can see). He is the proper object *of* faith. (Mk 11:22-24, Heb 11)
Human Words	Words, filled with faith, have power in-and-of-themselves, to create reality. This is a spiritual law.	Words are just verbal expressions of our beliefs and the intentions of the heart. *(Rom 10:10, Mk 7:20-23)*
Spiritual, not Material or Reasonable	Man is a spirit being, that possesses a soul and lives in a body. Knowledge of God or the Bible is only "spiritually understood," and truth "may even contradict human reasoning or physical evidence."	Man is not a spirit, but a material being *(Gen 3:19b, Isa. 31:3, 1 Cor 15:47-48)* that exists in a duality of body and soul or flesh and spirit. *(Mt 10:28, Rom 7:22-25)*. Human reason/logic are trustworthy *(Isa 1:18, 1 Pet 3:15, Acts 17:17)* in conjunction with faith, not in the absence of it. *(Heb 11, Prov 4:5-7)*
Humans were created to be gods	Humans were created in God's "class." Adam was created "the god of this world," a position legally transferred to Satan after the fall. Man's original status was "equality with God."	Humans were created in God's image, not His kind. We are not and never will be gods. *(Isa 43:10)* Adam wasn't legally god of earth, neither is Satan who is a rebel *counterfeit* "god" of this age. *(2 Cor 4:4)*
Believers are also God Incarnate	"The believer is as much an incarnation as was Jesus." Jesus lived as *a mere man* to pave the way for us to live like He did. Miracles came from the Holy Spirit, not Jesus.	Jesus is uniquely God incarnate. As God's only divine Son, He did what only God can do. The Father and Spirit worked through Jesus because the entire Trinity is involved in all of God's works.
Jesus was born again	Jesus died both physically and spiritually. He became sin, was separated from God, went to Hell and suffered in our place, and was then born again.	When Jesus died physically, He lived spiritually and went to Hades, the realm of the dead. He didn't literally become sin, He took upon Himself the consequences of sin. He never ceased being One with God.
We should speak words of faith like God	Words spoken in faith are inherently powerful. What we say, if we believe it, we get it. We should have mountain-moving faith, like God has, and call things into existence. We should claim to already possess, right now, what we want, even if our senses tell us otherwise.	Faith means trusting in God for the future, not claiming rights for the present. Faith is a spiritual gift *(1 Cor 12:8, 13:2)* and trust in God, not confidence in a spiritual law. *(Mk 11:22-24, Jn 14:1)* Faith is not denying our senses. Our words cannot make things real. Only God's word, unlike ours, always produces results.
God wants us to be healthy and wealthy now	Since Christ freed us from the curse of the Law, we are in principle now freed from all disease and poverty. Healing is assured in the atonement, we just have to "claim" the blessings. Failure to be healed or financially blessed is a result of a lack of faith.	Christ's redemption assures us of perfect health and wealth—in the resurrection. *(Rom 8:10-11, 23; 1 Cor 15:42-45)* Freedom from the curse means spiritual blessings now. *(Gal 3:13-16)* God heals people today when and as He chooses as a foretaste of those future blessings. *(Mt 8:16-17)*

Content borrowed heavily from Watchman Fellowship's *Word-Faith Movement Profile* [6]

Health and Wealth Gospel. It shouldn't even need to be said that God's desire is not that we live in extravagant wealth and indulgence. It's so unbiblical I'm not going to spend much time refuting it. If we read our Bible and have a heart for the lost and suffering we wouldn't even fall for it. It's antithetical to the gospel to have a self-centered life of indulgence. I want to cover the side more common today: health. They claim it's *never* God's will for us to experience illness, and if we do it's because we don't have enough faith and didn't "claim" the blessings available to us. So not only is it all about us, but God wants us to invest more dedication into our faithful focus on ourselves. It's *so* backwards! It's also taught that there is *no* good that can come from illness; it's always a bad thing, always the enemy. This isn't true and it leads to sick people believing they don't have enough faith and feeling desperation, or hopelessness, or that God doesn't love them. Prosperity preachers also teach that illness is an illusion and sick people are told not to even believe that they are sick. So Christians are willfully living in pure denial, and not getting the medical help they need. They also aren't using the illness however they can for God's glory and seeking Him throughout it. They're not even seeking Him in prayer for healing because, after all, they aren't *really* sick! It's a warped and twisted false thinking.

Illness is real. Because of sin the world is under a curse of death since the Fall. Humanity, which is a part of the physical world, is also under this curse of death. And every form of degradation and decay, including all illness, is an aspect of death. Illness is only possible because things break down, and there are harmful things that exist to cause these breakdowns. As long as we live in the physical body this side of the resurrection, we're subject to this. We need to learn how to give God glory through these trials, and let God use them to mold us into the image of Christ, rather than avoid and ignore these realities. Prosperity teachers never address the fact that every single human *still dies.* If we're to be fully healed of every illness today, because of what Jesus accomplished on the cross, then we should also not experience *any form* of death. Not just in the resurrection and the life to come, we shouldn't die—at all—if we were meant to receive *every* benefit in *this* life. But we still experience death, every single day we get older and our flesh decays a little bit more. *Age itself* is the evidence that all bodily healing isn't available to us immediately. Not a single prosperity preacher didn't age. If every benefit of the cross was to be immediately received through faith we wouldn't experience *any* of the consequences of sin, not *just* illness. *Death* will be the *last* enemy destroyed. *(1 Cor 1:26)*

Spiritual healing is available now. Isaiah 53:5 is often quoted by prosperity preachers. It reads, *"But He was pierced for our transgressions, He was crushed for our iniquities; the punishment that brought us peace was upon Him, and by His stripes we are healed."* The healing that Christ purchased for us is interpreted as: (1) physical healing, and (2) healing which we are to receive immediately—but only if we have enough faith in this. Here the emphasis is not on trusting in Jesus and the crucifixion for *salvation*, but on trusting in our physical healing, as though *this* was the purpose for which Jesus was crucified. But since there's still sickness in the Church it's taught that this is only because people don't have enough faith. They aren't thinking positive enough! If anyone has ever told you this, I'm sorry. It isn't true. You may have a very strong faith and a deep, persevering trust in Jesus, and a great relationship with Him, and *still* experience the hardships of living in a fallen world. Prosperity preachers try to argue that illness is always bad so God would never allow His children to become ill. Have you ever stopped to ask why they stop *there*? Why only illness and disease? The truth is because that's the *only* aspect of New Thought beliefs that can even be partially defended using any part of the Bible. Of course they still have to ignore most of the Bible to do it. But if only good things happen for true believers in the New Covenant why stop at disease? If God has guaranteed us total prosperity, and is willing to cure every disease, then why would He continue to allow us to get old? Why would He continue to let our bodies get arthritic, sluggish, and feeble? Why would He allow our minds to become less sharp and our memory and talents to diminish? Why would He still allow car accidents, tsunamis, tornados, home invasions, theft, abuse, murder, etc.? The Bible tells us that in the end there will be an increase in natural disasters, famine, pestilence, persecution, war, violence, etc. And for 2,000 years millions of Christians have endured persecution and martyrdom. Why would illness that kills God's people be somehow given this special pass from being a part of God's plan, but not martyrdom that kills God's people? Because it isn't true! Prosperity in this life is not guaranteed for us. Healing of the body in this life is not guaranteed for us. The biblical truth is that the healing the prophet Isaiah is referring to is *primarily spiritual* in nature. This passage is about the *forgiveness of sin.* Peter even told us this explicitly. The healing we receive through the gospel is not primarily physical, but spiritual. The healing we receive is primarily the forgiveness of sin, and our restoration to God, so that we might die to sin and live to righteousness.

---

1 Peter 2:24 He Himself bore our sins in His body on the tree, so that we might die to sin and live to righteousness. "By His stripes you are healed."

Is healing guaranteed in the New Testament? Nowhere do we find teachings like "the only reason you're still sick is because you lack faith that all illness has been dealt with already." Another biblical reason we know the Isaiah 53 prophecy was not intended to teach us all sickness was immediately abolished by the gospel is because there's many examples of people with great faith, even those with the gift to heal sickness in others, who *still* experienced sickness in the New Testament. Timothy still had frequent stomach illnesses *(1 Tim 5:23)*, and Paul had to leave Trophimus sick in Miletus. *(2 Tim 4:20)* Paul also suffered from poor eyesight that never fully recovered 100% after being blinded on the road to Damascus. This is what led him later to rely on Luke, the doctor, as his traveling companion, and for people to write for him. See (https://MPoweredChristian.org/Pauls-Thorn) for why I believe his poor eyesight was Paul's thorn in the flesh that he mentioned in 2 Corinthians 12:7. Even if you disagreed with me about what Paul's thorn was, no one can deny this passage contradicts the premise of the Prosperity Gospel. The entire point he is making is that he asked God to heal him of it three times and God told him *"No, my grace is sufficient for you."* God's reply was that his infirmity and trial was *part* of His plan for Paul's life. Paul goes on to share what he's learned from this experience. He now delighted in his weaknesses and difficulties, for the sake of Christ. This is the polar opposite of the Prosperity Gospel, which says that it is always God's will for us to happy, healthy, and wealthy, and to have a life of comfort. If it was important that Paul learn this lesson then it's important for us to learn it too! There *are* spiritual benefits to relying on God's grace during trials, including illness. Let's seek the long term fruit of letting God use hardships to make us more like Jesus, more than just the gain of immediate healing. Rather, let's earnestly plead for the latter without neglecting the benefit of the former!

---

2 Corinthians 12:7b So to keep me from becoming conceited, I was given a thorn in my flesh, a messenger of Satan, to torment me. [8]Three times I pleaded with the Lord to take it away from me. [9]But He said to me, "My grace is sufficient for you, for My power is perfected in weakness." Therefore I will boast all the more gladly in my weaknesses, so that the power of Christ may rest on me. [10]That is why, for the sake of Christ, I delight in weaknesses, in insults, in hardships, in persecutions, in difficulties. For when I am weak, then I am strong.

God does heal today, but doesn't always. The only universal, unchanging laws are those governed by God's own character. Spiritual *principles,* things generally true like "you reap what you sow," are subject to His will and they are true, but only in the *absolute* sense, not in the relative sense. In other words, they're true in the end, when all is said and done. There *are bad* people, who may receive good things in this life, but their end will be awful. And there *are good* people, who may suffer in this life, but their end will be joyous. So they *do* reap what they sow, but only in the final analysis, not necessarily during their earthly life. I *do* agree that Jesus's stripes *do* heal us physically, as well as spiritually. Jesus's atonement did accomplish everything needed to redeem us from every consequence and restore us to fullness and blessing in every possible way. But it's one thing to believe that, and trust in receiving that fullness in the resurrection and the life to come, and thinking we're guaranteed it now. If God heals today—and I do believe He still does—it's a generous gift and wonderful blessing; a gracious foretaste of the life to come. A gift to bless us and help encourage us to continue our story, or perhaps as *part* of our story. Job's illness season was the pinnacle of his testimony. So also was the paraplegic, the girl who bled for 18 years, and Moses's sister Miriam's leprous hand. But so was Stephen's martyrdom. We *should* keep asking for healing! We *should* have faith that God answers prayer! He *is* a good Father who gives good gifts to His children. But He never guarantees it to us. We're still sinners being saved by grace. And it's technically just. We shouldn't say we deserve to suffer *nothing* for our sins. If we suffer we share in Christ's suffering. God may hear our prayer and answer "no" or "not yet." We need to be okay with that, and trust in Him that there's a *good reason* for it. *That* is real faith— trusting in God even when things are difficult! Real faith is not believing in spiritual laws in order to get whatever we want in life. What's hard about that? What selfish, unsaved, wicked person is unwilling to do that? Who would be unwilling to believe, if all they had to do was believe and then they would receive whatever they believed for? If it were actually true it would be very easy to subscribe to that. It's the desire to be your own god. No, this is selfishness disguised as faith by Satan. Biblical faith is trusting in God, and in the gospel, and in all of God's promises, especially when it's difficult to do so.

GOOD PURPOSES of ILLNESS (and most forms of trials and suffering)	
1. To Increase Our Righteousness	Illness is part of the curse of death, which comes as a result of sin. 1 Corinthians 11:30 teaches illness / weakness can be a consequence of sin by receiving Communion with God without examining ourselves first. Illness can remind us of the necessity of always being godly and righteous.
2. To Increase Our Sanctification	Illness can be caused by demons and point to areas of spiritual defilement. Luke 13:16 teaches illness can be caused by Satan's access into a person's life. It's easier to procrastinate spiritual growth than physical health. Illness can cause us to be more deliberate in our efforts to be fully free and holy.
3. To Develop Our Relationship with God	It's easier to focus on worldy things than our relationship with God. Job 42:1-6 teaches illness emphasizes our weakness and vulnerability and need for God. Illness often causes us to take our eyes off of temporary worldly things and draw near to God for eternal things, meaning, and hope.
4. To Increase Our Spiritual Maturity	As 2 Corinthians 12:7-10 teaches, illness can help us learn to rely less on ourselves and more on God's grace. Think of how illness can help us become more like Christ by forcing us to dig deeper, grow, and mature.
5. To Glorify God In Perseverance	God is glorified in our desire to persevere in obedience to Him and by our trust in Him and in His promises. Our endurance through illness, while still loving Him and remaining faithful is a form of worship. (Unique Experience)
6. To Glorify God in Healing	Illness may be allowed specifically for the sole purpose of glorifying God by healing it. John 9:1-3 teaches God allows the consequences of sin to be used for good this way. Acts 5:16, 8:7 teach illness causes people to seek the Church for physical healing finding also spiritual healing, eternal life.
7. To Glorify God in Deliverance	Mark 16:17, Acts 5:16 and 8:7 teaches demons can cause illness and can be cast out by Jesus's followers. Illness can cause people to seek the Church to find healing. By exposing demons as real, and Jesus's authority over them, they can receive healing and the gospel for freedom and eternal life.
8. To Build Unity in Love and Maturity in the Church	James 5:13-18 teaches that healing happens when we come together to support, encourage, counsel, minister to, lay hands on, and pray for the healing of one another. Illness can be a tool that reinforces the necessity of, and greater blessings in, our unity in love and service to one other.

God doesn't enjoy us suffering any more than we do. He loves us. He didn't love Jesus's suffering on the cross either, but there was a greater purpose to it. As Section (J) explains Romans 8:28 says *all* things work together for the good. Illness is included in the "all things." God allows bad things that bear good fruit in the long run. There *are* benefits of illness and there are good reasons God allows it in this life. I'm not saying illness itself is good - it's not. I'm saying God can *use* illness for good. *Empowered* Christians recognize this tough truth. You definitely can and should pray for and believe in healing from God. You should also take advantage of every medical solution; that's good stewardship of the body. But you can't allow yourself to fall into despair if you or a loved one falls ill. God is sovereign and in control and if He decides to not heal it then we need to know there's a higher good to it, and we can, should, and need to, glorify God *through* it! Do this and you take away one more thing that Satan can use against you to damage your faith and the atmosphere of joy in your car! No, even in sickness, the joy of the Lord is our strength!

Suffering isn't good, but God uses suffering for good.

Illness can help our personal growth. The first four points in the table are all related to ways God can utilize illness to help us grow into the image and likeness of Jesus. These include: (1) increasing our righteousness, (2) increasing our sanctification, (3) developing our personal relationship with God, and (4) increasing our spiritual maturity. Illness is ultimately a consequence of the curse of sin. Just because we get sick doesn't mean that *we* have sinned, and are being punished for that specific sin. As in commit-a-sin-get-a-disease, never-sin-never-get-sick. We can all get sick regardless of how righteous we're being because we live in a fallen world and the body is still predisposed to decay. This isn't a direct causation, but it is a correlation. We need to be righteous anyway, illness can just help reminds us of this. Throughout the Old Testament God constantly used illness as punishment for sinning in His presence. If you doubt this just read Deuteronomy 28 where God describes the blessings of obedience and the curses of disobedience.

In 1 Corinthians 11:30 some in the church were eating and drinking the Lord's Supper in an unworthy way and Paul tells them that is why many of them were weak and sick, and why some have died. In James 5:13-18 the confession of sin, anointing with oil, and the earnest prayers of a righteous person offered in faith will restore the one who is sick. So, yes, you should rule out sin first. The same is true of the second point, it can help in our pursuit of holiness and sanctification; the third point, the strengthening of our relationship with God; and the fourth point, our growth into spiritual maturity. If you're living in willful sin you need to repent, confess your sins to God, restore your fellowship in the Body of Christ, trust in the gospel, and draw near to God. It's always possible God has loved you enough to allow sickness in your body to be a warning for you. Using it to help you realize there is a deeper spiritual problem that needs to be addressed. Sickness, in this regard, is not a curse, it's actually a blessing. It's an unpleasant experience that reminds us of our own mortality and can serve as a wake up call for us to get right with God and to meditate on Heaven and Hell.

Illness also has the potential benefit of helping us become more like Jesus. How? Jesus took on our human nature, our weaknesses, our infirmities, to become like us in every way, yet without sin. *(Heb 4:15)* One of the reasons He did this was to have a greater understanding of what we go through, by actually participating in the same struggle. Jesus calls us to "bear one another's burdens." *(Gal 6:2, 1 Cor 9:21)* How much more can we empathize with others' pain by experiencing our own. Illness is humbling. See Chapter 2, Section (G) for more on the necessity of humility. Illness helps us remain humble and to learn to lean into God and to trust in God, more than ourselves. As we examined in Chapter 1, Section (M), becoming like Christ is the chief goal, and enduring illness the way God would have us do has the potential to help us develop these attributes.

Illness can be used to glorify God directly. The remaining four points illustrate ways God can use illness to glorify Himself. The first is through the perseverance of His saints who love and obey Him through their trials. The best example of this point is Job, who's trial through illness and suffering is recorded in detail in the book of Job. God is glorified through the process of Job who never gives up faith in Him or curses His name. Job is an example to us of how we can prove to be faithful servants through our trial too. Satan's accusation in the first chapter was that Job only loved God because of the many blessings he had received. Satan charged that Job would curse God if he were to fall ill and lose his abundant prosperity. God responded with allowing him to take away his health and prosperity in order to test Job. God knew His heart and was confident that Job would persevere in his faith until the end. The very lesson that the book of Job was designed to teach us, the Satanic "Prosperity Gospel" tries to steal away from us.

The next two ways God can use illness to glorify Himself include: healing and delivering people. We need to always ask for healing because sickness may occur merely because God has allowed it to so that He could heal someone later for His own glory. An example of this is in John 9:1-3: *"Now as Jesus was passing by, He saw a man blind from birth, and His disciples asked Him, "Rabbi, who sinned, this man or his parents, that he was born blind?" Jesus answered, 'Neither this man nor his parents sinned, but this happened so that the works of God would be displayed in him.'"* So it's possible God will heal you, and that's exactly *why* you're sick—so that God could heal you, in the name of Jesus, and through your testimony be glorified in you! Of course if you are healed you are being called to evangelize and proclaim your testimony from the roof tops alongside the gospel. Here sickness is not a detriment, because of sin or lack of faith, but is rather an intentional opportunity for you to glorify God, and point people to Jesus, through your own unique healing story. An example of this in the early church is recorded in Acts 3, with the healing of the lame man becoming the springboard for Peter to proclaim the gospel to all the people in Solomon's Colonnade. Another reason for illness could be demonic oppression. Satan can oppress people, even godly people, and afflict them with illness. An example of this is the woman in Luke 13:16, who Jesus calls *"a daughter of Abraham whom Satan has bound for eighteen years."* This type of illness is not one that believers should seek to endure through. As we read in Luke 10:19-20 and Mark 16:17-18, Jesus's disciples have been given power and authority to cast out demons and heal the sick. God is glorified in the act of healing and delivering and in being a healer and deliver. And when we're healed and set free from oppression we also glorify Him with our gratitude, praise, and worship. And since healing and deliverance most commonly happens in conjunction with the rest of the Body of Christ these assist in the next.

Illness can be used to develop and expand God's Kingdom. Here the previous purposes all come together in harmony. The Church brings the gospel to people, many of whom may be sick and/or demonized, calls them to repentance, casts out their demons, and prays and lays hands on them for healing. If they're healed or delivered it's within the context of salvation through faith in Jesus and within His Church! Then in fellowship with the Church they continue to grow in their relationship, righteousness, sanctification, and spiritual maturity. Illness also has the characteristic of being a mutual enemy. Since it's always bad to be sick, we can unite in love against it. This provides servants of Christ the opportunity to love, serve, and care for the sick. Since people *can* get sick the Body of Christ *can* care for those who do. Which is actually *more* glorious to God? God healing someone with a contagious disease—or a person who's so driven by love for God they risk getting it to care for that person? I certainly pray for the former, but there's tremendous beauty in the latter. What a love! And this isn't a hypothetical scenario, it's the testimony of millions of Christians throughout the centuries. During the Black Plague and other pandemics the Church showed the love of Christ to the suffering this way. People came to Jesus because they saw genuine love through His people. It's okay to desire you, your loved ones, and everyone else for that matter, to be healthy, and to keep praying for this. I want to be healthy too! But if God permits illness by saying "no" to our prayers, it's for a good reason. It means our calling is to *use* it. It can benefit each of us individually as we grow in perseverance and become more like Christ, and be used for the continued growth of the Church. As we serve those in need, in the name of Jesus, we expand the Kingdom of God and we give the lost world what they really need: Jesus. And their primary need for Jesus is not their worldly needs but the redemption of their souls and life eternal with God. We can be a reflection of a joy and hope, when it makes no sense to the world to have joy and hope. They can see in us "the peace of God, which surpasses all understanding." *(Phil 4:7)* Don't let the false Prosperity Gospel keep you from fully making the best use out of a bad situation and attaining all of these benefits.

The Prosperity Gospel is not only false, it's in direct opposition to our true calling, as cross-bearing disciples.

Christianity is a God-focused religion; the Prosperity Gospel is a man-focused religion. Christianity points people to their need for Jesus; the Prosperity Gospel points people to *"the lust of the eyes, the lust of the flesh, and the pride of life."* 1 John 2:15-17 says these things are not from the Father, but from the world, and they are passing away. We're not to love these things. Don't let the atmosphere of your car be directed by *this* kind of faith, and focus your thoughts, beliefs, feelings, and behaviors on *these* kinds of ambitions. Think positive, focus on the glass as half full, and always be optimistic and eager to love and serve. However, don't do so *because* you believe thinking positive aligns you with spiritual laws so you can get more in this life. Do these for the right reason and heed the warnings in Matthew 6:19 and 13:22; 1 Timothy 3:3, and 2 Timothy 3:2. Fully embrace the peace, joy, contentment, and hope life with Christ and set your eyes on the life to come. Let your faith be based on trust in God, not trust in spiritual principles of prosperity.

---

1 Timothy 6:6 Of course, godliness with contentment is great gain. [7]For we brought nothing into the world, so we cannot carry anything out of it. [8]But if we have food and clothing, we will be content with these. [9]Those who want to be rich, however, fall into temptation and become ensnared by many foolish and harmful desires that plunge them into ruin and destruction. [10]For the love of money is the root of all kinds of evil. By craving it, some have wandered away from the faith and pierced themselves with many sorrows.

[11]But you, O man of God, flee from these things and pursue righteousness, godliness, faith, love, perseverance, and gentleness.

---

q. Rebuking the Enemy
You've been given the name and authority of Christ—use it against our adversary.

When Satan attacks, how do you respond? Attacks may be in the form of tormenting demonic oppression, as thoughts of false beliefs, or as toxic emotions. Whether a season of ongoing obvious attacks, or the occasional subtle attack, your response should be the same. He must be totally rejected and given no consideration at all. Respond to false thoughts with trust in the truth of God's Word. His accusations need to be dismissed. Accusations must be responded to with confidence in Jesus, the gospel, and your right standing with God because of it. Toxic emotions, which often accompany toxic thoughts trying to take us to a dark place, need to be cast away. Those thoughts and feelings need to be responded to, again, with faith in Jesus, the gospel, and your new identity as a born again child of God. Satan needs to win in the mind before he can win in our beliefs. And he needs to win in our beliefs before he can win in our emotions. And he needs to win in our emotions before he's able to establish a foothold there. And he needs a foothold there before he can establish a stronghold there to dominate in the future from. Get good at recognizing his attacks on each of these levels and fighting back against each of them in the name of Jesus and he will have no viable points of access in you.

How much power do we have over Satan? Jesus has all authority. In Matthew 28:18 Jesus says, *"All authority in heaven and on earth has been given to Me."* In Christ, we have as much as we need to be victorious, but we must have the faith necessary to access it and be deliberate in our desire to exercise our authority over him. If we don't, he will exploit our ignorance, fear, and faithlessness. During deliverance ministry sessions with clients, we include several activities that help identify how Satan has infiltrated a person's life, expose it, and remove it. These include curse breaking; identification, confession, and renunciation of sins; correction of false beliefs, teaching of biblical doctrine, pastoral counseling, inner healing, worship, declarations, Scripture, and biblical life coaching and guidance. Some deliverance ministries, what we might call "deliverance lite," focus on low-level demons, ones that might go by names like "anger, depression, addiction, or lust." They may cast them out using prayer without actually talking to them. This isn't bad, it's the easier way to go and probably the first thing to try. But there are deeper levels than these, demons whose name and assignment may be directly connected with demonic principalities, and other spiritual powers, who have greater power and influence. Powerful, life-controlling strongholds need to be exposed, unpacked, and dismantled. The method I was trained in by Reverend Bob Larson involves direct confrontation with demons. We do what Jesus did. We call them up to the host's consciousness, command them to reveal who they are, how they got there, how long they've been there, and what enables them to stay there. A well known conversation Jesus had with a demon is the demoniac of the Geresenes, recorded in Luke 8:26-33. Lest you think only Jesus had this ability, the seventy-two disciples in Luke 10:17 also testified that demons *submitted to them* when they confronted them in the name of Jesus. Jesus confirms this in verse 20. If demons *submitted* that means they were also confronted. As you might imagine, this isn't always a pleasant conversation; it's more like a terrorist interrogation. Demons are like parasites that don't want to leave their hosts and will resist unless thrown out. Sometimes the struggle is explosive. I'm not teaching you this so you'll rush out to do it; deliverance is an advanced area of ministry. It requires spiritual maturity and isn't for the faint of heart. Just you knowing it exists and is actually a lot more common than most people think, puts you ahead of the curve. It could even be happening to you, or people you know, often without them even realizing it. Unless we actually consider demons as a possibility and then diagnose it, we don't know if our illness, sinful thoughts, toxic emotions or behavior are actually being influenced by demonization. It's easier to just say "everyone deals with this" or "it's just the flesh." Anyways, I mention all this here because once you deal with demons *directly* you realize rebuking their thoughts and feelings is child's play. Once you've won a battle in a direct confrontation, and see them squirm under the power and authority of Jesus, it builds your confidence and puts things in perspective. The people who fear Satan the most are those who know and trust Jesus the least. But you don't have to experience a deliverance in order to believe and live with this truth: Satan and the demons are no match for Jesus! It's not even a fair fight! And if you need a little boost of confidence, check out Revelation 19:19-20 and 20:9-10 to see just how quick the final battle is!

So do all of Jesus's disciples have the authority to rebuke and cast out demons? Yes. Is it limited to only the "anointed?" No. Only those who went to seminary? No. Only those who are ordained ministers? No. Only those who have a job at a church? No. Only those with a special gift from the Holy Spirit? No. It's true of every person that's been born of God. The authority comes from Jesus, and it's received by anyone with the Holy Spirit in them. I teach every client this and they're taught to begin exercising authority over Satan themselves. The Church shouldn't rely on deliverance ministers exclusively. We're only shepherds and teachers, facilitators and mediators helping assist the Body to build up their own faith in Jesus. We work *together* to cast out, or to fight against, the attacks of Satan. I like that it's this way because our goal is not only to set people free. Our goal is to make disciples of Jesus and to advance the Kingdom of God. That means teaching you how to fish for yourself, so you can eat for a lifetime, not just giving you a fish so you can eat for a day. Learn to get free and stay free and help others do the same.

Ephesians 1:20 which He exerted in Christ when He raised Him from the dead and seated Him at His right hand in the heavenly realms, [21]far above all rule and authority, power and dominion, and every name that is named, not only in this age, but also in the one to come.

Luke 10:17 The seventy-two returned with joy and said, "Lord, even the demons submit to us in Your name." [18]So He told them, "I saw Satan fall like lightning from heaven. [19]See, I have given you authority to tread on snakes and scorpions, and over all the power of the enemy. Nothing will harm you. [20]Nevertheless, do not rejoice that the spirits submit to you, but rejoice that your names are written in heaven."

Mark 16:17 And these signs will accompany those who believe: In My name they will drive out demons...

Acts 5:16 Crowds also gathered from the towns around Jerusalem, bringing the sick and those tormented by unclean spirits, and all of them were healed.

Ours is a *spiritual* battle. I've heard stories of abuses of people dealing with demons. Ungodly people (identifying as Christians) who take it upon themselves to try to cast out demons by hitting or kicking them out of people, burning them, screaming or spitting at them, nearly drowning them in holy water, etc. These, and every other extreme external method are not only ineffective and unhelpful, it's downright demonic itself. As Ephesians 6 describes our struggle is *not* against flesh and blood, and we do not fight our enemy using physicality. Our weapons are spiritual and faith-based. Any person with a demon in them is an innocent victim any approach taken is to be gentle, loving, respectful, and considerate to the host person. This is what Jesus modeled, this is the heart of the true Church. It's possible to get aggressive, verbally and symbolically with the demon inside, but only once it has manifested and you know you're talking to a demon. However, care must be taken not to harm the host person in any way. The same is true in your own fight against the enemy. Don't beat yourself up either! This is a spiritual battle, it must be won in the spiritual realm, fighting with spiritual weapons. No amount of harm afflicted in an external way is going to help. Forget the horror movies, they're full of lies. The Bible, and the heart of God, is where our methodology comes from. If you are suffering from a demonic attack don't hurt yourself. You don't need to punish yourself, or do penance to atone for your sins. Take care of and love yourself. Jesus loves you. He already paid for your sins on the cross. Fight against Satan the way Jesus and the early church did: through faith in Jesus, in the gospel, in His authority and power, and in God's Word. This is how you'll win the war, and how you'll win each battle.

Have righteous decorum. When you're fighting or resisting some type of demonic attack, or even when talking or posting memes about Satan, demons, etc. always have *decorum*: a dignified and respectful propriety of behavior. We're a representation of God and must always do what's good, righteous, and proper. Some act like Jesus taught we should love one another, and even our enemies, but when it comes to demons we can be vile and vindictive towards them. I'm not saying we should love them, I'm saying we need to wage war in a self-controlled, righteous way. Yes, they're fallen beings, are in rebellion to God, and are doing evil and hurting people. But isn't that true of our earthly enemies too? It is. Now, demons are beyond repentance, so we're not using decorum in the hopes that they will repent and be saved. They're permanently lost and beyond salvation, but that doesn't mean we need to act demonic ourselves *towards* them. It's not about them, it's about who we are. Rebuke their lies, accusations, and toxic feelings. Embrace Jesus's authority that He allows us to borrow and use it to command them to obey our interrogation and then leave. Let's heed the warning in Jude 1:4-11 about our *attitude towards* demons. Jude wrote that it was *ungodly unsaved* people in his day that slandered demons. He said that their arrogant behavior was just as wicked, wrong, and ungodly as the demons'. Verse 9 says, *"But even the archangel Michael, when he disputed with the devil over the body of Moses, did not presume to bring a slanderous charge against him, but said, "The Lord rebuke you!"* He also warns us not to be arrogant in our own supposed authority. Let us exercise our authority over evil without losing our humility. Interestingly enough, in Zechariah 3:2, when God Almighty Himself is rebuking Satan, He also says the same phrase: *"And the LORD said to Satan: "The LORD rebukes you, Satan! Indeed, the LORD, who has chosen Jerusalem, rebukes you! Is not this man a firebrand snatched from the fire?"* It is good for us to say likewise. Always fight the good fight in ways that will glorify God! What exactly *is* a rebuke? A rebuke is simply a reprimand, an admonishment, or an intent to correct a fault using a stern reproof. It's confident, direct, bold, and firm, but it's not vicious, malevolent, sadistic, or violent. It's not wild, emotionally erratic, distempered, or full of curse words. Your rebukes to Satan (and all demons) should resemble the calm, orderly, and precise ways Jesus rebuked Satan:

Matthew 4:7 Jesus replied, "It is also written: 'Do not put the Lord your God to the test.'" [10]"Away from Me, Satan!" Jesus declared. "For it is written: 'Worship the Lord your God and serve Him only.'"

Matthew 16:23 But Jesus turned and said to Peter, "Get behind Me, Satan! You are a stumbling block to Me. For you do not have in mind the things of God, but the things of men."

---

r. Activations and Declarations
Warfare prayer isn't preparation for the battle against Satan, it *is* the battle.

Activation. To activate something means to do something to trigger it to run, or to set it in motion. A biblical example of this principle is found in 1 John 3:18 which says, *"Little children, let us love not in word and speech, but in action and truth."* It's not only the desire or decision to love, or even saying loving words, but the actual loving *actions* that matter most. If you were to move from just *believing in* loving others, to actually *doing* love towards others, this would be an activation of your love. You'd be activating your desire to love by putting it into action. The same is true if we're told to have faith, to share the gospel, to seek higher spiritual gifts, etc. Anything we're supposed to be doing, that we're not doing, needs to be activated. There are some who teach a different type of "spiritual activation" as though you don't have *access* to whatever it is, unless you activate it first. And often this requires *them*, or some type of incantation or new age mysticism - this type of "awakening" is unbiblical and demonic. We receive everything we need through the Holy Spirit, who's received by faith alone. The only activation you need to experience is based on *trust*—your trust in God's Word. All the truths and good works revealed in Scripture should be acted upon. It's not enough that we believe God's Word, our works must match our belief. Align your actions with what God's commands.

Declaration. A declaration is just an outward profession. It is the act of declaring something by confessing it with our words. Our words are meaningless without genuine faith in what we're saying. And both our words and our faith are meaningless without our actions supporting them. But combined with faith and action our words do have value. This is taught in Romans 10:9 and elsewhere. I'm not suggesting that our words have creative power in-and-of-themselves. See Section (P) where I thoroughly refute the false Word of Faith heresies in that regard. But, when a verbal declaration *does* have power behind it when: (1) it's declaring a biblical truth, (2) it's inspired and empowered by the Holy Spirit, (3) it's aligned with one's personal faith, and (4) it's aligned with right motives of the heart in service to God. It's not a creative power to do whatever *we* want it to do, but the power to do what *God* has *enabled* it to do. These declarations have the power of *His* Word behind it, because His *Spirit* is behind it. So it's good and fruitful for us to declare biblical truths. It's also beneficial to commit them to memory, to draw from during times of crisis, or to share with others. Also what we declare with our mouths requires a greater level of commitment of the will and holds us accountable. During your journey you'll encounter many obstacles, trials, tribulations, and different types of spiritual attacks. Your primary weapon is prayer. Your primary type of prayer will be between you and God (see Section M) and worship (see Section N). There's also Intercessory Prayer, which is prayer, *to* God, on behalf of others. These are vital weapons against the spiritual forces of evil. But there's another type of declaration/prayer.

Spiritual Warfare Prayer. Spiritual warfare prayer is not prayer *to* God. In a sense, it's not really even prayer either. It's really more like an active-declaration made into the spiritual realm—directed not to God, but to Satan. Not necessarily *to* Satan specifically, you're *not* praying to him. It's more like it's generically aimed at the spiritual realm. It's a type of prayer—as in it is *words spoken outwards*—to effectually change things in the spiritual realm. Unlike prayer to God, which is communication with God typically in the form of a request or a conversation, this is effectual. It's not a *request* to God, but a declaration "out *there*." It's less like "Lord, grant my request" and more like "Get behind me, Satan!" Warfare prayer is declaring biblical truths, as led by the inspiration of the Holy Spirit, motivated by the goal of the advancement of God's Kingdom. It's activated in the sense you have to believe and have faith that your declarations are true, offensive, and effectual. Declarations should be based on God's Word, so doing this *is* praying in the Spirit. God's Word is alive and powerful, and by aligning our words with God's Word they too become powerful, offensive spiritual weapons. Change your atmosphere with declarations! Let God's Living Word becoming a living part of your daily fight! Make God's voice, in your mind and spirit, LOUDER than Satan's voice anywhere you find it! I've provided a few examples of declarations below to illustrate what they look like but you can find more or create your own. For an entire book of warfare prayers and declarations, and the biblical basis for this, I recommend *Demon Proofing Prayers* by Bob Larson. (https://MPoweredChristian.org/Book-DemonProofingPrayers)

Hosea 6:5b I have slain them by the words of My mouth, and My judgments go forth like lightning.

Isaiah 11:4 He [*Jesus*] will strike the earth with the rod of His mouth and slay the wicked with the breath of His lips.

Hebrews 4:12a For the word of God is living and active. Sharper than any double-edged sword, it pierces even to dividing soul and spirit, joints and marrow. It judges the thoughts and intentions of the heart.

Ephesians 6:17 And take... the sword of the Spirit, which is the word of God. ¹⁸Pray in the Spirit at all times, with every kind of prayer and petition. To this end, stay alert with all perseverance in your prayers for all the saints.

Category	Biblical Basis	Declarations
Being an Overcomer	Romans 8:31 Romans 8:38-39	"If God is for me, who can be against me?" "Nothing can separate me from the love of Jesus Christ!"
Trusting in God's defense	Ephesians 6:13 Ephesians 6:16	"I stand and put on the full armor of God!" "I will extinguish every arrow of Satan through faith in Christ!"
Confidence in Justification	Ephesians 6:14 Colossians 2:9-11	"I am fitted with the breastplate of righteousness!" "I am perfected and made complete in Christ!"
Being/Feeling Loved	Romans 8:38-39 Ephesians 2:4-5	"Nothing can separate me from the love of Jesus Christ!" "God loves me and has given me life in Christ!"
Identity / Position	2 Cor. 1:21-22 Phil. 3:20, Gal. 4:7	"I have been established, anointed, sealed, and born again!" "I am a citizen of Heaven and an heir through God!"
Relationship with God	Romans 8:14-16 2 Cor. 5:18	"I am a child of God... a son/daughter of God!" "I am reconciled to God and am a minister of reconciliation!"
Feeling Fearful	2 Timothy 1:7 Psalm 23:4	"I don't have a spirit of fear, but of power and self-control!" "I will fear no evil, for God is with me and He comforts me!"
Feeling Anxiety	Psalm 46:1, 10 Matthew 6:25-34	"I will be still, knowing God is over all, my refuge and strength!" "I will not worry about tomorrow, for I know God is in control!"
Overcoming Temptation	Philippians 4:8 James 4:7	"I will focus on what is true, honorable, right, pure, lovely!" "I submit to God and resist the devil, and he will flee from me!"
Needing Direction	Psalm 32:8 Proverbs 3:5	"God teaches me, counsels me, and watches over me!" "I will trust in the LORD and lean not on my own understanding!"

s. Power to Overcome

Everyone in Christ has been given supernatural power by the Spirit, to overcome.

As you navigate your journey remember God has empowered you to overcome everything you're *supposed* to overcome. Every hard time, adversity, obstacle, or enemy before you, that you're *supposed* to be victorious over, you will be, if you trust in God for the victory and overcome it His way. Romans 8:37 reminds us every enemy before us, has already been conquered for us, by Christ who loved us. Trust in this, set your mind on this, let your thoughts and feelings be governed by faith in this. If you do, you'll tap into a reservoir of internal power the Holy Spirit is giving to those in Christ. God hasn't just plucked us from the grip of death, Hell, and Satan, and then left us to fend for ourselves. He's sovereignly guiding us, giving us the victory. Romans 16:20 reminds us He is our God of peace, that the grace of our Lord Jesus is with us, and Satan will soon be crushed under our feet. 2 Corinthians 2:14 affirms that God always leads us in triumph in Christ! 1 John 2:13-14 reminds us that we have *already* overcome the evil one. It's our faith, our trust, in the gospel, that has caused our new birth. 1 John 5:4 tells us, *"Everyone born of God overcomes the world. And this is the victory that has overcome the world: our faith."* So rely not on your own strength, but on God's! Outwardly we look like lambs, but we have the Spirit of the Lion of Judah on the inside! Psalm 54:4 and 7 says, *"Surely God is my helper; the Lord is the sustainer of my soul... For He has delivered me from every trouble, and my eyes have stared down my foes."* When trouble comes knocking, let it find an unshakeable faith in you! Ephesians 3:20 says, *"Now to Him who is able to do so much more than all we ask or imagine, according to His power that is at work within us..."*

t. Power to Endure
Everyone in Christ, has been given supernatural power by the Spirit, to endure.

A paraphrase of Ecclesiastes 9:11 could say: "The race is not given to the swift, nor the strong, but he who endures until the end." This reminds me of Aesop's fable, *The Hare and the Tortoise*. The rabbit mocked the turtle for being slow. The turtle challenged the rabbit to a race to prove he could beat him. During their race, the rabbit ran so far ahead he laid down to take a nap until the turtle could catch up. The turtle slowly and steadily plodded along, eventually catching up to the rabbit peacefully sleeping. By the time the rabbit woke he ran his fastest to catch up but still lost. The moral of the story: the race is not always to the swift. Slow and steady, enduring until the end, is a much more reliable and predictable model for success than a big, flashy burst off the starting line. The fleshly part of us will always be drawn to the flashiest churches and worship, the great revivals and miracles, the boldest or most entertaining preachers, and the provocative social and political news of the day. However, the true measure of Christian success is *longevity*. It's not he who makes the most noise and biggest flash that wins - it's the steady who persevere until the end that do. Now, I'm all for the great moves of God and ambitious efforts, but before you set your focus on such things make sure your foundation is strong. Don't be a rabbit. Don't run from major effort to long nap to major effort to long nap. Be a turtle. Slow and steady wins the race. Or, perhaps best, be a turtle that occasionally gets a rabbit's sprint! Get good at being consistent in the small things and God will give you opportunities to run ahead, because your steadiness will not be hindered. You will be ready to run, out of your excess spiritual energy, and you won't need to "nap" afterwards. The vast majority of guidance in God's Word is about our need to *endure* and persevere. To follow God and do what is right when it will be hard to do so. To walk the slow and steady race and trust God through it. As the previous section went into, God will empower you to conquer many enemies. And we know that we will conquer all of them, in God's time. Notice though, that I said God will empower you to conquer all of the things that you're *supposed* to be victorious over. Listen up. Do not miss this point: you're most likely not supposed to be totally victorious over every obstacle. You won't be healed of every disease. You won't avoid every tragedy. You won't be delivered out of every problem. It's these He hasn't called you to *conquer*. It's these He's called you to *endure.* Your race, in these situations, is a test of endurance. Will you trust in God over weeks, months, years? Will you keep walking, slow and steady, towards the finish line? Will you trust that He's going to, eventually, get you there? This is when our faith is tested most. Know it's coming and prepare yourself now. When the storms come you'll enter them with a very different mindset. The wind is raging, the waves are crashing, your boat feels like it's going to capsize, yet... Jesus is in the boat with you, sleeping. Do you trust Him? The Holy Spirit has given you everything you need to finish strong! Keep going. Keep holding on. Keep walking, slow and steady. God's got you!

James 5:10 Brothers, as an example of patience in affliction, take the prophets who spoke in the name of the Lord. [11]See how blessed we consider those who have persevered. You have heard of Job's perseverance and have seen the outcome from the Lord...

Colossians 1:10a so that you may walk in a manner worthy of the Lord... [11]being strengthened with all power according to His glorious might so that you may have full endurance and patience...

IV. Chapter Summary and Evaluation

Chapter Summary
Control the atmosphere in the car and your journey will be much more fruitful.

If your life's journey was like a road trip, what will you listen to on the radio? How will your choice affect your thoughts, what you focus on, and how you feel? Will you focus more on your destination, and the good thoughts and conversation in the car—or will you focus on the bad traffic, bad drivers, and road construction? The choice is yours. What will you let influence you? Will you crucify your old patterns of thinking, focus on your new identity in Christ, and your righteousness in Him? Will you remember your election, your salvation, how your sin can and cannot cause separation from God? Will you renew your mind daily to shift what you think about? You've learned right thoughts and beliefs will produce good feelings. You can feel how you want to feel by having a conqueror mentality instead of a victim mentality, being an optimist instead of a pessimist, and making gratitude the foundation of everything else. Often the hardest part of the journey is not *feeling* good, but through dedicated effort to focus on the right things you can influence your feelings. You can make your feelings, which are part of the flesh, submit to the Holy Spirit. With right thoughts and right emotions we can direct right words and right behavior. Control the atmosphere in the car and your doors remain locked. The enemy can still cause chaos on the outside, but your car will be full of the joy of the Lord! Philippians 4:11-13 says, *"I have learned to be content regardless of my circumstances. I know how to live humbly, and I know how to abound. I am accustomed to any and every situation—to being filled and being hungry, to having plenty and having need. I can do all things through Christ who gives me strength."*

Chapter 4 Evaluation

AFTER THOROUGH, CAREFUL EXAMINATION, RIGHT NOW:

	False		Partially False				Mostly True		True

I) I'm doing well at controlling my thoughts and beliefs .... | 1 | 2 | 3 | 4 | 5 | 6 | 7 | 8 | 9 | 10 |

II) I'm doing well at controlling my emotions and feelings .... | 1 | 2 | 3 | 4 | 5 | 6 | 7 | 8 | 9 | 10 |

III) I'm doing well at controlling my words and behaviors....... | 1 | 2 | 3 | 4 | 5 | 6 | 7 | 8 | 9 | 10 |

a) I've successfully identified and crucified my old patterns.. | 1 | 2 | 3 | 4 | 5 | 6 | 7 | 8 | 9 | 10 |

b) I live in peace and comfort, knowing I'm clothed in Christ | 1 | 2 | 3 | 4 | 5 | 6 | 7 | 8 | 9 | 10 |

c) The predominant way I think about myself is child of God | 1 | 2 | 3 | 4 | 5 | 6 | 7 | 8 | 9 | 10 |

d) I'm not fearful/doubtful that I'm not of the Elect in Christ . | 1 | 2 | 3 | 4 | 5 | 6 | 7 | 8 | 9 | 10 |

e) I'm not fearful/doubtful about losing my salvation .... | 1 | 2 | 3 | 4 | 5 | 6 | 7 | 8 | 9 | 10 |

f) I know what the unpardonable sin is, haven't committed it | 1 | 2 | 3 | 4 | 5 | 6 | 7 | 8 | 9 | 10 |

g) I'm close with God, conquering my sin, being led by Him.. | 1 | 2 | 3 | 4 | 5 | 6 | 7 | 8 | 9 | 10 |

h) I'm dedicated to, and continuing to, renew my mind daily | 1 | 2 | 3 | 4 | 5 | 6 | 7 | 8 | 9 | 10 |

i) I'd characterize my average daily emotions as very good .. | 1 | 2 | 3 | 4 | 5 | 6 | 7 | 8 | 9 | 10 |

j) I'm always in a constant state of gratitude towards God.... | 1 | 2 | 3 | 4 | 5 | 6 | 7 | 8 | 9 | 10 |

k) I'm never pessimistic in thought, attitude, and behavior .. | 1 | 2 | 3 | 4 | 5 | 6 | 7 | 8 | 9 | 10 |

l) I never think, feel, and act with a victim mentality .... | 1 | 2 | 3 | 4 | 5 | 6 | 7 | 8 | 9 | 10 |

m) My life is one that is full of prayer and intimacy with God .. | 1 | 2 | 3 | 4 | 5 | 6 | 7 | 8 | 9 | 10 |

n) I live my life always in a constant state of worship to God . | 1 | 2 | 3 | 4 | 5 | 6 | 7 | 8 | 9 | 10 |

o) My life is one of ongoing repentance and confession .... | 1 | 2 | 3 | 4 | 5 | 6 | 7 | 8 | 9 | 10 |

p) I understand the errors of Word of Faith and I reject it ...... | 1 | 2 | 3 | 4 | 5 | 6 | 7 | 8 | 9 | 10 |

q) In a godly way, I always rebuke the attacks of the enemy .. | 1 | 2 | 3 | 4 | 5 | 6 | 7 | 8 | 9 | 10 |

r) I overcome by knowing and boldly declaring God's truth.. | 1 | 2 | 3 | 4 | 5 | 6 | 7 | 8 | 9 | 10 |

st) I trust God is empowering me to overcome and endure .... | 1 | 2 | 3 | 4 | 5 | 6 | 7 | 8 | 9 | 10 |

Date Last Taken: _____

Questions for Reflection or Group Study:

1) Which of the three categories (thoughts, feelings, or behaviors) has most significantly hindered the peace and joy of your average daily atmosphere? Why do you think this is?

2) Pick a common negative behavior of yours that has been difficult to overcome. What thoughts are necessary to drive it? What are the negative feelings associated with it?

3) What section of this chapter did you struggle with the most? Why? Share your struggle. We need to explore, understand, and accept how we think and feel before we can change it. Then spend some time ministering to and praying for one another over things shared.

4) Has your faith ever struggled due to someone's illness? Did you feel like God was far away or didn't care? How does it feel knowing God is present, cares, and is using it for good?

5) Which of the false Word of Faith beliefs did you have? Why do so many evangelicals have these even though they're not biblical? How has your understanding of "faith" changed?

6) What area did you score highest in? Why? Could this be connected to a gift of the Holy Spirit you've received? How could you partner with someone low in this area to help them?

7) If you could fully control your thoughts, feelings, words, and behaviors, and make all of them submit to God, how would your walk with God and your life change?

8) Have you or someone you know ever struggled in your faith by thinking you'd committed the unpardonable sin or weren't of the elect? Does the truth change your atmosphere?

Explore Chapter 4 Deeper:

For additional resources related to the topics discussed in this chapter see our companion website at **https://MPoweredChristian.org/Road-Map-Book-Resources**

- Free printable pdf of this chapter evaluation for personal or classroom use
- List of related online courses, ecoaching programs, personal coaching services
- List of related videos, articles, and recommended books
- List of related live webinars and ways to ask questions

Notes/Reflections:

_____
_____
_____
_____
_____
_____
_____
_____
_____
_____
_____
_____
_____
_____
_____
_____
_____
_____
_____
_____
_____
_____
_____
_____
_____
_____
_____
_____
_____

To-Do List: _Date:_ _____

MY TASKS FOR **THIS UPCOMING WEEK...**

✔ **My Big 1-3:**
_____
_____
_____

✔ **For Personal Growth:**
_____
_____
_____

✔ **For Key Roles:**
_____
_____
_____

✔ **For Calling/Ministry Service:**
_____
_____
_____

✔ **Pray for/Request prayer about:**
_____
_____
_____

✔ **Learn more about:**
_____
_____
_____

✔ **Other:**
_____
_____
_____

CHAPTER FIVE

The NEW DIRECTION is VERY FRUITFUL

You'll know you're going in the right direction when you're moving towards the fruit.

Chapter Contents

I. The Significance of Fruit

There's a common saying that goes, "The road to Hell is paved with good intentions." This means that people often have a desire or intention to do good but what they *actually* do is a lot of bad. If you're not going in the *right* direction, it really doesn't matter how fast you're going, how efficient you're doing it, how popular you are while doing it, or how many accomplishments you achieved along the way. It's all an effort in futility. Direction is everything. It's immeasurably better to take a single, baby step in the right direction than it is to move mountains in the wrong direction. Yet, this is often what we focus on. How big the mountain was. How fast it was moved. How great and popular and amazing the accomplishments were. How foolish we can be, easily missing the forest for the trees. The right direction, God's direction, and your direction towards God, is very fruitful. Picture in front of you a main road and a highway, where you can either go right or left. How do you know which is the right way? What about every exit ramp later, off of each direction? What about all of the small roads off of exits, and so on? The Answer: Go in the direction with more good fruit on it. We can know with certainty that we are moving in the right direction if we are always seeking good fruit, moving in the direction of good fruit, seeing good fruit, planting good fruit, watering good fruit, growing good fruit, cultivating good fruit, and harvesting good fruit. Your map tells you how to get to the destination, but fruit is your compass. It will tell you which way is north.

a. What is Fruit

"Good Fruit" is a metaphor, for the produce of all effort, that glorifies God.

"Fruit" is a common biblical metaphor for produce. Not just produce as in plant vegetation, though it is that too. I mean produce, as in something produced, something that resulted because of production. Think about what the fruit on a tree is. It's the final results, the output, of all of the labor that came before it. It takes a lot of work to get fruit. It first took a living seed that had to be buried in good soil that wouldn't choke it so that it could sprout and then grow roots. It then needed water, nutrients, sunlight, and shade. It needed to strive upwards against gravity, break through the surface, and then survive the weather, insects, and other elements. It needed to grow and develop and get stronger and develop its trunk, branches, and leaves. And then, finally, after all of that effort, it has the proper foundation to grow fruit. The entire foundation is necessary to supply future nutrients all the way from the soil, up through the roots, up the trunk, and into the branches, to grow fruit. The fruit is the last stage of development. It's the final product. It's the result of all of the effort that came before it. So we should cherish it. But that doesn't mean that the only thing that matters is the fruit itself. Without the rest of the system it's impossible to get the fruit. So don't think you can shortchange the process and skip right to the making fruit part. No, the seeds, the roots, the trunk, branches, etc. are all part of the fruit process. Go in the direction that is *eventually* producing good fruit, even if it's only seeds, or trunks, or branches. Keep your directional eyes on the long term final fruit product, yes, but let your daily roles and goals be focused on the immediate pieces in front of you that you can directly influence.

Good fruit is another way of saying good deed, good produce, good result, or good outcome. Basically, good fruit is a metaphor for all that is good. All that is good according to God that is. Good fruit, as the Bible describes it, is all that is in accordance with God's will, or that which is an accurate reflection of God's character. There's a wide variety of different types of fruit, which we'll cover in detail in this chapter. But despite various shapes, forms, and colors, all good fruit has this in common: it brings glory to God in some way.

b. Expressions of God
Fruit is only good *if it* is an *accurate* expression of God's character and will.

Good fruit is based on who God is. God is the Judge. It is His character and will that determines what is good from what is evil. Good and evil don't exist apart from God. There isn't a good god and a bad god, a ying and yang opposite for everything. There aren't laws of the universe that exist outside of God. No, that which is good is only good because it is an accurate expression, or reflection, of God's character and will. In other words, it isn't good just *because*, as though it has its own internal worth. It's good because it is *like* God. And God sets the standard for what is evil as well. Evil doesn't exist apart from God either. Like in the movie Star Wars there's just 'the force' and you can use the good side or the dark side of the force. No, evil is just a name that we give to all that is contrary to the character and will of God. God is the standard of good. Sin is anything less than or contrary to that goodness. Evil is sin's extreme. Since God is love, then hate is evil. Since God is just, injustice is evil. Since God is holy, unholiness is evil. We can recognize these things, because we're made in God's image. But we don't determine them. We take it for granted as though "we're born knowing hate is evil and love is good." Intelligent animals don't. This knowledge is spiritual. It's the conscience.

We don't decide what is good and what isn't. God does. This is an important lesson to remember. History is filled with people who determined for themselves what is good from what is bad, and evil according to God is the inevitable result. The vast majority of evil is committed by someone who thinks they are doing what is good in their perspective. Hitler and Stalin believed they were purifying their countries for a socialist utopia. God and the rest of us see it for what it really was: murder and genocide. If we forget this lesson that we don't get to decide what is good and evil, we risk making the mistake of deciding for ourselves what is good and bad fruit. We risk trying to be our own judge. We might then decide that if something is good, whether because we say so, or even because God's Word says so, then we can just focus on *that.*

For example, the Bible teaches that God is love and love is good. If love is good, then anything *we* may think that is an act of love is good, right? However, what if what we, or someone else, calls love isn't good, according to God? The Bible says that homosexual relationships, and many types of incestuous

Eternal Fruit

Good fruit, built on the branch of Jesus and the gospel will last forever, but good fruit that isn't will eventually perish.

relationships are bad. But what if they are loving? What if a mother and her adult son love one another and want to be married? They claim to be in love, so it is good then? What then is our highest principle? Who decides? Do we go in the direction of "all love determines" or in the direction of "all God determines?" This creates a conflict. This will happen anytime we put a "good" thing above God. This is idolatry. Whenever we put a principle or value above God, and serve and chase *that fruit*, we will be misled and led astray to error and sin. Even "good" things are sinful if they are put above God. This is because God is the highest value, the highest good, the highest judge. If it is opposed to Him, it is evil regardless. Love, honor, trust, integrity, joy, peace, etc. these are all good *because* they are attributes of God. But apart from God, His character and will, they are not always good. Love—in incest—is not good, even though it *is* love (some argue), because it's opposed to God's will. He sets the standard. And neither is all honor no matter what. Hitler received honor. He was honored for being a great leader. But he wasn't a great leader, he was a horrible leader, a vile, genocidal maniac. Even though he received honor he was not honorable because he was opposed to God's will. So it is not the love, or the honor, themselves, that are the highest value, God is. It is only the love and honor that are in accord with God, that, now, become good fruits. As you progress through your journey in life, towards the direction of good fruit, you will be tempted by your flesh and by Satan, to aim for the good fruit. It's crucial that you not chase the fruits *themselves*, but rather, *God*—in the *direction* of the good fruit, according to Him. Don't let the fruits themselves be your desire, but the God of the fruits!

c. In the Kingdom Such as These
Good fruit can only come from good trees, which have certain attributes.

The fruit we're looking for during our journey, and should be growing, cultivating, and driving towards, is the fruit of the Kingdom of God. God's kingdom is everything operating under God's dominion, and everything influenced by that. Every being, whether spirit being (i.e. angel) or human being, can either be a part of God's kingdom, or a part of Satan's kingdom, the rebellion to God's kingdom. God's kingdom is not just where He reigns, and what He reigns, it's also *how* He reigns. God's kingdom is full of those with a particular set of attributes: beliefs, character traits, qualities, objectives, desires, and behaviors. Satan's kingdom is full of those with much of the opposite attributes. Another way of saying attributes could be fruit. As Jesus taught in Matthew 7:

> Matthew 7:15 *[Jesus]* Beware of false prophets. They come to you in sheep's clothing, but inwardly they are ravenous wolves. ¹⁶By their fruit you will recognize them. Are grapes gathered from thornbushes, or figs from thistles? ¹⁷Likewise, every good tree bears good fruit, but a bad tree bears bad fruit. ¹⁸A good tree cannot bear bad fruit, and a bad tree cannot bear good fruit. ¹⁹Every tree that does not bear good fruit is cut down and thrown into the fire. ²⁰So then, by their fruit you will recognize them.

As those who are mindfully moving in the direction towards good fruit we need to be aware of these attributes. We also need to examine ourselves regularly and make sure our attributes are in alignment with the attributes of those in God's kingdom. We need to be good trees that bear good fruit. And we need to be watchful for bad trees bearing bad fruit, that try to sneak into the Church, and into our lives, wearing sheep's clothing. Fruit is our compass. It will help us know which direction is the right direction.

In Chapter 1, Section (I) we learned of some of the attributes of those in God's kingdom. People who love goodness and truth, and those who want glory, honor, and immortality. Jesus's lesson in Matthew 13:41-43 gave us another description. Attributes of Satan's kingdom are those who cause sin and practice lawlessness. An attribute of those in the Kingdom of God is righteousness. The apostle Paul gives us another description of these attributes in 1 Corinthians 6:9-10. Satan's kingdom includes the wicked, the sexually immoral, the idolaters, the adulterers, those who commit homosexual acts, the thieves, the greedy, the drunkards, the verbal abusers, and the swindlers. None of these are in the kingdom of God, nor will they inherit the kingdom of God. In section (K) of Chapter 1 we learned how the new spiritual birth in Christ sets us on the right, and righteous, path. And it is our ongoing sanctification and submission to the Holy Spirit that continues us on this righteous course. One final very important attribute I'd like to mention here, the one most often overlooked, especially by religious legalists and modern-day "Christian" Pharisees. This lesson is recorded in all three of the synoptic gospels. *(Mt 19:13-15, Lk 18:15-17)* Jesus teaches us the right mindset and attitude of those in the kingdom of God, and the attitude we need to have should we desire to enter it.

> Mark 10:13 Now people were bringing the little children to Jesus for Him to place His hands on them, and the disciples rebuked those who brought them. ¹⁴But when Jesus saw this, He was indignant and told them, "Let the little children come to Me, and do not hinder them! For the kingdom of God belongs to such as these. ¹⁵Truly I tell you, anyone who does not receive the kingdom of God like a little child will never enter it."

Likewise, there is another lesson Jesus taught in Matthew 18 about what kind of personal attributes are greatest in the Kingdom of God. *(Mk 9:33-37, Lk 9:46-50)*

Matthew 18:1 At that time the disciples came to Jesus and asked, "Who then is the greatest in the kingdom of heaven?" ²Jesus invited a little child to stand among them. ³"Truly I tell you," He said, "unless you change and become like little children, you will never enter the kingdom of heaven. ⁴Therefore, whoever humbles himself like this little child is the greatest in the kingdom of heaven. ⁵And whoever welcomes a little child like this in My name welcomes Me.

In Luke 9:48 Jesus said, *"Whoever is the least among all of you, he is the greatest."* And in Mark 9:35 Jesus says, *"If anyone wants to be first, he must be the last of all and the servant of all."* So we see a very upside-down, backwards type of system in God's kingdom, very different from the kingdoms of this world. This is no accident. We know that Satan is the prince of this world and of its kingdoms. It is very clear that God desires in us a type of humbleness, a sense of innocence, a sense of awe in who He is, and an innocent childlike faith and trust in Him. If we're *only* after the fruit, the law keeping or the good deeds, we can absolutely forget this mindset totally. We can become legalists, religious lawyers, with strict adherence to God's laws of righteousness, even to a fault. Losing all sense of awe in God, all sense of mystery, all sense of *trust in Him*, and instead trusting in our own works. The mystery of the Holy Trinity, the cross, and the gospel all confront this, but we can still fall prey to this thinking so you need to watch out for it. The Kingdom of God is full of those like little children! Those who are humble, those who trust in God with childlike faith, those who seek to glorify God rather than themselves. Those who become greater in God's kingdom do so by becoming a lesser servant in the view of the world. This is the type of fruitfulness that you need to be moving towards.

d. Those Who Do the Father's Will
Our fruitfulness is built on the foundation of, trust in and obedience to, God's will.

In Hosea 6:6 God says, *"I delight in loyalty."* Our Heavenly Father considers fruitful behavior, and fruitful *people,* as those inline with His will. There's a way to be this, that's distinct from common examples we're more familiar with, things like loving your neighbor, helping the sick, providing to the poor, or praying with those struggling. These examples are fruits that have an external, worldly contribution to them. They *are* good. These are the kinds of things that can be seen, compared, measured, planned. God is calling us to do those kinds of things, but He's *also* calling us to do His will—regardless of what it looks like outwardly. For example, if God calls you to take a year off of everything you had planned just to fly halfway across the world, to travel on foot deep into the mountains of Peru, just to tend to the needs of and share the gospel with a single person, then it's good and fruitful for you to obey. If we focused only on *outward* matters, total numbers, statistics, etc. then we're more likely to be disobedient to God to do something like that by rationalizing that we can reach hundreds or thousands of people with our plans! I can be a bit of a pragmatist so I struggle with this too. Certainly a thousand people is better than one, right? Well, yes—unless it is God's will for you to go for the one! In this case, it is better for you to obey God's will, and do whatever He's calling you to do, than to do something else that *seems* to be more fruitful. The fruit here is trust in God, full surrender and obedience, even when it doesn't seem optimal to us. Our Father is looking for children who know Him, trust Him, and obey Him. And obedience is not hard when there is a relationship and trust there. The fruit the Father seeks is HIS will to be done, on earth as it is in Heaven. And fruitful people and actions are those done in obedience. Before we examine the different types of external fruit we need trust and obedience to be at the cornerstone of everything else. It is better to be obedient in what seems like a small thing than to be disobedient in what seems like a big thing. And this makes sense when we remember that our goal is to please God, not just to chase the fruit. Jesus said this desire is what makes us children of God in Mark 3:35: *"For whoever does the will of God is My brother and sister and mother."* This is an *internal* personal attribute, motive, attitude, and desire needed in you—first—*before* you worry about any type external behaviors and actions.

---

1 Samuel 15:22 But Samuel declared: "Does the LORD delight in burnt offerings and sacrifices as much as in obedience to His voice? Behold, obedience is better than sacrifice, and attentiveness is better than the fat of rams.

Jeremiah 42:6 Whether it is pleasant or unpleasant, we will obey the voice of the LORD our God to whom we are sending you, so that it may go well with us, for we will obey the voice of the LORD our God!

James 4:13 Come now, you who say, "Today or tomorrow we will go to this or that city, spend a year there, carry on business, and make a profit."... [15]Instead, you ought to say, "If the Lord is willing, we will live and do this or that."

1 Peter 3:17 For it is better, if it is God's will, to suffer for doing good than for doing evil.

II. Fruits of Righteousness

e. God's Law Legislated Fruit

The Law given to Moses made good fruit foundational, in the personal morality, and society governing, of Israel.

When God freed the Israelites from Egypt to create a new nation and a people for Himself, He didn't just provide a few recommendations for how they should live. Through Moses He gave them a brand new, entire ethical and legal framework to live by. This was a first of its kind. Called *Ethical Monotheism,* the people's ethics, or moral way of living, was governed according to a single God. The people being good, moral, and righteous was not just a *preference* to God, it was a necessity. The people being obedient to Him, putting Him first, being a morally good and just society, and loving and taking care of one another was the only permissible option. God would have it no other way. In Chapter 1, Section (J), I described God's Law, as well as the heart behind it, so take a look there for more about the Law of God in general.

Though God gave the Law in written form in the Bible's books of Exodus, Leviticus, Numbers, and Deuteronomy, ancient Jews compiled the many commandments of God into list format to create religious and legal systems. Since then many Christian ministries have also taken upon themselves to outline and categorize all of the 613 commandments given throughout the Law as well.[1] The Law included both positive commands, or things for them to do, and negative commands, or things for them not to do. The Law gave the requirement and encouragement of *good fruits,* for them to do, such as: (1) how to worship and celebrate God properly, (2) how to atone for sins, (3) how to have ritual purity, (4) how to offer tithes and offerings, (5) how to have a just legal system, (6) how to live morally righteous and just with your neighbors, and (7) how to honor God with your family structure and relationships. The Law also included the elimination of *bad fruit* such as: (1) not worshipping false gods, (2) not committing blasphemy, (3) not defiling God's temple, (4) not making offerings to God in pagan ways, (5) not doing things that created separation between you and God, (6) not being a bad steward of your resources, (7) not doing unloving, unjust, or immoral business dealings, (8) not having an unjust legal system, and (9) not having sinful sexual relationships. As you're looking for ways to be fruitful with your life a lot can be learned from studying the Law of God and how it was intended to govern Israel. It applied to all: individuals, families, kings, the entire nation. It applied to all situations: moral, physical, emotional, political, economic, military, legal, etc.

Today, in many countries we take a just system for granted, as though humanity has always had democracies and a system of justice where all people are equal before the law. But it hasn't always been. This is largely due to the influence of Christianity, the Protestant Reformation, the Renaissance, and the Enlightenment. God knew how wicked man and their laws were since the Fall. In Deuteronomy 4:8 Moses rhetorically asks the Israelites, *"And what nation is great enough to have righteous statutes and ordinances like this entire law I set before you today?"* The bottom line is this: fruitfulness is part is one with obedience to the Law of God. If you're not bearing good fruit you're probably in sinful violation of the Law, either to the letter of the Law or to the spirit of the Law. Now in the New Covenant through Jesus we're not under the Law, but under grace. Yet, we know that the Law *is* good and it can teach us about how to live fruitfully. When in doubt remember what Galatians 5:14 says about the law: *"The entire law is fulfilled in a single decree: 'Love your neighbor as yourself.'"*

Psalm 1:1 Blessed is the man who does not walk in the counsel of the wicked, or set foot on the path of sinners, or sit in the seat of mockers. [2]But his delight is in the Law of the LORD, and on His law he meditates day and night. [3]He is like a tree planted by streams of water, yielding its fruit in season, whose leaf does not wither, and who prospers in all he does.

---

f. In Keeping with Repentance
The path *to* good fruit begins with repentance, and the cessation of bad fruit.

Do good deeds and bad deeds cancel one another out? This is what Islam teaches. That on judgment day scales will be measured to see if all a person's good deeds outweigh their bad deeds. Most Christians know better than to buy this but perhaps we still subconsciously live this way. Don't many of us rationalize to ourselves I don't go to church or read the Bible but I still give to the poor. Or perhaps we compare our sins like this: I don't commit adultery or sleep around, all I do is watch a little pornography. Or perhaps we still use illegal, immoral, or ungodly means to get money but then donate some of that money to church. What about this - the workaholic who neglects the mental, emotional, or spiritual needs of their spouse and children but then tithes generously to the church. Is that God's will? Does the sin of the former action get cancelled out by the good of the latter action? The answer is no, it doesn't. In Deuteronomy 23:18 God says, *"You must not bring the wages of a prostitute, whether female or male, into the house of the LORD your God to fulfill any vow, because both are detestable to the LORD your God."* Here God makes it clear that it is not only the sin that is detestable to Him but also the wages earned by the sin. God wants nothing to do with it. The money earned through ungodliness is unacceptable to the Lord. You can't do something wrong and use the fruit of that to do good. It's unacceptable to God. In the fifth chapter of the book of Amos, God is rebuking Israel for being corrupt, unjust, trampling on the poor, taking bribes, and oppressing the righteous. He says in verses 22-24, *"Even though you offer Me burnt offerings and grain offerings, I will not accept them; for your peace offerings of fattened cattle I will have no regard. Take away from Me the noise of your songs! I will not listen to the music of your harps. But let justice roll on like a river, and righteousness like an ever-flowing stream."* (Amos 5:22-24)

God would not accept anything from them! Not their church services, not their money, not their prayer, not their worship—nothing! Don't think that there's nothing wrong with being wicked in one area of life while still trying to be good in other areas of your life at the same time and think that God is okay with that. We are either a good tree or a bad tree. We are either bearing good fruit or bearing bad fruit. We need to be truly repentant of our sinful lives. We need to produce fruit in keeping with repentance. Yes, there are many ways to produce good fruit. I've provided several tables of fruits over the next few sections to illustrate the big picture and outline their differences. I've identified separately fruits of repentance (Section F), fruits of inward character change (Section G), fruits of outward character change (Section H), fruits of biblical justice (Section I), and fruits of social justice (Section J). Each of these levels are progressive, each one building upon the progress of the previous levels. Fruit of repentance is the first level, it all begins there. Before trying to do good outwardly, like help the poor, stop living in sin inwardly, thinking and doing those things you shouldn't be. Before we can begin to grow in our ability to do more good we must first stop doing evil. Before we can start being a light in the world we must stop being darkness. Before we can start being a blessing to the world we must stop being a part of the curse. Fruitfulness begins with repentance.

Luke 3:8 *[John the Baptist]* Produce fruit, then, in keeping with repentance. And do not begin to say to yourselves, 'We have Abraham as our father.' For I tell you that out of these stones God can raise up children for Abraham. ⁹The axe lies ready at the root of the trees, and every tree that does not produce good fruit will be cut down and thrown into the fire." ¹⁰The crowds asked him, "What then should we do?" ¹¹John replied, "Whoever has two tunics should share with him who has none, and whoever has food should do the same." ¹²Even tax collectors came to be baptized. "Teacher," they asked, "what should we do?" ¹³"Collect no more than you are authorized," he answered. ¹⁴Then some soldiers asked him, "And what should we do?" "Do not take money by force or false accusation," he said. "Be content with your wages."

Matthew 7:19 *[Jesus]* Every tree that does not bear good fruit is cut down and thrown into the fire.

---

g. Inward Fruit First

Fruit begins within individuals, in personal private victory over sin, and in character growth and development.

When people ask how to be a good person or Christian they immediately go to helping the poor, giving tithes to the church, volunteering, or some other external thing. The culture today does the same with social movements, government social programs, climate change, etc. They immediately begin with *outward* behavior modification. The negative effects are multiplied when our focus is not even our own external behavior, but with *other people's* external behavior. External change is not the first thing the Church should focus on, especially not the external change of those *outside* the Church! This only contributes to the works-salvation and legalism mentality of false religions, and the world's hostility to the church. The Church then isn't best known for its loving marriages and families, but by its judging of outsiders.

We must first focus our change efforts internally. First to the innermost parts of the individual, then to the lives of individuals, then to entire churches, and so on. Prioritizing *individual* character, action, and behavior first, before directing it outwards. Stephen Covey, author of *The Seven Habits of Highly Effective People* said this: "The 'Inside-Out' approach to personal and interpersonal effectiveness means to start first with self; even more fundamentally, to start with the most inside part of self - with your paradigms, your character, and your motives. The inside-out approach says that private victories precede public victories."[2] I would argue that the inside-out approach is not only true of personal development and effectiveness, it's also true of creating great marriages, great families, great churches, great communities, great governments, great nations, and great societies. Before we can influence any kind of good change in these other places we must first start within ourselves. You cannot eat an elephant without taking a first bite, or walk a mile without taking a first step. If you cannot find love within yourself first, what makes you think you can find love in your marriage? If you can't control your

Change Spectrum

SOCIETY CHANGE (Fruits of Social Justice, The overall cumulative impact of Individuals, Communities, Systems)

SYSTEM CHANGE (Fruits of Biblical Justice, Creating Impact through Communities working together to change laws, bills)

COMMUNITY CHANGE (Fruits of Community Impact through Organized Local Action programs, Many individuals working together)

INDIVIDUAL EXTERNAL CHANGE (Fruits of *Outward* Behavior, Improved Marriages, Families, Influence on churches, businesses, neighborhoods)

INDIVIDUAL INTERNAL CHANGE (Fruits of *Inward* Repentance, Personal Private Victories, Character Growth and Development) All future change begins here.

own lust, anger, greed, etc., how can you help your kids, church, or culture to control theirs? If you don't put the needs of the poor person you drive by every day on the way to work above your own, how do you think you can influence politicians to put the needs of the poor above the needs of their political agenda? Change happens from the ground up, from the inside-out. The apostle Paul acknowledges this by saying that leaders need to have their own house in order first before they can lead others. 1 Timothy 3:4-5 says, *"An overseer must manage his own household well and keep his children under control, with complete dignity. For if someone does not know how to manage his own household, how can he care for the church of God?"* And how much more true is this in things larger than a local church? If we desire to have fruitful personal lives, marriages, families, churches, institutions, governments, legal systems, law enforcement, economic systems, nations, and societies we must begin first with fruitful individuals. We must begin with ourselves.

Inward Fruits (Individuals)

Good Fruit		Bad Fruit	
Love	Gal. 5:22	Hatred	Gal. 5:20
Joy	Gal. 5:22	Jealousy	Gal. 5:20
Peace	Gal. 5:22	Envy	Gal. 5:21
Patience	Gal. 5:22	Bitterness	Eph. 4:31
Goodness	Gal. 5:22	Malice	Col. 3:8
Self-Control	Gal. 5:23	Recklessness	Eph. 5:18
Faithfulness	Rom. 1:17	Faithlessness	Rom: 1:31
Righteousness	Rom. 14:17	Unholiness	1 Tim. 1:9
Hopefulness	Rom. 15:13	Greed	1 Cor. 6:10
Clear Conscience	1 Tim. 1:19	Depraved Mind	Rom. 1:28
Tender-Hearted	Eph. 4:32	Heartless	Rom. 1:31
Sober-Minded	1 Tim. 3:2	Insobriety	Gal. 5:21
Temperate	1 Tim. 3:2	Rage	Gal. 5:20
Humility	Col. 3:12	Pridefulness	Phil. 2:3
Lowly	Matt. 18:4	Conceit	Gal. 5:25
Contentment	Phil. 2:14	Covetousness	Ex. 20:17
Purity	1 Thes. 4:7	Lust	Col. 3:5
Sacrificial Love	1 John 3:16	Selfish Ambition	Phil. 2:3
Integrity	1 Kings 9:4	Deceitfulness	1 Pet. 3:10
Godliness	1 Kings 9:4	Ungodliness	1 Tim. 1:9
Obedience	1 Kings 9:4	Lawlessness	1 Tim. 1:9
Wisdom	1 Cor. 12:8	Foolishness	Mark 7:22
Fear of God	Prov. 9:10	Arrogance	Mark 7:22

h. Outward Fruit Flows
Inward fruit of the heart flows outwards through behavior.

Our inward fruits are the reflection of what kind of tree we are. If we are a good tree we will have good fruit, if a bad tree, then bad fruit. This first begins in the heart, which is another way of saying our thoughts, beliefs, emotions, desires, and will. And from the inward fruit of our heart flows outwards, through our attitudes, actions, behaviors, and habits. This is why we must not try to merely change our external habits or behavior. This is only treating the symptom. The root cause lies in the heart. Once the roots have been healed and restored, or dug up and replanted, then the rest of the plant will be healthy and bear good outward fruit.

Righteous outward works, whether driven by moral character or through the pursuit of love, justice, or goodness are always good, just as long as they are accompanied by right motives. Paul tells us in Galatians 5:23, *"Against such things there is no law."* These attributes and behaviors are naturally legal, naturally good; you cannot overdo them. Consider the ridiculousness of too much love, too much mercy, too much justice, too much integrity. The outward fruits are the outward behaviors that flow from these. These are the fruits we can witness and measure. Move in the direction of good outward fruit and away from bad outward fruit, both in yourself and in others you associate with. The outward fruit is your evidence of whether a person or group of people is good, whether or not a social program or political agenda is good, or whether a product or a service is good. Measure it by its fruitfulness! Sometimes the outward fruit is all you will have to go by. You will never have all the information but you can always make a wise and informed decision based upon the information that you do have. If you pursue things that have good fruit associated with them you can have peace of mind, and a clear conscience, knowing that you're being fruitful to the best of your ability.

Mark 7:21 *[Jesus]* For from within the hearts of men come evil thoughts, sexual immorality, theft, murder, adultery, 22greed, wickedness, deceit, debauchery, envy, slander, arrogance, and foolishness. 23All these evils come from within, and these are what defile a man."

Matthew 15:13 But Jesus replied, "Every plant that My heavenly Father has not planted will be pulled up by its roots.

Colossians 1:10 so that you may walk in a manner worthy of the Lord and may please Him in every way: bearing fruit in every good work,

---

On the following page is another table, this time of outward fruits. These are applicable to individuals as well as churches, businesses, communities, nations, etc. The fruits listed have a broad range of application. I don't specify every possible good thing you could do. Rather, I've given quite a few major themes of behavior. Instead of listing: (1) love your spouse and don't (2) commit adultery, (3) have homosexual relationships, (4) incestuous relationships, (5) sleep with prostitutes, (6) fornicate, (7) watch pornography, (8) lust, I just contrast sexual fidelity with sexual immorality, which *includes* all the above. Instead of giving specific examples like tithing, supporting the church, or helping the poor, I just list good stewardship, compassion, selflessness, and generosity. If you're just, humble, loving and serving others you shouldn't need to be told not to be racist, or to discriminate or oppress others. Examine each fruit closely and let the Holy Spirit guide you into personal evaluation and application. You will also have to sometimes choose not between good and evil, but between good and better. There is a spectrum to fruitfulness. It's both wise and good stewardship, to choose things that produce either more, or better, fruit than others.

Outward Fruits					
Good Fruit		**Bad Fruit**			
Sexual Fidelity	1 Tim. 3:2	Sex. Immorality	Gal. 5:19	Adultery	1 Cor. 6:9
Kindness	Gal. 5:22	Violence	Hab. 1:3	Murder	1 Tim. 1:9
Faithfulness	Gal. 5:22	Divorce	Matt. 5:32	Idolatry	Gal. 5:20
Gentleness	Gal. 5:23	Abuse	2 Tim. 3:2	Traitorous	2 Tim. 3:4
Self-Control	Gal. 5:23	Fornication	Deut. 22:21-24	Reckless	2 Tim. 3:4
Generosity	2 Cor. 9:11-12	Lover of Money	2 Tim. 3:3	Theft	1 Cor. 6:10
Compassion	Col. 3:12	Verbal Abusers	1 Cor. 6:10	Cursing Others	Rom. 12:14
Holiness	Col. 3:12	Crude Joking	Eph. 5:4	Unholy	2 Tim. 3:2
Forgiveness	Col. 3:13	Unforgiveness	2 Tim. 3:3	Rivalries	Gal. 5:20
Gracious Speech	Col. 4:6	Slander	Col. 3:8	Filthy Language	Col. 3:8
Loving Service	Eph. 4:12	Unloving	2 Tim. 3:3	Lover of Self	2 Tim. 3:2
Tender-Hearted	Eph. 4:32	Abortion	Ex. 21:22-24	Infanticide	Lev. 18:21
Honesty	Eph. 5:9	Lies	1 Tim. 1:10	Perjury	1 Tim. 1:10
Humbly Serving	Eph. 5:21	Selfish Ambition	James 3:16	Kidnapping	Ex. 21:16
Justice	Micah 6:8	Injustice	Hab. 2:12	Slave trading	1 Tim. 1:10
Merciful	Micah 6:8	Lacking Mercy	Prov. 21:10	Merciless	Rom. 1:31
Good Stewardship	Luke 12:42	Workaholism	Ex. 20:8-11	Bestiality	Lev. 18:23
Respectfulness	Rom. 12:10	Dishonor Parents	Ex. 20:12	Dishonor Poor	James 2:6
Modesty	1 Tim. 2:9	Debauchery	Gal. 5:19	Prostitution	Lev. 19:29
Hospitable	1 Pet. 4:9	Discord	Gal. 5:20	Divisions	Gal. 5:20
Honest Business	Deut. 25:15-16	Swindlers	1 Cor. 6:10	Oath Breaking	Num. 30:2
Trusting God	John 14:1	Divination	Deut. 18:10	Sorcery	Gal. 5:20
Lover of God	1 John 5:2	Lover of Pleasure	2 Tim. 3:4	Blasphemy	Deut. 5:11

i. Biblical Justice

Fruit based on the just character of God, and His will for humanity, whom are each coequal bearers of His image.

The topic of justice has been distorted in postmodern culture, with new concepts such as social justice, environmental justice, distributive justice, etc. This is why I've chosen to make a distinction between *biblical* justice and social justice, which we'll cover in the next section. Biblical justice is based on two simple premises. First, all justice proceeds from God's character, who is just, and second, all of humanity was created by God and are coequal bearers of His image. God is the Creator, the author of all life. He's the judge of what is right and wrong and what is better or worse. He's the final authority on all matters of justice. Our desire for justice comes from being made in God's image with a conscience. We explored this in Chapter 1, Section (F). We have the ability to recognize, desire, and determine justice because God is just and He has made us to be just. It's through justice that we can rightly represent His image and likeness on the earth. It's through justice that we can model God's character by upholding His righteous standards. Our being just, individually and corporately, pleases and glorifies Him.

The second biblical premise is this: all humans are coequal as image bearers of God. For most of human history we have not operated under this premise. Ancient kings believed that they were the manifestation of the gods, or the closest to them. There would be a secondary ruling class underneath the king or emperor consisting of the priests, prophets, magicians, councils and heads of state, and heads of the militaries. The rest submitted to their will. There was no principle of equality under the law. Equality under the law is a Judeo-Christian concept. Even 20th century examples, dictators like Adolf Hitler, Joseph Stalin, Mao Zedong, Pol Pot, and Saddam Hussein ruled in a similar way.[3] Even present-day Communist regimes in Russia, China, and North Korea, and Islamic regimes in Iran and Saudi Arabia operate with a top-down, tiered justice system.[3] It's not a universal constitution that the people helped create, and all are equally subject to, but rather the prevailing will of the ruler or the ruling elite. In these last two examples the rule of law is governed by constitutions influenced by the concept of Islamic Sharia, which is prejudicial and unjust according to western standards, even when it is being universally enforced. This is especially true for women, Jews, Christians, homosexuals, and former-Muslims who leave Islam. For specifics about Islam/Sharia I recommend Dr. Bill Warner's work at (https://PoliticalIslam.com).[4] But lack of equal justice is not limited to kings, emperors, dictatorships, or flawed constitutions based on unbiblical doctrines. Even in democratic nations with a democratic constitution, such as India, there are still injustices ingrained into the culture. There the predominant religion is Hinduism, and with it long-held religious and philosophical beliefs intertwined into the social structure. These influence inequality from its historical *caste* system and the Hindu beliefs of karma and dharma that govern it. The Hindu caste system is a three-thousand year old social hierarchy system that divides people into four main categories, from high-level teachers and priests to low-level menial workers, and a fifth class, the untouchables. Imagine being born into *classes* still in the 21st century! Though significant strides have influenced reform, such as those of Mohandas Gandhi, the caste system still affects many in India, which has nearly one-sixth of the world's total population.[5]

By contrast, God's Word teaches that all humans are created equal and justice applies to everyone equally under God's Law. This is the foundation for justice: equality under God. There are only two classes: God's, and everyone else's! We examined the foundation of the Law in Chapter 1, Section (J). This would destroy *any form* of racism or classism. When asked which commandment was most important in Mark 12:28 the second half of Jesus's answer, after putting God first above all, was *"'Love your neighbor as yourself.'"* James 2:8 calls this statement *"the royal law found in Scripture."* Likewise, Paul quotes it in Galatians 5:14 and Romans 13:9, saying the entire law is fulfilled in keeping this one command. By loving our neighbors as ourselves we treat them as equal. This is the essence of biblical justice. Justice is not ensuring no one ever has difficulty. It's not guaranteeing everyone has equal prosperity, as taught in corrupt communist and socialist philosophies. The bad fruits of these philosophies is evident in the cruel dictatorships they've inspired and the poverty, suffering, and 100 million deaths in the 20th century alone![3]

Let's examine briefly one of the distorted forms of justice of the economic philosophy behind socialism/communism. The Robin-Hood philosophy, that it's okay to rob from the rich to give to the poor. Is this just? We know that theft is always bad fruit. It is unjust to steal from someone, period. Just because one person has ten apples does not mean that they earned them in an illegal or immoral way. Just because ten other people have no apples, doesn't mean that they are righteous or moral, or that it's not still theft to steal from the one to give one apple to each of the ten others. It's still unjust. The thief, and the other ten if they knew about it, would be the ones guilty of sin. Biblical justice is about equality of dignity as a person, equality of the same human rights, equality of protection under the law. The United States Declaration of Independence captures this perfectly stating: "We hold these truths to be self-evident, that all men are created equal, that they are endowed by their Creator with certain unalienable Rights, that among these are Life, Liberty and the Pursuit of Happiness."[6] Justice is having a level playing field and everyone equally accountable under the same standards to do what is good, fair, and right, without favoritism. Biblical justice is always tied to righteousness.

Isaiah 33:15 *[About God]* He who walks righteously and speaks with sincerity, who refuses gain from extortion, whose hand never takes a bribe, who stops his ears against murderous plots and shuts his eyes tightly against evil...

Deuteronomy 16:19 *[God]* Do not deny justice or show partiality. Do not accept a bribe, for a bribe blinds the eyes of the wise and twists the words of the righteous. [20]Pursue justice, and justice alone, so that you may live, and you may possess the land that the LORD your God is giving you.

Psalm 89:14 *[To God]* Righteousness and justice are the foundation of Your throne; loving devotion and faithfulness go before You.

Proverbs 21:3 To do righteousness and justice is more desirable to the LORD than sacrifice.

Amos 5:24 *[To God]* Righteousness and justice are the foundation of Your throne; loving devotion and faithfulness go before You.

j. Social Justice
The movement for social justice—is BOTH godly and demonic.

That's perhaps the best way I can introduce you to both ends of the spectrum on this one. On one hand, many fighting for social justice are trying to fulfill the royal law to love their neighbors as themselves. And they are striving to produce: (1) true biblical justice, and (2) good, godly fruit that shines the light of Jesus into the world, lifts humans out of despair, eases suffering, promotes restoration, and advances the Kingdom of God. These things cannot be faulted. They're good. The confusion is that these good, godly, good-fruit-bearing objectives are called social justice—alongside bad, demonic, bad-fruit-bearing objectives that are *also* called social justice. Because they both use the same name this requires us in the Church to have discernment and wisdom. We also need to be quick to listen and slow to speak, especially if we're on the cusp of judging and condemning another believer by assuming they support bad social justice when they're trying to encourage good social justice. It's always better to optimistically assume the best of others and ask more questions until you know otherwise. Learn their *specific* ambitions.

The first problem with social justice begins with its name. It's not really based on *pure justice*, which is the quality of being just; in other words, righteousness, equitableness, or moral rightness. Justice is conformity to this principle, as manifested in *personal conduct*, and the administering of deserved punishment or reward for such conduct.[7] For Christians, this is best expressed in biblical, i.e. God-ordained, justice within human society. Social justice is not about individual conduct. It's about inequality or inequity within a society's social framework. One organization put it this way: "Social justice is the equal access to wealth, opportunities, and privileges within a society."[8] It's about fighting for people or causes that might already have equal treatment under the law, technically, but perhaps not equity or fairness within society due to other factors, usually systemic dysfunctions. Let's contrast the two. An example of biblical injustice would be pre-Civil War United States where African Americans were slaves in large part because of their skin color. Their slave status had nothing to do with any of the biblically-just reasons a person could became a slave: (1) as a means of repayment for *their* debt, (2) as an alternative to *their* death or exile after their nation had been conquered during war, or (3) as a means of *their* voluntary indentured servitude as a type of live-in job for survival. And in all of these cases God commanded that slaves would be treated humanely and had rights under God. But in pre-Civil War America many were not treated humanely and their status as slave was only due to skin color, which made it easy to have class distinction, which is totally unjust. This also clearly violated the biblical principle we previously read from the Declaration of Independence. Some would define the abolition of slavery as good social justice because it was the concerted effort towards the restructuring of an entire social system. I would merely call it biblical justice, but abolishing slavery could be considered social justice. Either way, the effort was good fruit.

Isaiah 58:6 *[God]* Isn't this the fast that I have chosen: to break the chains of wickedness, to untie the cords of the yoke, to set the oppressed free and tear off every yoke? ^{7}Isn't it to share your bread with the hungry, to bring the poor and homeless into your home, to clothe the naked when you see him, and not to turn away from your own flesh and blood?... ^{9b}If you remove the yoke from your midst, the pointing of the finger and malicious talk, ^{10}and if you give yourself to the hungry and satisfy the afflicted soul, then your light will go forth in the darkness, and your night will be like noonday.

Social justice is the desire and effort to promote equality and fairness in social systems. This is a good thing, however, not all are going about this with godly motives and with the desire to create a society more according to biblical standards. We all want a better world but we don't all agree as to what exactly would make it better. Much of the social justice movement is led by unregenerate sinners who are being led by Satan to further *corrupt* the world—in the name of justice! Many of the social justice reformation movements are advocating for: (1) abortion on demand, (2) inequality/racism/reverse racism, (3) theft via wealth redistribution, (4) socialism, (5) powerful, centralized or globalized government, (6) moralization of sexual liberty, (7) gender liberation, (8) hostile matriarchal feminism, (9) religious syncretism, (10) radicalized secularism, (11) redistributive liberty, and (12) restrictions on freedom/expression of religion and speech. These are antithetical to biblical justice and undermine biblical standards for living.

Intersectionality. Additionally, social justice according to some, tends to focus less on what we could call biblical justice, and more so as the fight against the unfair distribution of goods, against the systematic oppression by the so-called dominant, and the pragmatic emphasizing of coalition-building among different "oppressed" groups.[9] In Chapter 4 we looked at the necessity of living with gratitude rather than ingratitude (Section J), optimism rather than pessimism (Section K), and a conqueror mentality instead of a victim mentality (Section L). The mindset of many in this movement is the exact reverse, with fierce intensity and dedication to focus on whatever it is they feel they lack and their perceived victimization. This is called *Intersectionality,* because what they lack in common is negated by their common ground of being a victim, which is where they all intersect. And their alignment with other different "oppressed" groups often aligns different groups of ungodliness up with one another with a common enemy and goal, which just so happens to usually include the Church and those that share its conservative values. An example of this is the 2017 Women's March in the U.S. where radical feminists, pro-abortion, and LGBTQ movements aligned with pro-Sharia Muslim groups to march against conservatives. In any other reality this would be impossible, because Islamic Sharia Law is a far worse—and even deadly—opponent to their causes than Christians or conservatives are. Nonetheless these groups are forming alliances under the name of social justice to influence and change society. This is bad fruit anyways from a society's moral compass perspective, but it takes on another dimension from an end times perspective. Consider also how Satan is preparing the groundwork to one day use all of these philosophies and political alignments to create the perfect environment for the Antichrist to rise up and utilize them on a global scale. Righting these "injustices" will be thought of as just. Shutting down the "racist, bigoted, intolerant" churches will be the "good" thing to do. This storm is coming. So there's much bad fruit in this movement, too.

Justice must never be separated from righteousness.

A Caution. The mandate for Christians is to seek biblical justice in every way possible, including ways that involve improving the social structures of society. Our goal is to make them more just, more godly, more free. People must be free to proclaim and hear the gospel, and to follow Jesus in every way. The fruits of justice and righteousness begin in each of us individually, then from there they flow outward in our lives, communities, into our donations, voting, and service, and legislation. You should be aware that there is an effort to make social justice, even good, biblical, social justice, a more *centralized* part of what the Church is for. In extreme cases, this is being called "The Social Gospel." Herein the social aspects are being wrongly elevated as the *primary* thing for the Church to be doing. Or if not the primary thing then as a secondary aspect of equal importance. But let's be clear about this: social transformation of society is NOT the primary mission for

Christians! We'll look at the primary mission and purpose for Christians in Chapter 6, and the Church as a whole in Chapter 7. But simply put, we are fighting a *spiritual* fight and our mission and purpose are primarily spiritual. The Church is *holy*, which means "called-out" of the world. We can and should influence the world as much as possible but our mission is to help advance God's Kingdom by calling more people out. We're in the spiritual redemption and restoration business—not in the world-fixing business! We're in the business of bringing lost prodigals to the Father and the Lost to the Savior. We're bringing the spiritually hungry to Jesus, the Bread of Life, not to physical food alone! Do both if you can, but the former is weightier. *(Matt 4:4, Jn 6:22-58, Lk 12:23)*

We're in the spiritual redemption and restoration business—not in the world-fixing business!

Because of the complexity and diversity of needs and aims within the social justice spectrum there is opportunity for much good or evil. Another warning is necessary. Satan is using the love we have for our neighbors against the Church, by using the social justice movement to infiltrate the Church and distort important beliefs and behaviors of Christians. These are unbiblical and harmful beliefs that are still working towards the aim of good fruit, so they're subtle. Many have snuck in, and need to be exposed. A statement was put together by a group of influential Christian leaders called *The Statement on Social Justice*. It's online at (https://StatementOnSocialJustice.com). This reminds us of our need to "stand firm on the gospel and avoid being blown to and fro by every cultural trend that seeks to move the Church of Christ off course."[10] This website summarizes and refutes some of the unbiblical beliefs from the social justice movement that have, unfortunately, already been embraced by some Christian churches.

III. Fruit as Evidence of Saving Faith

Contrary to the false religions that teach salvation-by-works, Christians are saved by God's grace through faith in Jesus alone. However, that does not mean that works, i.e. good fruit, don't play any role in salvation. Good fruit doesn't *merit,* or help us *earn* salvation, but it does help reveal whether or not we are saved. It is evidence of our salvation. When we're saved and born again we receive the Holy Spirit, and with His presence comes the fruit of His Spirit. The fruit of the Spirit is the natural outflow of God's character. If His presence is in us our character and life will bear fruit as a result.

Proverbs 11:30a The fruit of the righteous is a tree of life...

k. Loving Mercy, Walking Humbly
Good fruit means loving mercy and walking humbly with God.

What is "good?" In Micah 6:8 God defines good for us. He says it's to act justly, love mercy, and walk humbly with Him. We've already examined what justice is in sections (I) and (J). We've examined humility throughout this book already, especially in Chapter 2, Section (G). But what about loving mercy? This is lacking in the hearts of many. Mercy is compassion or forgiveness shown towards someone, when it is within one's will to punish or harm them. If we are saved by ourselves, or our own good deeds, then we wouldn't have the same level of appreciation for mercy. The most legalistic religions and cultures are also the most cruel *because* people get the punishment that they do deserve. Christianity is built on the foundation that *Christ got* what we deserve! And we received the blessings that He deserved! Without mercy none of us has anything. We survive and prosper daily only through God's mercy. Naturally, as a response to this, we should have abundant mercy in our hearts towards others, too. This lesson was taught powerfully by Jesus in His parable of The Unforgiving Servant in Matthew 18:21-35. Because we have been forgiven of so much we need to extend this mercy and forgiveness to others. Even when they rightfully deserve punishment, and it's in your power to punish them, give mercy anyways. Shine brightest!

> Matthew 18:33 *[Jesus]* Shouldn't you have had mercy on your fellow servant, just as I had on you?'... [35]That is how My heavenly Father will treat each of you unless you forgive your brother from your heart."
>
> Micah 6:8 He has shown you, O mankind, what is good. And what does the LORD require of you but to act justly, to love mercy, and to walk humbly with your God?
>
> James 2:12 Speak and act as those who are going to be judged by the law that gives freedom. [13]For judgment without mercy will be shown to anyone who has not been merciful. Mercy triumphs over judgment.

l. Works Without Faith
Good works, without faith in Jesus, are *still* good works, though not supreme.

We're saved by faith, not works. See Chapter 2, Section (H) for more on that. But this does not mean that good works are not still good, *even if* they are done without total truth, knowledge, or faith in God. It's good to love your neighbor as yourself. It's good to help those in need. It's good to bring healing to the broken. It's good to bring a word of encouragement to the downtrodden. It's good to live just and to fight against injustice. These things are good even when they are done by non-Christians, or by bad Christians, or even by people who hate God! We should praise all secular and other interfaith religious efforts that do real good in the world. Remember section (J) of Chapter 4—the gratitude mindset. Think of the glass as half full, half good, at least in that particular good work. Now, they *still* need Jesus! But don't focus on and despise them for what they *aren't* doing right. Rejoice in what they *are* doing right! People aren't all or nothing. They are many little beliefs, many little pieces of who they are as a person, and many little actions. If they're doing any good at all then encourage that aspect of their activity without endorsing their other beliefs or actions. You should be able to recognize and endorse all that is good and best. Be careful though not to create partnerships that compromise your ability to spread the gospel. Remember, the best fruit we can give the world is the eternal fruit found in the gospel. Some churches align themselves with secular or interfaith social programs that want their assistance or money but want them to remain silent when it comes to matters of faith or politics. It's a mistake to enjoin ourselves with such things. *Any* good work that ultimately *suppresses* your *primary* objective is NOT a good work! So, rejoice in all good being done, in any form you find it, any place you find, by anyone or anything. However, reserve the majority of your time, talent, and treasure for that which is more aligned with your highest values, which should be Christ and gospel-centered.

m. Examine Your Motives
Be mindful of your real motivations, for doing good, so they're primarily for God.

We've already examined many of the attributes of good trees. We've examined how it's not enough to just want the final output, the fruit. We must be a good tree. It's an error to think we can accomplish any type of good fruit without first being a good tree anyways, as though we could shortchange the process. As though God only cares about the ends, and not the means. No, who we *are*, is just as important, if not more, than what we do. But what we do quite often reflects who we are. This is not always the case, though. There are certainly those who take care of their elderly parents, which looks like a good work on the outside, but God knows that in their heart they only do it for the inheritance. Greed, not love, is their motive. In Philippians 1:15-18 Paul says that there were people who *were* preaching, the *true* gospel, *but* their motive was envy, rivalry, and selfish ambition. So nothing is off limits. Even proclaiming the glorious gospel itself can be done in a way that results in a bad fruit. Nonetheless, his response in verse 18 was this: *"In every way, whether by false motives or true, Christ is preached. And in this I rejoice. Yes, and I will continue to rejoice,"* It is good, when good happens, even if by wrong motives.

Our Heavenly Father considers fruitful behavior those works that are inline with His will, done with a good motive. Well, as we've seen, the outward good is still good even if done with wrong motives. There is an extrinsically good outward aspect to it. If it wasn't good *at all*, for someone or something, then it wouldn't even be a good fruit. But when it comes to the *personal benefit* for the individual doing those outward acts, they will only be rewarded by God if they have pure motives. Jesus tells us in Matthew 6:1-21 that if we do good, righteous acts in the world—He uses the examples of giving to the needy, prayer, and fasting—but do so for the motivation of being esteemed by other people for being a religious or good person, then we've *already* received our reward. In other words, we didn't do it for God, to get closer to Him, but for the praise from the world and we've already received that praise. But if we do these things in secret, as though they're only for God, then we will store up for ourselves treasures in Heaven.

Example (Free Market). In the world good things will be done by people with bad motives. You need to accept and even expect this. Many do good while led by wicked intentions; Paul tells us to rejoice in the good. A system of good results being caused even by people with bad motives is one of the things I like about the economic system of capitalism, also called the Free Market. Business owners, or their employees, may be led to work purely by greed and their lust for money and possessions. But their bad motives are irrelevant when it comes to the success of the business. They won't earn any money unless they *first* satisfy the needs and wants of their customers. They have to first serve other people, and their needs, before they receive any money in return. And if the customers aren't satisfied, and *also* feeling like they're getting the better deal of the exchange, then they won't return and the business will die. But it's not only about the customers either, who are likely just as worldly, sinful, and greedy. If the business owner and employees don't *also* feel like they get what they want, in order to own a business, or to work in one, then the business will close and no one will benefit. So all parties need to benefit out of the entire enterprise otherwise it will eventually crumble. ALL parties could be motivated by greed and selfishness, and yet they must all serve one another's interests in mutual exchange in order for any needs to be met. The good of trade is ultimately accomplished despite all of it! If the market is truly free, it forces people to take care of one another.

Remember, it's not always wicked motivations. They may be just sinful, or may not even be inherently sinful, just natural, fleshly. At times we will be, too. This is why we must examine ourselves. You may start a good activity, for the right reasons, and then get consumed or distracted by the other perks of the activity. Maybe you started going to the soup kitchen to serve the less fortunate but then found yourself going a lot more often because of that cute volunteer there. Or you got into the worship band to use your talents to praise God, but then you started to find yourself really craving the spotlight and the admiration of your talents by others. But God knows why you really do what you're doing. Remember though that it's not all or nothing, you can have both. It's okay if you meet a cute volunteer while serving together, or to be complimented and appreciated for sharing your musical talents. Do it *for* God *first* and then just have gratitude to God for the additional blessings from fruitful activity. Enjoy all of the wonderful aspects that living a life of good fruit offers! Just keep an eye on your motives. Keep them in check. Remain confident of your *main motivation* for the reason that you're doing something.

n. Jesus is the Vine
Only good fruit, that is connected to the vine (Jesus), has any eternal significance.

In Chapter 2, Section (H) I went into detail about how we're saved by faith alone, and not at all by our good works. We looked at John 15:1-8, where Jesus describes Himself like a vine, with all of us as branches, and our good deeds as fruit coming off of our branches. One of the provocative statements Jesus says here, multiple times, is that without Him we cannot even bear good fruit! He says apart from Him we can do nothing! Now we've already explored several different ways that unsaved people can still do good things, and even wicked people with bad motives can still do good things, so what is Jesus saying here? He's saying that those good things that people can do, they won't *last,* without Him. They don't have *eternal* significance without Him. Those deeds are good in the same way that my dog obeying my commands is good. Or helping an elderly woman across the street is good. They're relatively good, but not absolutely good. They're temporarily good, at that place and time, but that is all. At the end of days, in the final analysis, those things won't matter. They don't affect the bottom line eternally. For us to produce truly good fruit, fruit of eternal significance, our fruit needs to be connected to Jesus. Jesus said that unless we are branches that *remain* in Him, we cannot bear any good fruit at all. We are utterly fruitless unless we're already a branch that is first in the vine (Him)! And it is only those already in Him by faith alone that are in the vine. Then, and only then, can we bear fruit. So, as you strive in your journey towards the fruitful direction never forget this truth. This is why the gospel needs to be at the center of all the other good works that we do! Because we want our fruit to count.

John 15:1 "I am the true vine, and My Father is the keeper of the vineyard. [2]He cuts off every branch in Me that bears no fruit, and every branch that does bear fruit, He prunes to make it even more fruitful... [4]Remain in Me, and I will remain in you. Just as no branch can bear fruit by itself unless it remains in the vine, neither can you bear fruit unless you remain in Me. [5]I am the vine and you are the branches. The one who remains in Me, and I in him, will bear much fruit. For apart from Me you can do nothing. [6]If anyone does not remain in Me, he is like a branch that is thrown away and withers. Such branches are gathered up, thrown into the fire, and burned.

---

o. Only the Foundation Survives
Only good workmanship, built upon the true foundation (Jesus), will survive.

Along the same line of thought as the previous section, here is a parallel truth: the only works—the good deeds, the projects, the businesses, the missions, the callings, the time, talents, and treasures—that are built on the foundation of Jesus will survive. EVERYTHING else will go up in flames! Here one day and then gone the next. Most of the billions of things we spend our lives focusing on will vanish in an instant one day. Only that which in some way points back to Jesus and the gospel and glorifies God will remain. Jesus equates Himself and His words as the rock and foundation in Matthew 7:24-27. This is the point that Paul is driving home in 1 Corinthians chapter 3. The Catholic Church has mishandled and twisted this Scripture for millennia falsely teaching that it supports their erroneous doctrine of purgatory. But Paul is talking about *works*, not people. And about a fire that burns up the *works*, to determine which works of Christians will survive in the end. Works that we build on a different foundation, other than Christ, will perish entirely. And works we build on the foundation of Christ, but with workmanship not actually *for* Christ, will also be burned up. The believer still on the foundation of Christ will survive, but their works won't. They will be saved, but only as if through the flames. Finally, it is the believer both on the foundation of Christ, who is then building good works that also glorify Christ upon that same foundation, that will stand, both the person and their works. Let us then strive to not only be upon Christ, our firm foundation, but also to build much good work upon that foundation that will last for all eternity!

---

1 Corinthians 3:10 By the grace God has given me, I laid a foundation as an expert builder, and someone else is building on it. But each one must be careful how he builds. [11]For no one can lay a foundation other than the one already laid, which is Jesus Christ. [12]If anyone builds on this foundation using gold, silver, precious stones, wood, hay, or straw, [13]his workmanship will be evident, because the Day will bring it to light. It will be revealed with fire, and the fire will prove the quality of each man's work. [14]If what he has built survives, he will receive a reward. [15]If it is burned up, he will suffer loss. He himself will be saved, but only as if through the flames.

---

p. Works-Based or Assisted Salvation
Remember, your good works do not earn, merit, or help assist in your salvation.

As you live a life of abundant fruitfulness you will encounter Christians who have wrong beliefs about fruitfulness. It's inevitable. The more we do good works the more you're going to serve alongside people who believe they are helping to merit their salvation through good works. The Catholic Church and other "Christian" groups may refer not only to good *deeds* assisting but also: (1) observance of the commandments, (2) observance of aspects of the Torah like Sabbath-keeping or dietary restrictions, (3) having to do penance for sin, (4) added human traditions, (5) purgatorial atonement, (4) indulgences for remission of purgatorial punishment, (6) prayers to, or help on our behalf of Mary or angels or patron saints, (7) obeying other supposed prophets, (8) avoiding every new conspiracy - every new form of the mark of the beast, or not saying God's "true" name the right way. Many believe we need external help to "*merit* for ourselves the graces needed to attain eternal life."[11] I cannot possibly list every bad example I've seen, but deny every single *addition* to the gospel! Nothing else can be added. Faith alone. And if you don't find it in this book then it isn't necessary. If we must *already be in* Jesus, the Vine, to have any fruit, then obviously our fruit cannot help us get or stay in the Vine!

q. Faith Without Works is Dead
Any faith that is alone, without good works as evidence of it, is a dead faith.

Believe it or not there are "Christians" who claim to love and believe in Jesus who think they have zero obligation or duty to *do* anything. No evangelism, no missions, no service in their community, no church attendance or participation, no or very little financial contribution to the things of God, no good deeds at all. They claim that to *do* anything is to try to earn or merit salvation. This is a wicked perversion of the truth. We are called and created to do good and genuine faith is evidenced by action. That action will be good fruit that testifies to their faith. In Matthew 5:16 Jesus said, *"Let your light shine before men, that they may see your good deeds and glorify your Father in heaven."* Our fruit is evidence of who we are and what we care about. A lack of desire to actively love others is a sign of still being unsaved! Jesus said in Matthew 7:19, *"Every tree that does not bear good fruit is cut down and thrown into the fire."* The apostle James encountered Christians who were ignoring the needs of those in their church and directly rebuked this type of fruitless faith.

James 2:14 What good is it, my brothers, if someone claims to have faith, but has no deeds? Can such faith save him? [15]Suppose a brother or sister is without clothes and daily food. [16]If one of you tells him, "Go in peace; stay warm and well fed," but does not provide for his physical needs, what good is that? [17]So too, faith by itself, if it is not complemented by action, is dead. [18]But someone will say, "You have faith and I have deeds." Show me your faith without deeds, and I will show you my faith by my deeds. [19]You believe that God is one. Good for you! Even the demons believe that—and shudder. [20]O foolish man, do you want evidence that faith without deeds is worthless? [21]Was not our father Abraham justified by what he did when he offered his son Isaac on the altar? [22]You see that his faith was working with his actions, and his faith was perfected by what he did. [23]And the Scripture was fulfilled that says, "Abraham believed God, and it was credited to him as righteousness," and he was called a friend of God. [24]As you can see, a man is justified by his deeds and not by faith alone. [25]In the same way, was not even Rahab the prostitute justified by her actions when she welcomed the spies and sent them off on another route? [26]As the body without the spirit is dead, so faith without deeds is dead.

Titus 3:14 And our people must also learn to devote themselves to good works in order to meet the pressing needs of others, so that they will not be unfruitful.

r. Loving Father Who Rewards
Salvation is a *gift*, received by faith—Heavenly rewards are *earned*, by good fruit.

Yes, you read that right! Good fruit that grows on the branch, that is in the vine of Jesus, built on the foundation of Jesus, earns us rewards! I outlined some of these eternal rewards in Chapter 1, Section (O) when I talked about Heaven on Earth in the life to come. It's important to keep the main thing the main thing, remember section (M) in this chapter about examining our motives? Don't chase heavenly rewards to the exclusion of a relationship with God, higher love, justice, righteousness, etc. You don't want to let selfish desire rule in you at all, and that includes heavenly earnings too. But if you keep things in balance, then yes, you should also know that your good works will merit you rewards! As Jesus says in Matthew 6:20 and 19:21 we can *"store up for yourselves treasures in Heaven, where moth and rust do not destroy, and where thieves do not break in and steal."* We will all be equal in one sense, equal in status as children of God, but our rewards will be different, based on our merits. So let this be another incentive for you to press in when it's difficult, to bear good fruit with your life.

1 Corinthians 3:6 I planted the seed and Apollos watered it, but God made it grow. [7]So neither he who plants nor he who waters is anything, but only God, who makes things grow. [8]He who plants and he who waters are one in purpose, and each will be rewarded according to his own labor... [14]If what he has built survives, he will receive a reward.

2 Corinthians 5:10 For we must all appear before the judgment seat of Christ, that each one may receive his due for the things done in the body, whether good or bad.

s. Proof of Being Jesus's Disciple
Your good fruit, is proof of your being Jesus's disciple, by actually following Him.

Jesus said in John 14:15, *"If you love Me, you will keep My commandments."* 1 John 2:4-6 makes it this crystal clear by saying, *"If anyone says, "I know Him," but does not keep His commandments, he is a liar, and the truth is not in him. But if anyone keeps His word, the love of God has been truly perfected in him. By this we know that we are in Him: Whoever claims to abide in Him must walk as Jesus walked."* I've heard Christians claim to know Jesus while living in sin. Or they try to follow *some* of the examples Jesus gave while ignoring many important commandments about righteousness God revealed in the Old Testament. Whenever we try to follow the "red letters" alone and not the entire Bible we're trying to dissect the Holy Trinity! To be Jesus's disciple means to also be obedient of everything God has said anywhere else, too. Jesus was totally obedient to the Father—and to be a disciple of Jesus means for us to be obedient like Him! During the Ten Commandments, in Exodus 20:6 God said I will *"Show loving devotion to a thousand generations of those who love Me and keep My commandments."* And Jesus never taught His disciples to only follow His commandments alone and not also God the Father's commandments. In fact, in warning the Church about the false prophets who would come in Jesus's name and infiltrate and deceive the Church He said they would do that very thing specifically! In Matthew 7:21 Jesus says, *"Not everyone who says to Me, 'Lord, Lord,' will enter the kingdom of heaven, but only he who does the will of My Father in heaven."* You see, obedience to the Father's will *is* Jesus's will. You cannot divide the Holy Trinity. To obey God is to obey God. Fruitfulness is part of discipleship. As you pursue a life of fruitfulness in faith know you're also proving that you're Jesus's disciple. And the loving devotion of God will be with you and be truly perfected in you.

Matthew 7:21 *[Jesus]* Not everyone who says to me, 'Lord, Lord,' will enter the kingdom of heaven, but the one who does the will of my Father who is in heaven. ²²On that day many will say to me, 'Lord, Lord, did we not prophesy in your name, and cast out demons in your name, and do many mighty works in your name?' ²³And then will I declare to them, 'I never knew you; depart from me, you workers of lawlessness.'

John 8:31 *[Jesus]* So He said to the Jews who had believed Him, "If you continue in My word, you are truly My disciples."

John 15:8 *[Jesus]* This is to My Father's glory, that you bear much fruit, proving yourselves to be My disciples.

---

t. Sanctification
Good fruit, internal and external, is evidence that you're being sanctified.

Romans 6:21 What fruit did you reap at that time from the things of which you are now ashamed? The outcome of those things is death. [22]But now that you have been set free from sin and have become slaves to God, the fruit you reap leads to holiness, and the outcome is eternal life.

Tough trials will come during your journey. You may go through situations where you have greater doubts in your faith, stumble into sin, wrestle with God. You may start to fall back into bad old patterns, or into bad new ones. Your memory of what God did in your life in the past will help you rebound back. Remembering how He delivered you from your old life will help you remember that it wasn't all in your mind. Your faith wasn't an illusion, something you were just indoctrinated in as a child. No, it was real! God is real. He *changed* you! Something happened. You had a powerful encounter with the Living God and it changed your course. Or He prevented you from going the wrong way, the way of sin and despair that others around you went into. Your good fruit will help remind you to stay the course. If you're still in a state of righteousness and victory now, your good fruit will help give you confidence as an outward sign that you *do* belong to Jesus. If you're starting to bear bad fruit now, this can act as an outward sign to remind you that you're drifting back in the wrong direction, or need to change something in your life. Maybe a fruitless relationship, business, church, lifestyle, habit. Your fruit, both the internal and external, can be a useful guide for you. It is an outward reflection that you *can* see, of your inner spiritual condition that you *can't* see. Use it as your compass...

IV. Chapter Summary and Evaluation

Chapter Summary
You'll know you're going in the right direction when moving towards the fruit.

You've got your new map. You're a new car, with a new driver, going in a new direction. Just follow the road, right? Not quite. Many of us will have to cover a lot of distance. There will be natural disasters, potholes, road construction, demonic attack, major illness, famines, pandemics, emergencies, unpredictable setbacks, children and grandchildren, job losses or changes, household or family dynamic changes, church leadership and mission focus changes, political or economic changes, and a variety of other things that come. It will not always be easy to know how best to handle the change that comes. And the *specifics* of what will come and how to handle those situations are also yet to be determined. But I can promise you this, you can figure it all out, sometimes much easier than most people realize, by measuring the fruitfulness of your options.

Let's consider an example. At the moment of this writing there is a global pandemic due to the highly contagious and deadly Covid-19 coronavirus. Many government-imposed restrictions have been set to reduce the spread of the virus causing businesses to close, many to lose their jobs, social distancing, families and churches meeting only virtually, etc. What should you do? How should you feel? What should you focus on? I'm using this time of isolation to hunker down and finish this book and doing only virtual counseling. And you should continue to be fruitful as well! You should continue to be a reflection and disciple of Jesus, who was a servant, healer, and shepherd. If you work in the medical field, in the church, or any field that is still open, and still *serving people,* great, keep doing what you're doing—in the name of Jesus! Treat not only their physical needs but also their spiritual needs. And if you're not, you can still pray for those who are sick, and for the protection of those serving the sick. And you can pray for God to eliminate this virus, and to use this season to draw people to Jesus through their trials. Rather than focusing on what stinks about this situation, be humble, be grateful, be optimistic, and seek God's voice to guide you in the unique ways that you play a role and serve others and be a blessing to them. If you were laid off it might include finding temporary work in a field that is overwhelmed right now. God may steer you to work, and to people in that work, that you may not have encountered otherwise. God is always working, keep your eyes open, there are opportunities everywhere!

This is also a season of quietness. Many people are not as consumed by their work, career ambitions, or consumerism. Sports games, concerts, bars, nightclubs, movie theaters, and many social outlets are all closed. Husbands, wives, and children are all home spending more time together. Forgetting the time-consuming activities that we've all become accustomed to, we're now having to remember the simple life like that of our ancestors. Much good fruit can come from this in the restoration of families. And in individuals, this is an opportunity for many to reconnect with God and reevaluate their lives. While some are on Facebook complaining about what they don't have you could be repenting, studying your Bible, developing your own knowledge, faith, and inward fruitful character. You could be evaluating the outward fruit in your personal life, marriage, parenting, career, church attendance, tithing, etc. Maybe you've been trusting so much in faith alone that your life hasn't been that fruitful, and this is your opportunity to change that. You could use this time of self-reflection to examine your own motivations in the thoughts, emotions, behaviors, and activities that consume you most. You could be on the internet learning more about your local community, identifying its needs in the way of biblical or social justice. You know your Heavenly Father will reward you for every good fruit built on the foundation of Jesus, so move towards it and let it bloom!

Chapter 5 Evaluation
AFTER THOROUGH, CAREFUL EXAMINATION, RIGHT NOW:

False   _Partially False_   _Mostly True_   _True_

Statement	1	2	3	4	5	6	7	8	9	10
a) I use fruitfulness to know I'm going in the right direction..	1	2	3	4	5	6	7	8	9	10
b) Fruit is good only if it expresses God's character or will	1	2	3	4	5	6	7	8	9	10
c) God's Kingdom is full of those humble with childlike faith	1	2	3	4	5	6	7	8	9	10
d) I'd rather be obedient to God than do what I think is best .	1	2	3	4	5	6	7	8	9	10
e) I know God's Law, it helps me make good choices in life ...	1	2	3	4	5	6	7	8	9	10
f) I've repented of all personal sinfulness and live righteously	1	2	3	4	5	6	7	8	9	10
g) My personal private life is bearing good inward fruit	1	2	3	4	5	6	7	8	9	10
h) My personal public life is bearing good outward fruit	1	2	3	4	5	6	7	8	9	10
i) I seek justice in everything, everyone is equal under God .	1	2	3	4	5	6	7	8	9	10
j) I support everything that blesses society and people in it.	1	2	3	4	5	6	7	8	9	10
j) I'm knowledgeable/cautious with Social Justice movement	1	2	3	4	5	6	7	8	9	10
k) I forgive everyone and I extend mercy to everyone	1	2	3	4	5	6	7	8	9	10
lp) There's no part of me that thinks my works help save me .	1	2	3	4	5	6	7	8	9	10
m) All current good deeds are done only with right motives...	1	2	3	4	5	6	7	8	9	10
n) We can bear no good eternal fruit without Jesus	1	2	3	4	5	6	7	8	9	10
o) Everything, not on the foundation of Jesus, will be burned	1	2	3	4	5	6	7	8	9	10
q) Faith without works (fruitful life) is a dead unsaving faith .	1	2	3	4	5	6	7	8	9	10
r) I'm more concerned with treasures/rewards in Heaven.....	1	2	3	4	5	6	7	8	9	10
s) Others would characterize my life as a disciple of Jesus....	1	2	3	4	5	6	7	8	9	10
t) The Holy Spirit has/is changing my life to bear more fruit.	1	2	3	4	5	6	7	8	9	10
IV) I will use fruitfulness to help me make decisions in life......	1	2	3	4	5	6	7	8	9	10

Date Last Taken: _____

Questions for Reflection or Group Study:

1) Why do you think people struggle with either a works-based salvation (saving ourselves with good works), and a faith-based salvation, without any good works at all?
2) Why do we focus on the lack of or bad fruit of others instead of ourselves? What area of your own life within your control, if you focused on improving fruit there, would make a major difference in your witness as a disciple of Jesus? How could you start tomorrow?
3) Prior to this chapter what would you think of first as the _main_ "good fruit" for a Christian? What fruit do you think is most significant now? How has your perspective changed?
4) See table of _Inward fruits_ (p. 240). Which good fruit has God sanctified and improved in your life most? Share your journey of overcoming, praise God together in gratitude.
5) Which bad fruit is still most prevalent in your life? Explore and share your struggle. Which do you need prayer for most? Read James 5:15-16. Confess your sins. Pray for one another.
6) See table of _Outward fruits_ (p. 242). Do the same. Which good fruit has God sanctified and improved in your life most? Which bad fruit do you still need prayer for the most?
7) Pick an area of biblical injustice or social injustice that is prevalent where you are, that you're most passionate about. Describe why this is an important issue to you and God.
8) Name a _specific_ area of biblical or social justice lacking, that you, your family, small group, or church, have the ability to do something about. What could you do to help?
9) Plan out a very small project that could be done together in the next two weeks.

Explore Chapter 5 Deeper:

For additional resources related to the topics discussed in this chapter see our companion website at **https://MPoweredChristian.org/Road-Map-Book-Resources**

- Free printable pdf of this chapter evaluation for personal or classroom use
- List of related online courses, ecoaching programs, personal coaching services
- List of related videos, articles, and recommended books
- List of related live webinars and ways to ask questions

Notes/Reflections:

_____
_____
_____
_____
_____
_____
_____
_____
_____
_____
_____
_____
_____
_____
_____
_____
_____
_____
_____
_____
_____
_____
_____
_____
_____
_____
_____
_____
_____
_____

To-Do List: Date: _____

MY TASKS FOR **THIS UPCOMING WEEK...**

✔ **My Big 1-3:**
_____
_____
_____

✔ **For Personal Growth:**
_____
_____
_____

✔ **For Key Roles:**
_____
_____
_____

✔ **For Calling/Ministry Service:**
_____
_____
_____

✔ **Pray for/Request prayer about:**
_____
_____
_____

✔ **Learn more about:**
_____
_____
_____

✔ **Other:**
_____
_____
_____

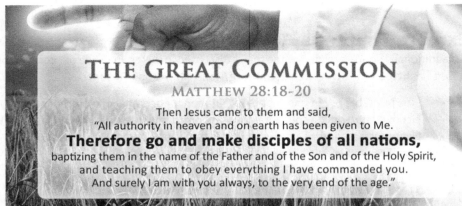

THE GREAT COMMISSION
MATTHEW 28:18-20

Then Jesus came to them and said,
"All authority in heaven and on earth has been given to Me.
Therefore go and make disciples of all nations,
baptizing them in the name of the Father and of the Son and of the Holy Spirit,
and teaching them to obey everything I have commanded you.
And surely I am with you always, to the very end of the age."

MPOWERED
CHRISTIAN

CHAPTER SIX

OUR MISSION AS DISCIPLES

You're a disciple of Jesus whose mission is to make more disciples of Jesus.

Chapter Contents

I. Seeing the Big Picture

a. Fruit is Only the Byproduct
Good external fruit is a byproduct—not your primary purpose, mission, or goal.

This needs to be taught! After the previous chapter it should be abundantly clear that we are to be fruitful. And if we're not then there's something wrong. Yet, this is not *why* we're here. Jesus didn't save us and leave us here so that we could cure the world of things like poverty. He told the disciples in John 12:8, *"The poor you will always have with you,"* so we know that the world will always have poor people. He didn't leave us here so we could *fix* every sin, injustice, and evil in the world. In the very last chapter of God's Word given to the Church, in Revelation 22:11 Jesus says, *"Let the unrighteous continue to be unrighteous, and the vile continue to be vile; let the righteous continue to practice righteousness, and the holy continue to be holy."* So not only will they continue He doesn't even tell us to try to fix them. And when Jesus describes the signs of the end of the age in Matthew 24 He says there will be wars, persecution, and multiplication of wickedness, that the love of most will grow cold. Please be optimistic but not naive.

Jesus's three and one half year ministry and the first few decades of the early church in the New Testament do not model for us efforts to overthrow the Roman government, legal, or political systems to make them better. They were told to pray *(Mt 5:44)* and bless *(Rom 12:14)* those who persecuted them, and in Romans 13 to submit to the governing authorities. The Church has had a positive impact on world history, but we're not going to fix the world and it isn't our job to. As long as people are not in the Kingdom of God they're still in the kingdom of darkness and under the influence of the prince of this world, Satan. The only way to fix the world is to save and sanctify every person in it. Therefore, the highest way for us to bring restoration to the world is to bring people to Jesus!

Think of it this way. Let's say I gave you an important letter with the mission to hand deliver it to someone in another country so you have to plan for that and take a long journey to get to them. Along the way to the second airport, you see an elderly woman get into a bad car accident and she needs your help to get to the hospital. You decide to stay with her for the night to keep her company because her family lives out of town and won't be able to get there until the following day. A few days later you're in a different city for the night and you see a homeless man and the Lord puts it on your heart to buy him dinner and take him shopping for a few things. Then on Sunday you visit a church nearby. After service you hang out and talk with people and find out that a young woman has been struggling with alcohol and depression since her divorce. You spend some time ministering to her needs, praying with her, and counseling her. All of these examples are good fruit. They are not a waste of time, they're exactly what God wants you to be doing. But remember your primary mission is to deliver the letter! And you're *always* doing that.

The external fruit-bearing things you do to bless others will change throughout your journey but your primary mission stays the same: to deliver the letter. One way to remember the sequence is to look at what Jesus said to the rich young man. He didn't tell him to give everything he had to the poor and then dedicate his life to helping the poor. He told him to give his possessions to the poor *then* to follow Him. Helping the poor was the temporary activity, following Jesus was the permanent activity. Following Jesus (and doing the things that a follower of Jesus does) is our primary mission. Helping the poor, and fruitful activities like that, are what we do *while* doing our primary mission.

Matthew 19:21 Jesus told him, "If you want to be perfect, go, sell your possessions and give to the poor, and you will have treasure in heaven. Then come, follow Me."

---

b. Remembering Our New Map
We are the holy "called-out" ones, who are no longer of this world.

We can and should influence the world for good, but this is a byproduct of being righteous, not the reason we've been called out of the world. As a born again child of God we're new creations. We're not of this world. We don't have the same maps as the people in the world. We're not going in the same direction as the people in the world. Yet, how easy it is for us to get caught up in the same activities as the world. Our hobbies are the same. Our TV and movies are the same. Our music is the same. Even our church services are worldly nowadays, with worship more in common with a drug-induced rock concert than a holy and religious celebration and time of communion with God. All this designed to entertain the goats rather than feed the sheep. See Matthew 25:31-46 if you don't get the reference. But before you get the wrong idea about me I'm not a total Puritan. I'm not saying that you need to live in a convent and only read the Bible all day long. There are plenty of ways to enjoy worldly non-Christian things, that are innocent enough, that a discerning and balanced amount of them won't pollute your walk.

However, there are certain domains or spheres of life that we need to be more cautious about. Areas where it's better to play it safe and stick with the fundamentals, not straying too far off from the straight and narrow. One of those areas is how we do *church*. What we think the *point* of church is. We'll cover that in Chapter 7. The other main area is how we do *discipleship*. What we think it means to be a disciple of Jesus, and what a disciple actually *does*. This has changed quite a bit over the years, influenced by the *outside* culture, so we need to get back to the basics. God hasn't changed, Jesus hasn't changed, the Bible hasn't changed, but church and discipleship have—why? Because the church is being influenced by the world! It's trying to keep up to stay relevant. We're not supposed to be relevant to the every desire of people still in Satan's kingdom.

The unsaved do not need the church to be relevant in *every* way, just in the matters of the soul. We need to be relevant and relatable, understandable, accessible. Able to bring Jesus to the needs of their heart and mind. But the ability to do that transcends culture. They need to be called out of where they are and led to Jesus! They don't need a church and a Jesus that fits into *their* map—they need the new map! We have something different, on purpose, and it's exactly what the world needs. Let us remember this when we're putting together discipleship programs and planning church activities. Our activities shouldn't be primarily fruitful activities that secular or non-Christian people and organizations are doing. Things like poverty relief programs. The whole unsaved world is concerned with things like poverty. If the entire unsaved world is consumed with these types of social concerns that is all the more an indication that it isn't the primary mission of the Church. Rather than just feeding the poor—give them Jesus! And if you can fill their bellies while doing so, even better! Jesus prayed this to the Father about the Church. It reminds us of how we should expect to see ourselves in the world and what our purpose is. We exist so that the world may believe in Jesus!

> John 17:14 *[Jesus praying to the Father]* I have given them Your word and the world has hated them; for they are not of the world, just as I am not of the world. ¹⁵I am not asking that You take them out of the world, but that You keep them from the evil one. ¹⁶They are not of the world, just as I am not of the world... ¹⁸As You sent Me into the world, I have also sent them into the world... ²⁰I am not asking on behalf of them alone, but also on behalf of those who will believe in Me through their message, ²¹that all of them may be one, as You, Father, are in Me, and I am in You. May they also be in Us, so that the world may believe that You sent Me.

Give them Jesus so they can receive eternal life—and just meet their temporary needs *while* doing it!

c. Treasures in Heaven
Your mission, lifestyle, goals, and objectives should be eternally-minded.

Get your eyes off of the treasures of this world. Focus on the people. Even more so, focus on the deepest parts of people. Their deepest spiritual needs. Align your objectives in the world with God's objectives in the world. Does God want to abolish poverty? Disease? Climate damage? Then He would have. Remember the long term goal of why He created humanity: to have a people for Himself that know Him and enjoy Him for eternity. For this to happen Jesus and the gospel must permeate the hearts and minds of people. This is eternally significant but might not bear fruit from a worldly perspective immediately or even at all in this life. Focus on the eternal rewards described in Chapter 1, Section (O). Remember the lessons you learned in Chapter 5, Section (N), only fruit connected to the vine (Jesus) has eternal significance, and Section (O), only good workmanship built upon the true foundation (Jesus), will survive. Set your focus on and pursue such things. Everything else is temporary and needs to take the back seat!

Matthew 19:29 *[Jesus]* And everyone who has left houses or brothers or sisters or father or mother or wife or children or fields for the sake of My name will receive a hundredfold and will inherit eternal life.

---

d. Fruit Can Be Unloving
God's way may seem bad, unkind, or unloving, to those still in rebellion to God.

Fortunately, many of the good, fruitful things that we do will also be seen by the rest of the unsaved world as good to them, too. People usually won't fault you for having a loving marriage, raising your children right, helping the poor, serving the vulnerable, helping animals, fighting for justice or equality. But this won't always be the case. In fact, if the world doesn't dislike what you're doing, at least a little, you're not preaching that people are sinners that need to repent and Jesus is the only way to avoid Hell! Because this will be offensive to people still living in sin who don't know Jesus. When you don't join in the same sinful activities, join in the cursing and gossip, use your wealth for God's Kingdom rather than hoarding it for yourself to keep up with the Joneses, they may feel judged, whether you've intentionally judged them or not. Many in the LGBTQ community accuse Christians, who see their beliefs and lifestyle as sinful, as being bigoted or hateful.

One example of this, that went far beyond feelings, to be made a national example of, is Jack Phillips. He is a Christian bakery owner who declined to bake a wedding cake for a homosexual couple, was accused of discrimination and has been fighting legal battles as a result since 2012. The first court battle cost him 40 percent of his business and prompted him to lay off six of his 10 employees. He said he also endured death threats and his shop was vandalized. After getting all the way to the U.S. Supreme Court and winning in 2018 you'd think his troubles were over. But the *same day* the Supreme Court announced it would hear Phillips' case against his state of Colorado, a transgender person requested a cake be made to celebrate the anniversary of their transition. He declined to make a cake celebrating something that counters his religious beliefs. Once again the activists and the State of Colorado targeted him to make an example out of what will happen to Christians who take a stand for beliefs going against sinful cultural tides.[1]

Of course not all will be threatened with our businesses being forced to close, endless legal battles, death threats, vandalism, violent or social persecution, etc. but we're all likely to offend, hurt feelings, risk relationships, and suffer other consequences. We can—and need to—speak the truth *in love*—always—but some will hate you and be vindictive anyways. Jack Phillips was a sweet, gentle man that had no problem with the same homosexual couple who had bought traditional cakes from his bakery for years. Another example is Dr. Michael L. Brown, a prominent evangelical leader dedicated to advancing social and cultural revival, who has openly stood against the rising influence of LGBTQ activism. He's always approached the subject with the heart of pastor and a demeanor of gentleness, love, and compassion for all people. To my knowledge, he is never filled with rage or hatred, but only love and concern for those struggling with sinful sexual temptation. In fact he is well known for his positive demeanor, with homosexuals, atheists and others who often call in to his radio show to discuss their disagreements. They often comment their appreciation for his always-in-love approach and demeanor. Nevertheless, he has still been put on the Southern Poverty Law Center's "Hate Watch" list and has been branded and targeted as a dangerous hate-filled bigot and homophobe.[2]

The same will be true for anything else you do in righteousness or in mission on behalf of the biblical Jesus. It isn't politically correct and it will upset and offend. But you need to remember that just because people accuse you of being filled with hate, or of being bigoted, homophobic, racist, Islamophobic, xenophobic, white nationalist, close-minded, etc. doesn't mean that you are. Your own conscience needs to testify of your innocence in those accusations. Your allegiance is to Christ and to God's Kingdom, not to the world and Satan's kingdom. Yes, you are to love all neighbors but this doesn't mean that they will always *feel* loved. Sometimes you will do the most loving *right* thing and people will still *feel* hated by you. They may *feel* judged, betrayed, criticized, angry, or mad but that doesn't necessarily mean you've done wrong. If your neighbors house is on fire and they are unaware of it, the most loving thing you can do is kick their front door down, grab them out of bed, and drag them to the front yard! This might not *feel* loving to them, but it is! They may prefer for you to send a gentle text message instead. One that tells them you love them and that if they would be open to it sometime if they would please consider leaving wherever they are and meeting you wherever you are. That may be more gentle, but if their house is on fire it's not more loving! Love cares enough that you're willing to make them mad at you, even though you'd prefer they weren't mad at you. That you love them enough that you're willing to get punched and scratched by them while dragging them out of a burning building! Now, you can't force anyone into the Kingdom of God but our activities do need to show them this *urgency*.

If your primary activities, on behalf of Jesus, never upset, you're operating out of *fear*—not love.

II. Our Primary Mission

e. Jesus Reigns With All Authority
There's two opposing kingdoms, but Jesus's reigns, and has greater authority.

If bearing fruit is not the main focus for us, then what *is* our primary mission? We're going to look at seven different aspects of our primary mission, though they're all very closely related. But before we get into them you need to understand what authority is. Authority is not the same thing as power. German sociologist Max Weber said that "power is the ability to exercise one's will over others." "Power is an entity or individual's ability to control or direct others, while authority is influence that is predicated on perceived legitimacy." (Weber 1922) Authority refers to accepted power, that is, power that people agree to follow. Weber identified three different types of authority, two of which are relevant to us now: charismatic and legal-rational. Charismatic authority is based on a leader's personal, dynamic qualities.[3] Jesus fits into this category because of who He is and how He leads. We willingly submit to His authority and follow Him because He is the model leader that we all look to and want to become like. This is even God's plan for us, to become just like Jesus, as we looked at in Chapter 1, Section (M).

Legal-rational authority resides in the office itself, not the person. Examples of this are the office of President or the role of police officer. It's not the person that has authority, but the position itself. Their power is legitimized by established rules, regulations, or laws.[3] Here's an interesting point: both Jesus and Satan fall into this category. Here's why. There's a natural consequence to sin: separation from God. As God separated fallen beings from Himself, an alternative kingdom was established as a result. After the Fall, humanity also came under the dominion of this other kingdom. Think of it like God deciding to establish a two-government system in the spiritual realm on earth. His own Kingdom, and then another, of which someone would become leader over. Because Satan initiated and led both the angelic and human rebellions against God, he's chief among sinners, naturally assuming this role. Jesus called Satan "the prince of this world" in John 12:31. Him being the prince isn't an honor that was bestowed to him by God, but a dishonor. In fact, he is intentionally called a prince—and not a king. His authority is not based on who he is, like charismatic authority. The authority lies in the office itself, the office that *God* established when He permitted an alternate kingdom to continue to operate alongside His. A time will come when Jesus will forever destroy that alternate kingdom, but in the meantime He's expanding God's Kingdom into it and conquering its territory. In the same verse, John 12:31, Jesus said that now, he [the prince of this world] would be cast out. So Jesus's arrival, and to an even greater extent His crucifixion and resurrection, marks an era when Satan's authority has been superceded and surpassed by Jesus's. Hebrews 2:14-15 says that Satan is the one who holds the power of death and is the captor of all people, who are held in slavery by our fear of death. But then it also says that Jesus, by His death, might destroy him [Satan], and free us. 1 John 3:8 confirms this saying, *"This is why the Son of God was revealed, to destroy the works of the devil."*

Satan has authority over all sin and all who sin. They're in bondage to him, because of their sin, and he's well aware of it. He tells Jesus in Luke 4:6-7, *"'I will give You authority over all these kingdoms and all their glory," he said. "For it has been relinquished to me, and I can give it to anyone I wish. So if You worship me, it will all be Yours.'"* But Jesus knew that both His authority and His power already exceed Satan's, even before the resurrection. He not only had greater authority and power Himself, He even extended it to all of His disciples during His ministry. In Luke 10:19 He tells them, *"See, I have given you authority to tread on snakes and scorpions, and over all the power of the enemy. Nothing will harm you."* This is true for all of us as well. Whoever we allow to influence us is given authority over us, and with that authority comes power over us as well. As we move forward and examine these seven aspects of our primary mission let us keep this truth in view: Jesus reigns with all authority in Heaven and on earth! But remember that humans have free will to sin, and whenever we do, we give Satan authority and power over us in that area. But every part inside of ourselves, as well as every part of the outer world that we go in the victory of the cross and in the authority of Jesus, a shift takes place there in the spiritual realm. God's Kingdom expands and Satan's kingdom shrinks! Jesus reigns right now from Heaven and He is in the process of destroying all other dominions, authorities, and powers. His reign will continue this way until all His enemies have been put under His feet, which will happen on the Last Day.

Matthew 28:18 Then Jesus came to them and said, "All authority in heaven and on earth has been given to Me."

Ephesians 1:20 ..when He raised Him *[Christ]* from the dead and seated Him at His right hand in the heavenly realms, [21]far above all rule and authority, power and dominion, and every name that is named, not only in this age, but also in the one to come. [22]And God put everything under His feet and made Him head over everything for the church, which is His body, the fullness of Him who fills all in all."

1 Corinthians 15:23 But each in his own turn: Christ the firstfruits; then at His coming, those who belong to Him. [24]Then the end will come, when He hands over the kingdom to God the Father after He has destroyed all dominion, authority, and power. [25]For He must reign until He has put all His enemies under His feet. [26]The last enemy to be destroyed is death. [27]For "God has put everything under His feet."

Colossians 2:10b Christ, who is the head over every ruler and authority.

f. On This Rock I Will Build

1) The Apostle Peter isn't the rock and foundation of the Church—Jesus is.
2) It's faith in Jesus's divine Messiahship, that enjoins us to HIS *spiritual* Church.
3) It's our mission to proclaim these two truths to others in the world.

How did Jesus establish the church? Who or what was the church built on? Where is the true church now? How does a person officially join it? The crucially important passages below, and how we interpret them, give us a lot of this information. This is yet another area that has been greatly and falsely distorted by the Roman Catholic Church. The passage below, nearly single handedly, contains the core argument for why they believe they have the entire authority of Jesus's Church on earth. For centuries they've claimed to be the one true church and every other view is considered heretical, and denomination estranged. It's belief in their authority that gives them permission to knowingly introduce other unbiblical doctrines, because their magisterium and popes are considered just as authoritative as the Bible. But if they're wrong about the single verse below then their entire Roman edifice crumbles like a house of cards. And they are wrong.

Matthew 16:13 When Jesus came to the region of Caesarea Philippi, He questioned His disciples: "Who do people say the Son of Man is?" [14]They replied, "Some say John the Baptist; others say Elijah; and still others, Jeremiah or one of the prophets." [15]"But what about you?" Jesus asked. "Who do you say I am?"

[16]Simon Peter answered, "You are the Christ, the Son of the living God."

[17]Jesus replied, "Blessed are you, Simon son of Jonah! For this was not revealed to you by flesh and blood, but by My Father in heaven.

[18]And I tell you that you are Peter, and on this rock I will build My church, and the gates of Hades will not prevail against it.

[19]I will give you the keys of the kingdom of heaven. Whatever you bind on earth will be bound in heaven, and whatever you loose on earth will be loosed in heaven."

The Roman Catholic Church's position is this: *Peter,* himself, is the rock that Jesus built His church on. He, alone, was given the keys of the kingdom of Heaven. They claim that Jesus established the Church, intending a single head to lead it, an office with authority. Since Peter was a bishop (leading church elder) in the city of Rome, this same authority was then passed down to every subsequent bishop of Rome since Peter. Called Roman pontiffs—or popes—the Catholic Church claims to have an unbroken chain of popes going back to Peter. Whenever a pope has made an official decree *ex cathedra* (from the seat of Peter), it has Apostolic authority, and is considered infallible (papal infallibility). Every follower of Jesus must ask: Is this what Jesus *meant* and *intended*?

Son of God. Peter was wise to recognize that Jesus was the Christ. But that particular insight was not new. In fact Peter's brother Andrew claimed this about Jesus before Peter had even met Him! We read in John 1:40-42, *"Andrew, Simon Peter's brother... found his brother Simon and told him, "We have found the Messiah" (which is translated as Christ). Andrew brought him to Jesus."* Many thought Jesus was the Christ prior to Peter's profession of faith here. Peter said something else though. In verse 16 he said, *"you are the Son of the living God."* It is *this* revelation, that actually touches on the unique divine nature of the eternal Word of God that became a man, that was divinely inspired by the Father. See, this wasn't Peter being a perfect leader who Jesus decides to build everything on. He wasn't. Peter was a good but flawed man who Jesus calls Satan just four verses later in Matthew 16:23. And then in the following chapter is the transfiguration of Jesus. Peter being Peter doesn't know what else to say so he blurts out and rambles on that they should put up shelters for Him, Moses, and Elijah. God the Father speaks out of Heaven and *literally interrupts him* saying, *"This is My beloved Son, Listen to Him!"* All, including Peter, fell facedown in terror. The Bible is clear. The focus is never Peter—it's about Jesus!

Matthew 17:1 After six days Jesus took with Him Peter, James, and John the brother of James, and led them up a high mountain by themselves. ²There He was transfigured before them. His face shone like the sun, and His clothes became as white as the light. ³Suddenly Moses and Elijah appeared before them, talking with Jesus. ⁴Peter said to Jesus, "Lord, it is good for us to be here. If You wish, I will put up three shelters—one for You, one for Moses, and one for Elijah." ⁵While Peter was still speaking, a bright cloud enveloped them, and a voice from the cloud said, "This is My beloved Son, in whom I am well pleased. Listen to Him!" ⁶When the disciples heard this, they fell facedown in terror. ⁷Then Jesus came over and touched them. "Get up," He said. "Do not be afraid."

The emphasis in both these passages is that Jesus is the Son of God. Jesus tells Peter he wasn't given this knowledge by man, but by inspiration from the Father. The Holy Spirit revealed it to Peter. He had faith. His eyes were spiritually opened by God. It is this— faith—in Jesus, as the Son of the living God—that is the rock, that Jesus built His Church on. It's not Peter, himself, that Jesus's Church was founded upon, as though everything hinges on Peter. No, it's personal faith—as led by the Spirit of God, in Jesus as the Son of God—that everything else hinges on. Peter's not the focus here - Jesus is! Always!

Who's the Rock? What about the phrase, *"you are Peter, and on this rock I will build My church."* Since the name *Peter,* given to Simon, means rock, is Peter the "rock" here? This is what the Catholic Church teaches.[5] But no, these are two different words. The Greek reads you are *Petros* and on this *petra* I will build My church. "*Pétros* (Strong's 4074) is a stone (pebble), such as a small rock found along a pathway. *Pétros* is an isolated rock, such as a man may throw. *Pétra* (Strong's 4073) then stands in contrast, as cliff, boulder, or projecting rock." Jesus essentially says "you are pebble, but on this cliff (of the statement you just made) I will build My Church."[4] They're likely all standing on a cliff and Jesus is just doing a play on words with his name. Catholic apologists will argue that Jesus originally spoke in Aramaic, supposing Jesus said Petra in both places, with an Aramaic version of Matthew written first that changed when it was converted to Greek.[5] Whatever early church evidence there is to support a belief in an earlier Aramaic version,[6] we do not *have* it so this is all purely hypothetical! It's pure conjecture! The Greek version is the one that was widely circulated and accepted, *guaranteed* to have actually existed and to have been inspired and preserved by the Holy Spirit. This is the version biblical people get their doctrines from. Plus, if Jesus wanted the entire Church to be built upon Peter why not just say upon *you* I will build my Church and *you* will lead it?

Death Proof? Jesus also says *"the gates of Hades will not prevail against it."* (v.18) Hades is the realm of the dead, not Hell. I've heard people wrongly quote "gates of Hell" here. (Though that's also true! :)) *(Mt 11:23; Lk 10:15, 16:23; Rev 1:18, 6:8, 20:13-14) Death itself* will not prevail against what He built! Rome's Church is not exempt from death. They experience death like everyone else. The Church Jesus built isn't an *earthly* institution of steeples, composed of human organizations, magisteriums, and canon laws. No, it's a *spiritual building* composed of all God's born again children now *exempt* from death!

What did Peter think? Did Peter himself believe that he was the rock and leader of Jesus's Church? Keep in mind the Catholic Church's *entire* case for even having a pope position - at all - hangs upon these two verses, Matthew 16:18-19. That's it. No other Scripture suggests, even vaguely, that Peter was believed to be the final decision maker and head of Jesus's Church. Much less that this headship would continue in perpetuity for thousands of years by people far removed. If Jesus had given Peter this supreme appointing, as the head of the entire Church, there would be evidence of it in Scripture, right? Yet, we find the exact opposite! First, we find that the account of Jesus saying this to Peter wasn't considered very important to the apostles. How so? This discussion is recorded in both other synoptic gospels: Mark 8:27-30 and Luke 9:18-20. Yet, the last controversial part about Peter being the rock and the one getting the keys is *only* recorded in Matthew's version! It's not rephrased or anything—it is *totally* left out completely! The authors didn't think it was significant enough to remember or make sure it was recorded. Not even in Mark's gospel, which has traditionally been believed to be written by John Mark, Peter's companion in Rome, written on behalf of Peter providing Peter's unique perspective. If essentially "Peter's" version of the gospel doesn't include it maybe it's not revealing information so significant the entire Church should be built upon it.

What does Scripture say about Peter's leadership? Because Peter denied Jesus before His crucifixion he doubted his role at all in the new church after the resurrection, perhaps even going back to his old fishing career. However, before His ascension Jesus reinstates Peter as part of His Church in John 21. But he doesn't say this whole thing is built upon you Peter, or I've put you in charge of my church Peter, or anything like that. He simply says, *"Feed My lambs, Shepherd My sheep, Feed My sheep."* (v.15-17) If Peter is the leader why does Jesus tell him not to worry about His plans for John and to just follow Him, twice. (v.19, 22) Jesus commissioned Peter to *follow Him*, not be the *head for Him*. Jesus is clearly the Head of His Church. They are *His* sheep! Peter is being told to follow Him and be a shepherd—not to be *His Vicar* on the earth! Peter alone isn't Jesus's representative on the earth—all Christians are. We see Peter being a leader in Acts 1:15 suggesting they select a replacement for Judas, but he doesn't choose the replacement himself. They decide as a group it's a good idea and then threw lots for it. I'd argue that God never really appointed apostleship here anyways. I believe the evidence suggests Jesus planned on using the Apostle Paul as Judas's replacement all along. We also see Peter stepping up as a leader in Acts 2:14 in his sermon at Pentecost. But none of this is really the issue. Christians all know and agree that Peter was *a* leader—the question is whether or not he was *the* leader. Peter doesn't imply he thinks this at all in either of his letters. In 1 Peter 1:1 he identifies himself as "Peter, in 1 Peter 5:1 as "an apostle of Jesus Christ" and a "fellow elder," and in 2 Peter 1:1, "Simon Peter, a servant and apostle of Jesus Christ." Peter saw himself as an apostle and an elder, not as the chief pontiff over everyone else. Remember what I said about the difference between Petros and petra? Peter himself would remember who the *rock* of the Church was built on, right? Peter had this to say about Jesus in his letter below. Not only does he not claim a headship status, or refer to himself as the rock, he's very clear about *who* the rock and foundation is. Jesus is the rock—not him! Notice how this is *all* about us *believing in Jesus* as our foundation.

---

1 Peter 2:4 As you come to Him, the living stone, rejected by men but chosen and precious in God's sight, [5]you also, like living stones, are being built into a spiritual house to be a holy priesthood, offering spiritual sacrifices acceptable to God through Jesus Christ. [6]For it stands in Scripture: "See, I lay in Zion a stone, a chosen and precious cornerstone; and the one who believes in Him will never be put to shame." [7]To you who believe, then, this stone is precious. But to those who do not believe, "The stone the builders rejected has become the cornerstone," [8]and, "A stone of stumbling and a rock of offense."

What did others think? Did the other apostles see Peter having greater authority after Jesus said this to him? Where they upset he was second in command? Did they think he was greatest among them? No, if he was, they had no idea! On their *final* trip to Jerusalem, where Jesus would be killed, John's and James's mother went to Jesus, while traveling on the road, to request that her sons would sit at his right and left. She requests *them* to be the next highest after Jesus. Odd request if everyone, especially them two, already knew that Peter would be the leader. But they didn't know this, in fact it says that the other ten (including Peter) were indignant with them for seeking for special privileges above the others! Jesus doesn't set them all straight and clarify that Peter is going to lead either. Rather, He does the exact opposite. In Matthew 20:24-28 it reads, *"When the ten heard about this, they were indignant with the two brothers. But Jesus called them aside and said, "You know that the rulers of the Gentiles lord it over them, and their superiors exercise authority over them. It shall not be this way among you. Instead, whoever wants to become great among you must be your servant, and whoever wants to be first among you must be your slave—just as the Son of Man did not come to be served, but to serve, and to give His life as a ransom for many."* Jesus doesn't tell them He's chosen Peter to be first. He even says "whoever wants to be first among you." He makes it clear that His Church will not have that type of worldly lordship type of authority to it. What Rome does now - having the entire world bowing down to a man because of his position as head of the church is the exact opposite of this! Nevertheless, the apostles continued to dispute over who is greatest among them, happening again the *night before* the crucifixion at the Last Supper. After Jesus tells them one of them will betray Him, it stirs them to question among themselves which of them was going to do it. Then in Luke 22:24 it says, *"A dispute also arose among the disciples as to which of them would be considered the greatest."* Again, they are all equals arguing over who will be considered greatest among them. No one thought Peter was greatest having been designated as the rock and head of the church!

What about the other apostles and disciples in the early church? We see in Galatians 2:9 that the apostle Paul recognized Peter as a pillar of the Church—but right alongside James and John. No hint of Peter's superiority. He also wasn't above public rebuke right to his face, of which Paul admits to doing in verse 11. And it wasn't over an insignificant matter either. He was being a total hypocrite and leading others astray into error! It was over the very heart of the gospel, salvation by faith alone, and the unity of Jews and Gentiles by faith apart from the works of the Law! *(Gal 2:9-21)* An error the Catholic Church *still* commits—having learned nothing from Peter's error! Fortunately, Peter did. In the first ecumenical church council at Jerusalem, recorded in Acts 15, they came together to discuss this matter concluding that Paul had been right. Peter shares his testimony and opinion among the other apostles and elders. *(v.6-11)* But Peter isn't the final authority. Rather, it's James, who church history records as bishop of Jerusalem, which was the entire Jesus movement's headquarters, that had the final say. In verse 19 he concludes the council saying, *"It is my judgment, therefore, that..."* and then that was it!

Keys of the Kingdom / Binding and Loosing. But didn't Jesus give Peter the keys of the kingdom of heaven? Wasn't Peter alone told first that whatever he binds on earth will be bound in heaven, and whatever he looses on earth will be loosed in heaven?

Doesn't he, or the office of chief Pontiff, hold these keys now? What does it mean to have the keys, or to bind and loose? No, Peter nor the head pontiff office holds the keys -Jesus does. In Revelation 1:18 Jesus says, *"I was dead, and behold, now I am alive forever and ever! And I hold the keys of Death and of Hades."* They weren't given to Peter, or to the office of pope, they were given to the entire Church as a whole. And this is only because the Church is the *Body* of Christ, and *He*—Jesus—still holds the keys. The same is true for the promise to bind and loose, which was not only given to Peter but to the rest of the apostles and the entire extended Church led by His Spirit. Binding and loosing were *judicial* terms that meant either to *legislatively declare* one thing to be prohibited and unlawful, or forgiven and having been restituted for. The apostles here aren't *deciding* for themselves what will be good, that it then becomes as such in heaven. As though Jesus has ordained us humans to declare God's rulings. Rather, it's the other way around. The Holy Spirit is guiding the members of the true Church. If we're each led by the Spirit of God, and come together in unity to declare a ruling, we will adjudicate and discipline members of the Church on earth just as it's already been determined in Heaven. It's not us determining what *shall* happen in the spiritual realm—it's us coming into agreement on earth to reflect the reality of what is so. This is why Jesus is present, via the Holy Spirit in us, in all godly prayer asked in unity in His name. This is modeled in Matthew 18:15-20, shown below. Importantly followed by a lesson in verses 21-35 about forgiveness.

Matthew 18:15 If your brother sins against you, go and confront him privately. If he listens to you, you have won your brother over. [16]But if he will not listen, take one or two others along, so that 'every matter may be established by the testimony of two or three witnesses.' [17]If he refuses to listen to them, tell it to the church. And if he refuses to listen even to the church, regard him as you would a pagan or a tax collector. [18]Truly I tell you, whatever you bind on earth will be bound in heaven, and whatever you loose on earth will be loosed in heaven. [19]Again, I tell you truly that if two of you on the earth agree about anything you ask for, it will be done for you by My Father in heaven. [20]For where two or three gather together in My name, there am I with them."

The Church on earth isn't to let people have a false sense of security in salvation, doctrine, or behavior. The Church needs to adequately convey the spiritual reality of how things really are in order to edify the Body. We aren't to tell people they're forgiven and right with God when they're still unrepentant and living in rebellion. Catholic priests who absolve (declare forgiven) a Catholic of their sins without knowing the person and identifying genuine repentance is actually doing the *exact opposite* of this principle. An example of this binding used correctly is in 1 Corinthians chapter 5, where Paul commands the church in Corinth to excommunicate the incestuous Christian from their congregation until he repents of his sin. Here Paul "binds" him, retains his sins, and delivers him over to Satan. But Paul tells the church if he repents to "loose" him, forgive him of his sins, and accept him back into fellowship. He models this in 2 Corinthians 2:10. He tells all of us do this, examining ourselves before partaking of communion in 1 Corinthians 11:27-32. It's also in John 20:22-23 where Jesus said, *"Receive the Holy Spirit. If you forgive anyone his sins, they are forgiven; if you withhold forgiveness from anyone, it is withheld."* We are to operate the visible expression of the Church so it reflects the spiritual reality.

How does Jesus want His Church to operate? Does He want a "pope" a human Vicar to represent Him? No. Jesus rebuked the religious of His day for their self-centered love of honor and esteem among people. Jesus isn't okay with *any* of His followers doing this. But to think that He approves of, and established, a

A Note on Binding & Loosing

 These same two words are also commonly used during spiritual warfare to enforce our authority, in Christ, over demons by binding (restraining) them. *(See Matt 12:22-30)* However, the use of these words for that purpose (which I do, too) doesn't change that Jesus's intent in Matt. 16/18 was legislative.

main-center-of-attention human Vicar of Himself to be recognized as a holy emperor, and be honored this way on a global scale, is not only antithetical to what He taught, it's arguably blasphemous. The same is true of people acting like prophet authoritarians or pastor superstars. Jesus's vision of His Church is for it to be equals. Not in role, we have different roles, some more public facing or leading, but we're all equally children of the Father. Jesus would hate what false religion and worldly people have done in His name with His supposed approval. Jesus rebuked the scribes and pharisees of His day for doing the same things! He says in Matthew 23:5-10 and 12, *"All their deeds are done for men to see. They broaden their phylacteries and lengthen their tassels. They love the places of honor at banquets, the chief seats in the synagogues, the greetings in the marketplaces, and the title of 'Rabbi' by which they are addressed. But you are not to be called 'Rabbi,' for you have one Teacher, and you are all brothers. And do not call anyone on earth your father, for you have one Father, who is in heaven. Nor are you to be called instructors, for you have one Instructor, the Christ... For whoever exalts himself will be humbled, and whoever humbles himself will be exalted."*

Why have I taken the time to refute the Catholic Church's beliefs? (1) Because there are 1.2 billion Catholics worldwide. (2) As fellow believers in the true Jesus we need to avoid believing their errors and to witness the full truth to them. Catholics have faith in a false religious system of *works*, built on Peter, Mary, and tradition—rather than *faith in Jesus* alone and God's Word alone. It is Holy Spirit-inspired personal faith in Jesus alone, as the eternal Son of God and Savior, and the Gospel, that enters us into His Church. His Church is not a man-made earthly institution made of buildings, magisteriums, legislation, etc. as taught in the RCC. His Church is the global, invisible, spiritual collection of every person that's been born of the Spirit of God through faith alone! Proclaiming this truth is a primary mission of disciples of Jesus and needed to make disciples of Jesus. On *this* rock Jesus has built His Church and the gates of Hades will not prevail against it!

g. Lights Amidst Broken Roads
Your mission is to be a light that shines bright, and attracts other light-seekers.

John 1:9 calls Jesus *"the true Light who gives light to every man."* In John 8:12 Jesus said, *"I am the light of the world. Whoever follows Me will never walk in the darkness, but will have the light of life."* Jesus called Himself the Light, and His disciples sons of light. In John 12:35-36, after telling them He was going to die, Jesus said, *"For a little while longer, the Light will be among you... While you have the Light, believe in the Light, so that you may become sons of light."* In Matthew 5:14 Jesus calls His disciples the light of the world. In Jesus's Parable of the Ten Virgins in Matthew 25:1-13 He describes His disciples as those who keep their lamps filled with oil so that their light doesn't go out. In Luke 12:35 Jesus tells us, *"Be dressed for service and keep your lamps burning."* This metaphor is also used in three other ways. First, in our sanctification, because the more intimate we are with the light then the less darkness there will be in us. Jesus says in Luke 11:35-36, *"Be careful, then, that the light within you is not darkness. So if your whole body is full of light, and no part of it in darkness, you will be radiant, as though a lamp were shining on you."* Second, both in us and in others, the light will expose all of the darkness at the end of time. In Mark 4:22 Jesus says, *"For there is nothing hidden that will not be disclosed, and nothing concealed that will not be brought to light."* (Mk 4:21-25, Lk 8:16-18) Third, is in our ability to either attract or repel others. The brighter we shine the more that those who love darkness will feel repelled by us. In John 3:20 Jesus says, *"Everyone who does evil hates the Light, and does not come into the Light for fear that his deeds will be exposed."* However, those who love the light will be drawn to it - like moths to a flame! In Revelation 1:20 Jesus's metaphor for individual churches is lampstands. Individual churches are places where individual light-bearers gather to shine brighter together. One of your primary missions is to be a son and daughter of light, of truth, of righteousness. So seek and eliminate all darkness inside of you, then partner up with other lights and pursue all activities that allow you to bring some light into every other dark place. By doing so we illuminate the world and attract to us God's other children being called to the light.

Matthew 5:14 You are the light of the world. A city on a hill cannot be hidden. [15]Neither do people light a lamp and put it under a basket. Instead, they set it on a stand, and it gives light to everyone in the house. [16]In the same way, let your light shine before men, that they may see your good deeds and glorify your Father in heaven.

Philippians 2:14 Do everything without complaining or arguing, [15]so that you may be blameless and pure, children of God without fault in a crooked and perverse generation, in which you shine as lights in the world [16a]as you hold forth the word of life...

---

h. Empowered For A Purpose

The power and gifting God gives you, isn't *itself* the mission, but is *for* the mission.

2 Peter 1:3-4 says the divine power of God has been given to us for everything we need for life and godliness, to partake in the divine nature, and escape the corruption in the world caused by evil desires. So one of the primary ways - and purposes - we've received power is to be victorious over sin and become sanctified. To take from the previous section, we're given power in order to become bright lights. So any of you who say that you cannot overcome your sinful desires you haven't embraced this truth. Before worrying about growing in *outward* power - healings, miracles, prophecy, etc. you need to focus on growing *inwardly* by being righteous! That's where your faith, prayers, and mission need to be focused first, and where God's power in you needs to be directed first.

After this, the next reason we're given power is as a sign of legitimacy and God's endorsement backing up the teaching we're giving and the life we're living. Hebrews 2:3-4 says *"This salvation was first announced by the Lord, was confirmed to us by those who heard Him, and was affirmed by God through signs, wonders, various miracles, and gifts of the Holy Spirit distributed according to His will."* (Heb 3b-4) This is also why Jesus did the miraculous. The signs were signs that pointed to His credibility, and to testify of His authority. In John 5:36 Jesus compared His ministry with John the Baptist's, which was mainly about repentance of sin. Jesus was calling people to do more than just repent, He was calling them to trust in Him with their lives. He says, *"But I have testimony more substantial than that of John. For the works that the Father has given Me to accomplish—the very works I am doing—testify about Me that the Father has sent Me."* He made greater claims so He did greater works. In John 10:25 He says, *"The works I do in My Father's name testify on My behalf."* And in 10:37-38 He says, *"If I am not doing the works of My Father, then do not believe Me. But if I am doing them, even though you do not believe Me, believe the works themselves, so that you may know and understand that the Father is in Me, and I am in the Father."* And in John 14:11 Jesus said, *"Believe Me that I am in the Father and the Father is in Me--or at least believe on account of the works themselves."* So it should be very clear that miracles are given to help people believe. They help people cross the bridge of their unbelief. Their faith is still needed, as is their ongoing repentance, their voluntary submission to follow Him, and their personal trust in Him. But God chooses to bless some by giving them a little miracle to help their faith along. And He blesses others by giving them greater faith to believe even without the miraculous intervention. Both are good, they're just different. But a miracle isn't the true gift - eternal life with God is! A miracle is just a gift that helps get some there.

Despite what my cessationist brethren believe, I don't believe God is done doing miracles, or done using us to do them either. I don't believe that there was an official close of the miraculous at the end of the first century, nor one at the end of the official formation of the Bible. The testimonies to the contrary are too numerous. And the Bible gives every indication that it would continue, and no indication that it would cease. This is the more biblical stance. The Church has been given all kinds of spiritual gifts which we'll touch on later. For now, I want to focus on the *purpose* of such gifts. My cessationist brethren will appreciate what I have to say on this. After all, it's the wide amount of false teachings and abuses in the charismatic world that have led many to be cessationist in the first place. The point is this: all the miraculous power, signs, and wonders, are not a means to an end themselves. They are not our goal. They are not our purpose. If church or revival services, or prayer meetings, are centered around such things, they're failing. If people are only showing up to be healed and could care less about Jesus and how to follow Him they're failing. Our *purpose* is not to do physical healing, deliverance, prophecy, etc. These are secondary aspects, ancillary functions given to help us in our efforts towards our primary mission: to preach the gospel, make disciples of Jesus, edify and grow the Church, and advance God's Kingdom on earth!

If you're given the gift of healing don't heal someone in the name of Jesus then let them leave without giving them the gospel! You need to share with them the true healing that they need: healing from sin. Maybe they're already a believer in which case they're likely still in need of greater spiritual healing. If you're given the gift of prophecy or words of knowledge about a person, do not share your revelation and give them a meaningful encounter without giving them an opportunity to accept Jesus as their Lord and Savior! As though just telling someone something about their life generically is what prophecy is for. It's not. Prophecy is intended to grow or edify the Church. Giving someone a word of knowledge—without contextualizing it in relation to Jesus—isn't biblical prophecy - it's mediumship! One last example, let's say you're given the gift of encouragement. Don't just give an encouraging word, an optimistic perspective, or just tell them that God loves them, without also telling them how Jesus can give them the peace that surpasses all understanding! I see this by even prominent evangelists. Running around telling people God loves them without defining who God is (to distinguish Him from false beliefs about God), how He has love(d) them—via the cross—or a call to action (what they should do in response to that love?). Don't stop at the superficial level and also don't get the secondary gifts become the main thing. If the Lord gives you an opportunity to heal someone's body, give them direction in life, or be encouraged - great - but don't see that has the main thing you're there to do. It's not! You're not a healer, prophet, or encourager who's sometimes a disciple of Jesus—you're a disciple of Jesus who's sometimes a healer, prophet, or encourager! Always seek the higher opportunity and look for the next level to take a person to. Your gifting, or whatever that presenting opportunity is, may allow you to have influence one way but then look for how to take them beyond that. Love the whole person and try to meet their deepest need. If a stranger and likely unsaved, then the need is easy to identify: they need to hear the gospel, and to repent and believe!

Take a look at what the Apostle Paul says about *why* God gave him the power of the Spirit of God for signs and wonders. It was so he could (verse 19) fully proclaim the gospel of Christ, and (verse 20) preach the gospel where Christ isn't known. Then after preaching to them, it was in order to (verse 18) lead them to obedience, so that they (verse 16) would become an acceptable offering to God, sanctified by the Holy Spirit. The purpose of power, signs, and wonders is to first help us preach and fully proclaim the gospel, then make obedient disciples of Jesus, and then to edify and sanctify God's people.

Romans 15:16 to be a minister of Christ Jesus to the Gentiles in the priestly service of the gospel of God, so that the Gentiles might become an acceptable offering to God, sanctified by the Holy Spirit. [17]Therefore I exult in Christ Jesus in my service to God. [18]I will not presume to speak of anything except what Christ has accomplished through me in leading the Gentiles to obedience by word and deed, [19]by the power of signs and wonders, and by the power of the Spirit of God. So from Jerusalem all the way around to Illyricum, I have fully proclaimed the gospel of Christ. [20]In this way, I have aspired to preach the gospel where Christ was not known, so that I would not be building on someone else's foundation.

---

i. Ambassadors For Christ
Your mission as Ambassador for Christ is to deliver the message of reconciliation.

---

2 Corinthians 5:18 All this is from God, who reconciled us to Himself through Christ and gave us the ministry of reconciliation: [19]that in Christ God was reconciling the world to Himself, not counting men's trespasses against them. And He has committed to us the message of reconciliation. [20]Therefore we are ambassadors for Christ, as though God were making His appeal through us. We implore you on behalf of Christ: Be reconciled to God. [21]God made Him who knew no sin to be sin on our behalf, so that in Him we might become the righteousness of God.

The Apostle Paul summarizes our mission concisely here. God is reconciling sinners to Himself through Christ, and He has committed to us this message of reconciliation. We are ambassadors for Christ, as though God were making His appeal, to them, through us! Did you know that's what you are - a letter messenger? Did you know that's your mission - to deliver that message? You have no control what they do once they get the message. Whether they accept the invitation wholeheartedly, or just throw it in the trash. Your responsibility is that they get it. You may get opportunities for follow-up, to further influence their decision. If you're anything like me follow-ups are much easier than the first drop-off. But once you've dropped off the invitation the ball is in their court. Now they're responsible for how they respond from that point forward. You've done your part.

We sometimes write people off beforehand, but this is a mistake. It might be because of fear of approaching people, fear of failure, or fear of rejection. Or maybe it's pessimism, assuming they won't accept Jesus anyways, right? Perhaps it's just good old-fashioned laziness or busyness? These are common ones. We've filled our lives with too much time-waster activities or other meaningful-but-not-eternal activities that we don't have time for eternal activities. Or maybe it's pure apathy, a lack of concern? We shouldn't be apathetic about anyone going to Hell. Examine yourself and if it's this one you need to extinguish it immediately because it's wicked. Or, your lack of effort could be driven by our primary human need for comfort. We all need to feel mostly comfortable, and we have specific activities that provide us a controllable measure of discomfort for variety. We have no shortage of excuses when it comes to avoiding doing uncomfortable things. Especially uncomfortable things with little guarantee of instant success and a decent likelihood of upsetting someone. But remember, you don't have to make them go to the banquet—you just have to make sure they get the invitation! In Matthew 22:9, Jesus, speaking in a parable says, *"Go therefore to the crossroads and invite to the banquet as many as you can find.'*

Remember what we learned about in Chapter 4, Section (K) about optimism? Don't assume people will say no. I won't even tell you what they say happens when you assume! Assume, rather, they will say yes until they say no. Plus, a no right now isn't the same thing as a no forever. Many of us said no for a long time before we said yes! And thank God that He never gave up on us and neither did the people praying for us and those who kept sharing the gospel and watering the seeds in us! I recall a story shared by Pastor John Ortberg of an account of almost writing someone off. He met a man at a banquet. He was Jewish but had no involvement in that faith beyond age twelve. He was thrice-divorced, and had only been to a unitarian church a few times. He thought to himself if he had to assess on the basis of one conversation who was as far away from faith in Christ as could be, it would have been this guy. Nonetheless, he invited him to come to their church, though he thought he'd never see him again. But the next Sunday he was there, sitting in the front row! Afterwards, they talked and he discovered that he had never read the New Testament before. He gave him one. The man started waking up early to read 20-30 pages every day. And he kept coming back every week. They talked and he was thinking about making a decision for Christ but it would've been a costly thing for him because of his heritage—his family told him if he became a Christian, he'd be dead to them. But he finally said yes to God. He said the last time he saw him he was with a friend. The man threw his arms around him and said to his friend, 'I want you to meet the person who helped bring me to Jesus.' He recalls, "I almost missed doing that because I almost said no for him."[7]

j. Preach the Gospel To All Creation
Your mission is to verbally communicate the Gospel to those in your influence.

Mark 16:15 And He *[Jesus]* said to them, "Go into all the world and preach the gospel to every creature.

There's an often quoted saying attributed to St. Francis of Assisi: "Preach the Gospel at all times. When necessary, use words." However, St. Francis never actually said this. It's also a false dichotomy between preaching the gospel and living consistent with it.[8] They aren't mutually exclusive, they go hand in hand. But this isn't the biggest problem with this phrase, or why people use it. They're suggesting it's possible to preach the Gospel in a way that *usually* won't require words—which is total nonsense! Basically this is a way of spiritualizing the fears and excuses we looked at in the previous section. It's a way of avoiding witnessing, being disobedient to the clear teaching of Scripture, all while sounding wise and super-spiritual at the same time. But it's like telling teachers to make sure students learn their ABC's, and when necessary, use letters. The letters *are* the ABC's! And the gospel *is* words! You can't preach the gospel without using words! It's impossible. You can *reinforce* the message of the gospel by having a loving spirit and good character and good deeds along with it, but you can't leave out the actual message.

What exactly *is* the Gospel? The Greek word we get the phrase 'gospel' from is *euaggélion*. It's where we get the words evangelism and evangelical from. It literally means "good news." In the simplest of terms, the gospel is good news that one can share and another can hear about. This is why Jesus can preach the gospel in Matthew 4:23 and 9:35, even though it was near the beginning of His ministry and the crucifixion and resurrection hadn't occurred yet. The good news, at that time, was the arrival of God's Kingdom to earth via Jesus's presence. The Bible even records Jesus in Mark chapter 1, verse 15 saying, *"The time is fulfilled... the kingdom of God is near. Repent and believe in the gospel!"* So, there are many types of gospels i.e. types of good news. The eternal Word of the only God becoming human and living among us is good news. Him voluntarily dying on a cross in our place to pay for our sins is good news. Him conquering sin and death and bodily rising back to life in a transformed eternal body is good news. Our spiritual rebirth and eternal salvation received by faith and trust in Him alone is good news. Our adoption by God the Father into His family is good news. Our victory over sin, death, Hell, and Satan is good news. So what is *the* - capital g - Gospel? It's all of this! Though the gospel could be expanded greatly, or consolidated greatly, it shouldn't be condensed too much. Reread the previous list. I summarized the gospel in 6 sentences that could be read in under a minute. The gospel includes all of the good news we could share about who Jesus is and what He did, though there are certain points that are most important to communicate first. The Apostle Paul gave us this summary:

> 1 Corinthians 15:1 Now, brothers, I want to remind you of the gospel I preached to you, which you received, and in which you stand firm. [2]By this gospel you are saved, if you hold firmly to the word I preached to you. Otherwise, you have believed in vain. [3]For what I received I passed on to you as of first importance: that Christ died for our sins according to the Scriptures, [4]that He was buried, that He was raised on the third day according to the Scriptures... [11b]this is what we preach, and this is what you believed... [17]And if Christ has not been raised, your faith is futile; you are still in your sins... [19]If our hope in Christ is for this life alone, we are to be pitied more than all men... [22]For as in Adam all die, so in Christ all will be made alive. [23]But each in his own turn: Christ the firstfruits; then at His coming, those who belong to Him.

Gospel-Sharing Tips. So what might a basic gospel presentation look like? There are innumerable ways to witness so please know there's no perfect one-size-fits-all approach. Feel free to learn about many ways, or create your own. I've seen some better than others. I'm not a fan of any "soul-winning" type of cookie-cutter scripts where you just walk up to a stranger and launch into a mini speech and prayer over them without their consent or engagement. The gospel isn't a shotgun to shoot at a person's face, it's good news to hand deliver to their heart. We're not after souls, as though a soul is trapped in a person and needs to be sprung out. Souls are people, and people are complex. They're individuals with different thoughts, emotions, backgrounds, etc. Each person has different things contributing to their reluctance. Jesus didn't treat people with an impersonal shotgun approach. He interacted with people and spoke to where they were. Your mission is also not to deliver a garbled up piece of the message to as many people as possible. Your mission is to deliver the full message! It's better to approach witnessing with a genuine love and interest in each individual, and be willing to invest time. If someone is willing to give you 5-10 minutes, or longer, you have more opportunity to make a lasting impact. You'll also have more reason to believe any confessions of faith you get will be genuine. Better one person who seems to be really getting it, having a real encounter with God, than ten who may be half-heartedly telling me what I want to hear! Review the Parable of the Sower in Matthew 13:1-9. It's good to spread the seed everywhere, but if a little extra care helps you know which people are currently "good soil" even better. Maybe you'll get the opportunity to really help someone break through barriers holding them back. In a real conversation you're also in a better position to speak to their deeper needs like personal, emotional, or intellectual concerns they may have.

There's one ministry's approach I like a lot. I've used it in the U.S. and even with the rural tribes of Mozambique in 2019. It's a good starter formula that anybody can use. It's also good as a simple foundation you can add to later with other approaches or methods, based on new things you learn, or other knowledge or experience, based on wherever they're coming from and things they bring up. The basic formula is to engage someone in a friendly dialogue, ask them questions, and then guide the conversation through: (1) personal conviction of their sin, (2) the Law of God, (3) the Gospel, and (4) invitation to accept Jesus as Lord and Savior. You start by asking a number of simple ice breaker questions, like if they know what happens when we die, or if they think that they're a good person. If the latter for example, then follow it up by telling them you have a test to find out and ask if they want to take it. You then guide them through a few quick questions, based on the Ten Commandments, like whether they've ever told a lie before, stolen anything before, used God's name in vain before, or looked at someone lustfully before. Each step ultimately discovering that they're not a good person according to God's standards, and they are a guilty sinner. Then you tell them that you're not judging them, but by their own admission they are a liar, thief, blasphemer, and adulterer at heart. Then ask them - innocent or guilty? Ok.. Heaven or Hell? Helping them to realize that if God judges them by these standards, and you've only looked a few of the many laws of God, then they would not go to Heaven but to Hell. Then, ask them if they know what Jesus did for them? Using the metaphor of God's courtroom, you then explain how there they are standing there guilty about to be condemned. And their fine is enormous - billions of dollars! They would never be able to pay it in ten lifetimes. Then Jesus gets up from behind the Judge's bench and walks around, stands next to them, and pays their fine on their behalf! This is what happened on the cross. Their fine, their sin debt, was paid in full by His sacrifice. Tell them He got what they deserved and they get what He deserves: righteousness, glory, and eternal life. If they are willing to repent and turn away from their sins, and put their trust in Jesus, and what He did, they will be forgiven of all of their sins, their entire debt will be wiped out, and they will inherit eternal life with God! All they need to do for this to happen is to believe in Jesus and receive Him as their Lord and Savior. And then ask them so when do you think you'll do that?

For video samples of this approach being used check out Ray Comfort of Living Waters. (https://www.livingwaters.com/watch) They also have an affordable evangelism school and personal workshops if you'd like to go deeper in your study and practice. When you ask someone when they'll do that, maybe they will choose to do it right then! This is great, and it's totally *their* choice! I've experienced this. It's a wonderful moment and it totally makes you want to share the gospel with more people! But maybe they will not be ready just then. Ask them if they will give this some thought. If they agree to do so, and most do, they are more likely to, since their conscience will hold them to their word. Ask them if they have a Bible at home. You've planted a seed. Sometimes we're planting a new seed, sometimes our efforts are just watering someone else's seed, and sometimes we get to witness the harvest. Maybe they will have follow up questions. Maybe you'll know the answers and can dialogue with them. Or if not volunteer to find out for them, and ask for their number or email. Invite them to come sit with you at your church. Give them your number or email and tell them they can email you any questions or prayer requests they have later. This way you're not only evangelizing you're also initiating discipleship. Doing this you're also growing yourself by becoming a mentor and helper to someone else. By doing this you begin moving into the next primary mission: to make disciples.

Acts 1:8b *[Jesus]* ...you will be My witnesses in Jerusalem, and in all Judea and Samaria, and to the ends of the earth.

Romans 10:14 How then can they call on the One in whom they have not believed? And how can they believe in the One of whom they have not heard? And how can they hear without someone to preach? [15]And how can they preach unless they are sent? As it is written: "How beautiful are the feet of those who bring good news!"

---

k. Make Disciples
Your mission is to make disciples of Jesus, that know, follow, and obey Him.

Matthew 28:19 Therefore go and make disciples of all nations, baptizing them in the name of the Father, and of the Son, and of the Holy Spirit, [20]and teaching them to obey all that I have commanded you.

Your mission isn't just to tell people about Jesus, or even to congregate with others in His name—it's to make disciples of Him! A disciple is a convinced and committed adherent. It's someone who knows, follows, and obeys. Obviously you can't force people to obey Jesus, but you can be obedient yourself and you can preach and teach others so they know their obedience is critical. The goal of discipleship is to look and act like the one we follow: Jesus. Think of ourselves as mini-Jesuses! Remember the What Would Jesus Do (WWJD) bracelets? This is more than a catch phrase - it's a lifestyle.

Discipleship is a Process. I think discipleship is lacking in the Church for two main reasons. The first reason is this: we've treated discipleship like a *program* instead of a *process.* Many churches will have something like a 4-week discipleship program, and it's likely a knowledge based, teacher-led classroom. This isn't necessarily bad, but it could be better. You don't learn how to become an obedient, committed, Spirit-led follower of Jesus, or begin living it out in 4 weeks. It takes time. Years. We become like Jesus over time. It's a slow process requiring refinement, dedication, maturity, practice, and growth. It's not something you graduate from just because you completed a class. You *never* finish becoming more like Jesus because He is all we could ever hope to become! So there's always deeper you could go. I'm further along than many and I can tell you that I'm far from anywhere close to Jesus! Also, you could've completed an 8-year Ph.D's worth of discipleship classes and still not be a *good* disciple. You could know all the right answers to the questions and still not be obedient. You could have all the head knowledge and still be spiritually and morally bankrupt. You could have the prestigious degree and still be completely self-centered rather than Jesus-centered. In fact, you could pass a test about faith and not even have faith. And all this is assuming your discipleship class tests its students for competency anyways. Most probably don't. "Disciple" is not a *credential*—it's an *attribute*. It's not something you learn and complete—it's something you become!

"Go and make disciples" is a command. The second reason I think discipleship is lacking in the Church is we're overly culturally sensitive, reactive, and fearful of doing anything that could be perceived as too religious or works-focused. There are influential leaders and movements that reinterpret Jesus's words to, "Go and make disciples" and change them to "*as you are going*, make disciples." The imperative then changes. In the former, the *reason* we are going, at all, is *to* make disciples. It's the *reason* we're going to all nations. The Great Commission. In the latter, we are going, for whatever reason of our own, and as we do we are to make disciples. Now, some are using this to mean that we should be witnessing and discipling people *everywhere*. If that's the reason for your phrase shift it could be okay, because the net result is more evangelism and discipleship, not less. But I've seen others who are using this strategy a different way. They're using it intentionally to water down Jesus's command. To soften it and make it seem less works-based, less religious—less like our primary purpose and mission! As though He intended for us to go about our lives however we feel like and just make some disciples as we're doing that! As though Jesus didn't model for us intentionally traveling around to towns and villages *in order to* proclaim the gospel and make disciples! As though the book of Acts didn't model for us an intentional effort to be on mission to new cities in order to proclaim the gospel and make disciples there! Don't dilute your view of "go and make disciples" in a way, that then, necessarily, also dilutes your view of evangelism. The problem with this phrase change fundamentally is that it's an attempt to put us in control first. So we're choosing the primary direction that we're going, and then making disciples is a secondary thing we just add in as convenient. This is backwards. God's driving this car, not us! We're dead to ourselves and now live for Christ! Make disciples as you are going—as well—but first and foremost, go and make disciples intentionally on mission.

Curriculum. *Educational* discipleship curriculum is fine if students are taught the process of becoming a disciple. I believe education is important. I've dedicated much of this book to educating you. But I hope I've also given practical, applicable direction too. It's not enough to just learn things, you have to apply them! You have to live them out. It should also be testable, where knowledge can be tested, but more importantly, *fruit* can be tested and measured. Where students grade themselves, and maybe even one another. We all tend to have blinders on, easily seeing the flaws of others but not our own. But those around us will tell us if we're as loving, just, generous, thoughtful, or dedicated as we think we are or desire to be. Most people that go into relationship counseling think their partner is the problem, but what does their partner say? Do they agree all problems in the relationship are their fault? Nope! Curriculums should also be applicable. Don't just learn how evangelism is biblical, or how to do it - *actually* do it! Go witness! All too often we learn and learn and learn and never do. Disciples do. For many of us, myself included, learning is easy, doing is hard. But we must strive to do. We must go and make disciples. And in the process of doing this, we *become* better disciples.

Luke 14:27 *[Jesus]* And whoever does not carry his cross and follow Me cannot be My disciple... [33]In the same way, any one of you who does not give up everything he has cannot be My disciple.

---

l. Advancing the Kingdom of God
Your mission is to advance God's *spiritual* dominion everywhere you can.

In Chapter 1, Section (J) a passage is shown from Mark 12 where Jesus sees that the scribe He's talking to rightly understands the purpose and heart of God's Law. He tells him he's not far from the Kingdom of God. In John 3:3 Jesus teaches us that no one can see or enter the Kingdom of God unless He first regenerates us spiritually with His Spirit in us. This is described in greater detail in Chapter 2, Section (D). We need to remember that the Kingdom of God is not the Church. Neither the lowercase-C church, which is the outward organization of believers. Nor is it the capital-C Church, which is the universal collection of all born-again believers. The Church is the Bride of Christ, and the Body of Christ. The Church is *part of* the Kingdom of God. The Kingdom of God is also different from, but includes, the realm of Heaven and the heavenly angels. It could be argued that if we described the realm of the Third Heaven *only* it might be better described as the Kingdom of *Heaven.* The Kingdom of *God* is everyone and everything that is under God's dominion. It's everything He is actively King over. This includes the Kingdom of Heaven but also every part of earth under God's dominion. Though He is sovereignly King over all, He's not principally King over all. We still have Satan, the prince, who is governing things differently on earth, in a way that is not with God's endorsement or approval. Probably the best known Scripture of this is in the Lord's Prayer in Matthew 6:10 where Jesus tells us to pray, *"Your kingdom come, Your will be done, on earth as it is heaven."*

Jesus said in John 16:33, *"In the world you will have tribulation. But take courage; I have overcome the world!"* But if the world has been overcome then how can it give us tribulation? It's because while both are called "world" two different things are being described here. The world—*material* world—will give us tribulation, but the world—

spiritual world—has already been conquered by Jesus! Or, the outer-physical-natural kingdoms of earth will still give us tribulation, but Jesus has already overcome the inner-spiritual forces in the world. In Acts 14:22 they told the disciples, *"We must endure many hardships to enter the kingdom of God."* Jesus said He's sending us out like lambs among wolves. *(Lk 10:3)* Yet we also know we have the Spirit of the Lion of Judah living in us! Your primary mission is not to strive in an uphill battle for victory in the material world. Your primary mission is to advance the Kingdom of God in the spiritual realm. Using the metaphor from Section (G) of this chapter, we are to advance the Light. The world is full of darkness and everywhere we advance the Kingdom of God it becomes brighter!

God's Kingdom on Earth? Am I saying that our mission as Christians to advance God's Kingdom is *only* spiritual advancement or just *primarily* spiritual advancement? Primarily. There is a concerted effort by many evangelicals to bring material aspects of this world under God's dominion now. One such philosophy is called the "seven mountains mandate." The idea is that there are seven mountains or spheres that are the most influential shapers of society, with the greatest impact on the way people think and behave: Education, Religion, Family, Business, Government/Military, Arts/Entertainment, and Media. There is nothing wrong with trying to influence godliness in these areas and in fact is a duty of good stewardship and a fruitful use of our time. A caveat though, and it begins with the word mandate. We do NOT have a mandate to change the social systems of the world! We have a mandate to deliver the message about Jesus and make disciples. The natural consequence of a society that is full of disciples of Jesus will be a changed system. Remember what you learned in Chapter 5, Section (G). Real change begins with transformed individuals. Now of course if you are in a position of leadership or influence in some important sphere of society by all means then do so. Pray about it, perhaps God has put you there for that very purpose as a unique calling. But this is not a mandate for the whole Church, and it has become for many a distraction from their real mission.

Some have even gone so far off the deep end that they teach *dominion theology* "that Christians should, and eventually will, take control of the government." That we are commanded to have dominion over everything. Another false variation is called *Kingdom Now Theology,* which teaches that it's our duty to "take back" the earth from Satan and subdue it for Christ.[9] Extreme versions even teach that we need to gain control first in order to usher in the return of Jesus, who won't return unless we do. Despite their twisting of Bible verses to support it, none of this is true, biblical, or good. Fact: God is in control. Fact: The world is going to get worse, not better, despite what we do to preserve its decay and influence pockets of good. Fact: Jesus will return when the Father has decided and we will not cause it to happen, nor are we to know when it will happen. *(Mt 24:36)* But Jesus *did* say the gospel would be preached in all the world first! It's our prayerful *request*—not our mandate to *cause*—God's Kingdom to come, on earth as it is in Heaven! The primary way we are to live on mission, consistent with this request, is by transforming individuals with the gospel to live consistent with being a disciple of Jesus.

Matthew 24:12 *[Jesus]* Because of the multiplication of wickedness, the love of most will grow cold. ¹³But the one who perseveres to the end will be saved. ¹⁴And this gospel of the kingdom will be preached in all the world as a testimony to all nations, and then the end will come.

III. Running the Race

Hebrews 12:1b Let us run with endurance the race set out for us.

m. Good and Faithful Servant
Be a good and faithful steward, over everything that God has entrusted you with.

In His Parable of the Talents in Matthew 25:14-30 Jesus teaches a lesson about what He expects of His disciples. I did a sermon short/video on it.[10] But to summarize, the master will be out of town for awhile so he gives his three servants talents (a measure of money) to steward it for him. Two of the servants invest their portions and double his investment, the third servant buries his portion in the ground. When the master returns he praises the first two, calling them good and faithful. He puts them in charge of many things and welcomes them into his joy. The third servant is then called wicked and lazy. His portion was taken from him and then he's thrown into the outer darkness, language to indicate Hell! The lesson behind the parable is that we've all been entrusted with a variety of things that belong to the Lord and we're responsible for how we steward them. It isn't just our money but our spiritual gifts, abilities, personalities, experiences, roles, vote, influence, etc. How we live and what we do with all of it! Jesus paints a portrait of the same opportunity being received by two very different types of servants. The first two servants love and trust their master. They care about what He cares about. They *feel entrusted* to get this responsibility, and are eager to please their master. The third servant hates, distrusts, blames, and even slanders the character of his master. He *feels fearful* to have this responsibility, is self-centered, and neglects to do anything good with it. The master calls the first two good and faithful and the last one - get this - not less good, but wicked and lazy! You've been entrusted! It's your mission as a disciple to run the race in such a way that you're rewarded at the end for being a good and faithful servant!

n. The BEMA Judgment
All born again Christians will appear there and receive what they've earned.

Throughout this book I've told you to fix your eyes on the prize at the end of the race. This will keep you from getting distracted by the pleasures of this world and get taken off course into sin or fruitlessness. It will also help you enjoy the pleasures of this world in a way that glorifies God, keeping you from turning anything into an idol that your life is too centered around. This reward ceremony doctrine, also found in Chapter 5, Section (R), is from 2 Corinthians 5:10, *"For we must all appear before the judgment seat of Christ, that each one may receive his due for the things done in the body, whether good or bad."*

Jesus describes all judgment events occurring after His return in Matthew 16:27, *"For the Son of Man will come in His Father's glory with His angels, and then He will repay each one according to what he has done."* This Judgment is not the same as the Judgment that determines whether people go to Heaven or Hell. Most Christians who have ever lived have already died and are already in Heaven with Jesus before His second coming. When Jesus returns, all who belong to Him, either dead or alive, will be transformed and meet Him in the air. *(1 Thes 4:16-17)* The Church is already officially separated at His return and appear glorious with Him in the clouds, as the Church does in Revelation 7:9-17. It is later, after the Antichrist, False Prophet, and Satan, have been defeated and cast into Hell, as described in Revelation 19:20 and 20:10, that the Great White Throne Judgment in Revelation 20:11-15 takes place. It's here when the rest of humanity will be judged. As Matthew 25:32 says, *"All the nations will be gathered before Him, and He will separate the people one from another, as a shepherd separates the sheep from the goats."*

Those of us confidently in Christ do not need to fear appearing at that Judgment. So we need not have any fear of Hell, we've already inherited Heaven. 1 John 2:28 reminds us to, *"remain in Christ, so that when He appears, we may be confident and unashamed before Him at His coming."* Yet, we should still be concerned about this Judgment! Not in fear but earnestness. We still need to run the race to be judged well. We want to appear, as Romans 2:16 says, *"...on that day when God will judge men's secrets through Christ Jesus..."* and be rewarded for *good* stewardship rather than be ashamed for all that we could've done and didn't do! Romans 14:10 assures us that all Christians *do* appear at this Judgment. In order to distinguish this Judgment from the Great White Throne Judgment that determines whether people inherit eternal life this has been called the Bema judgment. The Greek word *béma* (pronounced bay'-ma) just means a step, raised place, by implication a tribunal, a throne. It's a platform that someone would walk up to receive judgment, from a tribunal chair (throne) where rewards and punishments were given out. It is part of your mission as a disciple of Jesus to do good things in the Body now so that you reap rewards later at the Bema Judgment. It's also part of your mission to positively, rather than negatively, influence how your brothers and sisters in Christ do there too.

Romans 14:10 Why, then, do you judge your brother? Or why do you belittle your brother? For we will all stand before God's judgment seat... [12]So then, each of us will give an account of himself to God. [13]Therefore let us stop judging one another. Instead, make up your mind not to put any stumbling block or obstacle in your brother's way.

o. Rewards for Performance
At the Bema Judgment, you'll receive eternal rewards, based on your performance.

In Chapter 1, Section (O) I described some of the rewards we could earn at the BEMA Judgment. In Chapter 5, Section (R) we learned how God is a loving Father who rewards, and in Chapter 5, Section (O) how only what's built on the foundation of Jesus will *survive*. Yet, in the name of Jesus, we may do things that focus on fruitfulness (good works) and still receive a reward for it. For example in Luke 14:12-14 we read, *"Then Jesus said to the man who had invited Him, "When you host a dinner or a banquet, do not invite your friends or brothers or relatives or rich neighbors. Otherwise, they may invite you in return, and you will be repaid. But when you host a banquet, invite the poor, the crippled, the lame, and the blind, and you will be blessed. Since they cannot repay you, you will be repaid at the resurrection of the righteous."* As good as this is we're doubly blessed for caring after those in His Church. In fact, I think Scripture suggests even unsaved people may be blessed for doing things that help people because they belong to Jesus. It's my optimistic hope that some names have been graciously entered into the Lamb's Book of Life and have a better outcome on Judgment Day because they've done good for the Kingdom of God. For more information about this topic along with deeper study, visual slide show, group Bible study, and questionnaire, see our *Prioritize Your Life Series*, Course #2 - *Prepare for the Bema Judgment*. (https://MPoweredChristian.org/Prioritize-Your-Life). In the meantime, receive and bless those who belong to Jesus and those who are righteous! Keep your eyes fixed on your mission as a disciple, and on earning your heavenly eternal rewards at the Bema Judgment, and you'll run the race well!

Matthew 10:40 *[Jesus]* He who receives you receives Me, and he who receives Me receives the One who sent Me. [41]Whoever receives a prophet because he is a prophet will receive a prophet's reward, and whoever receives a righteous man because he is a righteous man will receive a righteous man's reward. [42]And if anyone gives even a cup of cold water to one of these little ones because he is My disciple, truly I tell you, he will never lose his reward."

Colossians 3:23 Whatever you do, work at it with your whole being, for the Lord and not for men, [24a]because you know that you will receive an inheritance from the Lord as your reward...

---

p. Enduring Tribulation
Your endurance, through the tribulation, is an important *part of* your mission.

Tribulation is not just something we have to deal with as disciples of Jesus. It's a necessary and important part of our mission. As much as I desire to live an easy life too, the easier our lives are the more we're probably falling short in this area. As a relatively healthy, educated, middle-class American in the twenty-first century who's endured very little persecution I struggle with this as do many of you. Many of us haven't been drafted into a war to fight for our religious freedom, had to hide our faith publicly under Islamic or Communist regimes, or flee our homes or countries due to religious persecution. But many have since the first century, and in a weird way they've been blessed by it. I wish for none of these things for any of us, but we can appreciate that their faith has been tested in the fire and shown approved! They are perhaps more confident than we in their faith and salvation. By just *remaining alive and Christian* they're continually storing up treasures in Heaven to be received at the Bema Judgment. Imagine that—by just *living* they're earning rewards! If we're not enduring tribulation then we must be *intentional*. We don't have to move somewhere where we'll be persecuted, but we do need to live with the same level of dedication to Jesus. *Know* that you won't fall away when it gets tough! Get tough now! On your own—be proactive! Your dedication can be evidenced by your level of commitment to our primary missions we've already gone through, which if lived out fully, will bring about a much less comfort-based life.

I do believe there's what we may call a capital-T Tribulation to come, a period of several years of increased difficulty just before the return of Jesus. But there is also a lowercase-T tribulation too. Regardless of your eschatological (end times) perspective and where you stand on the millennial period, the Bible *still* describes the *entire* period from the first coming of Jesus to the second coming of Jesus as "the great tribulation." Enduring this period and coming out of it with faith in Jesus intact is our calling.

Revelation 7:9 After this I looked and saw a multitude too large to count, from every nation and tribe and people and tongue, standing before the throne and before the Lamb. They were wearing white robes and were holding palm branches in their hands... [14b] "These are the ones who have come out of the great tribulation; they have washed their robes and made them white in the blood of the Lamb."

---

q. Perseverance of the Saints
The refinement of your faith - during tribulation - confirms your salvation.

Enduring tribulation is a necessary and important part of discipleship. But knowing *that* we will is different than knowing *why* we will, as in the purpose and benefit of it. Jesus described one type of false Christian as seed sown on the rocky ground in His Parable of the Sower in Matthew 13:20-21. They are those who hear the word, receive it with joy, but remain only for a season, falling away when tribulation or persecution comes. Paul reminds us in Romans 5:3-5 to rejoice in our tribulation because tribulation produces perseverance; perseverance, character; and character, hope. And through hope we receive God's love poured into our hearts through the Holy Spirit. It's our perseverance —in our faith in Jesus—that shows us approved. It's not enduring tribulation alone that saves, it's perseverance of our faith in Jesus, through tribulation, that does. 1 Peter 4:12 says, *"Beloved, do not be surprised at the fiery trial that has come upon you, as though something strange were happening to you."* It's the refining fire of tribulation that tests what we're made of, like a blazing fire consuming a piece of coal. It's our faith in Jesus that enables us to persevere through the fire / pressure and come out like a radiant diamond!

Mark 13:13 *[Jesus]* You will be hated by everyone because of My name, but the one who perseveres to the end will be saved.

Colossians 1:23 if indeed you continue in your faith, established and firm, not moved from the hope of the gospel you heard, which has been proclaimed to every creature under heaven...

---

r. Witnessing in the Last Days

The Great Tribulation is the final refining fire, to test the whole world.
It's also the Church's final test of perseverance, and final opportunity to witness.

There will come a period of great tribulation just before the return of Jesus. The person known as the Antichrist will come to power. You may encounter false teachers who deny this doctrine saying the name 'The Antichrist' is not in the Bible. This is true. The name, or rather *description*, antichrist comes from 1 John 2:18, 2:22, 4:3, and 2 John 1:7. It's used to describe the attributes of anything anti (*against*) Christ. So all demons and many people and systems fit the description of being a lowercase-A antichrist. We may use the uppercase A-Antichrist to refer to this singular individual who is the *epitome* of all lesser antichrist archetypes who come before him. He's the worst of them. He's not called 'The Antichrist' in Scripture. He's called "the lawless one" *(2 Thes 2:8)*, the "man of lawlessness" and "son of destruction" *(2 Thes 2:3)*, the one who causes the "abomination of desolation" *(Matt 24:15)*, the "beast" that comes up from the abyss *(Rev 11:7)*, the horn (king) with eyes like a man and a mouth uttering great boasts *(Dan 7:8)*, the king who exalts himself and speaks blasphemies against God *(Dan 11:36)*, and multiple descriptions in Daniel's prophetic vision in Daniel 8:23-25. He's the beast who assembles the kings of the earth and their armies against the One seated on the horse (Jesus), and against His army in the final battle. *(Rev 19:19)* He's given all power and authority from the dragon (Satan). *(Rev 13:2, 12:9)* He'll be accompanied by a second beast, another man called The False Prophet. He'll look like a *lamb*, meaning he'll be a religious figure resembling Jesus, but will speak like a dragon (Satan) with blasphemous lies. He'll also perform miraculous signs that successfully deceive people and cause them to worship the first beast. *(Rev 13:11-15)* I also examine some of these topics and verses in Chapter 1, Section (P); Chapter 3, Sections (F) and (H); Chapter 5, Section (J), and Chapter 6, Section (N).

There always has and always will be great and diverse speculation about when and how these events will occur. My opinion is that a third Jewish temple, designed using the specifications from the vision in the book of Ezekiel, will be built in Jerusalem *prior* to the rise of the Antichrist. *(Dan 9:24-25)* I think this will be built by Orthodox Jews but Zionist Christians will support the effort. The Antichrist will come out of the *North* (Asia Minor/Turkey), as a political and military leader and religious syncretist, with an agenda of unifying nations and religions. Many Muslims will believe him to be their end times Islamic leader, the Mahdi, the 12th Imam. He'll help establish a peace treaty between Israel and its Muslim neighbors ushering in a period of increased global peace, but it won't last. The False Prophet will be an imposter Islamic Jesus who will claim to not be God or to have been crucified or resurrected. His goal will be to first convince Christians to stop believing in *him* as the biblical "Son of God" Jesus, and for all to submit to and worship the Antichrist person. All who refuse to worship the image of the Antichrist will be killed. *(Rev 13:15)* Despite popular conspiracy theory rhetoric, the Bible teaches that it's the False Prophet figure that requires people have the "mark of the beast" on their right hand or forehead. *(Rev 13:16-18)* This identification—which is *specifically connected* to the ability of people to buy or sell goods—is received only through public allegiance to the Antichrist first. So lest we fear every new thing as the potential mark it's not going to be vague. It will look like this: Deny Jesus as the Son of God and worship the Antichrist person—or be killed! And you won't be able to legally buy and sell goods if you don't worship the Antichrist by taking his mark.

The total tribulation period will be 5-7 years. The Antichrist will set up the abomination that causes desolation in the temple, and his true colors come out. *(Dan 9:26-27, 11:29-31)* Wars, famines, pestilence, plagues, and increased global persecution will occur for 1,290 days, and then a final greater outpouring for 45 days, for a total of 1,335 days. *(Dan 12:11-12)* During this time, Jerusalem and Israel will be trampled on by the nations for 42 months, but two powerful prophets of God will preach the truth in Jerusalem. *(Rev 11:2-3, 7; 13:5)* During this the 7 seals and 7 bowls of God's wrath described in Revelation 6, 8, 9 and 11 will be poured out. I don't believe there will be a pre- or mid-tribulation rapture of the Church. See my *Prioritize Your Life Series*, specifically Course #3 - *The Truth about the Rapture and the Tribulation* (https://MPoweredChristian.org/Prioritize-Your-Life) for my thoughts on this. If I'm wrong and we get raptured out first, great! But whether you agree or disagree the main takeaway is this: if pre- or mid-tribulation rapture proponents are wrong then the Church will be here during all of this—so we'd better be ready! It's far better for us to be mentally and spiritually prepared to endure and witness during all of this than to be blindsided when we're forced to go through it. We must be prepared to endure! The tribulation is also our last and greatest opportunity to preach the true

Christ and the gospel! The darkness during this time is going to get very, very dark. However, that just means that the light in us is going to shine that much brighter!

Revelation 13:7 Then the beast was permitted to wage war against the saints and to conquer them, and it was given authority over every tribe and people and tongue and nation. [8]And all who dwell on the earth will worship the beast—all whose names have not been written from the foundation of the world in the Book of Life belonging to the Lamb who was slain. [9]He who has an ear, let him hear: [10]"If anyone is destined for captivity, into captivity he will go; if anyone is to die by the sword, by the sword he must be killed." Here is a call for the perseverance and faith of the saints.

IV. Chapter Summary and Evaluation

Chapter Summary

You're a disciple of Jesus, whose mission is to make more disciples of Jesus.

Motivational speaker and coach Tony Robbins said, "You can't hit a target if you don't know what it is."[11] Yet, many press forward in life without any clear direction. We have our new maps so we know our destination. We've got our compass of fruitfulness to know if our day-to-day travels are going in the right direction. Yet without a clear vision and mission we're going to struggle searching for purpose. We need to remember the big picture, who we are, and what our primary mission is. You're a disciple of Jesus who's mission is to make more disciples of Jesus! This truth should be the foundation at the forefront of all activity, allowing everything else to take the backseat. All good fruit is good, but it's still only a byproduct. A lot of people do good—they aren't all followers of Jesus. And sometimes fruit can feel bad or unloving to people just because they aren't a follower of Jesus. As you venture forward in your journey, be a bright light amidst dark broken roads, focused on your mission to proclaim Jesus and the gospel! Faith in Jesus as the eternal Son of God is the only true rock the true Church was built on. Be confident that Jesus reigns with all authority in Heaven and on Earth. Remember that you've been empowered by the Holy Spirit, but *for* a purpose - to be an ambassador for Christ, reconciling the lost to God, preaching the gospel to all creation, making disciples, and advancing the Kingdom of God on earth! Run the race. Be eager to store up treasures in Heaven and to receive the eternal rewards for good performance at the Bema Judgment. Prepare yourself now to be strong and ready to persevere until the very end, dedicated to being a witness for Jesus no matter what tribulation comes! Commit yourself today to being a good and faithful servant every day to steward your mission well!

Chapter 6 Evaluation
AFTER THOROUGH, CAREFUL EXAMINATION, RIGHT NOW:

Scale headers (columns 1–10): False, Partially False, Mostly True, True

a) Doing good deeds is not my primary mission 1 2 3 4 5 6 7 8 9 10
b) My mission is to give people Jesus, in a fruitful way........... 1 2 3 4 5 6 7 8 9 10
c) I'm more concerned with eternal than worldly treasure 1 2 3 4 5 6 7 8 9 10
d) I'm willing to do what's right, anticipating consequences . 1 2 3 4 5 6 7 8 9 10
e) Jesus is the highest authority, but sin gives Satan authority 1 2 3 4 5 6 7 8 9 10
f) The foundation of the Church is Faith in Jesus as Son of God 1 2 3 4 5 6 7 8 9 10
f) The RCC has no legitimacy as "Christ's Church" or authority 1 2 3 4 5 6 7 8 9 10
f) Our mission includes witnessing biblical truth to Catholics 1 2 3 4 5 6 7 8 9 10
g) The Light in me shines bright; I attract others to the Light 1 2 3 4 5 6 7 8 9 10
h) The Spirit's power is for sanctification & assisting mission 1 2 3 4 5 6 7 8 9 10
h) My spiritual gifts are for *assisting* my primary missions..... 1 2 3 4 5 6 7 8 9 10
i) I'm fulfilling my mission as an Ambassador for Christ........ 1 2 3 4 5 6 7 8 9 10
j) I'm fulfilling my mission as a Gospel Evangelist................. 1 2 3 4 5 6 7 8 9 10
k) I'm a Disciple and fulfilling my mission as a Disciple Maker 1 2 3 4 5 6 7 8 9 10
l) I'm fulfilling my mission as God's *spiritual* Kingdom Builder 1 2 3 4 5 6 7 8 9 10
m) I'm a good and faithful steward over everything I have 1 2 3 4 5 6 7 8 9 10
no) My performance will be judged well at the Bema Judgment 1 2 3 4 5 6 7 8 9 10
p) I'm confident I'll endure tribulation faithfully for Jesus 1 2 3 4 5 6 7 8 9 10
q) I see the value of hard times, I use them to refine my faith 1 2 3 4 5 6 7 8 9 10
r) I'll stay aware of end times events so that I'm prepared 1 2 3 4 5 6 7 8 9 10
r) I'm ready to be a witness for Jesus during the Tribulation 1 2 3 4 5 6 7 8 9 10

Date Last Taken: _____

Questions for Reflection or Group Study:

1) Prior to this chapter what did you think was the primary mission for Christians? How has your perspective changed? What mission stands out most in your mind right now?
2) The three external missions are: 1) preaching the gospel to all creation, 2) making disciples of Jesus, 3) advancing the Kingdom of God.
   a) Which have you personally neglected the most? Why? (Pick one)
   b) Which is most lacking in your church, community, country, other? Why? (Pick one)
   c) Which one do you think is the most important to act on? Why? (Pick one)
3) Name a *specific* way, that you, your family, small group, or church, could do a mission right away. What will you do and why? How can you get it started this week?
4) Describe a painful tribulation you've gone through. What did it teach you? How have you grown as a person and become more like Jesus as a result?
5) Imagine the Great Tribulation begins next year. What will you do this year to prepare for it spiritually, mentally, emotionally, and physically? What should change or improve?
6) Imagine you're in the Tribulation. The world is in chaos and the visible Church is beginning to be persecuted. What mission do you focus on? Where do you spend your time/energy?
7) What does it mean to be a disciple of Jesus? How could we be/make better disciples?
8) What are some ways we can bear fruit/good works without failing at our real mission?
9) How can we balance *seeking* spiritual gifts/empowerment with the *purpose for* them?

Explore Chapter 6 Deeper:

For additional resources related to the topics discussed in this chapter see our companion website at **https://MPoweredChristian.org/Road-Map-Book-Resources**

- Free printable pdf of this chapter evaluation for personal or classroom use
- List of related online courses, e-coaching programs, personal coaching services
- List of related videos, articles, and recommended books
- List of related live webinars and ways to ask questions

Notes/Reflections:

To-Do List:
Date: _____

MY TASKS FOR **THIS UPCOMING WEEK...**

✔ **My Big 1-3:**

✔ **For Personal Growth:**

✔ **For Key Roles:**

✔ **For Calling/Ministry Service:**

✔ **Pray for/Request prayer about:**

✔ **Learn more about:**

✔ **Other:**

CHAPTER SEVEN
THE AUTO CLUB
(The Church)

Church is the unity and collaboration of Jesus's disciples

Bonus Throughout: Tips to have an Empowered Church

Chapter Contents

I. Who and What is the Church

The word "church" has several different meanings and is used in multiple ways. In this section we'll examine the similarities and differences of four of the most common expressions used by Christians. Throughout the book we've already used all of these so I'll be brief here and just provide a summary of the main points you should know. The original Greek word that we translate in English to "church" is *ekklésia* (ek-klay-see'-ah) which means an assembly or congregation. It can also refer to the whole body of Christian believers. The word *ekklesia* originally comes from the Greek words *ek*, meaning "out from and to" and *kaléo*, "to call." The implication is that people are called out from the world and towards God, with the outcome of now being the Church. The English word "church" isn't a direct translation of *ekklésia*, which could refer to any kind of assembly of people. It comes from the Greek word *kyriakos*, meaning "belonging to the Lord." The Greek word for "Lord" is *kyrios*, which is what Jesus's disciples called Him.[1]

a. The Global Church
All who have been born again by the Spirit of God and now belong to Jesus.

Throughout this book you may have noticed some of the time I capitalize the C in Church and other times I don't. This isn't a typo. I like to do this to distinguish the *Global Church* from the word church being used locally or generically, in which both cases I'd spell church with a lowercase *c*. For example, if I were to say "Hey, are you going to church this weekend?" I'd use a lowercase *c* because I'm referring to a specific church, a single group or building. An example of a generic usage would be something like, "I really think the church is struggling to influence the morality of culture these days." I'm really just referring to the entire Christian world and I'm using the word church which kind of represents the public face of Christianity. Often when people speak of "the church" they mean one of these two things. Either a specific local church, or the public face of all of Christianity, as represented by church buildings and the people that meet in them.

The uppercase C Church is very different. By this I mean the Global Church. I don't mean all of the church *buildings* in the world either. I mean all of the born again Christian *people* in the entire world. This also includes all the saints in Heaven. The global Church is all people, everywhere, at any time in history, who now belong to Jesus. *This* is Christ's Church. In Chapter 6, Section (F) *On This Rock I Will Build*, we looked at when Jesus declared that He was building His own Church in detail. He said in Matthew 16:18, *"I will build My church, and the gates of Hades will not prevail against it."* It's important that we remember that *this* is the true Church! The true Church is not our buildings or any of our public representation of it on the earth. The true Church is *spiritual.* Only God knows who is truly in this Church, because you must be born again to be a part of it. Even if every single public gathering in the entire world was disbanded, every church building was torn down, and every single Christian was isolated in their own homes, there would still be a global, universal, spiritual Church that would be visible to God.

Acts 20:28 Keep watch over yourselves and the entire flock of which the Holy Spirit has made you overseers. Be shepherds of the church of God, which He purchased with His own blood.

Ephesians 5:23 For the husband is the head of the wife as Christ is the head of the church, His body, of which He is the Savior. [24]Now as the church submits to Christ, so also wives should submit to their husbands in everything. [25]Husbands, love your wives, just as Christ loved the church and gave Himself up for her [26]to sanctify her, cleansing her by the washing with water through the word, [27]and to present her to Himself as a glorious church, without stain or wrinkle or any such blemish, but holy and blameless.

---

b. The Elect in Christ
The corporate collection of all God foreknew, chosen in Christ, before the world.

We've discussed "the elect" a few times already in Chapter 1, (Summary); Chapter 2, Section (E); and Chapter 4, Section (D). We're not elected before we're born. We *become* (or prove to be) one of the elect through faith in Christ. If you're born again, you are part of the global Church, and prove yourself to be one of the Elect in Christ. Remember how *ekklésia*, the word we translate "church" from, means the "called out" ones? The word we translate "elect" from is *eklektos* (ek-lek-tos). See the similarity? Elect means select, chosen out from, out of a personal preference or intention.[2] The entire global Church is the elect. This is called "*corporate* election," though some believe in *individual* election. We are the ones chosen in Christ to be saved through Him. By referring to us as "The Elect" it gives us a different perspective: God's. By identifying as the Church, the ones that have been called out of the world, there's greater emphasis on us. *We are* the Church because *we* believed and trusted in Jesus. We *became* the Church. By describing us as the Elect, the emphasis is that we're the ones *God chose!* He foreknew us and had us in mind before everything else happened. Long before we were born to later have faith. We're the ones He came to die for. God foreknew our *future* selves *before* we were born! It's more special. More personal. It reminds us that God knows us, more than we know ourselves, on many levels. He knows us from all of our pasts, yes, and all our most intimate parts now, but He also knows all of our future potential and even the eternal version of us!

Romans 8:29 For those God foreknew, He also predestined...

Colossians 3:12a Therefore, **as the elect of God**, holy and beloved... [15]Let the peace of Christ rule in your hearts, for to this you were called as **members of one body**.

c. The Body of Christ
All a part of Christ, playing their unique role, within an integrated spiritual whole.

When we're born again by the Holy Spirit, we're baptized, submerged into Christ's spiritual body. In a mystical sense we're all connected through the same Spirit. This body metaphor helps us to understand why what any one of us does affects all the others. As 1 Corinthians 12:26 says, *"If one part suffers, every part suffers with it; if one part is honored, every part rejoices with it."* There should be no division in the body, but rather care and concern for one another. As 1 Corinthians 12 and Romans 12 teach, we all need one another. We are one body and each member belongs to one another. The Holy Spirit hasn't given any one single part of the body everything they need alone, and no part is greater than the other parts. Each person is given a certain portion so that in the unified whole that the fullness of the body is realized. All harkening back to the relational aspects of God from Chapter 1, Sections C & D. Colossians 2:19 we're reminded of our need to remain connected to Christ, our head. It's from Him the rest of the whole body, knit and held together by its joints and ligaments, grows as God causes it to grow. The term *Church* represents how we're all collectively called out and from the world. The term *Elect* represents how we're all individually chosen by God and uniquely special. But the term *Body of Christ* represents how we're an integrated spiritual whole. It captures our unique individuality, calling, and purpose, as well as our connection to a larger whole, with a common calling and purpose. Seeing these simultaneously shifts what we think the local church is for and how to best utilize it. This affects our individual journey and how we cooperate with others on their journeys, while working towards a common vision.

Colossians 1:24b in regard to Christ's afflictions for the sake of His body, which is the church.

1 Corinthians 12:12 The body is a unit, though it is comprised of many parts. And although its parts are many, they all form one body. So it is with Christ. [13]For in one Spirit we were all baptized into one body, whether Jews or Greeks, slave or free, and we were all given one Spirit to drink... [27]Now you are the body of Christ, and each of you is a member of it.

Romans 12:4 Just as each of us has one body with many members, and not all members have the same function, [5]so in Christ we who are many are one body, and each member belongs to one another.

d. The Local Congregation

The "local church" is the physical, visible expression of the "true Church" of Jesus.

The "local church" is the physical, visible expression of the "true Church" of Jesus, which is spiritual and invisible. The local congregation of believers is where the capital C Church is shown to the world. It is also where the other three expressions take shape. The capital C Church are the called-out ones. How can people claim to be *called out* of the world and *to* somewhere if they don't go *to* somewhere different together? They can't. The local congregation is also where the elect come together. It's our togetherness that confirms our election. The letter of 1 Peter is sent by Peter to the exiles scattered throughout the Roman world, including Pontus, Galatia, Cappadocia, Asia, and Bithynia. He calls them *all* the *chosen* (elect) according to the foreknowledge of God the Father. *(1 Pet 1:1-2)* At the end of his letter, in 1 Peter 5:13, he sends greetings to them from the church in "Babylon" (i.e. Rome) those *chosen* (elect) together with them. He addresses all local congregations of believers as members of the global Church and of the elect. Our own local congregations, and through local congregations in general, is also where we most express our individuality alongside our unity with other members of the Body of Christ. It is through public gatherings of believers that we're able to best unite, complement, love, and serve one another.

---

1 Corinthians 16:19 The churches in the province of Asia send you greetings. Aquila and Prisca greet you warmly in the Lord, and so does the church that meets at their house.

Hebrews 10:24 And let us consider how to spur one another on to love and good deeds. ²⁵Let us not neglect meeting together, as some have made a habit, but let us encourage one another, and all the more as you see the Day approaching.

II. Basic Function - Community, Maintenance, Repair

Now that you have a better understanding of what it means to be the Church we will look at the *functions* of the Church. Remember these are functions of the Church as a whole, the uppercase C Church, but they'll be manifested primarily through its local congregations, or lowercase *c* churches. There are the *basic functions* of the Church and then there are what we may describe as *higher callings* of the Church. We'll examine the basic functions first. These are all centered around community, maintenance, and repair.

e. Road Map Refinement
Church can help members have a Christian worldview through ongoing refinement.

The first basic function of the church is road map refinement. Just as the first chapter of this book was about making sure you have the right road map, the first function of your local church is about making sure you have the right road map. Everything your local church provides—weekly church services, sermons, worship time, Bible studies, life groups, discipleship programs, pastoral counseling, community service—are all to help you think, believe, and behave according to the new map. This is not to say that everything that *could* be said was in the first chapter of this book. Obviously much more has also been said in the last five chapters, and all of this content could be expanded on much more. But I tried to make sure that the most important things were at least mentioned in the first chapter. That's the point of a map. It's not a step-by-step guide. It's a broad overview of the largest and most important landmarks so that you can *see* the whole territory clearly. Local churches should be doing the same. They may not emphasize everything you think is important, or focus on what you want to learn more about every week, but they should be centered around the main things. If they do this the members will have a biblical Christian worldview and see the other things happening in their lives through this perspective. Members' road maps should be getting ongoing refinement through their local church.

Hopefully this book has just been a helpful resource that broadly surveys the landscape of Christian beliefs and life, probably shedding light in some new ways, and maybe filling in the gaps with greater depth on some things you had already known a little about. My hope and prayer is that your local church already teaches on many of these things I've covered to some extent. Of course some things I go into greater detail on, for example a survey of religious worldviews and false religions, are likely not covered. And that's okay. But if the gospel, salvation by faith alone, God's triune nature, Jesus as God and man, God's glory, righteousness, or our mission to make disciples aren't, then that's a major problem! If you've been in a church for a long time but much of this book, specifically those points that I've emphasized heavily and repeatedly, are *brand new* to you, then that's a problem. Examine your church closely and make sure it's a good, biblical church. Also know that they could be well-intentioned but just be a younger church, lacking experience or in need of support. Our ministry, *MPowered Christian Ministries*, provides interim pastor and church consulting services and is available to help.

f. Owner's Manual Review
Church can help members regularly read, study, and ultimately know, God's Word.

The next basic function of the church is to be a conduit between God's people and His Word. God's Word is provided to sanctify us *(Jn 17:17)*, make us wise *(Ps 19:7)*, help us believe *(Jn 20:31)*, instruct us *(Rom 15:4)*, guide us *(Ps 119:9)*, and give us spiritual life *(Mt 4:4)*. In the ancient past the role of preaching and teaching God's Word was even more significant because very few had a copy of God's sacred Scriptures themselves. God's decrees were communicated through prophets and His truths were read and explained by teachers of the Law. By the time of the early church they had moved away from using parchment (animal skins) to papyrus as a more affordable way to copy manuscripts. Churches could acquire Old Testament Scriptures or the writings of the Apostles, make copies, and then read and teach from them to the rest of the congregation. The invention of Gutenberg's printing press in the 15th century inspired and coincided with the birth of the Protestant Reformation and the desire for the Bible to be translated into the common language and be available to all. Since then it has been much more freely accessible.

This transition brought both good and bad consequences. People could now read God's Word for themselves which caused many to abandon the Roman Catholic Church along with many of its unbiblical beliefs and practices. Many found a more personal relationship and devotion to God themselves, through the Word, because there was no longer the false belief that it was necessary or more beneficial to go through the Roman religious system as the official intermediary between the people and God. These were all good things. However, the increased access to the Bible, along with the belief in *Sola Scriptura* (Scripture alone) did open the door to a surplus of differing interpretations of Scripture. This inevitably led to Christian denominationalism, and worse still offshoot Christian cults twisting the Word to support heretical doctrines. Because of these and increased individual Bible reading, the need for knowledgeable preaching and teaching became even more important. This is essential to ensure that Christians are using sound methods of biblical interpretation, forming right beliefs, and arriving at conclusions consistent with historical Christian orthodoxy. Teaching the importance of reading, studying, and knowing the Bible is one of the primary basic functions of the local church.

Acts 6:2 So the Twelve summoned all the disciples and said, "It is unacceptable for us to neglect the word of God in order to wait on tables. ³Therefore, brothers, select from among you seven men confirmed to be full of the Spirit and wisdom. We will appoint this responsibility to them ⁴and devote ourselves to prayer and to the ministry of the word."

Romans 15:4 For everything that was written in the past was written for our instruction, so that through endurance and the encouragement of the Scriptures, we might have hope.

1 Timothy 4:13 *[Paul to his protegé]* Until I come, devote yourself to the public reading of Scripture, to exhortation, and to teaching.

g. Car Club Meetings
Church can unite members for community, fellowship, sacraments, prayer, mission.

Community. At last we've arrived at the point where we'll start learning how the local church is like an auto club. It's awful that many Christians think church is a place you go to. Perhaps this is because we've haven't fully gotten away from Rome's way of doing things, treating church like a religious building you *go to*—rather than a group of people you're *a part of.* Perhaps it's been made worse by modern influence that has encouraged this wrong way of thinking. Our churches are now full-fledged service businesses, even with services and functions offered at set times. Perhaps it's because many of us go to *be served* rather than to serve. We go to receive something rather than to be a part of something. And those who work in churches often think of it like a job as well. They're there to serve and *give* to those who come - like a service business! Both are viewing the institution *transactionally*. Perhaps because we treat church like any other service business, our concern as a consumer is finding one that meets all our preferences. If we find one that does we're willing to drive farther to go there. Compare this mindset with the early churches which were small gatherings that met in people's homes. They were small, intimate, and within walking distance. The first church buildings didn't start to appear until the early 200s.[2] All these reasons contribute to how we see what church is and what it's for. It's not meant to be an auto repair shop, but rather an auto club!

Jesus's Church, and all of its local expressions, were not intended to be something to go to but something to be a part of. Something transformational that you *belong* to. Transforming not only individuals, and the group as a whole, but also the communities the groups are located in. Churches weren't intended to be places where a few gifted give and everyone else receives. They were intended to be communal—all give, all receive. Everyone plays a role, an important role. Everyone is an important part of the body, not just the head and mouth. Jesus didn't intend the "hands" to go look for a church designed to accommodate the personalities and desires of hands. It's the unity-within-diversity that is its strength and glory! The left-brained, logical, rational together with the right-brained, creative, charismatic. The young and old learning from one another. The mature and immature; the educated and uneducated; the experienced and inexperienced. The deeply spiritual with the deeply intellectual. Everyone growing as a result. It's the environment not suited for people looking to *be* served, to get or do what *they* want. The environment that intentionally puts *everyone* out of their comfort zones so we're all challenged to grow in ways God desires us to grow. Different perspectives aren't shunned, they're discussed. Through empathic listening by people who appreciate diversity of thought, all coming together to pursue spirit and truth, in a win-win synergistic pursuit of God's glory! The church is to be like an auto club that has a diverse group of people all united around a love for a common interest. In this case, it isn't cars — it's Jesus! He's the one thing that unites everyone, and He's more than enough!

Throughout this chapter we'll look at some of the ways churches can pursue the right atmosphere for these benefits. One of the basic functions of the church is community. Though we may not always fully appreciate or utilize this aspect of the church most know that it's more available. Many Christians deal with their personal struggles alone even though the church was expressly created so we don't have to! Most people also struggle for a sense of community and contribution, a sense of belonging, a sense of being a part of something important, something greater than themselves. This need is often met in unhealthy ways. God has provided the Church to meet this need! It's a shame that many are much more passionate and invested into their political party, sports teams, dependent relationships, or other clubs or hobbies. These things could be fine to enjoy or could be fruitless, purposeless idols that consume way more of us than they should. Which community are *you* most passionate about and invested in?

Fellowship is an important aspect of local church community. Fellowship is any social gathering for the purpose of building community bonds. It could be meals, outdoor outings, social events, lighthearted games, music and dancing, comedy shows, theaters, or plays. Or anything else, in the presence and spirit of the Lord, that helps members form a sense of belonging and relationship building with one another. Fellowship was an important part of early Israelite community. God created a fellowship offering which was an animal offering, first sacrificed to God, that was then eaten and enjoyed together by the community. A fellowship offering was also called a peace offering or an offering of thanksgiving. It was a meal shared together in gratitude to God. The Sabbath (sundown Friday to sundown Saturday) was a time specifically set aside every week where no working or labor or trip taking or cooking was permitted. Food preparation was done prior to sunset. The Sabbath was an ideal time for people to spend time with God and their families and communities to share food, stories, music, worship, and time together. This activity is harder to do for us not having a weekly Sabbath day, by living separately and farther from one another, and viewing "church" as something we go to rather than something we're a part of in our own neighborhood. However, we can still keep the spirit of fellowship alive and well if we're creative and intentional.

Sacraments are an essential part of Christian community. While they have been given to the whole Church their most common expression will be within the local assembly. A sacrament is something set apart for a sacred purpose. While many *institutions* are sacred (marriage for example), and *activities* are sacred (prayer and worship for example), in the church there are only two things given sacrament status within the Protestant tradition: Baptism and the Lord's Supper. This is because only these two rites have the following three distinguishing features: (1) they were instituted by Christ, (2) Christ enjoined (i.e. directed or imposed by authoritative order or with urgent admonition) them to His followers, and (3) they were bound up with Christ's word and revelation in such a way that they become "the expressions of divine thoughts, the visible symbols of divine acts." By these criteria these two are the only New Testament sacraments.[3]

Baptism, from the Greek *baptizo*, means to dip/submerge in water, and is a ceremonial rite of one's faith and public acceptance of Jesus as Lord and Savior and initiation into His Church. Jesus gave a clear command to do this just prior to His ascent into Heaven in Matthew 28:19 which reads, *"Therefore go and make disciples of all nations, baptizing them in the name of the Father and of the Son and of the Holy Spirit."* An example of this in action is only ten days later, on Pentecost, the first day of the new Church, in Acts 2:37-38 which reads, *"Brothers, what shall we do?" Peter replied, "Repent and be baptized, every one of you, in the name of Jesus Christ for the forgiveness of your sins, and you will receive the gift of the Holy Spirit."* For more on baptism see Chapter 1, Section (K).

The Lord's Supper is a distinctive rite of Christian worship instituted by Jesus on the night before His crucifixion. It's a "religious partaking of bread and wine, which, having been presented before God the Father in thankful memorial of Christ's inexhaustible sacrifice, have become (through sacramental blessing) the communion of the body and blood of Christ."[4] Jesus gave a clear command to do this as recorded in Luke 22:19-20 which reads, *"And He took the bread, gave thanks and broke it, and gave it to them, saying, 'This is My body, given for you; do this in remembrance of Me.' In the same way, after supper He took the cup, saying, 'This cup is the new covenant in My blood, which is poured out for you.'"* (Lk 22:14-23, Mt 26:26-29, Mk 14:22-25) The Apostle Paul instructs the church at Corinth to properly observe this sacrament in 1 Corinthians 11:17-34. He says in verse 26, *"For as often as you eat this bread and drink this cup, you proclaim the Lord's death until He comes."* This also happened on the day of Pentecost, the verse shown at the end of this section, referred to there as "the breaking of bread." For my personal views on Baptism and Lord's Supper and my Lord's Supper wall art visit MPoweredChristian.org.[56] Church communities are the ideal place to celebrate sacraments.

Prayer is another purpose and benefit of the communal aspect of the local church. Prayer connects us both to God and to one another. "Prayer requests" are an opportunity to share our challenges with others and to let them share theirs with us. Simply asking someone if they have prayer needs is an invitation into their lives. It can touch someone tremendously to know you care about them and are willing to not only hear about their problems but also to earnestly petition God on their behalf. This helps you be a better disciple of Jesus. We can also benefit ourselves from sharing our burdens with others and having them pray to God for us. God's Word is clear that when we come together in prayer in Jesus's name it's effectual and powerful. Another aspect is communal prayer, meaning praying together as a group, which offers additional spiritual benefits. This can be a Holy Spirit-led activity that has the potential to be very spiritually rewarding and fruitful. Many churches will have a "prayer time" where the church leadership meets for group prayer on a specific day or time, and other members are welcome to join. Many churches will also have an intercessory prayer team, consisting usually of volunteers, that are available to pray for members. Small group meetings are also a great and less intimidating environment for both group prayer or finding out the prayer needs of individuals. All of these are great, but I'd like to suggest an additional option. That *all* church members be encouraged to meet and pray for others. Perhaps even a regular activity where everyone in a service meets someone they don't know for this purpose. Churches should intentionally create opportunities for strangers to meet, exchange names with one another, each talking about their lives for a few minutes, and praying for one another. This is *proactively directing it* rather than just suggesting it. This initiates not only prayer but also relationship building, increased fellowship, and discipleship.

Vision and Mission. What unites an auto club, or really any kind of club, organization, or group, is a common vision and mission. Each local church should have a vision of why they exist and what they want to help cause to happen. They should also have a mission describing what they do to help accomplish this. It should be specifically created by them and for them and get everyone on the same page. All members should be involved in its creation so there is emotional investment. All new members should be taught about the vision and mission in a way that helps them engage with it. Church orientation for new members should be *part* class teaching about the church's history and mission and *part* discipleship mentoring, learning about the new member and helping them align *their* values and goals with the church's. Church visions and missions should be like a constitution, built upon their statement of faith, with those being a foundation that directs everything else they do. As challenges arise in the future, everyone, including leaders and elders, should submit to it like a governing authority over the whole body. While there should be an elected and/or hired leadership there should also be a level playing field where all members have a voice. Churches shouldn't be a top-down hierarchy where a single leader or a small board dictate their terms to the majority, i.e. "my way or the highway." This would contradict the entire point of the local church as a Jesus-headed, Holy Spirit-led congregation of believers united for a common purpose. Rather, the congregation should be seen as a living organism—a *body*! It's not about what one or a few want, to the exclusion of the others, it's about what's good for the health of the whole body. Sometimes the Lord introduces conflict not to divide but to guide! It's through Holy Spirit-led unity and collaboration we will thrive!

Acts 2:41 Those who embraced his message were baptized, and about three thousand were added to the believers that day. [42]They devoted themselves to the apostles' teaching and to the fellowship, to the breaking of bread and to prayer... [44]All the believers were together and had everything in common. [45]Selling their possessions and goods, they shared with anyone who was in need. [46]With one accord they continued to meet daily in the temple courts and to break bread from house to house, sharing their meals with gladness and sincerity of heart, [47]praising God and enjoying the favor of all the people. And the Lord added to their number daily those who were being saved.

h. Fruit Delivery Services
Church can help members be more fruitful in the community, through collaboration.

As I documented throughout Chapter 5 being fruitful is an important part of the Christian life. When it comes to external fruit we may have a heart to support important causes and serve those in our community but that doesn't always equate to action. We're often negatively influenced to inactivity by excess laziness or procrastination, or a lack of discipline, motivation, money, time, or energy. Other factors that cause inaction are too much pessimism, or not seeing enough results from our efforts. There's also a lot of news and people in the world who will spend the vast majority of their time focusing on reminding the rest of us how bad things are and how they're only getting worse. The optimistic, selfless, problem-solvers are always going to be outnumbered. On top of this, the world's a broken place with a lot of problems and suffering in it. Even when we're ready to make a difference in some way it can be overwhelming trying to decide where, when, and how. If we spread ourselves too thin, by contributing a little bit into a lot of different areas of need, it's harder to get excited and motivated. It's hard to feel motivated when you're not sure your small efforts are really making a difference. If you go the other way, contributing all your resources to a single cause, you will feel like you're making a significant impact. However, because there's so much attention focused in one specific area it's often harder to decide which cause to focus on, leading to procrastination getting started or a blind eye to all other needs. Once a decision's been made there may still be an ongoing internal dialogue about whether you chose the right cause.

These doubts and concerns will never fully go away. Mindfulness of these concerns allows us to reevaluate our priorities from time to time. This is a good thing; it's good stewardship. These concerns aren't meant to be dismissed - but *managed.* I hope this book helps you better survey your options and learn how to prioritize them. The entire metaphor of the car that needs to change first, and *during,* the journey is a reminder that before we try to fix the world we need to start with fixing ourselves and work outward from there. By picturing the fruitful roads ahead, whenever going in the right direction, we're reminded to keep evaluating which direction we're going in. By realizing not all fruitful activities are eternal—or part of our *actual* mission as disciples—it can help us prioritize activities that are *only* good, from activities that are good, eternally significant, and part of our primary mission. Our primary mission as disciples of Jesus were covered in Chapter 6. We'll also cover the primary mission of the Church, what I'm referring to as *The Higher Calling* of the Church, in Section *III* of this chapter. But for right now let's just talk regular fruit. If, as individuals, the road ahead is very fruitful, then as the Church, which is just a collection of individuals, the road ahead is also very fruitful.

Churches are in the best position to help their members be truly fruitful with their lives. The local church can help individual members be much more fruitful through collaboration in a variety of ways. By coming together in a concerted effort of teamwork nearly all of the causes of inaction we addressed at the outset of this section are minimized. Because the pool of resources, when combined together, is much deeper, the impact of the efforts are also much greater. This helps with motivation by feeling like you're making a difference, and in much less time. Churches can have systems, schedules, and roles in place to help plan and organize. Specific long or short term projects along with objectives, goals, and deadlines established help to motivate people, prevent procrastination, and cultivate teamwork and synergy. Pessimistic voices can be uninvited, drowned out, or inspired by the many unified and thus louder, optimistic ones.

Choose Fruit Collaboratively. Church leadership or a service committee shouldn't always choose their preferred causes or service projects for the whole church to do. Nor should there be a fixed project that is listed as a permanent ministry or fixture of the church, as though it communicates "*this* is what *we* do." At least, not unless the entire church voted for that thing, is highly engaged and passionate about it, and there are clear objectives. Because without these it won't fully engage all members. This is a wasted opportunity to build community and foster true synergy. Uninterested members are then left to either dispassionately help anyways, or independently seeking ministries, nonprofits, and causes to support elsewhere. This *isn't bad*, but it does lead to those many causes of inaction. The net result is Christians who belong to a church but their heart's not fully engaged or investing as much as it could in the activities their church is involved in. Volunteering and tithes suffer because they're at conflict with the heart. Decisions should be decided democratically. Larger churches may want leadership to predetermine a handful of appropriate options to choose from that are inline with the vision and mission of the church for everyone else to vote on. Perhaps a person highly passionate about each cause could be given the option to be that causes spokesman and "pitch it" to the people. Or there could be a rotating schedule so everyone's causes get an opportunity to be on the calendar. Or money could be set aside for when major tragedies/opportunities occur. Then the church can respond to it right away with everyone engaged to bless their community in an immediate, relevant way. The possibilities are endless. What matters most is that the entire church is involved to determine which causes to pursue and invest in so a collective is fully and highly engaged. When churches fail to choose causes that their members engage with they then have to struggle the rest of the time trying to *get* them engaged. This is wasted effort! It's not the church administration's duty to *get* members interested in what *they* planned. It's their duty to *coordinate* activities that the rest of the Body is being led by the Spirit to do! If these project causes rotate around then that'll be much easier. There will be an unspoken spirit of generosity that says if I support this cause that they're passionate about, later they will support my cause that I'm passionate about. We don't want our churches full of members that are emotionally divided and not united in common mission. If members are totally and fully engaged emotionally, mentally, physically, spiritually—and united— churches would be on fire and their communities would witness the impact of their light!

i. Routine Maintenance
Church can help members maintain their minimum spiritual requirements.

Typical routine car maintenance includes things like replacing the oil, replacing the oil and air filters, topping off the fluids, checking tire tread and air pressure, making sure lights work, and checking the engine for major noises or signs of problems. This type of quarterly maintenance isn't going to repair mechanical problems nor will it detect any but the most obvious. However, it's still an important routine that helps take care of the oil, which is the lifeblood of a car, and helps to catch major, common, and easy-to-spot problems. Occasional church membership and attendance does the same thing for our spiritual life. According to a 2014 Pew survey among Evangelical Protestants less than 70% attend a religious service at least once per week with some 20-40% only go from twice a month to a few times a year.[7] We may include the occasional wedding, baptism, or child dedications in this category as well. These are specific occasions when the church may be sought out regardless of whether there is a deep emotional relationship tie or not. It may be the Easter and Christmas services, and the occasional service when the need arises, that provides *some* sense of limited connection that keeps some from completely abandoning the faith. This small sampling of Bible reading, public worship of God, communal prayer, listening to preaching from God's Word, sense of community, and momentary focus on Christian things acts like a topping off of the spiritual fluids. It's far from optimal but it may be the bare minimum to keep their car's head gasket from blowing! People might even experience conviction or inspiration by the Holy Spirit during these services that helps direct them or sustain them all the way until their next maintenance check. This basic but vital role of the church helps keep some from total independence and eventually derailing. Of course routine maintenance offers little in terms of actual renewal of the car. They're just not looking under the hood long enough, not enough critical attention given to all the moving parts, to fix anything broken or prevent breakdowns in the future, much less be optimized for maximum performance.

j. Vehicle Repair
Church can help members by providing them support during crisis situations.

There are car enthusiasts who treat their cars like babies. They're always fixing them up, detailing and keeping them in pristine condition, modifying and upgrading parts, and giving them regular tune-ups for high performance capability. But there are others who see their car as a commodity. As long as it stays in one piece and gets them from point A to Z they're content. They don't want to do anything with the engine and motor but use them, unless something breaks, and then they'll take it to the mechanic. There are some who treat their faith this way. They don't really think about Jesus, the Bible, their personal walk, or the church—unless something breaks. Job loss, financial crisis, medical emergency, loss of a loved one, marriage problems, discipline problem with a child, struggle with addiction, family conflict, possible demonization, or some other problem that needs to be fixed. Then the local church pastor, pastoral counselor, deliverance minister, or family therapist gets a visit. How much better off they would be had they been getting regular maintenance! They might have caught it and restored it before it broke completely! But many aren't proactive. They don't foresee and anticipate problems and work on *prevention* of them. This takes maturity, wisdom, self-awareness, humility, behavior modification, discipline, and accountability. They just go about their way until the car gets broken and then seek help for repairs after. It's so much harder to fix problems once they're more broken. It's a shame we do this. It's not good to do things this way but at least it's good when there's enough of a connection/trust between them and the church that they turn to the church in their time of need. But we're all human. Some are active, engaged members of the church community, doing their best to be proactive, and problems can still come up. Either way the church is to meet these needs.

The church *is* in the restoration business because Jesus is! So regardless of how broken people and their situations are when they come to the church, repair is one of its basic functions. Repair the church provides comes through biblical counseling, gospel education, sin confession/repentance, personal and intercessory prayer, sacraments, ordinances, emotional support, community encouragement, and the guiding, power, healing, and comfort of the Holy Spirit. Every repair need that people have and bring to the church for support is an opportunity for them to surrender their situation to Jesus, who is the ultimate physician. It's also an opportunity for them to get the help they need for their immediate crisis while also hopefully learning of their greater need for more thorough and proactive future maintenance of everything else in their lives. Another area of repair comes via church support during inevitable member crises like when someone is sick in the hospital and needs anointing and prayer. Or if a loved one passes away and a funeral officiant or grief counseling are needed. The church is there to be a way for individual members to be supported, directly or indirectly, by the other members.

The six functions I've covered in this segment — Christian worldview refinement, Conduit for God's Word, Spirit-led community, Fruitful collaboration, Spiritual maintenance, and Crisis repair — are all basic functions of the church. These are the good deeds we should all be doing and the Lord calls us to do them together so we can support one another. But these basic functions of Community, Maintenance, and Repair are not the *higher calling* of the Church. We will examine those things in the next segment.

---

1 Timothy 3:15b *[We are]* God's household, which is the church of the living God, the pillar and foundation of the truth.

Titus 2:14* He *[Christ]* gave Himself for us... to purify for Himself a people for His own possession, zealous for good deeds.

III. Higher Calling - Family, Restoration, Missional Empowerment

The final segment of this chapter describes eight higher callings of the Church. By referring to them as higher callings I'm not suggesting that the previous six functions are less important, because they're not. I'm also not suggesting that these are necessarily more difficult, because they're not. Lastly, I'm also not suggesting that we should focus all or mostly on doing these things, rather than the basic functions, because I'm not. All fourteen are important aspects of the Church, difficult in their own ways, and are necessary functions we should be doing. I've segmented these into two categories for the following reason: churches tend to focus more exclusively on the basic functions— and they shouldn't! The eight higher callings we're going to go through are *neglected* in many evangelical churches. Several are *completely absent* and not on the radar at all! That's a shame! We need to get our priorities to align up with God's. As I mentioned in Section (H), just how there's a difference between bearing fruit and the actual mission of disciples for individuals, there's also a difference between bearing fruit and the actual mission of churches. It's even more important for churches to get this right than it is for individuals. It's much easier for churches with clear vision to teach their members than for members to influence their churches. Not impossible but easier. Because individuals in isolation will always struggle with unproductivity churches need to get their priorities straight so they can help empower their members to be fully engaged missional disciples.

k. Love One Another
Church can help members learn why, how, and practice, to love one another.

Love for many people is primarily an emotion. A feeling you have or don't have. Butterflies in the stomach. This isn't biblical. Love—or better defined, *sacrificial love*— is a verb. It's something you *do*. It's an action. Jesus showed us sacrificial love by dying for us on a cross. He didn't just tell us that He *would* die for us, He actually did. Our feelings of love toward Jesus proceed from what He did for us. Remembrance of His love towards us gives us feelings of love for Him. And He calls us to live sacrificially loving others, especially our church brethren, this same way! I'm with you - this is a very difficult teaching. None of us is living up to it, but we should be helping one another at least keep trying to! Not through harsh rebuke but gentle encouragement. By using techniques like positive reframes, or by volunteering to join others in doing loving actions, or even by reminding one another WWJD, or by citing a relevant Bible verse and inspiring each other to action. We're not going to learn this from the world, and certainly not be empowered by truth and the Holy Spirit in our efforts if we try using techniques from the world. I'm talking about transcending superficial love and *really, supernaturally,* loving each other.

I think relatively few churches really have the close-knit intimacy that Jesus calls us to have. Where if one just lost their job or dealing with a financial emergency, then others know about it and those able to bless them. I'm not talking about just the church pastor doing it on behalf of the church using money from donations, though I have seen this and it's the second best option. I think people should be actively engaged in helping *directly*. Why should the pastor or the "church" get the credit? Is it not better if a person experiences their actual brothers and sisters banding together to bless them? Knowing that it was *their* choice. Does this not also better help every one of those people become a better, more generous disciple, more connected with the people and their situation? Maybe some will choose to keep following up later with the family. Maybe they'll take more initiative, because what is being communicated is this: *we are* the Church! It's not the leadership's job to do everything. They are just members of the Body that are in a position to be full time helpers, but it's all the people that *are* the Body. It's the whole Body's duty to care for the whole Body! But it's not only financial things, it's all things! Marriages on the rocks, emotional problems, child discipline problems; gambling, alcohol, drug, or shopping addiction; whatever, you name it. People are so worried about being found out or talked about they're keeping their problems to themselves. Or pastoral counselors and prayer teams are the only people who know what's going on in people's lives. But it would be best if we were real community, where everyone barters services with one another, taking advantage of each other's strengths and compensating for each other's weaknesses. These may be exchanges of free things too like prayer, advice, referral, a shoulder to cry on, or an encouraging word. Remember the rule is to love your neighbor as yourself. And Jesus puts even greater emphasis on how *we* love our brothers and sisters *in the Church*. And talk is cheap. Everyone knows and parrots "the Golden Rule" but we need to live by it. There are churches that talk love all day but will then excommunicate you for disagreeing over nonessentials. Churches have an opportunity, merely by having people come together in the name of Jesus, to help members learn why they need to love each other, how to love each other, and to help them *actively practice* loving one another sacrificially. Everybody, not just the ambitious few. And all people need to be loved, not just the poor, elderly, etc. And all *can* love. The poor and the elderly have gifts to bless others too. Love like this won't happen if not intentional.

John 15:12 *[Jesus]* This is My commandment, that you love one another as I have loved you. [13]Greater love has no one than this, that he lay down his life for his friends.

1 John 3:16 By this we know what love is: Jesus laid down His life for us, and we ought to lay down our lives for our brothers. [17]If anyone with earthly possessions sees his brother in need, but withholds his compassion from him, how can the love of God abide in him? [18]Little children, let us love not in word and speech, but in action and truth.

l. Upholstery Replacement
Church can help members to fully renovate and restore their interiors.

The church can do a lot to really help transform individuals, marriages, and families. But if you'll recall, Chapter 2 taught us that only God, the Holy Spirit, can recreate our cars. Becoming born again is a miraculous, mysterious transformation that takes place when God enters our hearts and quickens us back to new spiritual life. I wanted to title this section "Total Renovation" but I don't want to leave you with the impression that the local church can make us into new cars. Whether we're transformed into a new car belongs to God alone, but the Church *can* help in the restoration of interiors. The Church *is* in the restoration business! The church can't make old cars into new cars, but it can help sanctify and reupholster new cars with bad interiors! Just because we're a new car doesn't mean we're free of bad drivers or passengers. The church can help us remove them. Just because we're a new car doesn't mean we don't have opened or unlocked doors. The church can help us close and lock them. We could still have false thoughts, false beliefs, toxic emotions, addictions, toxic relationships, or harmful behavior patterns. The church can help us identify these things, work through them, and overcome them. The church exists not just for us to help each other reach the bare minimum passing grade to get to Heaven! I hope you have greater ambition than that! As Ephesians 5:27 says Jesus desires for Himself a glorious church, without stain or wrinkle or any such blemish. Your desire shouldn't be for you alone to be blemish free, but all the others in the Body as well. This book is an example of my attempt to teach you some things that will help sanctify you. To help empower you in the process of renovating and restoring your interior. In this way I'm a fellow member of the global Church trying to help each of you, my brothers and sisters in the global Church. The Church can help one another in these ways and teach, edify, counsel, or serve one another to build each other up to become our highest potential. But your local church, which includes all the believers in your close circle of influence who you allow to minister to you, are able to serve you to an even greater degree. This is because of their proximity to you and the degree that you allow them in to your personal situations and trust, accept, and follow their counsel. Let's each strive for genuine Christ-likeness and help one another in our efforts.

m. Everyone is a Driver
Every Christian is *responsible* for *their* influence in the Global Church.

Pew Research found several reasons why self-identified Christians in America don't attend church. The top reason at 44% said they practice their faith in other ways. This was followed by 28% who said they haven't found a church they like, 15% don't have time to attend, 15% don't feel welcome at church, 14% don't like the sermons, and 13% have poor health or difficulty getting there.[8] LifeWay Research, however, did find good news. They found that 63% of churchgoers age 65 and older were completely committed to attending their same church in the future, and 50% of those under 35 were.[9] So is not attending church by "practicing faith in other ways" valid? Yes and no. If we're born again we're a representative of Christ's Church whether we belong to a local congregation or not. And yes we could still shine light in the world, spread the gospel, connect with God, pray, worship, read and study the Word, be fruitful in good deeds, and be on mission without a local church. We're *still* a car in the same auto club, driving in the same direction.

But is lone ranger Christianity really what Jesus called us to? No. As soon as we share the gospel with someone, and they believe and want to follow, is it not also our duty to invite them to join us in following? Or do we share the good news and then tell them to go and find a church and figure it out for themselves now? What if they end up in a heretical church! No, that's poor evangelism. It's not what we see in Acts. And when we get the opportunity to pray for someone, or to counsel someone, or to teach someone, or to disciple someone, are we not then two people meeting together in the name of Jesus? Once we're two people meeting in Jesus's name we *become a type* of church. And are not both people intended to share the gospel again and again? Yes. Multiplication is inevitable if we're truly living like disciples of Jesus. Being a part of a local church is inevitable if we are truly disciples. It doesn't have to be traditional church membership. A house church is still a local congregation. A traveling evangelist may not be firmly rooted in a single home congregation, but they're connected with the global Church. They also become a traveling church unto themselves. And they become a church planter who establishes churches elsewhere—and those they are firmly rooted in. The Apostle Paul modeled this. There was his home church, his *sending* church in Jerusalem, and then there were all of the churches he established and planted in Corinth, Thessalonica, etc. And Paul was a church unto himself during the journey. His church on the road became Barnabas, Mark, Luke, Timothy and his other traveling companions. When Paul went on to Macedonia he left Timothy to pastor the church in Ephesus. Timothy, who was like a son, was left to care for the Ephesian church Paul established, of whom Paul now became like a grandfather to. The Jerusalem church now becoming like a great grandfather to it.

We're all interconnected in the Body of Christ. If you're not connected *at all* with other humans that's a huge problem. For your own sake as well because you won't thrive on your own. Now, there are ways to be sanctified through isolation. Sometimes getting away from your old life of toxic behaviors, people, and influences can be cathartic and restorative. But in the long term it shouldn't stay this way forever. We must all graduate from this and go on to being a positive influence in the Body. Paul left his old lifestyle and Jewish connections, and was ministered to by Jesus for three years in isolation before beginning his apostolic ministry. He tells us in Galatians 1:16-18 that he didn't go to humans or to Jerusalem to meet the other apostles right away. He went to Arabia and then to Damascus, and didn't go to Jerusalem to meet Peter until after three years. But then he went on to connect with many and do much for the Kingdom. Let us do likewise!

LifeWay Research found some interesting conclusions about why Christians would consider leaving or changing their church. The top reason at 54% was that the church changed its doctrine. Now this might be a good thing depending on whether it was the member or the church that had the heretical beliefs. Other reasons included moving residences 48%, preaching style changed 19%, pastor left 12%, a family member wanted to change 10%, political views differed from theirs 9%, they didn't feel needed 6%, and relational conflict with someone 4%.[9] Hopefully, many are driven by good rather than selfish motives. People moving to a new area to pursue their calling there. People leaving because the preaching style changed from being gospel-centered, biblical and expository, to personal anecdotes and emotional fluff. Following their pastor left to a new church that's more biblical or one that utilizes every member so no one feels unneeded. Churches need to help establish strong interpersonal bonds between members so isolated relational conflicts are not a good enough reason to abandon the whole church. All of *us* need to be working to help create community. If any one person, knows why any other person, has decreased their attendance or left, they should take initiative as a mediator. It's up to each of us to maintain and increase the bonds of community.

Everyone is a driver. By this I mean that we're *all responsible*. What we do—or don't do—influences others in the Body. It's not the church's fault or the pastors fault if we're disconnected from others. If you're isolated that's on you. If you get burned by a person or a church it's up to you to make amends with them and/or find a new congregation to join. It's better to be a part of an imperfect congregation, and optimistically appreciate all that is good about it, than to pessimistically focus on all that is not good about it. None will be perfect. All of them are full of saved sinners trying to work through the sanctification process too—just like you! There's a saying: If you find the perfect church, don't join it, because if you do, it won't be perfect anymore! If you can't find a church examine your heart to see if you're there to serve them, or if you're looking to be served. *You* can serve in an imperfect church. In fact, the more imperfect they are the more *you* can bless *them*! If you do decide to isolate yourself it should be intentional, temporary, for good and wise reasons, and it should be a time where you are deliberately doing a lot of spiritual growth and maturing. It should be driven by purpose not emotion. Don't run away from church because of your old wounds—seek healing! Don't let the pain of your past prevent the success of your future! And if you know you'd get healed faster with others helping then stop isolating yourself. You're not being blessed by others, and they're not being blessed by you. You cannot learn to sacrificially love and selflessly serve people that you're unwilling to be around. You cannot proclaim the gospel to people if you're not talking with people. You cannot be a disciple of Jesus that makes disciples of Jesus if you're unwilling to connect with others. You *cannot advance* the Kingdom of God in isolation. Because we're all drivers, and we're all connected, everything you do affects others in one way or another. Just because another driver side-swiped your car a few miles back doesn't mean you shouldn't drive safely with others in mind going forward.

n. Everyone Should Be a Passenger
Every Christian should be deliberately actively involved in other Christians' lives.

Building off the principles from the previous section about how we're all drivers we all also need to be passengers. Chapter 3 explored many of the bad passengers that believers could be allowing to ride in their cars. Some of these examples included false religion, false spirituality, carnal compromise, and counterfeit Jesus's. We also looked at possible open doors believers could be leaving open including false beliefs, sinful behavior, emotional brokenness, or toxic relationships. Every one of us needs to remove these dangerous passengers and close these harmful doors. If you're a toxic person with a lot of junk in your own car you may have to focus on yourself first. You might not be much help to others yet. If you were to involve yourself in their lives *you* might just be a toxic relationship for them, bringing *them* down. So don't do that! But what about after you've cleaned up your car, once the Lord has delivered you from your garbage baggage? Now you've got your car together and your walk is strong. You're not perfect yet, but you've come a long way and you're steady. Now you can be a blessing without bringing toxicity or negativity to them. Now you're able to be a passenger in other people's cars!

Think about it. You know someone, a fellow believer who believes in and loves Jesus, but they've still got a lot of garbage baggage they're dealing with. They've still got bad passengers and opened doors—but they genuinely want to better their life. You should metaphorically get in their car! Now, get in with wisdom, perhaps gentleness, and not the front seat. You're not their Savior, you're a *helper*. Get in the back seat, gradually, and with caution. You want their permission to be there. Their trust, in you, in your character, your motives, and in your recommendations. From the backseat you can preach constantly which driver and passengers should be there. You can point out to them if they have a bad driver or passenger in the car and help them remove them. You can tell them that aspects of Jesus or the gospel they believe in aren't consistent with the biblical Jesus and gospel. If they believe and trust you, you're inviting in more of the true Jesus there. If they have sinful behavior you can help them recognize it and overcome it. If they have emotional brokenness you can help minister to them or walk alongside them and help them to get the healing they need. If they have toxic relationships you can help them separate from them or restore them into healthy ones. In these ways, you *partner* with them in their growth. Be prepared though, you need to wear the armor of God and go in prayed up, and having already cleaned up your own car first, knowing that you're going to deal with some spiritual warfare. Satan is in their life and he's *not* going to be happy about you coming in there and bringing more of God's presence and the Kingdom of God there. He will attack you *to* drive you away. You need to close your own doors first, otherwise you'll be trampled. Have patience with *them* because Satan may *use* them to do it. But if you go in *strong*, faithful, courageous you can really positively influence their whole situation. This is active discipleship. You may have had others do this for you. Extend it forward and advance the Kingdom of God—*within* people!

O. Spiritually Gifted Parts

The Body is being empowered with spiritual gifts for edification and expansion.

We're empowered by the Holy Spirit for lots of things. In Chapter 2, Section (N), I likened the Holy Spirit's power in us as a type of new fuel system that influences how we run and even what we run for. He empowers us to victoriously evict all of the bad passengers in Chapter 3. He empowers our emotions and attitude with the mindset of a victor to prosper, overcome, and endure, as seen in Chapter 4, Sections (S and T). He empowers us for personal sanctification, for private victory over sin, and for character growth and development, as seen in Chapter 5, Section (G). He empowers us to endure tribulation and not only persevere but witness for Jesus until the very end, as seen in Chapter 6, Sections (P, Q and R). In Luke 12:11-12 Jesus even tells us not to worry about how we will defend ourselves or what we will say in our hour of trial because, *"At that time the Holy Spirit will teach you what you should say."* And in Matthew 10:20 Jesus adds, *"For it will not be you speaking, but the Spirit of your Father speaking through you."* He empowers us in many great ways! Another way He empowers us is spiritual gifting.

Spiritual gifts are Tools, given to Parts, to be used to bless the Whole. The examples just given were somewhat internal and non-observational. They are forms of spiritual empowerment but not "spiritual gifts." The gifts are different in that they're *selective* spiritual endowments given for a specific purpose. They're *for* the mission. They're not given for us *individually*, meaning to use *for* ourselves, and to benefit *ourselves*. Rather, they are *tools*, given corporately, in order to benefit the whole. They are given *to* individuals *for* the whole. The Holy Spirit selects these spiritual gifts and gives them to individuals so the individual can use them in cooperative, collaborative ways to benefit the whole Body of Christ. While some people are given gifting to a higher degree, to affect the entire global capital C Church, the primary focus of the gifts is for the local congregation. The Holy Spirit gifts and empowers all of the members of the local assembly so we can accomplish everything necessary in our own immediate context. Each *Part* of the Body is uniquely gifted so that, collaboratively, they can all bless the whole Body.

A brief history. Christians have practiced the spiritual gifts from the beginning of the apostolic era but not much was written about them for the first 1,500 years. After the Reformation there was increased discussion about the role of the Holy Spirit in the Church but the focus remained on justification, piety, evangelism, and missions. As Gary Mcintosh notes, "rationalist religious writers interpreted spiritual gifts as just the natural talents that a person brought into the Christian life. To those looking at the supernatural from a naturalistic perspective, spiritual gifts were nothing but natural abilities with a touch of spiritual attitude."[11] However, others disagreed. John Owen, a church leader, theologian, and academic administrator at the University of Oxford, published a multi-volume book on the nature, personality, and gifting of the Holy Spirit in 1676. But it wasn't until the birth of the Pentecostal movement in 1906 that the spiritual gifts were given great attention.

There is common distinction between the spiritual gifts into one of three categories: speaking gifts, serving gifts, and sign gifts. Speaking/instructing and serving/ministry categories aren't as controversial. This is partly because many of these gifts have been reinterpreted in the church through naturalism. Gifts expressed in traditional skills that could be mistaken for natural talent, education, or experience. The third category - signs, wonders, and manifestations - are debated most because they're distinctly supernatural. If you haven't heard about, discovered, or developed any of these sign gifts, or the supernatural interpretation of some of the others, it's probably because your church doesn't believe that they're still in operation. This belief is called *Cessationism,* the belief that the gifts have ceased. The opposite, the belief that the gifts continue is called *Continuationism.* People who believe this are called *Continuationists.* Those who already practice and/or actively seek to experience all of the gifts are called *Charismatics.* This comes from the Greek words *charis*, referring to the grace provided by God in the desire and power given to us to accomplish His will, and *charisma*, referring to the gifts of blessing provided by God bestowed on us to help us edify and expand.

Spiritual Gift Assessments. Since the 1970s, several church leaders have developed lists of the different gifts and questionnaires to help determine what gifts people have received. *Spiritual Gift Inventories,* ranging anywhere from 14-25 different gifts, and *Spiritual Gift Assessments,* averaging 100-150 questions, have been used as standard practice in the Evangelical world for the past 30 years. Many churches have taken one of these originals and modified them for their own use, customizing the gifts and questions to accommodate their particular theological beliefs about the gifts. These can be a useful tool to help believers discern their spiritual gifts, however I would give several warnings.

Warning #1: No one sees themselves truly objectively. Most assessments consist of questions that you answer yourself from your own perspective, which has many limitations. For example, one question used to determine if a person has the gift of Discernment was, "I can readily distinguish between spiritual truth and error, good and evil." What if *they* think they can, but can't?! I know plenty of misguided people who believe they know and see everything as it is, who are ignorant and unbiblical. The fact that we answer questions like these ourselves limits their accuracy. We need to let our church and those around us help us determine where we're strongest and bring the most value.

Warning #2: Personal Preferences are not Spiritual Gifts. For example, the statement "I like to provide guidance for the whole person" is used in one assessment to help determine if a person has the gift of Prophecy. The problem is merely providing guidance is not prophecy. Your guidance may not be Holy Spirit-inspired at all. Your guidance could even be harmful or demonic! If you're not receiving direct revelation from God that proves itself reliable when tested how can anyone know you're not just giving your opinion? Even if you like giving guidance doesn't mean you're good at it or giving God's direction.

Warning #3: Most questions are too vague for accurate diagnosis. For instance, consider the previous example about providing guidance used to determine prophecy. Your guidance could equally be the gift of shepherding, encouragement, or teaching. Your enjoyment and proficiency of *general instruction* will get you into the right thrust of the role of "Guider" in the Body of some sort. So this could be helpful to get going in the right direction but it doesn't mean you've literally been spiritually gifted for that.

Warning #4: Natural Talents and Abilities are not Spiritual Gifts. Never demean and discount the living presence and power of the Holy Spirit by calling any natural talent or ability a spiritual gift. If we've been supernaturally endowed we will excel at it even if we don't enjoy it, or were previously poor at. There will also be immediate or gradual evidence of it in our life. For example, in 2012, before I decided to enter into ministry as a profession, I took an assessment and some of my lower scores were in evangelism and teaching. I had no real aptitude in these or any interest in them. But the Lord has continued to mold me the past eight years. I completed an assessment recently and scored very high in both of these areas. These weren't qualities I've always had, they were the result of allowing the Holy Spirit to guide me where He's calling me to serve. Examine your experiences since following Jesus wholeheartedly to see where He's been working in your life to use you.

Warning #5: Don't take the Holy Spirit out of your Spirituality. The Holy Spirit is personal, unlimited, and desires our trust, attentiveness, and obedience. (1) He's personal and He communicates with us personally. Don't make the error of believing in your theology that He's personal, and then live daily like He's not there or everything He does is like an impersonal force! Assessment results can make us go after certain types of assignments and stop trying to hear from Him directly for direction. (2) His power and gifting are unlimited. Even if your gifts were diagnosed accurately don't think for a minute that He can't dramatically increase the level of your gifting to supernatural heights, or give you brand new gifts to be used in a different way for different purposes. (3) He desires our attentiveness and obedience. People sometimes turn down opportunities to serve others saying "that's not my gift." This gives our "no" a spiritual sounding reason, but could just be an excuse. Don't rely on your test results to determine your calling or decisions. You can serve *wherever* there is a need in the Body! Continue to remain open to be used by God however He wants to use you. Rather than asking yourself "What can *I* do for God with *my* gifts?" we should ask, "How does *God* want to use me with *His* gifts He'll give me?"

Spiritual gifts in the church. I believe we should teach, and seek, *all* of the spiritual gifts whether we've experienced them firsthand or not because the Bible clearly teaches us to. Our trust is to be in God's Word not personal or anecdotal experience. Jesus told Thomas in John 20:29, *"Blessed are those who have not seen and yet have believed."* Believing in the gifts, I think, is a sign of faith. It is faith (trust) in what God's Word says even if you don't see it firsthand yourself. This does not mean you cannot have a healthy level of skepticism and proceed with caution. There are abuses by counterfeit charlatans and demonic deception by wolves in sheep's clothing so you should have your guard up. Remember what you've learned: examine the fruit! I will say this though. If you haven't heard about or experienced the gifts at all, it could be because you've insulated yourself too much from others who think just like you, you have of misunderstanding of how they operate, or it could be your disbelief. Just as Jesus is unreal and has no impact on the people who disbelieve in Him, the spiritual gifts are unreal and have no impact on those who disbelieve in them. And as Jesus is very real and life changing to those who believe in Him and pursue Him, the spiritual gifts will be very real and life changing to those who believe in them and pursue them. You should already believe all things are possible with God. Remain open-minded and teachable and allow for the possibility...

We can boil down two primary reasons the Holy Spirit gives spiritual gifts: For edification and for expansion. The first—edification—is to edify the Church, to educate it, to train it, to build it up, to sanctify it, to make disciples of Jesus. We'll look at that in Sections (P & Q). This is followed by the second—expansion—to expand the Church, to proclaim the gospel, to witness, to evangelize unreached areas, to plant churches, to advance God's Kingdom (Section R). Spiritual gifts are not given willy-nilly, for no good reason! They're given for a purpose—edification and expansion—and the Holy Spirit can give or take them away whenever He wants. To receive you must believe and then achieve! I think we also must live out the purpose *for* them. We don't get them and *then* do. No, we *do*, first, *then* get them to help us accomplish our goals. The power is for the purpose. The purpose of edifying and expanding the Church. If you aren't stepping out in faith, obedient to God's calling, and pursuing action you have no need for His gifting. Jesus said the Holy Spirit will speak through us *at that time. (Lk 12:12)* His promise is that we will be empowered the critical moment we need Him. Not before. Our giftings may be lying dormant waiting for us to activate them! So step out in faith, trust in the Lord, believe all things are possible through Him [Jesus] who strengthens you [including every gift]!

"To receive you must believe then achieve and need!"

As you review the table of gifts on the following page remember that the spiritual gifts are given primarily in the context of the local church. They are given to individual members/parts of the Body of Christ in order to grow the rest of the Body of Christ. You may receive gifts that go with you wherever you go. But you may also receive gifts as needed based on the needs of the Body! Based on the season or situation you're in, or the person you're speaking with, etc. So study them all, seek them all, grow in all ways. Don't avoid any, including the sign gifts. As Paul says in 1 Corinthians 14:1, *"Earnestly pursue love and eagerly desire spiritual gifts, especially the gift of prophecy"* and in 12:31, *"eagerly desire the greater gifts."* But don't make a salvation prerequisite or an idol out of any, like some wrongly do with tongues. Rather, 14:12 says, *"Strive to excel in gifts that build up the church."* For more read 1 Corinthians 12-14 and Romans 12. Remember, you'll inevitably abound in some more than others, and some more during different seasons of life or assignments. Keep listening, keep pursuing, stay flexible, stay obedient.

Spiritual Gift	Biblical Basis
Motivations (Inward Drives) - Grace given to each to express God's love & build up in particular ways	
Love (The Supreme Gift)	1 Cor. 13:1-13, 14:1; Rom. 12:10; 1 John 4:7-21; 1 Thes. 4:9-10; Lk 6:27-36
Faith	1 Cor. 12:9, 13:2; Rom. 4:20; Heb. 11; Mark 10:52
Showing Mercy/Kindness	Rom. 12:8; Matt. 5:7; Matt. 6:14-15, 18:33; Jam. 2:13; Luke 6:33-36
Encouragement	Rom. 12:8; Acts 11:22-24, 15:20-32
Hope	Rom. 15:13, 15:5, 14:17; Col. 1:5, 1:23, 3:16
Ministries (Service) - Ways God works within believers to serve and meet the needs of others	
Leadership	Rom. 12:8; 1 Peter 5:1-3; Luke 22:24-27
Helping/Serving	1 Cor. 12:28; Rom. 12:7, 16:1-2
Administration	1 Cor. 12:28; Acts 6:1-7
Teaching	1 Cor. 12:28-29; Eph. 4:11; Rom. 12:7
Exhortation/Preaching	Rom. 12:8; 1 Tim. 4:13-14; 1 Thes. 2:2-6 *(Gift of Encouragement but for action)*
Giving	Rom. 12:8; 1 Cor. 13:3; 2 Cor. 9:1-15 *(Blessed in order to provide abundantly)*
Word of Wisdom	1 Cor. 12:8, 2:1-14; Col. 1:9-10; Jer. 9:23-24 *(Divine revelation of God's ways)*
Craftsmanship	Exodus 31:1-6 *(Supernatural endowment with skills, abilities, not normal talent)*
Manifestations (Operations) - Demonstrations of God's supernatural power to aid in ministry	
Prophecy	1 Cor. 12:10, 12:28-29, 13:2; 14:1, 22; Rom. 12:6; 2 Pet. 1:21; 2 Sam. 23:2
Word of Knowledge	1 Cor. 12:8, 14:6; Acts 5:1-10; Matt. 9:4, Mark 2:6-8; John 1:45-50
Gifts of Healing	1 Cor. 12:9, 12:30
Working of Miracles	1 Cor. 12:10, 12:29, 2:4; 1 Thes. 1:5; Rom. 15:19
Distinguishing of Spirits	1 Cor. 12:10; Acts 16:16-18; Matt. 16:21-23 *(Not worldly discernment)*
Speaking in Tongues	1 Cor. 12:10, 12:28-30, 14:1-40
Interpreting Tongues	1 Cor. 12:10, 12:28-30
Divine Appt. Evangelism	Acts 8:26-39 *(Unique opportunities to evangelize, not communication skills)*

Description of Spiritual Gifts. If you're familiar with other Spiritual Gift Summaries you may notice several differences in mine. I believe they are *actually spiritual!* My first difference is that I exclude the fivefold ministry roles (apostle, prophet, evangelist, pastor, teacher) *(Eph 4:11)*, and any of the other roles *(Rom 12:28)*. Why? *Offices or Roles within the Church are not Spiritual Gifts.* These are not specific *gifts* given by the Holy Spirit to *do* something, they are roles or positions for members in the Body of Christ to hold or fulfill. Very different. A person could be primarily an evangelist in their role but still be given the gift of prophecy to help with their evangelism. Likewise, a person could be a helper or administrator in role but be gifted to interpret tongues. They may be a Shepherd/Pastor in role but be gifted with a supernatural degree of mercy/kindness in their heart. Roles are not gifts—gifts are *used in* roles. A man may be in the role of husband that doesn't mean he has the gift of husbandry. He may be given the gift of leadership in his husband role. And a person may have all the abilities to be a great husband but choose to remain single, like Jesus and Paul did. Just as a husband doesn't have the gift of husbandry, an apostle doesn't have the gift of apostleship. Apostle is a role. If someone is called to be an apostle, evangelist, pastor they will be empowered for that role. But the gifts they will be empowered with are from the same ones listed. The evangelist is not gifted with the "gift of evangelism." Neither are there gifts of apostleship or shepherding. These merely use the same gifts listed: teaching, encouraging, leading, serving, etc. Paul was one of the greatest evangelists and apostles. Yet, in 1 Corinthians 2:1-4 he says, *"I did not come with eloquence or wisdom... I came to you in weakness and fear, and with much trembling... My message and my preaching were not with persuasive words of wisdom, but with a demonstration of the Spirit's power, so that your faith would not rest on men's wisdom, but on God's power."* God's power—His spiritual gifting—*didn't* provide worldly wisdom, eloquence in communication, oratory excellence, commanding presence, unique apostolic skills, etc. I'd argue Paul did possess these attributes but *he* doesn't describe them as gifts. They are the same gifts of teaching, exhortation, etc. they're just elevated to a higher degree because of his *role* as apostle. Thinking only apostles get the gift of apostleship, etc. creates hierarchy in the Church and pigeon holes people into specific titles and jobs. I think we should get away from it. We'll examine roles later in Chapter 8, Section (E).

Motivations (Inward Drives). Another difference with my table is that these are often neglected. They're either not identified at all or some (Faith & Mercy) are listed alongside all the other gifts like they're in competition with them. (Most assessments highlight your top 3 highest ranking and suggest that you focus on those). But Paul made it clear in 1 Corinthians 13 that if you don't have the gifts of faith, love, or hope—and especially love— your other gifts are worthless! People in the Church need these giftings—the most—to be healed, edified and uplifted! If you have no other spiritual gift besides love you are still abundantly useful! Value, appreciate, and seek growth in all gifts in this category!

More-Spiritual, Spiritual Gift Descriptions. I've also reworded some of the gifts to get back to their original meanings. It's shameful how we've allowed a rationalistic, naturalistic reinterpretation of these gifts. For example, I have *Word of Wisdom* where others just say *Wisdom* and ask questions related to being a wise person. Now, I'm all for being a wise person according to worldly standards, *in addition to* spiritual wisdom, but this gift from the Holy Spirit has *nothing* to do with worldly wisdom. It's about receiving divine revelation that gives you understanding of God's ways. The entire chapter of 1 Corinthians 2 drives this point home! Peter's confession in Matthew 16 is an example of a word of wisdom. Same for the gift of the *Discerning or Distinguishing of Spirits,* which has nothing to do with normal discernment, making judgments about right and wrong. Examples include Paul identifying the demon in the medium in Acts 16:16-18 or Jesus identifying Satan speaking through Peter in Matthew 16:21-23. Another is the gift of *Prophecy,* which one assessment linked to the questions, "I enjoy hearing teachings about the Bible" and "I feel responsible to confront others with the truth." What?! Prophecy is a Holy Spirit-inspired divine utterance! Not just enjoying the Bible or confronting others. 1 Thessalonians 5:19-21 tells us, *"Do not extinguish the Spirit. Do not treat prophecies with contempt, but test all things. Hold fast to what is good."* Prophecies should be tested. Yet many are not only not testing them they're doing worldly thinking and calling it the gift of prophecy! Next is the *Word of Knowledge* which is receiving a divine revelation from God, about someone or something, that would've been unknowable by human means. An example of this is Peter knowing about Ananias in Acts 5. When you hear and share unknowable information with people it can give them faith in you (and God) and help open them up for healing, growth, or conversion. It's not just being a knowledgeable or well educated person by worldly means! Don't let people subvert the truth of the Bible and water it down so that it's less spiritual, less you need faith for, and easier to fit in to normal worldly life! It's better to have faith in them and have not experienced it personally than to pervert God's Word and change the meanings for unspiritual people. We can certainly *also* embrace non-miraculous variations of these things without labeling them spiritual gifts.

Non-Gifts. Lastly, I also excluded several of the supposed gifts that other assessments use. I covered a few of examples in my section about roles. Others I've excluded because, quite frankly, they're *not* described as spiritual gifts in the Bible at all. I'm not sure when these started but I think churches keep them around to help fill up job vacancies around the church. Examples include *Creative Communication* and *Music/Worship.* If you have the talent here, great, but the Bible doesn't teach that it comes from the Holy Spirit as a gift to build up the Church. These activities would just fall under the gift of *Helping / Serving*—and there's nothing wrong with that! Then there's a few I think are also falsely listed as spiritual gifts. The problem is the impression is given that only some are called to do these, *if* they're gifted or if they enjoy it. No! These include the gifts of: (1) *Evangelism,* no we're all called to evangelize; (2) *Hospitality,* no we should all be hospitable; (3) *Intercession,* no we should all intercede in prayer; (4 & 5) *Knowledge* and *Discernment,* which should be *"Word of Knowledge"* and *"Discernment of Spirits."* But *even if* these two were gifts of the Holy Spirit they apply to all as well. We should all have knowledge and discernment. Hopefully this book is helping you have more of both. Don't limit yourself—be empowered! I believe God is so much bigger than we think and that He will use you in greater ways than you can imagine! Examine the gifts in the table. Appreciate and grow in all in the *Motivations* category. Serve and share them with others in the *Ministries/Services* category. And eagerly seek all in the *Operations/Manifestations* category. Be "On Call" and let God use you for whatever He wills in any way that He wills!

p. Collaborative Discipleship
The Church *exists for* the purpose of edification, i.e. making disciples of Jesus.

The final three sections cover what spiritual gifts are primarily for. Discipleship is both an *inner* work (becoming a better disciple) and an *outward* work (helping to disciple others). Our giftings empower us to collaborate, or work together, in ways that use the gifts we've been given to help others become better disciples. And for them to help us become a better disciple. All the activities of disciples from Chapter 6 are also true for churches. If it's true for individuals then it's true for collections of individuals! Just as Christians get stuck in the mundane minutia of normal Christian life, local churches get stuck in the mundane minutia of normal church life. We go about life as though Sunday and maybe Wednesday is all any of us need or want. We're settling! We're not actively pursuing God's best. We're not forcing ourselves to go further in ambitious ways that would *require* us to be spiritually empowered, or to *depend* on the giftings of others to accomplish it. Our activities are way to unlike the churches in Acts which needed spiritual empowerment. We need to be intentional. Missional. Driven. It doesn't matter how filled our church services are, or how many programs are offered—are people becoming *better* disciples? Good fruit is a byproduct, not a mission. Lots of organizations do good but they aren't all spiritual operations ambitiously dedicated to changing the world for Jesus!

q. Collaborative Gospel Provision
The Church is to come together, in ways enabling the Gospel, to sanctify everything.

The truth of the gospel needs to be at the heart of everything we think, are, and do. Every individual, and every smallest part of the spiritual, emotional, mental, physical, relational, economic, career, etc. aspect of the individual needs to be permeated by the gospel. Its truth and reality need to be totally received, felt, and embraced in every domain. Brokenness needs to be healed. Sin needs to be forsaken and viewed with contempt. Minds, bodies, and souls need to be transformed. Marriages and families need to be healed, restored, strengthened, and made spiritually bullet proof. The reality of the gospel's sacrificial love needs to flow from transformed individuals into everything else. Single people need to remain celibate or enter into relationships seeking someone to sacrificially love and marry. Households, families, businesses, etc. need to transformed. The church has influence in all these areas. The question is whether or not we will all seek our *highest* potential and help one another do the same? Or will we settle for decent enough? Let us fully live out the effects of gospel reality and help our church community do the same! A church's collective sanctification is a collaborative effort. Our roles and spiritual gifts come together not only to change what we *do*, or our mission, but also what we *become*. If those gifted to teach are not teaching, those gifted to encourage are not encouraging, those gifted with faith are not inspiring, and those gifted to serve are not serving, many are not being built up. The pastor alone shouldering the entire load, should not, and cannot. Nor will the efforts of a few gifted people alone transform the whole deep enough. There may be prophecy, a word of wisdom, a word of knowledge, a deliverance, a healing, a leader's perspective, an intercessory prayer, an administrative responsibility, a financial blessing, an act of love, or a merciful act of kindness needed and these needs aren't being received. How much different would each of us be if a great percentage of our church *knew* us, knew what we needed, and were proactively just doing it as led by the Lord? And how much more valuable, needed, and significant would you feel if you knew you were directly helping many people in your church as well?

r. Collaborative Advancement
The Church, representing God's ever-expanding Kingdom, needs to keep advancing.

After church discipleship and sanctification it's about evangelism and church planting. A stronghold for God's Kingdom is planted, move on, repeat. We can't be complacent. The entire world could've been evangelized several times over already! How many church "missions" are short-term and fruit-centered, instead of long-term discipleship and evangelism centered? Our mission isn't to create third-world *dependents* that rely on us. It's to *empower them* for advancement! Churches have been, or perhaps *could* be, empowered by the Holy Spirit, but only *for* a purpose - to be an ambassador for Christ, to reconcile the lost to God, to preach the gospel to all creation, to make disciples, and to advance the Kingdom of God on earth! The world's getting darker and people will need focused and disciplined churches helping members be a loving, strong, and persevering witness until the very end. Commit yourself today to being a strong and positive influence for your local church and abroad, in whatever way you're able, to whoever you're able!

IV. Chapter Summary and Evaluation

Chapter Summary
The Empowered Church is the united vision and collaboration of Jesus's disciples.

We the people are collectively the Global Church, The Elect, the Body of Christ, of which He is the head. Local congregations are physical expressions of this, local clusters of individuals coming together. Our basic function is to be a community of believers that support and assist one another in our mutual edification, car maintenance and repair. Our higher calling, our true potential, is to be more like a close loving family, achieving total car restoration, coming together spiritually gifted and empowered in collaboration for our mission in the world. Our highest potential as disciples of Jesus is found not in what we do on our own but in what we can accomplish by working together.

"It's not so much that God has a mission for his church in the world, but that God has a church for his mission in the world" - Christopher Wright[10]

Chapter 7 Evaluation
AFTER THOROUGH, CAREFUL EXAMINATION, RIGHT NOW:

	False			Partially False			Mostly True			True
a) The "True Church" is every born again follower of Jesus…	1	2	3	4	5	6	7	8	9	10
b) As "Elect" I was foreknown by God and am valuable to Him	1	2	3	4	5	6	7	8	9	10
c) "Body of Christ" refers to us as an integrated spiritual whole	1	2	3	4	5	6	7	8	9	10
d) Local congregations are the visible expression of the Church	1	2	3	4	5	6	7	8	9	10
e) My local church helps me maintain a biblical worldview…	1	2	3	4	5	6	7	8	9	10
f) My local church helps me read, study & know God's Word	1	2	3	4	5	6	7	8	9	10
g) I'm helping my church be a transformational community.	1	2	3	4	5	6	7	8	9	10
g) I'm fully contributing to fellowship, sacraments, prayer….	1	2	3	4	5	6	7	8	9	10
g) I'm fully aligned with my church's vision and mission……	1	2	3	4	5	6	7	8	9	10
h) I'm fully engaged & contributing to my church's projects ..	1	2	3	4	5	6	7	8	9	10
ij) I support my church and their efforts to maintain & repair	1	2	3	4	5	6	7	8	9	10
k) I strive to proactively sacrificially love everyone that I can	1	2	3	4	5	6	7	8	9	10
l) The Church is called to pursue complete restoration………	1	2	3	4	5	6	7	8	9	10
m) As a driver I'm responsible for my influence in the Church .	1	2	3	4	5	6	7	8	9	10
n) I'm a passenger actively involved and discipling others……	1	2	3	4	5	6	7	8	9	10
o) I've been entrusted and empowered with spiritual gifts…..	1	2	3	4	5	6	7	8	9	10
o) I'm eagerly pursuing all gifts God would use through me ..	1	2	3	4	5	6	7	8	9	10
o) I'm collaborating my spiritual gifts to serve the whole Body	1	2	3	4	5	6	7	8	9	10
p) I'm collaborating with others to disciple and be discipled	1	2	3	4	5	6	7	8	9	10
q) I'm collaborating with others to sanctify and be sanctified	1	2	3	4	5	6	7	8	9	10
r) I'm collaborating with others to advance God's Kingdom ..	1	2	3	4	5	6	7	8	9	10

Date Last Taken: _____

Questions for Reflection or Group Study:

1) Local churches are Jesus's vehicle for transformation in the world. In what ways have you undervalued the role of the local church? What are some ways that you'll improve?

2) How would you rank your current/previous/prospective church in the areas of:
a) *Biblical,* b) *Community,* c) *Fellowship,* d) *Sacraments,* e) *Prayer,* f) *Vision/Mission,*
on a scale of 1-10? Which are they doing really well? What would you change and why?

3) How would you rank your current/previous/prospective church in the areas of:
a) *Love,* b) *Spiritual Gifts,* c) *Discipleship,* d) *Sanctification,* e) *Kingdom Advancement*
on a scale of 1-10? Which are they doing really well? What would you change and why?

4) Have you complained about, or left a church for, any of the reasons listed on p. 314-16? Did you focus on features of the church different from those listed in questions 2 and 3? Were you right to complain or leave—or wrongly too focused on non-essential things?

5) Describe some *specific* ways you're going to begin, now, to be more collaborative with your church in any of its key functions. How will you influence positive transformation?

6) What's your experience with spiritual gifts? Do you lean cessationist or charismatic? Why? Take a spiritual gift assessment and discuss your results. (See p. 318-24 and also 350-51)

7) What are some ways you could be *more collaborative* in the church towards the vision, mission, local causes, discipleship, healing/sanctification, or Kingdom advancement? How could you influence your entire church? What could change as a small group?

Explore Chapter 7 Deeper:

For additional resources related to the topics discussed in this chapter see our companion website at **https://MPoweredChristian.org/Road-Map-Book-Resources**

- Free printable pdf of this chapter evaluation for personal or classroom use
- List of related online courses, e-coaching programs, personal coaching services
- List of related videos, articles, and recommended books
- List of related live webinars and ways to ask questions

Notes/Reflections:

_____
_____
_____
_____
_____
_____
_____
_____
_____
_____
_____
_____
_____
_____
_____
_____
_____
_____
_____
_____
_____
_____
_____
_____
_____
_____
_____
_____

To-Do List: *Date:* _____

MY TASKS FOR **THIS UPCOMING WEEK...**

✔ **My Big 1-3:**
_____
_____
_____

✔ **For Personal Growth:**
_____
_____
_____

✔ **For Key Roles:**
_____
_____
_____

✔ **For Calling/Ministry Service:**
_____
_____
_____

✔ **Pray for/Request prayer about:**
_____
_____

✔ **Learn more about:**
_____
_____
_____

✔ **Other:**
_____
_____
_____

CHAPTER EIGHT

Same DESTINATION, Alternate ROUTES

You have a unique identity, calling, and mission to fulfill. And your story contributes to the grand narrative.

Chapter Contents

I. Discovering Your Unique Identity and Calling

Chapter Prelude. A few nights ago, as I was preparing to begin writing this chapter, I had an interesting, perhaps even prophetic, dream. In my dream I had finally gotten my dream sports car. I felt the sense that I had worked very long and hard for it and was finally reaping the fruit of my labor. I think it was a beautiful, new, black Lamborghini or a McLaren or something extravagant like that. It wasn't the exact car that was important; it was a feeling of pride of accomplishment that went with it that I remember. It was the kind of car that you just knew when you saw it. The kind that screamed "success" that very few people could afford and everyone thought was awesome. I had it pulled up at a family member's house. Though I was in the driver seat and it was definitely mine I don't remember having a recollection of having actually driven the car yet. So I decided to go for a quick drive. But when I got to the street it was having major issues. When I turned the steering wheel left the tires went right! It wouldn't accelerate properly. It was jumping through the gears! The brake and gas pedals kept alternating which would do which function! I can still picture this little small intersection I'm trying to drive in and I am spinning out and recklessly darting back and forth, going from 0-60 in 2 seconds to then slamming on the brakes to a screeching halt! Left. Right. Go. Stop. It was terrifying! I felt like the car was possessed! Oddly enough I made it back to the house and I still offered, right after this episode, to drive the rest of the family to wherever we were going. An offer they refused after having seen all of this. It was crazy I was still willing to drive it. I clearly had zero control over this car. The *reality* of the car was far from the *illusion* of grandiosity I had built up in my mind. I still wanted to have the appearance of success and the feeling of success. I had cognitive dissonance, which is what happens when you disassociate, or separate and compartmentalize things in your mind. This is done so that you can hold two contradictory beliefs, ideas, or values at the same time and not even realize it. This occurs so that we can be fully passionate about both things and not even realize that they totally contradict one another. The car was both a sign of my success and accomplishment and pride of doing well in life—as well as a sign of the fact that I had zero personal control or direction and am just being haphazardly thrown about.

When I awoke I immediately thought of this book which has used the car and driving as a consistent metaphor. And then it dawned on me that I was about to begin this chapter about personal direction in life. I gave a sly smile to God as I thought about the many creative ways He teaches us things and let Him know that I received the message. I actually thought that was the end of it but now He's bringing another part of my testimony to my mind to share with you. Many years ago I was at a crossroads in my life. This was before my call to ministry. I was working at an ad agency, and for the latter half of my nearly two year tenure, was leading a department of one that managed corporate client email marketing, website design, and other forms of internet marketing. I was earning income at the agency as an employee as well as through two small businesses of my own on the side. I had just finished getting Gazelle-intense, (a term Dave Ramsey fans will understand!), and getting debt free and rebuilding a fully-funded emergency fund again for the second time. In fact that's what brought me to the agency in the first place. I had been self-employed for years, and wanted to remain that way, but my savings had taken a hit during the years following the 2008 recession. I still lived responsibly but income wasn't always predicable. My savings dwindled down and a credit card was used to float me during income dips. A short-term contract job would help me quickly pay off my card, shred it, build my emergency savings back up, and get back to my *previous plan*. The long commute put like 25,000 miles a year on my car... at least until it got totaled when I was hit by a drunk driver. But I was a hustler, and determined. Even though I had multiple sources of income, and was making more money than I ever had in my entire life, my income vastly exceeding low monthly expenses, I still decided to buy the crappiest, 20-year old, egg-beater replacement car I could find. I think it was $1,500! Hey, it ran well and had A/C and that's all that mattered! I drove that eyesore for about a year until it needed an expensive repair and then I debated what kind of car to replace it with.

Now what I hadn't mentioned during the previous two years is that a lot more was changing than just my workplace and finances. At age 30, after 17 years of being a lukewarm Catholic, and then 13 years of being a lukewarm Protestant, the Lord began to convict and call me to Him. I began to attend church weekly and listen to hours and hours of audio Bible studies throughout my long commute. I was also coming to the conclusion that advertising and marketing was not as fulfilling or where the Lord was calling me. Since my early 20s I had always intended to make a difference in the world somehow, but thought owning a successful ad agency and influencing the world through it was the way I would do it. I began to pursue a more direct approach to helping people including a certification in life coaching. I also invested lots of time into Bible reading and study, listening to sermons online, and investing time into old passions of mine including health and fitness, personal productivity, life optimization, and personal empowerment. My relationship with God had also grown a lot. I stopped living in sin, stopped allowing romantic relationships and my career/business to be my idol, and began pursuing Him wholeheartedly. After realizing how centrally important He is, I officially dedicated my life to Him and declared that anything I do in the future to help people needs to *include* helping them understand their need for Jesus.

So what kind of car *did* I buy? Here's where my story came to a crossroad. I was ready for a nicer car. Though I could have just bought it with cash I didn't want to drain the savings I had just rebuilt. But I also really didn't want to wait another year to save up for it. I'd already driven an ugly cheap car for the past year. I thought to myself I could get my dream car which was a Mercedes Benz. It was sleek, fast, all black and chrome, with a chrome front grill. I thought, I deserve it. I've saved. I've been smart. My expenses are low and steady. My income is high and consistent. The problem? To get the one I wanted I'd need to get a car loan. Yep, I'd have to go back in debt! And I was seriously thinking about it. But I would be (sort-of) smart about it. I was going to get a five year loan but aggressively pay it off in two years. That's a reasonable compromise, right? I get my reward now and then hustle for two more years. What's two more years? I'm still *basically* debt-free besides a mortgage and now a car. And if I needed to I could always either sell the car or just pull cash out of savings and pay it off instantly. That seemed reasonable.

But there was one other problem: I would have to stay working at this job for two more years. It would be foolish and risky to be self employed again with this debt hanging over my head. And I couldn't afford this car if I left the job. So that was my dilemma. I could have my dream car, get some short term debt, and keep doing what I was doing, or get a cheaper but still upgraded car and be free and flexible to do whatever God calls me to do. I wrestled with which was the right decision for several weeks. I prayed about it. It wasn't just about a *car*—it was about *direction*. The car was a symbol. It represented what was most important to me. If I get the car it would control what my life would look like for the next two years. God was changing my perspective in many different ways and putting all kinds of dreams on my heart about a different career path focusing on helping people directly. I would basically be hindering or postponing that for two years if I get this car. But I really wanted the car! I remember thinking "Lord, I wish I knew *exactly* what you were calling me to for the future!" I remember thinking and saying to God: "Lord, I wish *you* would just make this decision *for* me!" That Sunday night, exasperated and sick of all the back-and-forth with it all, I decided I'm just going to get the car. It might be the wrong decision but I'm over all the indecision. I called my dad on the phone and said "I'm going to get the car. They have three slightly used, very low mileage versions of it at this dealership across state. Let's drive there this Saturday and I'll buy one of them." He agreed. Okay, it was the plan. I'm going to get the car.

Just hours later, early Monday morning the next day, I was laid off!

After the initial shock and upset I began to think with wisdom. About halfway on my commute home that morning I just broke out laughing. I looked up to Heaven and said to God "I guess you answered my prayer and made the decision for me!" (LOL!) It occurred to me that I had made the wrong call and He intervened to fix it for me. That's okay. It was a valuable lesson for me. It changed my trajectory. You may not be reading this book right now if that hadn't happened. I went home that same day on a new course and registered my company *MPowered Living, Inc.* and all of its subdivisions including *MPowered Christian*, later to become *MPowered Christian Ministries.* I share this part of my testimony not because it's the most exciting or interesting. I'm sure many of yours are much deeper and profound, more painful or traumatic, more miraculous or amazing. I share it because it's an example of how God's Will *will* be accomplished one way or another. And all of our experiences and decisions help form who we become and what we do. We're all navigating these roads of life in our own ways making lots of decisions, some good, some bad. Some decisions help us get the most of our lives and callings, some decisions hinder them in some way. But if we're trusting in God and always looking with wisdom for how He is moving and guiding us from the background then everything that happens has the potential to be seen for whatever good it brings to the bigger story. You may see a job loss whereas I see God intervening to set me on a right and very different course. Now I'm not immune to the emotional consequences of losses and setbacks. I *did* experience other emotions. I did feel grief and depression about the job loss; disrespected that the company didn't value me enough to discuss with me first other ways we could address their concerns; upset that they undervalued my talent and value; and even a sense of betrayal for all the sacrifice, long nights, and everything that I did for that employer. At one point during my first year there I had stepped up into a leadership role and had helped hold their entire internet marketing department together by a thread. But after the bitterness subsided I realized my heart was no longer fully in it the same way during the second year as it was during the first. God was already writing a different course for my life. I could sense it, and who knows maybe they could too. A new course was coming into focus before my eyes, it just wasn't very clearly defined just yet. And just so you know, I think it rarely ever truly is.

Every one of us has a unique identity. We're created as individuals, and are special, valuable, created with a purpose in mind. All of us can say to God and join in with David as he says in Psalm 139:14-16: *"I praise You, for I am fearfully and wonderfully made. Marvelous are Your works, and I know this very well. My frame was not hidden from You when I was made in secret, when I was woven together in the depths of the earth. Your eyes saw my unformed body; all my days were written in Your book and ordained for me before one of them came to be."* You are fearfully, wonderfully, and marvelously made! And your days were written and ordained already before you were born. God tells the prophet Jeremiah in Jeremiah 1:5, *"'Before I formed you in the womb I knew you, and before you were born I set you apart and appointed you a prophet to the nations.'"* Now it may not be your calling to be a prophet, much less a prophet in Israel to many nations like Jeremiah was. Your calling may not be like mine, to start a Christian empowerment ministry and eventually write a book. Nonetheless, you have a unique calling. God has a plan for you and you're intended to play a specific role and fulfill a specific purpose. And all of the things that are part of your unique story, are interwoven and interconnected throughout God's master narrative that includes all of our stories.

Most of us will get our official invitation into God's mission through our conversion. The day we were saved and gave our lives to Jesus we got a *general* idea of the direction we are to go in. That's when we got our new map. But you and I both know that a map is far from step-by-step directions! Especially if the journey is years or decades long!

What *exactly* we're supposed to do, our exact calling, our unique role? We never received that blueprint! You and me both. Key biblical figures like David and Jeremiah that I quoted from earlier played such an important role that God spoke to them directly. They received their calling like a personal visitation from the General himself. But for most of us we just accept our draft papers and show up for duty. We find out what our assignment is once already en route, or maybe realize it when already halfway through it! Sometimes we don't even realize experiences are part of our calling until we look back in retrospect. After all it wasn't the job loss alone that helped to carve my path. The financial problems with my business, the temporary contract job offer at the agency that was too good to pass up, even the hit-and-run by a drunk driver that totaled my car—all these pieces played a role! Thank God that He didn't let me focus on what was wrong but rather on what was right! I bet your story has similarities. Lots of experiences life would've been a smoother ride without, but you never would've gotten *right here* without them.

We don't so much as *receive* our calling as much as we *discover* our calling. We get it piece by piece. We discover it by reflecting backwards, inwards, and forewards. We discover it by closer examination of the situations we find ourselves in, by introspection into who we are as a person, by personal reflection of our past experiences and how they shaped us, and by the things God is currently putting on our heart for the future. This all makes it much more ambiguous and less clear. Much easier to misinterpret His will or to come up with numerous possible roads for us to take. But this needn't worry you! If God had an extremely specific calling for your life just trust Him that He would make it known to you in an obvious way, just as He did for David and Jeremiah. Not to mention Noah, Abraham, Isaac, Jacob, Moses, or John the Baptist. And if He *hasn't* made it razor sharp clear then it's because He has left our futures, at least for right now, *flexible* for us to follow the Holy Spirit's promptings of our heart. It's actually a gift! We can choose to enjoy the thrill of all this! I say "we" because He is *still* carving out my path. God-willing, this book isn't going to be the last thing I do! Choose to enjoy the spontaneity and variety of it all! Choose to enjoy the adventure and mystery of the ride!

a. You Are Part of the Body
You're an essential Part of the Body, with a purpose that contributes to the Whole.

Of all of the metaphors for the Church given to us in the Bible "the Body of Christ," covered in Section (C) of Chapter 7, is by far my favorite. I just love how it captures our individual roles in relation to the roles of the rest of the body. How we're all equally the body. How we're separate-but-integrated in many ways when it comes to our purpose. In regards to which spiritual gifts we receive and why. In regards to our unique roles and responsibilities and why. But it goes much deeper than this, I think extending all the way to our *entire* lives. It includes our actual *design*, why we are the way that we are, all of our personal experiences - everything! For example, I'm fulfilling the role of a teacher and pastor, and the role of a mind and a mouth in the body right now to you through this book. But beyond what I'm doing *right now*, parts of my life story, like those shared in the prelude of this chapter, are part of how I arrived here. Long before I was ever able to help anyone find direction in life I spent a lot of years trying to find my own! I wasn't a teacher then, I was a student. And in other areas of life, both before and now, I am a helping hand, a servant, a friendly smile, a son, a brother, a grandson, a client, a supporter. Each piece plays a very small role in many other people's lives, and everything else plays a role in mine. It's all interconnected. It's all important. All of my pain, struggles, challenges, defeats, and victories all influence who I now am, how I see the world, and how I teach. But the same is true for those who aren't primarily teaching. If you're a leader or a follower, an encourager or a prophet, an evangelist or a counselor, or whatever. All of who you are will go into it. You are more than just your role in the Church, more than just your spiritual gifts. Your painful past story that has become your testimony could be the trial that taught you how to trust in God that now makes you brimming with faith. That same painful story could've been the lesson you learned that makes you a wise teacher. Or a hope-filled person that's now a good encourager. Or it has helped you be a servant and a generous helper. You've got a story and that is all yours. It may share commonalities with a lot of other people, but how God is writing it and taking you through—and for what ultimate purpose for His glory—is distinctly *only yours!*

This book is a small part of my story. It contains many of the things I've learned and I hope it's a blessing to you. If it is then it will play a small role that contributes to you and a part of what God has done in my life will become a piece that lives on through you as well as everyone you influence and everyone they influence and so on. The same is true for everything you do. You may be a mouth that teaches others, hands that serve others, feet that bring the gospel to others, or whatever. So my impact, or lack thereof, in this work is totally dependent upon you! I'm relying on you!!! If you and everyone else like you reading this book does nothing with anything I've said my effort in writing this will contribute nothing in the long run. All of you determine if this will edify the Body or not. If it educates, edifies, inspires, blesses you in some way then I will be blessed by it in return. I pray it will - beginning with you! We tend to put the preachers and pastors on a pedestal in the church. But all but the most self-centered preachers know the real truth: if our *hearers* do nothing with what we preach then our preaching is useless! It's the hands and the feet of Jesus that actually gets things done. It's the word that is planted in the good soil that produces a crop. Even the best preaching in the world, if it falls on deaf ears will amount to nothing! It is the servants, the worker ants, who get the real work done. It's those who grind it out. It's those who love the Lord and serve wherever is needed so His will be done on earth as it is in Heaven. This is why all good leadership is servant leadership. If preachers don't value the actual serving, and aren't serving right alongside those they lead, then we have no business preaching! I don't know what your unique call is but I can promise you one thing: it matters! It matters more than you could ever possibly imagine. Whatever your calling is, its fruit is a fulfillment of the efforts of those who came before you, and a contributing factor to those who come after. You *matter* so, so much! You are an essential part of the body! Your roles, yes. Your gifts, yes. But also *you!* Your exact situation, your history, your experiences, your passions, your values, your relationships, your wisdom, your perspective, all of it. You were uniquely designed and God has a way that your life will glorify Him in a way that *only you* can do! The rest of us need you to discover your route!

---

1 Corinthians 12:15 If the foot should say, "Because I am not a hand, I do not belong to the body," that would not make it any less a part of the body. [16]And if the ear should say, "Because I am not an eye, I do not belong to the body," that would not make it any less a part of the body. [17]If the whole body were an eye, where would the sense of hearing be? If the whole body were an ear, where would the sense of smell be? [18]But in fact, God has arranged the members of the body, every one of them, according to His design. [19]If they were all one part, where would the body be? ...

[21]The eye cannot say to the hand, "I do not need you." Nor can the head say to the feet, "I do not need you." [22]On the contrary, the parts of the body that seem to be weaker are indispensable, [23]and the parts we consider less honorable, we treat with greater honor. And our unpresentable parts are treated with special modesty, [24]whereas our presentable parts have no such need. But God has composed the body and has given greater honor to the parts that lacked it, [25]so that there should be no division in the body, but that its members should have mutual concern for one another.

---

b. BE-DO-GO

A simple, practical framework to remember your primary and secondary callings.

In his book *More: Find Your Personal Calling and Live Life to the Fullest Measure*, author Todd Wilson lays out a simple and practical framework for our primary and secondary callings.[7] I think this framework is very helpful for helping us identify and narrow down our focus. I highly recommend the book. You can use my link to purchase it at (https://MPoweredChristian.org/Book-More). Wilson first identifies a primary or common calling that all Christians share in common, and then a secondary or unique calling specific to each individual. Using the phrase "BE-DO-GO" he breaks down each calling type into three parts. One of each for our common calling and one of each for our unique calling, with a total of six.

- *BE* - Represents our identity or design, the *way* that we were created by God.
- *DO* - Represents our mission or purpose, the things we were made *for*.
- *GO* - Represents our mission *field* or position.

Our primary or common calling is our "*Core*" Identity, Mission, and Position. Our secondary or unique calling is our "*Unique*" Identity, Mission, and Position.

- *Core Identity (cI)* - Disciple of Jesus, having His fullness maturing in you.
- *Core Mission (cM)* - Carrying Jesus' fullness to others making them disciples.
- *Core Position (cP)* - Wherever you are.

That should all sound familiar if you've already read Chapter 6, Our Mission as Disciples, which breaks down these things into greater detail. Regardless of how far along you are at identifying your unique calling remember this: your primary calling is more important! This is the one you are to always be doing and the one you have no excuses not to. I want you to get the most out of discovering and living out your unique calling but never sacrifice your core calling in the process. Your unique calling is secondary and is built on top of the foundation of your primary calling. Your personal calling is God's unique handiwork in your life, the way in which He is working through you, equipping you to play a unique role on earth. You're being uniquely used by God in both your primary and secondary callings. So what is your unique identity, mission, and position? This question we will explore in the next two sections.

- *My Unique Identity (uI)* - _____
- *My Unique Mission (uM)* - _____
- *My Unique Position (uP)* - _____

c. Your Values
Who you *are* can perhaps be best defined by what you value most.

Who are you *really?* By that I don't mean *what* are you. I already know what you are. You're a human being, created in the image and likeness of God. You're material and immaterial: body, soul, and spirit. We discussed that already in Chapter 1, Section (F). I mean *who* are you? What makes you unique? What about you is distinctly your own? These questions can be answered in many ways, each true in their own way, each highlighting different aspects of your existence. We'll explore a few of these ways over the next couple of sections. But first let me dispel a few myths. At our fundamental and deepest levels we are not defined by our experience. I'm not saying that the unique circumstances we were born into, or those we went through in life, had no impact on who we are now. Of course it has. But our experiences don't *define* us, or our uniqueness. They help *shape* it but they don't define it. For example, let's say you were one of the newborn baby girls in 1st century Rome that was unwanted and left abandoned to die in the wilderness. (This was their version of abortion) And let's say you were one of the many that 1st century Christians rescued and adopted. This would undoubtedly influence who you become later. Your experiences growing up would shape you. You're more likely to become a godly person but it's not guaranteed. Two different orphans could've had a similar upbringing. One grows up to become a pastor in the church, the other abandons the people and faith that rescued them and goes to worship the gods of Rome.

We're also not defined by our looks, talents, or personality. Just like experience these things will help shape our lives, but they won't define it. An attractive, charismatic, talented person may be drawn to the money, fame, and idolatry of Hollywood and be completely lost by moral corruption. Or, they could be characteristically unattractive and less talented but doing meaningful work in the service of others. And yet two other people may have been in a Nazi concentration camp and exposed to years of brutality and suffering. This may cause one person to be finally released to have been so hardened by the experience that they are now deeply troubled, cynical, and apathetic to humanity. But another person may have been so influenced by their experience to appreciate all life optimistically and eager to help anyone that is suffering. Our experiences shape us but they don't define us. What does is deeper. It's spiritual. We all have many things influencing who we become but at the end of the day it is our deepest values that define us uniquely the most. Our values are our principles or standards of behavior. Our values are those things that we consider to be most important in life. Your values have already greatly shaped your life, sometimes without us even realizing it. But our values are not external situations that we are born into, or external factors that we are born with. Nor are they external experiences that were imposed on us by others. Our values are our own. They are internal. Intrinsic. They are within. They are spiritually a part of you and you can discover what they are, and decide for yourself which will be most important.

Determining Your Values. If you want to quickly and effectively cut to the core of who you are as a person you need to discover your *highest* values. I have a simple virtual life coaching exercise program at MPoweredChristian.org basically designed to be like a one-hour private session with me to help you discover your highest values while offering additional techniques and insights. But here's a quick exercise to get an idea of your values on your own. Think of the things that you value. Some values others will esteem very highly but they will have little or no significance to you. Some people's values may even seem negative to you. Don't choose a value because you think it will look good or impress others. These are to reflect how you really feel in your gut. If you had money, freedom, time, etc. what would you do with it? Why? What is the underlying reason why you even want to have more money, freedom, time, etc.? I've listed a few values in the following table. There are hundreds more that could be added. Use these as just an example of the possible options and I left a few spaces to add your own in. Don't think about it long. Remember, don't pick what sounds good, what would impress others, or just all the "most Christian" sounding ones. I want what seems natural. I want the response of your gut instincts - not your analytical mind. There are other places where I want you to examine yourself, be critical, and judge yourself. This exercise is not one of those times. We want what the instinctual part of you would say about yourself. So set a timer to 60 seconds. That's all the time you get to finish the whole entire exercise. Scan the list with your eyes quickly and pick about 10! Maybe pick 2 per column? Stop when the timer stops. Which values jump out to you the most? What's important for you? Go!

List of Values

Achievement	Drive	Gratitude	Joy	Reason
Affection	Economy	Growth	Liberty	Recreation
Adventure	Ecstasy	Guidance	Logic	Relaxation
Beauty	Encouragement	Happiness	Love	Respect
Being the Best	Enjoyment	Harmony	Making Difference	Sacrifice
Belonging	Excitement	Health	Mindfulness	Security
Brilliance	Experience	Humor	Optimism	Sexuality
Certainty	Expressiveness	Hygiene	Organization	Spirituality
Charity	Faith	Imagination	Passion	Stability
Connection	Fame	Impact	Peace	Teamwork
Comfort	Family	Inspiration	Persuasiveness	Trust
Control	Fitness	Integrity	Playfulness	Truth
Creativity	Freedom	Intimacy	Piety	Victory
Dependability	Friendliness	Intuition	Power	Wealth
Determination	Generosity	Investing	Professionalism	Wisdom
Discipline	Grace	Justice	Proactivity	Youthfulness
_____	_____	_____	_____	_____

After the previous exercise you should have about 10 values selected. I want you to reflect on these values. They are an important part of who you are. Is there a common theme? Consider how these values have guided or influenced your life. How could they have shifted the way you've interpreted some of your life's experiences? Have each of these things always been a part of you? Another exercise you can do is rank them in order of priority. What are your Top 5? Top 3? Top 1? This will provide even greater insight into who you are as a person. Seeing which is most important, gun to your head, helps you understand why you prioritize certain things in your life a certain way. Remember, the primary goal at this junction isn't to _judge_ yourself right now. The goal is just to get a clearer sense of who you are. This exercise is about understanding, not judgment. Spend some time with yourself before moving on to the next section.

d. Your Personality

How you were uniquely wired is part of God's uniquely designed purpose for you.

Your personality is another important aspect of who you are. Unlike your values, which are more about *what* you are like, your personality is more about *how* you are like. It's your unique wiring. The way you just tend to behave. It's the way you approach life. The way you relate to others. These are the typical personality traits, behaviors, and tendencies that uniquely describe how you contribute to this world. There are a variety of personality assessments available. The best assessments are those that are not one-dimensional but understand that humans are beautiful, sophisticated, and complex beings. Good assessments attempt to understand people from a variety of different disciplines including psychological, social, behavioral, theological, cultural, economic, and physiological. Additionally, it's good to test yourself using a variety of assessments as no individual one will every be truly holistic and complete. Each one has its primary areas of focus as well as certain strengths and weaknesses. Some assessments are used primarily in clinical settings by mental health professionals to diagnose psychiatric and psychological disorders. These include the Revised Minnesota Multiphasic Personality Inventory (MMPI-2), Eysenck Personality Questionnaire, and Projective Measures like the Rorschach (Inkblot) and Thematic Apperception (TAT) tests. But for our purposes I recommend just using non-clinical assessments, those that are easy to self-administer, widely accepted, and are generally reliable, accurate, and insightful. These include:

- *Revised Neo Personality Inventory (Neo Pi-R), also called the Five Factor or Big Five Personality Test.* It measures personality along a continuum of opposing poles of Conscientiousness, Extroversion, Agreeableness, Neuroticism, Openness to Experience. If you take a college course in personality psychology this is the one you'll learn. Take for free at: (https://www.123test.com/personality-test/)

- *DISC Assessment.* Examines four areas of behavioral style - Dominance, Influence, Steadiness, Compliance. Can help determine value in a team, major strengths & weaknesses, motivations, time management, communication style, decision making. Learn more & take it for free at: (https://www.123test.com/what-is-disc/)

- *16 Personality Factor Inventory (16 PF).* Used to measure normal-range of anxiety, adjustment, emotional stability, and behavior problems by analyzing 16 different factors. Useful with career or marital counseling. Take for free at: (https://openpsychometrics.org/tests/16PF.php)

- *Myers-Briggs Type Indicator (MBTI).* Based on Carl Jung's theories which assigns people into 1 of 16 different personality types. Based on idea that for each of four psychological functions (attitude, perception, judging, lifestyle preference) we have a dominant trait. Take at: (https://www.123test.com/jung-personality-test/)

- *Keirsey Temperament Sorter (KTS).* Unlike the MBTI, the KTS focuses on actual behavior rather than how a person thinks and feels. Used to determine 1 of 4 primary temperaments that are then developed into 1 of 16 subtypes.

Methods I don't recommend. A popular way many try to learn about their personality is related to Astrology. These include Zodiac Signs, Chinese Zodiac, identifying yourself using birth signs or your personality attributes using birth or natal charts; Numerology (birthday, life path, attitude, personality numbers, etc.); Horoscopes of any type or frequency; studying Planet Retrograde, etc. Astrology as an occult practice dates back thousands of years. It is purely a spiritual belief system; it has no scientific credibility whatsoever. It is the result of the doctrines of demons who use belief in it to influence and guide humanity. It's use has been consistently shown to open up doors to the demonic. Throughout the Bible it is described as both sin and a defilement of spiritual purity. Some of these elements were mentioned in Chapter 3, Sections (F & N). The alignment of the stars or planets, during your birth or anytime, has nothing to do with who you are as a person, what you value, your personal attributes, or your future.

Perhaps you knew better than to trust astrology but what about this next one: the Enneagram. The Enneagram personality test, its use of types, as well as its subsequent levels of centers, instincts, development, and direction, is much more than a scientific instrument. Like astrology, it is a *spiritual* one—and one with occult origins as well! It has its roots in mysticism, witchcraft, Kabbalah, and automatic writing (a form of demonic divination). This has unfortunately been embraced by many in the Christian world. Exorcist Bob Larson said about the Enneagram, *"When the church denies the reality of spiritual warfare, it looks elsewhere for a more palatable substitute to overcome mankind's descent into spiritual entropy and demonic bondage. The Enneagram is the new Christian yoga, yet another attempt to take that which is historically and foundationally demonic and sanctify it by redefinition and clever semantics."*[1] Former professional astrologer and president of the Metropolitan Atlanta Astrological Society-turned-Christian apologist Marcia Montenegro wrote this about the Enneagram: *"The clear origin and purpose of the Enneagram is to initiate a Gnostic spiritual awakening to one's alleged true divine Self, which is in itself an occult initiation. This is the claim and goal of virtually all occult and New Age teachings. The purpose of such initiation is a shift in consciousness, a change in the way one views reality -- God, the world, others, and self."*[2]

Astrology, Enneagram, or any other similar forms of potentially harmful self-identification or unbiblical method of spiritual progress need to be abandoned. If you've been involved with these things I encourage you to test what I'm saying, investigate all things, learn more about the dangers of them, repent, and close their demonic doors into your life. But even methods I think offer value like MBTI aren't actually biblical themselves. They're secular at best. Carl Jung was a brilliant psychiatrist and psychoanalyst who was the father of analytical psychology. His work has been highly influential in many fields. However, his personal autobiography suggests that he was also battling *literal* demons of his own.[3] But as you should know by now, every idea, philosophy, and belief should be analyzed on *its own* merits. Valuable things can come from questionable sources. Remember what 1 Thessalonians 5:21 says, *"Test all things. Hold fast to what is good."*

Beware the Forer Effect. The Forer Effect, also called the Barnum Effect, is the phenomenon that occurs when individuals believe that personality descriptions apply *specifically* to them, despite the fact that they're filled with information that applies to everyone. This is one of the reasons horoscopes continue to be popular and trusted despite their lack of reliability or validity. In 1948, Bertram Forer gave a personality inventory to his students and then gave them each what he claimed was a unique personality profile. They all rated the profile as near excellent at describing them, despite the fact that they all received the same exact profile.[4] Studies have shown that the Forer Effect works best for statements that are positive. People are much less likely to believe a statement applies to them when it is negative.[5]

A Warning. In addition to the blind spot of the Forer Effect, remember we're all both self-conscious and self-centered to some degree. We like to hear good things about ourselves. This is not always bad but we need to be mindful of our ulterior motive. This can influence us to use personality tools and identities that always intentionally make us feel better - rather than being fully accurate diagnostically. We may also seek daily encouragement in these things without actually growing, improving ourselves, becoming more sanctified, becoming more like Jesus. We may also seek guidance from such tools, rather than the Holy Spirit, the Bible, the Church. Some Christians discourage using personality assessments at all because of the increased likelihood that people will be *too* defined by it, allowing it to cloud their understanding of who they truly are and their purpose in life. I disagree that there is no value at all in understanding your personality, but I do agree that it should remain a small contribution. Our security and personal worth needs to be found in our trust in Christ, not in knowing our supposed "true identity" via some assessment name, archetype, or number. Our deepest and truest identity as a human being is being created in the image and likeness of God. And after our rebirth our deepest and truest identity is an adopted child of God in Christ. These are the foundation, the frame, the structure and roof of our car, of who we *really* are. These things trump everything else! Personality assessments *may* merely help us better understand our *windows*, the differences and unique ways that we see out and relate to the world around us. And regardless of the personality we started out from, or where we are now, our goal is *still* to become more like Jesus. Our goal is not to be the best version of our supposed personality type. Our goal is to be like Jesus! The goal of understanding your personality, from a Christian perspective, is to be better able to identify and utilize your strengths in order to help the Body of Christ, while simultaneously working on your weaknesses, surrounding yourself with others who help compensate for them with their strengths. In this way the more we know about our personality the more it helps us toward this end.

Discovering Your Personality. If I had to recommend only one assessment that's free, most holistic, and most accurate, I recommend using the NERIS Type Explorer at (https://www.16personalities.com). In my opinion theirs is the best available. It will help you understand your own personality, and the underlying psychology involved. They keep the 16 letter acronym format introduced by Myers-Briggs and add an extra letter for a fifth scale. Instead of using Jungian concepts such as cognitive functions or their prioritization, which have proven to be unreliable because of their difficultly to measure and validate scientifically, they incorporate aspects of the Big Five personality traits, the model that dominates modern psychological and social research.[6] They measure:

- *Mind.* The degree to which you're more Extraverted or Introverted. This trait determines how you interact with your environment.
- *Energy.* The degree to which you're more Intuitive or Observant. This trait shows where you direct your mental energy.
- *Nature.* The degree to which you're more Thinking or Feeling. This trait determines how you make decisions and cope with emotions.
- *Tactics.* The degree to which you're more Judging or Prospecting. This trait reflects your approach to work, planning, and decision making.
- *Identity.* The degree to which you're more Assertive or Turbulent. This trait underpins the others, showing how confident you are in your abilities/decisions.

While each person is assigned a 4-letter+1 code the 16 types are each also arranged into 1 of 4 different *Role* categories, which identify typical goals, interests, and preferred activities. The *Roles* aspect captures the best of the Four Temperament system dating back to ancient Greece as well as modern versions of it like OSPP Four Temperaments Test, Keirsey Temperament Sorter, or Arno Profile. It aligns people into 1 of 4 role categories:

- *Analysts* - Logical and enterprising
- *Diplomats* - Compassionate and caring
- *Sentinels* - Hardworking and dutiful
- *Explorers* - Curious and fun-seeking

Furthermore, each person is also given a *Strategy* type. *Strategy* type identifies how you approach everyday situations and achieve your goals. I think this aspect captures the best parts of the DISC assessment. It aligns people into 1 of 4 strategy types:

- *Confident Individualism* - Private and self-assured
- *Constant Improvement* - Introspective and sensitive
- *People Mastery* - Confident and outgoing
- *Social Engagement* - Cordial and driven

So this one assessment captures a lot of the best aspects of the others. It's a useful tool for better understanding yourself and others, and for optimizing and utilizing your unique contribution capabilities. You can also retake the assessment, recording the differences in your history, so you can see what is consistent and what is fluid. I've found my unique Type and Strategy have fluctuated during different seasons but my Role hasn't.

Ministry tools. While exclusive to the Myers-Briggs categorical system you might find the book *Personality Type and Religious Leadership* helpful. You can purchase it at: (https://MPoweredChristian.org/Book-PersonalityTypeReligiousLeadership). When it comes to an affordable online tool to help bring teams together, using a variety of individual personality assessments, that are then integrated to better understand their group dynamics, check out (https://MindTrackers.com). For churches looking for more advanced assessment solutions check out (https://HealthyGrowingChurches.com). I think individual and team personality assessments, and their subsequent evaluation and optimization, could be valuable tools for identifying ways to build great balanced teams for synergy towards individual and Kingdom purposes.

e. A.P.E.S.T. and Other Roles
Know your ROLE, in the Body of Christ, as a leader or follower, and in which ways.

In Chapter 7, Section (O) I made a distinction between spiritual endowments given (i.e. spiritual gifts), and *roles* given in the Body of Christ. To be clear there *is* overlap. Anyone given a role of leadership in the body will of course be gifted to a higher degree in order to effectively meet the demand of that role. But it's important for us to know that our unique *roles* are the unique ways we have been called to serve others. Your dominant roles will help indicate your calling, as well as the extent of your calling to lead others. But just because you're called to a particular role type emphasis, or are gifted with a particular spiritual gift, doesn't necessarily mean that you're called to *lead* with that gift. For example, merely having the gift of prophecy doesn't necessarily mean you're called to lead others in the role of a prophet. In Section (A) I described how essential the entire Body is. I even make the point that leaders are nothing without followers who are inspired to action by their leadership. And if no one is a follower then no one is a leader! And if everyone is a leader then no one is a leader! The Body needs leaders, but it needs even more followers. By followers I don't mean people who follow without discernment, without question, without their own talents and abilities. Followers are not lesser in worth or even ability. Some followers may be equally or even more gifted with ability but are not the leadership type or possessing the desire to lead. Followers are just *servants.* And leaders should be servant leaders. If the Lord puts it on your heart, or puts you into a position of influence or leadership, know that you are still called to serve in *all other* ways. For every area we're called to lead we're also being called to be a servant/helper in every other area. For example, if I'm a pastor of a church and we go out to evangelize there will be another who has been specially gifted or is being called to lead in that area and I'd be a follower/helper. Your goal should be to be a servant in all areas you're able to bless the body and then step into leadership in any areas that the Lord is preparing and ordaining you for. But never discount just being a servant. It is the *saints* that do the work of the ministry—more than those in leadership.

> Ephesians 4:11 And it was He who gave some to be apostles, some to be prophets, some to be evangelists, and some to be pastors and teachers, [12]to equip the saints for works of ministry, to build up the body of Christ, [13]until we all reach unity in the faith and in the knowledge of the Son of God, as we mature to the full measure of the stature of Christ.
>
> [14]Then we will no longer be infants, tossed about by the waves and carried around by every wind of teaching and by the clever cunning of men in their deceitful scheming. [15]Instead, speaking the truth in love, we will in all things grow up into Christ Himself, who is the head. [16]From Him the whole body, fitted and held together by every supporting ligament, grows and builds itself up in love through the work of each individual part.

Verse 11 is where we get the A.P.E.S.T. acronym from. It stands for Apostles, Prophets, Evangelists, Shepherds (i.e. Pastors), and Teachers. This has been dubbed the Fivefold Ministry. Note that these *roles* are to, verse 12, *"equip the saints for works of ministry, to build up the body of Christ."* It is the collective body of saints that does the works of the ministry. Leaders are appointed to *equip them.* As verse 16 says, it is the whole body that builds itself up in love, all this through the work of each individual part. There is only one other portion of Scripture that highlights the different roles in the Church:

> 1 Corinthians 12:27 Now you are the body of Christ, and each of you is a member of it. [28]And in the church God has appointed first of all apostles, second prophets, third teachers, then workers of miracles, and those with gifts of healing, helping, administration, and various tongues. [29]Are all apostles? Are all prophets? Are all teachers? Do all work miracles? [30]Do all have gifts of healing? Do all speak in tongues? Do all interpret?

These verses teach us some important things about roles *within* the Church. Unlike Ephesians 4, the chapter of 1 Corinthians 12 was specifically about individual roles when it comes to spiritual gifting within the Body. An interesting difference is that evangelists and pastors aren't identified as a primary role here. Next, we see "Workers of Miracles" identified as a fourth type of role, and those with gifts of healing, helping, administration, and various tongues (which may include receiving words of knowledge or wisdom in addition to audible tongues and interpretation) as additional roles. We may conclude for a local church body to function at its highest potential it would have all of these parts.

Global Church Roles

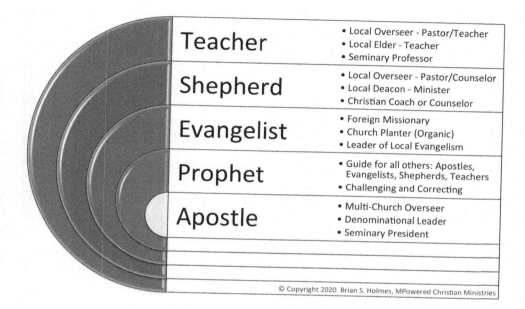

Teacher	• Local Overseer - Pastor/Teacher • Local Elder - Teacher • Seminary Professor
Shepherd	• Local Overseer - Pastor/Counselor • Local Deacon - Minister • Christian Coach or Counselor
Evangelist	• Foreign Missionary • Church Planter (Organic) • Leader of Local Evangelism
Prophet	• Guide for all others: Apostles, Evangelists, Shepherds, Teachers • Challenging and Correcting
Apostle	• Multi-Church Overseer • Denominational Leader • Seminary President

© Copyright 2020. Brian S. Holmes, MPowered Christian Ministries

Understanding the APEST roles. What about the role of Pastors and Evangelists? If they're intended to be official roles in the Church why aren't they mentioned in 1 Corinthians 12? Are the APEST roles *the* official roles? Paul acknowledges that these roles are much more flexible than many give credit. People (including myself) love to make systems, put things into fixed categories so we can have some order and wrap our head around things, but we should be more hesitant to do this when it comes to the Church. Some evangelical denominations assign titles or labels of apostle, evangelist, prophet, etc. This isn't unbiblical because we *do* see this modeled for us in the New Testament. For example several are described as prophets and teachers in Acts 13:1, Barnabas as apostle in Acts 14:14 and 1 Corinthians 9:6, Philip as evangelist in Acts 21:8, and Agabus as prophet in Acts 21:10. Yet others in the Church are okay with doing this for teachers, shepherds (pastors), and evangelists, but not for apostles or prophets today. *Regardless* of where you fall on this issue, I'm not sure that either of these is the *most* ideal way for us to think about these roles. Roles like apostle or prophet has the potential to go to some people's heads. It can also create a false hierarchy scenario that can mislead other members of the Body of Christ to think that only "official" people can do certain activities. Perhaps causing some to give too much authority or credibility to certain individuals whether or not they are sanctified or genuinely qualified, either spiritually or morally, to deserve such responsibility. Though I do acknowledge some people have extreme spiritual giftings and obvious callings in certain areas I think we're better off emphasizing the *roles themselves*, kind of like we do in business. For example in a business, individual *people* may come and go but the roles of manager and administrator continue to exist whether they're filled or not. The roles themselves are unchanging because they're based on need. The role could be filled by a certain person for a short season or maybe many years. It may be beneficial to think about the roles in the church the same way. We actually already do this with the church pastor role, just usually not the others. As though a role needs to be an official paid position with a title just to be filled—it doesn't! A role is merely a function assumed to meet a need. It may even be only an occasional need, regardless, it's needed and the church needs people to meet that need. And if no one does then the Body will have a deficiency. It will be lacking a vital body part!

But all this is less of a major issue anyways if we realize the roles themselves are much more fluid and can be met by multiple people in multiple ways. For instance, in 1 Timothy 2:7 Paul assigns three different roles all to himself: *"For this reason I was appointed as a herald, an apostle, and a faithful and true teacher of the Gentiles."* (Herald here is an evangelist or preacher). Paul calls himself an evangelist, apostle, and a teacher. He does it again in 2 Timothy 1:11. He doesn't rigidly force himself into only the apostle title and role, and then only do things that an apostle should do. No, he meets the needs wherever they are and goes wherever the Holy Spirit calls him to go! We need to do likewise! Didn't Paul also receive prophetic revelation from God and shepherd many in the faith? Yes, so we could equally identify him as prophet and pastor as well. All five! And in 1 Timothy 3, Paul tells Timothy to stay in Ephesus and appoint overseers and deacons in the churches, essentially giving him apostolic or chief authority over local overseers. And then in chapter 4 (shown below) Paul appoints Timothy to be a teacher, a preacher, and an exhorter (i.e. encourager/pastor). But he also tells him to do the work of an evangelist, and by doing so, fulfilling Timothy's ministry as an evangelist. So we see even in the lives of Paul and Timothy the APEST roles are not fixed and exclusive. They are fluid and adaptable depending on the needs of the Global Church and their Local Body.

---

1 Timothy 4:11 Command and teach these things... [13]Until I come, devote yourself to the public reading of Scripture, to exhortation, and to teaching... [16a]Pay close attention to your life and to your teaching.

2 Timothy 4:2 Preach the word; be prepared in season and out of season; reprove, rebuke, and encourage with every form of patient instruction. [3]For the time will come when men will not tolerate sound doctrine, but with itching ears they will gather around themselves teachers to suit their own desires... [5]But you, be sober in all things, endure hardship, do the work of an evangelist, fulfill your ministry.

Global Church Role Categories

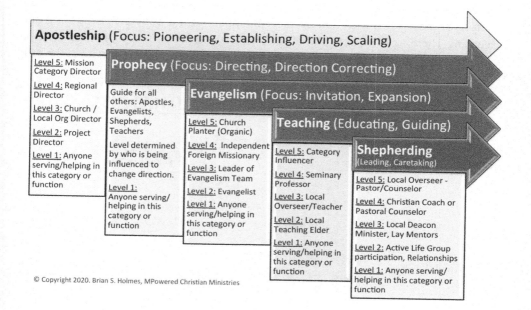

© Copyright 2020. Brian S. Holmes, MPowered Christian Ministries

I think it would be more helpful for us today to see these APEST roles more so as larger role categories. They are larger divisions of the work to be done by the Church. Of course my intention is not to take away from those who wish to keep each as a specific role or title. Rather, without *removing* that option, I'd like to *add* this option. Consider looking at each of the APEST roles as a role category that you feel most aligned with, most gifted in, and most called to. Serve in a *greater* capacity in those type of activities. You could be a level one in all, as needed by your local body, and let the Lord lead you towards a higher calling in one of them.

Other Types of Roles. What about other leadership roles mentioned in the New Testament, like that of Elders and Deacons? Paul provides the answers to this in his letters to his young protegé Timothy. Paul gives the qualifications for Overseers and Deacons in 1 Timothy 3. The Overseer role of the local church (*episkopon* in the Greek) is best understood as either a Pastor/Bishop or a church Elder. These would essentially be equal in their status of leadership, but the Pastor/Bishop would be a teacher and counselor, whereas an Elder would be a manager and supervisor. The Deacon role is that of a trustworthy servant, minister, or administrator. It's essentially an assistant manager type of role for overseers. They may be pastors or leaders in-training or just reliable members of the church without ambition to help lead, who just desire to serve in a higher capacity. And in 1 Timothy 5:17 Paul says, *"Elders who lead effectively are worthy of double* *honor, especially those who work hard at preaching and teaching."* Elders here is not the same word used for overseers (*episkopon*) who help officially lead the church, but elder (*presbuteros*) meaning older, presumably wiser and more mature. Again we see the fluid nature of these roles with non-overseer members of the Body also preaching and teaching. There are many both official and unofficial roles to be fulfilled, so that everyone in the Body of Christ is able to share their gifts, talents, and abilities in service to the rest.

Local Church Roles/Functions

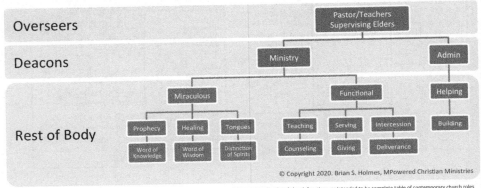

© Copyright 2020. Brian S. Holmes, MPowered Christian Ministries

*Not an exhaustive list of church functions, or intended to be complete table of contemporary church roles

In the chart above my goal is not to list every possible role, potential job type, or need in the local church. These could be vast and diverse and each local body will organize and distribute them as they deem best. It's merely to list those primary functions actually described in the New Testament. I hope it helps illustrate that the vast majority of the needs must be met by the Deacons and rest of the Body, which are primarily volunteer contributions. In a large local congregation there may be *many* departments, each one with its own pastor or supervising elder, and possibly also secondary deacons, assistant pastors, or other admin, etc. Either way, the fact remains that even within each of these departments it's the rest of the body that should be utilized for many of these functions. If you're an overseer or a deacon it's on you to recognize this truth and learn how to be a good *shepherd* of the flock under your stewardship by discipling all the others, encouraging them to discover their gifts and talents and share the best of themselves in service of the rest of the Body. The purpose of all management is to *manage* employees— not do the work for them. And if you're a lay member of the Body it's on you to learn of the ways leadership needs help, step up, and lend a hand however you're able to.

Lastly, important roles also include husband, wife, father, mother, child, family member, partner, citizen, soldier, representative, etc. Whatever situation you find yourself in where you have a unique role you need to steward those responsibilities well for Christ.

f. Embrace your S.H.A.P.E.

Embrace your unique Spiritual Gifts, Heart Desires, Abilities, Personality, Experience

In order to help you discover who God made you to be and how you may be best utilized in the church I recommend discovering and embracing your S.H.A.P.E. SHAPE is an acrostic developed by Pastors Rick Warren and Erik Rees of Saddleback Church in Southern California, in their books *The Purpose Driven Life: What on Earth Am I Here For?* and *S.H.A.P.E.: Finding and Fulfilling Your Unique Purpose for Life,* respectively. Their usage is now widely accepted and adapted throughout the evangelical world. You can purchase the books using my links at (https://MPoweredChristian.org/Book-SHAPE) and (https://MPoweredChristian.org/Book-PurposeDrivenLife). The S.H.A.P.E. acrostic stands for (S) Spiritual Gifts, (H) Heart, (A) Abilities, (P) Personality, and (E) Experience. Each of these five items alone can give you great direction when it comes to discovering your own unique calling. But when taken together as a whole they present a powerful interwoven theme that really helps reflect what God has and is doing in your life and shines light on the direction He is likely calling you to go in.

Spiritual Gifts. Your spiritual gifts are special abilities that God has given you, for Him to express His love through you. They are also given to empower you for a variety of reasons including serving others, edifying others, encouraging others, teaching others, witnessing to others, making disciples, and advancing the Kingdom of God. All gifts come from the same source, the Holy Spirit, and He apportions each of them according to His own will, and for a specific reason and purpose. Because of this, your gifts will help indicate in what ways He wants to use you in the Body. To learn more about the actual spiritual gifts see Chapter 7, Section (O), *Spiritually Gifted Parts*, beginning on page 318, where I spend significant time describing them. The rest of this section will be about discovering yours. Here's a few things to remember about spiritual gifts:

- Only believers have them. *(1 Cor 12:4-7; Jam 1:17)*
- Every believer is given at least one spiritual gift. *(1 Cor 12:7, 11; Eph 4:4-7)*
- The Holy Spirit decides which gifts you get. *(1 Cor 4:7, 12:11)*
- You can't earn or work for them. *(Eph 2:10, 4:7; Acts 8:20)*
- No believer has every gift, no gift is given to everyone. *(1 Cor 12:27-31)*
- You need to develop the gifts you receive. *(1 Tim 4:14; 2 Tim 1:6; 1 Thes 5:19)*
- It's sin to waste your gifts, not stewarding them well. *(1 Pet 4:10, 1 Cor 4:1-2, Mt 25:14-30)*
- Using your gifts honors God, matures you into Christ's likeness. *(Jn 15:8, Eph 4:13)*
- Love is the most important factor in using spiritual gifts. *(1 Cor 12:31-13:13)*

1 Timothy 4:14 says, *"Do not neglect the gift that is in you..."* And 1 Peter 4:10 instructs us, *"As good stewards of the manifold grace of God, each of you should use whatever gift he has received to serve one another."* Here are some tips to discover your spiritual gifts:

- *Experiment.* The gifts are given to help you accomplish Kingdom purposes.

Rather than trying to identify your gifts *so* that you can serve, serve in ministry in various ways to help with whatever is needed, and you'll discover that in some areas and ways you really flourish and shine more so than others.

- *Read and Study.* Study what the Bible says about spiritual gifts by reading it directly from Scripture. There are also plenty of books and sermons on the topic. Read and listen to both charismatic and non-charismatic sources for different perspectives.

- *Take Spiritual Gift Assessments.* See my warnings in Chapter 7, Section (O). Remember that most are skewed to reflect the doctrinal beliefs of the assessment maker, so it may be charismatic or non-charismatic, and to various degrees. Consider taking more than one assessment from different sources for greater insight. Non-charismatic assessments may not be properly identifying spiritual gifting in the same way but they will still highlight your (A) Abilities, so these may still provide personal direction either way.

- *Get Objective Opinions.* Ask others for input. Other people will often see gifts in us that we can't see ourselves. You might be seen by your church leadership, family, or friends as being particularly known for or good at certain things.

- *Consider the Spectrum.* On page 348 I showed a chart of global church role categories showing how we can all serve in a small way in every category even if we're not highly called in that area. The same is true of spiritual gift categories, of which there is a spectrum too. You don't need to have the gift of faith, an overwhelming degree of faith, to be *faithful*. Or the gift of spiritual wisdom to be wise. If possible pursue each gift's *attributes* to *some* degree.

Heart. Your heart represents your heart's passions that God has given you, ways that He expresses His love through you. It also includes all of those things you love as an expression of who you uniquely are. Your heart includes your desires, hopes, dreams, ambitions, affections, interests, and motivations. It's those activities or causes that you're most passionate about. Just like the Values Assessment in Section (C) you have certain subjects you're passionate about and others you couldn't care less about. By examining the passions of your heart you can gain insight into your own uniqueness, which will highlight areas God is calling you to. The three main spheres to examine are:

- *Role.* What kinds of roles are you most passionate about? What do you like to do? Which of the APEST categories on page 348 seem most appealing to you? Are you a strategic, entrepreneurial type that enjoys pioneering and innovating new things? Or do you prefer to evaluate current processes, diagnosing, correcting, and challenging their direction? Or perhaps you're a people person who prefers to work directly with others connecting, educating, or ministering to them?

- *People.* What kinds of people are you most passionate about helping? Are you drawn to a certain population or feel that you're uniquely qualified to help a certain demographic? Maybe it's infants, children, high school students, college age, older adults, young married people, business owners, single parents, families, men, women, prisoners, career-oriented people, widows, orphans?

- *Cause.* What kinds of causes are you most passionate about? What would you like to see changed in the church or in the world? Maybe it's victims of abuse, financial management, divorce recovery, sanctity of life, societal justice, drug or alcoholism recovery, disability support, homelessness, sexuality or gender issues, health or fitness, race relations, community issues, politics, economics?

I do want to remind you that your *primary mission* will remain the same, but your *secondary* calling can be very different. You might find, for example, that your heart passions inspire you find your unique calling in the area of helping high school age students (people) struggling with their sexuality or gender issues (cause). If you align with the apostolic category you may start your own ministry that focuses on helping the church better addressing this need nationally. If you align with the shepherding category you establish a support or counseling group aimed at this population in your local church so you can directly minister to the needs of struggling students in your own community. In accord with your primary mission all of this will be done in an evangelical way that helps the needs of the cause be met through the hands and feet of Jesus. You would meet their immediate needs through counseling with the transforming power of the gospel and bring yourself and Jesus to walk through their struggles with them.

Abilities. Your abilities are your natural talents that God gave you when you were born, things He wants to use for His glory. In addition to the abilities you were born with I would also include all of the learned skills you've acquired in life that now give you other unique ways to glorify God and bless others with. God permitted, enabled, and possibly orchestrated all of these abilities to come to fruition. They may well be part of your unique repertoire that God has used and will use in the future. If I was a pessimistic person I might look at my former career self-employed, doing advertising/design over 15 years wasting my time before finding my calling in ministry. However, I know God was shaping and molding me then for all I'm doing now. Starting a business can seem daunting to many but I knew exactly how to do it. And this book, from concept to writing to design to publishing is all my design. So was my ministry's logo, website, and everything else you see. What a tremendous blessing! If I had to pay others to do all of this I just wouldn't have been able to and I don't think any of this would've come to pass. What are your unique abilities? What vocations have you had? What education or knowledge do you have? What classes or seminars have you attended? How might those same skills be used for the Kingdom of God? Are you good at entertaining, recruiting, interviewing, researching, designing, analyzing, planning, managing, counseling, writing, teaching, speaking, translating, editing, promoting, repairing, cooking, music, research, accounting, technology, organizing, public relations, landscaping, decorating, business, marketing, motivating, recruiting, or teaching? You have unique inborn talents and learned abilities that should be directed at Kingdom purposes. To determine your top abilities of the 34 most common you could use the CliftonStrengths assessment (formerly StrengthsFinder 2.0) developed by Gallup. Learn more at (https://StrengthsFinder.com). You could also try the free tests at (https://123test.com). They have a Competency test, a Career test, a Work Values test, and a Team Roles test that will help you identify the common themes of your abilities and your preferred environments to use them in.

Personality. Your personality is the special way that God wired you, and His unique design of you, that causes you to navigate life and fulfill your Kingdom purpose in a certain way. Because your personality reveals how you prefer to relate to others it can identify ways God will use you. If God created you as an introverted, quiet, analytical and controlled person you would be highly out of your wheelhouse to pursue a highly sociable and public-facing leadership role requiring lots of decision making on the fly. This is not to say that God won't put you in situations where you'll have to trust and rely on Him, because He will. But these will be isolated seasons where He's developing your faith. Your entire life's calling won't be based on *consistently* working against the very best parts of you. Rather, they will be in accord with your natural personality and abilities, and reap greater potential as a result. Just make sure that you're not trusting in your own abilities rather than His presence, guidance, strength, and spiritual gifting—otherwise He may keep you running uphill! Lean into Him and *then* He will use the best of you! For more on personality see Chapter 8, Section (D), *Your Personality*, page 340, where I provide info and a series of tools you can use to identify your unique personality characteristics.

Experience. Your experience is the collective total of the things that you've gone through. This includes all of your past, both the positive and enjoyable, as well as the difficult and painful. God intends to use all of these things in great ways for His glory. Through your perseverance through them, your victory over them, your enjoyment of them, or the lessons He's taught you through them. Sometimes the experiences we find ourselves in, in life, are part of our spiritual gifting. In 1 Corinthians 7 Paul is giving advice to the church about marriage, singleness, and living with sexual fidelity. He calls the situation of being single and unmarried, and the ability to live as such in holy celibacy with sexual self-control, as a unique gift from God in verse 7: *"I wish that all men were as I am. But each man has his own gift from God; one has this gift, another has that."* God has used your experiences to stretch and mold you. Your experiences in a certain country, a in type of job, dealing with a type of illness, overcoming a certain type of tragedy, persevering through a type of challenge. In fact, it's your most painful experiences that you've had to go through, those you've resented or regretted the most, those you want to forget about—those are the one's God wants to use to help others! These are more "*your* story" and *your* contribution than the rest of the SHAPE. What you've gone through already, and come out the other end of, you can use to help others now.

II. Empowered for Your Individual Mission

g. Presence Over Purpose

It's better to sit at the Lord's feet, rejoicing in His presence, than to work for Him.

Let our daily prayer be like King David's in Psalm 51:11-13, *"Cast me not away from Your presence; take not Your Holy Spirit from me. Restore to me the joy of Your salvation, and sustain me with a willing spirit. Then I will teach transgressors Your ways, and sinners will return to You."* Remember the lessons from earlier chapters about how easy we are drawn to different types of naturalism and legalism. It is very easy to try to rely on our own strength and natural talent and then focus our efforts on doing religious works. This is even more true the more educated and equipped we become. After reading and absorbing this book you've learned a lot about many different aspects of Christianity. And if you've taken several assessments already you may get tempted to think you've got it all figured out. You know exactly what's true and exactly what to do with yourself. In one sense I'm happy you have that confidence. But in another sense I want to give you a warning. Don't let it go to your head! Don't ever let yourself "graduate" from needing God's guidance. Don't ever feel so confident knowing exactly what you should be doing that you don't still need to be led by God. Watch out for pride. James 4:10 reminds you to humble ourselves in the *presence* of the Lord and then He will exalt you. Also watch out for legalism (works-based mentality) trying to rear its ugly head. Works mentality is not only about salvation; it is also about everything we're *doing*. Remember presence over purpose! It's better to rest in God's presence than it is to leave His presence for the sake of doing works for Him. Do the latter without neglecting the former! Jesus regularly got away from it all to spend time in quiet communion with the Father. We see this in Mark 1:35, Matthew 14:23, and Mark 6:46. Luke 5:16 says *"He frequently withdrew to the wilderness to pray."* Remember from our Map God is relational and He desires to have a relationship with us. We need to remember this, and desire this too, and not be so consuming with *doing* that we neglect spending time in His presence. Presence *precedes* purpose. Time with God precedes service for God. This will also make your service more in-tune with God's will. Do you remember the lesson of Mary and Martha from Luke 10:38-42? (It's shown on page 192). Mary did the better thing. Perhaps we could learn from both of them and *continue* to sit at the Lord's feet *while* we serve Him.

The goal of prayer is the ear of God, a goal that can only be reached by patient and continued and continuous waiting upon Him, pouring out our heart to Him and permitting Him to speak to us. Only by so doing can we expect to know Him, and as we come to know Him better we shall spend more time in His presence and find that presence a constant and ever-increasing delight. - E.M. Bounds[8]

h. Get Regular Updates
Consistent refinement will help ensure you're taking the best alternative routes.

As you draw near to God regularly by putting presence over purpose you will be positioning yourself to better hear from God and let Him guide your life. You will know by your map if you're going in the right direction. The atmosphere of your car and your path's fruitfulness will confirm this, as well as your focus on your mission as a disciple of Jesus. In the grand scheme of things you can feel good about all that. But empowered Christians aren't settlers! We want to be more and do more! We want to achieve our highest potential! So how do you know if the alternate routes you're taking are ideal? I say ideal because they're all good. If you're going in the right direction and doing all the above all your options are good. The question is which is *best?* That's a better question than which is the *right* way and which is the *wrong* way? Or which way is the *good* and which is *bad?* Throw away that type of thinking. If you're doing the other things right it doesn't matter which alternate routes you take, they're all good. Whether you serve the homeless, help orphans, fight injustices, or help struggling marriages. Whether you're an evangelist and church planter or a local deacon minister and counselor. Whether you serve in ministry full time or do service that glorifies God in the secular world and contribute those skills and financial blessings to the church as a volunteer. But which route is ideal? Which is most optimal? Which route utilizes all the best parts of who you are in a way that most aligns them with the best possible outcome? I can't answer that for you, it's part of your journey to discover it. You should ask what your pastors, family, friends, and small groups think would be your ideal. Private life coaching can help provide guidance and it also has the benefits of being deliberate, goal focused, unbiased, and impartial. It's always beneficial to get objective third party perspectives because they'll see things that you can't. Plus, God is working and speaking through them, too.

But rather than grinding out day-after-day using the same old blueprint you got twenty years ago you need to consistently update it. Remember the old car GPS systems before wireless phones became the norm? You had to bring it inside the house and hook it up to your computer every so often to connect it to your computer's internet to update the software. This was necessary because things change. Roads are other physical landmarks are always being constructed or changed. New stores would open and others would close. New parks, malls, apartment complexes, and other things would get built which would all affect the roads and the GPS routes to get somewhere. Regular software updates were necessary so that your device didn't have an old, outdated map. I'll admit that I seldom took the time to do updates. It was a hassle! But then when I followed the GPS exactly and ended up at a dead end in the wrong neighborhood, instead of at the right location, I only had myself to blame. Your spiritual journey is the same way. You may have rightly heard or discerned from God at one point about what you should do and went in the right direction. You took the optimal route—at that time. But things change! The world, and everyone in it, and God's Kingdom, have continued to move and grow and change. You need to *keep* tuning in to God. Stay malleable. Flexible. Don't stubbornly persist in an old plan the Spirit no longer is behind. It's OK to change courses and take alternate routes. There's not only one good way! Take new assessments, or retake old assessments. Enter prayer asking how can I best serve you today, Lord?

i. Your Circle of Influence

Focus your time-energy-resources on things in your circle of control, and on increasing your circle of influence.

Zig Ziglar said, "Lack of direction, not lack of time, is the problem. We all have twenty-four hour days."[9] The sad truth is that most people spend way too much time, energy, and focus on things outside of their control. This only leads to fruitlessness, frustration, and depression. The world is a big place with a lot of things to be concerned about. It's okay to have these concerns, we just need to learn how to harness our energy and direct it with focus at those things we can actually do something about. The degree that you do, you'll be effective at influencing change. The degree that you don't, you'll be ineffective and not make much difference at all. It's the light concentrated on a single focal point that creates the powerful laser that can cut steel.

One way I find helps me to focus is by filtering my decisions through my circles. This concept comes from Stephen R. Covey in *The 7 Habits of Highly Effective People: Powerful Lessons in Personal Change.* I've quoted from him a few times already. This is a great book that has influenced me since I first read it in my early twenties. I highly recommend it for personal productivity in all areas of life, including efforts for the Kingdom of God. Purchase it using my link at: (https://mpoweredchristian.org/Book-7Habits). Picture in your mind three circles. The largest is your Circle of Concern. Within it is everything that concerns you. It may include national foreign policy, the economy, the weather, terrorism, natural disasters, the political views of others, the lives of politicians or celebrities, global poverty, large religious or political movements, and what's on the news. These things concern you, perhaps rightfully so, but there's nothing you can do to change them. Within your Circle of Concern is the smallest circle of the three, your Circle of Control. Within this circle is everything in your life you can directly control the outcome of. This may include things like your attitude, where you travel, what you buy, where you live, what you read, where you work, what skills you learn, where you go to church, how you serve there, and who you pray for. Your small Circle of Control is inside a slighter larger circle: your Circle of Influence. This circle contains things outside of your immediate control but still within your ability to influence some change. For example, it is within your ability to influence a loving marriage. You can't control whether your spouse will love you back, or treat you well, but you can influence them by what *you do*. You can be a loving person who says and does loving things towards them. That's within your control. By focusing on what *you* can actually do, rather than on things you have no control or influence over, like what others do, you can make a positive impact.

Multiply your Influence. You can make a greater impact by *working to expand* your Circle of Influence. Let's use the huge number of still Unreached People globally as an example. According to (JoshuaProject.net), a website that tracks global evangelism efforts, the number of unreached people groups is 7,410, which represents 3.19 billion people, or roughly 42% of the world's population![10] This is such an enormous problem in our Circle of Concern it seems impossible to do anything at all. And if we focus too much on those numbers it would lead to hopelessness. Rather, we need our concern for the unreached to inspire us to *action within* our Circle of Control. What *could* we do? Well, we can pray for the unreached daily. We can give to and support ministries and evangelical organizations dedicated to reaching the unreached. What about within our Circle of Influence? We could share our concerns with our family, friends, and small groups. They may decide to contribute to the cause out of their circle of control too! Maybe you could start a project with your small group to raise funds for the unreached? Maybe your small group could put together an effective presentation for the leadership at your church about ways the church could get behind the global evangelism efforts. It's the same for whatever your passion is for. Focus your energy and effort on what *you can* do yourself, and on expanding your circle of influence, and you can impact your larger circle of concern in significant ways you wouldn't have been able to otherwise.

j. Your Local Church and Community
Think global but act local. Your circle of influence begins first at home.

Chapter 5, Section (G), on page 239, I described a "Change Spectrum" demonstrating how we need to approach all change from the inside-out approach. We need to work on ourselves first. We need to work on individual internal change that bears the fruits of inward repentance, personal private victories, and other forms of character growth and development. That is within our circle of control. Then we can begin to effectively change externally through our outward behavior, and to improve our marriage, family, church, business, neighborhood, or community. These things are within our circle of influence. Throughout Chapter 7 we discussed many of the reasons and ways that the local church is *the* primary vehicle for effecting positive change in the world. Nowhere else will you find another *local* community dedicated to a shared vision and mission in the name of Jesus. And nowhere else will you have as much impact as a local community you're actively a part of. Because it is within your circle of influence you will have the greatest impact there. As your circle of influence expands you may gain greater leverage in other places: government, politics, business, denominational leadership, media, influential ministries, influential people, etc. But for the vast majority your local church is the best place for you to start serving as you're discovering your route. As you develop yourself, continue to refine your route, and expand your circle of influence, you'll be able to branch out and effect change in other ways. But your local church is still your "home base."

k. Living Intentionally
Be proactive. You're the co-pilot, "response-able," for navigation on your journey.

God is your Father, Jesus is your Lord and King, and the Holy Spirit is your navigating pilot on your journey. He will get you to your destination, the same destination as the rest of the Church. But you're not a passive passenger riding in the back the whole time, you're the co-pilot with the map in the front seat! In some ways He's driving, but in other very real ways you're driving. There's a back and forth going on. Sometimes He's driving and you're being asked to just obey and follow. These are the specific assignments that He needs you to do to accomplish a specific purpose. Other times you're driving. He gives you the wheel and says I'm not going to tell you exactly what to do. I'll whisper my will by My Spirit into your heart and you have to listen to it and do what you think is best. Why? Because we're in the process of being transformed into Christ's image! How can He know we're being molded properly if He has to micro-manage us every single decision and move we make? So you need to be proactive. You need to live intentionally. You need to realize that you're responsible. You're "response-able." Wake up every day deciding that you're going to be purposeful, and focused, and diligent. You're going to live every day like today is your last day before you meet Jesus!

l. Dream Big: Your Vision
Define your Personal Vision. What future are you ultimately working towards?

When trying to architect our own unique route in life it can seem complex and overwhelming. We need a way to narrow down our focus to a simple statement that is short, memorable, and useful to evaluate future concerns and opportunities by. Most businesses, nonprofits, churches, organizations, etc. use vision statements for this purpose. I think they can be helpful for individuals as well. You can create your own *personal* vision statement that helps you focus your unique calling. Here is an example of the vision statement of MPowered Christian Ministries, which doubles as my personal vision statement: *"Global revival by the Kingdom of God in every city."* This describes what my future objective is, and the future that I'm ultimately working towards. I want to see genuine revival throughout the entire world and I believe that will only happen through having the Kingdom of God fully representing the spirit of Jesus in every city. I don't just want a *church building* in every city, I want genuine born again disciples in every city, who by definition, would be sharing the gospel, making disciples, creating revival. A good church vision statement is that of Missio Dei Church in Cincinnati, OH: *"We are a gospel-centered, city-focused, church community."* Their statement is succinct and describes exact who and what they exist for and who they are focused on reaching. Good vision statements are simple and concise. They help *narrow* your focus. I like Habitat for Humanity's vision statement: *"A world where everyone has a decent place to live."* With a vision statement like this you know exactly what they're doing. The statement itself helps to narrow and focus all other objectives and activities. Let's say the president was given a great opportunity to partner in a project to *feed* the poor. Whether or not they decide to do it would be an easy decision if they just examine the opportunity in light of their stated vision. By asking the question: does this activity, that helps feed the poor, also help people in need to have a decent place to live? If the answer is "no" then however good the activity is, it's still a distraction from their vision. It doesn't help move the needle towards their objectives. Start thinking about what you would like to see happen in the world. If you could focus all of your energy on one thing what would it be? Start giving it some thought now and you'll get more help in the next few sections.

m. Start Small: Your Mission
Define your Personal Mission. Why exactly do you exist? What's your purpose?

As you reflect on what your own personal vision statement might look like, start to bring together all of the different pieces of your unique identity, calling, and mission from this chapter. Prayerfully pour over everything you've learned about yourself in your:

- BE-DO-GO primary and secondary calling assessments (Section B)
- Values assessment (Section C)
- Personality assessments (Section D)
- A.P.E.S.T. and other Roles assessments (Section E)
- S.H.A.P.E. assessments (Section F)

Also consider whether or not you have large ambitions, or the time and resources to pursue large ambitions right now. If you don't, that's okay, start small! Remember that you still need to put Presence over Purpose (Section G), to focus on your Sphere of Influence (Section I), and your Local Church and Community (Section J) first. Even if you have large ambitions—that's great, by the way—it's still best to start small and local. Get your feet wet first before jumping into the deep end of the pool. Make sure you're taking care of yourself and your household first before you venture out to try to conquer the world! You'll also learn a lot about yourself and refine your calling along the way.

For help putting your statements together I recommend the free Vision and Mission Statement Guide created by TopNonprofits at: (https://TopNonprofits.com/vision-mission/) There are more examples of vision statements there as well. But unless you have a church, ministry, or business please don't overthink this. Avoid getting paralysis by analysis! Remember the lesson from Section (H) about getting consistent updates. You can create a basic vision statement now and always change it later. The *point* of creating it is so that you can do a little work now putting it all together and not have to overthink every little decision later. This will help you set goals and measure your day by day tasks. Your vision should be quite broad. Keep it vague unless you really feel extremely confident about a specific direction the Lord is calling you in. And even then, your specifics will be defined in your mission statement. You could adopt and use mine for now if that helps. Just get something up so that you can use it to focus!

n. Your Mission Statement
Create a short, memorable statement that summarizes your mission priority.

Personal mission statements have been adopted by many top CEOs. William Arruda, author of a book on personal branding for executives says, "A personal mission statement is a critical piece of your brand because it helps you stay focused." He also says there is power in sharing it with others. "The more you share the more support you get to achieve your mission," he says. "Friends and mentors can support you or call you out if you're doing something counterproductive."[11] If successful executives use mission statements to focus themselves and achieve more, why shouldn't Christians do the same? In fact, many prominent Christian leaders do have mission statements. Some are very carefully crafted using information from assessments and deep introspection and care, while others consist of basic mantras right out of the Bible that we all already know and love. As you reflect on your calling and begin to craft your own mission statement, bring together all the different pieces of your unique identity and calling outlined in the previous section. Make sure your mission is inline with your sphere of influence.

Your mission statement will be closely related to your vision statement. Unlike your vision statement which is pretty broad in scope, your mission statement will be more specifically related to what you want to *do*, for *whom*, and *how* you will go about it. Your vision is *what*, your mission is *how*. For example, our vision statement, which is our objective, and what I'm working towards is: *"Global revival by the Kingdom of God in every city."* And our mission statement, which is what we do, and who/what we do it for, is: *"To mobilize disciples to advance the Kingdom of God globally."* I want global revival in every city and how I plan to help contribute to that objective is by mobilizing genuine disciples to do it. I can't do it all myself, but I can help train and prepare others to. That's my calling. So that focus drives everything else I do. Your mission doesn't have to be as vague or globally-minded as mine is. That's just part of the way that I'm wired, to think big that way. Yours could be much more specific. It could be related to just sharing the gospel, or just planting churches, or one aspect within any one of the APEST categories. It could be just helping in one demographic of the church, like discipling college age students, or in one cause like ministering to the homeless. Or it could be all about a specific city, or a specific need or cause within a single city. It's really up to you, there's no limitations or wrong answers. Just start with something now, and then revise it later as you go. *Especially* for *personal* mission statements it's meant to be a tool and a guide to help you focus on what the Lord has put on your heart. You'll likely change or tweak it many times over the years anyway. Remember, all tools like these are meant to be your servant, not your master. So just create *something.* It doesn't need to be perfect. Here's some tips below from TopNonprofits[12] using some examples[13] to get you started below. See the guide from the previous section for additional help.

MISSION
STATEMENT   **Action**   *Beneficiaries*   Service   Problem   *Cause*
EXAMPLES:

- **To** mobilize *disciples* **to advance** *the Kingdom of God globally* — Brian Holmes
- Make disciples. **Create revival.** — Our previous mission statement! See how it evolved?
- **To reach** *the valley for Christ* — Christ Church of the Valley (Peoria, AZ)
- **To lead** *people* **to become** *fully devoted followers of Christ* — LifeChurch.tv
- **Love** God, **Love** *People*, Make disciples — Highpoint Church (Memphis, TN)
- **Celebrating** *animals* and **confronting** cruelty — The Humane Society
- **Seeking to** *put God's love into action,* Habitat for Humanity **brings** *people* **together to** build homes, communities **and hope** — Habitat for Humanity
- **To love** God, and **love** *others* — Joel Manby, CEO of Herschend Family Entertainment

Other Mission Statements. I believe that a concise single statement version of your personal mission is most ideal and most important. It's the main thing that will help you focus on your unique calling in life, which is what this chapter is all about. If you only do one thing do that. That being said, it's also good if you want to draft a long-form version of your personal mission. This is more like a *personal* constitution, but instead of a bill of rights, with it is a list of personal values and objectives. These can be broken down into important categories or roles. It will include your Christian calling but not be limited to it, and will include all other important parts of who you are and what you want to do as well. You can list out your top values, highlight important aspects of your personality, APEST, or SHAPE. You could format it as a bullet list of general values or principles to live by, or write it out in paragraphs breaking it up into sections like Calling, Education, Health, Family, Career, Financial, Community. You could list out your Roles in life, like husband, wife, parent, son, daughter, leader, volunteer, board member, church member, neighbor, or friend and put some principles you want to remember to live by in those roles. Keep it to a single page. You can print it out or even frame it on the wall so you're more likely to read it regularly. Some people read their's every morning when they wake as a way to remind and reset their focus for the day. If you're married or have a family you could create a marriage or family mission statement as well. The point of all of this remains the same: to take the time to put the best of yourself into something that you can reference often and focus on later. Thereby helping you the become the best version of yourself by living it out. For help building one of these types of more thorough mission statements you can use the mission statement builder at (https://msb.FranklinCovey.com).

o. S.M.A.R.T. Action Plan

Have ambitious goals—broken down into projects with SMART milestones & tasks.

Bill Copeland once said, "The trouble with not having a goal is that you can spend your life running up and down the field and never score."[14] Andrew Carnegie gave advice I think every empowered Christian should take to heart: "If you want to be happy, set a goal that commands your thoughts, liberates your energy and inspires your hopes."[14] This chapter is about identifying your unique identity so you can embrace it, and your unique calling so you can chase it. Creating a unique vision and mission helps us narrow everything down to a central focus and objective. Once you've done that, deciding the alternate route to take, and have a general idea of the driving paths to get there, you'll next want to plan out your drive. Create some ambitious goals and then create a smart action plan to accomplish them. I'm not talking about things like "own a mansion" or "become famous." As empowered Christians we need to be driven by goals that increasingly glorify God. Proverbs 19:21 says, *"Many plans are in a man's heart, but the purpose of the LORD will prevail."* So what's on *His* heart that He has put on *your* heart? We have a big, amazing God so you should have big, amazing dreams, that you turn into big, amazing goals. I like what Dr. Martin Luther King Jr. said, "Human progress is neither automatic nor inevitable. Every step toward the goal of justice requires sacrifice, suffering, and struggle; the tireless exertions and passionate concern of dedicated individuals."[15] When in doubt of ourselves, what if we were to question our own fears in the way of Amy Carmichael? She once said, "If I fear to hold another to the highest goal because it is so much easier to avoid doing so, then I know nothing of Calvary love."[16] — Don't limit yourself!

But merely *having* a goal doesn't make it actionable. Many people have goals they never accomplish and never even make any progress towards. Hear me on this - if your goal doesn't have a plan and a deadline then it's not a goal - it's a wish! Andy Andrews said, "Intention without action is an insult to those who expect the best from you." God has put the hunger for those godly desires in you - don't insult Him by ignoring it! And don't you insult *yourself* either! I believe you have amazing potential, so believe in yourself. And even if you don't believe in yourself right now at least believe in the God who is working within you! If your goals are anything like mine they might seem like giant immovable elephants. But as the saying goes, "How do you eat an elephant? One bite at a time!" You might be thinking where or how do I start? The answer is to create a

SMART action plan. This means you don't want a vague "save the world" goal, neither do you want a long to-do list with thousands of items on it. You need to learn how to create thoughtful, long-term, forward-thinking game plans that will meet your long-term goals, but can also break down into smaller, short-term tasks that are easier to focus on. You'll accomplish this using a project management technique called *Chunking* which simply means that you will group tasks together into chunks that are more manageable. Really large goals should be broken down into multiple *projects*. Then each project will be broken down into SMART *milestones*, and those further broken down into SMART *tasks*. Once the action plan has been set up all you need to do is focus on the next single task and you can be sure that you're always moving the needle moving forward towards achieving your long term goal. Here's a simple diagram of this:

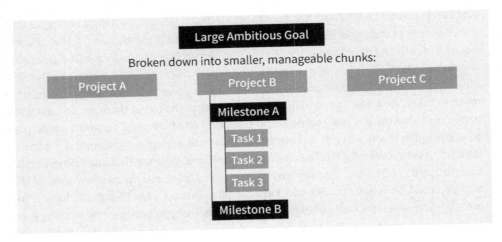

Refine your goal using chunking. Since I have no idea what your unique identity, vision, mission, and goals will be once you do this I'll just use my ministry's vision as an example for how it works. You've already learned the vision *I'm* working towards is to create global revival by the Kingdom of God in every city. That includes cities in the unreached world. Unreached cities are those with less than 5% Christians and less than 2% Evangelicals. This is 42% of the world's population, just under 3.2 billion people! How could we possibly work towards such an astronomically ambitious goal? Remember, just break it down into smaller chunks. First, those 3.2 billion people can be broken down into a much more manageable 7,410 different unreached people groups.[10] We're able to more effectively organize and prioritize around this smaller number. Some of these groups have less than 15,000 people in them so they could be quick groups to do first. When we take the total population of 3.2 billion and chunk it into separate populations of 50,000 people to raise up or send a missionary to each we would need less than 64,000 workers. By using the chunking technique we've taken a huge, unmanageable number, 3.2 billion, and organized it into 7,410 groups of people requiring 64,000 individual workers.

Let your vision and mission be your guide. The bigger your goals are the easier it is to get distracted by things along the way. Remember it's not the Church's mission to *convert* the entire world. Even if we brought the gospel to every living soul many will still reject it. This is also an example of how your *Mission* being very clearly defined will help you focus your efforts. To illustrate this consider how our ministry's unique mission influences the previous goal of reaching those unreached people groups. Our mission is *to mobilize disciples to advance the Kingdom of God.* We want the Kingdom of God present in every city, not just a church building. I'd rather have one authentic, born again and on fire disciple of Jesus than an entire church full of spiritually dead Pharisees. So I know my objective is not really to plant church buildings, but to inspire local disciple-making movements. The underground Church during its first 120 years likely grew to nearly a million strong! The underground church in Iran today is over three million! And China grew from three million adherents in the 1980s to an estimated 100 million today - all of mostly underground house churches! Our goal and execution strategies are influenced by our definition of "church." We don't need the financial or management capital to establish official church businesses. Of course the natural long term result, if Christianity is legal in these countries, would be that they would also have organized churches, but they're not absolutely necessary. We shouldn't slow the great commission to a grinding halt if it can't look the way it does in free, first-world countries. We only need to help spark, inspire, or assist in disciple-making movements with a *single* disciple, who can then witness to others and start growing organically using any of a variety of home-based microchurch models. That being the case, each of those 64,000 workers would then share the gospel and begin a new Jesus community that trains and empowers them to reach outwards. Let's say that one worker grows a microchurch of 30 people in the first year. Those 30 people could reach all 50,000 people in the *following* year if each person just intentionally shared the gospel with just five people per day - something that could be done in less than an hour. Imagine that! If each of those people did just their small part, the *entire* unreached world could be reached in only two years! And that's to mathematically personally connect with every single person. That's more than we in Christian societies do. If they even only do 1/5 of that they still reach 20% of the population *directly* and it's no longer an unreached people group! Likewise, you too can make an oversimplified strategy of your goal that "liberates your energy and inspires your hopes."

Create a real action plan. Get started breaking down your large goal in a simplistic way using round numbers, vague averaging, and an oversimplified mission strategy just to get your wheels turning. But the *more specific* you can get about your goals the more SMART you can be later about how to achieve them. So here's an example of how to plan your goal out. First, break it down into smaller manageable projects. Unless you have multiple teams working on this you should start your efforts by selecting, and then focusing *all* of our efforts on, a *single* project. In this case, a single unreached people group. Now we could start with the smallest, closest, or easiest to access group and embrace the *Snowball Effect*. This is when you start with the quickest, easiest tasks first. Since they're easy to complete and check off they quickly get the ball rolling, which then keeps picking up more and more snow as it rolls downhill. You then have a lot of forward momentum as you work towards the larger, more complex projects. But for the sake of this example I'm going to start with the hardest project just so you know this works either way. The Joshua Project ranks the *Shaikh* as the largest unreached people group. They are in Bangladesh and they have a population of nearly 134 million. Joshua Project has estimated, at a rate of 50,000 people per disciple worker, that the country needs 2,678 workers.[17] So that would be our objective, to either identify or send 2,678 workers and empower them to be effective. We then break this down into 2,678 territorial regions for each worker. Each person/territory would be considered a *Project*. Next, since we still have a pretty big list of 2,678 we should do some preliminary work in order to chunk these into useful categories. For example, we might do some broad research and find out that some territories have already been sent missionaries there by other missions organizations. Great! Let's assign those into a category. Then we might find that there other some other evangelical ministries that have gained traction by training indigenous disciples that already live there. Great, that's another category. So those specific projects would have milestones and tasks focused on monitoring their progress and seeing if we can do anything to partner with them and boost their progress. By so doing we have the opportunity to synergize and help one another! Maybe there are already Evangelical Christian churches, schools, orphanages, or ministries in some of these territories we could reach out to? Those could be other categories where we wouldn't have to start from scratch. Maybe they're interested in reaching their own community for the gospel but they need help discipling new leaders, educating, equipping, or empowering their members, or training in evangelism? Next, we might do some research to find out which of these areas are rural and third world, and which have internet access. If they have internet access we might be able to reach them remotely, either Christian disciples already there we could help, or even people directly with the gospel. Maybe some of the territories use a language that there isn't a Bible translation or other materials for yet. We may decide to deprioritize these and focus on them later. Or perhaps forward our research about these project territories to other ministries that specialize in the translation of Christian materials and outsource those to others more qualified to deal with their situation. If some of the project territories already have significant efforts in place and then we can add them to the "monitor" list and move on to the next one. Each Project territory will be evaluated individually and we would create an effective strategy that will be most efficient and effective for each one. But there would no doubt be common situations amongst them that would allow us to chunk them together. We could maybe find 2,678 churches in the U.S. or elsewhere to be a sponsor for each of our 2,678 project territories. Then they could be a co-managing partner and help facilitate the efforts. So we have a "Sponsored" category. So, based on all of that we may be left with 20 different categories of project territories. Now instead of 2,678 projects we have 20 groups averaging 130 projects each. Then those 20 categories could be sorted with a ranking system, perhaps based on saturation level or difficulty. Here, we may then decide to reintroduce the snowball effect strategy by beginning with the easiest or most efficient category first. And then we prioritize all of the projects within that category and begin doing one at a time, systematically. Every time you group something together because of some similarity in the situation it helps you better understand and have a grip on your larger goal. Every *single* task now is a step forward that will give you a sense of increased control over the whole project. All you have to do is focus on the next task. There are many approaches that could've been used in a process this big but I hope it's clear how you can take any large goal and break it down into smaller projects and tasks in a smart way. And if this strategy will work for a goal as big as reaching 134 million people with the gospel you can certainly use it for *whatever* your vision, mission and goals are!

Developing a SMART Action Plan. Once you've broken your larger goal into smaller projects, and then milestones, and then create individual tasks within those milestones. Not all tasks are created equal. Some tasks are too vague or too big. If a task can't be completed in a day it's too complex and it should be broken down into multiple tasks, so that all individual tasks remain simple and easily actionable. How you set up your plan is just as important as how you do it. Zig Ziglar says, "A goal properly set is halfway reached."[18] A helpful acrostic to remember about all goals (and I would add also all milestones and tasks within all goals) is that they need to be S.M.A.R.T. which stands for (S) Specific, (M) Measurable, (A) Attainable, (R) Relevant, and (T) Time-bound. Let me illustrate these five principles using a more simple people came to me all the time with as a personal trainer: weight loss. Their fitness program would include SMART goal setting. Clients would say to me things like "I just want to lose weight and get in shape." This is too vague to be actionable. How do we know if we're getting anywhere? How would we identify what needs to be changed? How can we stay motivated unless we have a way to measure and detect results?

- **Specific.** Your goals and tasks need to be specific. Consider the 5 W's. *What* exactly needs to be done? *Why* is this important? *Who* is going to do it? *Where* is it located? *When* does this need to be completed by?

   Example: "Lose weight" is too vague. How much weight exactly? 50 lbs. An ambitious yet safe weight loss program is a loss of 2 lbs. per week. So your goal will be to lose 2 lbs. per week for the next 6 months. It's important to look and feel good, lower blood pressure, and reduce symptoms of arthritis. You'll need to eat a healthy 1,500-calorie diet daily and do one hour of physical exercise 5 times per week, 3 with the trainer and 2 doing some form of cardio.

- **Measurable.** Your goals and tasks need to be immediately actionable and capable of being measured to quickly determine if a successful result was produced or not. This is necessary to assess your progress, meet deadlines, and keep up the excitement of getting closer to achieving your goal. Questions might include how much needs to be lost or gained? How will I know when this task has been completed?

Example: We will perform a body fat test every Monday. If you don't lose 2 lbs. per week then they either didn't follow the program or something in program needs to be modified. Measurement happens during the week daily. Were the daily calorie goals achieved all 7 days? Were all 5 workouts completed?

- **Attainable.** Your goals and tasks need to be realistic and doable. It's okay to stretch your abilities as long as it's still possible. If your tasks are unattainable they won't get completed. Break down all difficult tasks into smaller pieces that are each doable. Make sure to also address possible external constraints (people, resources, time) that would limit the ability to complete the task.

Example: A loss of 2 lbs. per week is an ambitious but physically attainable goal. There are ways to lose more than this but they're extreme, much less comfortable, and may add health risks. But if their goal was to lose 50 lbs. for a friend's wedding they're attending in 1 month they are setting themselves up for failure. It's better to accomplish a less-ambitious-yet-actually-attainable goal than to psyche yourself up to try to do the miraculous and fail miserably.

- **Relevant.** Your goals and tasks need to be relevant and meaningful to you or they will never stick. Goals or tasks that aren't compatible with your deeper values, human needs, and personal desires will eventually be abandoned. Are you the right person to do this? Is this a worthwhile task to do instead of other perhaps better or wiser alternatives? Is this the right time, place, and situation for this to goal to be sought after right now?

Example: You're currently unemployed with no emergency fund and debt piling up. The entire family is stressed and your relationships with your spouse, your children, and God are all being neglected and are at an all-time low. But you want to look good for your friend's wedding you're attending in a month so you hire an expensive personal trainer maxing out a credit card and invest all of your time and energy into losing weight. Even otherwise good goals can be unhealthily motivated, poorly prioritized, or unwise at the wrong time.

- **Time-bound.** Your goals and tasks need to have specific deadlines to help you focus your efforts. This is necessary for knowing if you're currently on track and where you are in your overall progress. Vague deadlines like "sometime this year" or "before I'm 35" don't cut it. Even *arbitrary* deadlines—if they are specific, attainable, and relevant—will provide motivation and accountability.

Example: Weekly weigh-in indicates the degree of success in meeting the weekly goal of 2 lbs. loss. A pound of fat is 3,500 calories which means a total loss of 7,000 calories. The weekly goal won't be met without meeting the daily goal loss of 1,000 calories. If the goal is to eat only 1,500 calories per day, and they eat three meals per day, their per-meal goal is 500 calories. If they focus on the SMART goal of eating 500 calories 3x day consistently it will pay off!

This example shows that this large goal is really quite simple once we apply a few SMART strategies to it. There's a weekly goal of 5 workouts, and then a daily goal of eating 1,500 calories, broken down into 3 goals of 500-calorie meals. The best way to ensure that the 6-month goal is actually reached is to be on top of your per-meal goal. Rather than thinking 50 lbs., 50 lbs., 50 lbs., and reinforcing this giant mountain in your mind that seems impossible to climb, we really just need to just trust in our plan and focus on achieving our next task: that next meal. All of your goals in life can be approached this way and I guarantee you will accomplish more! How liberating it truly is to free up all of that excess emotional energy spent on anxiety, fear, doubt, and other unfruitful things and focus it on productive things! Your big goals for the Kingdom of God are to be overcome in the same way. Chunk it down and get SMART with it! Your goal to quit pornography, smoking, drugs, or some other sinful vice in your life is to be overcome in the same way. Chunk it down and get SMART with it! Your commitment to dedicate yourself to God, repair a broken relationship in your life, get out of debt, become a loving spouse, a better parent, serving others more, reaching the lost, or ANY other type of goal in your life can be overcome the same way! Chunk it down and get SMART with it! Create a SMART plan to accomplish whatever it is you want to accomplish and just focus on the next task alone and let the stress of the rest of it all just melt away. God's got you.

p. Developing Discipline and Habits
Commit to daily renewal, improvement, self-discipline, and good habit building.

God has a plan to be glorified in a unique way through you. It's up to you to not let yourself get in the way of that. Commit, today, to continue developing into the best version of yourself. Your own unique way of being like Jesus. Your own unique way navigating this journey. It's true that if you continue to do what you've always done, you will continue to get the same results. Develop your emotional intelligence, learning how to recognize and manage your emotions will serve you well. Develop every dimension of yourself: spiritual, mental, physical, and emotional. Don't neglect any part. Work on all of them daily, even if for only 5 minutes. Check out the *Productivity Game* channel on YouTube for animated summaries of great books and practical tips. In James Clear's book *Atomic Habits*, order at (https://MPoweredChristian.org/Book-AtomicHabits), he outlines 'The Four Laws of Behavior Change.' If you want your new behavior to stick make it (1) obvious, (2) easy, (3) attractive, and (4) satisfying. Stack your good new habits with your good old habits. Position yourself for success. Lacking the self discipline to eat the junk food in the kitchen? Just have discipline during the one hour a week you're grocery shopping and you won't buy any to tempt you the rest of the week. Trying to resist the sinful temptations in your life and focus on your calling? Do the same thing. Position yourself for success, with that as the easy, obvious, satisfying option and you won't need crazy levels of self-discipline. Mike Hawkins said, "You don't get results by focusing on results. You get results by focusing on the actions that produce results."[19]

"We are what we repeatedly do. Excellence, then, is not an act but a habit." - Will Durant[20]

III. Chapter Summary and Evaluation

Chapter Summary

You have a unique identity, calling, and mission to fulfill. And your story contributes to the grand narrative.

Even though we're all traveling towards the same final destination we're all taking alternate routes. It's supposed to be this way, God made it so. It is through the vast diversity of His symbiotic creation that He is most fully expressed. We can either allow these differences to cause division through hostility, or we can allow them to cause unity through empathy. We could continue in the way of fallen humanity, allowing our differences to provoke us to war with one another. Banding together through group identity, with an "us vs. them" mentality. Or led by the Holy Spirit in oneness in Christ we could rise up to the challenge and show the world something very different. A Church united in love that embraces it's best through unity in diversity.

You, your unique identity, and your unique calling and mission are an important part of the grand narrative that God is writing through the ages. It's no coincidence that God says that those who will inherit eternal life have their names written in the *book* of life. I hope this chapter has helped you appreciate your uniqueness—the good, the bad, and the ugly! Even the bad and ugly aspects of our experience work towards the greater good. It's the tragedies of the fall that allow us to appreciate the joys of redemption. It's our shared experience of the many rough paths behind us that will allow us to truly appreciate the smoothness of the streets of gold up ahead.

Let's recap some of the things we went over in this chapter. In Section One you learned about *how* to discover your unique personality and identity. You, personally, and your unique story, are an important part of the Body. Your part is no less valuable than the most famous recognized names. Don't sell yourself short. The mouth needs the feet. If you're a foot be the best foot you can be. The dirty feet of Christ are sweeter than the lying mouth of the devil!

Remember the simple BE-DO-GO framework, and use it with your primary or common calling, and your secondary or unique calling. Your primary calling is the one that is common among all Christians. *Be* a disciple of Jesus, *do* - make disciples of Jesus, *go* - wherever you are. Your secondary calling is your unique calling, the special different way God will use your story by interweaving it into His grand narrative. You are to *be* the best version of your unique self, *do* those things the Lord has naturally and supernaturally empowered you to do well, and *go* wherever He calls you to go - what I call your alternate route. We explored many ways for you to learn about who you are. These include understanding and ways to determine:

- Your personal Values (what's uniquely more important about life to you)
- Your unique S.H.A.P.E.:
  - Your Spiritual Gifts (the endowments uniquely given you by the Holy Spirit)
  - Your Heart (the unique passions and desires the Lord's put on your heart)
  - Your Abilities (your unique natural talents and learned abilities)
  - Your Personality (the unique way God wired you to express His diversity)
  - Your Experience (your personal story that has helped mold who you are)

We also learned about a variety of roles, and how understanding roles it helps to illuminate the path of our secondary calling, because God calls us to steward well the roles that He places us in or calls us to. These include the roles of:

- The Global Church APEST (Apostle, Prophet, Evangelist, Shepherd, Teacher)
- The local church congregation (Overseer/Teacher, Overseer/Elder, Deacon)
- Personal roles like spouse, parent, child, or citizen.
- We looked at embrace APEST as role *categories*, rather than exclusive titles, and consider your SHAPE and affinity towards each of the categories.

With your identity and calling in mind we then moved on to look at some keys to being fully empowered for your individual mission. These include: (1) The necessity of presence over purpose. It's more important to have God with you than it is for you to work for Him. (2) Allowing yourself to get regular updates from God and letting Him alter and direct your plans. (3) Focusing your efforts on working within, and expanding, your Circle of Influence. (4) Beginning first with your local church and community. (5) Living intentionally. You're the co-pilot; your decisions to affect your direction, and you need to be proactive. (6) Dreaming big, about *what* you're called to affect the future *towards*, then developing your own personal Vision and personal vision statement to reflect this. (7) Then giving legs to your vision by developing your own personal Mission, *how* you're going to do it, and then developing your own personal mission statement to reflect this. (8) Principles of developing a SMART action plan including chunking, strategic project organization, and making sure goals and tasks are SMART (specific, measurable, attainable, relevant, and time-bound). (9) Being a disciplined person with good habits.

Chapter 8 Evaluation

AFTER THOROUGH, CAREFUL EXAMINATION, RIGHT NOW:

	False		Partially False			Mostly True			True

a) I am important and needed by others in the Body............

1	2	3	4	5	6	7	8	9	10

b) I am fulfilling both my primary and secondary callings....

1	2	3	4	5	6	7	8	9	10

cdf) Different Values and SHAPE make us unique and special

1	2	3	4	5	6	7	8	9	10

e) I understand APEST and categories and church roles ......

1	2	3	4	5	6	7	8	9	10

gh) I need to put God's presence first & get regular direction.

1	2	3	4	5	6	7	8	9	10

ijk) I'll live intentionally, focusing on my Circle of Influence...

1	2	3	4	5	6	7	8	9	10

Date Last Taken: _____

ACTIVITIES for Individuals or Study Groups:

1) What are your top 5 values, ranked from most important to least? (p.337, table on p. 339)
Top 1: _____ Why? _____
Next 4: _____
My values are centered around: _____

2) What's your personality type at 16Personalities.com? (p. 342-343) Test Date:_____
Type: _____ Code: _ _ _ _ + _ Role: _____ Strategy: _____
Strengths: _____
Weaknesses: _____
Significant insights: _____
_____
_____

3) What are your significant roles? (p.344) Who/what's in your circle of influence? (p. 356)
_____
_____

4) Which one of the 5 APEST categories fits you best? (p. 348) Why do you think this is?
_____
How could you embrace this? _____

5) What's your SHAPE? (p. 350) List your most significant items for each:
Spiritual Gifts (p. 322):_____
Heart Passions:_____
Abilities: _____
Experiences: _____
_____

6) What's your personal Vision Statement? (p. 358) _____

7) What's your Personal Mission Statement? (p. 360) _____

8) Chunk down your primary goal into an actionable project. (p. 362) Describe it:
_____

9) Describe how your project is SMART: (p. 366)_____
_____
_____
_____

Explore Chapter 8 Deeper:

For additional resources related to the topics discussed in this chapter see our companion website at **https://MPoweredChristian.org/Road-Map-Book-Resources**

- Free printable pdf of this chapter evaluation for personal or classroom use
- List of related online courses, e-coaching programs, personal coaching services
- List of related videos, articles, and recommended books
- List of related live webinars and ways to ask questions

Notes/Reflections:

_____
_____
_____
_____
_____
_____
_____
_____
_____
_____
_____
_____
_____
_____
_____
_____
_____
_____
_____
_____
_____
_____
_____
_____
_____
_____
_____
_____
_____
_____
_____

To-Do List: *Date:* _____

MY TASKS FOR **THIS UPCOMING WEEK...**

✔ **My Big 1-3:**
_____
_____
_____

✔ **For Personal Growth:**
_____
_____
_____

✔ **For Key Roles:**
_____
_____
_____

✔ **For Calling/Ministry Service:**
_____
_____
_____

✔ **Pray for/Request prayer about:**
_____
_____
_____

✔ **Learn more about:**
_____
_____
_____

✔ **Other:**
_____
_____
_____

Conclusion

The finish line at the end of the race is in sight!

When I began writing this book last year I never intended to write an entire book. I was praying about what I should create next, fully intending to give it away as a small, free, downloadable thing on my website. As I wrestled with what to make and what it should be about, I came face to face with several important questions. The first:

- If I could only teach *a single lesson* to someone what would it be and why?

I would give the most important lesson I could teach. There's thousands of things I could talk about but if I only have one opportunity to influence someone then the answer is simple: I'd give them the gospel! But maybe they already know it? They are on a *Christian* website after all. That doesn't matter. It's better to tell them again and reaffirm their faith, than it is to assume they know it already and then distract them even more by giving them other content of secondary importance. The gospel firmly planted in the soil of the soul can do infinitely more good than anything else I could teach. Plus, there's lots of people who call themselves Christians who have false beliefs and lifestyles that don't look like Jesus'. They might not even have the true gospel, after all many cults call themselves Christians. Or, they may have a correct knowledge of God and the gospel but other false beliefs that have distorted their faith, behavior, and relationship with God. Then I thought about all of the things that Christians often dispute with one another about. I'd start to list them but I'd like to finish the book this year! Many would rather play church and argue with one another over secondary issues, than live like Jesus, preach the gospel, and save the lost! Another thought came to me from the Lord:

- They need a road map that emphasizes the *most important* things, that if gotten wrong, would affect whether or not they make it to Heaven.

It seemed so simple. Yet, I have 100+ audiobooks and another 200 on my bookshelf and I don't think I've ever seen something like that. There's wonderful books, like *Mere Christianity* by C.S. Lewis for example, which I highly recommend if you've never read. (https://mpoweredchristian.org/Book-MereChristianity) But that's somewhat simplistic, and is really meant just to explain merely what Christianity *is* - not actually *prove* that's what the Bible teaches. I wanted something more definitive. More specific. Straight-forward. Brutally honest. Maybe even bold. Something more like an apologetic manual, a walk-through guide that doesn't pull any punches. It also needs to have tons of verse references throughout and even plenty of Bible verses right there so you don't even have to put the book down to look it up, or take *my word* for it—just trust in God's. So that was it. A simple map from A to B. Maybe 20 pages, right? So that's what I started to create. But as I wrote I kept running into complex topics that really needed to be unpacked and explained. How could I just say we're created in God's image without unpacking what that *really* means? I've seen that abused so much. How could I say we're saved by faith alone without also saying that if your life doesn't reflect God's righteousness through its works, and a willingness to lay it down for Jesus, then your faith is dead? How could I say we need to be born again without describing what that means, and how water baptism is important but it doesn't cause it? I reflected on the last few years ministering personally to hundreds, and doing apologetics to thousands, and thought of the many things I've seen Christians stumble in their faith over. It's a lot. I tried to address as many things as I could, and make it thorough enough to be persuasive, while still keeping it as brief as possible. The end result? A massive 70-page booklet!

During this time I continued to seek the Lord's guidance in prayer on how best to use it and what to do next. After all, if it was going to change lives at all then *I* needed to get out of the way and let Him lead this thing. He led me to do what I told you to do in the last chapter. I reflected on my SHAPE. What am I spiritually gifted in? I believe teaching and pastoring. What's my heart's passion? I want to create revival in the world by spreading the gospel and see it transform people and societies. What abilities do I have that are unique and special? I enjoy analyzing problems and creating solutions. I also enjoy research, writing, and graphic design. What's my personality and experience? I'm introverted, mission-focused, and in a season of my life where I have free time. And if I saw the benefit in doing so, I could live with isolation and dedicate myself to a large project. All the above providentially coincided with the fact that I felt the Church really needed what I felt the burning in me to create for it. After all, people having the map to salvation through Jesus isn't the only thing that's needed. There are plenty of saved-yet-kinda-lukewarm Christians. Revival won't be created if there's more of the status quo. We need fire! We need power! We need hunger! We need passion! We don't just need more *Christians*—we need *empowered* Christians! Then another revelation came to me:

- If I could only teach a single book worth of content, that would empower Christians to truly live out their faith, what's most important to know and do?

I felt the Holy Spirit guide me and I began to just let the thoughts flow through me. Within a few days I had eight pages of content, each focusing on a different category, with dozens of items listed on each of them. The book and its format was born! I didn't want to write a book, but it seemed as though the Lord was calling me to. At first it was going to be 180 pages, then 220, then 250, then 300, then certainly not more than 350, and then finally finishing it just shy of 400! I still can't believe it. But if you want empowered, on-fire Christians, you need to cover a lot of ground. It's not enough to just have the map to eternal life (Chapter 1), you need to really know how and have faith that God will deliver you. If you're fearful of losing your salvation you won't take risks, get uncomfortable, or be bold for God's Kingdom. Chapter 2 was born. But even born again Christians can be demonized, and get weighed down by all kinds of false beliefs and sinful behavior. Satan is actively trying to steal, kill, and destroy the Church. Chapter 3 is so necessary! But even with all the right beliefs and behavior, the real battlefield is the soul, which are the thoughts and emotions. Our own thoughts and feelings affect our behavior, and also our joy. We need to have the joy of the Lord, be mentally tough, have genuine faith, and be proactive, hence Chapter 4. We must also be fruitful and remember that we haven't been called to isolate ourselves from the world to stay holy, but rather to boldly enter the world of darkness and bring the light of Christ there (Chapter 5). But as we do that we need to remember not to get too distracted by the brokenness of the world and think it's our job to fix it. We need to remember that the war is spiritual, and our primary mission as Jesus's disciples is spiritual (Chapter 6). But we aren't to do it alone - this is why the Church was established. Our unity in this effort allows us to glorify God and build up one another as we work together in common purpose and mission (Chapter 7). And lastly, truly empowered Christians are self-aware. They're intentional and focused and disciplined. They know who they are and how God has been shaping them to be able to contribute in unique, effective, and fulfilling ways to the works that bring Him the most glory (Chapter 8). Let these eight core principles guide your life!

During your *entire lifetime*, the Lord is taking you through these eight steps you went through in this book. Right now, and every future season you go through, consider:

(Ch. 1)   Where am I going? What's most important to believe and focus on today?

(Ch. 2)   Am I new? Is my faith moving my entire life in the new direction today?

(Ch. 3)   Is there any evidence of garbage in my life for me to deal with today?

(Ch. 4)   Am I experiencing peace, joy and the fullness of the Gospel reality today?

(Ch. 5)   Does my life testify of my faith through abundant good fruit today?

(Ch. 6)   Am I being Jesus's disciple, following Him on mission in the world today?

(Ch. 7)   Am I contributing to, and on mission with, my church today?

(Ch. 8)   Am I finding ultimate fulfillment living out my unique calling today?

This Conclusion section began with a finish line, but the truth is finishing this book is not your finish line. In many ways you're still at your starting line! The next leg of your race begins tomorrow morning! Remember, it's not about what you *read* - it's about what you *do!* Your life will be accounted for one day by our Lord at the Bema Judgment. You'll be measured that day by how your testimony brings your Heavenly Father God glory. How much of your life will be built on the foundation of Jesus? Be sure to use the end of chapter evaluations to grade your progress. It's not about getting all 10's. It's about always moving to the *right*—consistently. Be intentional and proactive in areas you score poorly in, and dedicated to your progress. Seek the Lord for help, guidance, healing, restoration, growth, etc. and then develop a SMART action plan to improve. As you go about seeking the Lord's will, ask the same questions I did. If there was a single thing I could *learn* next, or a single thing I could *do* next, what should it be? Rise in the morning with the prayer: "Lord Jesus, how should I glorify you with my life today?" I'll leave you with this final thought from Psalm 16:8-11: *"I have set the LORD always before me. Because He is at my right hand, I will not be shaken. Therefore my heart is glad and my tongue rejoices; my body also will dwell securely. For You will not abandon my soul to Sheol, nor will You let Your Holy One see decay. You have made known to me **the path of life;** You will fill me with joy in Your presence, with eternal pleasures at Your right hand."*

Bibliography

Chapter 1: Recalculating... The Right Road Map

1. Piper, John, "What's the Origin of Desiring God's Slogan?," *DesiringGod.org*, 20 Sept. 2017, desiringgod.org/interviews/whats-the-origin-of-desiring-gods-slogan, Accessed 1 March. 2020.
2. Bristol Works, Inc., *Rose Bible Basics, What Christians Believe at a Glance*, Rose Publishing, Inc., 2010. p. 35.
3. Holmes, Brian, "What the Abyss is and Why Satan and the Demons are in it," *MPoweredChristian.org*, mpoweredchristian.org/blog/2020/02/what-the-abyss-is-and-why-satan-and-the-demons-are-currently-in-it/, Accessed 9 March. 2020.
4. Bible.ca, "What did early Christians believe about...? (Water Baptism in name of Father Son & Holy Spirit)," *Bible.ca*, bible.ca/H-baptism.htm#name, Accessed 19 March 2020.

Chapter 2: Rebuilt And Headed In A New Direction

1. GotQuestions.org, "Total depravity - is it biblical," *GotQuestions.org*, gotquestions.org/total-depravity.html, Accessed 2 June 2020.
2. Winger, Mike, "Brian Zahnd's False Gospel and Fake Jesus," *Mike Winger / BibleThinker.org*, 11 December 2018, https://youtu.be/QUNdh1u6774, Accessed 2 June 2020.
3. "VII: Cosmic Child Abuse," *American Gospel: Christ Crucified*, Free Preview released 7 April 2020, https://www.facebook.com/americangospelfilm/videos/601554273904923/, Accessed 2 June 2020.
4. Soronski, Jason, "What Does "Bible" Mean and How Did it Get That Name?," *BibleStudy-Tools.com*, 31 May 2019, biblestudytools.com/bible-study/explore-the-bible/what-does-bible-mean.html, Accessed 1 January 2020.
5. RW Research, Inc., *Rose Book of Charts, Maps, and Time Lines*, Rose Publishing, Inc., 2005.
6. Marlowe, Michael, "Third Council of Carthage (A.D. 397)," *Bible-Researcher.com*, 2012, bible-researcher.com/carthage.html, Accessed 1 January 2020.
7. Turner, Ryan, "Reasons why the Apocrypha does not belong in the Bible," *Christian Apologetics and Research Ministry*, 13 Oct. 2009, carm.org/reasons-why-apocrypha-does-not-belong-bible.
8. Stewart, Don, "Did the Ancient Jews, Jesus, and His Disciples Have a Fixed Canon of Scripture, or Was the Canon Still Open?," *BlueLetterBible.org*, blueletterbible.org/Comm/stewart_don/faq/books-missing-from-old-testament/question5-ancient-jews-canon-of-scripture.cfm, Accessed 1 January 2020.
9. Stewart, Don, "Does the Old Testament Apocrypha Give Evidence of Being Holy Scripture?," *BlueLetterBible.org*, blueletterbible.org/Comm/stewart_don/faq/books-missing-from-old-testament/question7-apocrypha-evidence.cfm, Accessed 1 January 2020.
10. Peters, Joel, "Twenty One Reasons to Reject Sola Scriptura," *CatholicApologetics.info*, catholicapologetics.info/apologetics/protestantism/sola.htm, Accessed 9 January 2020.
11. Wallace, J. Warner, *Cold-Case Christianity*, David C Cook, 2013.
12. HiSoMA-Sources Chrétiennes, *BiblIndex*, biblindex.mom.fr/presentation, Accessed 9 January 2020.
13. Bristol Works, Inc., *Rose Book of Bible Charts 2*, Rose Publishing, Inc., 2008.

Chapter 3: Dumping The Garbage Baggage

1. "Satan." *BibleHub.com*, biblehub.com/topical/s/satan.htm. Accessed 2 Feb. 2020.
2. "Lucifer." *BibleHub.com*, biblehub.com/topical/l/lucifer.htm. Accessed 2 Feb. 2020.
3. "Saboteur." *Merriam-Webster.com Dictionary*, Merriam-Webster, merriam-webster.com/dictionary/saboteur. Accessed 2 Feb. 2020.
4. "Sabotage." *Lexico.com Dictionary*, Oxford University Press (OUP), lexico.com/en/definition/sabotage. Accessed 2 Feb. 2020.
5. "Subversion." *Merriam-Webster.com Dictionary*, Merriam-Webster, merriam-webster.com/dictionary/subversion. Accessed 2 Feb. 2020.

6. "Monotheism, Pantheism, Panentheism, Polytheism, Animism." Ankerberg, John, and John Weldon, *Encyclopedia of New Age Beliefs*, Harvest House Publishers, 1996.

7. "Atheism." *Etymonline.com*, Online Etmology Dictionary, etymonline.com/word/atheism. Accessed 2 Feb. 2020.

8. "Gnosticism." *Theopedia.com*, Theopedia, theopedia.com/gnosticism. Accessed 9 Feb. 2020.

9. Smith, Joseph, *The King Follet Sermon*, churchofjesuschrist.org/study/ensign/1971/04/the-king-follett-sermon. Accessed 10 Feb. 2020.

10. Smith, C. Fred, *Shinto Profile*, Watchman Fellowship, Inc., 2019.

11. "Nicene Creed." *Encyclopedia Britannica*, Encyclopedia Britannica, inc., britannica.com/topic/Nicene-Creed, Accessed 14 Feb. 2020.

12. "Is Jesus the Archangel Michael?," *The Watchtower Announcing Jehovah's Kingdom*, Watch Tower Bible and Tract Society of Pennsylvania, 2010, wol.jw.org/en/wol/d/r1/lp-e/2010250#h=8, Accessed 14 Feb. 2020.

13. Wayne, Luke, "Did the author of the Quran understand the Trinity?," *CARM.org*, carm.org/did-the-author-of-the-quran-understand-the-trinity, Accessed 13 Feb. 2020.

14. Covey, Stephen R., *The 7 Habits of Highly Effective People*, Free Press; Revised Edition, 2004

15. Cherry, Kendra, "How Cognitive Biases Influence How You Think and Act," *VeryWellMind.com*, verywellmind.com/what-is-a-cognitive-bias-2794963, Accessed 19 Feb. 2020.

Chapter 4: The Atmosphere In The Car

1. Carson, D.A., *"Matthew," The Expositor's Bible Commentary, ed.*, Grand Rapids: Zondervan, 1984, p. 290

2. Jones, Clay, "What is the Unpardonable Sin?," *Equip.org*, 21 June 2013, equip.org/article/what-is-the-unpardonable-sin/, Accessed 8 March 2020.

3. Shutterfly, "Inspiring Gratitude Quotes," *Shutterfly.com*, 11 Dec. 2019, shutterfly.com/ideas/gratitude-quotes/, Accessed 17 March 2020.

4. BrainyQuote, "Viktor E. Frankl Quotes," *BrainyQuote.com*, brainyquote.com/quotes/viktor_e_frankl_131417, Accessed 18 March 2020.

5. Jones, David W., Russel S. Woodbridge, *"Health, Wealth, and Happiness: How the Prosperity Gospel Overshadows the Gospel of Christ,"* Kregel Publications, a division of Kregel, Inc., 2017.
   a) p. 22-23   b) p. 25   c) p. 27   d) p. 45-46

6. Bowman, Jr., Robert M., *Word-Faith Movement Profile*, Watchman Fellowship, Inc., 2019. watchman.org/profiles/pdf/wordfaithprofile.pdf

7. King, Paul L., "A.B. Simpson & the Modern Faith Movement," *HopeFaithPrayer.com*, hope-faithprayer.com/word-of-faith/a-b-simpson-and-the-modern-faith-movement-paul-l-king/, Accessed 16 June 2020.

Chapter 5: The New Direction Is Very Fruitful

1. GospelOutreach.net, "The Law: All 613 Commandments!," *GospelOutreach.net*, gospeloutreach.net/613laws.html, Accessed 3 April 2020.

2. Covey, Stephen R., *The 7 Habits of Highly Effective People*, Free Press; Revised Edition, 2004

3. Ranker, "List of Famous Dictators," *Ranker.com*, ranker.com/list/list-of-famous-dictators/reference, Accessed 7 April 2020.

4. Warner, Bill, PhD, "Sharia Law for Non-Muslims," CSPI, LLC, 2010, politicalislam.com/wp-content/uploads/2014/09/PDF-Look-Inside/Sharia_Non-Muslim_look_inside.pdf

5. USHistory.org, "The Caste System," *USHistory.org*, ushistory.org/civ/8b.asp, Accessed 7 April 2020.

6. USHistory.org, "The Declaration of Independence," *USHistory.org*, ushistory.org/declaration/document/, Accessed 7 April 2020.

7. "Justice." *Dictionary.com*, dictionary.com/browse/justice. Accessed 8 April 2020.

8. Pachamama Alliance, "What is Social Justice?," *Pachamama.org*, pachamama.org/social-justice/what-is-social-justice, Accessed 8 April 2020.

9. Molinari, Lori, "What Does the Left Mean by Social Justice?," *Heritage.org*, heritage.org/progressivism/report/what-does-the-left-mean-social-justice, Accessed 8 April 2020.

10. StatementOnSocialJustice.com, "Statement on Social Justice," *StatementOnSocialJustice.com*, Accessed 8 April 2020.

11. Slick, Matt, "A list of false teachings in the Roman Catholic Church," *CARM.org*, carm.org/catholic/list-of-roman-catholic-false-teachings, Accessed 9 April 2020.

Chapter 6: Our Mission As Disciples

1. Hutchinson, Bill, "Christian baker who won Supreme Court case in new cake-making legal battle," *ABC News*, August 16, 2018, abcnews.go.com/US/christian-baker-won-supreme-court-case-cake-making/story?id=57215854, Accessed 17 April 2020.
2. Southern Poverty Law Center, "30 New Activists Heading Up the Radical Right," *SPLcenter.org*, May 26, 2012, splcenter.org/fighting-hate/intelligence-report/2012/30-new-activists-heading-radical-right, Accessed 17 April 2020.
3. Lumen Learning, "Power and Authority," *LumenLearning.com*, courses.lumenlearning.com/sociology/chapter/power-and-authority/, Accessed 17 April 2020.
4. "Petros, Petra." *BibleHub.com*, "4074. Petros," biblehub.com/greek/4074.htm, Accessed 18 April 2020.
5. Catholic Answers, "Peter and the Papacy," *Catholic.com*, catholic.com/tract/peter-and-the-papacy, Accessed 18 April 2020.
6. Jones, Ron, "The Hebrew and Greek Gospels Written by Matthew the Apostle of Jesus Christ," *HebrewGospel.com*, http://hebrewgospel.com/Matthew%20Two%20Gospels%20Main%20Evidence.php, Accessed 18 April 2020.
7. Ortberg, John, *in the sermon* "Three Habits of Highly Contagious Christians," Willow Creek Community Church, South Barrington, Illinois.
8. Stanton, Glenn, "FactChecker: Misquoting Francis of Assisi," *TheGospelCoalition.org*, 10 July 2012, thegospelcoalition.org/article/factchecker-misquoting-francis-of-assisi/, Accessed 20 April 2020.
9. GotQuestions.org, "What is Christian dominionism?," *GotQuestions.org*, gotquestions.org/Christian-dominionism.html, Accessed 23 April 2020.
10. Holmes, Brian, Sermon "Good & Faithful or Wicked & Lazy?," *MPoweredChristian.org*, 30 August 2019, https://mpoweredchristian.org/sermons/good-faithful-wicked-lazy
11. Robbins, Tony, *QuoteMaster.org*, quotemaster.org/qd33601e3a72a0c733300801c3be4df9e, Accessed 24 April 2020.

Chapter 7: The Auto Club (The Church)

1. HELPS Word-studies, "Ekklésia," *BibleHub.com*, biblehub.com/greek/1577.htm. Accessed 28 April 2020.
2. Christianity.com, "A Look at the Early Church," *Christianity.com*, christianity.com/church/church-history/timeline/1-300/a-look-at-the-early-church-11629559.html, 3 May 2010, Accessed 30 April 2020.
3. International Standard Bible Encyclopedia, "Sacraments," *BibleHub.com*, https://biblehub.com/topical/s/sacraments.htm, Accessed 1 May 2020.
4. International Standard Bible Encyclopedia, "Lord's Supper," *BibleHub.com*, https://biblehub.com/topical/l/lord's_supper.htm, Accessed 1 May 2020.
5. "Baptism, Lord's Supper," *MPoweredChristian.org*, https://mpoweredchristian.org/what-we-teach/
6. "Lord's Supper Poster," *MPoweredChristian.org*, https://mpoweredchristian.org/wall-art-lords-supper
7. Pew Research Center, "Attendance at religious services among Evangelical Protestants by religious denomination," *PewForum.org*, pewforum.org/religious-landscape-study/compare/attendance-at-religious-services/by/religious-denomination/among/religious-tradition/evangelical-protestant/, Accessed 2 May 2020.
8. Weber, Jeremy, "Pew: Why Americans God to Church or Stay Home," *ChristianityToday.com*, 1 August 2018, christianitytoday.com/news/2018/july/church-attendance-top-reasons-go-or-stay-home-pew.html, Accessed 4 May 2020.
9. Smietana, Bob, "New Research: Churchgoers Stick Around for Theology, Not Music or Preachers," *ChristianityToday.com*, 6 July 2018, christianitytoday.com/edstetzer/2018/july/churchgoers-stick-around-for-theology-not-

music-or-preacher.html, Accessed 4 May 2020.

10. McDaniel, Lori, "Five Inspirational Quotes For Life On Mission," *NAMB.net*, 23 March 2015, namb.net/planter-wives-blog/five-inspirational-quotes-for-life-on-mission/, Accessed 4 May 2020.

11. Mcintosh, Gary, "Origin of Spiritual Gifts Profiles," *ChristianityToday.com*, 23 October 2017, christianitytoday.com/edstetzer/2017/october/origin-of-spiritual-gifts-profiles.html, Accessed 5 May 2020.

Chapter 8: Same Destination, Alternate Routes

1. Larson, Bob, "Beware the Enneagram," *BobLarson.org*, 16 July 2018, boblarson.org/beware-the-enneagram/, Accessed 15 May 2020.

2. Montenegro, Marcia, "The Enneagram GPS: Gnostic Path to Self," *ChristianAnswersForTheNewAge.org*, 11 March 2011, christiananswersforthenewage.org/Articles_Enneagram.aspx, Accessed 15 May 2020.

3. Lane, Christopher, "Carl Jung's Frightening Demons," *PsychologyToday.com,* 13 May 2020, psychologytoday.com/us/blog/side-effects/201005/carl-jungs-frightening-demons, Accessed 15 May 2020.

4. "Assessing Personality," *LumenLearning.com*, courses.lumenlearning.com/boundless-psychology/chapter/assessing-personality/, Accessed 15 May 2020.

5. Vohs, Kathleen D., "Barnum Effect," *Britannica.com*, britannica.com/science/Barnum-Effect, Accessed 15 May 2020.

6. "Our Framework," *16Personalities.com,* 16personalities.com/articles/our-theory, Accessed 15 May 2020.

7. Wilson, Todd, *More*, Zondervan, 2016.

8. Wellman, Jack, "'E.M. Bounds Quote' - '18 Quotes About Goals,'"*ChristianQuotes.info*, 28 December 2015, christianquotes.info/quotes-by-topic/quotes-about-goals/, Accessed 22 May 2020.

9. Mueller, Steve, "'Zig Ziglar Quote' - The 30 Most Inspiring Focus Quotes," *PlanetofSuccess.com*, planetofsuccess.com/blog/2016/inspiring-focus-quotes/, Accessed 20 May 2020.

10. "Global Statistics," *JoshuaProject.net*, joshuaproject.net/people_groups/statistics, Accessed 20 May 2020.

11. Vozza, Stephanie, *FastCompany.com*, fastcompany.com/3026791/personal-mission-statements-of-5-famous-ceos-and-why-you-should-write-one-too, Accessed 21 May 2020.

12. "Intro to Mission Statements," *TopNonprofit.com*, topnonprofits.com/vision-mission/, Accessed 20 May 2020.

13. Church Relevance Team, "50 Examples of Church Mission Statements," *ChurchRelevance.com*, 28 March 2013, churchrelevance.com/2013/03/28/50-examples-of-church-mission-statements/, Accessed 21 May 2020.

14. Sweatt, Lydia, "18 Motivational Quotes About Successful Goal Setting," Success.com, 29 December 2016, success.com/18-motivational-quotes-about-successful-goal-setting/, Accessed 22 May 2020.

15. Wellman, Jack, "'Martin Luther King Jr. Quote' - '18 Quotes About Goals,'"*ChristianQuotes.info*, 28 December 2015, christianquotes.info/quotes-by-topic/quotes-about-goals/, Accessed 22 May 2020.

16. Wellman, Jack, "'Amy Carmichael Quote' - '18 Quotes About Goals,'"*ChristianQuotes.info*, 28 December 2015, christianquotes.info/quotes-by-topic/quotes-about-goals/, Accessed 22 May 2020.

17. Frontier Ventures, "Progress Scale: 1 - Unreached," *JoshuaProject.net*, joshuaproject.net/progress/1, Accessed 21 May 2020.

18. Hogan, Matt, "'Zig Ziglar Quote' - Top 15 Goal Setting Quotes,'" *MoveMeQuotes.com*, movemequotes.com/top-15-goal-setting-quotes/, Accessed 22 May 2020.

19. Mueller, Steve, "'Mike Hawkins Quote' - The 30 Most Inspiring Focus Quotes," *PlanetofSuccess.com*, planetofsuccess.com/blog/2016/inspiring-focus-quotes/, Accessed 20 May 2020.

20. Durant, Will, "Will Durant Quote," *PlanetofSuccess.com*, planetofsuccess.com/blog/2016/inspiring-focus-quotes/, Accessed 20 May 2020.

Scripture Index

Note: This index doesn't include every single reference to a Bible verse or any of the various partial quotes throughout the book. This index includes many of the Bible verses written out in full within this book. (A few partial verses indicated using an "a", meaning the first half of a verse is shown, or "b" meaning the second half of the verse is shown). I hope you find this a useful reference guide!

SCRIPTURE ......PAGE

"These words I am commanding you today are to be upon your hearts. And you shall teach them diligently to your children and speak of them when you sit at home and when you walk along the road, when you lie down and when you get up. Tie them as reminders on your hands and bind them on your foreheads. Write them on the doorposts of your houses and on your gates."

Deuteronomy 6:6-8

Topical Index

Made in the USA
Coppell, TX
17 September 2022

83281871R10221